SONS OF SAINT PATRICK

George J. Marlin and Brad Miner

SONS OF SAINT PATRICK

A History of the Archbishops of New York
from Dagger John to Timmytown

IGNATIUS PRESS   SAN FRANCISCO

Cover photographs from the Archives of the Archdiocese of New York
Used by permission

Cover design by John Herreid

© 2017 by Ignatius Press, San Francisco
All rights reserved
ISBN 978-1-62164-113-1
Library of Congress Control Number 2016941443
Printed in the United States of America ∞

For our friend and colleague Robert Royal

CONTENTS

INTRODUCTION

Not long after becoming the tenth archbishop of New York, Timothy Michael Dolan responded to a reporter's question about how he was settling into the job by quipping that he had "already learned how to order a hot dog from the cart outside the cathedral".[1] It was a comment that won much affection for the new archbishop and furthered the sense that the Big Apple was now, as the *New York Post* had proclaimed, *Timmytown*. That is a very small example of what is necessary to fulfill the responsibilities of the job: the archbishop must know his city and be able to interact with its diverse people and media. And, really, it has always been so.

New York's first archbishop, the Irish-born John Joseph Hughes, became extremely skillful in his use of media, as we would say today, although his many memorable statements were not always as polished as Cardinal Dolan's.

A comparison of the first and tenth archbishops also makes clear two things that are at the heart of this book. As our title suggests, every one of the men who has served as archbishop of New York has been Irish either by birth (Hughes and Farley) or by heritage (Dolan and the other seven), and none has been at a further remove from his Irish roots than a second generation.

There is a single exception, and just a half exception at that. Thomas J. O'Connor, the father of Cardinal John J. O'Connor (archbishop from 1984 until 2000) was proudly Irish and Catholic, but the cardinal's mother, Dorothy Gumpel O'Connor, a Catholic convert at age nineteen, was the daughter of German (Prussian, to be exact) Jews. In fact, her father was a rabbi. Apparently Cardinal O'Connor was unaware of the fact, since it came to light only after his death. As the cardinal's sister, Mary O'Connor Ward-Donegan, said in 2014:[2] "That means my two brothers were Jewish, my sister was Jewish and I am Jewish. Of that I am very proud." Mrs. Ward-Donegan was referring to the matrilineal tradition in Judaism. She believes that her brother John, a tireless champion of Jews in New York and around the world, would have been very proud of his Jewish roots.

Since 1850, when the diocese of New York was elevated to archiepiscopal status, there have been thirty-two American presidents, forty New York governors, twelve popes, but just ten archbishops of New York. And (this is the second title clarification) we should make it clear here that this book is about *those* ten men, the ones who headed the archdiocese—the ordinaries, as they are known. We mention in passing some others who have held the rank of archbishop (the great Fulton J. Sheen, for example), and the first chapter traces the history of the New York diocese before 1850, but this book's focus in on the trials, tribulations, and triumphs of those ten ordinaries: John Hughes, John McCloskey, Michael Corrigan, John Farley, Patrick Hayes, Francis Spellman, Terence Cooke, John O'Connor, Edward Egan, and Timothy Dolan.

Not all of New York's archbishops have been headline makers, of course. Both Cardinal John McCloskey, the second archbishop, and Cardinal Edward Egan, the ninth, preferred to keep a lower profile than did, for instance, Archbishop Michael Corrigan, the third archbishop, or Cardinal O'Connor, the eighth. To some extent, this has been a matter of personal style, but in other cases, the public profile of New York's Catholic leader has been determined by the issues he has been forced to address. War, poverty, nativism, education, anti-Catholicism, and, more recently, matters of faith and morals have made it necessary for even the most publicity-shy archbishops to restate Church teaching clearly and to confront those who oppose that teaching.

It is unlikely in the contemporary media environment that Cardinal Dolan, and the men who will succeed him, will ever again be able to use the single medium of print to communicate with the faithful. Throughout the history of the archdiocese, printed appeals from New York's ordinaries, often read aloud by priests from the pulpits of every New York church, have given clear explanations of Catholic doctrine, thus fulfilling one of the key responsibilities of an archbishop. Today, communication between Church officials and the people is carried on mostly via mass media, especially television, and the Internet, and this happens in an era of shortened attention spans, which, despite the potential for much greater exposure of an archbishop's message, actually makes clarity in messaging more difficult. It is often the case that the message the media promote is an interpretation of what the archbishop has actually said, one crafted to appeal to constituencies (or the reporter's or medium's view of what the Church *should* be), even to gin up the sort of controversies that lead to further stories. This is one of the great challenges the Church has faced in the era of the New Evangelization.

But "messaging" is only one aspect of an archbishop's job. The media prefer to focus on any archbishop's positions that affect political debates, but most of the cleric's time is taken up in the management of Church affairs. Because these management matters are often of little interest to reporters, the stories reporters cover may make it seem to viewers and readers that archbishops are involved mostly in politics. An exception—at least in New York media—is Cardinal Dolan's recent decisions concerning the closing of parishes throughout the archdiocese, which became front-page news. But most of what Cardinal Dolan does on any given day is simply not fodder for media consumption.

As Reverend Thomas J. Reese, S.J., has written, "Bishops actually spend very little of their time on public policy." They are concerned mostly with "internal church matters in their own dioceses".[3]

This is true, and yet even in earlier times the public profile of the archbishop of New York, his visibility, has made him not simply a force in the world's media capital but a potential power broker as well. Writing in response to the appointment of Francis Joseph Spellman in 1939 (and using Manhattan to represent the whole archdiocese), the editor of the *Catholic World* noted:

New York is what it is reputed to be, a cosmos, a world on a narrow and not very long island. . . .

In a manner of speaking he [Spellman or any archbishop of New York] becomes the leader of the world, or at least of *a* world: and I hope I may say without undue exuberance that he has a greater opportunity to battle evil and to amplify good than any other one man except the Holy Father. There is no see in Christendom with such potentialities as New York.[4]

This may make the archbishop seem rather too much like Gotham's Batman, a fanciful comparison some in the media have made when Cardinal Dolan's ecclesiastical cape, his *ferraiolo*, flares out in the wind like wings. But there are, in fact, few other religious leaders in New York who have had or are likely to have the moral influence of its Catholic archbishop. How could he *not* wield such influence in a state of nearly twenty million souls, of whom about 15 percent are Roman Catholic? Whether this influence is currently waxing or waning is a matter for debate.

For many years, becoming the ordinary in New York usually involved earlier service in the diocese or archdiocese—a kind of apprenticeship. For instance, consider this sequence: Bishop John Dubois was the early champion of the future Archbishop John Hughes, who served as the former's coadjutor bishop, as Cardinal John McCloskey would receive his first episcopal appointment as Archbishop Hughes' coadjutor. Archbishop Michael Corrigan would likewise serve as McCloskey's coadjutor before becoming the ordinary, as Corrigan's right hand, the future Cardinal John Farley, would serve as Corrigan's coadjutor. Cardinal Patrick Hayes was the penultimate native New Yorker to head the archdiocese, and he had served with Farley at a Lower East Side church before becoming an auxiliary bishop for the five years prior to his being named archbishop. Then came the change.

Cardinal Francis Spellman was born in Massachusetts and had not served in New York prior to his elevation to the see in 1939. His old friend Eugenio Pacelli sent him to New York when Pacelli became Pope Pius XII. Spellman's successor, Cardinal Terence Cooke, *was* a native-born New Yorker—the last to become archbishop—and served in various roles in the archdiocese, including chancellor and auxiliary bishop. Subsequent archbishops—O'Connor, Egan, and Dolan—were born elsewhere, although Egan and O'Connor did have previous experience in New York: Egan as an auxiliary bishop and O'Connor as an auxiliary bishop of the Military Vicariate of the United States, which, until his appointment as archbishop of New York, counted New York as its home base. (The rechristened Archdiocese for Military Services is now based in Washington, D.C.) And here we do not address the number of secretaries and administrators who have served under the archbishops and have gone on to head up other dioceses.

Why the change? It seems clear that personality, education, and achievement now trump local experience. Timothy M. Dolan began his career in St. Louis, where he was born, educated, and received degrees from two Roman colleges as well as from Catholic University in Washington, D.C., where he also served as a secretary at the Apostolic Nunciature of the Holy See to the United States. He then returned to Rome as head of the North American College. He returned to St. Louis as an auxiliary bishop and from there became archbishop of Milwaukee. It is an understatement to say that the résumé he brought with him to New York is impressive, but it includes no experience whatsoever *in* New York, and *that* (Spellman excepted) is unique in the history of the archbishops of New York. No man comes to any archiepiscopal appointment without considerable experience and demonstrated achievements, but trends—in New York and elsewhere—indicate that it is no longer essential for him to have served any sort of apprenticeship in the archdiocese he will lead.

A modern American archdiocese is a bit like a great university, making archbishops rather like college presidents, which is to say they are almost constantly involved in financial management: facing shrinking endowments, diminishing revenues, and rising costs, necessitating engagement in aggressive fund-raising.

In the middle of the nineteenth century, the church in America went quickly into debt. New bishops undertook the business of building up their dioceses (constructing churches, seminaries, primary and secondary schools and colleges, orphanages, hospitals, and cemeteries), often with borrowed money. That debt, however, was somewhat mitigated by the rapid increase, via immigration, in the number of Catholics, whereas, in the twenty-first century, the Church spirals into even greater debt because so much of what was built in the nineteenth century and sustained in the twentieth has now become unaffordable. The Church is being worn down by burdensome regulations, soaring costs, priest shortages and scandals, and, above all, by diminishing income due to the movement of Catholics away from the old urban centers and by lapsing belief among the Catholics who remain. Some old Catholic neighborhoods in the archdiocese have been overtaken by corporate development; others have been sundered by "gentrification". It does not matter what the cause may be: when a parish church (and, possibly, school) that once served several thousand souls now serves several hundred, its relative costs remain the same or, more likely, increase because of inflation. Buildings must be maintained; heating bills must be paid. If there are not enough resident Catholics within the parish catchment, there is simply nothing an archbishop can do to fill the pews in a given church. And despite misinformation (or disinformation) concerning the wealth of the Roman Catholic Church, many parishes must be closed or consolidated if limited funds are to be stretched to cover the shortfalls of those other parishes where the census of practicing Catholics allows churches to operate in the black or nearly so. This is the reality Cardinal Dolan faced and why he had to act as he did in merging or closing so many parishes throughout New York.

New York's first and third archbishops were not elevated to the cardinalate, but all the rest have been. President Abraham Lincoln had hoped to see John Joseph Hughes receive the red hat from Pope Pius IX, but—although New York had been elevated to archiepiscopal status fourteen years before Hughes died in 1864—raising Hughes in what Rome still considered mission territory was considered premature. The first to receive the honor was Hughes' successor, John McCloskey, and that may have been in some measure due to the fact he was known well to so many in Rome, because he had received some post-graduate, post-ordination training there. At the time of our writing, America has nineteen cardinals, only nine of whom are under the age of eighty and thus would be qualified to vote should a conclave be held at this time. Of those nine cardinal electors, three will disqualify within a year, although new cardinals will surely be named to succeed them.

Among the duties of the archbishops of New York with the appointment to the cardinalate that almost comes with the job, none is more important than the role they play in the selection of popes.

As we note later, Cardinal McCloskey (not simply New York's first cardinal but America's first as well) was unable to reach Rome by ship in time to vote in the conclave that chose Vincenzo Gioacchino Raffaele Luigi Pecci as Pope Leo XIII. More recently, Cardinal Egan voted in the conclave that chose Joseph Aloisius Ratzinger as Benedict XVI, and Cardinal Dolan helped elect Jorge Mario Bergoglio as Pope Francis, and it is unlikely that Cardinal Dolan or any other American cardinal will ever again be late for a conclave.

As we were composing this introduction, the news came that Archbishop Emeritus Edward Cardinal Egan had died (March 5, 2015). For the nation and the world, it was the loss of a steadfast churchman and a man of ready wit and enormous personal dignity—a true Catholic leader. For the authors of this book, especially for Mr. Marlin, it was also the loss of a close personal friend. We had not only the great opportunity to interview Cardinal Egan on several occasions but, over dinners and through notes and phone calls with him, we had discussions on topics that ranged from Church history and politics to the cardinal's personal history and frank opinions about people and events in the Church throughout his nearly six decades as a priest. At Cardinal Egan's Requiem Mass, Cardinal Dolan said with sadness to Mr. Marlin: "You're going to have to revise your book." Indeed.

Cardinal Egan's body rests in the crypt in St. Patrick's along with the other eight archbishops who predeceased him, as one day Cardinal Dolan's body will, these ten extraordinary men awaiting the final trumpet blast and the resurrection that will join them and all the faithful in unity with the Blessed Trinity forever and ever.

George J. Marlin
Brad Miner
August 1, 2016

ACKNOWLEDGMENTS

The authors must express their gratitude to the following people, whose generosity and expertise made the writing of this book so much easier.

First of all, to the Reverend Michael P. Morris, chief archivist, and Kate Feighery, archival manager of the Archives of the Archdiocese of New York. Father Morris and Kate Feighery are as gracious as they are expert in their handling of researchers and the treasure trove of materials held in the archives and in the beautiful new John Cardinal O'Connor Memorial Library. Without their able advice and assistance we simply could not have written this book.

At the library at St. Joseph's Seminary, we were guided to the best published sources by chief librarian Barbara Carey and her staff.

Very special thanks to Barbara D. Marlin for the many hours she spent working on the manuscript and helping prepare it for publication.

We are grateful as well to our friend Linda Bridges, who read the manuscript, chapter by chapter, as it was being written. Her comments, corrections, and suggestions have been an enormous help to us.

PART I

Before the Beginning

Hard to Kill

Father Isaac Jogues, National Shrine of the North American Martyrs
(Auriesville, New York)

Old St. Patrick's Cathedral

About two hundred miles north of New York City, in the east-central part of the Empire State, is the area the Mohawks called Ossernenon. It was a center of seventeenth-century Catholic missionary activity in what would become the United States, and it was where Father Isaac Jogues was murdered, in the village of Auriesville, in 1646.[1] He was not the first missionary killed in North America, nor would he be the last. Seven other French Jesuits were also slain (between 1642 and 1649), and the eight are known collectively as the North American Martyrs. (The Native American saint Kateri Tekakwitha was born in Auriesville ten years after Jogues' martyrdom.)

Jogues had begun his missionary career in Quebec in 1636. On a trip south in 1642, he and his companions—some French, some from one of the native tribes of Canada—were captured by a Mohawk hunting party and taken to Auriesville, where Jogues and the other Europeans were tortured. Several of Jogues' fingers were gnawed and burnt off.

In 1643, Jogues was rescued by Dutch merchants (who later compensated the Mohawks with gold) and was taken to New Amsterdam (present-day Manhattan), which the Dutch had controlled since the 1620s. (Incidentally, the first European to see southern New York was not the English-Dutch—and Protestant—explorer Henry Hudson in 1609 but the Italian-French—and Catholic—Giovanni da Verrazzano in 1524.)

Historian William Harper Bennett describes the arrival of Isaac Jogues in New Amsterdam, where he was met, upon leaving the dinghy that brought him ashore, by the Calvinist domine Johannes Megapolensis:

> A bronzed, dark bearded face, lined and drawn with suffering, but in the eyes and expression "that peace which the world knows not of." Of the forefingers and the left thumb of his hands only the jagged red stumps remain. Every finger shows a partially healed wound and from all, the nails are gone.[2]

Megapolensis tenderly guided Jogues along the narrow, muddy streets, with the Jesuit "leaning on his arm, the bent broken figure in rags—partly Indian, partly European—that barely cover him".

Jogues would note a remarkable thing about this town (village, really). Out of New Amsterdam's population of nearly three hundred, there were just three Catholics: a Portuguese woman, an Irish man, and Jogues. Thus, when Jogues returned to France to recover his health, there were just two Catholics living in what would become America's largest and most Catholic city. (All in all, the residents of the town had, as the historians Edwin G. Burrows and Mike Wallace have written, a "claim to being the motliest assortment of souls in Christendom", and New Amsterdam was ramshackle.[3] It was less a colony than a temporary outpost.)

After a brief convalescence in France, Jogues returned, and not just to North America but soon back to Auriesville/Ossernenon. The Mohawks were impressed by his courage and dubbed him *Ondessonk*, "the indomitable one", which he was until his neck was hacked through with a tomahawk on October 18, 1646. All in all, it was not an auspicious beginning for Catholics in New York.

Writing in the middle of the nineteenth century, Father J. R. Bayley (private secretary to New York's first archbishop, John Joseph Hughes, and himself a future archbishop of Baltimore) lamented:

> Father Jogues' head was fastened to one of the palisades, and his body thrown into the Mohawk River. Thus perished the first [Catholic] missionary that ever visited our island. His memory was long cherished, even among the Iroquois ... and, though he has never been formally canonized, yet those who are laboring in the same field under more favorable circumstances, may justly invoke his intercession.[4]

Along with the other North American Martyrs, Father Jogues was canonized by Pope Pius XI in 1930.

Jogues' Dutch rescuers and their governing countrymen in Manhattan were notable for their tolerance. Another Jesuit captive rescued by the Dutch (again from one of the Iroquois tribes) a year after Jogues, Francesco-Giuseppe Bressani, was likewise treated with respect and honor in New Amsterdam. Bressani was given a letter of safe passage by Governor Willem Kieft. Unlike Father Jogues, however, Father Bressani died peacefully many years after his return to Italy.

In his retirement, Bressani wrote a memoir of his time in America (known as the *Breve Relatione*) in which he included the text of a letter he had written to his superior while still in captivity:

> I know not whether Your Paternity will recognize the letter of a poor cripple, who formerly, in perfect health, was well known to you. The letter is badly written and quite soiled, because, in addition to other inconveniences, he who writes it has only one whole finger on his right hand; and it is difficult to avoid staining the paper with the blood that flows from his wounds, not yet healed; he uses arquebus [a type of musket] powder for ink, and the earth for a table.[5]

He simply didn't know, he wrote, that a man could be so hard to kill.

Catholics were deeply indebted to the Dutch, although Dutch tolerance went only so far. It was the rule, even as Jogues and Bressani were affably conducted through New Amsterdam, that in New Netherland only one religion was to be practiced: Calvinism. No Masses could be said in the colony, and the turmoil of the late-Reformation period in the Netherlands was reflected in laws that essentially gave second-class status to all religions but the one established. This was especially true under the last Dutch governor (director general) of New Netherland, Peter Stuyvesant. That vaunted Dutch tolerance toward Catholics was in some measure due simply to the scarcity of Catholics.

Escorted cordially as those Jesuit missionaries had been, they were always being escorted *out*.

The English Come to Power

In 1664, Manhattan (from the Lenape word for "island of many hills") was seized by English forces, who renamed the Dutch holdings—from the lower Hudson River up to Albany (Beverwyck, the Dutch called it)—New York after James, Duke of

York, who in 1685 would accede to the throne in Great Britain as James II. His brother, Charles II, had given him New York "to rule as he pleased".[6]

In 1673, the Dutch retook New York and rechristened it New Orange, but this New World outpost was not considered as important back in the Netherlands as were certain spice islands in faraway Indonesia, for which ownership of New York was traded back to Great Britain in compensation—a fair trade then that seems in retrospect a terrible deal for the Dutch. Of course, they had profited considerably from Peter Minuit's purchase of Manhattan for sixty guilders from the Lenni Lenape tribe back in 1626. In any event, the British had effectively established themselves throughout the continent, from Protestant Boston to Catholic Baltimore.

The Duke of York surprised many in England when he converted to Catholicism in 1672, and he shocked many more in 1682 when he appointed an Irish Catholic, Thomas Dongan, as governor of the New York colony. Dongan served from approximately 1682 to 1688.

During Dongan's tenure, the first parochial school was built and the first Masses were said in Manhattan. But Dongan was not a parochial governor. He also formed New York's first legislature; issued a "Charter of Libertyes", which gave religious freedom to all New Yorkers; and appointed one of the Dutch dignitaries, Cornelius Steenwyck, as mayor of the city.[7]

It was impossible that the two ethnic communities could chart a course into the future that would not eventually be affected by the problems then simmering in Europe. And "liberal" though the policies of the Duke of York and Governor Dongan may have been, they were nonetheless class based. Whereas it was good to be a great landholder, it was less wonderful to be a poor New Yorker. Dongan may have been a decent fellow, but his responses to local controversies could sometimes be draconian.

When English laborers protested that the Dutch "cartmen"—sellers of firewood—had an unjust monopoly on the trade, Dongan began regulating the sale of firewood, with inspectors appointed to grade and measure each cord. This led those English laborers to begin America's first strike.[8]

Even then, New York was becoming something of a melting pot, and it was so aggressively oriented to commerce that the old European prejudices, including Protestant-Catholic enmity, seemed, for a short while, all but irrelevant.

Then Britain's Charles II died, a Catholic convert on his deathbed. His Catholic brother, James, the Duke of York, became King James II, New York became a royal colony, and the Charter of Libertyes was tossed out.

In France, Catholics began persecuting Protestants, there called Huguenots, many of whom fled to New York; there were two hundred Huguenot families in the city by 1688.[9]

Britain's Protestant leaders were alarmed by James II's refusal to enforce anti-Catholic laws and by the birth of his son, James Francis Edward, Prince of Wales—a *Catholic* heir to the throne. So they appealed to King James' daughter Mary, who remained staunchly Anglican. (She was the daughter of James' first wife; it was his second wife who had led him into the Church.) Mary was wed to her first cousin William of Orange, prince of the Netherlands—and also Protestant. Thus it was to them that the insurgents in what would come to be known as the Glorious Revolution turned to offer the British throne.

Dutch forces landed in England and carried out a short, nearly bloodless coup d'état. James II was deposed (fleeing to France without a fight), and the brief window of tolerance and opportunity for Catholics in Britain and New York fell shut. And, to boot, Catholics were thereafter banned from Great Britain's throne.

In 1686, shortly after his ascension, James II had reorganized the colonies along America's northeastern seaboard, from Maine to New Jersey, as the Dominion of New England, which the colonists interpreted as an attack on their well-established sovereignty.

Edmund Andros, who, as governor of the province of New York, had negotiated the final transfer of power over the colony from the Netherlands to Britain, became governor of the new dominion in 1686.

Discontent against the Andros administration and against Lieutenant Governor Francis Nicholson—Andros' replacement for Thomas Dongan and, in effect, his enforcer—first turned into open rebellion in Boston. On April 18, 1689, a well-organized mob attacked the governor's residence and took Andros into custody.

In New York, Nicholson did not learn of the Boston uprising until a week later, but when he did, he did his best to keep news of it—and of the revolution in England—from the citizens in Manhattan and the surrounding area. He failed. And there was news, too, of a war between England and its allies and France and its confreres (the Nine Years' War). In North America this became King William's War, involving England, France, and various Native American tribes. In short, the chaos avoided in England had spilled over to become chaos in the New World (and in much of Europe).

Although he was usually an able administrator, Nicholson's instincts could be authoritarian, his anger his undoing. Because Manhattan's defenses were weak, he attempted to confiscate arms and ammunition from private citizens, and—with the approval of his advisory council (made up of leading Dutch residents)—he sought new import taxes to raise money to shore up New York's military readiness. Both policies were unpopular in the extreme.

Also problematic for Nicholson was the fact that there was no standing military force under his control. Decentralized militias handled defenses in America and they rallied according to their own lights, not the government's. In one meeting with militiamen, Nicholson opined that he would "rather . . . see the Towne on fire than to be commanded by you".[10] The feeling was mutual.

Worst for Nicholson, who was Anglican, was the claim that he remained loyal to James II and had every intention of establishing Catholicism in New York.

Leisler's Rebellion

Enter one Jacob Leisler, who believed not only the Catholic rumor but also that Nicholson's remark about putting the torch to New York should be taken literally.

Around the first of June 1689, in order to "hinder and prevent bloodshed and further mischief", Nicholson imprudently gave the keys to the local powder magazine at Fort James (today the Battery) to a militia leader who demanded them. The militiaman gave the keys, along with the militia's backing, to Leisler, who quickly became the dictator of Southern New York, his influence spreading throughout much of New Jersey and Connecticut as well.

Leisler was a German immigrant, the son of a Calvinist minister. He had been in the employ of the Dutch West India Company as a mercenary when he came to New Amsterdam in 1660, but he later became prosperous as a fur trader. And he had a temper to match Nicholson's. In 1676 he got into a heated argument over theology with one of New York's best-connected ministers, Nicholas Van Rensselaer, implying that Van Rensselaer was acting against his religious superior. Leisler even brought suit against Van Rensselaer, and that led to the poor minister's arrest. But Leisler was determined to strike down the heretic, and he put much of his hard-earned money into Van Rensselaer's prosecution.

A trial was held, Van Rensselaer was acquitted (and reconciled with his superior), and everyone was happy, except Leisler, who had funded the trial and now forfeited that money and, indignity upon indignity, was forced to pay additional costs as well. Two years later (1678) while on a trading journey, Leisler was captured by pirates and had to pay them a considerable ransom to secure his freedom.

Still, he had the courage of his convictions, and when a destitute Huguenot woman and her son were to be sold as slaves to pay their debts, Leisler came forward to purchase them and free them. Indeed, he was so much affected by the plight of the French Protestant immigrants that in 1688 he was instrumental in establishing the town of Nouvelle-Rochelle, which we know today as New Rochelle, New York.

The mayor of New York at this time (who was also one of Nicholson's council members) was Stephanus Van Cortlandt. He began to carry out some of Nicholson's responsibilities, among which was the retention of Protestant office holders, according to the direct order of William and Mary. The anti-Catholic Leisler, now in charge of the city defenses, certainly had no objection to that. Yet he was incensed when Van Cortlandt sacked the city's collector of customs, who happened to be a Catholic. What angered him was not the religious issue but the assertion of authority by the mayor and his council—authority that had been given them by royal decree, although Leisler may not have known this.

What he did know was that Van Cortlandt's choice for customs collector was Nicholas Bayard, a member of the council and, like Van Rensselaer, a patroon—a member of the Dutch elite. Bayard was himself a former mayor, the brother-in-law of Peter Stuyvesant, and the father of the man married to Van Cortlandt's daughter. Bayard was one of the wealthiest men in North America. Leisler took a militia unit and captured the customs house. Bayard barely escaped with his life.

A convention of delegates from New York and New Jersey was called, and Leisler became head of a committee of public safety and was named commander in chief of New York. He was to serve "till orders shall come from their Majesties". Of course, those orders had already come. And there would be others.

In the meantime, Leisler sought to confirm the power he had seized by sending emissaries to England to place his case before the king and queen and to warn them of the imminent invasion of the colonies by the French.

In the seventeenth century, however, communications were unreliable enough to justify sending multiple messages in a distant crisis—the government of Britain not knowing who might be in charge at any given time anywhere in the colonies—and Leisler's men managed to intercept a decree sent to New York's leaders. The envelope bore Nicholson's name, but the decree itself was also addressed in "his absence to such as [shall] for the time being take care for preserving the peace and administering the laws". There was no doubt in the minds of the rebels and their leader who that person was, and Leisler took upon himself Nicholson's title, lieutenant governor, and began to collect taxes.

In order to consolidate his power and authority, Leisler appointed patroons and prominent English New Yorkers to key posts, just as Nicholson and Dongan had done, and, as if to demonstrate his warning about the French threat from Canada, he sent an armed force to New France, which succeeded only in proving that ad hoc military expeditions can easily fail and do so miserably. It was the beginning of the end of Leisler's Rebellion.

At the end of 1690, King William appointed a new governor, Colonel Henry Sloughter, of the dominion of New England and a new lieutenant governor for New York, Major Richard Ingoldesby—both no-nonsense military men. Sloughter, who had the legal Documents confirming his and Ingoldesby's appointments, arrived in New York after his lieutenant. In the interim, Major Ingoldesby had no success in convincing Leisler that he was to be replaced. When Colonel Sloughter arrived, Leisler claimed he could not know if Sloughter was really Sloughter. When it was confirmed that he was, Leisler attempted to negotiate, but the colonel would have none of that. Eventually Leisler came out of Fort James and surrendered.

Sloughter had Leisler and his closest companions thrown into prison. Leisler and another man, Jacob Milborne (Leisler's son-in-law and his partner in the suit against Van Rensselaer), were convicted of treason on April 17, 1691, and sentenced to be "hanged, drawn and quartered, and their estates confiscated".

Appeals were pending until Colonel Sloughter hastily signed death warrants for Leisler and Milborne, and they were executed on May 16. But their sentences were "commuted", which is to say that the men were simply hanged until dead, not hanged until *nearly* dead and then revived, only to be disemboweled and finally beheaded.

A Legacy of Prejudice

The significance of Leisler's Rebellion for Catholics in New York was twofold: They were effectively banned from holding public office, and, because of events in Britain, Ireland, the Netherlands, and France, they were strongly associated with sedition in the imagination of the Protestant rulers of America. European America was *Protestant* America, reflecting the rejection of Rome that had taken hold in the European nations from which most settlers had come to the New World in the 1600s. Catholic France (whose colonists had ended up mostly in Canada and the Mississippi valley) and Catholic Spain (Florida and the West) were enemies of the English, the Dutch, and the Huguenots, and they played in the minds of many generations of Protestant Americans the same sort of role the Soviet Union would play in the minds of both Protestant and Catholic Americans in the twentieth century.

Catholicism was a subversive and heretical force focused on world domination—or so the nativist script explained—and the best way to deal with Catholics was the way Britain had done through the Penal Laws it imposed in England, Scotland, and especially Ireland beginning with Henry VIII's First Act of Supremacy in 1534, by which he made England Protestant and himself head of the church.

Of course, similar laws (and laws that were effectively, if not explicitly, anti-Catholic) were already on the books in the emerging colonies. As we've seen, the Dutch settlers permitted no Masses in New Amsterdam. As of 1606, Virginia had made the Church of England its established church. As historian John Tracy Ellis has written, a "universal anti-Catholic bias was brought to Jamestown in 1607 and vigorously cultivated in all the thirteen colonies from Massachusetts to Georgia".[11] And American Protestants, otherwise contentious about their doctrinal differences, could find amity in a common dislike of Roman Catholics.

As Ellis writes, there are four points to keep in mind with regard to Catholics in prerevolutionary America:

> First, a universal anti-Catholic bias was brought to Jamestown in 1607 and vigilantly cultivated in all the thirteen colonies.... Second, [despite persecution] English and Irish [Catholics] ... clung to their religious faith. Third, the Catholic minority in their brief tenure of power in two colonies introduced the principle of religious toleration. Finally, the absence of domination by any one of the ... Protestant churches fostered the principle of religious freedom for all.[12]

Examples of anti-Catholicism are abundant and irrefutable:

In 1642, Virginia prohibited Catholics from entering the colony, as did the Massachusetts Bay Colony in 1647.

Cecil Calvert (Lord Baltimore), the Catholic founder of tolerant Maryland, was temporarily exiled from his colony in 1628 for refusing to acknowledge the religious supremacy of King Charles I. But he returned, and in 1649 Maryland published the Act Concerning Religion, better known as the Toleration Act, although not without irony. It allowed freedom of religion to all Christians who professed the Trinity. But it threatened a sentence of death upon anyone who denied the divinity of Jesus Christ.

The act held sway until Oliver Cromwell, the "Puritan Moses," "Old Ironsides"— the English Jacob Leisler—appointed a commissioner to oversee Maryland and rescinded the act. Upon Cromwell's death and the return of the British monarchy under Charles II, the Calverts returned to power in Maryland, and the act was restored.

But in 1692, the Catholic government of Maryland was overthrown, and the Church of England became the colony's established church. Anglicanism was financially supported to a great extent by onerous taxes levied against Catholics. Mass was prohibited, the sacraments were banned, Catholic schools were closed, and no Catholic could hold any elected or appointed political office. All this changed, of course, after the Revolution, especially when the Jesuit Father John Carroll was designated provincial superior (prefect apostolic) to America's missions.

In New York, meanwhile, in the aftermath of Leisler's Rebellion, King William ordered the Test Act of a generation earlier to be rigorously applied, which meant that all office holders had to "abjure their belief in transubstantiation and the veneration of the Blessed Virgin Mary and the saints".[13] In 1700 New York's Provincial Assembly passed the Act against Jesuits and Popish Priests, with its penalty of life imprisonment for any Catholic priest discovered in the colony.[14] The situation in New York had deteriorated so that conditions for Catholics were essentially those faced by any persecuted minority in a modern police state. (It is useful to recall that in only a few decades, England was officially Catholic, then Protestant, then Catholic again, and finally, and to this day, Protestant.)

This situation continued into the eighteenth century. In fact, the last legal restrictions were lifted only after the American Revolution and the ratification of the Constitution, with its First Amendment protections. There were, however, some places where American Catholics could dwell in relative safety all along. In the seventeenth century, William Penn welcomed Catholics into his colony, and Pennsylvania law tolerated all who believed in God.

After the Revolution, Father Carroll sent Father Ferdinand Farmer of Philadelphia to New York as its first vicar-general, although Father Farmer commuted, as we would say today, between the two cities. He was instrumental in building New York's first Catholic church, St. Peter's, but he was too ill to attend the dedication ceremony in 1785 and died in Philadelphia the following summer.

Even in the postrevolutionary period, anti-Catholicism was rampant. In 1788, no less a figure than John Jay—one of the authors of the *Federalist Papers* and the man who would become America's first chief justice the very next year—called upon the state legislature in New York to establish a religious test for political office, requiring that candidates renounce all foreign allegiances, including to the pope. To be fair, Jay also wanted the same restriction placed on those who gave fidelity to the Church of England. Jay was a Founding Father—both of the United States and of nativism.

Reflecting upon his four years as America's ambassador to Catholic France, Thomas Jefferson wrote to Horatio G. Spafford: "In every country and in every age, the priest has been hostile to liberty. He is always in alliance with the despot, abetting his abuses in return for protection of his own" (letter, March 17, 1814).

As the historian John Higham wrote, anti-Catholicism is "the most luxuriant, tenacious tradition of paranoiac agitation in American history".[15] Or, as historian Arthur Schlesinger Sr. put it, anti-Catholicism is "the deepest-held bias in the history of the American people".[16] Most succinct perhaps—and more focused on our own time—is the quip attributed to Daniel Patrick Moynihan: Anti-Catholicism is the "last acceptable prejudice".

This is not, as some commentators have suggested, a "lost" or "repressed" dimension of American history, although it is not inaccurate to say that it has not been sufficiently emphasized, principally because later generations of Catholics would succeed, assimilate, and consider themselves, for better or for worse, more American than Catholic.

In any case, it was into this landscape that Catholics came to New York in the great era of immigration in the nineteenth century—and among them priests and then bishops and, finally, archbishops. If some American Protestants had been tolerant of Catholics when Catholics were few (yet many had loathed even those few), imagine how the liberal minded and the nativist alike would react when war, famine, and intolerance in Europe began bringing Catholics to America in their hundreds, thousands, and millions.

The stories of the shepherds who guided those immigrants begin here.

The First Bishop: R. Luke Concanen, O.P. (1808–1810)

From an engraving by L. Hollyer

He just could not make it to New York.

The Right Reverend Richard Luke Concanen, an Irishman who had long been an agent at the Vatican for the Irish bishops, was appointed New York's first bishop in 1808 by his friend Pope Pius VII. He tried to get from Rome to Leghorn (Livorno) and thence to Naples, which finally he did, but, because of embargoes in force during the Napoleonic Wars, he was prevented from sailing to the United States by the French forces in possession of the city. Sixty-two years old and in fragile health, he died in Naples before he was able to board a ship for America.

Bishop Concanen was well known to John Carroll, America's first archbishop (elevated in the same *acta*—the bulls *Pontificii Muneris* and *Ex Debito Pastoralis Officii*—that gave New York to Concanen), because the two had shared a correspondence about the Church in America.

Carroll was essentially America's de facto primate, and his archdiocese comprised the whole United States. He suggested that the Vatican establish separate dioceses in America—specifically, Boston, Philadelphia, Bardstown (Kentucky), and New York—and recommended priests to head up these new sees—all but one, that is.

Carroll could think of nobody capable of handling the New York assignment. As he wrote to the prefect of the Sacra Congregatio de Propaganda Fide (more familiarly Propaganda Fide or just Propaganda, the Vatican office that is now known as the Congregation for the Evangelization of Peoples):

> It seems necessary that in the beginning the bishop of Boston should exercise jurisdiction over the territory ... [of the] diocese-to-be of New York. For none of the priests residing in that territory appear to me to be suited for the episcopacy. I therefore refrain from recommending anyone for that responsible post.[17]

Note that the soon-to-be archbishop put stress on *residence* in New York as key. He believed strongly that the best bishop for any diocese is one who knows the people and the problems in the area—and is known to the people. (Informally, he had raised the name of a priest in Baltimore, the Frenchman Ambrose Maréchal, but that went nowhere. Maréchal would become Baltimore's third archbishop in 1817.)

We do not know why Bishop Carroll did not suggest one of three fellow Jesuits then living and working in America: Leonard Neale (Carroll's own coadjutor and a native-born Marylander), Benedict Fenwick (also native born), and Anthony Kohlmann (who came from Alsace and had migrated to Washington, D.C.). Neale had become bishop coadjutor in 1808, the first consecrated in the United States, and was presumed to be Carroll's successor in Baltimore. We may also presume that the seventy-three-year-old Carroll needed Neale at his side. Father Fenwick was a Marylander and therefore known well to the bishop, although he was just twenty-six and newly ordained at the time Carroll needed a man for New York. (He would become bishop of Boston in 1825.) Kohlmann, on the other hand, was thirty-seven, which seems far too young for episcopal appointment in our era, but Bishop Jean-Louis Cheverus—the pope's choice to head up Boston—was only forty, and—although his appointment came a decade later—John England was named bishop of Charleston, South Carolina, when he was just thirty-four. In fact, Father Kohlmann, who was a talented administrator, was also well known to Bishop Carroll and Bishop Concanen, although perhaps not so well to Pope Pius VII. When Concanen's passage to America was delayed, Carroll sent Kohlmann to New York as administrator and vicar-general.

In any case, Pius VII believed he knew the right man for New York, and that was Concanen. Carroll was not consulted. Carroll had hoped to find a capable "New Yorker" very soon, but that was not soon enough for the pope, who was in a hurry to make appointments before the French army carried him off into exile. (Finding a priest from New York was no easy task, as America had only two seminaries, both in Maryland, and therefore few native-born New York priests. Thus, the episcopal appointments made for America, in addition to the Irish Concanen, were all European-born: Boston's Cheverus was French, Philadelphia's Michael Egan was Irish, and Bardstown's Benedict Flaget was French. Carroll and Neale were the only native-born Americans in this first hierarchy.)

And as the historian Monsignor Thomas J. Shelley has written, "Carroll was unhappy with the selection of Concanen to head the Church in New York, but Concanen may have been even more unhappy."[18] Although Carroll knew that the Irishman was passionate about Catholic missionary work in America, he was also aware that Concanen knew next to nothing about New York. And, after all, as the idea for the creation of a New York diocese was discussed, Father Concanen had seemed keen that his friend and fellow Irish Dominican John Connolly be the one chosen. But the election fell upon Concanen all the same.

Doctor No

When Pius VII chose him for the new post in the New World, it was not the first time Concanen had been designated for episcopal assignment. The previous pope, Pius VI, had tapped him in 1798 to become bishop and apostolic administrator of the unified Irish diocese of Kilmacduagh and Kilfenora, but the Reverend Dr. Concanen had declined the appointment owing to poor health. At that time he had written to a friend in New York,[19] the Reverend Dr. William O'Brien (of whom Elizabeth Ann Seton once wrote, "They say [he] is the only priest in New York"):

> Conscious of my inability for the awful Episcopal Charge, I have, from the very beginning, renounced the Appointment. Tho my resignation cannot be accepted till after the Election of the new Pope [Pius VI died in 1799], yet I have no room to doubt but it will be readily admitted; especially as I have forwarded and recommended to the Cardinals of the Congregation, a postulation received this week from the Canons and Priests of the two united Dioceses.... I am resolved to live and die in the obscure and retired way of life I have chosen from my youth.[20]

There is a problem with this statement. If illness were at that point the reason for Father Concanen's decision to decline to become a bishop in Ireland, why did he make reference to obscurity and retirement? In a later (1803) letter to Bishop Carroll,[21] he assures his correspondent that he will undertake any labor on Carroll's behalf *in Rome*, especially since Carroll's own agent there, a Reverend Mr. Connell, was ill and his "gouty indisposition may keep him confined". But then Concanen adds:

> I enjoy, thanks be to God, perfect health in my ripe age of 56 years; and continue to do the business in this Court of almost all the Prelates of Ireland, of some of the Apost. Vicars of England and the Mission of S. Domingo, Martinique, Holland, etc.; and therefore hope to prove active in Service.

Curious, perhaps, for a man who just a few years earlier was too sickly to head to Ireland on behalf of the Holy Father. Still, this is insufficient evidence to suggest that Father Concanen simply loved Rome too much to leave—Rome, where December temperatures are in the fifties, whereas in Kilmacduagh (or Manhattan) the winter temperatures regularly fell below freezing. (One historian has argued that Concanen, always concerned about his health, was actually inclined to accept the New York post because he thought the climate on America's eastern coast would be agreeable.[22] This is almost certainly not true.)

In any case, his letters to Bishop Carroll and others made clear his unhappiness about the New York appointment. Although, at sixty-one, he was a dozen years younger than Carroll, he was yet a decade and a half older than the other new bishops, and his frequent claims of illness must, if only in retrospect, be taken seriously. World travel at the turn of the nineteenth century was arduous and therefore, for some, dangerous.

Richard Luke Concanen had come to Rome via the great Catholic seminary, the College of the Holy Cross in Louvain, Belgium. As a young man seeking a proper education and priestly ordination, he was also a refugee. In his short biography of Concanen in the *Catholic Historical Review* in 1916, the Reverend Victor F. O'Daniel laments the fact that the place of the future bishop's birth is uncertain. O'Daniel speculates that it was "Connaught, in the ecclesiastical province of Tuam. Both the county of Galway and that of Roscommon have been given the honor of being the place of his birth."[23] (An 1872 book, *Lives of the Deceased Bishops of the Catholic Church in the United States*, suggests that Concanen hailed from Kilbegnet in Galway, where he was born on December 27, 1747.) Connacht (today the preferred spelling of Connaught) is almost certainly the correct Irish province, and Tuam, an archdiocese within Connacht, is surely the correct ecclesiastical province. Tuam includes Galway.

Historian Monsignor Thomas Shelley has written that Concanen was born in Kilbegnet, though he places it in Roscommon, "and was baptized the next day by a Dominican friar".[24] So what we may say with confidence is that Concanen was, as they say in Ireland, a "man of the West". There is no doubt (we have his own testimony about it) that he left Ireland in his late teens or early twenties to escape oppressive English laws that made his higher education problematic, although—because he came from a well-to-do family—his early education had been good. As O'Daniel phrases it: "Circumstances hostile to Catholic schools in Ireland at that period obliged the youth of the country to repair to the Continent for their education."[25] Many young Irishmen did so. Indeed, the Irish diaspora has millions of similar stories.

We know that Concanen must have excelled in his schooling at Louvain, because his later success in Rome as a Dominican friar was both rapid and remarkable. He arrived in Rome in June of 1769, in his twenty-first year. He was by then a member of the Order of Preachers, having made his initial profession of vows, at which point he also took on a new name, Luke, not given to him at baptism. We may assume that it was by this name that he was addressed (on those few occasions when the use of a Christian name was considered appropriate), since thereafter he was invariably referred to as R. Luke Concanen.

He was ordained a priest in Rome a few days before Christmas in 1770 and received a master of sacred theology degree in 1783. He gained what might have proved valuable administrative experience—had he ever reached New York—as subprior and prior of Rome's Dominican monastery, San Clemente, and as an aide to two heads of the Order of Preachers.

But what especially brought him to the attention of Propaganda—and of the pope—was his knowledge of America. It is not that he knew very much about New York, but that he grasped better than most the legal and spiritual sensibility of the new American nation. As we would say today, he "got" religious freedom in its specific American context. This, together with his long advocacy of American missions, Carroll's unwillingness to choose a candidate, and the pope's unwillingness to wait, made Concanen seem to be the only choice.

Monsignor Shelley quips that Concanen's advocacy for America's toleration of religion (in Concanen's words) "without preference for any [religion] in particular" would, a century later, probably have gotten him tagged as an *Americanist*.[26]

And as if the burden placed upon Concanen was not—from his point of view—already heavy enough, he was given still more authority by the Dominican Order. In an unprecedented decision, the Dominicans (themselves under a kind of siege amidst the ongoing Napoleonic Wars, and anxious to make quick decisions about various matters) invested Concanen with "the government of his Order in all the New World".[27] What made this extraordinary was the fact that upon becoming bishop of New York, he was, essentially, no longer under the direction of the Dominicans. But who else was there?

After his consecration, Bishop Concanen attempted to find passage to America, going first to Livorno and then to Naples. Perhaps a younger, haler, or simply more energetic man might—either through forthrightness or by guile—have found a way to make the journey. Bishop Concanen did not.

After failing in Livorno, he returned to Rome. More than a year passed, and he thought he might try traveling by land to France—even at the risk of being detained there—since ships were regularly sailing from there to America. And he might well have attempted this alternative, had word not come from Naples in the early spring of 1810 that ships bound for America were docked there and preparing to embark. So he hurried to Naples.

It seemed that here too his passage would be blocked, but American diplomatic officials intervened, and he was ready to set off on June 17, bound for Salem, Massachusetts. Then, within hours, that diplomatic victory was dashed, when French officials (still swept up in their Revolution's anticlericalism) discovered that his papers were not valid.

It was a shock for the bishop. And it may well have played a role in his death two days later. Bishop Concanen was buried in the Church of San Domenico Maggiore in Naples.

But as Edward Cardinal Egan wrote in 2006: "The story, however, does not end there." As it happens, Concanen was buried in an unmarked grave, which never seemed appropriate for the first bishop of New York. So in 1978 Cardinal Terence Cooke traveled to Naples to lay a plaque at the gravesite. Cardinal Egan tells the rest of the story:

> As they [Cooke and his New York entourage] were leaving the church, they met a Catholic Chaplain of the United States Navy whose ship was anchored in the harbor of Naples. In the course of their conversation with the Chaplain, they suggested that he might want to visit the tomb of the first Bishop of New York and see the plaque that adorned it.
>
> This the Chaplain did, and thus another of Bishop Concanen's successors knelt in prayer before his final resting place. The Chaplain's name was Reverend John J. O'Connor.[28]

And O'Connor, of course, was a future archbishop of New York.

The Second Bishop: John Connolly, O.P. (1814–1825)

Illustration from John Talbot Smith, *The Catholic Church in New York*

As mentioned earlier, Bishop Concanen would have preferred to have the See of New York given to his associate John Connolly. And in 1814 it was. The delay in making the appointment had to do with the pope's situation: he was a prisoner of Napoleon.

Father Connolly's journey in life closely parallels that of his late friend. Born in Ireland (but in the east, in County Meath) in 1750 (just three years after Concanen), John Connolly traveled to Louvain to the College of the Holy Cross, where, like his friend and sponsor Concanen, he distinguished himself both in scholarship and in administration.

But it should not be assumed that Connolly and Concanen were close friends at the time of the latter's death. Far from it. In part because of the Napoleonic Wars, the Church was in straitened circumstances, in terms of both leadership and finances, and the lingering in Italy of Bishop Concanen had placed an unwanted burden upon the Dominicans in Rome, who were required to support this man who for health and other reasons seemed unwilling ever to depart for his new assignment in America. Concanen often complained of poverty, but Connolly and the others suspected he was simply parsimonious: He had always had sufficient funds available to donate notable sums to the missions in the United States, and so it was thought that he had plenty of money to support himself in his too-long-delayed departure for his new assignment.

All this was mooted by Concanen's death.

Connolly himself did not immediately board a ship for America but first went back to Ireland, with the intention of making a last visit to family and friends and of recruiting at least a few priests to accompany him to the New World. He had been consecrated in Rome on November 6, 1814, but did not reach America until nearly a year later. In the meantime, Anthony Kohlmann, S.J., was doing his best—at Archbishop Carroll's behest—to keep a lid on New York until its first resident bishop could take up his duties in the city. Kohlmann was aided by Father Benedict

Fenwick, who had been ordained a priest the very year that New York became a diocese. (Fenwick would go on to become president of Georgetown, America's oldest Catholic college and in 1825 would succeed Cheverus as bishop of Boston.)

The Kohlmann Interregnum

Anthony Kohlmann was Alsatian, born on July 13, 1771, in the town of Kayserberg. Given the historical back-and-forth of Alsace between Germany and France, he grew up speaking both French and German. At this time, however, Alsace was French, and so Kohlmann was known as a *Kaysersbergeois*. According to one biographer, his path to the priesthood was both direct, in that it was an early ambition that not even the anticlerical French Revolution could dislodge, and jagged, in that in his religious profession he went from the Capuchins to the Sacred Heart Fathers, and finally to the Jesuits.[29] In the process, his journey took him from France to Germany, Austria, England, Russia, America, and finally Italy.

In this last stage of his journey, when he was a professor at the Pontifical Gregorian University in Rome (initially the Collegio Romano)—where he taught from 1824 more or less until his death in 1836—one of his students was Vincenzo Gioacchino Raffaele Luigi Pecci, the future Pope Leo XIII.

It may well be that Kohlmann wished to become a Jesuit from the start, but the order was undergoing a suppression—via a 1773 papal "brief" (*Dominus ac Redemptor*) by Clement XIV. The suppression, which would last forty years, affected most of Western and Southern Europe and the European colonies in South America and drove Kohlmann into Russia, then something of a safe haven for Jesuits.

Why the suppression? In the simplest terms, it was a response to the rising tide of the Enlightenment with its strong anticlerical bias, aimed especially at the Jesuits, who had become powerful—not least in education—and were thus a ripe target for secular leaders, who could more easily attack the "pope's men" than the pope himself. Indeed, Pope Clement suppressed the Jesuits more to placate secularist governments than because he had any true bias against the order.[30]

In the United States, Bishop Carroll was struggling with issues that arose from the suppression, specifically concerning the status of brother Jesuits who had come to the United States seeking to practice their ministries in a territory not directly affected by the suppression. In 1805, Carroll wrote to the Jesuits' superior general, then in Russia, concerning the status of sixteen men of various positions within the order (including some novices) who were residents in his diocese. He was directed to name a superior for the Jesuits in the United States.

Robert Molyneux got that job, and in 1806 he opened a novitiate at Georgetown.

It was in 1804 that Anthony Kohlmann, still a novice himself (because of his late entry into the Jesuit Order), came from Russia to Baltimore. From there he went to Georgetown to join Molyneux as assistant to the novice master. Father Kohlmann had become proficient in English during his time in England.

Back in Rome, Bishop Concanen wrote to Archbishop Carroll to suggest that he send someone to New York to deal with issues there—among them the organization of the new diocese—until he, Concanen, could make passage to America. His letter reached Carroll in September of 1808, but Carroll had already sent Kohlmann (with Benedict Fenwick) to New York.

Now in Manhattan, Kohlmann took over as rector of New York City's first and (in 1808) only Catholic church, St. Peter's. Mass had first been celebrated there in 1786, and, three years before the arrival of Kohlmann and Fenwick, Elizabeth Ann Seton had been received into the Catholic faith there. (The church still stands on Barclay Street in Lower Manhattan, although it was rebuilt in 1834.) Because New York was then the capital of the United States, diplomatic concerns prevailed over the widespread anti-Catholic feeling of the time and smoothed the way for the building of a church that could minister to French and Spanish dignitaries as well as the growing number of German and, especially, Irish Catholic immigrants. (On September 11, 2001, 215 years after its founding, St. Peter's became a staging point for medical and rescue efforts after the terrorist attacks on the World Trade Center, and it was to St. Peter's that the body of Father Mychal Judge—the first confirmed death that day—was brought.)

In a letter written shortly after his arrival in New York, Kohlmann described the lay of the land:

> The congregation chiefly consists of Irish, some hundred of French and as many Germans; in all, according to the common estimation, of 14,000 souls.... The parish was so neglected in every respect, that it goes beyond all conception.[31]

Kohlmann's most immediate response was to decide that he needed to build a new church—indeed, a cathedral—which he began immediately, with the approval of Archbishop Carroll, who suggested the name St. Patrick's.

More will be said later about the problem of trusteeism in New York's Catholic churches, but in this case Father Kohlmann had the approval of the city's Catholic laymen (principally the merchant and philanthropist Dominick Lynch and Andrew Morris, the first Catholic elected to city goverment)[32] and of the city's Protestant fathers, too, although this latter group suggested that the new cathedral be built outside the city. After all, for those within the then-current city limits, there was already St. Peter's (which at its inception in 1785 was also outside the city proper). So Kohlmann bought a large parcel of vacant land on Mulberry Street between Prince and Houston (pronounced by New Yorkers as HOUSE-ton) that was, as Father Kohlmann put it, "so very close to the wilderness ... that foxes were frequent visitors".[33] Today, of course, that intersection is in the heart of the area known as Nolita (North of Little Italy)—not really in the center of Manhattan, given that Manhattan has many centers.

The cathedral was designed by Joseph F. Mangin, the architect of New York's City Hall. The cornerstone of St. Patrick's was laid on June 8, 1809.

Three thousand people attended the dedication of St. Patrick's (today, Old St. Patrick's) on May 14, 1815, by Boston's bishop John Cheverus. Father Fenwick delivered the homily that day (being an American by birth, he was easier to understand than Father Kohlmann). Among his listeners was Mayor DeWitt Clinton.

Not long after the dedication, Father Kohlmann, in anticipation of Bishop John Connolly's arrival, returned to Georgetown. Father Fenwick took over as vicar-general for a year before also heading to Washington as president of Georgetown—his last step before succeeding Cheverus in Boston.

But now a significant anecdote concerning Kohlmann and Fenwick, before we turn to a historic event that caught up the former: A short time before the ground-breaking of Old St. Pat's, Fathers Kohlmann and Fenwick received a note from a woman in Greenwich Village requesting that they come to the bedside of a dying man. That would not have been extraordinary had the man not been the atheist Thomas Paine, the author of *Common Sense* and, more to the point, *The Age of Reason*—an anti-religious manifesto in which he wrote: "I do not believe in the creed professed by the Jewish church, by the Roman church, by the Greek church, by the Turkish church, by the Protestant church, nor by any church that I know of. My own mind is my own church."[34]

Could it be that the man who considered Christianity to be a "fabulous invention" desired to enter the Church before meeting his Maker? No.

As Peter Schineller, S.J. wrote for *America* magazine, the woman who summoned the priests—she had been baptized by Fenwick—had something other than salvation in mind:

> [She] had told Paine that only a Catholic priest could cure him. When the two priests arrived and started talking with Paine, they asked about his soul rather than his bodily pains. Paine, rationalist to the end, ordered them out of the room. According to the account of Fr. Fenwick, they were chased away by Paine and left, followed by blasphemies.[35]

And now a final story of Father Kohlmann before we turn to Bishop John Connolly's days in New York.

The Seal of the Confessional

Kohlmann had founded, and he and Benedict Fenwick had both taught at, the New York Literary Institution, New York's first Catholic school, erected on the site now occupied by the new St. Patrick's Cathedral. The area was then known as the village of Elgin.[36] Both men had done the work of priests: celebrating the Eucharist, baptizing babies, burying the dead, and hearing confessions. It was in this last capacity that Father Kohlmann became the center of an epochal court case in American history, an early demonstration of the nation's commitment to religious freedom.

No matter how many Protestants showed up to help dedicate a cathedral or elect a Catholic politician, there remained among them deep suspicion about the practices of the "popish" faith. So when a Catholic man, Daniel Philips, went to confession at St. Peter's and told Father Kohlmann that he had received some stolen jewels, and after Father Kohlmann returned those jewels to the victim (another St. Peter's parishioner, James Keating), the stage was set for a dramatic confrontation between Church and state.

Having received the jewels back by Father Kohlmann's intervention, Keating went to the police to let them know they could drop the case. But restitution does not erase the crime, and the police demanded that Keating identify the person who had returned his property. Keating admitted it was his church's rector.

Now official attention fell upon Kohlmann—first in police interrogation, then in a grand-jury proceeding, and finally in Manhattan's Court of General Sessions.

But before the trial, testimony from others revealed the names of the two men who had stolen the jewels, and from their accounts Philips' name emerged, so the prosecutor was willing to separate Father Kohlmann from the case.

The good priest was relieved—that is, until he met with the trustees of St. Peter's, some of whom were lawyers. They saw in *People v. Philips* an opportunity to establish a legal precedent, and they convinced Kohlmann to give testimony that would enable him to *refuse* to reveal Philips' name in court. There was a charade concerning contempt of court, but what the judges, the prosecutor, the defense attorneys, and the church trustees—everyone, really, except the thieves and poor Mr. Philips—were after was a decision about the inviolability of words heard by a priest in the sacrament of penance.

One of the defense counsels in the case was the Protestant lawyer William Sampson, an Irish immigrant who had suffered imprisonment and exile from England and Ireland for having defended Irish Catholics against persecution and discrimination. After the trial, Sampson wrote an account of the case under the splendid title *The Catholic Question in America: Whether a Roman Catholic Clergyman Be in Any Case Compellable to Disclose the Secrets of Auricular Confession.*[37]

Mr. Sampson successfully argued that if the tenets of a religion cannot be freely and wholly practiced, then the religion cannot be practiced, period. "The people of whose will [the Constitution] speaks", he told the court, "were not of any one church but of many and various sects all of whom had suffered more or less in Europe for their religious tenets, and many ... had unrelentingly persecuted each other." He continued:

> The Catholics, it is true, bore the hardest burden of all, but the others would be very sorry, I believe, to put aside our Constitution and resume their ancient condition. And God forbid it should be so.

In the court's unanimous decision, rendered on June 14, 1813, Mayor DeWitt Clinton, the presiding member of the court who had served in the U.S. Senate and would later become New York's sixth governor, wrote:

> It is essential to the free exercise of a religion, that its ordinances should be administered—that its ceremonies as well as its essentials should be protected. Secrecy is of the essence of penance. The sinner will not confess, nor will the priest receive his confession, if the veil of secrecy is removed.

This was the first affirmation of confessional privilege in American history.

In a later case, *People v. Smith* (1817), a Staten Island court found that the right to such privileged communication did not extend to Protestant clergy, since no actual *sacrament* of penance exists in Protestantism.

But the *Smith* case led to a New York law protecting *all* communication of a spiritual nature between clergy and penitents.

Bishop Connolly Arrives

The arrival of John Connolly in New York was not without controversy. He had been at sea for more than two months, and, with no means of communicating from the ship, he landed in Manhattan unannounced on November 24, 1815, and was met by nobody as he disembarked from his ship, the *Sally*. He must have lingered for a moment on an East River pier, wondering what to do. He might have hoped to be greeted by a delegation from the Friendly Sons of St. Patrick, but there was no one. He must have taken a carriage to St. Patrick's Cathedral, because John Murphy Farley, fourth archbishop of New York, tells us early in his 1908 history of the *new* St. Patrick's that Bishop Connolly arrived in New York and "that day took possession of his cathedral, the finest church in the city, and unequaled in the whole country".[38]

The new bishop, however, had not done his episcopal duty and notified Archbishop Carroll of his arrival. Indeed, the more appropriate entry into his new see would have been through the port of Baltimore, with a visit paid to his archbishop, and only then an overland journey to New York to take up his duties.

This discourtesy was not unintentional. Although the Irish in New York—those who were aware of Connolly's appointment—may well have welcomed his coming, it was well known in Rome that Connolly was considered by many Americans to be, as an Irishman, a British subject.[39] This was problematic, since America was fighting Great Britain in the War of 1812. News of Connolly's consecration had come just a few months after British troops had occupied Washington, D.C., and set the White House ablaze. Connolly, who as an Irishman was only too aware of the oppression of Irish Catholics by the English, may have regarded this attitude as absurd, but he was certainly aware of it.

Not only did Bishop Connolly not communicate with Archbishop Carroll, he also failed to send a collegial greeting to Father Kohlmann, who had administered the diocese for seven years. But it must also be remembered that Connolly was a Dominican and both Carroll and Kohlmann were Jesuits, and that their order was only just emerging from decades of suppression. As native-born Americans regarded Irish immigrants with suspicion, and the Irish regarded any cleric not Irish-born (Kohlmann principally) with suspicion, so the Dominicans looked down on the Jesuits—all in all, an unpleasant portrait of religious and cultural harmony, but confirmation to some extent of what Carroll had anticipated when news reached him of Connolly's appointment:

> Mr. Connolly is appointed, with whom none of us are acquainted; nor has anyone in this country been consulted. I wish that this may not become a very dangerous precedent, fruitful of mischief by drawing censure upon our religion, and false opinion of the servility of our principles.

Carroll was especially miffed, because in 1809 Bishop Concanen had assured him that "no arrangement of any importance regarding the Churches of the United States" would be made "without your previous advice and consent."[40]

Of his experience in Rome, of which it is claimed he "saved" Dominican properties from rampaging French troops, Connolly had written:

> By having obtained leave from the Republic to open that church after its suppression, and serve the public in it as chaplain and confessor, without any emolument, I have saved it from destruction, as also the convent and library.... It was to render this service to my order that I determined to stay here, if permitted by the Republic. This

city is in a deplorable state, owing to a great scarcity of provisions, particularly bread, and the number of robberies committed almost every night in the streets, houses, and even churches.[41]

As it happened, he also found conditions in New York in a deplorable state, if for very different reasons.

Fathers Kohlmann and Fenwick had done the very best they could, and they accomplished a lot: the sound management of St. Peter's Church, the construction of Old St. Patrick's Cathedral, and an increase in Mass attendance and confession; and the establishment of the Literary Institution as well as the introduction of schools and orphanages run by Ursuline nuns and, strange as it may seem, Trappist monks. But by the time Connolly arrived, except for the activities of the two churches, all this was gone—as were Kohlmann and Fenwick. And what those two had been unable to resolve—and we saw a bit of this in the story of *People v. Philips*—was the problem of trusteeism. There was also a priest problem, in terms of both their numbers and their discipline.

The Challenge of Trusteeism

The Catholic community in New York City had grown from the three people mentioned by Father Jogues in the 1640s to some fifteen thousand souls by 1815. There were just two churches and four priests in the city, and it was difficult for the priests to manage the churches effectively. Elsewhere in the state the problem of the priest-to-parishioner ratio, while not as great as in the big city, was exacerbated by the sometimes large distances a priest had to travel to visit his parishioners.

But it was not ratios or distances alone that led nonclerical Catholics to take control of the governance and ownership of their churches. As Canadian historian W. Barry Smith has written, these laymen were Americans caught up in the early years of the new republican democracy and well acquainted with the success of their (often hostile) Protestant neighbors:

> As familiarity grew, so did a sympathy for the manner in which the Protestant churches in the United States were governed, i.e., by the people who built the churches and called their clergy to serve them and determined their length of service. Thus, while Catholicism was still suspect at best in most Protestant minds, it learned from the very people who were its supposed enemies.[42]

The proximity to well-run Methodist, Presbyterian, and Episcopal churches was one reason Catholic laymen found trusteeism attractive, but it was only one of several.

Until the arrival of Connolly in 1815, there were no local bishops to oversee parish appointments. Archbishop Carroll often had no idea who might be presenting himself as a priest to the people in any given community throughout the United States. And, as noted, there were few priests available in any case. But there was also another dimension of Catholics' proximity to Protestants.

Anti-Catholicism, once enshrined in colonial law, was no longer de jure, but it continued to be a de facto problem. The very presence of priests in clerical garb was sometimes the occasion for enmity or even violence by nativists, and it was hard for lay Catholics to resist getting caught up in it themselves. It's not that they did not want priests, without whom they could not have access to the sacraments, except through heretical acts, but they did not want the priests too visible in leadership. This desire to protect their spiritual fathers may yet have contributed to a certain disrespect for them. As we will see, this would change dramatically beginning in 1842 with the elevation of John Joseph Hughes as New York's first archbishop.

In 1822 Pope Pius VII would condemn trusteeism in the bull *Ad futuram rei memoriam*, asserting that Church lands were Church lands, period, and could not be owned or run except by those in holy orders.[43] And laymen would no longer be permitted, as had been the case in the heyday of trusteeism, to hire and fire their church's pastors, although the tangle of ecclesiastical and civil law was such that trusteeism continued for some years.

And trusteeism had been part of New York Catholic history from the start. Ground was broken in 1784 for St. Peter's Church even before it had a pastor (having been incorporated under state law as owned by the Trustees of the Roman Catholic Church in the City of New York), and when Bishop Carroll appointed Father Charles Whelan pastor a year later (the city's *first* resident priest), the founding trustees were initially accepting. But Whelan soon acquired an ambitious assistant, Father Andrew Nugent, who was, like Whelan, a Capuchin. Both priests were also Irish, so there was no bone of contention there. But Father Nugent was apparently the superior preacher, and in 1786 the trustees fired Father Whelan and replaced him with Nugent. Carroll was horrified: "The unity and Catholicity of the Church is at end" were he to accept such a decision, he wrote to the trustees, adding that the Church in America "would be formed into distinct and independent Societies; nearly in the same manner as the Congregational Presbyterians of your neighboring New England States".[44]

Carroll would not regain control over St. Peter's until 1790—and would never eliminate the problem of trusteeism. Father Nugent was out, though, having run afoul of the trustees, and was replaced by William O'Brien—the priest who would bring Elizabeth Ann Seton into the Church.

Archbishop John Joseph Hughes would later write (1853) that trusteeism, in its more limited applications—regarded a priori—was not objectionable. Indeed, "no system could be less objectionable ... both to secure advantages to those congregations, and at the same time to recommend the Catholic religion to the liberal consideration of Protestant sentiment in the country."[45]

What made trusteeism anathema to Rome and the American hierarchy was exactly the issue raised by the firing of Father Whelan by the trustees at St. Peter's. Whatever other valuable contributions might be made by laymen to the life of the Church, the appointment of priests to their parishes by laymen or even their expression of preferences in the naming of bishops for dioceses was an intolerable affront to apostolic succession.

Bishop Connolly Takes Charge

One impetus behind the trustee movement was ethnic diversity, plenty of which was already evident in New York in 1815 when John Connolly began his decade of service. The Irish wanted Irish priests, the Germans wanted Germans, and so on— and they wanted their fellow old-countrymen with an intensity the melting-pot

Americans of later generations would not feel. "As Bishop Connolly quickly dis-covered," historian John Talbot Smith would write, "New York Catholics were mainly Irish, but they also included French and Germans with a sprinkling of other nationalities as well."[46]

Connolly also discovered that New York was not Rome. He had just three churches in his massive diocese (the two in Manhattan and one up in Albany) and fewer than ten priests. The diocese encompassed all of New York State and most of northern New Jersey.

Among that handful of priests were a few competent men. We've mentioned Benedict Fenwick. But there were also some itinerant priests—often refugees from France and Ireland—who had fled the oppression of revolution and legal discrimi-nation and were not fully accredited and sometimes taught a Catholicism that was borderline heresy, and occasionally over the border. But to communities of French and Irish, it was sweetness itself to hear the Gospel in their own language or accent.[47]

And there were priests who admired the assertiveness of lay trustees. One such cleric was Father Peter A. Malou, who ran afoul of Bishop Connolly right from the start.

Father Malou was born in Belgium in 1753 to a wealthy industrial family, mar-ried before he found his religious vocation (after the death of his wife), and became a political and military leader during and after the French Revolution, which he vigorously opposed. He ultimately became a Jesuit priest and served in Russia alongside Anthony Kohlmann, which is why he was tapped for New York in 1811, where he served for a time at St. Peter's. But he took the side of the trustees in a dis-agreement with Bishop Connolly, who suspended Malou's faculties, claiming—in part—that Malou was conspiring with French revolutionaries (a ludicrous charge, considering his history). Father Malou was not admitted back into ministry until Father John Power became diocesan administrator in the interim between the death of Connolly and the arrival of Bishop John Dubois.

Just before John Connolly settled in as bishop, several of his priests had been called to other posts (Fenwick back to Maryland, and the pastor of St. Mary's, the Albany church, Father Paul McQuade, to Canada), so Connolly was left with just two other priests besides Malou. And less than a month after his arrival in New York, Archbishop Carroll died, depriving Connolly of any guidance he might have received from the great man—assuming, that is, that he had wished to solicit it.

Letters in the archives of the Archdiocese of New York indicate that Bishop Connolly turned for help to Carroll's successor, Leonard Neale. For instance, when he received word from Archbishop Neale that crates of books and other eccle-siastical implements (including, presumably, vestments) had arrived in Baltimore addressed to him, Connolly expressed caution, since he did not know the Baltimore agents who had written to him requesting money, and since

> at this moment I am not in a condition to advance money for any person; as the
> Trustees of this congregation [St. Patrick's] have assured me two days ago, that they
> have not at present in their hands money enough to pay the Salary due to me for those
> three months last past.[48]

If and when he received this shipment, we cannot be sure.

In his history of the Church in New York, the Reverend James Roosevelt Bayley, then just ending his five years as secretary to Archbishop Hughes, gave in a footnote an eyewitness description of Bishop Connolly, given him by one Mr. Hart:

> Bishop Connolly was a small-sized man, very neat in appearance; lived first at 211 Bowery . . . afterwards in Broome Street, and finally at 512 Broadway, in which house he died. He was very simple in his manners, and most zealous in hearing confessions and attending the sick—singing high mass every Sunday without mitre or crozier. All the clergy then wore white cravats like the ministers.[49]

What Father Bayley does not say is that the bishop was altogether effective at his job. But he goes on to describe some of the difficulties Connolly faced with his trustees.

> Bishop Connolly was not lacking in firmness, but the great wants of his diocese made it necessary for him to fall in, to a certain extent, with the established order of things, and this exposed him afterwards to much difficulty and many humiliations.[50]

This meant, Bayley suggests, that he was a good missionary but not an effective administrator.

Distance and Time

Much of Bishop Connolly's journal—and, presumably, much of his time—was dedicated to correspondence. His record of the letters he sent (probably indicating that he had no secretary or copyist) includes notes on messages sent to other American bishops, to priests and bishops in Ireland, to officials in Rome, and to priests in other parts of his diocese.

He approved the establishment of new upstate churches, and by 1821 there were five: St. Mary's in Albany, which he inherited (and which had been founded by Father William O'Brien); St. John's in Utica (1819); St. Patrick's in Rochester (1820); Holy Family in Auburn (1820); and St. James in Carthage (1821). In 1822, Connolly made a visit to several of these congregations—his second since arriving in New York. (He had visited St. Mary's in 1816.)

In 1817, Bishop Connolly asked Mother Seton to establish a chapter of the Sisters of Charity in New York. Mother Seton was living in Baltimore, where she had established the Sisters of Charity in 1809. As the order's official history recounts:

> Mother Seton sent three Sisters to New York to care for orphaned immigrant children in the Roman Catholic Orphan Asylum. Popularly known as St. Patrick's Asylum because of its proximity to St. Patrick's Old Cathedral, this orphanage began with 5 orphans. . . . One year later it was filled to capacity. It served as a haven for children bereft of relatives and friends in a city where poverty, illness, and death were commonplace in the lives of the burgeoning population of Irish immigrants.[51]

This was the orphanage that had been founded and then abandoned by the Trappists a few years earlier. (It also became the site on which the new St. Patrick's would be built.)

Bishop Connolly also made free with recommendations to Propaganda about which new sees ought to be established in the United States, and he suggested candidates to head them. After he had been in New York for seven years, however, the staff situation in his own diocese remained bleak. In the *Catholic Almanac* of 1822, the clergy in the diocese—and, recall, this is all of New York State and much of New Jersey—were as follows: at St. Patrick's Cathedral were Bishop Connolly and Father Michael O'Gorman; at St. Peter's Church were Father Charles French and Father John Power; a Reverend Mr. Bulger was working in the vicinity of Paterson, New Jersey; Father Michael Carroll was at St. Mary's, Albany; Father John Farnham was at St. John's, Utica; Father Patrick Kelly was covering western New York; and Father Philip Larissy traveled the Hudson valley and made visits to Staten Island and Long Island.[52] That is a total of nine priests in five churches for thousands of square miles and tens of thousands of Catholic laymen. With the approval of Bishop Connolly, Masses were often said in private homes. But things were about to change—although, again, thanks mostly to the efforts of those laymen, who undertook the building of new churches in Brooklyn, on Long Island, and elsewhere.

The establishment of the Brooklyn Navy Yard in 1801 brought Irish tradesmen to the area. On most Sundays many were unable to travel over the East River and into Manhattan to attend Mass at either St. Patrick's or St. Peter's, so in 1822 Brooklyn's Catholics petitioned Bishop Connolly to approve plans for what would become St. James' Church: "In the first place," their plea read, "we want our children instructed in the principles of our holy religion; we want more convenience of hearing the word of God ourselves. In fact, we want a church, a pastor, and a place for interment." They got it all, with Bishop Connolly laying the cornerstone on July 25, 1822.[53] At the time of Connolly's death three years later, the diocese had nine churches. Bishop Connolly had ordained nine men to the priesthood, although he was unable to interest New York's Catholics in the establishment of a seminary, the idea of which, he noted, was greeted with an "almost invincible repugnance" by the laity.[54]

John Connolly, mourning the early deaths of two of those he had ordained, died at the bishop's residence on Broadway on February 5, 1815, and was buried beneath the altar at Old St. Patrick's.

Father John Power became administrator of the diocese and, with the rest of New York, awaited the arrival of a third bishop for the see. They would wait nearly two years.

The Third Bishop: John Dubois, S.S. (1826–1842)

Illustration from Smith, *The Catholic Church in New York*

Now came to New York one of the most extraordinary men ever to lead the diocese. He was also one of the most underappreciated by his largely Irish fellow Catholics.

To begin with, John Dubois had the extraordinarily bad fortune to have been born in France. To the immigrant Church in New York, adjusting to being under-appreciated in their adopted nation, a French bishop seemed like a punishment sent by Rome, and they almost never let Dubois forget it.

He was born in Paris on August 24, 1764 (as *Jean* Dubois), and was ordained a priest just two years before the outbreak of the French Revolution, whose anticler-icalism he fled—as did many other French priests.

Before the Revolution, he had been admitted to (and spent a dozen years at) the Collège Louis-le-Grand, which remains one of the best preparatory schools in France. Among his classmates were two leaders of the future Revolution, Camille Desmoulins and Maximilien Robespierre.[54] He also knew Jean-Louis Anne Made-lain Lefebvre de Cheverus, a younger student who would follow Dubois to America and become the first bishop of Boston. But Dubois' friendship with the six-years-older Robespierre would be the more important one.

As the future Archbishop Bayley of Baltimore would write in a footnote to his *Brief Sketch of the Early History of the Catholic Church on the Island of New York*, two years into the Revolution, Robespierre and Dubois met for breakfast, and "it was by his [Robespierre's] connivance that he [Dubois] was able to escape from France"—just four years after Dubois had been ordained to the priesthood at the age of twenty-three. He served briefly at the great Church of St. Sulpice, second in Paris only to Notre Dame and seemingly always under construction. (He became a member of the Society of St. Sulpice years later in America.)

Among the parishioners at St. Sulpice was Marie Lafayette, the wife of the great French hero of the American Revolution. She liked young Father Dubois, and, as anticlerical tensions rose in Paris ahead of the Great Terror, Madame Lafayette convinced her husband, the marquis, to craft a letter of introduction for Dubois, which in June of 1791 he secreted on his person as he fled France for the United States—using false papers, a necessity to ensure an outlaw safe passage to the New World.[55]

An Instant Success

One might have wondered how far the Lafayette letter would get Father Dubois. In fact, after his arrival at Norfolk, Virginia (and although he spoke no English), he was soon in residence at the home of none other than Senator James Monroe, future president of the United States. Monroe would leave the Senate a few years later in order to serve as ambassador to France, and no doubt Dubois was helpful to him in mastering French. Dubois learned English from Monroe's friend and neighbor Patrick Henry.[56] He also spent time in the home of Thomas Sim Lee, a Catholic who was twice governor of Maryland.[57]

Monroe, however, was no special friend of what he called the "Romish religion", but that, Dubois learned, was typical of his American friends. As Richard Shaw writes:

> Monroe was thoroughly gracious to him, yet continued to speak demagogically against the Roman Catholic priesthood. The Virginia newspapers expressed shock that "to the great scandal of Frenchmen and the law" some nonjuring priests [those loyal to the Vatican, not the Revolutionary government] were still functioning in France. This while he was invited to celebrate Mass in the courtroom of the State Capitol building.[58]

Father Dubois caught the eye of Bishop Carroll, who gave him a pastorate in Frederick, Maryland, in 1794. By 1808, Dubois was living in Emmitsburg, Maryland—where he joined the Sulpicians—and he set about to build there a much needed seminary and college.

Perhaps it was this, the beginning of his efforts to build what became Mount St. Mary's Seminary and College (or the fact that he was French), that kept Bishop Carroll from considering him for the new episcopate in New York. But by the time of Bishop Connolly's death, John Dubois (who had long since Americanized his Christian name) was acknowledged not only as a holy man and a diligent priest but also as a man who could all but move mountains. The construction of "the Mount" (with material, financial, and spiritual setbacks at every turn) and his spiritual guidance of Elizabeth Ann Seton and her newly founded Sisters of Charity, now also in Emmitsburg, tagged Dubois as the perfect man for New York in 1826, which was true—except, of course, for the fact that he wasn't Irish.

Father Dubois, however, was not Rome's first choice—or its second—which is why he had not been named bishop coadjutor toward the end of Connolly's life. But neither had anybody else. Leo XII now sat in Peter's throne, and it is uncertain exactly when Dubois' name crept up the list of candidates and reached the top. Among the others who received consideration were: the popular Irish priest John Power, who was then administrator of the New York Diocese, but who campaigned rather too vigorously for the appointment, especially through the pages of a Catholic newspaper he helped found and edit, the *Truth Teller*; the able Benedict Fenwick, president of Georgetown; and, closer to the decision-making, the great Anthony Kohlmann. But Kohlmann had no interest in returning to the diocese he had once managed, and it was he who suggested John Dubois.

It was Power's prodding of Kohlmann to choose *him* that drove Kohlmann to recommend Dubois.[59]

The pope did not designate Dubois until sixteen months after the death of Connolly, which had given New York's Catholic press ample time to anticipate the appointment of another Irishman, probably Power. The *National Advocate* demanded to know: "Who formed the congregation in New York, Irishmen or Frenchmen?" Why, the editorial continued, did the French "junta" in Baltimore decide so? "Will Irishmen permit it?"[60]

Father Richard Shaw, author of the luminous and definitive biography of Bishop Dubois, describes the scene as Father Dubois left the Mount to assume his duties in New York:

> Here, at a most dramatic moment, stood together the next three of the occupants of the See of New York. John Hughes, leaving for his own ordination ... and the sixteen-year-old John McCloskey was one of the boys seeing them off.... Hughes would rule as an archbishop.... McCloskey would become the first cardinal of the United States.[61]

Dubois' first stop on his way to New York was Baltimore, where on October 29, 1826, he received his episcopal consecration from the city's archbishop, Ambrose Maréchal.

Dubois in New York

The New York diocese was then in its eighteenth year, yet in those nearly two decades progress had been slow, especially in Manhattan. As Dubois would write to his friend Father Simon Bruté, he had found

> a large and increasing Catholic population, with only four priests [according to one census made in the month prior to Dubois' arrival, there were actually six Catholic clergymen], and without the means of providing more. The few churches were loaded with debt, and most of those who had the temporary management of them, under the title of trustees, by their carelessness and inexperience only rendered the matter worse.[62]

In other words, he came up hard against the ongoing troubles caused by trusteeism.

But there was also the matter of the recent success and great popularity of Father John Power, who the Irish Catholics of New York and the trustees of the city's churches had assumed would be Bishop Connolly's successor. It galled Dubois that the press in New York called him a "foreigner". For one thing, he had been in the United States for thirty-five years before coming to New York. For another, many of the very people raising the issue were themselves immigrants. So he sought to defuse the issue by pointing out that St. Patrick himself was a native not of Ireland but of Gaul (that is, of France) and by adding to his episcopal coat of arms both the motto of the United States (*E pluribus unum*) and the image of a shamrock.[63] But these gestures had little effect.

None of this, however, dulled Dubois' desire to get to know the people of New York and New Jersey, and during his first years as bishop he traveled indefatigably throughout the diocese. There were, of course, difficulties—most of them back in New York City.

In 1828 a group of Irish religious brothers had come to the city and presented themselves to Bishop Dubois as teachers ready to undertake the opening of two schools: one fee based, the other free (for the education of the poor). Dubois thought this a gift from heaven, as perhaps it was, but when lay trustees demanded control over the schools, the brothers decided there was too much risk—to their ministry and to their security—and, to Dubois' dismay, they packed up and returned to Ireland.[64]

By 1830, Dubois noted that there were 35,000 Catholics in New York City, but in the entire diocese—which still included all of the state of New York and most of northern New Jersey—there were 150,000. In just a few years, there would be 200,000, and although the number of churches and chapels had grown to thirty-seven, those places of worship were yet far from sufficient to serve the needs of the diocese's Catholic population.

Meanwhile, Dubois himself had just returned from a two-year sabbatical in Europe, which he had undertaken in large measure to raise funds in France, Spain, and Portugal for the diocese, but also to recruit priests—in Ireland!—and to visit Pope Pius VIII in Rome. But he had returned all but empty-handed, without money or new priests, and it seemed there was always some crisis needing his attention. If it wasn't a drunken priest or an irascible group of trustees, it was the slanders and libels of New York's nativists. As Father Richard Shaw writes, Dubois had to contend with (and in some way try to answer) "tales of dungeons under Cathedrals (including St. Patrick's in New York) and sexual orgies in convents and rectories". Dubois was urbane enough to understand that on balance it was best to ignore such filth and nonsense, and the calumnies "might have remained under store counters like pornography" were it not for the pugnacious Irishmen, who were "more temperamentally disposed to respond".[65]

The Bishop in Decline

In 1835, Bishop Dubois began to seek help in managing his diocese and made the odd request that Francis Kenrick, the bishop coadjutor of Philadelphia, be named his coadjutor in New York.[66] But neither Kenrick nor the Vatican had any interest in that, most especially because Henry Conwell, Philadelphia's bishop since 1819, was an irascible, even combustible man, and Kenrick had been put at his side for a reason.

The Diocese of New York—and really the whole of Catholic life in the United States—perplexed those in Rome, not least Pope Gregory XVI, whose instinct was to watch and wait before naming successors in any American diocese. In this case—and after much politicking from several American clergy, for and against various candidates—the European press leaked the news that the pope's choice had fallen upon Dubois' erstwhile Mount St. Mary's student John Joseph Hughes, a priest in Philadelphia.

And, indeed, he was Bishop Dubois' second choice, which is testimony to Dubois' open-mindedness, since, as we shall see in the following chapter, his judgment of Hughes' intellectual capacity was not of the highest order. But he surely saw that the young man's (Hughes was forty) abilities were a good fit with New York. Hughes was Irish; he was a fighter, a vigorous defender of Catholicism who was willing to engage anyone in debate; and he was thought to be a sound administrator and a man—much like Dubois in his youth—who believed in and thrived on hard work. And, perhaps most significant, Hughes was a merciless crusader against trusteeism.

At an 1837 synod in Baltimore, America's bishops agreed that Hughes was the right man for New York, and they communicated their opinion to the pope, who named Hughes to the coadjutor post on August 7, 1837. Dubois had not attended the gathering, presumably because of ill health. At the synod there had been support voiced for Francis Kenrick and, once again, for John Power—this time by people besides John Power.

Most of the rest of Dubois' story actually belongs in the next chapter, since the final four years of his life were dominated by the rise of John Hughes. But a little remains to be written here.

In the archives of the Archdiocese of New York is a note of congratulations written by Bishop Dubois to "My Dear Young Friend", a recent graduate of the Mount. Research makes clear that it was written to John J. Hughes. The message is one of fatherly tenderness and pride.

The letter is in stark contrast to the epitaph chosen by Dubois, who died on December 20, 1842, at the age of seventy-eight. Speaking of the Irish in general (and likely of Hughes in particular), he instructed that he be interred beneath the front steps of Old St. Patrick's, with this as his epitaph: "Bury me where people will walk over me in death as they wished to in life." One may see the plaque with those words at the old cathedral's entrance today.[67]

PART II

The Rise to Power

The Gardener

John Joseph Hughes
First Archbishop of New York
(1850–1864)

Photo by Mathew Brady around the time of Hughes' enthronement

Archbishop Hughes in his bier

New York's first archbishop, who would come to be known as Dagger John, was born in Annaloghan, in the diocese of Clogher, County Tyrone, Ulster, on Saturday, June 24, 1797. As John Hassard (Hughes' first biographer—perhaps one should say *hagiographer*) observed, June 24 is the feast of the Nativity of St. John the Baptist. On that very day in the United States, Spanish priests founded the mission of San Juan Bautista in California, and they read at Mass from the book of Isaiah (49:1–2, NAB), as surely Catholics in Ireland also did:

> Hear me, O coastlands,
>   listen, O distant peoples.
> The LORD called me from birth,
>   from my mother's womb he gave me my name.
> He made of me a sharp-edged sword
>   and concealed me in the shadow of his arm.
> He made me a polished arrow,
>   in his quiver he hid me.

Hughes would become a sharp-edged sword, a polished arrow—and to distant peoples, a dagger.

John Hughes (he would take his middle name only at confirmation—the custom at that time) came from a long line of farmers and weavers. His mother, Margaret McKenna Hughes, came from Brackagh in County Londonderry, in the far north of Ulster. His father, Patrick Hughes, came from Dernaved in County Monaghan, in the southernmost part of old Protestant Ulster; today Monaghan is part of Catholic Ireland.

Margaret and Patrick were blessed with seven children, of whom John was the third. Two of the children, however, Mary and Peter (the fourth and fifth), died in infancy and were buried in the family plot at Errigal Truagh, some miles to the east of the Hughes farm. The surviving children in addition to John were Michael, Patrick, Ellen (later Sister Mary Angela), and Margaret.

As we shall see, as archbishop, Hughes had a ready wit, often colored by a tinge of sarcasm, as when he recalled the beginning of his life in Ulster: "I had social and civil equality with the most favored subjects of the British Empire", he said. That is, he had this equality as an *unbaptized* person.[1] Once baptized as a Catholic, which he was on his fifth day of life, he lost that social and civil equality, although he gained, he believed, a moral and spiritual superiority.

Historian Michael Wood has referred to sixteenth-century (Tudor) England as a "police state", principally with regard to the treatment of Catholics by the new Protestant majority. (As previously mentioned, in the space of just a few decades, England was Catholic, Protestant, Catholic, and Protestant again. Eighty years after the death of Queen Elizabeth, the brief reign of the Catholic convert King James II had no effect on the official Anglican faith of the nation.)

Upon returning to the United States from a 2012 trip to England, Father Robert Barron noted the vitality of English Catholicism in the twenty-first century, but he also remarked that the period of Tudor persecutions is "still very much a living reality" there.[2] The context of Father Barron's comments is the issue of religious liberty, which Catholics lacked in Great Britain for hundreds of years and which remained a serious matter in the eighteenth century, especially in Ireland.

The sorts of persecution of Catholics common under the Tudors—torture and execution—had largely been replaced (until the brutal suppression of the Rebellion of 1798) with discriminatory penal laws enforced principally, although not exclusively, in Ireland. These laws were acidly described by the great English statesman Edmund Burke (born in Ireland to a Catholic mother and a Protestant father) as "a machine of wise and elaborate contrivance, as well fitted for the oppression, impoverishment and degradation of a people, and the debasement in them of human nature itself, as ever proceeded from the perverted ingenuity of man".[3] Catholics accounted for 85 percent of Ireland's population, but they owned just 5 percent of the land.

In the century before the birth of John Hughes, the Irish had risen four times in rebellion against Protestant Great Britain, and by the end of the eighteenth century, although there was peace, the Irish view of the English was at best wary, but more often actively hostile. And with reason: acts of criminal violence against Catholics were common.

John Hughes himself described being accosted by a gang of "Orangemen" (Protestants belonging to the Orange Order, founded in 1795) when he was fifteen: "Five bayonets were pointed at my breast; but when I told my name, the men let me go, saying, 'All right; we know his father.' "[4]

This incident notwithstanding, the history of Catholics under British rule, though not always directly applicable to Hughes, still provides a background to the beginning of the Irish exodus to America—and a key to the character of the man who would rise to become, arguably, America's greatest Catholic leader. Specifically, the Irish gangs in the Five Points section of Manhattan—just a few blocks south of Old St. Patrick's Cathedral—had their genesis in the Catholic-Protestant conflicts in the North of Ireland.

The Irish diaspora involved many millions of people (not all of whom came to the United States and Canada), which is nearly twenty times the current population of Ireland. As the old Irish ballad "The Green Fields of America" had it:

> So pack up your sea-stores, consider no longer,
> Ten dollars a week is not very bad pay,
> With no taxes or tithes to devour up your wages,
> When you're on the green fields of Americay.

It is no surprise that today Irish-Americans constitute one of the largest ethnic groups in the United States. (German-Americans form the largest ethnic group from Continental Europe.) Millions of immigrants have (and still do) come to America from all around the world for a host of reasons, but for the Irish, poverty, oppression, and famine were the primary reasons. As of 1790, there were approximately 400,000 Irish-Americans throughout the United States. More than half of them, like Hughes, were from Ireland's northern counties, although, unlike Hughes, the majority were Protestant Scots-Irish. (The "Scots" part does not mean they were from Scotland. Some were by heritage, but they were primarily Ulstermen by birth and residence.) Five percent of the total United States population at that time were Catholics and many of them had come as indentured servants.

Four hundred thousand may not seem like a tidal wave, but there were then just a little under four million inhabitants in the new nation, making the Irish a solid 10 percent, just a few percentage points less than Irish-Americans represent today. But as of 1790, the Irish had come in large numbers into the United States, and Irish Catholics were concentrated in large cities. In New York, they accounted for 15 percent of the population, and by the time John Hughes emigrated to America in 1817, the Irish were fully a quarter of the city's inhabitants. And the great surge of Irish Catholic immigration was yet to come. (The number of Irish immigrants to America between 1820 and 1830 was 54,338; between 1851 and 1860, the peak years of Archbishop Hughes' episcopacy, Irish immigration exploded to 914,119.)[5]

Back in Ireland, John Hughes' formal education had begun at a hedge school, an informal rural school. Less than a generation earlier, Britain's penal laws had forbidden Catholic schools, but Hughes received an education sufficient to advance him to a nearby grammar school (in Aughnacloy, Tyrone).[6] Still, by the time he left Ireland for America, unlike his countrymen R. Luke Concanen and John Connolly, he had not acquired enough education to win him acceptance into a seminary. But that was of not much consequence to Hughes at that time, because his call to the priesthood was yet in its early stages, although it was certainly forming in his mind, moving in his soul. Hassard quotes a recollection Hughes made to friends about being forced as a teenager to leave school to work on the family farm (this would have been at about the time his father and his older brother Patrick set off for America, in 1816), although it seems more likely that these were thoughts that formed in his mind after his arrival in America: "Many a time have I thrown down my rake in the meadow, and kneeling behind a hayrick, begged God and the Blessed Virgin to let me become a priest."[7] The comment was apposite, however, because he worked not only on his parents' farm but also on a nearby estate as an assistant to the gardener,[8] and these would turn out to be providential assignments.

Hughes Comes to America

At age twenty, John Hughes followed his father and older brother to America. He brought with him a substantial amount of bitterness toward the British and great hope for the Americans, whose country, he believed, was one "in which no stigma of inferiority would be impressed" on him simply because he "professed one creed or another".[9]

He was a young man of modest build, dark hair, and blue-gray eyes and tended to stand in a posture like a boxer, which made him seem larger. This was to the good, because, although America did welcome him, there were many fights ahead of him—not just with Protestants and nativists but with Catholic clerics as well.

Father Richard Shaw, Bishop Dubois' biographer, writes that Hughes' bitterness about British oppression of the Irish was not focused solely on English overlords or soldiers or Protestant gangs. He had contempt too for the priests who seemed to have no answer to the "Irish Question": "He judged that because they were doing nothing effective to this end they were to a good measure responsible for conditions in that hapless land. The young man who wanted to be a priest left his homeland solidly anticlerical."[10]

Perhaps. But one thing is certain: John Joseph Hughes arrived in Baltimore in 1817 with a chip on his shoulder and was largely past tolerating anybody's anti-Catholic attitudes or any Catholic's hesitance to defend the faith.

When John arrived in the United States, Patrick Jr. was working in the Baltimore area, although their father had moved to Chambersburg, Pennsylvania. (The rest of the Hughes clan would follow soon after.) John decided to stay with his brother and took employment as a gardener. But that work lasted only until the onset of winter, at which time both Hughes boys went to Chambersburg to be with their father. Chambersburg is in Pennsylvania's south-central region, close to the Maryland border and far enough south to be the only city in the Union to be torched by Confederate troops during the Civil War. Most of the settlers in what was then called the West were Scots-Irish, although Catholics had been in the area for thirty years before Patrick Hughes and his family went there. Chambersburg was the sort of American frontier town in which the first courthouse was also a tavern.

Emmitsburg, Maryland, and Mount St. Mary's Seminary were only about forty miles away, and at his earliest convenience young John Hughes traveled that distance to seek admission to the Mount, his decision to be a priest now clearly formed. There he found that, at twenty, he was not so young.

In an early (1864) book about Hughes, the anonymous author writes that upon John's arrival in Chambersburg, Patrick Hughes found him employment with a florist "to learn the art of gardening", but John was already well versed in that field from his time in Ireland and in the Baltimore area. The author goes on: "But having little taste for such pursuits, and feeling within himself a call to till and cultivate the 'Garden of the Lord,' he devoted his spare time to study, and as soon as his engagement expired, entered the Theological Seminary at Mount St. Mary's."[11] If only it had happened so quickly.

Father John Dubois, who was still the rector of Mount St. Mary's, no doubt admired the ambition of John Hughes, but he considered him far too old to be enrolled at the Mount—most first-year students there were in their teens (some in their early teens, and John McCloskey, Hughes' future successor to the See of New York, was just eleven when he entered the Mount, although in its secondary school, not the seminary per se). In addition, from Hughes' own description of his education among the hedgerows, Dubois considered him insufficiently prepared for the rigors of seminary study. So he turned him down.

In 1819, however, Hughes got a job nearby working for Mother Elizabeth Ann Seton and the Sisters of Charity at St. Joseph's School. Mother Seton not only hired Hughes as her gardener, but she listened to him describe his longing to be a priest, and she admired his passion for serving God. So she wrote to Dubois, suggesting that the rector give renewed consideration to Hughes' exceptional drive.

Dubois relented. How could he not, having received such a request from a woman he so greatly admired? (In a review of a biography of Hughes, one writer quipped that "Hughes' foes regard Mother Seton's intercession as her worst blunder, his friends believe it to be her first miracle."[12]) According to the Reverend Henry Brann, in his 1892 biography of Hughes, Dubois said: "All I can do is to give you work in the garden."[13] In fact, Dubois presented Hughes with a more complicated offer: He was to work as the gardener at Mount St. Mary's; he would manage the seminary's slaves (named Timothy and Peter);[14] he would live on the grounds in a cabin; and he would receive tutoring to bring him up to the educational level necessary to train for the priesthood. Dubois was skeptical that Hughes' obvious capacity for physical labor would be matched by any similar intellectual capacity.

For Hughes, it was clearly the beginning he needed, although the arrangement displeased him. Indeed, it angered him, and the anger stayed with him—as did his anger at the English and at ineffectual priests—for the rest of his life.

He found working with the slaves an especially odious task—not because he despised them, but because he found slavery repellent. (This did not stop him, for reasons to be discussed later on, from initially siding with the Southern states' objections to the election of Abraham Lincoln and the prospect of abolition.)

One night, when Father Dubois was out for a walk in the early evening, he saw a light burning in the cabin he had given to Hughes (a cabin that remains on the grounds of the Mount as a tribute to the seminary's most famous graduate). There he found Hughes intently studying a book. It may have been a Latin text (Father Brann's book says it was, and this is confirmed, to some extent, by the fact that Hughes would become a Latin tutor at Mount St. Mary's), but whatever it was— Church history, theology, philosophy, engineering—Dubois was intrigued enough to begin quizzing Hughes. The Irishman's responses were impressive—*under the circumstances*, Dubois may have thought—and so the future bishop relented and allowed the future archbishop to become a full-time seminarian in the new class beginning in the fall of 1820. At twenty-three, Hughes was half a decade older than most of his classmates.

Although Hughes had done a good job of preparing himself, classroom work could not have been easy at first. Whatever deficits he may have had were surely exacerbated by the fact that Dubois had yet to release him from his responsibilities in managing the seminary grounds. The younger students enjoyed poking fun at Hughes, especially when he was put in charge of study sessions, and some of his professors found him difficult to manage. He was diffident in the classroom—he was a naturally quiet young man—and some professors took this as a sign that he was struggling to grasp the more difficult material. But this was only in the beginning.

As monitor of those study sessions, Hughes had to deal with the more obstreperous students. On one St. Patrick's Day, a group of boys, led in their prank by the scion of a distinguished family, made an effigy of the great Irish saint, which they hoisted to a rafter in the study hall. Hughes looked up at the stuffed figure; then he looked straight at the ringleader.

"*O tempora, O mores!*" Hughes said drolly. "The son of a judge has become a hangman." After that, there were no more tricks played, although Hughes would be removed from his post as study-hall monitor, because his notion of discipline too often included "physical chastisement".[15]

Hughes was helped immeasurably by the tutoring of one of the Mount's most distinguished teachers, Simon Bruté, like Dubois a Sulpician priest and, like many other French priests in America, a refugee from the French Revolution (or, as in his case, from its aftermath). As a young priest, Bruté had been offered a position as chaplain to Napoleon Bonaparte, but such a post had little appeal for him. His dream was to be a missionary. And with his friend Benedict Joseph Flaget (future bishop of Bardstown, Kentucky, and then of Louisville), he came to America in 1810 and two years later joined the staff at the Mount, where he would remain until he was designated bishop of Vincennes, Indiana, in 1834. He and Hughes would remain close friends until Bruté's death in 1839.

It did not take long for just about everybody at the Mount, from the youngest student to Dubois himself, to see that Hughes was not only a fast learner and an excellent student but also, in his subdued way, an assertive leader, although sometimes also a bit—or more than a bit—belligerent. In part because of his real-world experience but also because of his age (now an asset), John Hughes had knowledge of things about which many at the seminary were uninformed.

When a fire on the mountain threatened the seminary, Hughes took charge, organizing everybody in brigades—students and faculty alike fell into line—to begin close-cutting the area around the buildings to deprive the fire of fuel; he even set a backfire to do the same and to change the path of the flames.

Had a time traveler come to tell students, faculty, and administrators that the taciturn but pugnacious Hughes would, in the coming half century, become America's greatest churchman, some would have doubted it, but most would not have been surprised, because they had all learned that John Joseph Hughes was simply relentless.

When yet another fire succeeded in destroying one of the Mount's buildings, Dubois sent the students out into neighboring villages and towns to raise the money necessary to rebuild what had been lost. Hughes found himself in a tavern near Hagerstown, Pennsylvania, trying his best, in his reserved manner, to drum up contributions for the cash-poor seminary, when a tipsy patron took exception to his "papist" faith. That's when young Hughes gave an early sign of the battling bishop he would become. Although in classes at the Mount he sometimes was unable to speak effectively, against this drunken Protestant he became the very incarnation of St. Malachy, the twelfth-century archbishop of Armagh who restored the Church's greatness in Ireland and whose eloquence was legendary. Proof of this is Hughes' great success in passing the hat that day. Throughout his life, Hughes was a formidable defender of the faith whenever he "got his Irish up".

Finally a Priest

John Joseph Hughes became a deacon in 1825. He took some time shortly thereafter to visit his family in Chambersburg, hoping to spend the whole of his seminary break with them. But it was not to be so. As it happened, the Bishop of Philadelphia, Henry Conwell, was on a diocesan tour that brought him through Chambersburg. When he met Deacon Hughes, the impetuous bishop immediately suggested that the young man accompany him on the rest of his journey. What better way than that to give the deacon practical experience?

The eighty-year-old Conwell (from County Londonderry) had been a priest in Ireland for more than forty years before emigrating to America. He became Philadelphia's second bishop upon the death of Michael Egan, but only after the see had been offered to Ambrose Maréchal (archbishop of Baltimore), John Baptist Mary David (who would become bishop of Bardstown), and Louis de Barth, who was then interim administrator in Philadelphia. All three said no, fearful of the battles then raging at St. Mary's Cathedral between Egan, his priests, and the cathedral's lay trustees.

When Conwell arrived to take up his post on December 2, 1820, he quickly set about making things worse.

The issue at St. Mary's was one that Archbishop Carroll had faced and that would cause Bishop Dubois so much annoyance: trusteeism, and in particular the hiring and firing of priests. Having come from Ireland, Conwell had no doubt with whom the responsibility lay, and it was not with laymen.

In the period between Egan's death and Conwell's arrival, the trustees at St. Mary's, with the acquiescence of Father de Barth, had assigned the Reverend William Hogan to be a priest at the cathedral. Hogan, also from Ireland, was a popular preacher and something of a social climber. Indeed, Bishop Conwell found his lifestyle utterly inconsistent with Church standards, and he suspended Hogan's faculties. (Hogan would eventually be excommunicated, convert to Protestantism, marry, and become a writer of anti-Catholic tracts.) That sent the trustees into a swoon. And they would fly into a rage when Conwell brought in as Hogan's replacement a Dominican, William Harold, who previously had been dismissed by Bishop Egan. The controversy would last for years and would eventually involve a newly ordained priest serving at St. Mary's, one John Joseph Hughes.

But that was all still ahead when Conwell took Deacon Hughes under his wing and set off with him in his travels to one parish after another. The bishop, happy to be temporarily free of the Philadelphia troubles, took the rest of the visitation as a kind of vacation, allowing Hughes to give the homilies at most of the Masses at which they officiated.

Hughes did well, although in a somewhat unorthodox fashion. He had prepared just one homily, so that's the one he gave everywhere he and Conwell went. And the elderly bishop was far too amused with what he called Hughes' "cuckoo sermon" ever to complain of the deacon's lack of creativity.[16] John Hassard goes so far as to suggest that by the end of the trip Conwell was so impressed with Hughes—if not specifically with his sermonizing—that he prophesied the deacon's future elevation to the episcopacy.[17]

Bishop Conwell had ordained Hughes a deacon, and on October 15, 1826, the feast of St. Teresa of Ávila, he ordained him a priest in St. Mary's Cathedral. This was just two weeks before Hughes' former preceptor and future adversary, John Dubois, was consecrated bishop of New York. Father Hughes was twenty-nine.

Much had been made about Hughes' age before his seminary training began. In the nineteenth century, most priests received ordination at about the age of twenty-three, as did R. Luke Concanen, but there were plenty of exceptions. John Connolly was twenty-seven, and John Carroll was thirty-four. But the real exception, at least among the future ordinaries of New York, was John Dubois. He was just seventeen when he took holy orders, and this may be one reason why Hughes had seemed to him too old, at twenty, to begin at the Mount.

Hughes' first assignment was as assistant to the Reverend Michael Hurley, the Augustinian pastor of St. Augustine's Church in Philadelphia, founded in 1801 (it would be burned to the ground during a nativist riot in 1844).

Prior to his priestly ordination, Hughes, who had spent time at St. Augustine's during his diaconate, had received a letter from Father Hurley suggesting that he prepare himself for ministry by writing out at least six months' worth of half-hour homilies, advice Hughes failed to take, but which would have been extremely help-ful on his travels with Bishop Conwell.

After Father Hughes had spent just a few weeks with Father Hurley, who gave him a crash course in the management of parish life, Bishop Conwell assigned the younger priest to Bedford in western Pennsylvania, the Appalachian town in which President Washington had set up his headquarters during the Whiskey Rebellion—the only time an American president has led troops in conflict.[18] Although Bedford is just two hundred miles from Philadelphia, the newly ordained priest considered it the end of the earth.

But before Hughes headed there, he had received another letter, a sweet one—well, *mostly* sweet—from his former seminary rector, John Dubois. The letter, kept in the Archives of the Archdiocese of New York, is dated October 26, 1826, which is to say, eleven days after Hughes' ordination and three days before Dubois' con-secration as bishop of New York (performed in Baltimore by Archbishop Ambrose Maréchal). Clearly, the soon-to-be bishop was aware of Father Hughes' assignment and was none too pleased about it. The letter is worth quoting at length (among other things, it may tell us a bit about the cadence of *le Père* Dubois' speech):

> My ever Dear Child and Reverend Friend
>
> I have not had a moment to answer your favour of the 22nd ... happy as I am to hear of your Ordination. I feel for the difficult situation in which you are going to be placed; more than for the flock which is to be entrusted to you.
>
> Reverend Mr. Heyden had not more experience than you when he went, and I think less steadiness of mind than you have, to go through the various duties belong-ing to it—still I must confess that it is much to be regretted that young priests should be sent out of the reach of Counsels, oftentimes out of reach of that Piscina [a basin for ablution] of penance which they need more than the 1,000 they have yearly to admitt [*sic*] to it, and out of the chance of cultivating talents yet in the bud, and Ecclesiastical knowledge which they have only tasted.
>
> But I must acknowledge that I know not how the Bishop, situated as he is, could get a more Suitable Person for that important station than yourself, and an old man would not do for a mission which requires activity and a Speculator in money would not [*assess*—word illegible] where disinterestedness is wanting to form a new Establishment.
>
> Look around you as far as your knowledge of the diocese extends and shew [*sic*] me one who would answer. I am far from thinking that the recall of Mr. Heyden to Philadelphia will be useful either to himself or to others—the air of Philadelphia may turn the head of one who, tho endowed with an excellent heart, is perhaps not insen-sible to public applause and may sacrifice to popularity more essential Virtues—you could have done there what he will do at least in the most essential parts, if you have not the best advice and examples near at hand, I think you would have stood against the danger of Influence—in the doubts you would have formulated near and far, the constant tides unavoidable in Country Missions would not [have] taken up your time and you could have improved both yr talents and yr knowledge. But I see that the poor Bishop was obliged to gratify the people for peace's sake—all I advise you to do is to try to prevail upon him to give you as soon as possible a Companion who will share in your Labours and Solitude.... Perhaps you could get your former messmate, Mr. [John] Riley [or Reilley, presumably a classmate from the Mount; a priest with whom Hughes would later serve at St. Joseph's in Philadelphia].

Meanwhile, since it is the will of God to place you in this Situation (for even the mistakes of our superiors are permitted by him)—act cautiously, pray fervently—watch carefully—and say as I did in my more awful situations with the great St Leo: [Dubois here adapts Pope Leo I's Latin phrase, which translated is] *And yet we do not despair nor lose heart, because we put our trust not in ourselves but in Him who works in us.*

Did the Bishop tell you that the black Woman [probably a slave at the Mount] had given you through mistake at least one shirt and handkerchief of mine and gave me one of each and a neck handkerchief belonging to you—leave mine in Philadelphia if you have enough. Otherwise I will leave yours there when I go through to be forwarded to you by the 1st opportunity—if you have not enough, keep mine and still I will send yours.

May God ever help you, my Ever Dear Child—let me hear sometimes from you, for nothing will gratify me more than to hear that you continue a faithful servt. of the Divine Master so that, if I do my part also, We may reunite one day where We can no more be parted.

Your devoted Servt. and friend and Father
John Dubois[19]

There may be retrospective irony in the fact that they would reunite within a decade, although in New York, not in heaven (where they hopefully now are together), and that reunion would not be paradise for either man.

Hughes took to his wide, mountainous parish with his usual energy, although there is very little known about his activities there, because he was called back to Philadelphia in a matter of months. He had been sent to Bedford to replace Father Thomas Heyden, whom Bishop Conwell had decided to bring to Philadelphia as a replacement at St. Mary's during the battle between the bishop and the trustees in the Hogan-Harold controversy. (While in Bedford, Hughes stayed with Heyden's parents.)

Conwell's plan was apparently to hold back Hughes, the man he now considered his protégé, almost as a general might secrete a cavalry division in the mountains, and then release him to descend upon the hothouse that was Philadelphia, and—at some point—deliver Hughes right into the roiling mess at St. Mary's, the enemy camp.

And, as if following the bishop's plan, poor Father Heyden almost immediately began begging the bishop to let him return to his parents in Bedford, even arguing with Conwell that John Hughes would be much the better man for so contentious a place as St. Mary's.[20] The bishop thought that an excellent suggestion (his plan all along, after all), although he had no intention of sending Heyden back to the mountains, or of putting Hughes directly into St. Mary's. He instead sent Hughes to be curate at St. Joseph's Church, Philadelphia's oldest (founded in 1733).[21] To serve at the only place in America where, a century before, Catholics had been legally permitted to worship was a matter of tremendous pride for the not-yet-thirty-year-old Irishman; to be back in Philadelphia less than four months after ordination must have been for him a stunning affirmation of his destiny. He would serve at St. Joseph's—with stints at St. Mary's—until 1832, when he would become founding pastor of St. John the Evangelist Church in Philadelphia.

But in 1827 Hughes' ascent was threatened by the lingering trustee issues at St. Mary's.

The Hells of St. Mary's

The bizarre Father Hogan having moved on to graze in what his bovine tastes told him were greener pastures, Father Harold became the rather confused focus for the trustees at St. Mary's, who continued to take a republican attitude toward Church governance. To them, Bishop Conwell remained a foreigner imposed upon them by a distant monarchy, and—although they were willing to defer on some matters to popes and bishops—the hiring, firing, and compensation of clergy were things they believed they had a right and a responsibility to keep for themselves.

Of course, Bishop Conwell would have none of that. He would shortly run into troubles over his handling of the controversy, the end of which was the suspension and then excommunication of Father Harold, but in the immediate dispute with the trustees, the bishop took the expedient of gathering his priests and essentially ordering them to sign a document supporting his actions against Harold.

John Hughes refused—at least at first. He certainly believed that it was his bishop's (any bishop's) right to censure and expel from ministry any priest whose actions dictated it, as, in Hughes' view, Harold's did. But he did not think it necessary for individual priests to be brought into the matter. In this belief he was supported and encouraged by his mentor, Father Bruté, among others. But the old bishop kept applying pressure on Hughes to fall into line, which Hughes finally did, albeit with trepidation.

And he was right to be concerned, because no sooner had the bishop's letter of condemnation of Harold, replete with the signatures of so many priests, been published, than John Hughes found himself, specifically and individually, sued by William Harold.

Harold was savvy enough to realize that there was little point in going after the doddering old bishop or the milquetoast diocesan administrator, Father de Barth; and of all the other names on the list of his persecutors, none was more noteworthy to Harold than that of the bishop's golden boy, Hughes, against whom he brought a defamation-of-character suit.[22]

Conwell must have felt vindicated by Harold's despicable and frivolous lawsuit, and, as if to bait the trap he thought he was setting for the trustees, he sent Hughes to St. Mary's as pastor, replacing Harold. The trustees' reaction was predictable: they vilified Hughes.

"I have no spite against anyone," Hughes wrote to Bruté, "but I have been sorely injured in this business."[23]

But although Hughes found himself in the middle of a Church-politics battle that he wanted nothing to do with, he did not respond by lashing out at either Harold or the St. Mary's trustees. He may have been considered by most Philadelphians to be on one side or the other in this battle, but he never saw it that way. His only position was the Church's position, which was at that point a casualty of this controversy that pitted laymen against the bishop. To Hughes, the trustees' premises were awry; until Americans learned to accept the distinction between the rough-and-tumble of politics—of republican democracy—and a hierarchical Church, they would not be proper Catholics. He never thought that laymen should be subservient to priests, bishops, or even the pope, but he would always insist that they be obedient in those realms that were uniquely the province of ecclesiastical authority.

Although he had lived in the United States for just a decade, he understood the American spirit. But that spirit could not be allowed to control Church governance or ownership, any more than it could reject or modify the Church's theology.

Once Hughes was ensconced at St. Mary's, however, the vilification abated, and he became again a much-respected priest. And he might have stayed on at St. Mary's for many years had the issue of trusteeism not loomed so large still. Conwell's moves may have sealed the fate of Harold, who quickly dropped his legal action against Hughes, but they had not at all resolved the issue of who was responsible for financial management at St. Mary's or any other church. For his part, Hughes decided to confront the situation head on. But he did so not by arguing at trustee meetings or by publishing letters in Philadelphia's newspapers; he did it by standing up in the pulpit one Sunday morning (June 17, 1827) and announcing to the startled parishioners, including many trustees, that because of their intransigence he had decided to return to St. Joseph's (i.e., to Bishop Conwell). As Father Richard Shaw writes, Hughes told them, in essence, that they— who justified their self-regarding power to hire and fire priests as nothing more than seeking worthy men for the job—were unworthy of *him*. So Hughes took his assistant and left, leaving the increasingly discredited Harold alone at St. Mary's. Father Shaw adds:

> It was a coup for which Hughes was singlehandedly responsible, winning for him the deepening affections of the old man (who afterwards began continually recommending to Rome that Hughes be made a bishop) and the wary respect of the public, who learned that this was a man far above the caliber of the clerical pygmies they thought were representative of the priesthood.[24]

Indeed, if it is not on the edge of blasphemy to say so, the reaction of the people of Philadelphia to Hughes was like that of the Galileans to Christ after he gave the Sermon on the Mount: "[F]or he taught them as one who had authority, and not as their scribes" (Mt 7:29).

Conwell, if he was surprised at all by Hughes' decision, welcomed him back to St. Joseph's and decided not to send any other priests to St. Mary's. For Conwell, however, this was the last hurrah. His dealings with the trustees, including compromises made with them, had been brought to the attention of Propaganda Fide in Rome, and he was summoned there to answer questions about the near chaos in Philadelphia, the upshot of which was the naming of a coadjutor, Francis Kenrick, and Conwell's effective retirement at the age of eighty-four. He would live for another decade, but he never again played a role in the life of his diocese.

Bishop Kenrick asked Hughes to found a parish and build a church, one that was to become the city's cathedral. That church was St. John the Evangelist, which opened in 1832. By all accounts, it was the finest ever seen in America. (Hughes also opened a Catholic school in the church basement.) A few years before, Hughes had spearheaded the foundation of a Catholic orphanage, also named for St. John, and the remainder of his time in Philadelphia was characterized mostly by outreach to Philadelphia's poor, sometimes in cooperation with the city's Protestants.

But his relations with Catholicism's separated brethren were not always amicable, even through almost always respectful. And his engagement with Protestants is very important in understanding why John Joseph Hughes would soon be tapped by Rome to become coadjutor bishop in New York. To be sure, Hughes was developing a reputation as a builder—as a man who could tackle the construction of churches, orphanages, and sodalities in aid of the faithful—and as a champion of Catholic orthodoxy as against republican-minded Catholic laity and priests, and as a priest above all loyal to the Church hierarchy. But in all this, important as it was, he was not entirely unique. What made the man stand out—indeed, what brought him fame—was his vigorous defense of Catholicism against the growing threat of anti-Catholicism and nativism in America. He was no longer the timorous seminarian.

John Hughes contra Mundum

Among Hughes' first attempts at what we may call public apologetics came in the form of an answer of sorts to a novel published in Britain that became a best seller in America. It went by various titles but is best known as *Andrew Dunn: An Irish Story*. Written by a Protestant, Thomas Kelly, it purported to be the story of a young Catholic's awakening to the horrible truths about the Catholic faith—and his salvific conversion to Protestantism.

In his spare time, Hughes wrote a reply (in novel form as well), arranged for its publication, and awaited the acclaim that would follow. But there are few accolades for any book that hardly anybody reads. Hughes sent a number of copies to Simon Bruté with the request that his mentor put them in the hands of those who might make the book better known. "I do not wish the thing to make noise," he wrote to Bruté, somewhat disingenuously, "because the Protestants will take alarm."

He needed not have worried. Bruté could not get through the book and never did give any copies away.[25]

But that was only a minor setback for John Joseph Hughes. His ability as a preacher was improving apace, and he soon began to receive requests from Catholic congregations that he travel to their parishes to preach. Among those visits was one to St. Peter's in Manhattan in 1829, and it may have been on that trip that he came to the attention of a Princetonian named John A. Breckinridge.

Breckinridge hardly fits our modern ideas about nativists, because he was something of an intellectual and very much a "liberal", which to him meant broad-minded. In fact, at that time, liberalism often meant a kind of republicanism (sometimes to the point of Jacobinism) and individualism, and liberals were thus suspicious of—if not frankly hostile to—ancient institutions such as the Roman Catholic Church. Breckinridge did not think of himself as a nativist, but he and others like him laid the foundations of mid-nineteenth-century anti-Catholicism. Liberalism, as such, was a meaningless concept to most people. But, in the words of Philip Hamburger of Columbia Law School:

> In the name of "Americanism" the nativists assailed the Catholic Church for seeking temporal power—an accusation substantiated by pointing to the extravagant claims of the Pope and some Catholic clergy [and refuted by Hughes]. More fundamentally, however, nativists also condemned the ... Church for asserting its religious authority over its own adherents, thus, allegedly, depriving them of the mental freedom necessary for American citizenship.[26]

A creedal faith, such as is professed by Catholics, was to the Protestant liberal establishment a religion of enslavement, from which its people were in need of liberation. This seemed especially so to some Presbyterians, such as Breckinridge, who in 1835 wrote that the Catholic Church "is anti-American and anti-liberal". And further: "The papal system cannot become liberal, and they [Catholics] will not renounce it; and here we join issue—here we fix our final opposition to it as anti-American, as well as anti-Christian."[27]

In response to this sort of statement, Hughes began a back-and-forth with Breckinridge in 1832 that, when first collected and published in book form in 1833, comprised more than three hundred double-column pages.[28] The two went at it, Breckinridge in Protestant periodicals and Hughes in Catholic ones, and by most accounts Hughes got the better of the argument—not that Reverend Breckinridge or his friends would have so conceded. But, given the temper of the time, few had thought a Catholic could even make a credible defense of this "foreign" doctrine.

Given his growing confidence as an orator, Hughes had initially wished for a face-to-face debate, but Breckinridge demurred. (They did eventually engage in a number of debates, but these occasions were diminished by descents into incivility and by raucous crowds that, apparently, were either not interested in reasonableness or were incapable of understanding the issues.)[29] An indication of how Breckinridge felt about the progress of the arguments may be intuited from one of the last letters the two exchanged (September 21, 1833), this one written by Breckinridge in Philadelphia, not at his home in New York:

> To the Reverend John Hughes,
> I have received with extreme regret your *verbal* reply to my letter of the 19th inst. in which you wholly decline my proposal to finish the pending Controversy in a public oral discussion.[30]

But Hughes believed he had won the day, and he saw no reason either to change the current format of the debate or, if Breckinridge refused that, to continue on at all. Probably both men were weary of the exchange, by then nearly a year in duration. Certainly, Hughes was pleased with himself for having avoided the temptation to return insult with insult:

> I have wounded no man's feelings; I have ridiculed no man's religion; I have injured no man's character.... I am proud to believe that, though a Catholic and a priest, I stand as high in public, even Protestant, estimation as Mr. Breckinridge himself.[31]

We recall that in the nineteenth century such public debates, carried on in newspapers or, if oral, reprinted in them, were among the era's most popular entertainments—and not just for the literati. The arguments Hughes made, both for the ancient tenets of his faith and for his (and, by extension, other immigrant Catholics') newfound loyalty to the United States of America, resonated equally in the Vatican's Apostolic Palace and in the mean streets of New York's Five Points neighborhood.

To be clear: Nativism was rising to become a force in American life, and Hughes saw it coming and intended to do his part to stop it. But he also believed that nativism was a virus not just among Protestants, whether bluebloods or hoi polloi. He saw in the agitation of trustees and dissident priests such as Hogan and Harold the same essential infection, one that would later become a very serious issue in the Church as the heresy (or near heresy) of Americanism.

Bishop Hughes

John England was an Irishman (born in Cork in 1786) who, at the age of thirty-four, became the first bishop of Charleston, South Carolina. Six years later, he had the extraordinary privilege of being the first Catholic priest to address Congress—in a two-hour speech that was, in part, a response to an anti-Catholic speech given some years before by John Quincy Adams—secretary of state at the time. But when Bishop England addressed Congress on January 8, 1826, President Adams was in the gallery, and by then the president had warmed to Bishop England and developed a spirit of religious tolerance, and the bishop had come to believe that Americans were ripe for evangelizing.

> They [Americans] are a well-disposed, religiously-inclined people: there is but one true Church, and that is the Roman Catholic; but how can they believe without evidence?—they have never received it. They must be instructed not abused. They must be expostulated with, not quarreled with. They are not obstinate heretics—they are an inquiring, thinking, reasoning ... I will add, a pious people.[32]

Bishop England's eminence in America was matched by his reputation in Rome, and while he was in the Holy City on an *ad limina* visit in 1833, the cardinal-prefect of Propaganda Fide, Carlo Maria Pedicini, approached him and asked for his opinion on which American priest would be the Vatican's best choice to succeed Edward Fenwick as bishop of Cincinnati. There are two under consideration, the cardinal explained: John Baptist Purcell and John Joseph Hughes. "If you can mention any particular, no matter how trifling," Pedicini said, "in which one seems to you better qualified than the other, I think a decision may be reached at once."[33]

England did not want to answer. He knew and admired both men and had no wish to pick one over the other. So he asked for time to think about it, probably hoping he could stall until it was time for him to return to Charleston. But Pedicini persisted.

And England relented. Well, he told the cardinal, "there is one point ... which may deserve to be considered. Mr. Hughes is emphatically a self-made man, and perhaps he would be on that account more acceptable to the people of a Western diocese than Mr. Purcell."

Pedicini was elated and hurried off to report to his dicastery and his pope, Gregory XVI. The next day, he caught up with England again. "Well, bishop," he said, "the question is settled. As soon as I told the cardinals what you said about Mr. Purcell's being a self-made man, they agreed upon him unanimously!"[34]

Obviously, this conversation was reported by Bishop England himself, who added that he at first thought to explain to the cardinal that he was mistaken—that *Hughes* was the man for the West. "But I reflected that it was no doubt the work of the Holy Spirit", and so he remained silent. Subsequent history may have proved

England's insight entirely justified, even though later on, when the New York episcopacy was in play, he was personally in favor of his friend John Power. Perhaps he even reflected that John Dubois, who was feeling his age and was actively seeking a coadjutor to help out in his declining years, would almost certainly put Hughes' name on his short list of candidates for that position. England may thus have figured that a Hughes passed over, as he now appeared to have been for Cincinnati, would be a Hughes diminished in stature in Rome.

In fact, Bishop Dubois' first thought was Bishop Kenrick, so recently named coadjutor to Conwell in Philadelphia, and he campaigned vigorously for Kenrick's appointment. But Philadelphia (which is to say, St. Mary's) was too riven to consider moving Kenrick anywhere.

John Power, now in his mid-forties, had done his best to make himself the popular choice of New York's Catholics. He was the vicar-general of the diocese, but, as we saw in chapter 1, he was also an almost embarrassing campaigner for a bishop's miter. And Dubois had no love for Power. As Monsignor Thomas J. Shelley wrote, "Both John Power and Thomas Levins ... rector of [Old St. Patrick's] ... criticized him harshly as an incompetent administrator",[35] and, sensing that neither Kenrick nor John Timon, another American priest he had recommended to Rome (although he had never met the man), was going to win Rome's approval, he thought to add the name of John J. Hughes. There was loyalty there, surely. And Hughes was Irish, after all.

Kenrick, who would not have accepted the New York bishopric had it been tendered (a "thorny crown", he called it), had suggested that he be transferred to Pittsburgh and that Hughes replace him as coadjutor to the nonagenarian Conwell. "Propaganda approved the plan in January 1836," Shelley wrote, "but Pope Gregory ... deferred action because he wished to give the U.S. bishops the opportunity to consider the proposal ... at their next provincial council, which took place in Baltimore in April 1837."[36] And all the bishops but one designated Hughes for the job. The only one to vote no was John England.

One other name considered at that council of bishops was Father Samuel J. Mulledy, S.J., president of Georgetown University. Among the first things bishop-designate Hughes did upon receiving confirmation of his episcopal appointment in November of 1837 (after sending a note to Dubois) was write to Mulledy to ask him to give the homily at his consecration at St. Patrick's on January 7, 1838. Mulledy apparently had other plans, but, as historian Vincent Peter Lannie wrote, "The newly acquired influence of the episcopal state was sufficiently convincing to eliminate the obstacles."[37]

Dubois officiated at the consecration, assisted by Kenrick and a familiar face at St. Patrick's: Benedict Fenwick, now bishop of Boston. According to Catholic practice, Hughes received a titular see: he became bishop of Basilinopolis, an ancient city in Turkey.

Also in the cathedral that day was John McCloskey, who—as has been pointed out since the very first accounts of Hughes' life—would deliver the eulogy at Archbishop Hughes' funeral twenty-six years later to the day. McCloskey did not know then that he would be chosen as Hughes' successor, although as Hughes' health declined in the 1860s, he feared he would be. Such apprehensions have often gone with the appointment.

In his letter to Dubois ahead of his consecration, Hughes had expressed his own deep concern about his prospects in New York. For one thing, he knew the general opinion among the laity had been in favor of Father Power. For another, although this was not mentioned, he had to dread the prospect of finding himself in a situation similar to the Kenrick-Conwell drama in Philadelphia. Most coadjutor arrangements are, as they say, fraught. But gentle Bishop Dubois, confident of his own authority—illness notwithstanding—and sure of Hughes' unending gratitude to him for the opportunities he had given the young Hughes back at the Mount, reassured his new coadjutor: "You surely could not suppose a moment that I would encroach upon the rights and privileges attached to that sacred office, and I have too great an opinion of your merit and affection for me to suppose that you would encroach upon mine."[38]

He was not wrong—not exactly—although he would come to believe he had been. He soon suffered the first in a series of strokes, which would lead quickly to Hughes' designation as apostolic administrator and his assumption of the powers necessary to act accordingly. Bishop Dubois knew he was diminished in capacity, but—despite his ischemic attacks—he believed himself capable of governance, and continued to govern until he died four years later.

The fundamental difficulty Hughes faced as he began his episcopal tenure would quickly become obvious to him: poverty—material poverty, including a paucity of priests and churches; and a certain weakness of spirit among the faithful, especially among lay trustees.

Changing New York—Forever

Even a few thousand poor Catholics, such as Bishop R. Luke Concanen might have found, had he made it to New York back in 1808, would have been one thing; what Hughes inherited was quite another. As he would write to Cincinnati's Bishop Purcell in 1838: "The people were too poor and for a long time the increase in their numbers only added to their poverty as emigrants [principally Irish and Germans] arrived in our port from Europe penniless."[39] And New York had yet to face the truly huge immigrant influx that would accompany Ireland's Great Famine of the 1840s and 1850s. (One million Irish would die of starvation in Ireland as a result of the famine, and a nearly equal number would come to the United States. The peak year was 1850.) During Hughes' time in New York, Catholicism went from being a minority Christian denomination to being America's largest.

It might be difficult in the twenty-first century to imagine the disruption this immigrant tsunami caused. (The recent flood of immigrants into Europe may give some idea.) To be sure, we have over recent decades seen immigration across the southern border of the United States that is unprecedented in absolute numbers, but not on a comparative scale. In fact, the impact on New York of Catholic immigration in the nineteenth century was far more dramatic. The term "melting pot" would not become common until the beginning of the twentieth century, and with good reason.

As we saw in Hughes' debates with John Breckinridge, nativism was on the rise among all classes of society. But, more or less along the lines Hughes outlined to Purcell with regard to poverty, the sudden rise in immigration was like kindling thrown upon flickering nativism, and it caused a social bonfire. Poor, mostly rural Irish flooded into Manhattan, Brooklyn, the Bronx (which was then part of West-chester County), and elsewhere in New York at a pace that economic growth and employment opportunities simply could not match. And unlike today—legal issues aside—there were few social structures to aid immigrants; few structures and, there-fore, little advocacy.

But there was the Church. And throughout his tumultuous reign as bishop and then archbishop (much of the tumult having nothing to do with him or the Church, but rather with the Civil War), John Hughes would accomplish astonishing things. As Monsignor Shelley wrote:

> The twenty-five years that he was the spiritual leader of New York's Catholics were the most significant in the history of the diocese. For better or for worse, no bishop or archbishop ... before or since has [had] as profound an impact on New York Catholicism as John Hughes. He inherited a rudderless ship with a mutinous crew and bequeathed to his successor the largest, wealthiest and most important archdiocese in North America.[40]

Of course, he also left that successor, John McCloskey, a mountain of debt and numerous administrative headaches, but the Hughes era was what it needed to be: a period of solidification and growth—both things that had been needed but not accomplished since 1808. What John Hughes may have lacked in administra-tive skill and financial capability was outweighed by his ability to identify prob-lems and seek to solve them. Few solutions to social problems are ever absolute or permanent, but the inventive mind of Hughes created institutions (among them, churches, a cathedral, orphanages, hospitals, immigrant-aid societies, schools, and a seminary) that helped New York's growing immigrant Catholic population better assimilate into American life. It is true that he did more for the Irish than for, say, the Germans, but all Catholics benefited from his efforts to show them and the larger Protestant population that they could be what nativists said they could not be: Catholic *and* American.

It is often assumed that John Hughes got his "Dagger" nickname because of his street-fighter personality, and there's some truth in this. But as he began to issue replies in the press to attacks coming from Protestants and nativists, and in printed versions of his sermons, speeches, and exhortations, there would appear with his printed signature a cross—a device most bishops have always used when signing documents by hand. In typography at the time, there was no cross avail-able to printers, so they used the closest symbol they had: the dagger. It looks like this: †. Of course, in other dioceses, bishops (and their printers) used the same symbol, but none of them was nicknamed Dagger. With Hughes, it seemed an appropriate association.

It was during his episcopacy—doubtless owing to the number of personal appearances he was obligated to make (but, perhaps, because of vanity as well)—that Hughes began to wear a scratch wig. This was not the powdered sort worn by men in earlier centuries, but more along the lines of a toupee, designed to blend in with his hair while covering bald spots. In photographs of Hughes, the wig is hardly discernible.

He had by now lost much of his brogue—another indication of his adaptability to American life. Shelley notes that he retained "just the slightest trace of a soft Irish accent".[41] He was, one might say, Irish in his bones but American in his skin. For many New Yorkers, this was sufficient to make him worthy of esteem; less so, however, for the diocese's clergy. As one contemporary witness described it:

> They had heard and approved of the great things achieved in Philadelphia ... [by Hughes]. But why was he sent to New York, when some See might have been found for him in Pennsylvania ... [and Father John Power], a man known and loved by all classes of citizens, might with so much profit have been placed at their head?[42]

There was enmity too from one of New York's most important newspapers, the *Herald*, and its peculiarly anti-Catholic Catholic founding editor, James Gordon Bennett.

Bennett was a Catholic immigrant from Scotland. As a teenager he had considered the priesthood and had attended a seminary in Aberdeen. At twenty-four he decided to emigrate. He became a schoolteacher in Nova Scotia, moved to Boston, where he got into the newspaper business, and finally settled in New York, where he worked for two papers before founding his own, the *Herald*, in 1835.

The era of yellow journalism was still several generations away, but Bennett's *New York Herald* may lay claim to being America's first newspaper to adopt what today we think of as tabloid (i.e., sensational) journalism. The purpose of popular journalism, Bennett said, was "not to instruct but to startle".[43] Advertisers had to pay up front—not the practice at the time—and most were happy to do so, since Bennett's shocking stories sent the circulation of the *Herald* soaring. Still in its first year, the *Herald* gave front-page coverage to the murder of a prostitute named Helen Jewett and the subsequent trial of a young client of hers, Richard P. Robinson. Before this, no American newspaper had ever given so much attention to such a sordid affair—and with so much lurid detail. Bennett took Robinson's side, and Robinson was acquitted of the crime, although he may well have been guilty.

In any event, the *Herald* quickly rose to become America's most popular and profitable newspaper.

Bennett had a peculiar relationship with Catholicism in New York and with the city's first archbishop. It is not uncommon to read in descriptions of Bennett that he was an anti-Catholic nativist, but he was actually anti-Irish. As a recent writer put it, "He harrumphed that Catholic rituals were pure poetry, especially episcopal consecrations, but to hold such a ceremony before the 'general run of New York Irish was like putting gold rings through pigs' noses.'"[44]

And then there was Hughes himself, who represented for Bennett all that was wrong with American Catholicism. As one pro-Bennett biographer has written:

> As the Know-Nothing sentiment grew, the Archbishop became more virulent, thundering against Bennett in press and pulpit—rival editors being foolish enough to print his fulminations. He also, in effect, excommunicated the aggressive editor—all of which helped the *Herald*. Undauntedly the editor continued his crusade, and went so far as to demand the separation of the Catholic Church in America from the rule of Rome. He wanted an American church free from the overlordship of the hierarchy.[45]

One may without difficulty imagine how such sentiments were received by John Hughes. According to Carl Sandburg, Hughes considered Bennett "a very dangerous man".[46]

The sparks began to fly between the two men the day after Hughes' consecration, when Bennett noted, as quoted previously, that having in attendance at the cathedral so many Catholics from all stations in society, "was like putting gold rings through pigs' noses."[47] All in all, it was an inauspicious welcome for New York's fourth bishop.

Bennett's attitude would never change; the attitudes of Hughes' clergy and pretty much the rest of nonnativist New York would.

Job One: Education

In 1858, two decades into his episcopacy, John Hughes wrote a memoir-cum-apologia of his time in New York thus far. It was in the form of a letter to his friend the Reverend Bernard Smith, O.S.B., an Irishman who taught in Rome at Propaganda Fide's Urban College. Although addressed to Smith, Hughes' missive was principally intended for the eyes of Cardinal Alessandro Barnabò, Propaganda's prefect.

This "letter", which in printed form (depending on the version considered) is some fifty pages long, is the archbishop's account of his goals and achievements over his (then) two decades in New York. In it, Hughes explains that he faced seven challenges:

> *First*—The mixed or divided government of the Church between the authority of the Bishop ... and that of Lay Trustees ...
> *Second*—The education of Catholic Children, under a system of protestant, or rather infidel, training established by law ...
> *Third*—The insufficient number of churches, their indebtedness, and the inability, as it seemed, of the Catholic Community to build more.
> *Fourth*—The absence of any provision for the training of Ecclesiastics.
> *Fifth*—The evils entailed on this Diocese ... as remote consequences of the Irish famine ...
> *Sixth*—The ruinous rebound of the Revolutions in Europe immediately after the famine [with] ... numerous refugees from several nations, who ... left nothing undone to overthrow all respect for religion ...
> *Seventh and lastly*—The prevalence of a faction calling itself "*Know-nothing*".[48]

This outline of sorts will serve as a road map—with detours—for the rest of the story of the episcopacy and archiepiscopacy of John Hughes. But rather than serially following his list, we will begin with education, the second and fourth points in his letter.

Bishop Hughes understood well, especially because of his own experience, the importance of education in helping immigrants rise out of poverty. So he set about to educate New York's Catholics—in primary and secondary schools and in seminaries.

Toward the end of the episcopacy of Hughes' successor, John McCloskey, the issue of Americanism arose, and it dominated in some sense the episcopacy of

Michael Corrigan and lingered into that of John Farley; we will have much to say about that in the next three chapters. But to start with, part of what gave rise to this "heresy" (if that is what it was) was the spirit of independence in America and the distance of former Europeans from the old countries, which among Catholics meant a great remove from Rome. America's political institutions were new (no matter to what extent they were derived from European and classical roots), and it seemed to many that American religion also ought to be new; a perfect example of this was the ongoing crisis concerning trusteeism. But on the positive side, there was also among Catholics a great desire to have clergy of their own: American priests trained in American seminaries. It would take some time for the Vatican to adapt to this model, which was actually very much the one the hierarchy used, although not exclusively, in Europe: Italian priests for Italy, French clerics for France. But first Rome needed to see and believe that America could produce the sort of men who were needed. And it did not take long for Rome to believe: first the Brooklyn-born McCloskey—educated at Mount St. Mary's, named coadjutor to Hughes in 1843 and his successor in 1864, and made the first American cardinal in 1872—and then the New Jersey–born Corrigan (also a Mount grad) followed throughout their careers the path of Americans for America. Localism—an Americanism that had no theological component—would become the rule.

But first New York must have its own seminary. Bishop John Dubois had made this a priority, but his efforts were frustrated by his inability as a fund-raiser (a problem nearly as important then as it is today) and by fate.

In 1832, Dubois purchased land on the west side of the Hudson River near the site of today's Tappan Zee Bridge. As work commenced on the seminary in 1834, Dubois hired the Reverend John McGerry, one of his successors at the Mount, as president, and one additional professor as well: the twenty-four-year-old McCloskey, fresh from his ordination at Dubois' hands. Classes began to be held in a house already on the property, and the students included John Loughlin, who would go on to become Brooklyn's first bishop.[49]

During construction of the new building, however, a fire started, and the site was damaged beyond repair. Dubois had no money to begin the job again.

Cornelius Heeney, a Catholic former business partner of fur magnate John Jacob Astor, offered a site he owned in Brooklyn, but he refused to deed ownership of the land to the Church until *after* the seminary's construction, so Dubois backed away.

When John Hughes was given the powers of the ailing Dubois in 1839, he found himself in possession of 460 acres in the tiny town of La Fargeville, New York, way up in the north-central part of the state, at the northeastern tip of Lake Ontario. Here Hughes founded St. Vincent de Paul Seminary, which within a year was closed—a complete failure due to its inability, so far from New York City, to attract students.

Hughes now looked closer to home and in 1840 found land in the Rose Hill section of the Bronx, then a lovely wooded area (and now home, lovely in a new way, to the New York Botanical Garden and the Bronx Zoo). This was the beginning of St. Joseph's Seminary, which remained at Rose Hill until the year of Hughes' death (1864). Rose Hill was also where Hughes would found St. John's College in 1841, with McCloskey as its first president. (This institution—later renamed

Fordham University—is not to be confused with St. John's University in Queens, New York, founded in 1870 by the Vincentian Fathers.)

When McCloskey succeeded Hughes as archbishop, he moved St. Joseph's Seminary up the Hudson River to Troy, New York, in Rensselaer County, where it would remain until Auxiliary Bishop John Murphy Farley (a graduate of the seminary at the Troy location) reestablished it in 1896 at its current location in the Dunwoodie section of Yonkers.

Hughes gave equal—if not greater—attention to the development of both primary and secondary education, because the need among immigrants, especially the Irish, was so great. According to Joseph McCadden, education professor at New York's Hunter College, at the time of Hughes' arrival in New York, "eight makeshift parochial schools, meeting in church basements or rented halls, had on register about 5,000 Catholic children. An additional 7,000 either lacked accommodation or made no effort to go to school."[50] As bad as that sounds, Professor McCadden's estimation of the extent of the problem may represent a substantial undercounting.

Aid had been given to these early Catholic schools by New York's Public School Society, but that had ended in 1825. After that year, the Society was still willing to educate Catholic children, but it intended to do so in its own very Protestant manner. At first, Catholics had no intention of enrolling their children in the Society's better-provided-for schools, believing that it was better not to go to hell than (perhaps) to go to Harvard. Elizabeth Ann Seton's half brother, Samuel Seton, worked for the Public School Society, attempting to convince parents in poor neighborhoods to allow their children to attend the Society's schools.[51] The Society even convinced the city's Common Council (which later became the Board of Aldermen and is today the City Council) to pass legislation making it "an offence [sic] in a minor to be found idle and uninstructed and subject to commitment if reformation did not take place".[52] By "commitment" the law meant that these poor children would be sent into the country to reside at a farm–labor school.

A few years before Hughes became bishop, what was probably New York's finest Catholic school, run by the Sisters of Charity and facing (Old) St. Patrick's on Mulberry Street, had burned to the ground. Dubois had gone miter in hand to the Society, asking that the children be accommodated in a nearby Society school and that he might have a say in the choice of teachers and textbooks. The Society said this would be *unconstitutional*, adding this remarkable contradiction: "religious and moral instruction is given in the schools entirely free from sectarianism".[53]

But the Society remained determined to bring Catholic children into its ambit—partly because the more students its schools had, the more money it would receive in support from the government, but also for the reclamation of the students' souls from papist captivity. As a matter of strategy, the Society invited Catholic laymen to join its board and even agreed to remove some books from its curriculum if something in the text offended Catholic sensibilities. Dubois could easily have said yes (or no), but he appears to have decided not to decide.

Governor William H. Seward, with whom Hughes would become friends (and who later brought together Hughes and Abraham Lincoln), was very aware of the plight of immigrant Catholic children in New York. Early in 1840, he told the state's legislators that more than twenty-five thousand immigrant children were not being educated, and he believed they should be allowed to learn from Catholic teachers if they were Catholic and in German if that was the language of their heritage. The point was to get them educated so they could become productive American citizens. Nativists who had supported Seward were outraged. (*His* nativists were anti-Catholic, to be sure, but they were also of the Anti-Masonic Party, which saw in Freemasonry an elite, anti-democratic, and un–American cabal.)

While Hughes was in Europe trying to raise money for the diocese, Father John Power, again vicar-general of the diocese (although this time *co*-vicar-general), sought to become a lobbyist in Albany, with money from the Common Council if he could get it, in order to seize the momentum caused both by the governor's speech and by the Society's overtures of compromise. Not surprisingly, the Catholic newspaper the *Truth Teller*, to which Power was a contributor, endorsed the idea of his mission, although the editors were educational separatists. But another cathedral priest, the Cuban-born Félix Varela—the other co-vicar-general—used his newly founded (1839) *New York Catholic Register* to campaign not for the sort of compromises Power was willing to accept (Society schools with some Catholic content—the deal offered to Dubois) but for an entirely separate Catholic school system, funded exactly as the Public School Society's system was.[54] When Power found both the *Truth Teller* and the *Catholic Register* uncooperative, he founded his own sheet, the *Freeman's Journal*. (The *Register* would soon merge with the *Journal*.) In the end, the Common Council refused to fund Power's lobbying, citing the same constitutional argument put forward by the Society.

It is important to pause briefly to recount the career of Father Varela. Although born in Cuba, he had grown up in Florida, and he had a remarkable facility for languages, so much so that he even mastered "Irish" (Gaeilge or Gaelic), the better to speak with New York's largest, poorest group of immigrants.

Varela received his seminary training in Cuba, lived in Spain for a while, and campaigned for Latin American independence. Barely escaping a death sentence for his political activity, he went to New York, where he spent most of the rest of his life. He was instrumental in the development of the *Baltimore Catechism* and was the founder of *El Habanero*, one of the first Spanish-language papers in the United States. For health reasons, he spent the last few years of his life in St. Augustine, Florida, where he died and was buried in 1853. In 1913 his body was returned to Cuba. In 2012, under the sponsorship of the Archdioceses of Miami and New York, Varela was designated by the Vatican's Congregation for the Causes of Saints as *Venerable*, an early step on the way to canonization.

But back to Bishop Hughes: It was not until six months after Governor Seward's speech of advocacy for Catholic education that Hughes returned from his European journey. He quickly assessed the various pros and cons of the education question, especially those put forward by his vicars-general, taking the side of Varela. (He went so far as to call Power a "Protestant priest".)

In a letter dated August 27, 1840, he wrote: "Whether we shall succeed or not in getting our proportion of the public money ... the effort will cause an entire separation of our children from those [Public] schools—and excite greater zeal on the part of our people for Catholic education."[55]

This was a fight Hughes would lose. The street fighter was punching too far above his weight. There were simply too many Protestants in New York and too much anti-Catholic sentiment, even with the governor's moral support. Hughes came to consider the Society nothing more than a "wicked monopoly which claimed to take charge of the minds and hearts of Catholic children", and history gives credence to the claim. Many of the Society's board members were little different from those who were, throughout New York and New England, engaged in abolitionist campaigns to end slavery but with no intention of ever sharing power or proximity with freed slaves.

Bishop Hughes wrote to Governor Seward and included a copy of his own jeremiad against the Public School Society: *Address of the Roman Catholics to Their Fellow-Citizens, of the City and State of New York*. Simply put, it was, in the words of Professor McCadden, a "scathing attack on [the Society] ... for its godless, anti-Catholic schools and on the [Common Council] for misusing the shibboleth of constitutionality and favoring the new sectarianism of infidelity".[56] Seward wrote back saying that he read the address with "lively satisfaction".

At the urging of Thurlow Weed, the political "kingmaker" who had helped secure five presidential nominations and who would become an even better friend to Hughes than Seward himself, the governor invited the bishop to Albany for discussions, news of which led the Society—still hoping to boost its coffers with Catholic enrollment—to offer all proposed texts for Hughes' review and to promise to drop *all* texts containing explicitly anti-Catholic material.

But Hughes was now firmly focused on the justice of public support for separate school systems, since to him the Society's schools were in fact Protestant. Had he been willing to compromise, there might have evolved in the United States a system of publicly funded parochial schools. Whether or not the bishop had it in mind, eventually, to try to obtain such a deal, events quickly spiraled out of control. Nativist Protestants and nativists of no particular religion began to attack any idea of accommodation for Catholics with regard to education. The Methodist Episcopal Church issued a statement reminding New Yorkers of the Catholic Church's intolerance, and specifically of "the revocation of the Edict of Nantes, the massacre of St. Bartholomew's Day, the fires of Smithfield, ... [and] the crusade against the Waldenses",[57] thus evoking incidents of violent Catholic anti-Protestantism from 1685, 1572, 1555, and 1487, respectively.

At the end of October 1840, several days of arguments began before the (now) Board of Aldermen. Hughes spoke for Catholic New York; able and experienced lawyers represented the Society. The Society's representatives carefully and cleverly argued that no one was disputing the importance of using the Bible in the educational process, but that simply meant that edifying biblical passages ought to be chosen by a committee of Protestants and Catholics, the results to be acceptable to both sides.

Hughes engaged in a stem-winder of a recitation of Colonial anti-Catholicism, arguing that the Society was reviving it. And at the end of his presentation to the aldermen, the bishop believed he had the best of the argument.

The board voted fifteen to one *against* him. Among other reasons Hughes lost was the widespread fear that a Catholic victory might lead to the sort of riot that had erupted in Boston six years before, during which nativist crowds had torched an Ursuline convent.

Hughes then began to use insult in return for injury, engaging in a campaign against the Society that, had things gone differently—had he incited massive

Catholic protests—might have properly been termed incendiary. "The Union is repealed!" he told one cheering crowd.[58]

Meanwhile, Governor Seward kept up the drumbeat for Catholic education in Albany. His superintendent of schools very publicly reaffirmed the principle—one evoking the argument offered before the Board of Aldermen by the Society—that the Christian religion ought to be part of every child's instruction, although his conclusion was that this implied state-funded Catholic schools. He put forward a bill to that effect.

There was so much politicking going on that there was grumbling on all sides about violations of the barrier between church and state. Father Varela felt it necessary to address the issue in the *Catholic Register* after handbills featuring a pro-Irish talk by the governor were left in the pews at St. Peter's: "The Church recognizes no political party, and the Ecclesiastical Authority is prepared to exercise its spiritual power, should in future any individual of any party whatever dare to perpetrate similar acts."[59]

Most people with any knowledge of New York political history know that Tammany Hall (or the Tammany Society, or Sons of St. Tammany—although the name actually derived from a legendary leader of the Lenape, Manhattan's first human inhabitants), the political organization founded in the late 1780s, was the center of activity on behalf of Irish immigrants. The Hughes era preceded the rise of William M. "Boss" Tweed, but the Tammany Society was very powerful in the 1840s, and a force with which Hughes should have allied himself. But he did not. Neither, apparently, did he in this case exactly approve the statement of Father Varela.

In the lead-up to legislative elections in 1841, Hughes, who had often and vigorously asserted that the Church had no business involving herself in politics, announced the formation of the Catholic Party (aka the Carroll Hall ticket—the Hall being a Catholic gathering place that would soon become the Church of St. Andrew): a slate of candidates offered as alternatives to both Tammany's Democrats and Seward's Whigs, although most of those on the Hughes slate were Democrats, and all were in favor of the bill that would have provided for funding for Catholic schools. The formation of an opposition party, even one largely in agreement with their positions, was intolerable to Tammany's "sachems", who voted to "rebuke, censure, and renounce" the bishop. James Gordon Bennett's *New York Herald* wrote of Hughes that "his impudent and atrocious attempt to convert his Church into a political faction" was an instance of the "worn-out impudence of priestcraft imported from Rome".[60]

The Catholic Party did not prevail, although the Democrats it supported won. Whether Hughes' foray into politics was appropriate is debatable, but it was not entirely ineffective, in that it demonstrated the sort of ad hoc organization the bishop could quickly put together—and the power he could wield. It also strengthened the bond between him and Seward. (Hughes may not have known at the time that Governor Seward had—almost at the time he had proposed it—quietly abandoned his support for a separate school system for Catholics.) But Seward's Whigs had mostly carried the day in 1841, and Hughes liked to joke with Seward that the bishop was now as subject to brickbats as was the governor.

Hughes had also underestimated the extent of *Catholic* opposition. Many of the city's Irish (exactly how many is uncertain) were actually opposed on principle to

Catholic schools. It was fine to have seminaries such as His Grace the Bishop of New York was establishing, and if folks wanted to send their children to a parochial school, that was their business. Hughes was already famous for his expansion of catechetical programs in churches; let him expand them further. But the ambition of many immigrant parents was focused upon seeing their children rise in American society, which is to say, *Protestant* society. They knew the ghetto and did not like it; they wanted their children free of it. They were Americans first and Catholics second.

In the end, a modified bill that established an elected school board for New York City passed into law, effectively ending the Public School Society's monopoly on education. But it also put into law a ban, still in existence, on state support for Catholic (and other religious) schools.

Whereas the history of the school controversy indicates that compromise of principles was mostly demanded of the Roman Catholics, some early deal between the Society and Bishop Dubois might, as suggested above, have led to the establishment of a principle that the state's interest in seeing *all* its citizens educated meant that it was appropriate to provide taxpayer support for both secular and parochial schools. Hughes had the same opportunity to make such an aid agreement. Had it been reached, of course, it might not have survived a challenge in the courts. In the end, the great school question resulted in nothing so much as an early example of what Father Richard John Neuhaus called the "naked public square": not just no Catholicism in public schools or even a denatured Christianity, but no religion whatsoever in public places.

Meanwhile, the controversy had left a lasting mark on Hughes' reputation. True, he became respected and even feared—a force with which to be reckoned. But for the remaining two-plus decades of his life, he would be known as a *politician*, a "charge" that was repeated so often (over his denials) that he could not escape it. Politicians sought his endorsement. As he later wrote, "I have often disclaimed this imputed political influence; but the more I disclaimed it, the more conviction to the contrary became strong and settled."[61]

And so, much of the rest of his episcopacy was spent in trying to raise sufficient funds to develop a separate Catholic school system, which he did. But his failed educational crusade had yet another consequence. He had undertaken the entire effort without consulting the diocese's trustees. He had shown Catholic New York exactly who the Church's leader was. The trustees were on notice.

The (Almost) End of Trusteeism

In the first chapter and in the discussion in this chapter of Hughes' time in Philadelphia, we saw the extent to which trusteeism threatened the Catholic Church in the United States. The roots of trusteeism—the system by which lay boards controlled the management of the parishes and dioceses to which they belonged, even insisting on hiring their own priests and designating their own bishops—were in the eighteenth century, when it made a certain kind of sense. There usually were, in a given locality, few priests and no bishop. Many Catholics—for instance, those in Buffalo, New York, who did not receive a priest until 1831[62]—had to devise ways of practicing their Catholic faith that elsewhere in the world had not been necessary in more than a thousand years.

Bishop Concanen knew very little about trusteeism and never witnessed it. Bishop Connolly was surprised by it and did his best to accommodate it. Bishop Dubois firmly confronted his trustees and was largely ignored by them. Bishop Hughes intended to end the practice entirely, and he came close to succeeding. Certainly he made clear to Catholics in his diocese and then archdiocese that this thing called the Church has a hierarchical structure, and, although he was an admirer of representative government, and in particular of America's republican democracy, that is not the way Holy Mother Church is organized and operates.

And we know from the archbishop's 1858 report to Propaganda that he considered his battle to end trusteeism the top item on the list of his goals and achievements. It is all but certain that officials in Rome were very much aware of the evils of trusteeism, but Hughes explained them anyway in the preface to his description of his actions against the practice. Whereas it was good that laymen should be involved in their churches, he wrote, trusteeism too often came down to this: If the trustees disliked a priest given to them by their bishop, "they respected, if you will, the authority of the Bishop in appointing him, for they were Catholics; but oftentimes refused him [the priest] the means of support because they were trustees."[63]

For Hughes, the problem cut to the heart of the faith itself: "I saw from the first moment of my entrance in the Episcopal office that religion could never take its proper and legitimate form and direction until this system ... should be modified or overthrown."[64] And Hughes had no intention of modifying it. He was all for overthrowing trustees.

To be sure, his traditionalist and hierarchical understanding of trusteeism—of the Church's essential authority over both discipline and proprietorship—was not the only way of looking at the issue. Clearly the trustees saw themselves as acting sensibly as Americans in exercising property and management rights that came naturally to them as purchasers, builders, and proprietors—as it had been in New York before John Connolly's arrival in 1815. Archbishop Carroll had done his best to administer the Church in New York for the three decades prior to Connolly's arrival, but what Connolly found was a Church (and churches) entirely built by laypeople. As Patrick Carey writes, it was unsurprising that the boards, having taken the initiative and financial risks involved in erecting churches, were reluctant simply to give over control—and not just of the property: "Lay initiative was likewise manifested when lay men and women became the spiritual supervisors of their communities, leading Catholics in prayer meetings, Bible readings, and other quasi-liturgical services, and helping to organize the religious instruction of their children."[65] In the Spirit of '76, you might say—"no taxation without representation"—trustees argued that to donate was to earn the right to administer. It was not exactly a case study in democracy, however, since boards of trustees were not elected by the parishioners as a whole, but only by the wealthy pew holders.

In some cases, trustees also had the backing of local law. Whereas the legal authorities in most jurisdictions were unwilling to consider regulating religious institutions, when and where disputes did arise, it was evidence of ownership (deeds, mortgages, trusts, and so forth) that judges and legislators looked to, favoring what was known as the "sectarian conception".[66] This could easily have been disastrous for the Catholic Church, since among all faiths in America it was the most centralized and hierarchical, the one with the least democratic structure. Simply consider what happened when Bishop Hughes asserted the Church's right to receive public funds for the support of education. And the fact that lay management and ownership were common among Protestant denominations made the Church's position especially perilous.

To what extent difficulties of a similar kind in Ireland—where the issue arose over Great Britain's assertion of the right to reject bishops appointed by Rome—affected American thinking is unclear, but as Professor Carey puts it: "The new age was republican."[67]

However much John Joseph Hughes admired the United States and the libertarian governance enshrined in America's Founding, he believed that his liberties derived not from consent of the governed but directly from God. The Declaration of Independence suggested this but did not accept the implications of it. Its God (reduced to "Nature's God") was too small. In Hughes' view, the Church had first claim to the hearts and minds of men: Irish, Italian, or German; Egyptian, Turk, or African—no matter how "hyphenated" these souls might become in America. All were God's children, and all were under the authority and spiritual direction of the Church that Jesus Christ bestowed upon Peter, the first pope. And, as Father Gerald C. Treacy wrote, "It is to the first Archbishop of New York that the honor is due of gaining the strangle-hold on the trustee adversary, and crushing with relentless force the foe that had continually disturbed the peace of the American Church from the days of Bishop Carroll."[68]

Hughes, an indefatigable fund-raiser, understood that if ownership was half of the problem of trusteeism (authority being the other half), he could make great progress against the trustee boards by personally eradicating the debt that troubled more than half of the city's Catholic churches. And "personally" here does not simply mean that he used Church funds to buy the churches: He put ownership of the churches into his own name.[69]

Hughes was aware that earlier attempts to rein in trustees had been only partially successful. In 1829, the First Provincial Council of Baltimore had decreed that bishops "thenceforth sponsor no church whose deed was not in their hands; ... that donations of the faithful did not establish title to [church property] ... and exhorted the bishops to use canonical penalties to bring trustees to terms".[70] A subsequent provincial council (1837) had issued similar instructions, but still Hughes found himself in New York facing trusteeism exactly as he had faced it in Philadelphia.

Purchasing properties was an efficient way to handle the most pressing legal problem, but it was not possible to find funds sufficient to buy all Church property in New York and northern New Jersey. So Hughes stepped forward boldly to establish his authority.

He had succeeded—although, as we saw, at a price—during the controversy over the school question, so he took a similar approach to trusteeism: instead of undertaking negotiations with trustees, he took his case directly to the faithful. In 1842 he called New York's first diocesan synod, where he educated (some would say, hectored) his priests about the chain of command, essentially: the Triune God, the one pope, followed by Hughes. Then he issued a pastoral letter: "In Regard to the Administration of the Sacraments, Secret Societies, and the 'Trustee System' in Reference to Church Property." The letter was widely reprinted in the press and read in churches.

The letter is addressed to "Venerable Brethren of the Clergy, and beloved Children of the Laity" from "JOHN, by the Grace of God, and the appointment of the Holy See, Bishop of Basileopolis [*sic*], Coadjutor to the Bishop, and Administrator of the Diocese of New York, Grace and Peace through our Lord Jesus Christ".[71] (A recent pastoral letter from Cardinal Timothy Dolan, titled "The Altar and the Confessional: A Pastoral Letter on the Sacrament of Penance", is addressed to "My dear friends in Christ".)

Bishop Hughes first thanks the clergy for their attentiveness during the synod—and for their "acquiescence". He reminds them that the statutes they discussed "are such as it is competent for the bishop to enact by his own sacred office, from which in fact their force is exclusively derived".[72] In two paragraphs he says all he needs to say to his priests; the rest of the twelve-page letter is his message to the laity about "the laws for the ecclesiastical discipline of this diocese". It is a history lesson.

It is true, he writes, that at times the Church has experienced persecutions—some violent, others by force of law—and that in such times of fight or flight it may have been necessary, especially when exile has caused Mother Church to seem distant, to tolerate a "departure from the ordinary laws and usages of the Catholic Church". There have been "privations, sufferings", and even martyrdom. But now, in "this happy country", that time of episcopal indulgence of error is at an end, and we must "return to the ordinary and regular discipline of the Church".[73]

The point of the letter is that the trustees had nobly done what needed to be done in the absence of ecclesiastical authority, but, should they persist in trusteeism, they would, by reason of failing in obedience to the bishop, become heretics. But Hughes was far too clever to begin with so obvious a point. Instead he first lists other liturgical and sacramental abuses, such as baptism in homes (with qualifications for distance for parents to travel or an infant's risk of death), and he emphasizes that traditional rules concerning confirmation, confession, and Communion will now be strictly enforced. Then he addresses matrimony, which he notes has been subjected to "abuses and sacrileges", most especially with regard to remarriage, which by his account happened often without a determination of annulment.

The letter evokes a Church all but utterly in disarray in terms of knowledge and enforcement of doctrine. When he emphasizes that Catholics proposing to partake of the sacraments (confession excepted) must be in a state of grace, one surmises that this may have been news to New Yorkers—that with regard to the statutes, he is the first to advise the "faithful at large of their existence". Marriage outside the faith (by implication a common practice) may be tolerated if and only if the Catholic partner is given full access to the sacraments and a pledge is given by the non-Catholic partner that the children born to the couple will be baptized in the Catholic Church and educated in the faith. "Without this condition, such marriages are not only disapproved but condemned and reprobated by the Church."[74]

The bishop makes clear that, under penalty of loss of access to the sacraments, no Catholic may be a member of any society or organization, public or secret (and New York was rife with both), whose principles are contrary to Church teaching.

Now he turns to trusteeism. "One of the most perplexing questions connected with the well-being of religion is the tenure and administration of ecclesiastical property." Here the trustees of the various churches in the diocese must have braced themselves for whatever was coming next, which was this:

We have known many trustees, and we have never known one to retire from the office a better Catholic or a more pious man than when he entered on it. But, on the contrary, we have known many, who, on retiring from that office, were found to have lost, not only much of their religious feeling, but also much of their faith; from whom their families have derived, perhaps, the first impulse in that direction which so many have taken, of alienation from the Church.[75]

Trusteeism: bad for the Church; morally fatal to the trustees. One can only imagine how this was read by the trustees themselves, most of whom had not entered into the building of churches and their administration with motives of profit, even if some enjoyed the power.

In his letter Hughes did not mention, as he would in his apologia to Propaganda Fide, that civil law required yearly election of boards of trustees, which led to canvassing for votes, and on election day to "scenes of scandal, strife, and violence, even to bloodshed, such as could hardly be surpassed in the unscrupulous political struggles of the wildest democracy".[76]

As he also pointed out to Propaganda, Hughes never singled out any individual trustees in his public statements.

In the end, he told his Roman confreres, "Hence, from that period, the trustees ... became docile and respectful towards the Episcopal authority ... [and] the whole system was overthrown, within a period of two or three years".[77] This was largely but not wholly true.

Churches with Irish priests and parishioners did mostly fall into line, but, as Monsignor Thomas Shelley observes, Hughes never overcame the trustees at St. Nicholas Kirche, a German congregation (in what is today Manhattan's Lower East Side): "It was only in 1908 that the trustees finally surrendered control of the parish to the archdiocese."[78] And non-Irish elsewhere resisted. Nativists also weighed in; they cared not at all for Catholics but relished the chance to attack what they considered a foreign power.

Bishop John Dubois died on December 20, 1842, and full control of the diocese, which had been John Hughes' de facto, now became his de jure. It was a transition of no difficulty for Hughes, since he had been fully in charge for four years. (It would be somewhat different eight years later, when, on July 19, 1850, Pope Pius IX elevated New York to the status of archdiocese, and the poor farmer's son from County Tyrone became Archbishop John J. Hughes.)

Hughes versus the Nativists

In 1843, Hughes put the parish of St. Louis in Buffalo under interdict—essentially what Bishop Conwell had done as a temporary measure against the trustees of St. Mary's in Philadelphia. Relations between Buffalo and the bishop were still strained when, in 1847, Buffalo became a separate diocese, with the Reverend John Timon, once considered by Dubois as a suitable coadjutor, designated as bishop. For a short time, a rapprochement seemed to be in place. But in 1851, the trustees and parishioners of St. Louis literally drove their new Jesuit pastor from the premises.[79] The church was again placed under interdict, and in 1853 Archbishop Hughes lobbied the New York State Senate for relief for Catholic parishes "by passing a property law which would provide for clerical ownership of church lands".[80] Nativists in the Senate, however, had exactly the opposite in mind.

Hughes had gone to Rome to participate in the ceremony that resulted from Pope Pius IX's survey of bishops on the question of the Virgin Mary's relationship to sin. This survey led to the bull *Ineffabilis Deus*, which established the doctrine of the Immaculate Conception. The pope made his infallible pronouncement on December 8, 1854.

Upon Hughes' return, he found himself at loggerheads over the property question with Senator Erastus Brooks, who had been elected in 1853 as a member of the Native American Party, aka the Know-Nothings. Brooks' position was that "the political state is Protestant ... [and] that other systems of faith are not in harmony with true civil and religious liberty."[81] The legislative bill that was proposed, and over which Brooks and Hughes debated in the newspapers, was called the Church Property Bill, and it essentially gave ownership of church property to laymen.

Nativism was born in the early years of the American republic. John Adams had advocated the Alien and Sedition Acts in 1798, and this may have been among the reasons he lost the presidency in 1800. The Acts were aimed specifically at German and Irish immigrants and made them liable to imprisonment at the whim of authorities for activities, including oral and printed speech, deemed anti-American. Also passed by the Federalist-controlled Congress in 1798 was the Naturalization Act, which increased from five to fourteen the number of years a person had to reside in the United States before becoming eligible for citizenship.

It was also true that, in some degree, Adams lost to Thomas Jefferson in 1800 because of the Constitution's three-fifths clause, which counted slaves in the national census. Since the census determined how many seats each state had in the Electoral College (as well as in the House of Representatives), this gave Southern candidates a distinct advantage in presidential elections.

The bitterness of the election of 1800 rippled forward throughout the next half century.

The spread of the nativist movement was rapid and remarkable, and it would be a mistake to look at Erastus Brooks' attacks on the Church in his debates with Hughes over the Church Property Bill as out of sync with popular opinion. With the possible exception of the first decade and a half of the twenty-first century, the period leading up to the Civil War was the most unstable and fractious in American history.

In New York City, for example, the painter and inventor Samuel F. B. Morse ran for mayor as a Nativist Party candidate in 1836, not long before the successful launch of his great invention, the telegraph. Two years before the election, he had been much in the public eye thanks to his anti-Catholic broadside, *Foreign Conspiracy against the Liberties of the United States*.[82]

And just a few years later, in the 1840s, nativist riots broke out in several American cities, not least in Philadelphia, where, in early May of 1844, a simple request from Bishop Francis Kenrick that the city's Catholic children attending public schools be allowed to read the Bible in the Douay-Rheims version exploded into riots during which two Catholic churches, St. Augustine and St. Philip Neri, were burned down. Bishop Kenrick closed all the Catholic churches in Philadelphia and called for calm.[83] Reading about this in the newspapers, Bishop Hughes remarked that

Philadelphia's Catholics "should have defended their churches, since the authorities could not or would not do it for them".[84]

And when nativist demonstrations were planned in New York in response to those in Philadelphia, Hughes went to see Mayor Robert Morris and told him the demonstrations ought to be stopped.

"Are you afraid that some of your churches may be burned?" the mayor asked.

"No, sir, but I'm afraid that some of yours will be burned. We can protect our own."[85]

Indeed, Hughes went further than that. He told Morris that "if a single Catholic church is burned in New York, the city will become a second Moscow", evoking the fires set by Napoleon's troops in 1812.[86] The mayor took notice, and he convinced the man recently elected to succeed him, the nativist James Harper, to convince the anti-Irish, anti-Catholic elements in New York not to rally.

In the *Freeman's Journal* a few days later, Hughes reassured his readers that if riots had broken out in New York, the "carnage that would have ensued is ... utterly beyond calculation".[87] He noted that every church in New York had been surrounded with thousands of Catholic defenders, "cool, collected, armed to the teeth", ready to take lives and sacrifice their own. As Monsignor Shelley quips: "The bishop's reflections hardly reflected the spirit of the Sermon on the Mount."[88]

As Shelley also notes, the bishop's assertion that thousands rallied in defense of churches (between one and three thousand per church, it has been suggested—with the largest number at Old St. Patrick's) may not actually pass a simple mathematical test. It's notable as well that no mention of such a deployment of defenders appears elsewhere in contemporary New York newspapers. The ad hoc organization and distribution of Catholic men as a military force would have been a labor worthy of Hercules—though Hughes was certainly up to it, especially since the diocese's priests were now fully behind him.

In any case, it seems clear that, whether through a show of arms or simply the threat of it, Hughes succeeded in quelling a riot. He would have somewhat less success in silencing State Senator Brooks.

Brooks thought nothing in his speeches and writing of mixing fact and fiction in describing the threat to America of its growing Catholic population—a threat best dealt with, he argued, by the republican expedients of disenfranchisement and divestiture. So he conjured up images of the poor French people "who voted to perpetuate the French dynasty ... [with] bayonets on one side of the ballot box and ... priests on the other".[89] (Napoleon Bonaparte had become first consul of France in 1799 and emperor in 1804, thus ending France's postrevolutionary democracy. By the time of Brooks' debates with Hughes, the French monarchy had fallen, replaced by the democratic Second Republic. The first president elected, however, was Louis-Napoleon Bonaparte, the former emperor's nephew, who affected a royalist coup d'état in 1851.)

The many exchanges between Brooks and Hughes—even more so than Hughes' earlier debates with John A. Breckinridge—were very popular with readers of the day, since the two men pulled no punches on matters of principle or personality. Hughes took their initial exchanges with deep seriousness—perhaps too much seriousness. Better was his very brief comment about the anti-Catholic Theodore Frelinghuysen, running mate in Henry Clay's 1844 bid (his third and final) for the presidency. "For myself," Hughes said of Frelinghuysen, "I look upon him as a sincere, honest, and so far as the two ideas can be associated, honorable bigot."[90] Hughes actually voted for Clay—the only vote he ever cast in a presidential election.

But Brooks was able to establish some facts about the amount of Catholic property held in Hughes' name: $5 million—the equivalent of more than $150 million in 2014 dollars. Hughes denied the figure. When Brooks cited forty-five properties valued at *more than* $5 million, Hughes took an awful drubbing in the press.[91] And the bill passed.

Hughes said he hardly minded. He was, after all, a priest. For him, property matters were trumped by spiritual concerns. In any case, the law was never enforced: the ownership of no Church property ever moved from ecclesiastical hands to those of laymen. And then the bill was quickly rescinded.

Rather, as in the school question, the defeat that became a victory was a boon. Hughes was busy building a parochial-school system, and now he could proceed with the construction of more churches, sure in the knowledge that Church property would not be forcibly divested. But just as the squabbles over education had made him the unquestioned leader of the Church in New York, the property question established him as a leading voice against nativism—perhaps the most important one in America.

The Bedini Incident

The rise and decline of nativism in America is an underappreciated story in the nation's history. The period in which nativism thrived—between about 1830 and 1860—was obviously one of rising sectional tensions, whose climax came with the secession of South Carolina in December of 1860 and the attack on Fort Sumter in April of the following year—the first shots fired in the Civil War. In all of this, slavery was the most important issue, and from the war would come both emancipation and, to a great extent, the end of nativism as a force in American public life.

It is not that ethnic tensions would disappear (consider the postwar rise of the Ku Klux Klan), but that for four years Protestant and Catholic soldiers, native and immigrant—and on both sides in the war—stood shoulder to shoulder in the fight, which had the effect of defusing the intensity of the xenophobia that was at the heart of nativism. Each of us must reflect upon the cost of a million casualties (625,000 dead; 412,000 wounded), but all will agree that the end of bondage and the diminishment of intolerance were both good for the American soul.

But in the decade before the Civil War, nativism was in its heyday, and it was visible especially and surprisingly (to Catholics anyway) in the reaction of the press and the people in June of 1853 to the apostolic visit to the United States of Archbishop Gaetano Bedini, recently appointed papal nuncio to Brazil.

Bedini came to the United States in part to present to President Franklin Pierce greetings and letters from Pope Pius IX, but also to consecrate bishops, open churches, and get a sense of Catholicism, *in situ*: as his Vatican instructions put it, "to observe the state of religion" in America.[92] The impetus behind the visit may well have been nothing more than the Vatican's recognition of the United States of America as an emerging power with a growing Catholic population. It may also have been a specific scouting expedition to gauge the readiness of a largely Protestant nation to accept the creation of a position—a permanent Vatican observer in Washington, D.C.—analogous to the one Bedini was on his way to Brazil to undertake. What it was *not* was part of a Catholic conspiracy to seize control of America, which is exactly how nativists presented it.

In this bizarre claim the press was aided by a former priest turned Protestant, Alessandro Gavazzi. Gavazzi told tales about Catholics every bit as lurid as those served up in *The Awful Disclosures of Maria Monk, or, The Hidden Secrets of a Nun's Life in a Convent Exposed* (1836), a bestselling forgery of anti-Catholic venom that became something of a nativist bible.

Gavazzi had been rabble-rousing in Canada when word reached him that Bedini would be arriving in New York on June 30, 1853. Gavazzi rushed south in order to shadow Bedini, traveling to nearly every place in the United States that Bedini visited, and dogging newspaper editors with a canine intensity to tell of the supposed crimes both of Bedini and of the hierarchy he represented. At one New York lecture given by Gavazzi before Bedini's arrival, Archbishop Hughes sat disguised near the rear of the hall. (He often did this.)[93] Still, Hughes and especially Bedini were unprepared for the scorn directed at the visitor from Rome.

Hughes had accompanied Bedini to Washington, D.C., where the mood was friendly, but when Bedini headed west—to, among other places, Virginia, Ohio, and the Minnesota Territory—Gavazzi was there stoking prejudice and warning of the Papist Menace. By the time poor Archbishop Bedini returned to Manhattan, he was in fear for his life. John Hassard writes that "crowds of foreign radicals gathered on the wharves to watch every departure" for Rio de Janeiro. It is unlikely those crowds included just republican foreigners. In the event, "at the suggestion of the mayor, the nuncio went secretly to Staten Island, and boarded the steamer from a tug boat as she went down the harbor. Archbishop Hughes was intensely mortified when he heard of these disgraceful occurrences." Indeed. Somewhat grandiloquently Hughes later wrote to Bedini that if he had been in New York, "we should have taken a carriage at my door, even an open one if the day had been fine enough, and gone by the ordinary streets to the steamboat on which you were to embark."[94]

In the context of Hassard's work, which we described at the start of this chapter as arguably being hagiographic, it is clear he believes Hughes would have done just that, as he might well have. It is likely, however, that he would have surrounded the carriage with Catholic bodyguards.

Slavery, War, and President Lincoln

Slavery was the issue of the day throughout the United States in the 1850s, and—in twenty-first-century parlance—we might describe Archbishop Hughes' view on the matter as *nuanced*. But, as one historian has observed, "Upon so controversial a subject as slavery, however, the position of [Hughes'] church had become one of studied silence."[95] The Ninth Provincial Council held in Baltimore in 1858 had frankly admitted that whereas slavery was roiling the nation, among America's prelates "there has been no agitation on the subject."[96] Hughes, at least, spoke out.

In the decade before hostilities erupted, Hughes had traveled to the South and to Cuba, where he was able to observe slavery firsthand. In an 1854 sermon at Old St.

Patrick's, he said plainly that "slavery is an evil." He also suggested that most slaves considered their lot better in the Americas than it had been in Africa.[97] He was not an abolitionist, and he never became one—not even after he accepted Abraham Lincoln's commission to visit European capitals for the purpose of gaining support for the Union cause.

But as the war over slavery began to seem inevitable, Hughes had only to listen to New York's Irish Catholics to understand that a substantial number of them were in sympathy with the Copperheads—that segment of the Democratic Party that opposed the war. ("Copperhead" was a Republican Party epithet aimed at these Democrats—i.e., they were *snakes*—who took the insult and turned it into their badge of honor, literally: on their lapels they wore copper pennies, which bore the image of Liberty on the obverse.)

The school question had tagged Hughes—to his dismay—as a politician, and his friendship with William Seward and Thurlow Weed cemented that assumption for many. And as the war approached, and as Hughes gave homilies that seemed neutral on the question of slavery, he began to be associated with the Copperheads himself. It was an association he neither wished for nor liked, especially when in 1860 Seward was tapped by President-Elect Lincoln to be America's next Secretary of State. Whatever Hughes believed in his heart, his public stance was bipartisan.

Seward had been among the leading candidates for the Republican presidential nomination in both 1856 and 1860, and Hughes had made a point of not endorsing him—not exactly, that is. "If the people of the United States shall think proper to confer on him the highest honor in their gift," the archbishop wrote in the *Freeman's Journal*, "I shall not heave a sigh or shed a tear.... But no vote of mine shall aid him."[98]

When Hughes was personally pressed by the antislavery senator Cassius M. Clay of Kentucky to "change your alliances", Hughes replied that it would not matter, since "Catholics vote as individuals in the free exercise of their franchise, with no direction from their clergy."[99]

One of Archbishop Hughes' combatants in his final years was the Catholic convert Orestes Brownson. Brownson had no hesitation in siding with Lincoln and the Union as the nation began separating into North and South, Blue and Gray. The national government in Washington, D.C., he wrote in 1861, "has never lost its legitimacy by any act of tyranny or oppression.... Rebellion against it, therefore, is not only a crime, but a sin." Historian Patrick W. Carey notes that as Brownson tallied a dozen Catholic newspapers, "he could count only two as decidedly loyal, two as occasionally loyal, one that strived to be on both sides." The rest were "secession sheets".[100]

For his part, Hughes accepted Brownson's anti-secessionist views but not the journalist's abolitionism. As mentioned earlier, Hughes was not a champion of slavery per se (even if he believed that the Bible justified the practice), but he thought it unlikely that Irish-Americans would support a war to end it, and in that he was both right and wrong. In response to Brownson, Hughes took to the *Metropolitan Record* with an essay titled "The Abolition Views of Brownson Overthrown", in which he made eight points: (1) the Church "has ever set her face against the slave trade"; (2) however, the Church accepts slavery where it is the law of the land; (3) slave owners are not guilty in such cases; (4) "the Master should treat his slaves with all humanity and Christian care and protection"; (5) property rights are *sacred*; (6) it is only military necessity (preservation of the Union) that justifies abolition; (7) caution must be sought in abolition, given that freed slaves would subsequently have no means of support, no places in which to live; and (8) emancipation would be likely to increase the "race problem", as blacks moved north to dwell in white communities.[101]

In this formulation, writes Walter G. Sharrow in the *Journal of Negro History*, "Hughes had come perilously close to establishing a Divine origin for the institution",[102] although there was a kind of Burkean conservatism in his attitude. In a pamphlet written back in 1852, Hughes had stated that the Church has "little confidence in theoretical systems which assume that great or enduring benefit [will] result from sudden or unexpected excitements, even of a religious kind".[103] And despite the bond that he would forge with President Lincoln, Hughes was deeply suspicious of what was then called Red Republicanism, which was the revolutionary spirit of the rebellions that had swept through Europe in 1848—what W.B. Yeats would later call the "The Seven Sages", "A levelling, rancorous, rational sort of mind / That never looked out of the eye of a saint / Or out of a drunkard's eye".

Hughes' refusal to condemn slavery and his states'-rights view were obviously in conflict with his stance against secession, whether or not he saw the contradiction. In just two years, this contradiction would make his embrace of the war and his encouragement of Irish-American enlistment ring hollow to many. Still, Hughes saw to it that the Stars and Stripes flew atop his cathedral, and this among other things brought him to the attention of the Lincoln administration.

Hughes' friendship with former Governor Seward, now Secretary of State Seward, led to one of the most significant opportunities ever offered to an American Catholic up to that point, when Lincoln asked him to serve as an envoy to the Catholic European capitals in search of their governments' support of the Union cause—or, at a minimum, their neutrality. Hughes was initially skeptical of the commission, but when Seward agreed that Thurlow Weed could accompany him on the journey, the archbishop threw himself into the mission with his usual passion. For him, the dissent of Catholic trustees against Church policy was of a piece with the Southern rebellion against the national government. Authority and union must rule above all.

Writing in 1917, Father Victor F. O'Daniel was effusive in his judgment of the success of Hughes' mission:

> It was largely through the Archbishop's efforts that France was prevented from following in the footsteps of England, and throwing the weight of her sympathies with the Confederate States. Wherever he traveled in Europe, he was accorded an honorable reception. He left nothing undone to promote the cause of the Union, and did much to enlist the sympathies of the Old World in the preservation of the American Republic.[104]

Only England was inclined to support the Confederacy. Some naval conflicts and a sense that a divided United States was less threatening to English interests than was a unified America encouraged some in Great Britain to support the Southern side, though Queen Victoria and her government remained neutral.

Upon his return from Europe, Hughes took to the cathedral pulpit and on August 17, 1862, gave what has become known as his "war sermon", as the *New York Times* called it. Most of what he preached that day was a recitation of his successes in Europe, and it was only at the very end that he lamented that New York's Catholics were, of necessity, drawn into war. "How long is this to go on?" he asked somewhat disingenuously. "As it goes on, it is affording a pretext for all the nations to combine against us; but even then, I say their interference should not be permitted, except in the way of benevolence; but, if with the sword, we should unite in setting them at defiance." If ever there were a straw-man argument, this was it. But the specter of English involvement was sure to stir the hearts of Irish-Americans, united in their hatred of their former oppressors. Hughes went so far as to warn that the United States could become another Poland, which, having been partitioned after the Congress of Vienna (1815), was even then in a war for its survival against Russia. "Every [American] state will become independent", Hughes claimed, "and render itself an easy prey to foreign powers." And now the call to fight:

> Volunteers have been appealed to, and they have answered the appeal; but for my own part, if I had a voice in the councils of the nations, I would say, let volunteers continue, and the draft be made. If three hundred thousand men are not sufficient, let three hundred thousand more be called upon, so that the army, in its fulness [*sic*] of strength, shall be always on hand for any emergency. This is not cruelty; this is mercy.[105]

Indeed, the archbishop said the people (and he meant young Irish and German immigrants) should insist on being drafted. How else was the Union to bring the horror of war to a close? How else to do God's will?

The homily had the desired effect, and Messrs. Lincoln and Seward could hardly have been more pleased. However, the draft that was about to begin—and which would draw large numbers of immigrants into the war—was a very flawed system. And it would coincide in the new year with one of the finest expressions of charity in American history: the Emancipation Proclamation.

The Draft Riots of 1863

Although the Thirteenth Amendment to the United States Constitution would forever outlaw slavery (involuntary servitude) in 1865, Abraham Lincoln believed it was necessary *during* the war to free the three million slaves living in the Confederacy. It is not necessary here to detail the controversies surrounding the Proclamation, except to note its effect upon public sentiment in New York, especially in the light of the Enrollment Act, passed by Congress on March 3, 1863, just two months after the Emancipation Proclamation.

The trouble with the draft, which provided fewer than 5 percent of those serving in the Union army, was its embrace of a terrible inequity: it allowed rich men to pay poor men to take their places in ranks or simply to pay $300 to the government to free themselves from the obligation to serve. These two options were known as substitution and commutation. Commutation was an especially cynical policy, since it was designed to keep the substitution price low. America was a huge nation, with—at the time—just thirty-four states; most of the land west of Missouri (one of the four slave states that fought with the Union) was still governed as territories. And note: $300 then was equal to nearly $6,000 today. A conscript could take his $300 and simply head to California, for instance. The Golden State had joined the Union in 1850, but it was never actively involved in the war, and a deserter could easily go unnoticed in the Gold Rush–crazed state.

Had the price of commutation been set higher, however—at $1,000, say (a price many wealthy men would still have been willing to pay)—it was feared that the price for substitution would rise also, and to the point where the incentive to desert would have been too high.

Even so, substitution probably would not have been as great an issue in 1861, when everyone in the North expected a quick Union victory, as it became after the numbers of dead and wounded grew alarming over two years of war. News of the Battle of Gettysburg, an uncertain victory for the North, reached New York in the first week of July 1863, and even though it turned out to be the "high-water mark of the Confederacy", as historian John Bachelder later dubbed it, the slaughter, which nineteenth-century newspapers were not shy to report, was shocking: dead, wounded, missing, and captured amounted to nearly fifty thousand—and in just three days of fighting.

Now New York's immigrants felt like scapegoats. Not only were they cannon fodder; they expected blacks to flood into New York City, where nobody doubted they would undercut the already atrocious market for unskilled workers. And so it was that ten days after Gettysburg (and two days after the draft began), Manhattan exploded in what became known as the New York City Draft Riots.

The mood in New York had long been sour about the war, and because of the Southern cotton that moved through the city's ports, there were many Confederate sympathizers. At the end of the week in which emancipation was proclaimed from Washington, Mayor Fernando Wood had called upon the Board of Aldermen to "declare the city's independence from Albany and from Washington", a move that "would have the whole and united support of the Southern States".[106]

Writing in his *Quarterly Review* several months after the riots, Orestes Brownson had no doubt about who the primary perpetrators were: "The immediate actors in the late riots in this city, got up to resist the draft and to create a diversion in favor of the southern rebellion, were almost exclusively Irishmen and catholics [sic]."[107]

It has often been asserted that the riots ceased after the city fathers appealed to Archbishop Hughes to speak to the rioters and to request that they desist. Hughes certainly did that, after which the arson, looting, and lynching (of several African-American men) did cease. (One thousand people died in the unrest.) But in several scholarly accounts of the riots, no mention is made of Hughes' role, and it is likely that the rioters' passions had been spent and that remorse was settling over the immigrant community. Not to mention that federal units from Gettysburg had been diverted from the chase after Robert E. Lee's Army of Northern Virginia and had been sent to quell the riots. The troops entered the city on the third day of the riots and were in no mood to tolerate what they took to be an assault on the honor of their military service. Typical of the more pious accounts of Hughes' peacemaking is this from a modern New York journalist:

A then-dying Archbishop Hughes summoned the leaders of the rebellion to meet with him. However disturbed he might have been that the Irish were being called on to do so much of the dying in the struggle against the South, he supported the war and was totally opposed to slavery, having preached against it since his ordination as a priest in 1826. He told the riot leaders that "no blood of innocent martyrs, shed by Irish Catholics, has ever stained the soil of Ireland" and that they were dishonoring that impeccable history. The riot leaders went back to their neighborhoods, and the violence melted away. The riot saddened the dying archbishop: he felt he had failed as a prelate.[108]

Hughes was ill—no doubt about that. But it is far from certain that he had any regrets about his quarter century of episcopal leadership.

The Death of the Archbishop

On January 4, 1864, the *New York Times* reported:

> His Grace Archbishop Hughes expired at his residence in Madison-avenue, last evening, at 7 1/2 o'clock, after a lingering illness, in which he suffered much, but endured with fortitude. He has been failing in body for more than a year past. During the past Summer he has been continually under the care of his physicians, Drs. Clarks and Wood. [In ...] December he was first confined to the bed of sickness from which he was never to arise. His decease, although apprehended, was not considered imminent until last Thursday, when he commenced [to fail] rapidly, and, indeed, came so near his end that rumors of his death were circulated and generally believed. He received the last Sacraments of the Church, and shortly after became speechless, but still retained his consciousness.
>
> He remained in that state until yesterday afternoon, when a change for the worse occurred, and growing weaker and weaker, be breathed his last at precisely 31 minutes past 7 o'clock. He was surrounded in his last hours by his family, his physicians and the following Catholic clergymen: Bishop McClosky [*sic*], Albany; Bishop Laughlin [*sic*], Brooklyn: Vicar General Very Reverend Father Starrs; Reverend Dr. Nelliger, Father McNerney, Private Secretary to the Bishop, and other members of the clergy. The consolations of the Catholic religion and friendship were administered by the clergy present.[109]

Referring to the end of the Draft Riots, the *Times* notes that Hughes "was confined to his bed by sickness, but he announced that if the people would meet him at his residence he would address them from the balcony". (By this time he had taken up residence on Madison Avenue, near where the new St. Patrick's was being constructed.) "An immense assembly gathered there at the appointed time, and he spoke to them as announced, requesting them to obey the laws, to assist in enforcing obedience if necessary, and if wrong had been done to seek redress through the proper channels, and not by riots and turbulent outbreaks."[110]

Harper's Weekly, in its issue of January 16, 1864, took a slightly less favorable view of the archbishop's balcony speech to the rioters:

> His last notable effort was his speech to the Catholics of New York, at the time of the riots of last July. This speech was sharply and, we think, justly criticized. Its

intent was good; but we thought at the time, and must think still, that it contained some highly objectionable features. We apprehend that the mental, as well as the physical, strength of the Archbishop was impaired when he made this speech, which we are confident was heard or read with regret by the best and wisest of his friends. Apart from this speech, conceived and delivered when the venerable prelate was not his old self, we think it would be difficult to point to a single important act in his long administration that was not wise and politic, and which, viewed from his own standpoint, was not right and honorable. He died as he had lived, a true man, and a sincere Christian.[111]

That is a reasonable sentiment from a secular magazine.

Historical memory is not long—at least if the one to be remembered does not leave a legacy, whether of fame or infamy. John Joseph Hughes may well have been the archdiocese's greatest leader, but when one looks at present-day New York there are few streets or buildings or organizations named for him, and by that measure he may be forgotten. His legacy, however, is everywhere. It suffices to give one very grand example.

Several years before the outbreak of the Civil War, Hughes began to think of his legacy and decided that the best thing he could leave the People of God was a new cathedral—one worthy of their ascending prominence in American life.

It was the genius of Hughes to have chosen acreage for the cathedral that the Church already owned and had since the beginning of the century. In 1810, Father Anthony Kohlmann mentioned this parcel of land in a letter to a friend in England, in which he proclaimed that the new Diocese of New York (*Neo-Eboracensis*) was already so far advanced:

> as to see not only the Catholic religion highly respected by the first characters of the city, but even a Catholic [Jesuit men's] college established, the house well furnished ... in the ... improvements made in the college for four or five hundred dollars.... The college is in the centre not of Long Island but of the Island of New York, the most delightful and most healthy spot of the whole island, at a distance of four small miles from the city, and of half a mile from the East and North rivers, both of which are seen from the house; situated between two roads which are very much frequented, opposite to the botanic gardens which belong to the State. It has adjacent to it a beautiful lawn, garden, orchard, etc.[112]

Amazing to anyone in the twenty-first century contemplating Manhattan ("the Island of New York") is that Kohlmann was describing the real estate now occupied by St. Patrick's Cathedral, from which views of *both* the East and the Hudson Rivers are now blocked by skyscrapers. (The Hudson is the "North" river in Kohlmann's letter—that was a translation of the Dutch name, au courant until the start of the twentieth century.) It has been a very long time since one could see either river from St. Patrick's—even from its spires.

In addition to the Jesuit school and chapel Kohlmann refers to (St. Ignatius), the site (and building) had also been occupied by a Trappist Monastery between 1813 and 1815, and, beginning in 1841, by the Church of St. John the Evangelist, built by Bishop Hughes. Hughes later built the Catholic Orphan Asylum nearby, which gave the Church more property in the area and provided the archbishop his first opportunity to work with architect James Renwick. (Renwick's partner, William Rodrigue, married Hughes' sister Margaret.) The orphanage sat just north of the future cathedral, which grew up beside it.

All this land was far from the city center ("four small miles", as Kohlmann put it), which is why many called the archbishop's decision to build there "Hughes' Folly". But Hughes knew that Manhattan could grow in one direction only: north.

John Joseph Hughes laid the cornerstone of the new cathedral on Sunday, August 15, 1858—the feast of the Assumption. The archbishop's health had not yet begun to fail, but he surely knew that this building would become his most lasting legacy. As his activities during the Civil War would show, the groundbreaking for St. Patrick's was far from his last accomplishment, but it may well be considered his greatest.

The war would bring the construction of St. Patrick's to a halt, guaranteeing that Hughes would not live to see it completed, although he and Renwick had finished the design, so the archbishop was able to see the cathedral in his mind's eye.

That day some 60,000 came to watch Hughes officiate. But on the later day (May 25, 1879) when Cardinal McCloskey dedicated the cathedral, there were in attendance two hundred priests and a hundred choirboys marching in procession. "The throng of onlookers was so thick—100,000 strong, by one estimate—that all the city's [horse-drawn] streetcars were diverted north to accommodate the crowd." Downtown Manhattan was described as "depleted".[113]

Hughes took a dagger and marked the cornerstone with a Cross. Very fitting for the man born on the feast of John the Baptist, for which—as noted at the beginning of this chapter—the liturgy includes this quote from Isaiah: "He made of me a sharp-edged sword / and concealed me in the shadow of his arm. / He made me a polished arrow, / in his quiver he hid me."

Archbishop Hughes had created a Catholic presence in New York that had the effect both of shining light upon the darkness in which many Catholics lived and of bringing many Catholics out of that darkness. He built churches, schools, and seminaries, and he encouraged religious orders to come to New York to undertake teaching and nursing. In his memoir letter written to Propaganda in 1858, he noted that in the archdiocese's Catholic schools there were 12,938 pupils being taught by 316 teachers. Nearly $2 million had been invested in education, with the largest expenditure for "female high schools".[114] He mentioned the six churches, not counting Old St. Patrick's, that were operational but "burthened" with debt when he came to New York City in 1838. He admitted that debt remained a problem, but he added that since then eighteen churches and "six large chapels attached to as many Religious Communities" had been constructed. Three more were under construction as he wrote his report.[115]

Despite his best efforts, however, just sixty priests were working in the city, when one hundred fifty would hardly have been enough.

His greatest regret is that so many Irish immigrants—who streamed into New York after Ireland's Great Famine (*An Gorta Mór*), especially between 1845 and 1851—continued to live in dire poverty. "For these evils," he writes, "it is not in our power to provide a remedy."[116]

At the laying of the cornerstone of the new St. Patrick's, which was otherwise a paean to those who had already donated to St. Patrick's and a plea for the funding necessary to complete construction, Archbishop Hughes answered the question he knew was on the minds of some Catholics and many Protestants (dignitaries of the various denominations were among the throngs that day)—a question that was essentially the one Judas asked when Mary of Bethany anointed Christ with expensive ointment: *Why build a cathedral when that money could provide for the poor?*

> When they tell you this, do not forget the charity that is due to persons; but as for the argument itself, laugh it to scorn. And say, that the building of cathedrals and churches was, in all ages, intimately connected with and conducive to the support of the poor, until the period when the first predecessors of those who accuse you, actually spoiled and ruined, so far as human agency could accomplish it, the plan of Christ for the protection of the poor. Say to them, that the first lady in christendom [*sic*] that ever witnessed what we now call "pauperism," was Queen Elizabeth— that her father was the robber of the poor in suppressing churches, monasteries, and cathedrals in Catholic England. That, except as used in the Gospel, *beati pauperes*, the word pauper was unknown in the modern languages of christendom, until the period just referred to; that it is creditable to her woman's nature that Elizabeth sympathized with the poor, and that, after one or two homilies addressed to her parliament on the subject, she was, in very desperation, compelled to introduce, almost to the shame of Christianity, human laws forcing men to support their own destitute brethren. Compulsion was necessary; the law of charity in the Gospel, as prescribed by our Lord, had become inefficient, and apparently obsolete; and it was requisite to invoke the same human legislative authority, which is divinely instituted for the punishment of crime and the protection of society, in order to make Christians "love each other," or at least to pay something into the public treasury to prevent men from dying of starvation. Has all this resulted in benefit to the poor? ... Say to them, finally, that if they were guided by the large, and may I not call it divine, instinct of the Catholic religion, they would consider the poor of future generations as well as of the present. And in that view they would regard with certainty the erection of this cathedral as a head-fountain, sending out its living waters of faith and charity on all sides, and as a great nursery for cultivating the principle of charity among the generations that are to succeed us.... *Nisi Dominus custodierit civitatem, frustra vigilat qui custodit eam.*[117] [Unless the LORD builds the house, those who build it labor in vain (Ps 127:1).]

As ever, Dagger John.†

But the last word about Hughes cannot come from him. In his funeral oration for the archbishop, John McCloskey—to whom Hughes had often turned when a difficult assignment needed delegating (and who is the subject of the next chapter)—summed up the career and character of John Joseph Hughes. McCloskey, then Bishop of Albany and in a somewhat panicked state that soon he would be named successor to Hughes, began by describing for the mourners the high points of the archbishop's administration, before turning to the thing that made Hughes such a formidable man.

He says "there was one trait that distinguished our great Archbishop most particularly." He then names four: "It was his singular force, and clearness, and vigor of intellect, his strength of will and his firmness of resolution." But McCloskey adds that Hughes was also a gentleman and a gentle man.

The genuine impulses and feelings of his heart were all impulses of kindness and of pity. He knew no selfishness. He despised everything that was mean and little.... And we have this to say in conclusion, that if ever there was a man who ... impressed upon us the sense and the conviction that he had been raised up by God, was chosen as His instrument to do an appointed work, and was strengthened by His grace and supported by His wisdom for the accomplishment of the work for which he had been chosen and appointed, that man was Archbishop Hughes. He was, from the beginning until the end, clearly and plainly an instrument in the hands of God.[118]

3

The First

John Joseph McCloskey
Second Archbishop of New York
(1864–1885)

Photo by Mathew Brady around the time of McCloskey's
consecration as bishop, ca. 1844

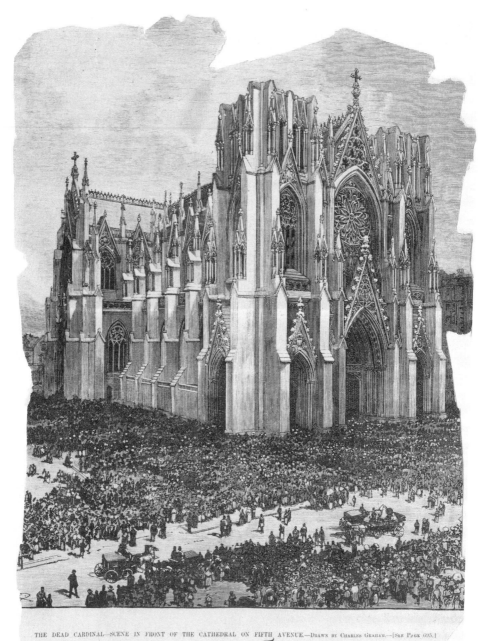

THE DEAD CARDINAL—SCENE IN FRONT OF THE CATHEDRAL ON FIFTH AVENUE.—DRAWN BY CHARLES GRAHAM.—[SEE PAGE 695.]

Harper's Weekly, October 24, 1885: Cardinal McCloskey's funeral

John McCloskey, New York's second archbishop, was a man of firsts: the first native New Yorker to be ordained a priest, the first native American to become archbishop of New York, the first American archbishop to be elevated to the cardinalate, and, therefore, the first American eligible to participate in the election of a new pope. (Unfortunately, McCloskey arrived in Rome too late to sit in the 1878 conclave that elected Leo XIII in just three ballots.)

The main secondary source on John McCloskey's life is a biography supposedly written by his former secretary, the future Cardinal John Farley. But *The Life of John Cardinal McCloskey: First Prince of the Church in America: 1810–1885*[1] has been described by the eminent priest-historian John Tracy Ellis as unworthy of credence. The book, he says, was not actually written by Cardinal Farley at all; it was written by Monsignor Peter Guilday, who told his friend Father Ellis that Farley's secretary, the future Cardinal Patrick Hayes, "had 'castrated'—his [Guilday's] own word—the work".[2] Indeed, it is a tangle: His Eminence (Hayes) editing His Eminence (Farley) "writing" about His Eminence (McCloskey)—all in the somewhat hagiographic style of episcopal biographies of the late nineteenth and early twentieth centuries. (And all these men were at work, essentially, as McCloskey's successor, Archbishop Michael Corrigan, lay dying.)

Perhaps there is a dearth of writing about John McCloskey because he was much less controversial than his predecessor John Hughes. As Michael Glazier and Monsignor Thomas J. Shelley have written (1997): "Temperamentally, the quiet, peace-loving McCloskey was the exact opposite of the assertive and confrontational Hughes."[3] In a much earlier (1905) account, McCloskey is described as, "in temperament ... the very contrary of his patron [Hughes]. Delicate of build, of a sound constitution, yet without surplus vigor and energy, all his life [he] was forced to husband his physical resources, to avoid unusual strain, and to make up for heroic effort by the persistent and well-regulated labor of each day."[4]

Farley's "castrated" book—the *only* full-length biography of McCloskey—is at least a guide to the *outline* of Cardinal McCloskey's life. But make no mistake: for reasons we shall explore, John McCloskey has not inspired historians the way his predecessor has or the way Cardinal Timothy Dolan excites journalists today. Sometimes it seems that McCloskey is an obscure footnote—or even a bungled reference.

An example of the latter appears in two mentions of Cardinal McCloskey in an interesting biography of Thomas Ewing Sherman, son of Civil War hero William Tecumseh Sherman. The younger Sherman—against his father's wishes—converted to Catholicism and became a Jesuit priest.[5] According to the Jesuit author of the biography, General Sherman was a friend of the cardinal (as well as of Archbishop Ryan of Philadelphia and Archbishop Purcell of Cincinnati—in Sherman's home state, Ohio), and it was to McCloskey that the Protestant general wrote, around 1880, urgently requesting that he dissuade Thomas from entering the priesthood. McCloskey could not and would not do so, which left the old warrior deeply bitter.

The trouble is, the index of the biography identifies McCloskey as "McCloskey, Cardinal William George." William George McCloskey was, like John McCloskey, born in Brooklyn (but he was not of the cardinal's immediate family), and he also went to Mount St. Mary's Seminary in Maryland. He eventually became bishop of Louisville, Kentucky, but he never became a cardinal. Listing him as one is a surprising error, though probably due to carelessness on the part of the editor or the indexer, not of the author.

And there is more to the story. General Sherman's bitterness was manifest in an interview he gave to a Midwestern reporter, to whom he flatly stated that Cardinal McCloskey had "betrayed him." The reporter wired McCloskey for comment, and the always subtle cardinal replied: "General Sherman's letter to me was marked 'Private and confidential.' "[6] Such taciturnity is admirable, but it is another reason why McCloskey has not excited the imagination of historians.

Early Life and Education

John McCloskey's parents were both Irish: Patrick McCloskey and Elizabeth Hassen (sometimes Harron[7]) hailed from towns in the parish of Banagher, County Londonderry (or Derry, as Catholics prefer to call it), and emigrated to Brooklyn in 1808,[8] the year the Diocese of New York was created. Their marriage had been opposed by the local priest, a Father O'Reagan, on grounds of consanguinity: Patrick and Elizabeth were cousins. A note in the archives of the Archdiocese of New York, in one of the files marked "Materials Used in the Life of Cardinal Mc-Closkey", states that Patrick and Elizabeth were "*at least* second cousins" (emphasis added) and identifies Elizabeth's parents as John Hassen and Ann McCloskey,[9] which could mean the cardinal's parents were actually first cousins. Second-cousin marriages were uncommon in nineteenth-century Ireland but not unheard of, whereas first-cousin marriages were forbidden by the Church. In any case, Patrick and Elizabeth (with aid from their parents) fled from Banagher to the city of Derry, where they were permitted to marry, and from there they went to Brooklyn.

In about 1900, a ninety-one-year-old woman who was living in Brooklyn, but had grown up in Ireland, recalled that back in Banagher, not long after the future cardinal was born, a letter arrived from America containing a lock of the baby's hair. Farley notes that a Mr. Stewart, the nephew of the elderly lady, Miss McVey, said of his aunt's reminiscence: "She says in those days an American letter was a very rare thing to see." It may have seemed a portent of remarkable things to come for the child.

Stewart also noted in passing that after Patrick McCloskey and Elizabeth Hassen were married at the cathedral in Derry, they spent the night aboard the ship that would convey them to America; it began its voyage the very next morning.[10]

On May 6, 1810, two months after John was born (probably at the McCloskey home in Brooklyn), his parents took him in a rowboat across the East River to have him baptized by Father Benedict Fenwick, S.J., at St. Peter's in Manhattan. St. Peter's was at that time the closest Catholic church to the McCloskeys' home—indeed, it was the only Catholic church in the city, and the only one to which they could reasonably go. Old St. Patrick's ("then styled 'The New Church out of Town' "[11]) was under construction, but it would not be completed until 1815, the year Bishop John Connolly took up the reins of the new diocese. But as of 1810, as Cardinal Farley points out, apart from St. Peter's, "there was a priest in the missions of New Jersey, a church with a resident pastor in Albany, another at Utica, another at Carthage, and a numerous body of Catholics in Buffalo."[12]

The McCloskeys would repeat this pilgrimage to Manhattan nearly every Sunday until 1817, when the family moved across the river to settle on Murray Street near

City Hall. Later, after the death of Patrick McCloskey in 1820, Elizabeth moved with the children to Bedford in Westchester County. Exactly when the McCloskeys moved to Bedford is unclear, although it was likely no earlier than 1822.

The Farley biography mentions that McCloskey had sisters but seldom refers to them by name. McCloskey's letters to them (cited by Farley) always begin simply, "Dear Sister". *The Life of John Cardinal McCloskey* states quite specifically that one sister died at the age of eighteen on March 8, 1835. We later learn that her name was Elizabeth and that she is buried alongside another sister, Mary; their mother was later buried nearby. From an account of McCloskey's consecration as coadjutor bishop of New York in 1843, we learn that in attendance that day with his mother was a sister named Margaret. Some genealogical sources indicate that John Mc-Closkey also had a brother, William, possibly born in Ireland (although that is very unlikely), who in old age was living with a daughter in Albany. Another citation claims that Patrick and Elizabeth McCloskey had thirteen children!

The cardinal had nieces, one of whom was named Ann Theresa Mullen. She married the New York politician "Honest" John Kelly, a head of Tammany Hall, whose nickname was not given in earnest. Their nuptials were almost certainly around 1880, at which point Kelly, whose second marriage it was, was in his late fifties. And, since Ann Theresa's maiden name was Mullen, she had to be the daughter of one of the cardinal's married sisters, although not Elizabeth, who died in 1835, of whom Farley writes: "Shortly after he had left home [for Mount St. Mary's, in September 1821], his sister started for the convent school at Emmitsburg."[13] The Farley chronology is imprecise, to say the least. One source states that Elizabeth was "already in residence at Mother Seton's school in Emmitsburg".[14] Given the age at which students went off to "seminaries" and "convents"—which were often combinations of primary schools, secondary schools, colleges, and institutions for the education of priests and other religious—it is likely that Miss McCloskey was not even a teenager in 1821, which is when John headed to the Mount. But the dates in Cardinal Farley's biography seem to suggest the Elizabeth was four years old when she was in school with Mother Seton.

The genealogical picture is fleshed out somewhat in an article about Cardinal McCloskey's funeral that appeared in the *New York Times* on October 16, 1885, which mentions that the funeral was attended by "the dead prelate's four nieces", who are named "Mrs. John Kelly, Miss Mullen, Miss McCloskey, and Mrs. Cleary, and by the latter's husband and Dr. and Mrs. L. L. Keyes". But in New York's archdiocesan archives there is a file containing papers, including financial records, pertaining to the late cardinal's estate. One "invoice" from the Calvary Cemetery Office (266 Mulberry Street), dated February 23, 1886, reads as follows:

> Rec'd from Most Rev. M. A. Corrigan
> Fifteen thousand dollars
> to be paid to Mrs. McCloskey
> of Cleveland, Ohio and her children.

The *Times* may have been wrong in its report on the funeral in identifying the McCloskey niece as *Miss*, or the Calvary Cemetery may have been wrong in calling her *Mrs.* We do not know the role this McCloskey niece played in the cardinal's life, but the money he left to her upon his death is the equivalent of several hundred thousand dollars in today's currency.

Finally, on the matter of Cardinal McCloskey's siblings, we know—from one note among the papers about McCloskey's life that Farley/Hayes/Guilday collected—that Father Benedict Fenwick, who baptized John McCloskey, "subsequently baptized other memers of the McCloskey family", although how many others we do not know.

The future cardinal's first teacher was his mother, Elizabeth, known as Bettie, and she would remain a close—if not his closest—confidant until her death in 1845, not long after McCloskey became coadjutor bishop to Archbishop Hughes. References are made to John McCloskey's enrollment, at a very early age, in a Quaker school in Brooklyn, but he began his more formal education at the age of five, when he attended a school run by a former Irish actress, Mrs. Charlotte Melmoth. Her name is often misspelled Milmouth; it is so spelled in Farley's biography, which may be because of correspondence between then Bishop Farley and Thomas F. Meehan, a Brooklyn-born writer who was managing editor of the *Irish-American* and a contributor to the *Catholic Historical Review*. In response to a request from would-be biographer Farley, Meehan jotted down some things he knew about McCloskey's early life. In one such note, he asked if facts about "Mrs. Milmouth" were known to the bishop. No doubt Farley did know of her, since Cardinal McCloskey often credited her with his own clear enunciation, a quality of his speech that was universally admired.[15] In a brief biographical typescript about McCloskey's early life in the archives of the Archdiocese of New York, the typist—probably Father Guilday—laments that "we have been unable to ascertain" the identity of McCloskey's female teacher. Both Farley, especially, and Hayes probably knew her name; they just had not told Guilday at that point, and none of them knew how to spell her name properly.

At the zenith of her career, Charlotte Melmoth had been "the Grande Dame of Tragedy on the Early American Stage", but for many years before that, she had struggled even to survive. At one low point, she had been reduced to posing as a fortune-teller. She lived in a nonstandard arrangement with a "husband", Samuel Jackson Pratt, a former clergyman who used the stage name Courtney Melmoth; Charlotte traveled and performed with him in England and France, and she came to know Benjamin Franklin in Paris. At the end of the eighteenth century, she left Pratt and immigrated to the United States, and she quickly established herself as a leading light in American theater. In 1812 she opened the school John McCloskey attended on Carroll Street in the Red Hook section of Brooklyn. At some point, she found anew the faith of her youth and after her death was buried in the cemetery adjacent to Old St. Patrick's.

After the McCloskeys' move from Brooklyn, then a village ("thoroughly Dutch and Lutheran")[16] of about ten thousand, to Manhattan (whose population was around a hundred thousand), John was enrolled at a Latin school run by one Thomas Brady. McCloskey's time there was notable for three things: (1) Brady's determination that his young pupil would one day become a lawyer; (2) the death of Patrick McCloskey during this period; and (3) the decision that young John's education should continue at Mount St. Mary's in Maryland.

Since settling in the United States, the senior McCloskey, by training either a chemist or a clerk, had been employed by Hezekiah Beers Pierrepont (d. 1838), a distiller and early Brooklyn real-estate magnate. Pierrepont made gin under the brand name Anchor.[17] But it was as a land developer that he made his fortune and fame. The fame is still enshrined in an eponymous street, which runs along the south side of the Brooklyn Public Library; the fortune came mostly from building houses and selling lots in the neighborhood Pierrepont dubbed Brooklyn Heights, America's first true suburb.[18]

Why the McCloskeys decided to move across the East River into lower Manhattan is not known for certain, although Cardinal Farley sensibly suggests it was because in the city "Catholic educational facilities were greater."[19] It is certain that after the family's move Patrick McCloskey continued to work for Pierrepont during the last several years of his life. In effect, he was, as we would say today, a reverse commuter.

Looking through archival material and published articles about Cardinal McCloskey, one cannot fail to notice how much respect so many people had for him from very early on—even, it seems, when he was just a boy. As the historian Francis Beauchesne Thornton has written:

> It is interesting to note that, beginning with his baptism by the future Bishop Fenwick, John McCloskey was intimately associated with many of the most important figures in the early American Church. It was largely through them and their appreciation of the boy's personality and talents that John's way was made easy in achieving the great responsibilities and honors that came later in life.[20]

As we mentioned above, the schoolmaster Brady was determined that his pupil would become a lawyer, as Brady's own sons and some of McCloskey's classmates did, but there were other men watching over young John who did not agree. One was Richard Riker, who had several times been the district attorney of New York and who, during a hiatus in his public service, had been co-counsel for the defense in the famous confessional case of 1813 (*People v. Philips*). Riker, along with lead counsel William Sampson, had "ably defended Father Kohlmann in the celebrated case".[21] Both men were Protestants, and Riker was also a Freemason, yet he was interested in the future of the Catholic John McCloskey. Exactly why is uncertain. Perhaps because of a friendship with Pierrepont, or perhaps he had a son studying with Brady. In any case, he told Mrs. McCloskey:

> I will not advise you not to put your son to the study of law, but I will say that there are more young lawyers starving than are making a living honestly. They begin with the best intentions, but they must work. All kinds of cases come to them, and all kinds are taken by them. The temptations are very great, too great for many to resist. If you can put your son to some thing else, I would advise it.[22]

The most important voice weighing in on this discussion, however, was probably not Brady's or Riker's or even Mrs. McCloskey's, but Cornelius Heeney's.

Heeney was arguably New York's most prominent Catholic layman. He had been a force, along with Father Kohlmann, in building Old St. Patrick's (Heeney and a partner purchased and then donated the land), and he became John McCloskey's guardian after the death of Patrick.

Heeney, another Irish immigrant, had come to the United States in 1784 and become an employee of John Jacob (Johann Jakob) Astor, the fur trader who became America's first multimillionaire and was one of the richest men in the world. (Astor's net worth at the time of his death in 1848 was the equivalent of billions in twenty-first-century dollars.) When Astor retired, Heeney became a part owner of the retail section of Astor's fur business and accumulated a substantial fortune of his own.[23]

The probably apocryphal story is told (even today on the website of the Brooklyn Benevolent Society, which he founded) of Heeney's arrival in America:

> On entering the Delaware River the ship on which Heeney had sailed was struck by lightning and wrecked. Some oystermen, dredging nearby, rescued the passengers, and for this service they demanded from each the sum of $1.00. A friendly Quaker, who some say was a fellow-passenger, others a mere looker-on, lent the dollar to the impecunious Irishman. Asking the name of his benefactor, that he might, when able, repay him, Heeney received the reply: "Whenever thou seest a fellow-creature in want of a dollar, as thou art now, give it to him, and thou shalt have repaid me."

Thus were established the frugality and charity that characterized his life.

We do not know how it is that young McCloskey became Heeney's ward, but we know that he did and that, one day in the summer of 1821, John was brought by his mother from Brady's school to the Prince Street orphanage, where Heeney was waiting with none other than Father John Dubois, president of Mount St. Mary's College. The McCloskeys had aspirations that young John might attend either Columbia or Georgetown, but it was Heeney's opinion that the boy would find the Mount more congenial to his disposition. At just eleven years old, McCloskey was not yet being proposed for seminary studies but was sent simply for the solid education in the advanced moral curriculum Dubois had organized.[24]

Farley writes:

> The Cardinal often related that Father Dubois, placing in his hands an open Breviary, asked him to translate the passage before his eyes. The result of this brief examination was not satisfactory, but he was assured that whatever defects he had would be remedied at the "Mountain."[25]

It may well be that Patrick McCloskey had so impressed Hezekiah Pierrepont that the latter told Heeney, his best Catholic friend, about the talented immigrant family, and it may be that Heeney even spoke of the McCloskeys to Astor or Riker, and that the family's friendship with priests at St. Peter's—including Benedict Fenwick, Anthony Kohlmann, the contentious John Power, and Peter Malou (whom we discussed in chapter 1)—brought them, and especially young John, to the attention of other members of New York's elite. But credit for setting John McCloskey on the path to the priesthood and all that followed may mostly belong, in spite of himself, to Thomas Brady. Surely Bettie McCloskey could see that her son was exceptionally smart, and no doubt Mrs. Melmoth had confirmed that impression.

But it would have been in Brady's Latin school that true tests of the boy's intellect began to be given and the results found to be impressive. It was his growing mastery of Latin, the language of Mother Church, that revealed something special about the boy to Father Dubois. The same thing had happened with John Joseph Hughes and had helped Dubois overcome his doubts about Hughes' intellect and agree to the Irishman's admission to the Mount. In whatever way the McCloskey boy mangled his translation of the breviary, it was likely due to the differences between classical and ecclesiastical Latin, between the Latin of Virgil and that of Aquinas. Dubois would have recognized this.

What Dubois saw was a brilliant boy, of just the right age and temperament—clay that he, Father Simon *Bruté*, and the other teachers at the Mount could shape into a true Catholic scholar, and that is what McCloskey became, albeit a strangely reluctant one.

At the Mount

John McCloskey matriculated at Mount St. Mary's in September of 1821, traveling to Maryland by steamboat and stagecoach.[26] In all, he would spend most of the next dozen years in Maryland, first as a college student—essentially what today amounts to high school and undergraduate university studies—and then as a seminarian. It would not be the end of his education.

Although more than a dozen years apart in age, McCloskey and John Joseph Hughes began their student days at the Mount separated by only a year. Hughes, of course, had been living on the property as gardener and slave manager for a time before he became a seminarian in 1820, and McCloskey was just beginning his secondary education, but their paths crossed early on. Hughes was a Latin tutor at the Mount, after all.

Whether or not John McCloskey was as frail a boy as his few biographers have suggested, he was certainly not a robust or boisterous youth. As we shall see, he was involved in a serious accident after his graduation from the Mount (but before he began his seminary studies), and it may be that his weakened condition then—and the effect it had upon his destiny—has been read back into the story of his childhood. Few nineteenth-century children reached their teenage years without having suffered through serious illnesses, and many children died. Those diseases and deaths had an effect upon the spirit of the age, so much so that the word *melancholy* might easily be given to the age itself.

On the other hand, if you could reach even ten years of age without having contracted typhoid, diphtheria, scarlet fever, or tuberculosis—or if you got one of those diseases but did not die from it—you had a real chance of growing strong and living a full life.

Cardinal Farley quotes a history of Mount St. Mary's (the "Mountain", he always calls the place) in which John McCloskey's arrival there is noted:

> The future Cardinal was a frail, delicate lad, and it was hoped that the Mountain air would strengthen him. He won the admiration and esteem of his teachers and the respect and love of his collegemates by the piety and the modesty of his character, his

gentleness, and sweet disposition, the enthusiasm with which he threw himself into his studies, and his prominent standing in class. He grew strong physically, too.[27]

At this time there were about one hundred boys at the college, and McCloskey was certainly in the student body's top tier. An 1824 report card of sorts indicates that he had a child's piety and then details his standing in his school subjects:

Religion: more attentive than formerly. 3rd. Latin: Excellent. 2nd. French: Applies and succeeds. Geography: excellent; attention and improvement. Rational arithmetic: excellent; seems to have a peculiar talent for studies of this kind. Behavior: Much better than formerly; much improved; unexceptionable. Temper: Mild but easily led away and artful when led away. Influenced by example. Generally mild and amiable. Application: Very good. Excellent manners. Engaging.[28]

Upon his graduation from the college in 1825, the fifteen-year-old McCloskey wrote an essay on patriotism (possibly the text of a speech), which was an exposition on a famous line of the Latin poet Horace: "Dulce et decorum est pro patria mori." (It is sweet and fitting to die for one's country.) The manuscript of seven pages is the sort of document that, in terms of handwriting, style, and content, demonstrates how superior nineteenth-century education was to ours today. McCloskey's scope reaches from the ancient Roman ideals of liberty, as found in the works of Cicero, to then-recent American history in the achievements of George Washington and "Montgomery". Apparently McCloskey was referring to Richard Montgomery, an Irish-born former British soldier who joined the Continental Army during the American Revolution and died in 1775 while leading an unsuccessful invasion of Canada, and who, McCloskey wrote of him,

though not by birth an American, rather than see the rights of an innocent and unoffending people trampled upon by a British tyrant, chose to hazard his own life in defense of their liberty. And to his lot, alas, it fell to perish in the conflict. But who is there, acquainted with the circumstances of this man's death, will say that it was not sweet? Where is he within whose bosom beats a heart whose every pulsation tells him that he is a freeman, that would not be eager to meet a similar fate, to die the protector of his country, to die a Montgomery?

As we have seen, John Joseph Hughes would soon become embroiled in debates about the Americanism of Catholics, and he might have offered young McCloskey's essay as proof of the esteem for and dedication to the United States of which a Roman Catholic teenager was capable. Young McCloskey concludes:

But where is the American that can be else than patriot? The graves of our forefathers admonish us that all these blessings and all the happiness which we now so peacefully are enjoying, are but the fruits of their labors and the reward of their patriotism, and that the continuance of these enjoyments can only be procured by following their example.[29]

McCloskey stayed on at the Mount to study philosophy until July of 1826, when he returned to the family farm near Bedford, New York.[30] It was there that fate intervened.

The Accident

That John McCloskey was to be a lawyer seems to have been the opinion of nearly everyone—perhaps even him. It may well have been in his nature to be compliant with the opinions of others (Riker notwithstanding), and it appears that with his undergraduate studies at the Mount completed, he had no thought of entering the priesthood. The call had not yet come.

His health and fitness were, at sixteen, sufficiently robust for him to participate in the management of the McCloskey farm. In a sepia-toned photograph taken when he was in his teens, possibly upon his graduation from the Mount, he has the sides of his hair slicked back and looks askance with an expression that seems forlorn. His eyes, which we know were blue, convey both intelligence and wariness. His wide lips and broad mouth are turned slightly down, and he has a slight dimple in his chin. The downturned mouth is seen in nearly every photo taken of him at every age, as if he were uneasy and possibly unhappy. In the schoolboy photo, his nose seems flatter and his lips fuller than in later photos, suggesting that he was not yet through puberty.[31]

He remained in Bedford for the rest of 1826 and through the summer of 1827. There is no record of exactly how he spent that year, except that he did work of one sort or another around the farm. And then one day, early in the winter of '26–'27, he suffered a serious accident that would change the course of his life. Here is how the accident is described in Farley's *Life of John Cardinal McCloskey*:

> A farmhand employed in drawing logs near the house, left his ox-team and loaded wagon unattended. John, who was then in his eighteenth year was passing by, and seeing no one about, got up on the wagon and started to drive the team. His lack of skill frightened the oxen and with a lurch the wagon was overturned and he was buried beneath the logs. When found, he was unconscious and remained in that state for several days.

McCloskey was confined to his bed for many weeks, and during the first days after he was found, perhaps by the farmhand who had left the wagon unattended, he was unconscious. He had almost surely suffered a severe concussion and must have been badly bruised in many places, possibly including his spine. He was also blind for several days. According to the modern understanding of concussion, there are three levels:

> Grade 1: no loss of consciousness, transient confusion, and other symptoms that resolve within 15 minutes;
> Grade 2: no loss of consciousness, transient confusion, and other symptoms that require more than 15 minutes to resolve;
> Grade 3: loss of consciousness for any period.
> Days or weeks after the accident, the person may show signs of the following: headache, poor attention and concentration, memory difficulties, anxiety, depression, sleep disturbances, light and noise intolerance.

> The occurrence of such symptoms is called "post-concussion syndrome."[32]

But despite any short- or long-term damage the accident may have caused, he was back at Mount St. Mary's in the autumn of 1827.

In later years John McCloskey insisted that while still at the Mount as a college student, he had not seriously considered the priesthood. He recalled, though, a conversation with the man who was president of the Mount between 1826 and 1829, Father Michael de Burgo Egan. As McCloskey was ready to head home to Bedford in 1826, Egan told him: "Remember this, John: if you once had a vocation and lose it through your own fault, you will have to answer for it."[33] He did remember.

The cardinal would later say that the accident was a matter of Divine Providence. He experienced something of what Giovanni di Pietro di Bernardone did after he suffered the thirteenth-century version of post-traumatic stress disorder during Assisi's interminable wars with Perugia. Out of Bernardone's recovery came a new dedication to Christ, and the man whose father had nicknamed him Francesco (the Frenchman), after the nationality of his mother, became St. Francis. So McCloskey too saw things suddenly in a perspective he had not had before the accident. The call had come. He answered.

First he told his closest advisor and confidante:

> Till then, I had never spoken openly to my mother of my intention to study for the priesthood and she felt that it was too delicate a matter to discuss with me directly. I knew, however, how much it would delight her, if she were convinced that I had, of my own accord, made up my mind to embrace that holy state. She said to me, after a moment's reflection: "John, you see what a priest has to suffer and how often he is treated ungratefully." She alluded to the trustee war, then waxing to its height. It was altogether a stormy time for priests and bishops in New York. She concluded with these words: "Now you see what you have to expect if you are a priest; so I hope you have well considered the step you propose to take."[34]

Mrs. McCloskey was prophetic.

John McCloskey's spiritual advisor at the Mount was Simon Bruté, who had played a similar role during John Hughes' preparation for the priesthood. (By this time Hughes was serving as a priest in Philadelphia.) But if Bruté was McCloskey's mentor, St. Francis de Sales (1567–1622) was his model. Among other things, de Sales was known as a gentle conciliator in the aftermath of the Protestant Reformation, and the great saint's book *Introduction to the Devout Life* must have had considerable influence on the young seminarian.[35]

McCloskey's journals from his seminary days show a student in pursuit of organization, if not to say regimentation. As he records his thoughts about meditation (*contemplation*, we might say today), he breaks down the process of preparation and practice into logical, numbered steps deemed necessary for meeting God in thought. He concludes:

> Conclusion consists of three things: 1, To thank God for having permitted us to appear in His presence; 2, to ask God's pardon for distractions and neglects committed in so holy an exercise, and His blessing on our resolutions for the present day; 3, to make the *bouquet spiritual* ... [which] consists in taking one or two of the thoughts which have struck us in prayer, which in the sight of God we think most useful to us, and to repeat them frequently during the day. Finis.[36]

Cardinal Farley notes that these journals (now apparently lost) are filled with a wide range of jottings, "among them paragraphs on Genius, Railways, Silver Mines, Poets, Art, Glass, Byron and many extracts from [Edmund] Burke, who seems to have had quite an influence upon John McCloskey's mind". The conservatism that Burke saw in what he called "prejudice and prescription" is visible in one of McCloskey's notebook entries—as are echoes of the Declaration and the Constitution:

> It is this happy nature which contributes in so eminent a degree to the preservation and promotion of that peace and harmony which should at all times and in all places exist in society. But our best and happiest and most virtuous dispositions, will, when permitted to exceed those limits, which the laws of God and his divine Religion have prescribed for them, immediately be divested of their commending quality and degenerate into so many vices. For vice is nothing more than an excessive indulgence of our own natural propensities—A due regard for the opinions of men and well regulated desire to please, so far from being opposed to the maxims of the Gospel, are, on the contrary, both commendable and praiseworthy. But when the alternative once presents itself either of offending man or of offending God ... hesitation would be criminal. Every nerve should be braced and every power both of mind and body exerted to its utmost, in order to bear up against the torrent of ridicule and abuse however headstrong and prove ourselves triumphantly superior to its fury and its violence.[37]

But above all there are echoes of de Sales, especially the saint's how-to discussion on meditation, or mental prayer, "a thing much neglected nowadays".

> Exercise your ordinary imagination, picturing the Saviour to yourself in His Sacred Humanity as if He were beside you just as we are wont to think of our friends, and fancy that we see or hear them at our side. But when the Blessed Sacrament of the Altar is there, then this Presence is no longer imaginary, but most real; and the sacred species are but as a veil from behind which the Present Saviour beholds and considers us, although we cannot see Him as He is.[38]

Lost Time

Now a peculiar thing happens: an apparent interlude in McCloskey's time at the Mount. Cardinal Farley (with Hayes and Guilday) is forced to deal with a passage in *The Story of the Mountain*, by Mary E. Meline and Edward F. X. McSween, historians of the seminary. They note in their book that Father Bruté, who kept a personal record of comings and goings at the Mount, observed on August 15, 1829, that, as they paraphrase him: "John [Cardinal] McCloskey returned to the Seminary this year, having tried his vocation outside."[39] Farley writes that "a reference from Dr. McCaffrey's notes has been misplaced in the chronology."[40] But that will not do.

The McCaffrey to whom Farley refers is the Reverend John McCaffrey, who was rector of the Mount from 1838 to 1872. The entire paragraph from *The Story of the Mountain* from which Farley quotes is this:

> Father *Bruté* intimates in his notes of Aug. 15, 1829, that the divinity course was then two years at the Mountain and one at Baltimore, that is three years in all. *As we saw, the College lost two priests and two masters within the year. John* [Cardinal] *McCloskey*

returned to the Seminary this year, having tried his vocation outside. There were nineteen Americans and ten natives of Ireland in the Seminary here, and one, an American, in Paris. Five were ordained this year and two left. Dr. McCaffrey's notes tell us that. [Emphasis added.]

But from whose notes did the observation about McCloskey come—Bruté's or McCaffrey's? Farley may be hoping it was Father McCaffrey, because Bruté's reputation for probity and accuracy was legendary.

This is important because of what comes next in Farley's own chronology: that in 1829 McCloskey asked Bishop Dubois (as head of his home diocese) for an *exeat*—a decree that, under the usual circumstances for such an order, would transfer a priest from one diocese to another. It seems an entirely odd request to be made by a seminarian, unless he was asking to be allowed to transfer to another seminary. To be sure, there was another nearby in Baltimore (another St. Mary's— America's oldest seminary), to which Meline and McSween confusingly refer in the paragraph quoted above. McCloskey may have wished to go there. But why? There's no evidence of any difficulty at the Mount between him and other students or faculty.

Farley wants to treat the "return" of McCloskey in 1829 as, perhaps, actually referring to the Mount graduate's "return" in 1827 after his accident, to begin anew as a seminarian. It could be just a miswritten citation by McCaffrey—a seven may easily be mistaken for a nine. Yet it is not as if Farley simply breezes past the "having tried his vocation outside" part, because his very next observation concerns the exeat, which he does not attempt to explain. Instead, he gives what amounts to a literary shrug of the shoulders. We do not know even if McCloskey wished to go elsewhere or if the Mount wanted to send him elsewhere—or if McCloskey was requesting to be freed from such preliminary vows as he may have made in the first year or two of his priestly education.

An intriguing bit of evidence that may have something to do with the exeat mystery comes from the Bedford Historical Society. On its website, in a description of the Bedford Library, formerly the Bedford Academy (opened in 1807 and closed in 1902), the society states that John McCloskey was a student there. In response to an inquiry by the authors of this book, the society provided photocopies of pages from the *History of Bedford Academy*, published in 1877. The pages provided include a list of the Academy's distinguished former students and the statement:

> Among the pupils that have gone out of this institution may be found ministers of nearly all religious denominations. Bedford Academy has the honor of having had the distinguished Catholic Cardinal, John McClosky [*sic*], as a pupil. He is the highest dignitary of the Roman church in America—the first and only Cardinal in this country.[41]

It may be that the young McCloskey—because of either homesickness or doubt about his vocation as a priest—decided to take time off (perhaps to undertake prelaw studies, as Thomas Brady thought he should), during which period he took classes at the academy. There may be an altogether different reason, but it is difficult not to take that provocative phrase, "having tried his vocation outside", at face value.

It is also interesting to note that among the earliest financial backers of the academy was the lawyer Richard Riker, who, as we have seen, took an early interest in McCloskey.

We do know that McCloskey was at the Mount (as a very young undergraduate) through 1826 and then back there in the fall of '27 to begin his seminary studies. Since (if McCaffrey did not miscopy the date) the exeat was not applied for until 1829, it may be that McCloskey's time at Bedford Academy came in either 1828 or 1829. Then again, since the reason for the exeat request is not known, McCloskey may simply have taken summer-school classes in Bedford during breaks from the Mount between 1822 and 1826.

It is certainly intriguing that Farley/Hayes/Guilday skipped over this part of the cardinal's education, almost as if the authors were unaware of it.

It was Father John Power—writing on behalf of Bishop Dubois to Father Francis B. Jamison at Mount St. Mary's on January 20, 1830—who refused the exeat. This makes it appear as if it was the seminary that had sought the exeat, whether for its own reasons or at McCloskey's request. Power's phrasing suggests that he (Power) would have approved Father Jamison's application had he felt free to do so, but Power believed that Dubois (who was away in Rome) would not have given permission, and so Power felt compelled to refuse the request. This is as reported in the Farley biography,[42] although there is a slight problem with the dating. Farley refers to Father Jamison as rector of the Mount in 1830, but in fact he did not serve in that capacity until 1833.[43] He may have undertaken McCloskey's exeat in some other role he played at the Mount. In any case, it was to Jamison that Power wrote, and Power's side of the correspondence does not supply answers to any of our questions. He wrote:

> If he [McCloskey] were my subject properly speaking, indeed I would not *refuse him to Mt. St. Mary's*, but as I only hold the place [as vicar-general] to another [Dubois], I feel myself bound to keep as near to his [Dubois'] wishes and intentions as I possibly can.[44] [Emphasis added.]

Power adds that he believes that Jamison will now "relinquish a demand which I am free to say is but just on your side". But what does this mean? By "just", Power seems to suggest that Father Jamison was within his rights to ask for the exeat. Might this mean that John McCloskey had violated seminary rules, perhaps simply by returning to Bedford when he should have been in Emmitsburg? We may never know the answer.

In any case, by 1831, McCloskey was actively recruiting young men for the Mount, "making our College known to many who enjoy high literary reputation" and making them aware of the importance of the priesthood.

From this point forward in the life of John McCloskey, there was no second-guessing his vocation.

Father McCloskey

Upon finally graduating from the seminary, John McCloskey was ordained by Bishop Dubois at Old St. Patrick's on January 12, 1834.[45] A report extrapolated from McCloskey's own recollection describes the scene:

> A furious snowstorm was raging, making it impossible for his friends to be with him;
> the dusky reaches of the church were almost deserted. While the wind rattled the
> windows, drowning the soft hiss of gas jets, John knelt in the luminous sanctuary
> for the long ceremony of ordination. The weather had also kept the usual throng
> of priests away. Except for the acolytes and the ministers at the altar, Bishop Dubois
> moved through the Mass unattended by his usual retinue.[46]

The author of the quote, Francis Beauchesne Thornton, was born in 1898 and may
never actually have heard hissing gas lamps, so one may reasonably surmise, since
his only cited source is the Farley biography (which makes no mention of cathedral
lighting), that Thornton was either exercising poetic license or had access to the lost
McCloskey diaries (or some other unnamed resource).

Although hardly educated in medical matters, Cardinal Farley makes his own
interesting speculation about that day:

> At the time of his ordination few thought that he would live long. Always frail in
> health, the accident of 1827 had left its trace, and no one suspected at the time that the
> young priest would live beyond the Scriptural three score years and ten.[47]

But neither Farley nor any other historian describes the young priest as limping,
sallow faced, or sickly in any way. Much has been made of the accident—perhaps
too much.

McCloskey's first parish assignment was at Old St. Patrick's. He did there what
all priests do: he said Mass, baptized babies, performed weddings, and heard confessions. He was also chaplain at Bellevue Hospital. Bellevue was not known then—as
it is today (and incorrectly)—as a psychiatric hospital, which has always been just
one among a range of medical specialties at which the great institution excels.
(It may be that the association with psychiatry is merely a misuse by Americans:
substituting "Bellevue" for "Bedlam", the famous psychiatric facility in London,
England—and the name "Bedlam" is itself a corruption of "Bethlehem Royal Hospital". After sixteenth-century excesses at the then asylum, "Bedlam" became a
word meaning "madhouse".) At Bellevue, Father McCloskey would have made the
usual "sick calls", which meant distributing Communion to the bedridden, giving
comfort to a child with a broken leg, and, in extremis, administering the last rites.

But these assignments—and his time at the cathedral—were brief, because, as
was noted in the previous chapter, Bishop Dubois tapped McCloskey to be vice
president of the diocese's first seminary, under construction in Nyack, New York.
As we also noted, however, the project—and Dubois' hope for a local seminary—
was destroyed by fire in August of 1834.

His future now uncertain, McCloskey petitioned "to be allowed to help in the
work of caring for the sick and dying"[48] during the cholera epidemic then devastat-
ing New York. Dubois was having none of that, especially because, apparently like
everybody else, he "knew" that the young priest was "frail in health".

But around this time McCloskey had also asked to be allowed to go to Rome for
further study, perhaps leading to a doctorate, and this option Bishop Dubois now
seized upon, the better to get his young priest into the presumably more healthful
environs of Central Italy and the warmth of the Tyrrhenian Sea. The bishop did

have some doubts in the matter, but they were overcome by the intervention of
Cornelius Heeney, who assured him that Mrs. McCloskey would "bear all the
expenses" of the young priest's journey to Europe.[49] Cardinal McCloskey himself
would recall many years later that his departure for Rome fulfilled a promise made
to him as a boy by Bishop John Connolly:

> I remember as though it were yesterday, his once placing his hands on my young
> head and telling me that if I ever wished to become a priest, he would send me to the
> Propaganda.[50]

McCloskey also found it somewhat amusing, looking back, that a part of the reason
he was sent to Rome was concern about his health. Everybody thought he was "so
feeble" that "my friends thought I would not return. Providence spared me beyond
expectations."[51]

McCloskey set sail for the northern French port city of Le Havre on November 3, 1834, arriving there exactly one month later. In the company of an American Protestant physician named Willet, McCloskey headed first to Rouen, then to
Paris, Lyon, and Marseilles, and from there through various Italian coastal cities to
Rome, where they arrived on February 8, 1835.[52] The travelers reached the summit
of a hill outside Rome from which they could see, in the distance, the dome of St.
Peter's. The significance of the moment was not lost on the young priest:

> There stood the city which had been visited by St. Peter and St. Paul, and in which
> they surrendered their lives in testimony of the faith they had there established. My
> eyes now beheld the same scenes on which theirs had often rested; the same sky, the
> same hills, the same plains, the same mountains. I now beheld the city from whose
> gates had gone forth victorious armies to conquer the world. They had trodden the
> same soil which I was treading, perhaps the very spot on which I stood had been sig-
> nalized by some of their achievements.[53]

Visiting St. Peter's the next day, he is disappointed that, at ground level, one cannot grasp the magnificence of the great basilica. Then he recalls some lines of Lord
Byron: "Thou seest not all, but piecemeal thou must break / To separate contemplation, the great whole" (*Childe Harold's Pilgrimage*).

McCloskey came to Rome bearing a number of written introductions to men
in top positions in the governing Curia as well as letters from Bishop Dubois and
others to various Vatican dignitaries.[54] His intention was to study at the college of
the Sacred Congregation for the Propagation of the Faith (Propaganda Fide), and so
among the first illustrious men he sought out was Monsignor Angelo Mai, former
head of the Vatican Library (and a renowned philologist), the secretary of the Propaganda college. As it happened, Mai was away when McCloskey presented himself, so McCloskey met instead with Father Karl-August von Reisach, the college's
rector of studies. Both Mai and Reisach would later become cardinals, the former
in 1838 and the latter in 1855. McCloskey and Reisach would become friends, and in
1864 Bishop McCloskey would write to Cardinal Reisach plaintively after the
death of John Joseph Hughes, begging unsuccessfully that the mantle of archbishop
of New York not fall upon him.

For now, Reisach and Mai saw to it that McCloskey was given a place to live in the recently revived Pontifical Irish College (Pontificio Collegio Irlandese), the Pontifical North American College not yet having been established. The plan was for McCloskey to live there while attending classes at the Pontifical Gregorian University—not at the Propaganda, as he had expected—with the eventual reward of an advanced degree in theology. The Gregorian, as it is called, was at that point often called the Roman College. It had been founded in 1551 by Ignatius of Loyola, and his Jesuit order would be the on-again, off-again administrators of the college, renamed *Gregorian* after Pope Gregory XIII moved the college to grander quarters a generation after its founding. As he began his studies there, John McCloskey was surely aware that ten of its alumni had become popes.

Soon after he arrived in Rome, the twenty-five-year-old American wrote to his venerable bishop back home in New York that, to him, the Eternal City was just that. His words might have formed an essay he would never have thought to write while at the Mount, "Why I Am a Catholic":

> Rome is still the City of the soul; the Mother of arts; the Parent of our religion. Pregnant as are her crumbling monuments and hoary ruins with classic and historic associations, every temple and almost every shrine seems fraught with lessons to the Christian far more affecting in all that is instructive, all that is sublime in the history of our religion. Seated in her libraries you can converse with the earliest and most venerable Doctors of the Church, and gather the most precious knowledge amid the vast and various treasures which they open to you. And emerging from the study to mingle in the realities of life, you can, if you will, discover new sources of instruction and edification as well as of pleasure at almost every step. Indeed I can never be too thankful to those who encouraged me in my desire of going abroad.[55]

In that same letter, McCloskey tells Bishop Dubois that his rooms at the Convent of Sant'Andrea della Valle (which adjoined the Irish College) are spacious and that he comes and goes as he "would in a house of my own". He attended two lectures each day at the Gregorian: one on moral theology and the other on dogmatic theology.

> In addition to this I attend what is called an Academy of the Sapienza, where students, principally clergymen who have already finished their course, discuss controversial questions, to which they always come prepared, as being proposed a week previously. Scripture and ecclesiastical history, I study privately.[56]

Sapienza Academy (today University) was founded in 1303 by Pope Boniface VIII.

In a letter addressed simply to "Dear Sister", he described the course of a typical day:

> I rise at six; say Mass at the Church of the Gesu; walk to the Roman College; hear the lectures; return to my room; study till dinner—the company are the members of the religious community with which I live. After dinner I chat a while with my companion, a young Irish clergyman. In the afternoon I return for lectures; take a short walk; visit the Blessed Sacrament in some of the many churches near at hand; return in the evening before the Ave Maria, i.e., sundown; study till supper, and, after an hour or more of reading, retire for the night.

The Church of the Gesu is the Chiesa del Santissimo Nome di Gesù all'Argentina (Church of the Most Holy Name of Jesus at the "Argentina"—not the South American country, but a derivation from *Argentoratum*, the Roman name for the city of Strasbourg). The Argentina is the motherhouse of the Jesuit Order and is located near the Gregorian.

There was another, very special reason why Rome was a revelation for John McCloskey: it was thoroughly Catholic. Growing up in New York, he had lived with a sense of being in a minority in the midst of a hostile majority—sometimes very hostile. In Rome, he was in the cradle of Catholicism, walking daily not simply through the city's beautifully exotic streets and among ruins of an ancient culture, but in the living, breathing epicenter of the one, true faith. Mother Church held him in her arms. There were no apologies to be made, either in the sense of making excuses to antagonistic Protestant America or in the sense of evangelizing for the faith. In Rome, the Church was the sun: she was everywhere, warming everyone, and all revolved around her.

McCloskey's connections to people in high places—which seem always to have existed for him—served him well in Rome, securing for him the friendship and patronage of eminent men. Among them (courtesy of his friendship with Father Simon Bruté) was the elderly French cardinal Joseph Fesch, prince of France, a member of the Imperial House of the First French Empire, and the uncle of Napoleon Bonaparte. It was Fesch who blessed the marriage between his nephew and Joséphine de Beauharnais prior to their coronation as emperor and empress in 1804. Six years later, after Napoleon's marriage to Joséphine—who had proven unable to give him an heir—was annulled, Fesch celebrated the nuptial Mass between Napoleon and Marie-Louise of Austria. Fesch was a great patron of the arts, and his home at the Palazzo Falconieri contained a large library, to which McCloskey was welcomed *sans cérémonie.*[57]

Above all, there was McCloskey's renewed acquaintance with Father Anthony Kohlmann, S.J. Father Kohlmann, who had been the first administrator of the new Diocese of New York two decades earlier, had moved to Rome and occupied a chair in theology at the Gregorian; he acted as McCloskey's spiritual advisor during the young priest's sojourn in Rome.

Among McCloskey's closest friends in Rome was another Frenchman, Father Jean-Baptiste Henri-Dominique Lacordaire, a follower of the ultramontanists Louis de Bonald, Joseph de Maistre, and Félecité Robert de Lamennais. Lacordaire represents, at least to some extent, the then-emerging search for balance between political democracy (what, in the context of the Enlightenment, can only be called *liberalism*) and an almost authoritarian Church—a liberal Caesar and a conservative God. He was a champion of the separation of church and state as the best way to protect the interests of the Church. Lacordaire and his companions had journeyed to Rome to seek what they assumed would be the approval of their efforts by Pope Gregory XVI, but the pope actually condemned many of their views in an 1832 encyclical, *Mirari vos* (*On Liberalism and Religious Indifferentism*).

Lacordaire's response was swift and instructive: he recanted. And one day when he and McCloskey were talking, Lacordaire said of his love for Rome, "*Parce qu'elle m'a arraché de l'Abîme.*" (He loved the city—and the Church—"because she snatched me from the Abyss.")

His friendship with Lacordaire was likely McCloskey's first serious encounter with what would become known as Modernism, which would prove to be a serious issue toward the end of McCloskey's episcopacy and would truly haunt that of his successor, Michael Augustine Corrigan.

Return to America

When McCloskey returned to America in 1837, it was without the advanced degree it was assumed he would achieve, but this had no effect upon the rest of his meteoric ecclesiastical career.

Back in New York, he again stayed briefly at the rectory of Old St. Patrick's. His former guardian, Cornelius Heeney, petitioned Bishop Dubois to send him to St. James' Church in Brooklyn, but it was the old story anew: the trustees there had their own man in mind.

And so it was that the twenty-seven-year-old Father John McCloskey was assigned to St. Joseph's Church in Manhattan, at Sixth Avenue and Washington Place. As Monsignor Shelley describes it, "Founded in 1829, St. Joseph's was the Mother Church of the Catholics in Greenwich Village and the fifth oldest parish in the whole archdiocese."[58]

Coming in as rector for his first true parish assignment, Father McCloskey found himself embroiled in the same old scourge of trusteeism. Shortly before his appointment, the previous pastor, Father James Quinn, had been transferred to Troy, New York—essentially because of disrespect he had shown to Bishop Dubois. Quinn had been replaced by Father Constantine Pise, who had been McCloskey's classmate at the Mount. The St. Joseph's trustees expressed their indignation at the Pise appointment in a long letter dated September 7, 1837, in which, according to Farley, "all the vicious elements of trusteeism are plainly visible":

> The phrases "inherent right," "free agents," "privileges," "legal meetings," etc., are flung back and forth and confuse the point at issue. It is a dreary letter at best.[59]

The high-minded Pise had already resigned.

McCloskey had actually arrived at St. Joseph's in August, and so bitter was the battle between the bishop and the trustees that for the next six months not a single parishioner ever called upon the new rector. When he gave his homilies at Mass, the pews were nearly empty. As Thornton would write, "Undaunted and serene, the pastor continued Sunday after Sunday with his beautifully crafted sermons on human respect, poverty and humility."[60] Later it would be said of him that though he would not fight, he would conquer. And eventually the parishioners of St. Joseph's came to admire, trust, and even revere him.

It was at exactly this moment that his former schoolmate and tutor from Mount St. Mary's, John Joseph Hughes, was made coadjutor bishop of New York, and Hughes began to look to McCloskey whenever he had a new and difficult project in need of leadership. In 1840, he named the reluctant McCloskey president of what would become St. John's College in the Fordham area of Westchester County, today part of the Bronx, and rechristened Fordham University. McCloskey would spend two years leading the college, while also attempting to minister to his flock at St. Joseph's.

When Bishop Dubois died in December of 1842, Hughes succeeded him, and in less than a year the new bishop recommended the reluctant McCloskey to be his own coadjutor.

"Reluctant", in fact, is the word that not a few have chosen with reference to the steps in McCloskey's rise in the Church, not least McCloskey himself. Some of that hesitancy, shyness, or fear—whatever it was—may have been the result, at least in part, of the health issues that seemed to follow him. Of McCloskey's short tenure at St. John's College, Francis Beauchesne Thornton claims that the "position turned out to be damaging to John's health". Then came the appointment as coadjutor, which, Thornton continues, "very probably [was] to Father McCloskey's dismay".[61]

When we consider his mysterious absence from the seminary a decade and a half earlier and the way the man himself expressed reluctance, dismay, or hesitation about each new increase in responsibility, it is hard not to conclude that John McCloskey was a man of little ambition but great dedication. But sickly? He lived to be seventy-five.

Surely weighing on his mind on March 10, 1844, as he was being consecrated by Hughes as coadjutor bishop of New York (and titular bishop of Axieri), was the knowledge that he would likely be named Hughes' successor when the time came. That conviction can only have been fortified by his assumption that his Roman connections, many of whom were now close advisors to cardinals and even to Pope Gregory, would keep him in mind as a priest whose loyalty to the Church was beyond question. New York was not yet considered the preeminent American diocese—its status as an archdiocese was still more than five years in the future—but those with vision in Rome cannot have failed to see the former mission in New York on its way to becoming a see every bit as important as any other in the world, save Rome itself. And if asked which priest showed the greatest promise as a leader in the American Church, many in Rome would have named the man they considered the most cultured, well-spoken, godly American they knew, and that was not John Hughes. Hughes, they knew, was the right man for that time, but McCloskey was a cleric who was the best kind of man for any time.

Unlike the sparsely attended Hughes consecration of six years before, the elevation of McCloskey was witnessed by a crowd inside and outside the cathedral estimated at between seven and eight thousand people. And, as previously mentioned, according to a reliable account, Bettie McCloskey was one of those people at St. Patrick's the day her son became a bishop, as was her daughter Margaret. It was doubly good that they were there: to celebrate his consecration and his thirty-fourth birthday.[62] And it was good that the consecration took place when it did, since Mrs. McCloskey would die not many months later.

Bishop McCloskey

Again, it may simply be a reaction to the difference in style between Hughes and McCloskey that led Farley to write:

To the superficial observer of a life so quietly passed in the service of God as that of Cardinal McCloskey, it would seem in reality that it was almost devoid of incident; that it was a life hidden within the Tabernacle with the Lord to Whom it had been consecrated; and that he himself, instead of being a leader in the stirring incidents of these first three years of his episcopate, was rather guided by the current of events which swept through the New York diocese at this time. But, that he was observant of every detail of the crises which came upon the Church is evident from his letters and from the part he played in all the great movements of these years. He took no public part in the crisis brought on by the Native-American Movement of 1844, or in the excitement caused later by the Church Property Bill; but he was by no means a silent spectator during these years when the Church was almost at the mercy of a band of fanatical politicians. More and more the strong mind of John Hughes began to depend upon his quiet and far-seeing coadjutor and suffragan.[63]

But Bishop McCloskey was more than just an observer of crises, even if he did not engage in public debates with nativists or Protestants. His esteem rose directly in proportion to his presence among Catholics in the diocese. He traveled widely after his appointment, and his reputation for piety led many to seek his friendship and counsel.

Among those was Isaac Hecker, whom McCloskey would bring into the Church and who would go on to found the Paulist Fathers. Hecker's intent was to evangelize America, with the goal of converting the entire nation to Catholicism. Shortly after baptizing Hecker, McCloskey was also instrumental in bringing into the Church no less an American intellectual figure than Orestes Brownson, whose New York–based publication, *Brownson's Quarterly*, gave both delight and displeasure to Hughes and McCloskey.

Brownson had a habit of careening from liberalism to conservatism in his search for Truth, and his criticisms of both laymen and clergy with whom he disagreed could be caustic. He was a convert whose passion for the Faith was white-hot. As biographer Patrick W. Carey would write, Brownson believed Rome

was the antidote to individualism and no-churchism, twin evils in American society. The Catholic Church was the only viable option for him personally, and as he made evident later in his career, it was the only reliable support for freedom as well as authority within American society.[64]

Not a few others came into the Church through McCloskey's steady encouragement. Curiously, though, McCloskey was not of a mind to receive converts quickly. Farley notes:

He never liked to see them come in "crowds," as he once said; and he had the born Catholic's fear of the reforming element so strong sometimes in the newly converted. Not that he condemned such a spirit, but the danger was always present of their forming new schools and tendencies.[65]

At the Sixth Provincial Council of Baltimore, held in May of 1846, Bishop Hughes announced his intention, provided that the council (and Rome, of course) approved, of dividing New York into "three separate bishoprics", the new ones to have their sees in Albany and Buffalo. The newly elected Pope Pius IX created the new dioceses on April 23, 1847, and John McCloskey was sent to Albany as its first bishop. (Just fifty-four when elected pope, Pius IX—Pio Nono, the aristocratic Giovanni Maria Mastai-Ferretti—would reign for more than thirty-one years. He would initiate the First Vatican Council, in 1869, and, of course, give a red hat to John McCloskey.)

In Albany the situation was not dissimilar to the one that John Connolly had found upon his arrival in Manhattan three decades earlier. Although Dubois and Hughes had imposed some discipline upon the churches up north (and their trustees), many parishes in the new diocese were still disunited and contentious—not just in Albany but also in Oswego and Utica. The story is told of the arrival in Albany of a delegation of laymen from Utica who were unhappy with their pastor, Francis Patrick McFarland. Presenting themselves before McCloskey, they demanded that McFarland be transferred to another parish. McCloskey sat silently as they presented their bill of indictment, such as it was. When the trustees were finished, McCloskey assured them that their "petition shall be granted shortly". No doubt the men were amazed both at their own apparent eloquence in making the case against their pastor and at their new bishop's alacrity in acceding to their demand.

Recalling the vocal training he had received from the actress Mrs. Melmoth, one can imagine the effect upon the trustees when McCloskey arose and said: "I have just received from Rome a bull appointing your pastor Bishop of Hartford."[66] Then he left the room, after which the delegation hurried home to Utica to spread the good news about *their* pastor's being elevated to the episcopate.

Meanwhile, in Buffalo, relations between the bishop, John Timon, and trustees in the new diocese there were so contentious that Archbishop Gaetano Bedini was asked to intervene, which he did on behalf of Timon, and his action helped to inflame the so-called Bedini Incident described in the previous chapter.

Farley writes of the early years of the seventeen that McCloskey would spend in Albany:

> The flock entrusted to him contained over sixty thousand souls, scattered from Kingston on the Hudson to the St. Lawrence. Often he had to administer the Sacrament of Confirmation in humble sheds and in tanneries; and yet, as he himself often declared, never did he feel himself nearer to God, and nearer to Christ, than during these early apostolic days of his episcopate.[67]

Among the projects Bishop McCloskey took on was the building of a proper cathedral for the new diocese. He and Bishop Hughes laid the cornerstone for the Cathedral of the Immaculate Conception on July 2, 1848, "with over ten thousand people watching in the rain".[68] The building was completed in just under five years, and most of the construction was undertaken by an immigrant workforce, mostly Irish. The cost was $250,000 or, as the cathedral's website calculates it, "$6.5 million in today's dollars". McCloskey's experience with the building of Immaculate Conception would benefit him when the time came to finish the work on the new St. Patrick's in Manhattan that Hughes would begin in 1858.

During the legislative battle over the 1855 Church Property Bill, Bishop McCloskey provided now-Archbishop Hughes with invaluable intelligence about the debates raging in the state capital. Even so, the efforts of Hughes and McCloskey were to no avail, and the bill passed. However, as mentioned earlier, ownership of churches was never transferred from the Church to trustees, and the bill was eventually repealed.

It was a stimulating and busy time for John McCloskey, and there are few references in letters or other documents indicating that he suffered in any way from mental or physical stresses owing to any condition of ill health. But he became very anxious in 1864 after the death of Archbishop Hughes, because he knew only too well whom Rome was likely to call on to take up the reins of the Archdiocese of New York.

One newspaper account cited by Farley (but not footnoted) summarizes McCloskey's years in Albany:

When he went to Albany, the town contained four Catholic churches.... The remainder of his diocese contained about forty churches, and had less than that number of Catholic clergymen.... The Catholics were much scattered over the territory, were far from being wealthy as a body, and it must be acknowledged in some of the districts there existed a great prejudice against them.... After a service of seventeen years in the diocese, there were 113 churches, 8 chapels, 85 priests, 15 students for the Ministry, 3 academies for boys, 6 orphan asylums and 15 parochial schools.[69]

Or as Father John Talbot Smith summarized:

Before his administration ended in 1864 the Catholic population increased to 230,000. As in the metropolis, all things had to be done for the new diocese, and money was scarce. The temper concealed in the delicate frame of Bishop McCloskey showed itself by the manner in which he conducted the work of religion. He travelled about his wild diocese, administering the sacraments in halls, tanneries, and private houses, organizing his people, and laying strong foundations. He succeeded in building a handsome cathedral, in raising the number of the clergy to one hundred, the number of churches to one hundred and twenty, and of schools to twenty-seven, besides introducing religious communities into the diocese, and helping in the work of founding the Seminary at Troy.... His success as an administrator, his kindly manners, his devotedness, and his piety, no less than the fact that he was a native and diocesan of New York, all combined to suggest him as the fit successor to Archbishop Hughes.[70]

Archbishop McCloskey

Hughes died on January 3, 1864. As the archbishop of New Orleans, Jean-Marie Odin, wrote a few months later, "No sooner had God called to his eternal reward the good and greatly lamented Dr. Hughes, than all eyes were turned towards Albany to find him a successor."[71] This, of course, Bishop McCloskey dreaded. He wrote to his old friend from Rome, Karl-August von Reisach, now Cardinal Reisach and a close advisor to Pope Pius IX, pleading that this cup might pass from him. The letter begins:

Your Eminence will pardon me, I trust, if, presuming on the kindness and condescension shown me in the past, I now venture to have recourse to you in a moment which for me is one of deepest anxiety and fear. Your Eminence, as a member of the

Sacred Congregation de Propaganda Fide, will have learned, most probably before this reaches you, that among the names commended through the Sacred Congregation to the Holy See to fill the vacancy caused by the much lamented death of the illustrious Archbishop of New York, my name unfortunately is placed first on the list. Now I write to implore your Eminence in case there should be any danger of my appointment or of my being transferred from Albany to New York to aid me in preventing it, and to save me from the humiliation and misery of being placed in a position for the duties and responsibilities of which I feel myself, both physically and morally, wholly unfit and unequal.[72]

Can he actually have believed this last part about himself? Perhaps because of his "history" of supposed infirmity one might credit as convincing an argument about physical unfitness. But what were his moral deficits?

He goes on to suggest others who, he says, would be more fit for the job and then to apologize to Reisach, who—powerful though he was (Camerlengo of the Sacred College of Cardinals)—is not, McCloskey acknowledges, among those charged with filling the empty see. His letter should have gone to Cardinal Alessandro Barnabò, the head of Propaganda Fide. But, Bishop McCloskey said, he did not wish to be too forward in assuming that he actually was in the running to be New York's second archbishop.

Now it might be argued that Bishop McCloskey was following some protocol, real or imagined, by which a man about to be elevated to great responsibility turns away the laurel, as Caesar three times refused the crown offered by Marc Antony. But the sentiments he expressed in the letter to Reisach seem all too real. He writes that he is sincere "when I say that I possess neither the learning, nor prudence, nor energy, nor firmness, nor bodily health and strength, which are requisite for such an arduous and highly responsible office".

But, in the end, he undercuts whatever seriousness there is in his plea to be passed over by admitting that, "once the decision is made and the Holy Father speaks, there remains for me nothing but silence. His will is in all things to me a law." And on May 6, 1864 (fifty-four years to the day after McCloskey's baptism by Benedict Fenwick), the pope made it official. On August 27, the reluctant McCloskey was installed as the second archbishop of New York. And for all his alleged lack of "energy", "firmness", or "bodily health and strength", he would ably and vigorously serve the archdiocese for the next two decades.

When McCloskey learned that his fate had been sealed by Pius IX, he left for New York City that very evening, on the night boat from Albany. He was accompanied on the journey by Father John Conroy, vicar-general of the Diocese of Albany. At the Hudson River dock in Manhattan they were met by McCloskey's secretary, Father Francis McNeirny, who had gone down to the city ahead of them. The trio would be the first, second, and third men to serve as Albany's spiritual leader. It was a gathering reminiscent of the day at the Mount in 1826 when Father John Dubois left to be consecrated as bishop of New York, with John Hughes (on his way to his first parish assignment) accompanying him in the carriage, and the young student John McCloskey happily waving as he saw them off.

For Bishop McCloskey himself, the move back to New York at the height of the Civil War was unsettling. Even more disturbing was the appearance the very next morning at his residence at 218 Madison Avenue of a deranged woman who loudly proclaimed—to McCloskey himself—that she was the new archbishop's mother. When McCloskey introduced himself, the woman was undaunted and demanded to be given a bedroom in the house. The police were summoned, and she was led away. Later, at the police station, as McCloskey gave a formal statement about the episode, the guileless desk sergeant commented that the woman might be an impostor, but: "She tells a pretty straight story for a crazy woman."

When the woman was brought up from her cell to face the formal charge against her, she pleaded with McCloskey: "Don't leave me here with these rascals! They tried to ruin me"—clearly an allegation of sexual assault. McCloskey turned to the desk sergeant and with the slightest smile said: "Yes, she tells a *very* straight story indeed."[73]

With characteristic modesty, the new archbishop spoke to a gathering of distinguished New Yorkers that had been organized a few months after his installation:

> How sacred and important is the trust; how manifold and grave the responsibilities which that preferment imposed; no one can know and feel more deeply than myself. It were enough to say that I have been called to succeed that illustrious prelate to whose memory such an affectionate tribute has just now been paid, to be made fully, even painfully, conscious of the magnitude of the task which is set before me; enough to remember that I have become the successor of Archbishop Hughes, the first, and, as future history will doubtless record, the greatest Archbishop of New York; enough to remember this in order to be convinced not only how far short I must fall of the measure of his goodness, but also of the great disproportion there exists between the weight of the burden imposed and the strength of the shoulders by which it must be carried.[74]

The first task the archbishop took on was the completion of the new St. Patrick's Cathedral, whose construction had been begun by Hughes in 1858 but had been brought to a standstill by the Civil War. John McCloskey truly did admire his illustrious predecessor and would have agreed with the assessment by Monsignor Florence Cohalan, writing of the decision to build the great cathedral, that it "received more criticism and ridicule than anything else he started, [but] remains to remind us of the vision, courage, and perseverance that marked his administration".[75] Thus, bringing the cathedral's construction to completion was nearly a sacred duty for Archbishop McCloskey.

The deal made by Hughes with architect James Renwick had called for a white marble church of "suitable magnificence" to be built on a budget of $850,000. A comparison of 1858 dollars to today's inflated currency gives us little comprehension of the boldness of Archbishop Hughes' vision: a straight calculation suggests an amount no less than $225 million in 2015 dollars, but that cannot possibly be right. The 2012–2015 renovation of St. Patrick's undertaken by Cardinal Dolan—no new construction, just repair and cleaning—was projected to cost $180 million. The cost of building New York's Freedom Tower—constructed on the footprint of One World Trade Center, one of the buildings destroyed on September 11, 2001—exceeded $4 billion. In any event, that initial $850,000 was insufficient to bring Hughes' dream to completion, and Archbishop McCloskey found much of his time and energy devoted to fund-raising. He would labor tirelessly for the next fifteen years to complete the project.

While he was attending the Second Plenary Council in Baltimore in 1866, and just before he was about to speak to the archbishops, bishops, and priests assembled (including Baltimore's archbishop, James Gibbons, who would become America's second cardinal), McCloskey was handed a telegram informing him that Old St. Patrick's Cathedral on Mulberry Street had been gutted by fire.[76] He might have left that instant for New York, but he went ahead and gave his planned address. When Archbishop Gibbons discovered the news that the telegram contained, he asked McCloskey how he was able to carry on as if nothing had happened. "The damage was done," he said, "and I could not undo it." (In his eulogy at McCloskey's funeral nineteen years later, Gibbons would add that McCloskey said in summary: "We must calmly submit to the will of Providence.")[77]

The result of the fire was not, however, the demolition of the damaged structure and the transfer of the Old St. Patrick's staff to other New York parishes, but the immediate decision to restore the cathedral's interior, which was accomplished in just two years.

From this point forward, McCloskey became the archdiocese's master builder. It is not the purpose of this chapter to detail the various edifices and institutions for which he was responsible, but Father Smith, always good at summaries, gives the highlights:

> The Catholic population had increased by 1885 to 600,000; they were served by 285 diocesan priests and 119 convent priests; their schools and charities were managed by 300 brothers and 2,000 nuns; the churches numbered 176, the chapels 60, and mass was given at 38 missions which had no churches; eight orphanages sheltered 2,000 children, and thirteen industrial schools trained 5,000 poor children; three homes for the aged supported 700 inmates, six hospitals were in operation, and 43 conferences of St. Vincent de Paul with 1,000 members looked after the scattered destitute. And behind these figures stood a unity of feeling and action that bespoke the perfect health of the whole body; the administration moved without a hitch; and every day the Church itself came into greater prominence through events of various kinds, most of them connected with the quiet, silent Archbishop himself.[78]

Few construction projects can have more long-term benefit for the People of God than the building of seminaries. As we have seen (and as Father Smith alludes to in the passage quoted earlier in this chapter), a Mass may be said in a warehouse and confessions heard in a Catholic home, but none of the seven sacraments may be administered without a priest. Archbishop Hughes had made several attempts (Nyack, Lafargeville, Fordham) to found a seminary, but none had succeeded until, in 1862, he bought a failed Methodist college in Troy, New York, a town that sits along the Hudson River in Rensselaer County, approximately 150 miles north of New York City. This former college became St. Joseph's Seminary and became operational the year Hughes died. The seminary Hughes had established at St. John's (Fordham) was also called St. Joseph's, as would be the great and permanent one that Archbishop Corrigan would open at Dunwoodie in 1896.

As bishop of Albany, McCloskey had served on a board set up by Archbishop Hughes that included brother bishops from Boston and Hartford charged with staffing the new seminary. Part of the reason Hughes had shuttered the seminary at

Fordham was his conclusion that there simply were not enough sound theologians among New York's clergy to educate would-be priests properly, and it struck McCloskey that it would be best to look to Europe, specifically to the great university seminary in Louvain, Belgium. McCloskey wrote to the Bishop of Ghent, Louis-Joseph Delebecque, and the bishop promised to find the right men for the job. As Henry Gabriels (himself one of the first men sent from Belgium to New York) would write four decades later in his history of the seminary:

> Having so large a supply of university-bred theological scholars in his diocese, he fixed his eyes on a number of them, fit by their character, their talents, and their academical [sic] success to be placed in charge of so important a mission.[79]

The first head of the seminary was a Belgian already in New York, the Reverend Louis J. Vandenhende. His appointment was soon followed by the arrival of a number of priests who came directly from Belgium, including the twenty-six-year-old Father Gabriels, who crossed the Atlantic with Father Charles Roelants and Father Peter A. Puissant, coming first to Manhattan to receive the new archbishop's blessing, and then taking the ferry north to Troy. Father Gabriels would become rector (president) of the seminary, serving in that capacity from 1871 to 1891, and eventually bishop of Ogdensburg, New York, on the American-Canadian border.

Still there was no building project more critical to McCloskey, to New York City's faithful, or to Catholics throughout the United States than the completion of St. Patrick's cathedral. This undertaking in the beginning really was an act of faith. Archbishop Hughes had chosen land long owned by the Church (since 1810) in a part of the great, growing city that was not yet "Midtown," as we refer to it today, but an outpost on the city's northern periphery. The Jesuit college built there early in the nineteenth century had been a country school at a time when New York was more village than metropolis. Some called the archbishop's decision "Hughes' Folly", but he knew—as did others with foresight—that the city had only one direction in which to grow, and that was north.

But Hughes had also embarked upon the project without the funds necessary to complete it, and that was a most singular act of faith. God, he was sure, would provide. By the time ground was broken in 1858, war was looming, and so was the possibility that construction would have to cease because of a lack of funds. Hughes told the *New York Times* in 1860 that, whether or not the work was ever completed, he would "never allow the laborer to be defrauded of his wages in carrying out the work".[80] Therefore, when the money ran out, the work stopped. In all, it would take thirty years to complete the job, from the laying of the cornerstone to the raising of the Gothic spires in 1888. (Actually, the process of bringing the cathedral to its present state—and it was under extensive renovation as this book was being written—was not fully completed until construction of the Chapel of Our Lady, more commonly known as the Lady Chapel, in 1906.)

Among the ways Archbishop McCloskey sought to fund the completion of St. Patrick's was through what has become known as the Great Cathedral Fair, which ran for a month, beginning on October 23, 1878, and closing on November 30. According to Archbishop Farley's account, "Forty-five parishes of the Diocese were represented at the fair by parochial tables."[81] In the end, more than $170,000 was raised, as was the cathedral's profile in the minds of New Yorkers. The *Times* called the cathedral "the noblest ecclesiastical building ever erected in this City, or in the United States".[82]

Cardinal McCloskey

By that time, John McCloskey had received the cardinal's red hat. There were a number of reasons why he was the first American to receive that honor.

He had been called to Rome by Pope Pius IX in 1869 to attend the First Vatican Council, the first ecumenical gathering since the sixteenth-century Council of Trent. This new council met in St. Peter's Basilica between December 8, 1869, and October 20, 1870. It is likely that the pope's invitation to Archbishop McCloskey was due in large measure to the advice of Cardinal Reisach, McCloskey's old friend from his student days in Rome.

The headline issue addressed by the council was papal infallibility, and McCloskey's views on the matter were typical of churchmen from around the world. He believed in it unreservedly, but he was deeply concerned about a formal declaration of the doctrine.[83] In the more ultramontane areas of Europe—in nations that were solidly Catholic and had been ever since Christianity took hold in Europe— the doctrine hardly raised an eyebrow, with the possible exception of France, still reeling in postrevolutionary uncertainties. But in America, where nativism still held sway among many otherwise sensible people, a formal declaration might be seized upon as ipso facto evidence of the utterly foreign and antidemocratic nature of Catholicism.

When it came time for a vote, however, McCloskey embraced the doctrine as part of the Magisterium, and his support was not unnoticed by Pio Nono, who would elevate him to the cardinalate in 1875. As we noted earlier in this chapter, those with vision in Rome had realized that the most cultured, well-spoken, godly American they knew, was John McCloskey.

It was time for an American cardinal. President Lincoln himself had urged the pope to choose one, believing that it would help raise awareness in Europe and Latin America of the growing importance of the United States in world affairs. Lincoln's request was ridiculed by some in the Vatican, but not by Pio Nono.[84] And even the naysayers recognized that New York was the logical place to start, if the Holy Father believed it was appropriate to elevate an American to the cardinalate. When official notification came on March 15, 1875 (the news had been leaked earlier and had already appeared in several journals in Europe and America), McCloskey was humbled but this time was not in a state of fear and trembling about his new position. Archbishop of New York or Cardinal Archbishop of New York—it would make little difference in his day-to-day administration of the archdiocese.

When the sixty-five-year-old McCloskey was presented with the cardinal's biretta on April 27 at Old St. Patrick's by his old friend Archbishop James Roosevelt Bayley, the eighth archbishop of Baltimore, his mind must surely have gone back to the days when he and Bayley had become friends. Bayley, the nephew of Elizabeth Ann Seton (Mother Seton to history), had been an Episcopal minister in Harlem, but his conversations and correspondence with McCloskey had convinced him to "cross the Tiber", and he had been ordained a Catholic priest in 1844. Now here they were some thirty years later: the leader of the nation's oldest Catholic diocese presenting the red hat to the nation's first cardinal. (Archbishop Bayley had gone to Baltimore after serving as the first bishop of Newark, New Jersey. He was succeeded in that position by Michael Augustine Corrigan, who would succeed McCloskey in New York.)

It was traditional that at some point a man upon whom the red hat was bestowed would travel to Rome to receive it from the hands of the pope. In McCloskey's case, the opportunity did not arise until Pius IX had been succeeded by Leo XIII.

When Pio Nono died, on February 7, 1878 (he was the longest-reigning elected pope in history), the cardinals of the Church began to make their way to Rome for the conclave that would choose his successor. McCloskey left for Rome at his earliest convenience, but—like his friend Paul Cullen of Dublin—he arrived too late to participate in what turned out to be a very short conclave (just three ballots), which chose Cardinal Vincenzo Gioacchino Raffaele Luigi Pecci as Leo XIII. A month later, the new pope presented cardinalitial honors to McCloskey, at which point the new prince of the Church was able to visit the Roman church of which he was now cardinal-priest, fittingly the ancient Santa Maria sopra Minerva, the Dominican church and convent that had been the haunt of New York's first two bishops, R. Luke Concanen and John Connolly.

It happened that while McCloskey was in Rome, former President Ulysses Grant was also there, and Cardinal McCloskey had the pleasure of introducing the president to the pope. John Russell Young, Grant's secretary, wrote:

> As the representative prelate of the Catholics in the United States, His Reverence, Cardinal McCloskey, immediately called on General Grant, and under the auspices of the Cardinal and [the] rector of the American College of the United States in Rome, the ex-President was received by His Holiness Leo XIII. The interview was of a most agreeable character, and left a very pleasant impression on the General. Of course this reception, highly flattering as it was to the distinguished head of our party, was not to be considered as partaking of a religious character. It was simply a visit of respectful courtesy of Americans to the highest dignitary of the Catholic Church. The manners and habits of Leo XIII are of the simplest character, free from all pomp and parade, and those who had the honor to be present at the interview were struck by the quiet ease, dignity and impressiveness of His Holiness.[85]

This is especially interesting inasmuch as the pope was a member of the Italian aristocracy.

Leo would reign until 1903. The combined papacies of Pio Nono and Leo covered fifty-seven years, during which time America had fifteen presidents.

The Final Years

At this point in the story of John McCloskey, little remains to be told. In the Farley biography, there are just forty pages (out of 388) to go, covering the final seven years of the cardinal's life. Farley and others acknowledge that McCloskey's years as a cardinal were marked by a retreat from public activities, in large measure because of health problems that were, after 1880, all too real.

Michael Corrigan was brought over from Newark to serve as coadjutor arch-bishop of New York on October 1, 1880, which gave the forty-one-year-old Cor-rigan an opportunity to ease himself into the job that he would inherit and that, unlike McCloskey, he very much wanted.

Cardinal McCloskey was able to preside at the opening of the new cathedral in May of 1879, and his "last great burst of joy" came on January 12, 1884, when his golden jubilee (the fiftieth anniversary of his ordination) was celebrated throughout the archdiocese. To mark the occasion, Leo XIII sent a bejeweled chalice.[86]

The cause of Cardinal McCloskey's death is uncertain. Farley writes that it "may surprise many to learn that it was only during the last ten years of his life that Car-dinal McCloskey felt the need of a physician's care". Several sources suggest that, perhaps on his way to the conclave of 1878 or in Rome at that time, the cardinal had contracted malaria—or that he had suffered with the disease for some number of years, and his death was caused by a relapse. *Wikipedia*'s entry on McCloskey says so and cites the Farley biography as its source, but that book makes no mention of malaria. McCloskey's own doctor attributed the persistent fever the cardinal suf-fered throughout 1885 to a cold caught in Rome. After leaving Rome, McCloskey had traveled to Dublin, an altogether better place to catch cold, but from whatever cause, John McCloskey died on October 25, 1885.

A fair summary of his career was offered by the eulogist at his funeral, Arch-bishop James Gibbons of Baltimore, who in a year would become America's second cardinal:

> I shall not attempt to enumerate the Institutions of religion, charity, and learning which have sprung up in this populous diocese during the Cardinal's administration of one-and-twenty years. We may form some estimate of the development of Catho-licity when we consider that the number of churches has increased during that period from seventy to one hundred and seventy, and the number of the clergy from one hundred and fifty to four hundred....
>
> He has left you two precious legacies of his love, and first, the legacy of a pure and unsullied life, as Priest, Bishop, Archbishop, and Cardinal. He never tarnished the surplice of the Priest nor the rochet of the Bishop, nor the pallium of the Archbishop nor the scarlet robes of the Cardinal. After spending upwards of half a century in the exercise of the ministry, he goes down to his honored grave without a stain upon his moral character. He leaves you another precious legacy in the person of his gifted successor. When Moses died, says the sacred Scripture, the people mourned for him thirty days. And Josue, his successor, was filled with the spirit of wisdom, because Moses had laid his hands upon him; and the children of Israel obeyed Josue as Moses had commanded them. The dying Cardinal laid his hands in benediction on his suc-cessor, and that benediction of the expiring Patriarch will be as fruitful to the son of his adoption.[87]

It would remain to be seen if Michael Augustine Corrigan would fulfill Cardinal McCloskey's legacy.

A final fact about the episcopal career of John McCloskey: In 1873, on the occa-sion of the feast of the Immaculate Conception, he consecrated the archdiocese to the Most Sacred Heart of Jesus. That so austere, reserved, and rational a man as John McCloskey would embrace such a popular a devotion illuminates the depth of faith that sustained him throughout his life. Without devotion to Christ and His compassion, McCloskey believed, mankind had little to hope for. As he had explained it in a pastoral message on November 15, 1873:

> There is a moral darkness overspreading the earth. The light of Divine Faith, the only true light to guide our footsteps, has become obscured. In some places it is burning dimly, in others it is wholly or well-nigh extinguished. Yet, men are seen to "love the darkness rather than the light, for their ways are evil." They have risen in open revolt against God and against His Christ; against the supremacy of His dominion over the minds and consciences of individuals and of nations. The most essential truths of His revelation are rejected; the holiest mysteries of His religion are scoffed at and denied; the very life of Christianity is threatened. Irreligion, indifferentism, unbelief, with their attendant train of evils, abound on every side....
>
> It is fitting also that you should join in this act as a public profession of your faith especially in all the great mysteries of redemption, which have their most expressive symbol, as well as their living source and centre, in the adorable Heart of the God-man, the "Word made flesh, and dwelling among us."
>
> You will offer it, besides, as an act of reparation for the daily outrages and insults, the sacrileges and impieties, the indifference and unbelief, which so grievously afflict and wound this divine Heart, so tender and compassionate, so patient, charitable, forgiving, notwithstanding the ingratitude and wickedness of men.
>
> But above all, you will seek to consecrate your own hearts to the Heart of your dear Saviour.

The past as prologue.

4

The Roman

DOMINUS PETRA MEA

Michael Augustine Corrigan
Third Archbishop of New York
(1873–1902)

Photographer and date unknown

Archbishop Corrigan as a boy

Michael Corrigan was born in Newark, New Jersey, in a house at 174 Market Street near the corner of Broad on August 13, 1839. His mother was Mary English Corrigan of County Cavan in Ulster. His father, Thomas, was a native of County Meath (in Leinster Province) and had trained in Ireland to be a cabinetmaker—an indentured one, according to one historian.[1] His parents had emigrated from Ireland a year apart and met in Newark, where they were married on July 31, 1831. Michael was the fifth child (baptized at home on September 15, 1839)—and the fourth boy—in a family that would eventually boast nine children: eight boys and one girl, Catherine, who was the firstborn.[2]

Michael received his first Communion at the Cathedral of St. Patrick in Newark on September 14, 1851.

His education began at home, where his mother did her best to instruct him and his siblings in rudimentary learning. In 1846 Michael began studies at the Plane Street school of Bernard Kearney, who happened to be his godfather. There were no parochial schools in Newark until at least 1850. At the age of fourteen, Michael was sent to St. Mary's College in Wilmington, Delaware.

St. Mary's had been founded in 1841 by one Patrick Reilly, and the school had a quarter-century lifespan, closing in 1866. While Corrigan was there, he had the honor of receiving confirmation from Bishop John Neumann of Philadelphia. Neumann was an immigrant from what is now the Czech Republic. He had come to New York in the spring of 1836 and presented his credentials (a record of his priestly studies in Bohemia) to Bishop John Dubois, who ordained him pretty much on the spot. Neumann had joined the Redemptorist Order in Baltimore in 1840 and was a pastor of a small church in Elkridge, Maryland, from 1849 to 1851. In 1852, Pius IX tapped him for the episcopacy in Philadelphia, where he served until his death in 1860. He was canonized by Paul VI in 1977. The only American man ever to be named a saint, Neumann was known for his concern for the poor and his saintly simplicity, manifest in the possibly apocryphal claim that in his twenty-four years in America he owned just one pair of boots. All this was years in the future as the bishop laid his hands upon the future Archbishop of New York, so the moment may not have seemed auspicious to either Corrigan or Neumann.

In the fall of 1855, Michael Corrigan enrolled in Mount St. Mary's, as had John Hughes and John McCloskey. He was admitted in no small part because of a letter of recommendation from Newark's first bishop, James Roosevelt Bayley, which read in part:

> He is a good boy and I believe very attentive to his books; I therefore recommend him to you with a great deal of confidence. If he should turn out a good priest one of these days so much the better.[3]

Young Corrigan would not disappoint his bishop.

Unlike Hughes and McCloskey, however, he did not receive his seminary training at the Mount, initially spending just two years there. In 1857, the eighteen-year-old left Emmitsburg to accompany his twenty-five-year-old sister, Catherine, on a grand tour of Italy. Their father, Thomas, was now a prosperous owner of a wholesale and retail grocery business and a liquor store (and possibly a tavern),[4] and he could afford to send his children on the sort of journey that would broaden their view of the world and, it was hoped, have a positive effect on Catherine's poor health.

The two left New York on the *North Star* and sailed to Southampton and from there by various transports to Paris and four other French cities; then through Italy (although not to Rome), ending the first leg of their travels in Palermo, Sicily, on the Tyrrhenian Sea. Following two months' respite there, they went north and, finally, to Rome. On June 29, 1858, Michael boarded the *Fulton* in Paris and sailed back to New York. Catherine stayed on in the French capital.[5] John A. Mooney, a contemporary who would help produce a published tribute to Archbishop Corrigan shortly after his death, described the young man Michael had become:

> With genial good humor he was full to overflowing—joyous. Though bashful, he was fond of companionship, and made agreeable acquaintances in all places. His faith was firm, soulful, lively; and his piety, like that of his sister, ardent. To brother and sister, the real world, the most beautiful world was that one made up of the tombs of Christian martyrs, confessors, virgins; of altars grand or mean—altars of perpetual sacrifice; of grottoes, fountains, valleys, hilltops, reminiscent of the glories, the sorrows, the joys, the mercies of Immaculate Mary.[6]

Whether such a description may have come to Mr. Mooney from the archbishop himself we do not know.

What shaped Michael Corrigan's vocation to the priesthood is also uncertain. His discernment may have begun during his education under the Catholic teachers Bernard Kearney and Patrick Reilly, or it may have peaked during his European sojourn with his sister, although it seems most likely that it was his time at the Mount—to which he returned in 1859 to complete his undergraduate studies—that motivated him to seek holy orders.

> Whatever had been his natural inclination, it was only now that, assured of a vocation, he told his parents of his intention to aspire to the priesthood. Bishop Bayley, to whom he and his family were well and most favorably known, forwarded the youth's plans; and provision was made for his entrance into the [North] American College, which the hierarchy of the United States, in union with Pius IX, purposed opening at Rome in the fall of the same year.[7]

The North American College (or simply the NAC, pronounced *knack*) had been established in part to be a kind of incubator of bishops—a place where talented Americans might be not only educated but also closely observed by officials of the Roman Curia, who at that time were not entirely happy with the results of episcopal recommendations made by the emerging American hierarchy. The College itself was housed in buildings at the Dominican Priory of Santa Maria sopra Minerva, which (as detailed in this book's first chapter) had formerly been the residence of the first two men appointed to head the see of New York, R. Luke Concanen and John Connolly.

The college had been the brainchild of Gaetano Bedini, whose controversial visitation to the United States had sparked protests and violence among nativists. Among the reasons Bedini thought the College essential to the Church's future in America was the necessity of controlling "the development of an unhealthy nationalism among the native clergy who would soon predominate".[8] About that he was correct.

At the College, Michael Corrigan "manifested a more than usual piety, a notably scholarly disposition, the ability to master languages, and some capacity for leadership".[9] Of course, he had never been anything other than a superb student.

But his time at the NAC was notable for a quite remarkable irony—in the sense of events in which outcomes are all but the opposite of the expected. Although the first rector of the College was the future bishop of Louisville, William McCloskey (again, no relation to Cardinal John McCloskey), the first functional head of the school was Father Bernard Smith (an Englishman, who was a good friend and confidant of Archbishop John Hughes). But Smith apparently spent neither time nor effort in running the school. He was a figurehead until William McCloskey arrived in March of 1860, and Smith saw himself as merely a placeholder. The true operational head of school was a fourth-year seminarian from Rome's Urban College (or Propaganda), the American Edward McGlynn. As we shall see, the arc of the lives of McGlynn and Michael Corrigan would collide: the former a leading light of liberal Americanism (in part, that nationalism that Bedini had feared), the latter its staunchest opponent—not enemies exactly but definitely combatants. In the matter of this later conflict, many (perhaps *most*) historians have taken McGlynn's side. As one has rapturously written, in the era of "Rum, Romanism, and Rebellion," McGlynn "could dream of modernizing the American Catholic Church, leading it to shake off medieval trappings and old-world control, and leading the U.S. to genuine unity".[10] That seems contrary to the historical facts and to overestimate both McGlynn's intentions and his abilities. It also underestimates Corrigan's fidelity to the Church and the virtue of such fidelity.

In a letter home to the Corrigans in New Jersey, Michael wrote of the visit to the new college by (now Blessed) Pius IX on January 29, 1860:

> You should have heard the three times three hurrahs we gave His Holiness when he praised our own [George] Washington. The guards came running to the spot, thinking a revolution had broken out.[11]

Winston Churchill quipped that "history is written by the victors", and many twentieth- and twenty-first-century historians read history from their own "progressive" perspective—whether their progressive liberalism is political, economic, or theological. And as one has written about Corrigan:

> Although [he] was a man who earnestly sought sanctity by prayer and asceticism throughout his life ... he seemed unable to translate private piety into public probity. He was almost pathologically prone to fear of ubiquitous conspiracies. In reacting to these perceived plots he equivocated, he dissembled, he utilized spies against those he thought were undermining the Church; he condoned dubious loyalty oaths and then made them the criterion for promotion; he did many things that were unworthy of an archbishop.[12]

Of course, as the saying goes, you are not paranoid if the conspiracies are real.

Father Corrigan

Not unlike the case of John McCloskey, Michael Corrigan's health presented difficulties, at least in his youth, and usually concerned his vision. In photographs of him
as a young priest, although rarely in later episcopal portraits, he wears spectacles,
and as a seminarian in Rome he was known for wearing green-tinted sunglasses, the
better to combat the "Roman heat and glare".[13]

Corrigan's scholarly life was all but unrelenting: when he was not studying specifically academic requirements of the College, he was traveling throughout Italy,
visiting pagan and Christian sites, learning the history of those places, and even
studying the engineering methods by which they had been constructed. His progress
through the seminary curriculum was quick, as was his path to ordination. Although
his studies had begun in 1859, he was ordained a deacon on March 21, 1863, and
then elevated to the priesthood on September 19 of that same year. He was ordained
a deacon, fittingly, on the feast of St. Rose of Lima, the first saint of the New World,
and on the day after his ordination to the priesthood at the Church of St. John Lateran in Rome by Cardinal Costantino Patrizi Naro, Father Corrigan celebrated his
first Mass at a church used by the NAC, its altar dedicated to Our Lady of Guadalupe,
patroness of the Americas. It was just the end of his fourth year as a seminarian.[14]

In June of 1864, Corrigan received his doctorate of divinity, albeit with a heavy
heart. His beloved sister, Catherine, had died shortly before Michael received his
advanced degree. She had traveled again to Italy to recover her health, but she was
beyond the help of physicians and sunshine. Because she was afflicted with a constant cough, we assume she was a victim of tuberculosis, known in the nineteenth
century as *consumption*. After time in the Eternal City, at which point she was also
revisiting a desire to enter the religious life—a desire she had nurtured for many
years but had, mostly for the sake of her mother, put aside to help Mary Corrigan
at home—Catherine began to sense that death was upon her. She decided to return
home, so she traveled back to France.

She had come to Italy in the company of another brother, James, who would
also enroll at the NAC, so now she said farewell to him and her favorite brother,
Michael, and in the company of a French nun (also a trained nurse) headed, we
presume, toward the northern port city of Le Havre. She got no farther than Meaux
(in the Ile-de-France region), the site of a great cathedral and the home convent of
Catherine's traveling companion, who was a sister of the Hospitallers of St. Augustine. Catherine was given a bed at the convent, and she asked to be allowed to make
her profession as an Augustinian sister. This was an extraordinary if not unprecedented request, so the bishop of Meaux was consulted, and he not only agreed but
came in person to give the happy news to Catherine. As John A. Mooney wrote:
"Her rare virtues were known to him."

And so Catherine became Sister Amélie. Shortly thereafter she received Viati-
cum, and several hours later she died. It was Candlemas 1864, the feast of the Purification of the Blessed Virgin. Many years later, in July of 1900, returning from his
last *ad limina* visit to Rome, Archbishop Corrigan would visit his sister's grave in
the convent cemetery.

In September of 1864, his Roman education completed, Father Corrigan returned
to Newark to begin his extraordinary career. Bishop Bayley, obviously recognizing

Corrigan's academic stature, appointed him to a professorship of dogmatic theology and Sacred Scripture at Immaculate Conception Seminary at Seton Hall College, founded by Bayley in 1858 and named by him after his aunt, Mother Elizabeth Ann Seton. The appointment was a life-changing moment for Michael Corrigan.

In a year, he would become vice president of the college, and four years later, president, but it was his meeting and friendship with the man he had succeeded, Father Bernard McQuaid, that would profoundly affect Corrigan's future.

Corrigan and McQuaid

Bernard John McQuaid has been described as the "Grand Old Man of American Catholicism", although more often in far less complimentary terms. When he left Seton Hall, it was to become the first bishop of Rochester, New York. He had been a Union chaplain in the Civil War and briefly a prisoner of the Confederacy. With Bishop Bayley he had helped found Seton Hall, and Bayley had made him vicar-general of the diocese in 1866. When Michael Corrigan arrived at the Hall, McQuaid took him under his wing, and it was from McQuaid that Corrigan got an education in the Americanism controversy that would explode onto the world stage a generation later. Although McQuaid was sixteen years older than Corrigan, he would outlive his protégé by six years. When McQuaid died on January 18, 1909, the bells of Rochester's St. Patrick's Cathedral pealed eighty-six times in commemoration of the years of the bishop's life.[15]

McQuaid was fiercely proud to be an American and, as the son of Irish immigrants, believed in the promise of a poor man's ability to rise to prominence from the humblest of circumstances, as his certainly were. His mother died at a young age, and his father was killed in a bar fight, so young Bernard grew up in the Catholic orphan asylum in New York City founded by Bishop John Hughes. McQuaid attributed his later success to the care of the Sisters of Charity, who ran the asylum.[16] He began the process of priestly formation at the minor seminary in Chambly, Quebec, and completed his training at St. John's Seminary in New York (also, of course, founded by Bishop Hughes). Archbishop Hughes ordained him at Old St. Patrick's in 1848. Hughes would ever after be his hero, and McQuaid did his best to be a second "Dagger John".

> The McQuaid-Corrigan relationship developed at Seton Hall and so highly did McQuaid esteem the mind and administrative talents of the young Corrigan, that rightly or wrongly, McQuaid later would claim credit for Corrigan's advancement.... After 1880 [when Corrigan became coadjutor to Archbishop McCloskey], Corrigan was technically McQuaid's superior, but to the very end it remained the relationship of a former teacher and his pupil with McQuaid playing the role of friend, advisor and trusted confidant, who always encouraged Corrigan to act clearly, boldly and decisively.[17]

For better or worse, we might add.

In 1868 James Corrigan, now ordained, returned from the NAC and replaced his brother as head of Immaculate Conception Seminary, which helped Michael balance his duties as president of Seton Hall with his responsibilities as vicar-general of the Newark Diocese.

Bishop Corrigan

James Roosevelt Bayley, a Catholic convert like his famous aunt, was clearly destined to take on greater episcopal tasks, and after ten years in Newark he was named to the See of Baltimore on July 30, 1872. He was reluctant to leave Newark but was confident in the man who would replace him: the thirty-three-year-old Michael Corrigan. He was the 131st man and the youngest elevated to the episcopacy in the United States.

Corrigan would spend eight years in Newark, and nearly all of it was "under the shadow of the great depression" that followed the Panic of 1873.[18] Known at the time as the Great Depression, it was a nearly worldwide phenomenon. The causes were many, including the failure of banking houses in the wake of wars (the Civil War in America, the Franco-Prussian War in Europe), and the effects were seen in unemployment and strikes and, most significantly for an American Catholic bishop, in a sudden decrease in the pace of immigration to the United States. Nonetheless, the population of Newark expanded over the course of the decade from just over 900,000 to just over 1.1 million. Newark was at least as ethnically diverse as New York City.[19]

Throughout his years in Newark, Bishop Corrigan kept a journal of his activities. It shows that he was a peripatetic leader, visiting every Catholic community in the state and doing his best to standardize the practice of the faith.

> The journal therefore focuses upon the administration of the sacraments, church and parish building, parochial education, the proper conduct of the liturgy, and the provision of adequate clergy. Despite the hard times, it reflects a tale of rapid growth.[20]

It also reflects the bishop's successful administration during this troubled period.

When Corrigan took over in the summer of 1872, there were "116 priests, 67 churches, and 48 missions" in the diocese. When he left in 1880 to become coadjutor to John Cardinal McCloskey in New York, Newark had "184 priests, 142 churches, and 40 missions".[21] It is natural that, as the number of parishes increased, the number of missions would decline.

As noted elsewhere in this book, it took some time throughout most of the nineteenth century for communications to be exchanged between Rome and the United States. Bishop-Designate Corrigan notes in his journal that it wasn't until March 15, 1873, nearly eight months after Bayley's move to Baltimore, that official confirmation (in the form of a bull) of his appointment to Newark was received by Archbishop McCloskey, who promptly notified Corrigan by telegram. As seems always to have been the case with those elevated to the episcopacy, Corrigan was reluctant to accept. He ferried across the Hudson to McCloskey to protest, but, as he writes: "In an interview with His Grace, I stated my difficulties and objections to assuming the Episcopal burden, which, however, he overruled."[22] One can imagine the ever-reluctant John McCloskey smiling patiently, understanding perfectly, and explaining clearly to the young man that, in obedience, there simply was no escape from the call.

On the third Sunday after Easter (May 4, 1873), Michael Augustine Corrigan was consecrated as the spiritual leader of his home diocese by Archbishop Mc-Closkey, assisted by Bishop John Loughlin of Brooklyn and William McCloskey of Louisville. Archbishop Bayley returned for the service, as did Bishop McQuaid. A week later, the new bishop had the pleasure of performing confirmations at St. John's, the church of his boyhood, and on it went for the better part of the next decade. His journal records visits during the first year of his episcopacy from Seton Hall (where he continued to live[23]) to Raritan, Morristown, and Newton; to Franklin Furnace to see the miners and to Jersey City to bless relics of St. Eusebius. He went to Paterson, Bergen City, Elizabeth, and scores of other cities, towns, and villages, where he baptized, confirmed, gave the Eucharist to, listened to the confessions of, married, ordained, and buried the Catholics of New Jersey.

Corrigan's leadership was marked by an indefatigable quest for order and a zealous exercise of personal power and authority. It would serve him and the Newark diocese well; less so in New York after his move there. The impression given is of a classic micromanager. As one account of his tenure in Newark puts it:

> Because of the Bishop's patiently acquired habit of method, it would cost only the time used in copying to detail here every public act of his industrious life in Newark: pastorals, ordinations, the laying of corner-stones, receptions of religious, dedication of churches, confirmations, retreats, marriages, meetings of diocesan committees, letters open or quasi-private, speeches in Latin or English, instructions and sermons. Of all the priests of the diocese, secular and regular, he personally compiled a list, with the dates of appointment, change of place, absence or death. The progress of the ecclesiastical students he recorded with equal care: where and what they were studying, their rank in class, and their date of ordination. Warned by his early experience, he had taken simple measures to control the finances of every parish in the diocese. Through the annual reports he first exacted from the pastors, at a glance he could tell the income and the debt of each church subject to him. Receiving all reports and comparing, he exercised a proper control over the finances of the diocese as a whole, and over each part. The annual baptisms and marriages, church by church, he also made a note of, doing all this work with his own hand. At any minute he could take a view, general or particular, of his charge. Theologian, legist, rubricist, he was also an archivist. So well was this recognized, that Archbishop Bayley, entering the see of Baltimore, sent for Dr. Corrigan to put in order and to systematize the records of that comparatively ancient see.[24]

How long he spent in Baltimore whipping things into shape is unstated.

On April 7, 1880, Corrigan noted in his journal a meeting of bishops of the archdiocese at Cardinal McCloskey's residence, where they proposed a *terna*, a list of three candidates to become the ailing McCloskey's coadjutor. Corrigan himself appears to have prepared and sent the final document, in Latin, to the cardinal. Clearly, his name was on the list.

Still, there follows in his journal for the summer of 1880 the usual detailing of visitations to churches, discussions with pastors about finances, and the rest of the business of being a bishop, and there is no hint of a move to New York until an entry on September 28, the import of which is that

> a cablegram from Rome brought the sorrowful news that the Holy Father [Leo XIII] had appointed the Bp. of Newark Coadjutor to the Archbishop of New York. *Ehu! Anni mei in gemitibus!* [Alas! My years are wasted away in sighs!][25]

The quote is from Psalm 30:11 (Vulgate).

The journal then picks up again the catalog of visits and duties, until the very last entry.

On the afternoon of Sunday November 7, 1880, the bishop laid the cornerstone for St. Rose's Home for the Aged in Newark. It was a cold, windy day, and Corrigan notes that few people attended the ceremony and that "it was as much as one could do to keep Mitre on one's head." And then, in a sentence clearly added in New York, he notes: "On the Tuesday following, I left for New York." But what makes the last entry so poignant is another Latin quote (this one from Philippians 1:6): "*Qui coepit in vobis opus bonum, Ipse perficiet usque in diem Christi Jesu.*" (He who began a good work in you will bring it to completion at the day of Jesus Christ.) This is the same quotation Father Corrigan had cited in his journal upon receiving news of his appointment as the second Bishop of Newark.[26]

The Roman in New York

The forty-one-year-old coadjutor archbishop of New York came into America's premier Catholic see with much experience but few solid connections among New York's clergy. Cardinal McCloskey had two vicars-general, the Monsignors William Quinn and Thomas Preston, both well established and used to handling administration on their own, the cardinal having ceded an increasing number of responsibilities to them over time. Both men were older than the new coadjutor archbishop by at least fifteen years. Monsignor Preston was also the archdiocesan chancellor—essentially the cardinal's lawyer. So, Archbishop Corrigan watched and waited, learning, weighing, and evaluating the structure and personnel of the assignment that became his full responsibility only on October 10, 1885. Before he died, however, Cardinal McCloskey did ensure that Corrigan got a particular education about the peculiarities of New York. These included:

> the consecration or dedication of churches, ordaining of priests, administration of other sacraments, laying of corner-stones, pontificating on solemn feasts. Lesser duties were also committed to him: attending college and convent commencements, preaching at church celebrations, speaking at public or private functions. Important duties, too, he fulfilled, such as the carrying on of official correspondence demanding more than ordinary privacy or care.[27]

Writing in the second volume of his history of the Church in New York, Reverend John Talbot Smith could not resist foreshadowing the Corrigan tenure:

> A change in administration was needed, as Tennyson expresses it: "Lest one good custom should corrupt the world." It was felt among the well-informed that Archbishop Corrigan would provide the change without the usual ill-effects involved in a peaceful revolution. He had been trained in Rome, which was a distinction thirty years ago, and is always an advantage to an ecclesiastic; and, as a native, he understood his own country and people, and had influential connections everywhere. Had the contemporary prophet declared in the year 1885 that his reign would witness greater troubles than in all the preceding years, that dangerous dissensions, from which the past had been entirely free, would arise to aid schism, and that no part of his career would henceforth be free from strife, such a prophet would have been laughed at; and yet the prediction would have been literally true.[28]

Among the important tasks initially undertaken by Archbishop Corrigan was his assignment by Cardinal McCloskey to attend a meeting in Rome called by Pope Leo XIII in 1883 to discuss the agenda for an upcoming plenary council in Baltimore.[29] At that Third Plenary Council, held from November 9 to December 7, 1884, Corrigan represented not only his ailing cardinal but, for the first time in a very public forum, the interests of the so-called conservative side in the "great crisis" of domestic Catholicism: *Americanism* (known throughout the world more broadly as Modernism, except in France, where it was known, rather paradoxically, as Americanism).

As stated earlier, this issue would dominate Archbishop Corrigan's tenure. As loyal as he was to Rome, his response to Americanism probably ruined his chances of succeeding McCloskey to the cardinalate.

But at that plenary council, he became known as a man thoroughly familiar with "doctrine, morals, canon law, rubrics, on forms of procedure, and on methods of administration, being expert in all, expert without pretension".[30]

In the lee of the storm that would break, Corrigan took from the council ideas concerning issues that seemed to him utterly uncontroversial but that would later mark him in the minds of some as a leader of the "reactionaries" and "ultramontanists": support of parochial schools; support of ethnic parishes; support of Roman primacy.

Catholic Education

In the chapter on Archbishop Hughes, we saw how Dagger John campaigned to guarantee funding for Catholic schools by the state of New York. He failed. But he, Cardinal McCloskey, and Archbishop Corrigan believed that educating Catholic children in a religious environment—taught by nuns, priests, and properly catechized laymen, with curricula to include religious studies—was an essential responsibility of the Church. How else to ensure that these American children would become responsible citizens as well as saints destined for heaven?

Yet at that Third Plenary Council there was strong disagreement about just those premises, including the question of whether Catholic schoolchildren should even attend Catholic schools. Because of Hughes' failed attempt to arrange state funding of Catholic schools (thanks to the tepid support of Governor William Seward and New York's legislators), the archdiocese had for several decades been building parochial schools. Yet in Poughkeepsie, New York, in 1873, Father Patrick F. McSweeny had entered into an arrangement with that city's school board to lease two Catholic school buildings in his diocese to the secular board for $1 per year, as long as the Sisters of Charity would be among the teachers and no religion would be taught during class time. (Prayers were said before school hours actually began, and the Catechism was studied after hours.) Despite complaints from some Catholic leaders in New York, the so-called Poughkeepsie Plan was in force for more than two decades. In Minnesota, Bishop John Ireland would adapt the concept in what became known there as the Faribault-Stillwater Plan, so named for two towns in which the Poughkeepsie model was put in place. To Father McSweeny and Bishop Ireland, these arrangements were the essence of common sense. They allowed financially strapped Catholic schools to survive, even as they lessened the financial burden on secular boards of education. To many other Catholics, however, the idea was anathema. Nuns teaching secular curricula did not make the educational environment sufficiently less secular.

At the plenary council, Ireland gave an address titled "The Catholic Church in Civil Society" (or, in some sources, "The Church—the Support of Just Government", possibly because the former title seemed more appropriate when published along with other speeches in a later [1905] book, *The Church in Modern Society*). Much of his address employed generalizations and boosterism about the compatibility of Catholicism and Americanism—Americanism here in the sense of loyalty to the foundations of republican democracy in the United States. Yet there were hints of the nascent Americanist heresy too.

Whereas Bishop Ireland did maintain that the "repudiation of the divine origin of society and of government leaves no choice for the State between anarchy and despotism", he also insisted that the "State is sovereign in the administration of temporal affairs, and in the practical methods of government: in these the Church has no voice."[31] This was not the position of Pope Leo XIII (or his predecessors), and some at the council and many in the press "found it difficult to reconcile Ireland's claim for Catholicism as a defender of liberty with Pius IX's Syllabus of Errors".[32] As we shall see, Pope Leo would address this, and some other ideas raised at the council, in an 1899 apostolic letter (often misidentified as an encyclical) directed to Baltimore's Cardinal James Gibbons, *Testem Benevolentiae Nostrae* (*Testimony of Our Benevolence*—and carrying the English subtitle, *Concerning New Opinions, Virtue, Nature and Grace, with Regard to Americanism.*)

The council approved a statement encouraging the development of Catholic schools in American dioceses, but not a few bishops were less than enthusiastic about it, and some failed to implement it.

At this same time, Archbishop Corrigan also carried out the exchange of letters between the Church in America, the American government, the papacy, and the Italian government over the preservation of the North American College in Rome. As one of the College's first graduates, this was of special importance to Corrigan. The background was this: A new anti-clerical Italian government chose to enforce statutes long on the books related to the seizure of property (for revenue and other purposes), and these actions led periodically to conflicts with the Church, especially with regard to any Vatican property subject to foreign ownership or influence. This connection to foreign "missions" explains why the Church was represented in Italian courts by Propaganda Fide. On January 29, 1884, a case was decided by the highest Italian judicial body (the Court of Cassation) that gave the city of Rome the right to confiscate the NAC (along with other Propaganda properties), and in March the government announced its intention to do just that. Corrigan wrote to Secretary of State Frederick Frelinghuysen, a New Jerseyan, who "was no stranger to Corrigan".[33] President Chester A. Arthur was asked to intervene (Corrigan met with the president to discuss the issue), which Arthur did with King Victor Emmanuel III, mostly through the good offices of the American minister in Rome, William Waldorf "Willy" Astor.[34] We recall that Cardinal McCloskey's family had an early professional connection to the Astor family through a former associate of John Jacob Astor, Cornelius Heeney, who had become the future cardinal's guardian after the death of McCloskey's father.

With the further intervention of Pope Leo XIII, the Italian government agreed to exempt the NAC from its land grab, and the pope quickly acted to place the NAC wholly outside the scope of secular government actions by naming it a pontifical college on October 25, 1884.

That particular crisis passed by quickly and successfully, but the conflict over Catholic education in America would linger. And it was not just a matter of whether Catholic children should attend public or parochial schools. At the Third Plenary Council it had been decided that a new national Catholic university be founded. At first, Archbishop Corrigan was not opposed, especially if that designation were to be given to his beloved Seton Hall. It was not. Instead, the sentiment grew that this new institution should be built from scratch, and this idea troubled Corrigan, more so when Washington, D.C., was chosen as the site for the Catholic University of America. Georgetown College was already there, as was America's political class, whose proximity could hardly help the new school avoid further near occasions of Modernism.

It has been suggested that, during the process of decision-making about the proposed Catholic university, Corrigan engaged in duplicity, although the historians who say so admit to expressing assumptions, largely because there is no direct evidence to support the case for deceit. In his book about Corrigan's role as leader of conservative Catholicism, former Jesuit priest Robert Emmett Curran writes of Corrigan's growing opposition to Catholic University, its proposed location in the nation's capital, and his decision to resign from the university board. "It is difficult not to conclude that Corrigan was being less than honest with [Cardinal James] Gibbons and the board members."[35] This was because Corrigan had accepted a place on the board, despite his disappointment with the bishops' rejection of Seton Hall (a sensible option for matters of operational efficiency and monetary savings) and his later decision to sign on to the petition that went to Rome seeking the Vatican's final approval of Washington, D.C.

Why then would Corrigan have pulled back not only his own participation in guiding the new university but also his archdiocese's financial support? Curran was not convinced by Corrigan's suggestion that he, who had never thought that a national university was necessary, was truthful in telling Gibbons he needed money from his own parishioners and major donors to support the construction of a great archdiocesan seminary in New York—that would become St. Joseph's at Dunwoodie. Yet it seems clear that this was indeed one reason why Corrigan declined, but there is another.

It is odd that in a book that is to some extent a defense of the Americanist position Professor Curran (of Georgetown University) would ignore the fact that Corrigan was becoming increasingly uneasy with trends in the American church (as was Pope Leo). It is one thing to disagree with Archbishop Corrigan's (or the pope's) stance concerning Americanism, but quite another *not* to see it as a reasonable influence on many of the actions Corrigan took in the last decade of his life. Actions follow from premises. And it hardly seems fair to demean Corrigan because he deported himself dispassionately by not revealing to his friends, among whom Gibbons must be counted, his doubts about the direction they were heading. His thinking evolved, but he did not engage in adversarial confrontations about it with other members of the hierarchy, because it was not in his nature to do so.

The debate about Americanism will be dealt with shortly, but it is important to note here that at the Third Plenary Council, the word was not used, although its elements were becoming clear, at least as we look back on them. With time, however, opposition would build and controversy would not increase, and so it was in the 1880s, as specific and legitimate needs of American Catholics would diverge to a greater or lesser extent from the direction defined by the traditions of Rome.

Still, there is here an expression of Corrigan's detachment from the tumult in New York, America, and Rome. A priest-historian who was the archbishop's contemporary summed up the problem:

> His courtesy and gentleness smoothed the exercise of authority, and complainers and petitioners found him ready to listen to their longest protests. He believed in the prompt and vigorous use of his episcopal power, and he expected as prompt obedience. Not until sharp experience had taught him, was he able to appreciate the modifications that circumstances introduce into ancient traditions. He fell foul of the most thorny questions, and never could understand why they did not yield to his simple fiat. He knew little of the times in which he lived, of the temper of the people, of the currents of thought and feeling dominating the American world. Nor did he care to know. He kept away from the public eye, content with just his diocese, his regular and busy life, and the intimacy of a few friends. He had little taste for the delicate and useful methods employed by Cardinal Gibbons in dealing with the interested public; for Archbishop Ireland's open and candid assault on an enemy, or vigorous instruction to inquirers, he had no little distrust. It was against his will that he became involved in matters of national and international interest. He kept away from all movements that did not originate in his own diocese and could not be controlled by diocesan powers.[36]

There was about the man a kind of innocence, and it did not always serve him well.

Dunwoodie

Much more may be said about the lasting impact of the Third Plenary Council, but we turn now to another, lasting contribution to Catholic education made by Archbishop Corrigan: the building of St. Joseph's Seminary in the Dunwoodie section of Yonkers, New York, just a few miles north of the Bronx.

As we saw in previous chapters of this book, various attempts had been made to create a diocesan seminary in the vicinity of New York City, but none had succeeded as the archbishops would have wished—until, at the Fifth Diocesan Synod, held in November of 1886, Corrigan announced his intention finally to get it right. He believed that the current location of the seminary, up the Hudson River at Troy, was inconvenient and the physical plant insufficient for the proper education of priests. So he bought sixty acres of rocky ground in lower Westchester County atop what was known then as Valentine Hill. George Washington had used Valentine Hill as his headquarters before the Battle of White Plains in 1776. The cost of the property was more than $60,000.[37]

Archbishop Corrigan laid the cornerstone on May 17, 1891. A remarkable eighty thousand people attended the groundbreaking, and a crowd nearly equal in number had to be turned away at Grand Central Depot and other stations, because the New

York Central Railway was simply overwhelmed by the demand. All the details for the laying of the cornerstone were handled by a Committee of Arrangement headed by Monsignor John Murphy Farley, who would become archbishop upon Corrigan's death.

The seminary was completed five years later:

> The vigil for the veneration of the sacred relics to be deposited in the altars was begun Sunday evening, August 9, 1896, in the Sisters' [of Charity, who took care of "domestic arrangements"] chapel, and was observed during the whole night. On the following morning, at six o'clock, the Archbishop consecrated the main altar under the patronage of St. Joseph, placing there the relics of St. Honoratus, St. Agatha, St. James the Greater, and St. Vincent de Paul. The altar of the Sacred Heart was then consecrated and the relics of St. Severinus, St. Julia, St. Ambrose, and St. Alphonsus Ligouri were placed therein. The consecration of the altar of the Assumption was reserved for the consecration of the chapel proper, which took place in 1898. Immediately after the ceremonies, the Archbishop celebrated the first Mass on the high altar of the chapel.[38]

The future Cardinal Farley addressed Archbishop Corrigan on that day, and his remarks were titled "Wisdom Hath Built Herself a House" (see Prov 9:1). "Your Grace," he said to Corrigan, "this must be for you one of the most consoling days of your life." The Irish-born Farley then waxed eloquent about what he saw in his mind's eye: "the spirits of your eminent and illustrious predecessors in this See— McCloskey, Hughes, Dubois, Connolly—with the whole host of holy patrons of the churches and institutions of this diocese ..." Monsignor Farley then launched into one very long question:

> Who can doubt that as they laid at the feet of the Lamb, this latest, and greatest, gift of a grateful clergy and people, this future home of piety and learning, who can doubt, I say, that these holy patrons and prelates united their prayers and pleadings with those that fill the hearts of all the prelates and priests and people here today, that the Eternal Father would pour out upon this seminary and upon all who shall dwell herein, the fullness of His blessing; that the Great High-Priest may make intercession for those who are to be made after His likeness here; that they may be most perfect models; that the Holy Spirit may diffuse upon the souls of the young Levites soon and for centuries to come to fill these noble halls with His light and His grace; that as generation after generation of young priests goes forth from these sacred precincts, they may bear away with them the fullness of His wisdom and understanding, and counsel and fortitude, and knowledge, and piety, and the fear of the Lord?[39]

But make no mistake, grandiloquent as Farley could be, as Corrigan's vicar-general, he was remarkably effective, and no example proves the point so much as the fact that Farley, "by his energy and tact", undertook a successful effort to raise $250,000 and effected the "legal discharge of the whole debt of the new seminary."[40] That money would amount to approximately $6 million in today's currency.[41]

The edifice of Dunwoodie was designed by William Schickel and Company in the Renaissance style with stone quarried from Valentine Hill itself. It is a fitting building to house an institution that soon became known as the "West Point of

Catholic seminaries" for its rigorous curricula and rigid discipline. And it is worth noting here that Archbishop Corrigan was responsible for overcoming Protestant resistance to the construction of a Catholic chapel at the United States Military Academy at West Point.[42] Most Holy Trinity Chapel opened in 1900 on a hill overlooking the Hudson River and is the oldest of the religious houses in continuous use on the base.

Reading the names of the first seminarians, administrators, teachers, and patrons of Dunwoodie, one sees that almost without exception they were Irish (the few exceptions were French, principally because Archbishop Corrigan recruited French Sulpicians as faculty), and it is not difficult to understand why German and Italian Catholics felt some resentment toward the sons of St. Patrick, believing the Irish to have a virtual stranglehold on Catholic life in New York.

The Question of Ethnicity

Those Germans and especially the Italians, however, had a friend in Michael Augustine Corrigan. Irish immigrants were, by the time of Corrigan's episcopacy, becoming reasonably well situated in American life. Mediating institutions, such as Tammany Hall, had arisen to aid the Irish in the process of assimilation, and, like McCloskey before him, Corrigan had no problem with that. German immigrants had, more than any other group, tended to keep moving westward, where they became the dominant immigrant group in a number of Midwestern cities. Indeed, from the 1880s onward, the majority of German speakers in New York City were Jewish immigrants.

Italians were another matter entirely.

The number of Italians who flooded into America between 1880 and 1920 was in excess of four million. Most came from Southern Italy, the Mezzogiorno, including Abruzzo, Campania, Calabria, Puglia, Sicily, and Sardinia, among other regions.[43] As one scholar has written: "These immigrants were poor *contadini* or peasants, traditional, and lacking sophistication."[44] They were just the sort of Catholics who alarmed nativists and established Catholics alike and were the focus of much of the interest among some Church leaders to see them quickly Americanized. Archbishop Corrigan, in part because he was a fluent Italian speaker, believed that it was essential to bring talented, properly educated, approved Italian priests to New York, as quickly as possible, to provide the spiritual guidance and cultural leadership that were lacking in the archdiocese's growing Italian community.

And there was no immigrant community quite like New York's Italians. As Father Stephen Michael DiGiovanni explains in his book *Archbishop Corrigan and the Italian Immigrants*, these immigrants were as diverse as the communities they had come from:

> Most Italians who arrived in [America] ... were illiterate and ignorant of the customs and language of America, often speaking only the dialect of their province or town. They, therefore, settled in colonies in the larger cities, forming "Little Italies," composed of other members of their family and province, re-creating, as best they could, their village life with its customs, language, and relationships.... [They] had no real national identity, unlike other immigrant groups. They identified themselves, not as Italians, but as Neapolitans, Sicilians, or Abruzzesi.[45]

As Father DiGiovanni points out, this insularity, such as it was, explains the remarkable fact that nearly half of these immigrants returned to Italy between 1882 and 1896,[46] a pattern that would continue, albeit at decreasing levels, into the first decade of the twentieth century.

Catholic practice in the Mezzogiorno was a peculiar mix of the traditional Catholic faith and folk elements, and some of the first priests who came with the immigrants also approached Catholicism in nonstandard ways. Not a few of these clerics had actually fled Italy, with charges of sexual license trailing them. This led the Vatican to require, first, that any Italian priest leaving for America first obtain the proper exeat from his bishop, and, later, that the exeat be accompanied by both a letter of commendation from Italy, an acceptance from an American bishop, and, finally, an approval from the Holy See.[47] But whatever their approaches to Catholicism might be, when they arrived in America there was no support system available to aid them or other Italians—none initially, in any case. And Corrigan had informed Rome that "of the 50,000 Italians in New York and vicinity, only 1,200 ever went to Mass, even though they easily could have done so."[48]

Corrigan was among the American bishops who agreed with the Vatican judgment that the best way to help Italian immigrants was to establish aid societies here and in Italy and to have Italian-speaking priests in more-or-less Italian parishes. But other bishops disdained the idea. Much as they had worried that the papal declaration of infallibility in 1870 would leave their American Protestant brethren aghast, they now worried that bringing Italian nationals in to administer Italian parishes would strike many as an attempt by the then very Italian Vatican to colonize America.

Corrigan recognized, however, that the rapid assimilation of Italians was both unlikely and unwise. In fact, he

> believed it necessary to retard the process of Americanization as much as possible, since too rapid Americanization could demoralize the immigrants [and] ... the shock of being forced to shed one's language, ... customs, and traditions might result in the immigrants' shedding of their Catholic faith as well.[49]

Indeed, and superficially conforming to the belief that he was a behind-the-scenes schemer, Corrigan wrote to the Vatican's Archbishop Camillo Mazzella, S.J., a friend from his student days in Rome, who was close to Pope Leo, that America's liberal bishops (specifically naming John Ireland as leader of the clique) were, in their approaches to education, immigration, and episcopal recommendations "encroaching on the rights of bishops, and assuming to speak for the entire United States, in matters in which they had no rightful authority", which clearly put them in the position of ignoring and therefore undermining Roman power.[50]

One thing about which Corrigan and Ireland could agree was their opposition to the position of a German layman named Peter Paul Cahensly, who had the approbation of the Vatican (or so it seemed to the Americans) for his plan to ensure that in America, where Catholicism was an immigrant faith, international bishops be named to dioceses where one particular immigrant group dominated. Needless to say, the American hierarchy was slack jawed at the suggestion, since this had been the reality way back in 1808, when the episcopacy was first expanded out of Baltimore, but since then capable Americans had been educated in American (and some Canadian and European) seminaries. In fact, officials in Rome had learned well the ongoing issues that arose whenever Americans sensed that foreign influences were at work behind the scenes in ecclesiastical politics. Foreign-born priests who spoke the native languages of immigrants, yes; bishops from overseas to administer foreign-language dioceses, no.

But as was so often the case during this period of America's Catholic adolescence, the reasons for agreement (as between Corrigan and Ireland) were superficial. Ireland wanted to assimilate Catholics so they could fully embrace the benefits of citizenship. Corrigan sought to ensure that Catholics remained Catholic, and he believed that whereas American Catholics were blessed to be free to practice the faith, the trends in secular America were increasingly in opposition to Catholic belief. It was essential that Catholic teaching never be compromised in any entente with Americanism—in either sense of the word.

Throughout the rest his life, Archbishop Corrigan stayed in close communication with Rome about the needs of Italians in New York. He welcomed into the archdiocese Mother Frances X. Cabrini and her Missionary Sisters of the Sacred Heart, who founded orphanages and schools for immigrant children. She and the archbishop did not always see eye to eye, but they always worked closely together. The indefatigable Cabrini went on to found sixty-seven charitable institutions throughout the United States and was proclaimed a saint in 1947.

The McGlynn Episode

It was one thing for an archbishop to struggle to bring immigrant Catholics into a more standard practice of the Catholic faith, but quite another to deal with the non-standard practice of the faith by American-born Catholics, especially those among the clergy, which is what Archbishop Corrigan was forced to do in the case of his former tutor at the North American College, Father Edward McGlynn.

Stated simply, Father McGlynn was—on a wide range of issues—a social activist, and it seems right to suggest that at times his version of the social gospel diminished the importance of the gospel itself, and the "social" part often amounted to socialism. He was part of a group of New York priests, including Richard Burtsell, the man who would become his chief defender in controversy, who believed Catholicism was the best faith for America, because—unlike the various Protestant sects—the Church saw Man not as wholly depraved but as wounded by Original Sin yet capable of reform, and so the Catholic faith was the natural leader in effecting social change. In some ways, this made McGlynn and his confreres (known collectively as the New York Accademia[51]) not unlike the compassionate missionaries, such as Elizabeth Ann Seton, who had earlier done so much for America's poor and sick. But the ambition of this latter group was also political, and it was the collision at the crossroads of politics and religion that so frequently, between the 1860s and the turn of the century, got McGlynn especially into serious trouble. He and all the Accademians were thoroughgoing Americanists, although they went further than those in the hierarchy who shared some of their views.

Earlier in this chapter we noted that McGlynn, two years older than Michael Corrigan, had briefly stood in as de facto head of the infant North American College in Rome, where he came to know the future archbishop. Neither man could have imagined in 1859 that decades later they would become combatants on opposite sides of what each believed was a battle for the soul of the Church.

Father Burtsell kept a diary in which a note from 1865 gives a clear sense of what he, McGlynn, and other reform-minded priests saw as their goal:

> We have the country whence a new activity may spread throughout the whole Christian world. A little more democracy would be of use. We agreed also that the most oppressive mystery of our faith is the promise of never-ending happiness. Eternity oppresses the mind, accustomed to the variety found in time. We can hardly look forward to an eternal existence with pleasure. Annihilation seems almost desirable.[52]

As one historian sympathetic to McGlynn writes: "With such convictions it *was* inevitable that conflicts should have early arisen between ... [the Accademians] and the chancery."[53] It was a bitter conflict, although one usually carried on with notable civility.

Early on McGlynn had clashed with Cardinal McCloskey over the influence of Tammany Hall. For McGlynn, the poor should look to the Church for aid and not to a corrupt political machine. McCloskey, of course, had different views, and, as noted in chapter 3, one of his nieces was married to Tammany's Chief Sachem. McGlynn was also opposed to Catholic education, although not just because it ghettoized Catholic children, as some others held, but because schools were expensive to build and operate and McGlynn thought the money would be better spent on uplifting poor people's bodies and spirits. He also believed that education "was the proper realm of the State".[54]

For his public statements on such matters—made at Cooper Union and other popular New York City venues—McGlynn was called to a meeting with Cardinal McCloskey, who ordered him to cease engaging in politics. Serially, McGlynn would agree to stop editorializing on subjects not approved by the Church and in ways that seemed to question Catholic teaching, and, serially, he would feel compelled to do so anyway. He traveled abroad without permission and became embroiled in Irish nationalism and active in the New York mayoral campaign of the reformer Henry George. All this was coming to a head as Cardinal McCloskey's health was declining and his newly minted coadjutor archbishop was still settling in.

The George candidacy happened at a time when the Church, in Rome as much as in New York, was rigorously evaluating the question of labor, especially in terms of labor unions. Some unions—the Knights of Labor is an obvious example— seemed to be organized in ways—with odd rituals and secret meetings—that suggested affinity with Freemasonry, a fraternal organization the Church had been condemning since Pope Clement XII's 1738 encyclical *In Emenenti*, and—at the time of Corrigan—culminating in Leo XIII's *Humanum Genus* in 1882.[55] The admixture of socialism and, essentially, occultism, and a revolutionary spirit in politics (George, McGlynn, and others were in solidarity with the Fenian movement in Ireland), was taken in Rome to be among the most formidable challenges the Church faced in the world.

But, as Father John Talbot Smith wrote (1905) just two years after Corrigan's death, to regard either Corrigan or McGlynn merely through the controversies of the last decade or two of their lives is a mistake.

> Prelate and priest were good men, true priests.... It was most strange that any set of circumstances should have placed these two noble priests in grave opposition, particularly when neither sought nor desired the contest. The initiative came from outside, from the Prefect of Propaganda, Cardinal [Giovanni] Simeoni.[56]

This is at least half true. While it is certainly the case that the lives of McGlynn and Corrigan deserve consideration beyond New York's liberal-conservative Kulturkampf, Cardinal Simeoni's involvement was hardly causative in the controversy. McGlynn took positions on issues that clearly contradicted Catholic doctrine, and he did so in the democratic spirit of the times. And on several occasions when Simeoni wrote to Cardinal McCloskey suggesting actions to be taken with regard to McGlynn's case, McCloskey simply ignored them. Archbishop Corrigan, on the other hand, was more ready to enforce discipline, which he did after McCloskey's death in 1885.

McGlynn was for several decades the pastor of St. Stephen's Church on East Twenty-Eighth Street in Manhattan, a populous but poor parish, where he was beloved of his mostly Irish parishioners as a *soggarth aroon*, Gaelic for "precious priest".[57] Yet in all his time there, he never built a Catholic school, which went some way toward alienating him from both McCloskey and Corrigan,[58] and which firmly identified him with the Americanists.

But the most serious fissure came when McGlynn began his campaign on behalf of Henry George in 1886. George was a believer in what he called the Single Tax or land value tax (LVT), which would apply only to the value of owned land, so that the more one owns—presumably, the richer one is—the more one pays. By not taxing wages or production, but only the value of the property in which wages are earned and goods produced, economic activity would not be affected—or so George hypothesized. He also hoped that big landowners, because of the tax burden placed on them, would end up divesting much of their property, which would lead to more equitable distribution of land. George's magnum opus, *Progress and Poverty* (1879), was placed on the Vatican's *Index Librorum Prohibitorum*.

In fact, there are a number of versions of Georgist theory, and it can be difficult to grasp. However, we have help from George himself via a letter he wrote to Pope Leo XIII after the publication of Leo's most famous encyclical, *Rerum Novarum*, in 1891.

Briefly, *Rerum Novarum* (Of new things, or Of revolutionary change) was Leo's response to emerging economic changes, one of which was the rise of socialism. The pope addressed property rights and the relationship between management and labor, and defended private ownership and condemned government ownership of the means of production. In Leo's vision, employers and workers, Church and state must work together, each in its sphere seeking justice. In its most stirring passages, *Rerum Novarum* gives special attention to the most perplexing economic problem of all: poverty.

Among other remarkable aspects of the document is that even as the pope condemns communism and praises private property as a principle of natural law, he holds out a hand to modern liberalism—understood in the nineteenth-century sense, as allowing for free associations and limited intervention by governments in the economic life of nations. Although Leo does not use the word in the encyclical, *Rerum Novarum* is the birthplace of what has come to be known as *subsidiarity*, arguably the most important principle of Catholic social teaching.

Henry George, thinking the pope had written the encyclical as an attack on him (and as a reproof of Father McGlynn), wrote an open letter to Leo called "The Condition of Labour". It was doubtless sentences such as these in *Rerum* that caught George's eye:

> They assert that it is right for private persons to have the use of the soil and its various fruits, but that it is unjust for any one to possess outright either the land on which he has built or the estate which he has brought under cultivation. But those who deny these rights do not perceive that they are defrauding man of what his own labor has produced. For the soil which is tilled and cultivated with toil and skill utterly changes its condition; it was wild before, now it is fruitful; was barren, but now brings forth in abundance.[59]

To this Mr. George stated that, whereas he too believed in private property, he considered property to be solely what a man *produces* from his own efforts, so that "if he cultivates grain he acquires a right of property in the grain his labour brings forth. But he cannot obtain a similar right of property in the sun which ripened it or the soil on which it grew."[60] And this had often been restated by Father McGlynn in ways clearly opposed to Catholic doctrine. For instance:

> God has made ample provision for the needs of all men during their residence upon earth, and that involuntary poverty is the result of human laws that allow individual to hold as private property that for which the Creator provided for the use of all.[61]

And this was a fairly mild statement in comparison with some others. The *New York Times* of February 27, 1883, reported that at one rally the previous summer Father McGlynn had said: "If I had to choose between Landlordism and communism, I would prefer the latter."

Although not a few historians *have* suggested that the pope *did* write the encyclical in part as a reaction to George's ideas, especially as steered into a Catholic context by Father McGlynn, more recent studies demonstrate that any causative connection is unlikely.[62]

Rerum Novarum did, however, begin the process by which McGlynn's reputation and his priestly faculties were restored. And much restoration was necessary, because in the aftermath of his disobedience to Corrigan's order that he not campaign for Henry George, the archbishop had distributed, with Cardinal Simeoni's blessing, a condemnation of George's theories (although it did not name him), which was read aloud at Masses in every parish. He had also, in fact, begun to consider excommunicating Father McGlynn. Simeoni called McGlynn to Rome in January of 1887 to answer for his actions, and McGlynn had refused to go. Half a year later, on July 4, 1887, Corrigan announced the excommunication.[63] The suspension of McGlynn's priestly faculties remained in place until 1892, because

Archbishop Corrigan refused (despite large protests by St. Stephen's parishioners and some of the city's labor unions) to reinstate him, *unless* McGlynn submitted to that call to Rome. (Those protests were vehement, and according to one historian, a friend of Corrigan kept his yacht at the ready in case the archbishop was forced to flee from a mob.[64])

What few seem ready to acknowledge is the remarkable arrogance of both McGlynn and George. When McGlynn learned that Corrigan had not read George's *Progress and Property*, he (and George) were aghast and flooded the archbishop's office with the whole of the George corpus (the aforementioned book and all his articles and pamphlets), confident that Corrigan would see the light.[65] Given that the archbishop already knew exactly what George believed, he ignored the documents. The self-regard of the politicians was of little concern to Corrigan, who kept his attention clearly focused on Catholic teaching, not to mention on his administrative and pastoral responsibilities, of which the McGlynn affair was a small, if irritating, footnote.

And Corrigan gave as good as he got. In remarks made to his priests, gathered for the Fifth Diocesan Synod a few weeks after the mayoral election, the archbishop revealed the depth of his knowledge of Georgism. Speaking of certain economic theories inimical to the Church (and acknowledging the exploitation of workers as an irrefutable fact), he used the following illustration:

> Who would burrow the earth to draw forth its buried treasures, if the very mine he was working were at the mercy of the passerby whom its riches would attract? Who would watch with eagerness the season when to sow and to reap, and to gather the harvest which is the very fruit of his labors, if he is told that those who stand by the wayside idle are equally entitled to its enjoyment?[66]

Here was a bold defense of private property and ownership that balanced economic theory with a Catholic view of human nature in a way that Pope Leo would soon expand upon in *Rerum Novarum*.

At the heart of McGlynn's defiance was a belief in the independence of the clergy—a belief at the heart of Americanism, then and now—which was anathema in Rome. We know of no other similar case of insubordination. Consider: Cardinal Simeoni had ordered McGlynn to come to the Vatican to discuss the reasons Archbishop Corrigan had suspended him from ministry, and McGlynn refused. Not long after, McGlynn received a summons to Rome from Cardinal Luigi Jacobini, Vatican secretary of state, and McGlynn refused—again. Then on January 17, 1887, Pope Leo himself formally requested McGlynn's presence, and McGlynn again said no. At one point, McGlynn told Corrigan that his refusal had nothing to do with defiance but, rather, with his own poor health, the financial issues involved, and the necessity of caring for the children of his deceased sister. This was clearly dissembling. As he himself would write later in an article for the *New York Daily Tribune* (February 4, 1887):

> I deny the right of Bishop, Propaganda or Pope, to punish me for my actions as a man and a citizen in the late municipal canvass, or in other political movements. I deny their right to censure me, or to punish me for my opinions.

It may be that these serial refusals of filial obedience were taken at the Vatican as an indication that Corrigan had lost control, if not of his clergy as a whole (he had not), then certainly of some, and of one priest in particular, because the archbishop received notice that McGlynn's case would thereafter be handled personally by the pope.[67] The key to understanding how this became problematic, especially after Corrigan told the press that the matter was out of his hands, may be the archbishop's decision to excommunicate McGlynn. It cannot have pleased the pope that the matter, being after all in "his own hands", suddenly found it complicated by the severest possible ecclesiastical penalty.

It must be noted that Archbishop Corrigan did his position no favors when he allowed a petition to be circulated among the clergy for their signatures that amounted to a loyalty oath. Many signed, but several prominent priests, including Monsignor John Farley, the archbishop's strong right arm, refused to put their names on the document.[68]

The case dragged on until the end of 1892, at which point the Vatican's first apostolic delegate to the United States, soon-to-be Cardinal Francesco Satolli, had taken up residence in Washington, and his summons to McGlynn was finally answered. McGlynn submitted a lengthy treatise to Satolli that attempted to show that, even if the economic theories of Henry George were not entirely in concert with Catholic teaching, they were also not *directly* contradictory. Satolli, wishing to bring the whole affair to an end, accepted McGlynn's arguments and reinstated him in ministry. McGlynn wrote for publication a mea culpa in which he praised *Rerum Novarum* and claimed that he had never intended to dispute any positions held by the Holy See, "but whatsoever word may have escaped me not conformable to the respect due to [the Holy See], I should be the first to regret it and to recall it."[69] McGlynn also finally agreed to visit Rome, where he had an audience with Leo XIII in 1893.

Corrigan, Gibbons, and just about every member of the hierarchy in the United States had opposed the appointment of an apostolic delegate, although Corrigan had accepted Satolli's appointment once it had been announced. (Despite Satolli's actions with regard to McGlynn, he and Corrigan were sufficiently reconciled so that Satolli officiated at the opening of St. Joseph's Seminary in Yonkers. Time in America moved him dramatically from support of liberals to the shelter of conservatives.[70]) But, as always, there had been fear that the appointment of a permanent Vatican representative would be read by non-Catholic Americans as part of an insidious Roman plan to subvert American sovereignty, and protests reached Rome from both liberals and conservatives. To Pope Leo it must have seemed that in so many ways his sons across the Atlantic were both obstreperous and rebellious. In fact, a permanent embassy of the United States to the Holy See did not exist until President Ronald Reagan established it in 1984.

McGlynn's restoration had been made without a formal notification to Archbishop Corrigan of the decision. But the archbishop, as weary as everyone else of the protracted conflict, eventually welcomed McGlynn back to ministry; he sent him up the river, so to speak, to St. Stephen's Church in Newburgh, New York, the Hudson River community sixty miles north of New York City.

McGlynn died on January 7, 1900, and Archbishop Corrigan was at his funeral to pronounce "the last absolution".

Corrigan's Stand against Americanism

Until now, we have spoken of Americanism without defining it in detail. In part, this is because, as one historian has put it, "Americanism is one of those elusive and subtle terms that defies definition, and there have been ... as many Americanisms as there have been Americanizers."[71]

Archbishop Corrigan's understanding of Americanism, and his opposition to it, had its genesis in his natural affection for Catholicism's Roman heart and was reinforced by his long friendship with Bishop Bernard McQuaid, Americanism's most implacable enemy. McQuaid not only understood Americanism; he also knew many Americanists, including the New York priests who formed the Accademians. He had also been a close friend of Father Isaac Hecker.

McQuaid believed that America's Protestant ethos, with its emphasis on personalism, was likely to collapse upon itself and that the choice all Americans would then face would be between "Rome and Voltaire", between Catholicity and skepticism.[72]

Scholar Glen Janus provides an excellent description of the character of the Americanists' position in the 1880s: "[They] believed in a messianic role for America in world affairs, as well as a Catholic 'manifest destiny,' whereby American Catholicism would be the model and catalyst for the revitalization of European Catholicism."[73] This seemed quite clearly to place the Vatican on the outskirts of evangelization.

McQuaid and Corrigan had been surprised and disappointed with the outcome of the Third Plenary Council. Both men expressed their concerns to Rome. In matters of parochial schooling and in the council's directive that clerics remove themselves from politics, the practical outcome was less than satisfactory and called into question the integrity of those who had approved the council's recommendations yet expended little or no effort to implement them. In the case of John Ireland in St. Paul, Minnesota, the bishop was actively subverting the council's instructions.

Ireland's Americanism was nothing if not ambitious—truly on a grandiose scale—and was characterized by:

> an obsession with how the Catholic Church looked in the modern age, its public image, was ever present, and was probably stronger than his genuine sympathy for modernity. In the visionary style of the romantic, and not unlike Isaac Hecker, his ultimate hope was the creation of a neo-Christendom centered in Washington. If he could succeed in converting the American nation to the Catholic Church, then Catholicism would encircle the globe on the wings of American expansionism.[74]

Compare this with Archbishop Corrigan's support for *Roman* Catholicism:

> The liberal bishops "never denied that there were differences between their approach to Catholicism and that of the conservatives [such as Archbishop Michael Corrigan of New York]. They were generally friendlier toward Protestants than the latter and more willing to reconcile the Church with democracy and science without fearing that they would undermine their faith." In addition, liberals tended to be less literal "in their interpretation of the pope's authoritative, [but] non-infallible teachings." They also "desired a greater degree of de-Romanization than the conservatives did

in the operation and policies of the American Church … and stressed the importance of developing active [social] virtues far more than did the [more tradition-bound] conservatives. Yet they denied that these differences were anything more than methodological" and vehemently protested their orthodoxy and loyalty to the pope and the church.[75]

Among the paradoxes of the time is that Bishop Ireland, unlike, say, Father McGlynn, was not a supporter of radical politics. He was a thoroughgoing and vocal supporter of the Republican Party. Still, the spirit of the council (also the spiritual counsel coming from the Vatican) was opposed to clerical involvement in politics, and this Ireland, like McGlynn, simply ignored. And this and other matters of substance were what led Leo XIII to issue *Testem Benevolentiae Nostrae*.

The letter was addressed to Cardinal James Gibbons of Baltimore and dated January 22, 1899. The title more-or-less translates as "Witness to our goodwill". In it the pope criticizes the Americanist heresy, although without citing any Americanist documents.

What he does cite is an edict from the Second Council of Orange (a town in Southern France), in 529. Orange was one of several councils that sought to suppress Pelagianism, which asserted that salvation was attainable without grace. Leo quotes thusly:

> For if any persuades himself that he can give assent to saving, that is, to gospel truth when proclaimed, without any illumination of the Holy Spirit, who gives unto all sweetness both to assent and to hold, such an one is deceived by a heretical spirit.

And in summarizing the reports he has received about doctrinal developments in the United States, the pope attempts to make clear what he is attacking: "From the foregoing it is manifest, beloved son, that we are not able to give approval to those views which, in their collective sense, are called by some 'Americanism.' "

Leo quoted no American expressions of the heresy, because the matter actually came most forcefully to his attention via a French translation of a biography of Father Isaac Hecker, whose conversion to Catholicism had been helped along by Cardinal McCloskey and who had founded the Paulist order (the Missionary Society of St. Paul the Apostle), which was dedicated to evangelizing Americans using new forms of popular communications: principally lectures and print media.

Hecker was far from being a Pelagian; he believed in the action of the Holy Spirit in matters small and large, and he was certain that the Church's message could be brought home to Americans if presented in the right way. Although Hecker was younger, John Henry Newman considered that they were joined in the same effort—Newman through the Oxford Movement in England. Hecker was baptized by Bishop McCloskey in 1844 and in 1849 was ordained a priest (in the Redemptorist Order) in London by Nicholas Wiseman, then coadjutor bishop of Westminster, who had played a key role in Newman's conversion to Catholicism.

To be sure, there was something of the utopian about Hecker—at least in his background. He had spent six months at the transcendentalist, experimental, and socialist Brook Farm commune shortly before his conversion to Catholicism. He believed strongly that America was lost without religious practice, and for him that

could only mean becoming a minister of some sort. He met with a leading Anglican prelate in New York and then with Archbishop John Joseph Hughes, who
almost succeeded in driving Hecker away from the Church. What saved him was
his friendship with Orestes Brownson, who, in the middle of Hecker's search for a
spiritual home, became a Catholic himself, although, as the married father of eight
children, obviously not a priest. This convinced Hecker to overcome his doubts
that a "foreign" church could ever become the proper force to bring Americans
to Christ.

Hecker founded the *Catholic World*, a monthly magazine, and attended the First
Vatican Council as an advisory theologian.

The biography of Hecker to which the pope reacted was not, per se, the book
written by Hecker's close Paulist associate, Father Walter Elliott, but a version of
it published in French in which the translator, Comptesse de Ravilliax, took considerable liberties. But this was even more the case in the introduction to the translation by one Abbé Félix Klein, whose encomia to the separation of Church and
State went far beyond anything Father Hecker advocated. Hecker sought no compromise of Catholic doctrine. And how far the French edition differed from the
original may be deduced from the imprimatur given to the American edition—by
Archbishop Michael Corrigan.[76] But when the stilted French translation appeared
and began receiving extensive and enthusiastic attention, the pope decided he had
to act.

To be sure, popes would soon abandon active hope that modern nation states,
even in Italy, where once the pope had also been a temporal ruler, would remain
Catholic states in their foundation. Historically, they had been Catholic states (thus
Christendom), but by the end of the nineteenth century the divorce was complete,
and *Testem* may be seen as a last, ultimately futile, plea on behalf of the once unassailable belief that faith should not just rule men's hearts but should define their laws
as well. It was that, but it was also, as Leo made clear, a warning that Catholicism is
not, especially doctrinally, itself a democracy. No Catholic cleric, from deacon to
cardinal, may present his *personal* views as consonant with the Magisterium, unless
they are so. When those views contradict the Magisterium, they are heretical.

Leo was willing to acknowledge the many ways the Church had adapted herself
to different times and places, but he stressed that Church teaching never changed.

> But, beloved son, in this present matter of which we are speaking, there is ... a greater
> danger and a more manifest opposition to Catholic doctrine and discipline in that
> opinion of the lovers of novelty, according to which they hold such liberty should
> be allowed in the Church, that her supervision and watchfulness being in some sense
> lessened, allowance be granted the faithful, each one to follow out more freely the
> leading of his own mind and the trend of his own proper activity. They are of opinion
> that such liberty has its counterpart in the newly given civil freedom which is now the
> right and the foundation of almost every secular state.

Now it may be that Archbishop Corrigan should not have taken a triumphalist
posture following the publication of the pope's apostolic letter, but he did. He
wrote a thank-you note to the pope that was widely reprinted in American newspapers from coast to coast. For many Protestants and inattentive Catholics, *Testem*

came across as a condemnation of that other Americanism, the patriotic kind, and so Corrigan's praise of it was guaranteed to raise hackles. And the majority of America's Catholic hierarchy were angry at the New York archbishop's finger wagging at what many bishops considered a "phantom heresy". The subheadline in a story in the *San Francisco Call* of May 1, 1899, proclaimed:

> So-Called "Americanism" Is Denounced by the Prelate. CALLS IT A MONSTER. Pleased His Holiness Has Rooted Out "This Cockle From the Field of Wheat."

Then, before reprinting the text of Corrigan's letter to Leo, the article notes that just about every other bishop, archbishop, and cardinal of note have "solemnly protested to the Pope that the errors which he had designated as 'Americanism' had no place in the American Roman Catholic church". Thus was Corrigan's praise presented as sycophant.

Corrigan had written in part:

> We receive and accept for ourselves, our clergy and, for the communities and congregations which with us work for the salvation of souls, as well as for all, *Testem benevolentae* [sic]. We accept it and make it our own, word for word, sentence for sentence, in the same identical sense in which your Holiness, following the tradition and wisdom of all Christian antiquity, intends it, and wishes that it *should* be understood by us. In its regard we shall never make, nor shall we ever permit that others depending from us, either directly or indirectly, should make any reservation or tergiversation. Your Holiness has spoken. The question is therefore ended.

It was not ended, of course, but in the years remaining to him, Michael Corrigan allowed the controversies to fade away.

They might have been inflamed and burned longer had Corrigan known at the time the extent to which Ireland and the Americanists had sought to undermine him in the pursuit of their goals. In a letter he wrote to a friend in Rome, regarding the program by which the Americanists had used Italian and French media to promote their agenda, Ireland observed:

> I pray that the origin of American letters to the *Moniteur* be never suspected by him [Corrigan] or her [Ella Edes, Corrigan's Roman agent]. Caution the abbe Boeglin against her inquisitiveness. You may smell from them [the American letters] a western fragrance.... My Roman sojourn taught me diplomacy, a branch neglected at the time of my theological studies.[77]

Perhaps it bears mentioning that prior to his death, Archbishop Ireland saw to the burning of all his private papers.

But this moment of triumph for Michael Corrigan, as the nineteenth century drew to a close, had also cost him a great deal in terms of energy and peace of mind. One of history's greatest popes, Leo XIII—who would die at ninety-three in 1903 having written more than eighty encyclicals, the last dozen *after* he turned ninety—had heeded the archbishop of New York's warnings about Americanism and acted accordingly, and for this Corrigan's episcopal brethren in the United States would never really forgive him.

The Lord Is My Rock

Archbishop Corrigan's final years were spent in relative peace, "in freedom from the dissensions, and from press criticism".[78]

At a celebration for Corrigan at the Metropolitan Opera House, organized by Bishop John Farley, now his coadjutor and soon-to-be successor, many dignitaries from New York and the nation gathered to pay tribute to the man whom they praised not only as New York's leading religious figure but also as its first citizen. Secretary of War Elihu Root, who would become secretary of state in 1905 and United States senator from New York in 1909, said of Corrigan that he had been "a great conservative force, maintaining the social order of civilization against all socialistic and anarchistic attacks, maintaining the rights of property, on which our homes and the rewards of honest toil, and the hopes of honorable ambition, all depend".[79]

The archbishop's last years were, despite failing health, not spent in idleness. In yet another demonstration of his loyalty to Rome and his affection for Pope Leo, he planned to send a delegation of laypeople and priests to the Vatican to participate in celebrations surrounding the pope's silver jubilee in September 1902. Bishop Farley "reported to Corrigan that the pontiff very much wanted the archbishop to lead the pilgrimage ... [implying] that the red hat might be at the end of the journey".[80] If so, it would not have been the first time elevation to the cardinalate was awarded to an "elderly" prelate for his service to the Church.

In the last year of the old century, Archbishop Corrigan began several additions to New York's cathedral church. He built a small alcove/chapel dedicated to St. John the Evangelist in honor of the four ordinaries of New York who preceded him: John Connolly, John Dubois, John Hughes, and John McCloskey.[81] More significant was his role in the creation of the cathedral's Lady Chapel.

Money for the chapel came from the family of banker Eugene Kelly, who had died several years before. Kelly had been born in County Tyrone and in 1834 had emigrated to the United States, where he became successful in New York and California, amassing a considerable fortune and becoming a trustee of St. Patrick's. The Kelly family has its own crypt beneath the cathedral sacristy.[82] Archbishop Corrigan, the Kelly family, and a consulting architect from Columbia University rejected the plans of the firm of James Renwick, the cathedral's original designer, in favor of the proposal of Charles T. Matthews. The chapel was completed in 1901.[83]

Corrigan died on Monday, May 5, 1902, from complications of pneumonia that flared up after he fell during the previous winter and broke a blood vessel in his foot[84] while surveying the progress of construction in the Lady Chapel.[85] He had seemed to be recovering from the illness when a single, massive heart attack felled him. This "elderly", frail, and failing man was just sixty-three.

Sixty thousand came to file past his coffin, and his funeral was among the largest ever held in New York to that point. Archbishop Patrick John Ryan of Philadelphia delivered the homily, and the principal celebrant at the requiem Mass was Corrigan's old friend and sometimes adversary Cardinal Gibbons.

Perhaps the archbishop's face in death (his body was placed on a catafalque at the front of the sanctuary and tilted feet down to give mourners a good view of his countenance) displayed the quality that his contemporaries noted could never be (and never was) caught in photographs or paintings of Michael Augustine Corrigan—what one writer (after the English writer Matthew Arnold) called "sweetness and light".[86] For some it was an expression of saintliness.

One of his harshest critics has written that Corrigan's "efficiency and aptitude for organization had left the archdiocese much better fitted to meet the needs of the largest Catholic population in the country".[87] Yet no good deed goes unpunished.

> The surveillance of dissidents, the front page controversies, the loyalty oaths, and the pressure tactics of the Corrigan administration had left a bad taste in the mouths of New Yorkers.[88]

That was certainly true of the New Yorkers who were dissidents.

It seems fair to say, however, that among Catholics loyal to the Magisterium, there was no bitterness whatsoever. Writing in the *Philadelphia Press*, the hard-nosed investigative reporter Elisha Jay Edwards extolled the archbishop as possessing the "peculiar distinction of ... seeming to be young always and at the same time ... mature", a quality Corrigan had throughout his life. By way of comparison, we might suggest that he was not unlike Joseph Ratzinger, Pope Benedict XVI. As Edwards wrote:

> He [Corrigan] was able to turn, after a day's labor at his residence, not to lighter, but to different things, and to become on the instant the profound scholar, the real academician.[89]

In his homily, Archbishop Ryan saw his good friend Michael Corrigan as the apotheosis of his two predecessor archbishops: he had the "invincible courage" of Hughes and the "marvelous prudence" of McCloskey.

> The late Archbishop might be regarded as belonging to the class of Cardinal McCloskey, yet, when principle was at stake, the lamb became a lion, and he was found as fearless as ever was Archbishop Hughes. *Dominus petra mea*, the Lord is my rock: because he leaned upon God, because his motives were supernatural, he worked with the inspired intrepidity of God. *Dominus petra mea* was the motto of Moses the meek, and Moses the unconquerable. The Archbishop was a rock, gentle, yielding, mossy on the surface; but beneath all that gentleness strength and power and immovability of principle were found.[90]

Archbishop Ryan was referencing Corrigan's archiepiscopal motto, and it was a fitting one at nearly every stage of Michael Augustine Corrigan's life.

The Builder

John Murphy Farley
Fourth Archbishop of New York
(1902–1918)

The Easter Parade, 1903

Shortly after the death of Archbishop Corrigan, rules to recommend a successor to a vacant see laid down by the Third Plenary Council of Baltimore in 1884 were invoked. The board of consultors, which was made up of Corrigan appointees and "permanent" rectors of archdiocesan parishes, met to compile a *terna* (a list of three clerics) deemed suitable for consideration by the Vatican. The bishops of the other dioceses in New York State and the archbishops of the United States also submitted lists of nominees. The pope, of course, had the final say on the selection and could discard the recommendations if so inclined.

During the consultors' deliberations, the recommendation that the next archbishop should be someone from outside New York State was rejected. The ordinary of the Diocese of Brooklyn, Bishop Charles E. McDonnell, was ruled out because he was viewed as having been too close to Corrigan both personally and politically. The three men eventually agreed upon were known to all the board members, with Auxiliary Bishop John Farley in first place, followed by Monsignor Joseph Murphy, and the Reverend Dr. Patrick McSweeney. New York's bishops and other American archbishops also agreed upon Farley as their top choice.

Farley attracted wide support because he was known to have a different personality and temperament from the man he had assisted for the previous seven years. Farley was cut more in the Cardinal McCloskey mold.

Vatican insiders, the American hierarchy, and New York's clerics knew that while Farley was a loyal, hardworking, and prudent priest, he had not always seen eye to eye with his late boss. Farley had positioned himself as a moderate during Corrigan's battles with Archbishop Ireland and Cardinal Gibbons, the Knights of Labor, and New York City mayoral candidate Henry George.

He disagreed with Corrigan's belief that the Catholic University of America would be a breeding ground for Americanism. As secretary of the Catholic University board, Farley was most supportive of the university and received a letter of thanks from Cardinal Gibbons for the help he "gave to remove the obstacles to its success".[1]

Farley also believed that the new St. Joseph's Seminary in Yonkers should not sacrifice intellectual training in favor of spiritual formation. He was not jubilant when Corrigan hired a French order, the Society of St. Sulpice—the order Bishop John Dubois belonged to at the beginning of the nineteenth century—to manage the seminary. He argued that there should be "a higher grade of intellectuality" and said to his archbishop, "I do not see why, if we could build a million dollar seminary, we could not provide a staff of professors." Reacting strongly, Corrigan dismissed his auxiliary bishop's argument, saying, "We may get better professors perhaps—but I think that the result will be a lower grade of priests."[2]

As for the McGlynn affair, Farley urged his archbishop to be more evenhanded. "In Rome," Farley told Corrigan, "they give celebrets [a kind of visa to say Mass anywhere] to people compared with whom McGlynn ... is an angel."[3]

Farley cautiously separated himself from Corrigan on the Americanism issue, not in New York but in Ireland. In an 1892 trip to the land of his birth, he told an audience, "those timid souls [who] feared that [the] newborn spirit of liberty ... might be detrimental to the faith of St. Patrick were far at fault.... Liberty rightly understood is the most faithful ally of the Church."[4]

Bishop Farley's fellow priests judged him to be a leader who could calm the waters in the archdiocese and end the clerical factionalism—and the Holy See agreed. In August 1902, the Vatican told him he was to get the job, and it was publicly announced on September 25, 1902.

Early Life

The fourth archbishop of New York was born in 1842, the youngest of four children to Philip and Catherine Farrelly in the town of Newton Hamilton, in County Armagh, Ireland. (John eventually changed the spelling of his family name to Farley, the way it was pronounced in New York. For consistency, Farley will be used throughout this chapter.)

John's parents, who owned a small farm and produce shop, died when he was a child, and his uncle Patrick Murphy took on the financial responsibility of supporting and educating the Farley orphans. Murphy had the means, having emmigrated to New York in 1830, where he went on to own and operate a successful furniture-manufacturing plant.

The Farley siblings grew up forty miles from Belfast, near a mountain overlooking the Irish Sea. The area was controlled by Protestants, but, thanks to the British Parliament's passage of the Act of Catholic Emancipation in 1829, Catholics no longer had to meet in secret to celebrate Mass or educate children.

The future cleric attended village schools, and at the seminary high school, St. McCartan's College in Monaghan, he was well trained in Greek, Latin, and mathematics.

In 1864, at the age of twenty-two, John decided it was in his best interest to leave his homeland and join his uncle in New York. Patrick agreed to continue supporting him, and John enrolled in St. John's College (later known as Fordham) in the Bronx—which had been founded by Bishop Hughes in 1841 and turned over to the Jesuits in 1846. John was devoted to the study of the English language, developed a fine writing style and enjoyed writing poetry. At the end of the academic year, he ranked number one in his class and won eight of the nine academic prizes.

Certain he had a priestly vocation, John transferred to the provincial seminary in Troy, New York. Recognizing that John was a top-notch student, Archbishop McCloskey selected him in 1867 to continue his education in the fledgling North American College (NAC) in Rome. It was an extraordinary time to be in Rome, and during his three years of study, John witnessed a lot of history in the making. In the secular world, the decades-long struggle—which had several times burst into armed conflict—over the unification of Italy was drawing to a conclusion. And in the Church, the historic First Vatican Council would be convened on December 8, 1869, during Farley's third year in Rome. Thanks to McCloskey, Farley had the good fortune of viewing the council from a ringside seat. While listening to the sophisticated debates over the question of papal infallibility—which was declared in July 1870—John came to appreciate the need for a cleric to have strong academic training.

Because McCloskey invited John to accompany him to the various papal committees on which he served, the seminarian was able to observe prelates in action, and he studied the inner workings of the Church's governing bodies and various Church-sponsored charitable and educational institutions.

John was ordained by the Vicar of Rome, Cardinal Costantino Patrizi Naro, on June 11, 1870. The young priest, well versed in theology, Church history, canon law, and commonsense Church politics, sailed for New York on August 1.

Seven weeks after Farley's departure, on September 20, the Italian Nationalist forces broke through the Porta Pia, forcing General Hermann Kanzler, the commander of the pope's army, to surrender the city of Rome to King Victor Emmanuel. A defiant Pius IX excommunicated the invaders and imprisoned himself inside the Vatican.

Farley's first assignment in the archdiocese, at age twenty-eight, was as curate at the Church of St. Peter in the New Brighton section of rural Staten Island. Two years later, after McCloskey's secretary, Monsignor Francis McNeirny, was named titular bishop of Rhesaina and coadjutor with right of succession to the Diocese of Albany, Farley was tapped to fill the vacancy. (It was at this time that he changed the spelling of his name.) His receiving this post, which he was to hold for twelve years, so soon after his ordination confirmed that McCloskey had been impressed by this young immigrant during their time spent together at the Vatican Council.

Farley did not disappoint his archbishop. He proved to be a first-rate administrator with fine, methodical habits. As secretary, he organized McCloskey's schedule and handled routine matters. He also had the ability—some call it an Irish gift—to say no to favor seekers with grace and kindness.

When McCloskey became the first American prelate elevated to the College of Cardinals, it was Farley who directed the arrangements for the cardinal-elect to receive his red biretta at Old St. Patrick's Cathedral from the archbishop of Baltimore, James Roosevelt Bayley (a cousin of Franklin D. and the nephew of Elizabeth Ann Seton) on April 27, 1875.

Three years later, in March 1878, Farley traveled with McCloskey to Rome to meet the new pope, Leo XIII.

In January 1884, the year before McCloskey's death, the ailing cardinal informed Farley that the Holy Father had named him a papal chamberlain. This was indeed a great honor because at that time the rank of monsignor was rarely granted to American priests, particularly those in their early forties.

In August 1884, Cardinal McCloskey named Farley pastor of St. Gabriel's Church, a working-class parish on East Thirty-Seventh Street in Manhattan. Farley, believing that "the best contribution the Catholic Church could make for good citizenship in America was to provide that combination of religious and secular studies which trained the whole man and not merely his intellect at the expense of his will",[5] would devote much of his eighteen-year pastorate to enhancing St. Gabriel's parish school.

Thanks to the many contacts Farley had made during his time in the chancellery, he was able to raise sufficient funds to complete the church spire, pay off the mortgage, renovate the school, and build a parish hall.

The pastor strove to make St. Gabriel's the social and religious center of its East Side neighborhood. He and his assistant priests visited each family in the parish every year. The parish hall was an important component of his outreach plan. The hall served as a home for the lay Catholic societies and a venue for social events, particularly dances for teenagers.

In 1891 McCloskey's successor, Archbishop Corrigan, appointed Farley vicar-general and chairman of the archdiocesan school board to succeed the late Monsignor Thomas Preston. He was promoted to domestic prelate in 1892, and two years later Pope Leo XIII bestowed on Monsignor Farley the Church's highest nonepiscopal rank (just below auxiliary bishop): protonotary apostolic.

To impress upon the city's elected officials the size and importance of the archdiocese's parochial-school system, Farley organized an exhibit that explained the classroom work and displayed student projects. There was a huge parade that included thousands of schoolchildren and their teachers.

On December 2, 1895, Farley was named the first auxiliary bishop of New York and titular bishop of the ancient see of Zeugma. He had initially been named Corrigan's coadjutor with right to succession, but the archbishop, arguing that this appointment would make the Holy Father look bad in the United States, convinced him to rescind the honor. Since the position of coadjutor was not uncommon throughout the early history of the Church in America, when it was still considered missionary territory by the Vatican, it is difficult to explain Corrigan's action. It would not be unfair to suggest that the autocratic archbishop, while dependent on Farley, was suspicious of his loyalties and feared that the popular and competent cleric could overshadow him.

In 1898, to celebrate the silver jubilee of Archbishop Corrigan's episcopal ordination, Farley began a drive to pay off the $300,000 mortgage on the two-year-old St. Joseph's Seminary at Dunwoodie. As we wrote in chapter 4, he succeeded and was able to present to Corrigan at the jubilee celebration a bank notification stating that the mortgage had been satisfied.

When Archbishop Corrigan died, on September 15, 1902, Farley took up the reins of the Archdiocese of New York. He had to wait eleven months, however, before receiving the pallium from the apostolic delegate, Archbishop Diomede Falconio. The delay was attributed to a frail and ailing Pope Leo XIII, who died on July 20, 1903, at the age of ninety-three, history's oldest and third-longest-reigning pope.

John Murphy Farley, the last foreign-born archbishop of New York, brought to the office unprecedented diocesan experience. As a close collaborator with his two predecessors and as notary to the Third Plenary Council and secretary to the council's committee for the Catholic University of America, he possessed incredible knowledge of both the archdiocese and the Church in America as a whole. This experience would serve him well in an archdiocese that was facing significant challenges and changing demographics at the dawn of a new century.

The Church in America at the Turn of the Century

In the last decades of the nineteenth century and the early years of the twentieth, Catholic immigrants flooded the nation. So great was the influx—some nine million in all—that the Catholic Church became the largest denomination in America.

There was, however, a marked difference in the origins of this new immigrant population. Unlike earlier waves, which consisted primarily of Irish and Germans, many of those arriving in the new wave were coming from eastern and southern Europe. Political upheavals in these regions prompted hundreds of thousands to look to America as the land of hope. The creation of the dual Austro-Hungarian monarchy, racial animosities, and jealousies caused a mass exodus from the Balkans. Following the unification of Italy, the battle over papal property and the incompetence of the new centralized government caused thousands to flee their homeland. Emperor Napoleon III's defeat in the Franco-Prussian war and Bismarck's anti-Catholic Kulturkampf drove the faithful from France and Germany to "seek a newer world".

Selected Catholic Immigration to United States[6]

	1871–1880	1881–1890	1891–1900	1901–1910	1911–1920
Austro-Hungary	46,230	134,000	232,000	553,000	239,000
France	4,000	15,000	4,000	26,000	18,000
Germany	175,000	400,000	105,000	36,500	10,000
Italy	27,000	130,000	390,000	802,000	275,000
Poland	4,000	78,000	190,000	608,400	250,000
Ireland	180,000	300,000	40,000	10,000	70,000

The U.S. Catholic population, which totaled 8.9 million in 1890, had catapulted to 16.3 million by 1920 and represented 20 percent of the total U.S. population.

As Poles and Czechs settled in Chicago and Detroit, Italians in New York and Boston, Hungarians and Slovaks in Pittsburgh and Cleveland, and Ukrainians in other parts of Pennsylvania, they centered themselves socially and politically in family, parish, and neighborhood, reflecting the basic principle of Catholic social thought—subsidiarity.

Immigrants happily gave their hard-earned nickels and dimes to local pastors to build magnificent parish churches, whose architectural style reflected the places of worship in the Old Country. These grand structures that stood out in tenement-filled neighborhoods also reflected the gratitude these immigrants felt toward an all-loving God who they believed had permitted them to escape to the shores of America.

Because of this tremendous growth in the number of non-English-speaking Catholic immigrants, local bishops implemented policies that permitted the establishment of national-ethnic parishes as opposed to the traditional territorial parishes. Polish, French, Slovak, Italian, and German parishes sprouted up throughout America's inner cities. This type of church brought together people who shared a language and an ethnic culture. Parishioners were loyal to their local churches, and they identified and introduced themselves to others by the names of their parishes.

These parishes provided vital services for immigrants trying to find their way in the new land. The parish organized social activities for its flock through the Holy Name Society, the Women's Sodality, and Communion breakfasts. The pastor got children off the streets and out of gangs by organizing sports played in the parish yard and dances held in the church hall. Parish activities helped build parishioners' self-confidence—immigrants were treated as special persons with God-given abilities and not as victims. As Michael Novak put it, "The Church taught the immigrants to work hard, to obey the law, to respect their leaders and to concentrate on private, familial relationships."[7]

The parish school also provided an essential service for immigrant children. The teaching nuns, brothers, and priests taught discipline—both moral and physical. They taught benevolence, forgiveness, and atonement through the Catechism and by marching students to weekly confession. Parish schools instilled a moral compass in hundreds of thousands of immigrant children.

While New York City experienced an immigrant population boom during this period, growing from 3.4 million in 1900 to 5.6 million in 1920, there was little growth in the archdiocese during the Farley administration. In 1902 its Catholic population stood at 1.2 million; in 1905 and in 1910, 1.20 million; and in 1920 the total was 1.33 million. The city population grew 64 percent while the archdiocese grew only 8 percent.

This is because most of the Catholic population gains in the city were in two boroughs—Brooklyn and Queens—that were outside the boundaries of the archdiocese. The population of the Brooklyn Diocese grew 173 percent, from 300,000 to 800,000 between 1890 and 1920.

The primary reasons for this growth in the outer boroughs were cheaper housing and the construction of the subway system, which made it feasible to commute longer distances to workplaces, particularly in Manhattan.

The Farley Administration: First Stirrings

Archbishop Farley's first task after taking the reins of office was to calm the clerical waters. He was committed to reuniting his clergy, who had been badly split during the controversial Corrigan years.

To achieve this end he adopted the style and approach Cardinal McCloskey had exercised. Farley did not seek a national profile and declined to lead any charges in national Church or political battles. Instead, he devoted his time and energies to meeting the needs of his clergy and his flock.

Unlike Corrigan, Farley was not a public lightning rod. He worked quietly behind the scenes and was acknowledged by his priests as a firm yet understanding boss.

One of his first steps to heal clerical wounds was to persuade the Vatican to name eight domestic prelates. This was a heavy lift, considering that there were fewer than two dozen priests throughout the entire nation who held the rank at that time. Nevertheless, Farley's request was granted, and he parceled the new designations out to deserving clerics, including some who were perceived as Corrigan opponents. Bestowing these honors was Farley's way of rewarding faithful service and sending the message to a subset of his clergy that their days of exile were over.

Reacting to the naming of this unprecedentedly large contingent of monsignors in New York, Archbishop Patrick Ryan of Philadelphia jokingly said to Farley, "I understand, Your Grace, that since your recent visit to Rome, half of your Diocese has become purple and the other half blue."[8]

Farley held recollection meetings with a different group of his priests every month. This gave him the opportunity to pray with them and to get to know them better.

Newly ordained priests cut their teeth in rural parishes. Farley, whose own first assignment had been in Staten Island, believed it was important for young clerics to get a sense of how struggling folks in the countryside lived and worked before transferring them to bustling inner-city parishes.

Over time Farley's outreach to his clergy healed the wounds and brought the turmoil of the Corrigan years to an end. As a result, at Farley's death in 1918, the long-time rector of St. Patrick's Cathedral, Monsignor Michael Lavelle, was able to state proudly that Farley left behind "no faction or clique".[9]

While Farley kept in place many of his predecessor's appointments to administrative posts, he came to rely on three priests in particular to oversee the day-to-day affairs of the archdiocese:

- Michael Lavelle (1856–1939). The monsignor served as vicar-general from 1902 to 1918 and rector of the cathedral from May 1887 until his death in 1939. Ordained in 1879, Lavelle spent his entire clerical life assigned to the cathedral. He is the only priest buried in the crypt below the altar in St. Patrick's who is not a bishop or an archbishop.
- John J. Dunn (1869–1933). Ordained in 1896, he was a capable administrator with business savvy. During the Farley regime, he was named executive director of the Society for the Propagation of the Faith in 1904 and chancellor of the archdiocese in 1914. On October 28, 1921, he was consecrated as Archbishop Hayes' first auxiliary bishop.
- Patrick Hayes (1867–1938). Ordained in 1892, he was Farley's alter ego and his successor as archbishop.

After skillfully reuniting his clergy, Farley turned his attention to the parishes and parochial schools. While the total Catholic population of the archdiocese was basically unaltered during his tenure, the ethnic composition was experiencing significant changes. Fluent in Italian, French, and Spanish, he personally reached out to the new ethnics. He permitted the building of ethnic parishes and created special committees to cater to their needs.

Farley was particularly focused on the Italians, whose population in the archdiocese swelled from 133,000 at the turn of the century to 500,000 in 1918, building upon the work Archbishop Corrigan had begun. Knowing that many had abandoned the faith after the unification of Italy, Farley was keen on expanding the numbers of ethnic-Italian parishes, which stood at eighteen in 1902. By the time of his death, there were thirty-eight Italian parishes and thirteen Italian chapels. The number of Italian priests serving in these parishes grew from fifty-two to seventy-four.

To help ethnic children at once maintain their faith and compete for their piece of the American dream, Farley devoted much time to raising the funds required to renovate and expand the Catholic educational system. Fifty new parish schools were opened, and total enrollment doubled.

Unlike his predecessor, Farley was an enthusiastic supporter of the Catholic University of America. His devotion to education was best summed up in Monsignor Lavelle's 1919 monograph on Farley: "He was impregnated with the conviction that Catholic education is the greatest of all evangelizing forces, and he fostered everything that promised to strengthen and diffuse Catholic scholarship."[10]

To encourage and identify vocations among teenage boys, Farley completed in September 1903 the construction of the minor seminary begun by Corrigan. It was located on Madison Avenue between Fiftieth and Fifty-First Streets on land the archdiocese bought for $350,000 from the Catholic Asylum, which moved to a new facility in the Kingsbridge section of the Bronx.

Father Patrick Hayes came up with the name of the minor seminary, Cathedral College, and was named the first president of the school. Classes were held six days a week, and students attended for six years—four years of high school and the first two years of undergraduate studies. It was not a boarding school, because Farley believed it was important during the formative teenage years that students live at home and "grow up under the influences of home virtues and parental supervision".[11]

St. Joseph's Seminary and the Modernist Crisis

Archbishop Farley had a warm spot in his heart for the major seminary, often called Dunwoodie. He expanded the facility, adding a new three-story dormitory to accommodate the growing number of students. He also spent as much time as possible at Dunwoodie, meeting with the seminarians and the faculty and attending to their needs. And over time his efforts paid off.

When St. Joseph's officially opened in 1896 it housed 96 seminarians. When Farley took office in 1902 there were 155, and at the time of his death in 1918 there were in attendance 267 candidates for the priesthood.

Because Farley had more in mind for Dunwoodie than building projects, his legacy includes a battle for control of the seminary and plenty of backroom intrigue that led to a clash with the Vatican during the Modernist crisis.

When Archbishop Corrigan had floated the idea of hiring the priests of the French Society of St. Sulpice—the Sulpicians—to run Dunwoodie, there was much grumbling among his clergy. The most vociferous objections came from Farley, who questioned, perhaps unjustly, the scholarship of the order priests. There were also widespread complaints about the proposed contract, which was to turn over ownership of Dunwoodie to the Sulpicians.

Despite the opposition, Corrigan insisted on executing his plan, albeit with significant changes in the contract. He sent one of his priests to negotiate directly with the order's superior general in Paris; among the results of those negotiations, the ownership clause was dropped, and it was agreed that either side could cancel the contract for any reason with one year's notice.

Before the designated first rector, Father Charles Rex, was to take charge, he came down with tuberculosis and was forced to enter a sanatorium. To calm Corrigan, who feared that a liberal might get the position, the ailing cleric recommended an American-born member of the order who was slated to teach moral theology at Dunwoodie, Father Edward R. Dyer.

Farley was not a fan of Dyer; they had clashed over policy matters when Farley was an auxiliary. However, shortly after Corrigan died and before Farley was named to succeed him, Father Dyer was named U.S. vicar-general of his order, moved on to Baltimore, and turned the reins of Dunwoodie over to Father James F. Driscoll.

Driscoll was perceived as tilting to the left and in 1901 was falsely denounced by confreres to the Sulpicians' superior general as being a heretic. His friendship with the controversial French biblical scholar Father Alfred Loisy, who was to be excommunicated in 1908, did not help Driscoll's reputation.

Farley actually got along with Driscoll, because they agreed on one goal: to make Dunwoodie a leading center for Catholic scholarships in the United States. And together they succeeded. Catholic historian Father Thomas J. Shelley, in his history of Dunwoodie, concluded, "The credit for Dunwoodie's high academic reputation is due largely to Farley and Driscoll who together created a favorable atmosphere for teaching and learning."[12]

While Farley and Driscoll were collaborating in New York, a storm was brewing four thousand miles away in the Vatican that would eventually engulf Dunwoodie and leave a dark cloud over the Farley administration.

When the cardinal-patriarch of Venice, Giuseppe Sarto—a priest renowned for his pastoral works—was elected pope in August 1903 and took the name Pius X, most Vatican observers expected a low-key transitional pontificate after the twenty-five-year activist, albeit conservative, reign of Leo XIII.

Rome's chattering class could not have been more wrong. Pius moved fast to reorganize the Curia, codify canon law, reform the rules for seminaries, and revise the breviary and liturgical music.

The pope also threw down the gauntlet to the Modernists, who he believed synthesized all the current heresies.

Modernism was a movement led by a group of Catholic intellectuals who were striving to reinterpret and renovate Catholic dogma to reflect the findings of contemporary science and philosophy. Some went so far as to twist Church truths to complement current opinions. "The logical outcome of Modernism", British Catholic historian Michael Davies has observed, "is that there is no God; there is no life to come, and Revelation means man talking to himself, for the Modernist man has no God outside himself.... Man replaces God as the center of reality."[13]

The leading Catholic Modernist George Tyrrell (1861–1909), who was expelled from the English province of the Society of Jesus and stripped of his priestly powers in 1906, summed up the thinking of the movement in these words: "it is *always* and *necessarily* we ourselves who speak to ourselves and who (aided no doubt by the immanent God) work out truth by ourselves."[14] In other words individuals, not the Magisterium of the Church, determine what is true about their Catholic beliefs.

To stop this movement in its tracks, Pius released a *Syllabus Condemning the Errors of the Modernists* (July 3, 1907), which reprobated sixty-five propositions drawn from its leading intellectuals.

The pope followed this up with the encyclical *Pascendi Dominici Gregis* (September 8, 1907), in which he denounced Modernism, evolutionism, and immanentism.

Pius X laid out rules to combat the Modernist heresy, including "the exclusion from seminaries and colleges of directors and professors in any way imbued with Modernism". He also called for the creation of "episcopal vigilance committees to supervise publications and clergy conferences".

To suppress further the spread of errors, Pius X ordered, in *Sacrorum Antistitum* (September 1, 1910), that all "clergy, pastors, confessors, preachers, religious superiors and professors in philosophical-theological seminaries"[15] take an oath against Modernism.

Back in New York, Archbishop Farley followed the pontiff's struggle against Modernism and tried to be supportive. For instance, after Pius condemned the Third Republic in France for its 1904 de-Christianization laws that forbade Catholic priests and nuns to teach, forced the closing of two thousand schools, confiscated Church property, and renounced the 1801 Napoleonic Concordat, Farley publicly defended the pope's actions.

To raise awareness of the injustices being perpetrated by the French government, Farley organized a "Stand Up for Religious Liberty" rally in 1905 at Manhattan's Hippodrome Theatre.

The newly opened Hippodrome, which was located on Sixth Avenue between Forty-Third and Forty-Fourth Streets and held 5,300 seats and two circus rings, was the largest theater in America. The rally attracted more than thirty thousand Catholics. Prominent laymen who denounced France's persecution of religious orders and the government's seizure of monasteries, convents, and shrines made worldwide headlines.

Many observers were convinced that the rally had an impact on the leaders of the Third Republic. In its aftermath, the anti-Catholic crusade subsided, and many of the new laws were not enforced. The Vatican "recognized that there had been a worthy exercise of episcopal prudence and influence in America carried out with devoted zeal yet pregnant with excellent effect for the cause of the Church".[16]

After the publication of the *Syllabus Condemning the Errors of the Modernists*, Farley, as metropolitan, and all the bishops in his province signed an August 31, 1907, document addressed to Pius declaring their gratitude and fealty:

> The decree recently promulgated is a magnificent monument to the office of the Supreme Teacher and evokes from our humble hearts feelings of the liveliest joy and gratitude ... [and] these same sentiments are unanimously shared by the faithful of the Province of New York.... While none among us, as far as we know, is inbred with these disastrous errors, nevertheless, we ... hasten to assure Your Holiness of our immediate and steadfast adhesion to this most opportune decree. We condemn and proscribe all and each proposition condemned and proscribed ... and, moreover, we have taken effective measures to preserve the doctrine and discipline of our Churches, schools, and Seminaries from the dangers indicated in the new decree.[17]

Because he had covered his bases on the Modernist issues, and knowing that the New York Catholic community was not exactly a hotbed of radicalism, Farley went about his business of building up the intellectual reputation of Dunwoodie, unaware that a series of events between 1905 and 1909 was to put his administration under the Vatican's microscope.

The problems began when the Sulpicians in Paris, reacting to the Third Republic's anti-Catholicism, chose a new superior general, Father Jules-Joseph Lebas, who was much more regal than his predecessors. He began to impose tougher teaching and publishing standards on members of the order.

One Dunwoodie teacher who came under fire was Father Francis Gigot, a noted biblical scholar who had joined the faculty in 1904. Angry that his superiors in Paris had held up the publication of his latest book, he threatened to resign from the order.

In 1905, while Rector Driscoll was trying to manage the Gigot situation, he was approached by two members of his faculty, Father Francis P. Duffy and Father John Brady, with a proposal to publish the first Catholic theological journal in the

United States, whose purpose would be to guide American priests through current Church controversies.

Driscoll, who liked the idea, presented it to Farley, who heartily approved the project. The archbishop, who never pretended to be a great scholar, respected scholarship and was a strong proponent of expanding the philosophical and theological training of his priests in particular and the Catholic population in general.

This belief also explains why, at about the same time, he had set in motion the production of the *Catholic Encyclopedia*, which would be published in fifteen volumes between March 1907 and April 1914.

The *Encyclopedia* was intended to provide "authoritative information for the entire cycle of Catholic interests, action, and doctrine".[18] Farley promoted subscriptions and personally invested $5,000 into the enterprise and wrote several of the *Encyclopedia*'s entries.

Farley was so excited and impressed by the hard work and dedication of the editors and the hundreds of contributors that, against the advice of senior counselors, he permitted the editors to be their own censors. This was a risky decision considering the doctrinal battles being waged by the Vatican.

Nevertheless, the project was a great success. The distinguished French religious historian Georges Goyan (1869–1939) hailed the *Encyclopedia*, saying it "marshaled the Catholic intellectual forces of the modern world, as the Crusades had marshaled the Catholic military forces of the Middle Ages".[19]

When it came, however, to the theological journal, which was to be called the *New York Review*, Farley was not as lucky as he was with his *Encyclopedia*.

The first sign of trouble was when Rector Driscoll went to his Sulpician superior, Father Edward R. Dyer, and informed him of the venture. Father Dyer was angry because Driscoll had not first sought his approval before going to Farley. He also could not share Driscoll's enthusiasm, fearing the anti-Modernist winds blowing west from Europe. He argued that it was not a prudent project—that it could backfire and harm the order.

Dyer bluntly told Driscoll that Farley "is no more aware than a child about the topics to be treated in the new review. He would like to be a Cardinal and if a word of disapproval should come from Rome, he would abandon the review completely and pounce upon the editors".[20]

Dyer insisted that Farley publicly take full responsibility for the *Review* in order to protect the Sulpicians. The archbishop was perturbed, but he relented and in a letter dated March 31, 1905, wrote, "You may state that I wished the review to be undertaken, that it is to be conducted by the Fathers of my Seminary, and that it be connected with the Seminary, and that the Fathers may consider themselves responsible to me in all that concerns it."[21]

The brochure announcing the review stated that it was to publish articles by renowned Catholics "to keep the readers informed on most recent developments of religious questions ... [because] the strides made in scientific and historical research during the past half century have forced upon us the consideration of new problems, and have rendered necessary the restatement of many theological problems".[22] The list of twenty-nine contributors included George Tyrrell.

The *New York Review: A Journal of the Ancient Faith and Modern Thought* made its debut in June 1905. And while its content was applauded in many circles, Driscoll's superior house in Paris was not impressed and demanded prepublication review of all articles and the rights of censorship. This did not sit well with the rector's confreres, and on January 9, 1906, five Dunwoodie Sulpicians, including Father Driscoll, announced that they were resigning from the order and had accepted Farley's invitation to be incardinated in the archdiocese.

With this move, Farley achieved his long-term goal of ridding himself of the Sulpicians. With only one member of the order left at Dunwoodie, Farley exercised his right to cancel their contract. This action did, however, have consequences.

A livid Father Dyer accused Farley of underhanded tactics. He wrote a 160-page memo that stated his version of events and made sure it was leaked to appropriate parties. He also filed a complaint in Rome. Following the advice of Cardinal Gibbons, Dyer consulted with the prefect of Propaganda, who was not happy with what he heard.

To add more fuel to the fire, the Sulpician procurator general, Father Marie François Hertzog, handed over the Dyer memo to Pope Pius. The pope, who until that time had been in the dark about the matter, was most perturbed that during Archbishop Farley's recent visit to the Vatican, he had not informed him of the situation, and that Farley "has left the rebels in the Seminary".[23]

Because several of the "rebels" were also editors of the *New York Review*, and despite the fact that the journal defended the pope's war on Modernism and viewed it "as the beginning of a more glorious period of Catholic intellectual activity",[24] the journal fell under suspicion.

On January 15, 1908, the apostolic delegate to the United States, Archbishop Diomede Falconio, sent a three-page handwritten letter to Farley, calling his attention "to an advertisement of the books by Rev. George Tyrell which has appeared in the *New York Review* V. III, Nos. 2 and 3, September, October, November, December 1907.... As your Grace may easily see such an advertisement appears to be a violation of both the letter and the Spirit of the recent Encyclical on Modernism ... reproduced in the same number of the *New York Review*!"[25]

The apostolic delegate went on to warn Farley that writers who favor Modernism should not be published and that, to avoid controversy, all proposed articles for publication should be reviewed and approved by the archbishop. "In confidence," Falconio added, "... it has made no favorable impression in Rome to see the *Review* articles contributed not only by Rev. Fr. Tyrell but also [other suspected Modernists].... I have thought it my duty to call your attention to these facts in order that Your Grace ... may avert future displeasures."

This letter did not sit well with Archbishop Farley, even though he had been tipped off in May by the rector of the North American College, Monsignor Thomas Kennedy, that Rome had "heard some very harsh criticism of the *Review*".[26]

In a handwritten reply dated June 22, 1908, Farley shot back at Falconio. "In regard to the conduct of the *New York Review*," Farley wrote, "... your informant is in error in some of the charges against the review."[27]

Farley pointed out the factual errors and explained that Tyrrell and other authors were in good standing when their articles were published. As for the Tyrrell book advertisement, Farley stated that it was "an accident which the managing editor, who is responsible for it, deeply regrets".

Farley went on to defend the reputation of four New York priests studying at the NAC whose loyalties had been questioned. One of them was the Reverend John J. Mitty, who would later become a professor at Dunwoodie and eventually archbishop of San Francisco.

While Farley's reply overall was a firm refutation of the apostolic delegate's charges, he made this concession in a postscript: "Every article which is to appear in the review in the future will pass through my own hands and that of my diocesan censors before going to print."

Back at Dunwoodie, the *Review*'s managing editor, Father Driscoll, remained confident that the journal and his colleagues would survive the storm. To show that he was a team player, he wrote to Farley in March 1908 that he was in receipt of the new Italian *Catechism on Modernism* and had commissioned a translation and was seeking permission from the European publisher to print an American edition.[28]

Driscoll's optimism was short-lived. Under pressure to clean house, in June 1908 Farley ordered the closing of the *New York Review*.

In the official announcement, the editors pointed out that the journal had never "been made the object of official condemnation"[29] and blamed its demise on lack of financial support. This was nonsense. The *New York Review* was the victim of clerical intrigue and jealousy.

Driscoll, who now thought the worst was behind him, was to discover he was sorely mistaken.

In January 1909, Farley received word from the Reverend William Hughes, a New York priest who worked in Washington for the apostolic delegate, that Falconio had informed Rome that eight priests in the archdiocese were promoting Modernism. While names were not mentioned, fingers pointed to Dunwoodie teachers. Hughes told Farley that "they are a source of offence and complaint to the Holy See and a deadly injury to the prestige of our diocese".[30]

During a June 1909 visit to Rome, Farley knuckled under. He informed his top deputies that he intended to fire Driscoll, Gigot, and Duffy. But then the usually decisive archbishop wavered and sent word to New York that only Driscoll was to be ousted.

To contain the damage, Farley personally handled the public disclosure of the Dunwoodie shakeup. He lamely lectured Driscoll, who had offered to resign after the *Review* was shut down the previous year, that "an important seminary like ours suffers more than others would from unfavorable reports about teachings and only a change of some kind can remove the outside impression whether well-founded or not."[31]

The execution of Farley's plan began on September 5, 1909. At a special meeting of the Dunwoodie faculty, he persuaded its members to approve a resolution that thanked Driscoll for his years of service and pointed out that he had handed in his letter of resignation a year earlier.

The official statement from the archdiocese published in the September 18, 1909, edition of the *Catholic News* said Driscoll was leaving "in order to devote his energies to other fields of priestly labor". Father Driscoll was appointed pastor of St. Ambrose parish and later St. Gabriel's in New Rochelle, where he died in 1922.

To ensure that there would be no more Modernist charges against the seminary, Dunwoodie devolved into an institution that did not place much value on scholarly achievement, and its teaching staff became known for its mediocrity.

One telling sign of things to come: When Farley's favorite project, the *Catholic Encyclopedia*, was completed and it was suggested that his seminarians be permitted to acquire sets, he declined to give his assent, saying, "It would be too much of a distraction."[32]

Looking back on this sad episode, the noted Catholic historian Father Thomas J. Shelley made this astute observation: "It would have taken a leader of stronger character than John Murphy Farley to resist the anti-Modernist panic in the Catholic Church. As the winds of repression reached a gale force in 1908 and 1909, Farley reverted to the habits of a lifetime and decided that the better part of valor was to imitate the willow not the oak."[33]

The Hundredth Anniversary of the Archdiocese

Archbishop Farley's troubles with Rome did not interfere with his centenary plans for the archdiocese in 1908. Farley intended to show off and celebrate one hundred years of progress and the mighty presence of the Church in New York, as well as the inroads made by Irish Catholics in business and political circles.

The festivities began on Sunday, April 26, with Masses of thanksgiving in every parish. The next day, Masses were said in the churches for schoolchildren. That evening, receptions were held in the mansions of well-to-do Manhattan Catholics to honor the archbishop and visiting dignitaries.

On Tuesday, April 28, a Solemn Pontifical Mass was sung at St. Patrick's Cathedral. The main celebrant was Cardinal Michael Logue, the primate of Ireland. Logue was the archbishop of Armagh, the see once held by St. Patrick.

The sermon was preached by Cardinal Gibbons, who traced the history of the archdiocese and its achievements. Gibbons described how, when the Diocese of New York was founded in 1808, it had just one church, three priests, and fifteen thousand faithful. Over the ensuing century, it had been split into eight dioceses "with 1,546 churches, 2,710 priests, 583 parochial schools with 251,383 pupils and about 3,162,309 people".[34] The gentle Gibbons also spoke in glowing terms of the man with whom he had often clashed, Archbishop Michael Augustine Corrigan. The late Archbishop Corrigan, Gibbons said, was "a man of many-sided attainments: so learned in speculative theology yet so practical; so courtly yet so humble; so gentle yet so strong. He was a man of most methodical habits, never wasting a minute, and was eminently conspicuous for administrative ability. In all questions affecting canon law and church history as well as the venerable traditions and usages of the Apostolic See, he was an authority and a living encyclopedia among his colleagues."[35]

To a packed cathedral, with those in attendance including a majority of the U.S. hierarchy, eight hundred priests, and over six thousand laypeople, Farley read messages from distinguished personages. President Theodore Roosevelt congratulated Catholic New Yorkers for their "general impulse to higher patriotism given by the way in which the celebration was conducted".[36]

After the Pontifical Mass, there was a luncheon at Cathedral College. That evening, back at St. Patrick's, there was Solemn Vespers, an evening prayer service of thanks. The apostolic delegate presided, and the archbishop of St. Louis, John Glennon, preached. On Modernism, Glennon stated:

> You have heard much of the recent encyclical of the Holy Father on Modernism.... You have heard how it purposed stifling all mental activity, all spirit of inquiry, all further search for the truth; how it must produce atrophy of the spiritual sense.
>
> The truth is that the encyclical is first of all a defense of the divinity of Christ, a defense made with all the more spirit because the denial in these latter days was heard in the home of His friends; in some instances even from those who, as His priests, had sworn to serve Him and proclaim that divinity unto all men.[37]

Ironically, the former rector of Dunwoodie, Father James Driscoll, who participated as an assistant during the ceremony, found himself sitting next to his nemesis, Archbishop Falconio.

To close the week of celebration, a four-hour parade commenced on Saturday, May 2. Fifty thousand Catholic laymen marched from Washington Square up Fifth Avenue past the cathedral and a reviewing stand that held 3,500 people.

To commemorate the centennial, a fundraising campaign commenced to raise $850,000 to pay off the debt of St. Patrick's Cathedral. Thanks to the leadership of Monsignor Lavelle and the cathedral's board of trustees, which included two former New York mayors, William Grace and Hugh Grant, the goal was met in less than two years.

Satisfying the mortgage cleared the way for the cathedral to be consecrated on October 5, 1910. Archbishop Farley presided over the ceremony; Cardinal Gibbons celebrated the Pontifical Mass along with two concelebrants, Cardinal Logue and Cardinal Vincenzo Vannutelli of the Vatican. More than fifty thousand watched outside as Farley blessed the cathedral's outer walls. The Mass and ceremony took five hours and brought three cardinals together under the roof of the cathedral for the first time.

One year later, on October 30, 1911, the Vatican announced that three archbishops residing in the United States were to be elevated to the College of Cardinals: Archbishop Farley, Archbishop O'Connell of Boston, and, to the surprise of many, the apostolic delegate, Diomede Falconio, O.F.M. The Italian-born Falconio had been ordained a Franciscan in Buffalo, New York, in 1861, and had served in parishes until summoned to Rome in 1881. He had returned to Washington as the pope's U.S. representative in 1902.

The cardinal–secretary of state, Rafael Merry del Val, a close friend of O'Connell, informed the cardinals-elect that for the first time Americans were to receive their red hats from the hands of the pope.

Farley traveled to Rome with a large entourage of New Yorkers on the S.S. *Kronprinzessin*, whose captain hoisted the papal flag over the ocean liner.

While in Rome, Farley resided in the North American College, where, on November 27, 1911, he received the formal notification of his nomination as a cardinal-priest. Two days later Pope Pius X conferred on Farley the red biretta and the cappa magna, the red cape with a long train. The next day, November 30, he received the wide-brimmed red galero.

Pope Pius assigned Farley the Dominican church of Santa Maria sopra Minerva as his titular church in Rome. Farley formally took possession of the church on

December 10 and celebrated a Solemn High Mass. (A Dominican church was chosen to recognize the fact that New York's first two ordinaries, R. Luke Concanen and John Connolly, had been members of that order.)

When his returning steamer, the S.S. *Berlin*, docked at the Hoboken, New Jersey, piers on January 18, 1912, Farley was greeted by tens of thousands of people of every faith. The boat that took him to Lower Manhattan's Battery was decorated with red bunting and was accompanied by a flotilla of similarly trimmed boats.

After disembarking, the cardinal was driven up Broadway in an open carriage to St. Patrick's. During the five-mile trip, he was greeted and cheered by more than five hundred thousand people who lined the streets.

Upon entering the cathedral, Farley kissed a cross presented to him and took his place in the procession, which started up the center aisle accompanied by the solemn antiphon from the liturgy of the hours, "Ecce sacerdos magnus, qui in diebus suis placuit Deo"—"Behold the great priest, who in his days pleased God."

Thanking the well-wishers gathered in the cathedral, the cardinal, as Professor Francis Thornton put it, "with praiseworthy humility, constantly insisted that the honor was due to their efforts, rather than his own importance".[38]

Cardinal John Farley was formally installed as cardinal archbishop of New York by the apostolic delegate on January 25, 1912. Afterward a private reception was held at the Catholic Club, followed one week later by a huge reception at the Hippodrome for the general Catholic population.

In addition, Farley was honored by leading non-Catholics at a Waldorf-Astoria reception. The New York City comptroller, Herman Metz, served as master of ceremonies, and tributes were made by Governor John Dix, Mayor William Gaynor, and other political luminaries.

President William Howard Taft's letter, which was read to the audience, said: "I regret I am unable to be present at the dinner for Cardinal Farley on his elevation to the highest rank of the Roman Catholic Church. The non-sectarian character of the dinner is an indication of the great progress we have made in mutual tolerance and brotherly cooperation. Please present my compliments to Cardinal Farley, with whose friendship I have been honored for many years."[39]

Farley in the Public Square

Cardinal Farley was not a Church leader who relished throwing bombs from the steps of St. Patrick's into the public square. "There are two types of Americans," the *Tablet* of London reported, "those who get into the papers and those who keep out. Cardinal Farley belongs to the latter and distinguished minority. He does not seek the public; but they seek him. He does not keep a press agent but he keeps New York sympathetic and reverent to the faith."[40]

While it was true that Farley was not a publicity seeker, he did speak out publicly when necessary to explain and defend the teachings of the Church.

In the first year of his administration, after a public symposium on divorce was held in New York that argued for the easing of laws to terminate marriage, the archbishop accepted an invitation from the Hearst Syndicate of newspapers to state the Church's "views on the great national disgrace".

In his essay, which was published in the *New York American* as well as other Hearst papers in November 1902, Farley made it clear that the family is the basic unity of society; hence the state must "remember that it exists not so much [as] a society of individuals [but] as a corporate unification of many families.... Disrupt the unit by permitting divorce and you weaken the very foundation of the state".[41]

After explaining Church doctrines and quoting extensively the pope's position, which he had personally heard articulated in Rome, Farley unabashedly concluded that divorce is

the black pall of the basest degradation that hangs heavy over the land. No regard for the sacred character of marriage [means] woman is a chattel, a commercial commodity, bought and sold in open market. The result can easily be imagined—the mental and physical deterioration of the race; stagnation and paralysis of every high and holy effort; no sense of human responsibility here or hereafter.

May this our own nation learn wisdom from the past, and bend every effort to cut out of our body politic this parasite of divorce, which, we are ashamed to say, has taken hold on many of our homes. May public sentiment become such that over every American fireside all may read: "What God has joined together let no man put asunder."[42]

The article raised many eyebrows nationally, and Hearst Syndicate managers were pleased with the archbishop's effort. In a letter to Farley, the publisher of the *New York American* thanked him and said, "It was by all odds the ablest setting forth of the great Divorce evil that we have yet printed."[43]

From time to time, Farley quietly lobbied for Catholic politicians. In March 1913 he wrote a letter to William D. Guthrie, one-time presiding partner of the law firm Cravath and president of the New York City Bar Association, pushing Michael Mulqueen for the position of judge of the New York Supreme Court. "My interest", Farley wrote, "is based on my knowledge of the gentleman's character.... I have never heard all these years anything detrimental to his high standing." After listing Mulqueen's services to Church organizations, the archbishop concluded, "I shall be much indebted to you for any interest you may be pleased to take in Mr. Mulqueen's case."[44]

Mulqueen did not get the judgeship, but in 1916 he was named a Knight of St. Gregory by Pope Benedict XV for his service to the Catholic Club, and in 1920 Governor Alfred E. Smith appointed him a commissioner of the state board of charity.

While visiting California in 1912, Farley granted an interview to a group of reporters and made some comments that he may have later regretted. "Farley: I Do Not Believe in Woman Suffrage" was the headline in the November 9, 1912, *Los Angeles Examiner.*

When a reporter pointed out that California had equal suffrage, Farley replied: "I am opposed to it because I think my mother and my sister have their true place in the home, and that it is best for them and all women to leave to men politics, and so far as possible the affairs of government. St. Paul said that woman shall be subject to the man, and that is pretty good authority."

"Would you call equal suffrage a fashion?" asked the suffragist reporter.

"A fad rather", said His Eminence. "I do not believe it will last."

"But women have changed since the days of St. Paul," ventured the other suffragist interviewer, "and conditions of life are vastly different now."

"Has woman changed so much?" asked the cardinal. "I challenge that. A thousand years ago there were great women, brilliant women in the great Catholic universities' professorships. You do not know that? Oh yes, that is a part of our history. I doubt if women have changed much fundamentally."

"Do you believe women are inferior to men intellectually?"

"Well, I should not say that. They have not had the same opportunities as men, but I would not want to be put down as saying they are inferior intellectually. That is delicate ground. On the other hand, I would not commit myself to the statement that they are the intellectual equals of men."[45]

Farley's comments did not sit well with the women reporters then, and one could only imagine the outcries if a high churchman made similar remarks today.

Several weeks later, back in New York, Farley invited a reporter from the Los Angeles Catholic newspaper *The Tidings* to interview him for its Christmas issue. He told the reporter that although it was a busy season for him, "the recollections of my recent visit to your hospitable city are still so recent, and so filled with pleasant memories, that I cannot refuse a request from your edition. You see I am quite at your mercy."

In this interview, Farley stuck to safer turf and gave his views on socialism.

"Socialism", he said, "is the hope of present-day pessimists." He went on:

From a religious standpoint it is ... dangerous. In fact it has to be, because it must destroy religion, if it would succeed. It must get rid of the idea of a personal God. The notion of God implies the idea of the future life, of moral responsibility, of a divine and not a handmade morality. All these notions are absolutely at variance with socialism. The reason of it is quite plain. Socialism must make its appeal to the materialist. It makes happiness here on earth the end of man; it makes him responsible only to the state which shall be the guide of his moral acts. Such a basis of ethics can only succeed on the ruins of Christian ethics....

In practice the socialists and the capitalists are in great measure quite alike in their hatred for religion. Religion torments the conscience, when unfair and unjust methods of gain are resorted to.... The rich man's selfishness, his desire for pleasure and enjoyment make him the enemy of religion.

So too is it with the poor man.... Granting that the poor man has a grievance, which as I said happens, he nevertheless is often moved by selfish motives. He wants to get as much as he can, whether he gets it justly or not.... Therefore he must try to rid himself of an uncomfortable morality, and consequently religion must go....

Each side is selfish, and the consequence is that we [are in] a sort of class war. The only way to overcome the difficulties between capitalism and labor is by education of the conscience. Without that, we cannot hope to succeed. Only the man who has a high notion of his duties to God and his neighbor can overcome the natural selfishness of man. And these are the men who must solve our present difficulties. These are the men who will be just in their dealings, and fair in their treatment of their employees.

"You mean that we must have a little more of the true Christmas spirit, your Eminence?" asked the reporter.

"Yes: we have to extend the Christmas feeling over the entire year. We have got to remember always that the Infant Jesus, who was born on Christmas Day, died to save us all, that He taught us we are all brothers, having the same origin, and the same end, and that we should as a consequence love and help each other."[46]

When the New York Jewish community asked Farley to speak out against Czar Nicholas II's pogroms in Kiev, Russia, he gladly agreed. The executive secretary of the American Jewish Committee, Herman Bernstein, in a letter to Farley dated November 13, 1913, conceded that the Jews had received very little help from the U.S. State Department and thanked the cardinal for demanding that Czar Nicholas II withdraw the false murder charges brought against them. "Be assured", he wrote, "that the Jewish people everywhere will deeply appreciate your broad sympathy and your willingness to come forward and express your protest against this despicable evidence of bigotry and race hatred."[47]

When it came to protecting the interests of the Church from conniving politicians, the cardinal was most vigilant.

In March 1915, he kept a close eye on legislation introduced in the New York Assembly, the lower house of the state legislature, to permit the property of religious and charitable bodies to be taxed.

When asked to join other religious leaders in publicly protesting, Farley declined, saying he had already made his objections known privately to Albany power brokers and had been assured that the bill would get nowhere in the legislative session. "It seems", his spokesman Bishop Hayes told other opponents of the proposal, that it had been "introduced in order to force the issue into the [state] constitutional convention".[48]

New York's constitution mandates that every twenty years voters must decide at the ballot box if there should be a convention to revise or amend the constitution, or both. If the vote is affirmative, then delegates are elected throughout the state at the next general election.

In April 1914, the voters had approved, by a very slim margin—153,322–151,969— the convening of a convention, and in November they elected 168 delegates.

Farley was worried about the convention, and his concerns were well founded. On May 4, 1915, an amendment to Article 3 of the state constitution was proposed calling for the abolition of tax exemptions. It read:

> No tax exemption on real estate shall be granted to any church, society, or school under church direction or ownership, nor to any cemetery association, or public or private institution of any character not owned by the federal, state, county or municipal government, but all such property shall be taxed proportionately to its assessed valuation, the said tax to be applied to the general fund of the city, county, or state by which it is levied. The legislature shall enact such statutes as are necessary for the enforcement of the foregoing provisions.[49]

Warned by Manhattan attorney George Gillespie that "casual conversation of the [convention] members indicates that some favor this amendment",[50] Farley jumped into action.

He formed the Committee on Catholic Interests, whose members included laymen and clerics from every diocese in New York State. Its purpose, Farley stated, was to "prepare to meet any possible attack in the convention of taxation of church property, of church education, or of Catholic Charities".[51]

At the organizational meeting it was agreed that prominent Catholics in each locality should reach out, "directly or indirectly, to the delegates to the convention, by individual appeals to their fairness on the merits of our position".[52]

Because a large subset of delegates to the convention were Progressive Republicans and were not big fans of the Church or of her members who controlled local political machines, the mission of the Committee on Catholic Interests was not an easy one. Its statewide efforts, however, paid off. The tax amendment never made it out of committee. The final revised constitution that went before the voters in November 1915 was decisively defeated, 901,462 nays to 400,423 yeas.

In 1917, Farley led another group, this time made up of Catholics, Protestants, and Jews, to change the Revenue Act of 1916, which imposed a federal estate tax, and to oppose a proposed federal estate-tax law that included "no exemptions of bequests, legacies, or gifts for educational, philanthropic, charitable, or religious purposes".[53]

Every member of New York's congressional delegation was warned how much these bequests and gifts meant to New York hospitals, schools, universities, museums, and public libraries and how such laws would cause bequests to decrease and endanger the future operations of those institutions.

Feeling the heat, U.S. Senator James W. Wadsworth, Republican of New York, wrote to Farley that he had "been convinced for a long time that bequests to charitable ... institutions should be exempt from inheritance taxes, federal and state.... I urged such an exemption, and I shall continue to urge it whenever appropriate revenue legislation is before the Senate."[54]

Farley and his national allies eventually prevailed, and charitable bequests are exempt from estate taxes to this day.

Church vs. State

The comptroller of the City of New York, William Pendergast, approved in 1910 a request from the Bureau of Municipal Research to investigate the finances of private charitable institutions, particularly those that received public funds. The bureau, an independent organization founded in 1906 by progressive good-government types (aka "goo-goos"), was created to monitor governing bodies in New York City.

Convinced that the primary purpose of the investigations was to go after Catholic institutions, Archbishop Farley decided to co-opt the bureau's mission and ordered an independent audit of Catholic charities in both the New York and Brooklyn Dioceses. The firm that conducted the audit—and charged $83,000 for its services—Patterson, Teele and Dennis, reported in its management letter that it did not find any evidence of misuse of public funds. The report did recommend that a uniform accounting system and operating procedures be designed and that all 120 of the charitable institutions in question be directed to implement it.

These recommendations were blessed by the city comptroller, and the Bureau of Municipal Research was ordered to cease its investigation.

Reviewing the activities of the bureau, the New York State commissioner of charities, Michael Drummond, made these comments in a pamphlet he penned, titled *The Truth about the Attack on the Charitable Institution*:

The cause of humanity, charity and economy [was] not advanced one step. The installation of the new accounting system, an afterthought, was simply a move to cover the
failure of the attempt to prove that the institutions of the Jews, the Protestants and the
Catholics were dishonorable.

   To the contrary, I assert and know that they are among the most useful, honorable
and blessed agencies for the care and help of suffering humanity.[55]

To improve Catholic services and oversight further, Farley created an umbrella
group called United Catholic Works. But this plan to coordinate Catholic charitable institutions was not good enough for reformers led by John Mitchel, who took
over city hall on January 1, 1914.

   John Purroy Mitchel (1879–1918), an Irish-Spanish Catholic, was born in the
Fordham part of the Bronx. After graduating from Columbia University and New
York Law School, he was appointed an investigator specializing in municipal
corruption. The headlines he made in that job catapulted him into the office of
president of New York City's Board of Aldermen in 1909. Although he was a
registered Democrat, his loyalties lay with the goo-goos, not with Boss Charles F.
Murphy's Democratic Tammany Hall. And in the 1913 race for mayor, Mitchel,
running as the Fusion candidate, decisively beat Democrat Edward McCall,
receiving 57 percent of the vote.

   Like many reformers, Mitchel was overzealous in his drive to implement scientific formulas to govern people. He did not understand his diverse ethnic constituencies and managed to antagonize many of them, particularly Catholics.

   Itching to extend government's power and "willing to accept any brawl that
followed", the mayor commenced an investigation of the city's private charitable
institutions.

   Leading the charge was the newly appointed commissioner of charities, John
Adams Kingsbury, tasked with setting and enforcing city regulations. He appointed
a board of goo-goos to investigate privately managed childcare institutions.

   One member was Kingsbury's top lieutenant, Deputy Commissioner William
Doherty, who held a grudge against the Sisters of St. Joseph who ran the orphanage
in which he had grown up. Kingsbury later said that he selected Doherty "because
he was a Catholic and might be able to cope with the opposition of the Catholic Church".[56]

   The official report concluded that twenty-six of the thirty-eight childcare centers
investigated did not meet approved standards. Of the twenty-six that failed, twelve
were Catholic. The report also concluded that the state board of charities (SBC), which
had oversight power and had approved all the charities, was incompetent and corrupt.

   Reacting, Mayor Mitchel put pressure on the Republican governor, Charles
Whitman, to establish an independent commission to investigate the SBC and the
Kingsbury charges against the various orphanages.

   Whitman, afraid of tarnishing his progressive credentials, gave in to Mitchel
and exercised the power granted to him under Section 6 of the executive law (the
Moreland Act), which empowered the governor to create independent commissions to investigate the affairs and actions of any "state government department,
bureau, board or commission with a goal of documenting and exposing mismanagement, fraud or wrongdoing".[57]

The Moreland Commission on charities, chaired by a leading goo-goo, Charles Strong, president of the City Club, possessed subpoena power and could question witnesses under oath. The commission, however, was not guided by the ordinary rules of evidence. This meant that hearsay evidence and opinions could be sought.

Cardinal Farley and his advisors were convinced that Strong's commission could turn into an anti-Catholic witch hunt, which could result in government subsidies' being eliminated or tax exemptions' being revoked. This view was confirmed by the distinguished lawyer William Guthrie, who in a letter to Bishop Patrick Hayes, dated December 27, 1915, wrote that after chatting with the commission's general counsel, John Bowers, he had concluded "that the principal grounds of attack are based upon Catholic institutions and that there is evidently a determination to restrict the field of denominational activities".[58]

In another letter dated the same day to Judge Morgan O'Brien, the head of the Committee on Catholic Interests, Guthrie warned that "Catholic interests ought to be carefully looked after in the [Strong Commission], for its origin is undoubtedly anti-Catholic".[59]

The hearings began in January 1916. Not only were they biased, but the well-staged proceedings provided plenty of fodder for the tabloids. A paid publicity agent fed the papers one-sided information and made horrible accusations about conditions at the orphanages without offering any supporting data. The most outrageous and false charge was that the children at Immaculate Virgin Mission on Staten Island were fed from the same dishes as the pigs. A headline the next day read, "Orphans and Pigs Fed From the Same Bowl."[60]

To counter the half-truths, innuendos, and deliberate falsehoods, the Church went on the offensive.

Father William Farrell of the Brooklyn Diocese was encouraged to write a rebuttal in the form of an open letter to Governor Whitman. The eleven-page document blasted the malicious commission and closed with these words:

> This Strong Commission in its course to date has made itself thoroughly distrusted, and the press reports almost daily disclose what appear as a lack of judicial impartiality, as well as a nasty anti-Catholic animus.
>
> The exploitation of Doherty's Committee, with its abusive and violent descriptive adjectives, is an unseemly farce.
>
> The whole thing should come to an immediate end, and in its stead there should be a committee of the legislature with power to completely investigate the entire charity problem of the city; the societies pushing this discredited investigation, who themselves exist on the contributions of the benevolent; the Department of Public Charities in all its ramifications; the private institutions and hospitals receiving public money; and the State Board of Charities. Then and then only can the full knowledge of the facts be secured, proper legislation to cover the situation be enacted and a real settlement reached.
>
> If the Governor will give personal attention to this important and, as it has been conducted, painful subject, as set forth above, the public can look for impartial action, know the truth about the entire matter and the crooked can be made straight.[61]

Shortly after Farrell's letter was released, an anonymous reply in pamphlet form appeared all over the city. It was a collection of vile and inaccurate headlines and misleading editorial comments from around the country. The publication aroused a storm of protests, particularly when it was revealed that its author was Edward Moree, an officer of the State Charities Association.

A livid Monsignor John Dunn, the chancellor of the archdiocese, ordered that Farrell's letter be printed as a pamphlet. Over seven hundred thousand copies of *A Public Scandal* were distributed on March 15, 1916; they were given out after every Mass at every church in the New York Archdiocese and the Brooklyn Diocese. Father Farrell went on to write three more pamphlets that were widely distributed.

Sensing that the tide was turning in the Church's favor and against the investigation, Mayor Mitchel tried to change the subject by claiming there was a Catholic conspiracy to discredit the Strong Commission. To support his accusations, the desperate mayor ordered wiretaps on Father Farrell and Monsignor Dunn.

When the wiretapping became public, there was a huge outcry. The Thompson Commission, which was investigating public utilities in New York State was given additional authority to get to the bottom of this new scandal.

The mayor, who was subpoenaed to appear, lost his cool before the Thompson Commission. He insisted that there was a conspiracy and said that he would not tolerate religious interference and "that, as Government shall not lay its hand upon the altar of the Church, so the Church shall not lay its hand upon the altar of Government. And let me say that while I am mayor it will not".[62]

Monsignor Dunn and the others who had been wiretapped appeared before the Thompson Commission the day after the mayor and said under oath that the tapes were "forged insinuations". The attorney of the Thompson Commission destroyed the city's case during cross-examination and stated, "The mayor could not indict a yellow dog on such testimony."[63]

A Brooklyn grand jury, on May 23, 1916, indicted Commissioner Kingsbury and his legal counsel, William Hotchkiss. The mayor escaped indictment by one vote. The grand jury also discovered that Kingsbury had approved the distribution of the Moree pamphlet.

When it handed down the indictments, the grand jury declared: "If, as does appear, they [Mr. Mitchel and Police Commissioner Woods] approved of the conduct of those who were responsible for the tapping of the wires in question for no other purpose than to furnish counsel in personal and private litigation with information, and to gratify curiosity, and not for the detection or prevention of crime, the conduct of the Mayor and the Police Commissioner merits the most severe condemnation."[64]

Two months later, Monsignor Dunn, Father Farrell, and two laymen were indicted for perjury and conspiracy to obstruct justice. The defendants were found not guilty, however, because the charges were based on tampered wiretapped recordings.

Charges against Kingsbury and Hotchkiss were later dismissed on the dubious grounds that even though the wiretapping had occurred, the actions had not been committed with "bad faith or evil intent".[65]

The mayor, who hated the Church, now despised even more her leader Cardinal Farley, who had outmaneuvered him. In a letter to Bishop Hayes, Bishop McDonnell, the ordinary of Brooklyn, gleefully reported on the mayor's disposition.

I met a gentleman this noon who tells me that Mayor Mitchel is as mad as a bull in a
china shop at His Eminence.... Whenever he hears mention of the Cardinal's name,
he loses his head and swears at him, how he would like to tear the scarlet robes to
pieces. How much there may be in this statement I cannot say, but his actions and
declarations in the press lead me to believe that there may be much truth in the tale.[66]

Despite all the hoopla, the conclusions and recommendations of the Strong Commission were relatively mild. Strong rejected the Kingsbury claim that Catholic
childcare institutions were "unfit for human habitation". It did, however, endorse
the recommendations of the Kingsbury Commission. Farley accepted many of the
recommendations and laid the groundwork for the creation by his successor of
Catholic Charities.

In the end, the cardinal and New York's Catholic population got the last laugh.
In November 1917, Catholics came out in full force to vote Mayor Mitchel out
of office. He was soundly defeated by Democrat John F. Hylan, with 78 percent of
the votes cast against him. In a letter to the apostolic delegate, Archbishop Bonzano,
dated November 17, 1917, Bishop Hayes happily wrote:

I know that you must have heard from His Eminence of our glorious triumph over
the enemies of the Church in New York at the recent election. The defeat was more
overwhelming than the most sanguine could have anticipated. Our good Catholic
people have been heartened by the result and, without exception, ascribe it to prayer.[67]

One year later, Governor Whitman—grandfather-in-law of future New Jersey
Governor Christine Whitman—lost to a kid from Lower Manhattan's St. James
parish, Alfred E. Smith.

Farley, the Missions, and World War I

While studying in Rome, the young John Farley had learned how the fledgling
Church in America during the nineteenth century had benefited from the financial
aid of many Europeans and South Americans. The United States was considered
mission territory by the Vatican, and international support was encouraged to help
build the presence of the Church.

To show his gratitude, Archbishop Farley took an active role in promoting
financial support of the missions in the Pacific and in Latin America.

At his urging, the national office of the Society for the Propagation of the Faith
moved from Baltimore to New York in 1903. An archdiocesan branch of the society was opened in 1904.

Under Farley's guiding hand, total U.S. annual contributions rose from $3,800 in
1903 to $70,000 in 1908 to $250,000 in 1918.

After the Catholic Foreign Mission Society was founded in 1911 by Father James
Walsh of Massachusetts, Father Thomas Frederick of North Carolina, and Sister
Mary Rodgers of Boston, Farley gave them the money to open their motherhouse
in Ossining, New York, on a knoll dedicated to Mary. Hence, they became commonly known as Maryknolls.

The first man to enter the Ossining seminary was Francis Xavier Ford of Brooklyn. After ordination he traveled to China, where he spent the rest of his life

preaching the gospel and was named a bishop in 1935. In December 1950, he was arrested by the Chinese communists. Accused of being a spy, he was tortured and died in 1952 in a prison in Canton.

President Woodrow Wilson, reelected in 1916 on a peace platform and on the slogan "He kept us out of war", took the nation into war less than a month after his second inauguration.

Tired of German violations of American neutrality, Wilson appeared before Congress on April 2, 1917, and delivered a war message. Four days later, the president signed legislation that approved a declaration of war against Germany and its allies.

To avoid any misconceptions about the Church's stand on the war, the U.S. Catholic bishops published this statement:

> Moved to the very depth of our hearts by the stirring appeal of the President of the United States and by the action of our national congress, we accept wholeheartedly and unreservedly the decree of that legislative authority proclaiming this country to be in a state of war.... We stand ready ... to cooperate in every way possible ... to the end that the great and holy cause of liberty may triumph.[68]

America's senior and most beloved prelate, James Cardinal Gibbons of Baltimore, also spoke out forcefully on the obligation of American Catholics: "The primary duty of a citizen is loyalty to country.... It is exhibited by an absolute and unreserved obedience to his country's call."[69]

The Church took an active role in ministering to Catholic troops and created the National Catholic War Council (NCWC), which raised millions from parishes to help meet the costs of providing spiritual services. In addition, the Supreme Knight of Columbus, James Flaherty, received approval to establish a Catholic version of the YMCA. The Knights set up more than 250 facilities overseas and 350 domestic ones; these clubhouses provided recreational, spiritual, and social aid to Catholic soldiers.

Over 1.1 million Catholics put aside ethnic animosities and allegiances and joined the armed forces. While the Catholic population in 1917 represented about 15 percent of the nation, more than 20 percent of the troops who served during the war were members of the Church.

In New York, Cardinal Farley took an active role in promoting and providing various services for Catholics in uniform. He created a New York branch of the Catholic War Council, and he sponsored a national drive to raise money to finance the activities of the council. The goal of $2.5 million was easily surpassed; in fact, the total hit $5 million.

Farley opened a Soldiers' and Sailors' Club on Thirtieth Street in Manhattan to accommodate and entertain troops on leave. He also established a Young Women's Catholic Patriotic Club on Lexington Avenue and a Catholic hospital dedicated to caring for shell-shocked patients.

When Farley heard that the number of Catholic chaplains permitted to serve would be unfairly limited because outdated religious-affiliation census numbers were being used, he complained by telegram on June 13, 1917, directly to the secretary of war, Newton Baker. He advised the secretary that "justice demands at least that distribution should be made on the same basis for all. I respectfully ask that you see to it that justice is done in this matter..."[70]

Secretary Baker replied two days later, promising that "some equitable solution of the problem can be reached."[71] In response, on June 19 the cardinal sent a letter thanking Baker and reminding him

> that in my judgment the War Department could render no greater service to the Catholic soldiers enlisted or to be enrolled in the National Army, than by providing an adequate corps of chaplains of their faith. These men will do their duty with greater spirit and enthusiasm when fortified by the presence of a priest. When they face the dangers of battle, they want to be at peace with God. The priest of God can only bring this peace to their souls, and only one who knows the Catholic heart can understand what it means to the Catholic soldier to have the priest at his side in battle.[72]

Farley's position was to prevail, and the Church in America was able to supply more than enough priests to minister to the needs of Catholic soldiers.

The Holy See announced on November 24, 1917, that it had created a nonterritorial U.S. Military Diocese that was to be headquartered in New York at 142 East Twenty-Ninth Street. Farley's auxiliary bishop, Patrick Hayes, was named Episcopus Castrensis, "Bishop of the Camp"—in other words, he was to be the ordinary of the new diocese.

Upon taking office, Hayes divided the nation into five vicarates, and he appointed one vicar-general, located in France. With the financial help of the Knights of Columbus, he was able to increase the number of Catholic chaplains from 16 to 1,023 by the war's end. New York supplied 87 priests—far exceeding its quota of 49.

Cardinal Farley not only encouraged his priests to join the armed services, but he also urged his flock to support the war by buying Liberty Bonds. In a speech he gave to the Catholic Club, he described the role Catholics had played in previous U.S. wars and told his listeners that "this war is in defense of the democratic principles of government under which we have lived and prospered." Congratulating them for the success of the club's Liberty Bond drive, he said, "You have your Liberty Bonds, diplomas of a school record of sacrifice and patriotism."[73]

On July 8, 1918, the three American cardinals, Farley, O'Connell, and Gibbons, issued a joint statement asking all Americans to pray three times daily "for the guidance of our rulers, the unity of the nation and the welfare of heroes". In the appeal, which was entitled "Fight and Pray", the cardinals declared, "If we fight like heroes and pray like saints, soon will America overcome mere force by greater force and conquer lust of power by the noble power of sacrifice and faith."[74]

One priest who became a chaplain was Father Francis Patrick Duffy, who had served for fourteen years (1898–1912) as a popular philosophy teacher at Dunwoodie and was a founding editor of the ill-fated *New York Review*.

Duffy became the chaplain of the famous "Fighting Irish" Sixty-Ninth Regiment from New York, led by Colonel William "Wild Bill" Donovan, who was awarded the Medal of Honor. Duffy was the poster face for chaplains in the war, and he was decorated by the American, French, and Canadian governments.

It is worth noting that Duffy was not a favorite of either Cardinal Farley or Bishop Hayes, and if they had suspected he was to achieve great fame in France, they might have kept him on as pastor of Our Savior Church in the Bronx.

Duffy, who was boisterous and aggressive and who towered over Farley and Hayes, appears to have rubbed them the wrong way. But apart from any personal dislike, the *New York Review* crisis would have colored their attitudes toward him in any case.

There is ample evidence to confirm this contention. In March 1913 the Canadian apostolic delegate had sent a letter to Farley concerning Father Duffy, who was a native of the Diocese of Peterborough in the Province of Ontario. "I should wish", Archbishop P. F. Stagni wrote, "to consult him as to the merits of certain priests proposed for that vacant See, whom he very probably knows, and I should be grateful if Your Eminence would tell me, if his judgment on such a grave matter would be of such conscientious and judicious character that reliance could be placed upon it."[75]

In a reply dated March 4, Farley gave this startlingly blunt assessment and recommendation:

> He is a priest of good parts and very intelligent; but as to his judgment in the matter of the choice of a bishop, I should hesitate to attach much weight to his opinion. He has shown for years a strong leaning towards the liberal tendency of the time called Modernism. He may give intelligently his recollections of the priests of the Diocese of Peterborough, but it is very many years since he lived there. As he has been attached to this diocese as student and priest for more than fifteen years, I should think his knowledge and experience of the clergy of Peterborough would not be of much value.[76]

When Patrick Hayes became archbishop of New York, he appears to have maintained the grudge. In March 1933, the year after Duffy's death, Colonel Donovan, who had been the unsuccessful Republican candidate for governor of New York in 1932 and who served as chairman of the Father Duffy Memorial Committee, wrote Hayes concerning the erection "of a memorial to commemorate the life of this wonderful priest and soldier". Donovan outlined the fund-raising plans and invited the cardinal to become a member of the group, which included Governor Al Smith, General Douglas MacArthur, and other notables.[77]

Hayes, replying in a letter dated April 3, 1933, declined the invitation and went on to say, "While I appreciate the thoughts which animate the proponents of the memorial to the late Father Duffy, I am of the opinion that it is hardly an opportune moment to launch such a movement.... I should not like to see such an appeal made to the public in view of hard and cold experience."[78]

One year later, the New York City commissioner of the Department of Public Markets, Antoinette DiNapoli, sent a letter to the cardinal's secretary stating that although she "had been informed that His Eminence Cardinal Hayes no longer had any interest in a memorial to Father Duffy ... will [you] be so kind as to advise me who the Chairman of the Committee is?" She received this terse reply from Father John Casey: "I wish to inform you that His Eminence, the Cardinal, is not in charge of the proposed memorial for the late Father Duffy. I really do not know who is handling this matter."[79] Frankly, this is disingenuous, because "Wild Bill" Donovan was not a man one was likely to forget, particularly in New York Catholic circles.

Despite Cardinal Hayes' attitude, the money was raised, and the statue, which stands to this day in Times Square, was to be unveiled at 3:00 P.M. on Sunday, May 2, 1937—the birthday of Father Duffy.

At an event that notables from around the nation were expected to attend to honor America's best-known Catholic priest, Cardinal Hayes declined to give the main address. In a letter to the chairman of the dedication committee, he said, "While appreciating your very courteous invitation ... I regret very much to say it will be impossible for me to accept, due to the fact that some time ago I made two very important engagements for that day. It would not be possible to cancel them." Hayes designated Monsignor Lavelle to represent the archdiocese.[80]

Farley's Last Illness

Throughout America's involvement in the First World War, Cardinal Farley was visibly ailing. In May 1917, he underwent surgery, followed by a slow recovery. The apostolic delegate, Archbishop John Bonzano, wrote to Bishop Hayes that he had apprised Pope Benedict of Cardinal Farley's condition and expected the Holy Father to contact Farley "to cheer His Eminence and aid him on his road to recovery".[81]

The cardinal was able to carry on his duties for several months, but by the spring of 1918 he began to weaken and contracted pneumonia. He made his last public appearance in May at the consecration of a new cemetery, Gate of Heaven in Hawthorne, New York.

By August he was confined to his bed, and to escape the summer heat he convalesced at a home in Orienta Point, Mamaroneck, in Westchester County.

In regular reports to the apostolic delegate, Farley's secretary briefed him on the cardinal's condition. On August 25, 1918, he wrote that there appeared to be some improvement.

> Today the Cardinal's appetite returned. We gave him some champagne, and after that he took a dish of oatmeal, an egg and a cup of tea, remarking that it was an old-fashioned breakfast. At noon he had another glass of champagne, some soup with an egg, and another egg with a piece of bread and butter. This was most encouraging. He is much stronger and not quite as restless. He slept for two hours this afternoon and has been somewhat restless since. I have just come from his bedside where I have been assisting the sister for the past hour and a half in quieting him.[82]

While Farley's lungs were clearing up, the physicians were now concerned about his weak heart. "Powerful heart stimulants" did not appear to be helping his recovery.

Cardinal John Farley died on September 17, 1918, in the sixteenth year of his administration. Fifty cars accompanied the hearse that contained his body on the drive from Westchester County to St. Patrick's Cathedral. Tens of thousands lined the route to bid him farewell. More than five hundred thousand viewed his body in the cathedral.

More than ten thousand people—including three cardinals, forty-two archbishops and bishops, and twelve hundred priests—attended the Solemn Requiem Mass on September 25, 1918. Cardinal Gibbons presided; Archbishop Bonzano was the main celebrant, and the bishop of Rochester, Thomas Hickey, delivered the homily. After the Mass, Farley was laid to rest in the crypt below the cathedral's main altar.

Bishop Hickey eulogized the cardinal as "a true leader of men, simple in his manners, a personification of faith, hope and charity, a master in administration and in gathering about him zealous and efficient priests for the management of this greatest diocese in the world".

Hickey also commented on the war, reminding the mourners that the nation needed "a solid foundation of victory in the great war to assure the rights of free people". He further stated that "the great agency of the Catholic Church had stood behind the President in the country's patriotic and relief movements [and] the foremost among the leaders in this cause was Cardinal John Farley of New York."[83]

6

The Bureaucrat

Patrick Joseph Hayes
Fifth Archbishop of New York
(1919–1938)

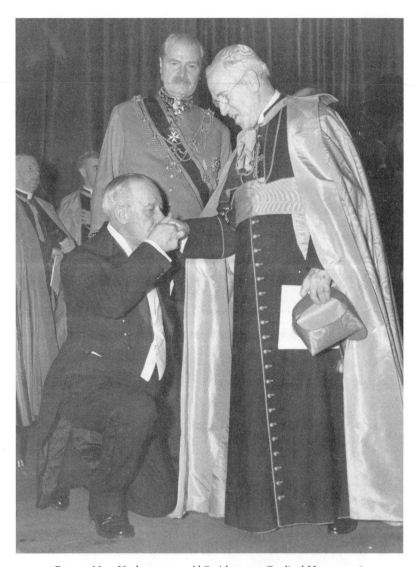

Former New York governor Al Smith greets Cardinal Hayes, 1938

Choosing a new bishop for an open see was streamlined by Pope Benedict XV in 1916. He abolished the procedures established by the Third Plenary Council, under which Farley had been proposed in 1902. Under the new rules, a list of three candidates was to be sent to Rome by the bishops of a given province every two years. Patrick Joseph Hayes was at the top of the last list compiled before Farley's death.

It appears that Farley had lobbied for Hayes. In his homily at Cardinal Farley's Requiem Mass, the apostolic delegate, Archbishop John Bonzano, told the faithful in St. Patrick's Cathedral that it was Farley's "earnest wish" that Hayes succeed him.

Although the ever-ambitious cardinal archbishop of Boston, William O'Connell, floated his own name as a candidate, the Holy Father, amidst the chaos of World War I—which would not draw to a close until a month and a half after Farley's death—made the sensible choice and turned to Hayes.

On February 16, 1919, the Vatican officially announced the Hayes appointment. He was installed by Archbishop Bonzano at the cathedral on March 19, the feast of St. Joseph. Monsignor Joseph Mooney, the administrator during the interregnum, welcomed Hayes on behalf of the clergy of the diocese, and New York Appellate Court Judge Victor Dowling spoke for the laity. Hayes insisted that the ceremony and festivities be low-key because it was Lent. On May 8, he was invested with the pallium by Archbishop Bonzano.

The fifth archbishop of New York was very different from his predecessor. He was shy, not a scholar, and not a great orator (he rarely spoke from the pulpit), and he had very little pastoral experience. He avoided publicity, had no interest in attending social events or courting New York's power brokers and elites, and he strove to avoid the political arena.

When it was announced on March 6, 1924, that there was to be a papal consistory solely to elevate two Americans to the College of Cardinals—Patrick Hayes and his school chum, George Mundelein—the New York cardinal-elect insisted there be no public fuss. He left quietly for Rome on a steamer, received his red hat, celebrated Mass at his titular church in Rome, Santa Maria in Via, and left for home seven weeks later as quietly as he had come.

Upon his arrival in Lower Manhattan, he had no choice but to participate in the parade in his honor from city hall to St. Patrick's, but he insisted on no great parties or fancy receptions. Reflecting on his elevation to the College of Cardinals, he told his fellow New Yorkers: "My thought is one of deepest gratitude for the honors given to one so humble, who would choose rather to serve in the ranks than in a superior position. But God called me, and in response to the command of the Holy Father, I came to receive the high dignity with chastened soul.... In this moment of joy my soul turns in prayer, gratitude, and affection to the glorious country of which I am proud and happy to be a citizen."[1]

Hayes, who rarely accepted social invitations but instead worked at his desk late into the night, changed his policy after he received his red hat. "I'll make the rounds," he explained, "so they won't think success has gone to my head."[2] After several weeks of making appearances at various events, however, he suddenly stopped, insisting he was "too busy".

Comparing Hayes with his former boss, historian Charles Morris observed, "Farley seems to have been a well-balanced man, with many friends, while Hayes was narrow, cautious and constrained."[3] The noted New York Catholic historian and longtime seminary teacher Monsignor Florence Cohalan (1908–2001) described Hayes this way:

> [Hayes was aware] of his own limitations, and [had] an understandable desire to avoid unnecessary involvement in areas in which he was unsure of himself and had no special interest and competence.... He had all and more of Cardinal Farley's caution and Archbishop Corrigan's lack of interest in matters that lay outside the immediate concerns of a diocesan bishop. He was in fact a man of narrow range who had one major, overriding, and almost exclusive interest, Catholic Charities, to which he was drawn by a strong natural attraction, by experience, by his recognition of its great and growing importance....
>
> Though he was less gifted than any of the preceding archbishops, he had strengths of his own. In his chosen field, in which he felt entirely at ease, he moved with a sureness of touch, a clear view of his goals, a grasp of principles, an eye for detail, a talent for organization, and an unwearied interest that made him a resounding success.[4]

Early Life

Patrick Joseph Hayes was the first archbishop of New York who was a product of the streets of Manhattan.

The first of two sons, Patrick was born on November 20, 1867, to Irish immigrants from County Kerry. The Hayes family lived at 17 City Hall Place, a street in the notorious crime-and-poverty-ridden Five Points neighborhood in Lower Manhattan. Patrick was baptized at St. Andrew's Church on Duane Street on the feast of Christ's Presentation in the Temple.

After his mother, Mary Gleeson Hayes, died in June 1872, Patrick's longshoreman father, Daniel, remarried, and his second wife gave birth to a daughter. Finding it difficult to support a household with three children, Daniel asked his sister-in-law, Ellen Gleeson Egan, and her husband, John, to bring up Patrick in their home. The Egans, who lived in a tenement on Madison Street and owned a grocery store, were delighted to take Patrick in, and they provided a fine home life for him.

Since St. Andrew's parish did not have a grammar school, Patrick attended the one at the neighboring Transfiguration parish. In 1883 he entered the Christian Brothers' De La Salle Institute on Manhattan's Second Street. The small, shy Hayes was a good student who took seriously his religious instruction. He was often protected from schoolyard bullies by a large German-American lad, George Mundelein, who came from future governor Al Smith's home parish, St. James on James Street. Mundelein, who would be a lifelong friend of Hayes, was destined to become the first cardinal archbishop of Chicago.

Both Hayes and Mundelein were enrolled in La Salle's accelerated program and completed their studies in three years. In 1886, the two pals went on together to the Christian Brothers' Manhattan College, then on Broadway at 133rd Street. Hayes was elected president of Manhattan's student organization.

After graduation in 1888, Hayes, as his aunt Mary would proudly say, "got the calling" and entered St. Joseph's Seminary in Troy. Mundelein studied for the priesthood at St. Vincent's Seminary in Latrobe, Pennsylvania.

Recognizing that Hayes was one of the star pupils in his class, Archbishop Corrigan ordained him two years ahead of his confreres, on September 8, 1892, so he could receive additional theological training. Corrigan wanted to send Hayes to the North American College in Rome, but Hayes declined that opportunity in order to be closer to his aging aunt and uncle. Instead, he went to the Catholic University of America in Washington, D.C., where he earned a licentiate of sacred theology.

He was called back to New York in 1894 and had the good fortune to be assigned as curate to St. Gabriel's parish, where Monsignor Farley was still the pastor.

Farley, impressed by the young priest's work ethic and attention to detail, took Hayes under his wing and taught him the ways of the archdiocese. Little did Hayes know that he and his mentor were to be close collaborators for the remainder of Farley's life.

After Farley was consecrated an auxiliary bishop in 1895, he named Hayes his secretary. Appointment to this position, which Hayes was to hold until 1903, not only was a great honor for the twenty-eight-year-old, who had been a priest for only three years, but also revealed Farley's confidence in his protégé.

Hayes was named chancellor of the archdiocese in 1903, soon after Farley became archbishop. He was also appointed president of the newly established minor seminary, Cathedral College, which was structured to educate prospective priests for six years—four years of high school and the first two years of undergraduate studies.

As chancellor, Hayes proved to be an able manager. He reorganized the administrative arm of the archdiocese. He made it his job to acquaint himself with every priest in the archdiocese and to visit every parish. At the preparatory seminary, he spent time with every student, kept track of their progress, and identified talented men on the road to ordination.

When Farley was elevated to the College of Cardinals in 1911, it was Hayes who organized the celebratory events and accompanied him to Rome for the consistory.

Hayes collaborated with Farley in advancing the publication of the *Catholic Encyclopedia*. He penned several entries and contributed several articles to the *Catholic University Bulletin* and the *North American Review*.

Pope Pius X named Father Hayes a domestic prelate in 1907, and in 1914, while traveling with Farley in Rome, Hayes learned that he was to be named auxiliary bishop of New York and titular bishop of Tagaste. Getting a second auxiliary for a U.S. see was unheard of at the time, but the cardinal had managed it, and on October 28, 1914, Hayes was consecrated by Farley and two co-consecrators, Bishop Henry Gabriels, ordinary of the Ogdensburg Diocese, and New York's other auxiliary, Bishop Thomas F. Cusack.

In July 1915, Hayes replaced Cusack as pastor of St. Stephen's on East Twenty-Eighth Street, where Edward McGlynn had once been pastor. He was, however, unable to devote much time to his parish duties because of Farley's declining health and America's entry into the First World War.

To serve American Catholic troops, Pope Benedict XV announced in November 1917 the creation of a military ordinate and appointed Hayes the bishop ordinary of the armed forces. This diocese was to include bases throughout the United States and wherever in the world American Catholic soldiers, sailors, and chaplains were stationed.

Additional wartime duties for Hayes included serving on the executive committee of the National Catholic War Council and as director of United War Work.

These two groups coordinated the activities of the fifteen thousand Catholic organizations that contributed to the war effort.

As bishop-chaplain, Hayes visited military camps throughout the nation and spent plenty of time in Washington, D.C. He became acquainted with many Protestant leaders as well as federal and state elected and appointed officials. He hit it off with the assistant secretary of the navy, fellow New Yorker Franklin Delano Roosevelt, and the two became good friends.

Bishop Hayes was scheduled to travel to Europe in the fall of 1918 to visit troops at the battlefront but was forced to cancel when news reached him that the ailing cardinal was close to death. At 4 A.M. on September 16, Hayes administered extreme unction to his confrere. Shortly afterward, Farley became unconscious, and he died peacefully the following day.

Farley and Hayes had collaborated for twenty-four years. Farley had become so dependent on his auxiliary that he refused to let him go when he was told in December 1915 by the apostolic delegate that Hayes "has been presented as 'dignissimus' on the terna for the vacant See of Los Angeles–Monterey".[5] It was made clear that Farley could "not be deprived of so valid and able an assistant".[6]

Archbishop of San Francisco, Edward Joseph Hanna sent Farley a letter apologizing for proposing Hayes' name for the California see. "That I could willingly cause you pain is unthinkable for my affection for you is great", Hanna wrote. "That I brought grief to you causes me sorrow and I humbly [seek] pardon."[7]

Archbishop Hayes and Catholic Charities

Archbishop Hayes' primary talent was administration, and he used his skills to bring the archdiocese into the twentieth century.

As auxiliary bishop, Hayes had been at the center of the ruckus with the city and the state over the conditions of private charitable institutions, and he had learned a lot from that experience. He realized that the lack of supervision over the 175 Catholic charitable enterprises throughout the archdiocese—which included twenty-six hospitals, twenty childcare institutions, twenty-four day-care centers, and five homes for the aged—could mean trouble.

Accordingly, at the annual diocesan retreat for the clergy in 1919, Hayes announced that he had hired a group of professionals to take a survey of the missions, policies, practices, organization, finances, and accounting procedures of all the diocesan charitable and social institutions and facilities. The directors of the project were to be John Lapp, LL.D., who was noted for his survey of Ohio recipients of state pensions and social insurance; the Reverend Robert Keegan, who had been the archdiocesan secretary for charities; and the Reverend Bryan J. McEntegart, who had been a priest for only two years but had an academic background in social work. (McEntegart went on to be the head of the Catholic Near East Welfare Association, rector of the Catholic University of America, bishop of Ogdensburg, and bishop of Brooklyn.)

Later in the year, at a meeting of the four hundred key employees of Catholic charitable works, Hayes outlined the purpose and scope of the study. He made it clear that the undertaking was to be a constructive one and not a "gotcha" investigation.

The aim, he declared, "was to learn the full scope of the work carried on through the churches, agencies, and institutions, the methods used, the limitations felt, and the improvements needed".[8]

The questionnaire that was sent out during the winter of 1919–1920 was designed to gather information on childcare, hospitals, relief, delinquency, recreation, and other activities. The recipients of the survey must have grasped immediately the importance of the project. The Catholic Charities Diocesan Survey stationery, which listed the directors and committee members and gave the address of the project as 375 Lafayette Street in Lower Manhattan, also stated in bold print:

> Under the Supervision of
> The Most Reverend Patrick J. Hayes, D.D.
> Archbishop of New York

The completed surveys, which had to be filed by February 15, 1920, were analyzed by forty-two employees. The two-hundred-page general report that was presented to the archbishop revealed three key weaknesses in the status quo:

1. There was a lack of coordination or understanding between agencies operating in the same field.
2. In a great many places, there was a lack of sufficient funds to carry on the work according to the ideals of those in charge.
3. In every division, there were great uncovered areas where charitable works were needed.[9]

The study also determined that combined total annual revenue for charities was $6.8 million, of which $2.6 million came from subsidies from the New York State government.

To fix this flawed hodgepodge and to eliminate inefficiencies and duplicative services, the committee recommended that all the agencies be united under a central diocesan office "to do the work which was formerly neglected, to improve that which was poorly done, to extend Catholic services and influence wherever [they were] needed".[10] The other significant recommendation was to design a fund-raising program that would involve the laity to help finance these agencies and institutions.

At the June 12, 1920, meeting of the Federated Catholic Societies, Archbishop Hayes, as keynote speaker, announced that he had ordered a complete reorganization of the 175 service agencies under the supervision of a new entity, which had already been incorporated: The Catholic Charities of the Archbishop of New York, which was to be located on East Twenty-Second Street. Hayes would serve as president and Father Keegan as executive director. There were to be six divisions—health, families, children, social action, protective care, and finances. Each would be headed by a director, who would have supervisory authority over all the agencies within the division.

When he began his efforts to unify Catholic philanthropic activities, Hayes wrote down the some of the program's postulates and purposes:

God is Charity
Roof of the Homeless
Heal the Sick
Save the Boy
Protect the Girl
Charity is Kind[11]

To maintain the new Catholic Charities' Catholic identity, to avoid letting it become an adjunct of the government, and to ensure that relief did not become "a state or city function without any higher ideal than an economic or social one", Hayes immediately implemented the fundraising recommendation by establishing the Archbishop's Committee of the Laity.

To meet the goal of securing 100,000 pledges of financial support, Hayes divided the archdiocese into 16 districts. A priest-manager for each district was charged with identifying a thousand laymen who would commit their time, talents, and treasure to securing pledges from their fellow parishioners. The organization of the parishes was a great success. The annual goal of $500,000 to aid Catholic services was easily met, and more than 233,000 people made pledges. In the first three years, more than $2.6 million was donated by Catholic laity. The number of pledgers would grow annually until the Depression struck in 1929.

To strengthen further the bond between the Church and the needy and to relieve overcrowded hospitals, Hayes encouraged religious sisters and laywomen to visit the sick and the poor at their homes. He promoted a new religious congregation known as Parish Visitors, founded by Mother Mary Teresa Tallon. Women trained in social work at the School of Social Service of Fordham University went out day and night, dressed in simple dark clothes, and visited the sick and the needy in the city's tenements.

To avoid abuses in the system, trained professionals were hired as administrators and planners to coordinate and consolidate services in each division. The finance division carefully monitored spending. The result was that administrative costs were kept at about thirteen cents for every dollar raised. In other words, eighty-seven cents of every budgeted charity dollar was spent directly on the needy. By any standard, this was an excellent ratio.

Hayes not only enkindled his people's hearts for Christlike service, but his Catholic Charities became the model for the nation. In its 1920 annual report to the New York state legislature, the state board of charities described the formation of Catholic Charities as "the most significant and important event of the year in the field of charitable work".[12]

Hayes the administrator thrived when he was studying reports, creating new committees and programs, and examining plans and proposals to expand diocesan facilities. Believing that "general literature has of late degenerated swiftly and terribly" and that "the country is deluged with obscene and immoral publications",[13] he founded the Cardinal's Literature Committee, which twice a year released reviews of recently published books. The Catholic Theatre Movement, founded by Cardinal Farley, continued to publish its views on new Broadway plays. Hayes also supported the work of the Legion of Decency, a national organization founded in 1933, which gave guidance to the faithful on motion pictures.

He encouraged the Legion to move its headquarters from Chicago to New York in 1936.

Other organizations in the archdiocese that received his approval were the Catholic Lawyers Guild (1927), the Catholic Interracial Council (1934), the Legion of Mary (1935), the Association of Catholic Trade Unionists (1937), Dorothy Day's Catholic Worker Movement (1933), and the Catholic Youth Organization (1936).

Hayes and Dunwoodie

As for archdiocesan construction projects, Hayes continued his predecessor's expansion plans and opened sixty-five parishes during his tenure; the Great Depression slowed the momentum significantly, however, and he opened only five during the last nine years of his life. Parish schools totaled 178 when he took office and 218 at the time of his death.

Sadly, one school in which he had lost all interest was St. Joseph's Seminary, Dunwoodie. It has never been exactly clear why he had such a dislike for the place. Historian Monsignor Cohalan speculated that he turned on Dunwoodie because many of the faculty opposed his appointment as archbishop. Others have contended that Hayes thought the facility was too lavish and wanted it to be run more economically.

Upon taking office in 1919, he canceled Cardinal Farley's expansion plans and appointed a procurator, Father John J. Donovan, who was charged with the task of slashing the budget to the bone. Donovan, who had Hayes' solid backing, bullied the rectors and the faculty and imposed draconian cost-cutting measures.

Cleaning services were severely cut, leading to an invasion of rats and mice. The food budget was emasculated, and the quality of meals was so bad that many seminarians fell ill. During the winter, temperatures in the dormitory rooms fell to 38 degrees because Donovan made drastic cutbacks in coal purchases. Many students became ill, and several contracted pneumonia. The library budget was slashed to $500 a year for all purchasing, processing, and maintenance of books.[14]

Complaints to the archbishop from the Sisters of Charity, who managed Dunwoodie's housing staff, and from the rector, John Chatwick, that "the habitable conditions of the seminary [have] been for the majority of the seminarians unbearable",[15] fell on deaf ears. And in 1922, when the rector could not put up with the conditions anymore and offered his resignation, it was accepted. Donovan's reign of terror was to go on for the remainder of the Hayes administration and beyond; he was to stay in the job until 1940.

Hayes had such a low regard for Dunwoodie that, unlike Farley, he spent very little time at the facility and almost no time with his seminarians. When the Vatican cardinal–secretary of state and future pope Eugenio Pacelli visited major U.S. sees in 1936, Hayes was the only ordinary who did not take Pacelli to visit his seminary. The students were only able to wave at Pacelli's passing car when he was on his way to Joseph Kennedy's home in nearby Bronxville.

During one of Hayes' rare visits to Dunwoodie, he was appalled to find grounds littered with cigarette butts and issued an order forbidding smoking. Massive disobedience forced the rector to urge the cardinal to rescind the command, which he did reluctantly.

Despite these awful living conditions, the number of applications to the seminary was unprecedented. By 1931 there were more than three hundred seminarians in residence. The facility was bursting at the seams, but Hayes refused to build additional dormitories.

Though Hayes may have had no love for his seminary, it was still a great period for vocations. In the nineteen years he was archbishop, a record-breaking 656 priests were ordained—an average of 34 a year. The average ordained in the twenty-first century has been fewer than 5 a year.

Indeed, it began to appear that the archdiocese actually had too many vocations. By the late 1930s, Cardinal Hayes was ordaining so many seminarians, about fifty a year, that he did not know where to place all of them. He contacted various pastors and asked them if they needed an extra curate.

A report titled *The Present Problem of Increased Vocations*, written in 1933 by Father Arthur Scanlan, who served as Dunwoodie's rector from 1931 to 1941, caused Hayes to reduce enrollment by about 30 percent by the time of his death. His successor, Archbishop Spellman, continued the reductions, and in 1940 scores of seminarians were booted out because of low academic standing; only eighteen were ordained that year.[16]

The Politics of the Jazz Age and the Rise of Al Smith

The city of bright lights, champagne, and silk hats—that was New York in the 1920s. Walking down Broadway for the first time in 1921, British journalist G. K. Chesterton considered the colorful neon display and proclaimed: "What a glorious garden of wonders this would be to anyone who was lucky enough to be unable to read."

During the Roaring Twenties, Tammany Hall reigned supreme in New York thanks to its gifted leader, Grand Sachem Charles Francis Murphy.

Murphy, who ran New York City politics for a generation, was instinctively conservative. He was also a pragmatist who understood the needs and cultures of the city's diverse immigrant neighborhoods; his machine was built on meeting those needs.

The reign of Boss Murphy begat Al Smith, and it was Smith who, as governor of New York, managed to implement a state agenda that embodied the principle of subsidiarity.

Al Smith was born on the Lower East Side, in the shadow of the Brooklyn Bridge, on December 30, 1873. Upon the death of his father, a manual laborer, the thirteen-year-old Al dropped out of the St. James parish grammar school to take on various menial jobs to help support his penniless family.

For Smith, like so many of his time, the Catholic parish served as the spiritual, social, and educational center of life. The nuns and priests instilled in him a love of God, family, neighborhood, and country as well as a belief in the dignity of work.

After spending long hours rolling fish barrels at the Fulton Fish Market (in later years he would boast that his alma mater was FFM), Smith would spend his leisure time participating in parish plays and oratory contests. And it was at these activities that he caught the eye of a Tammany Hall district leader named Tom Foley.

Hired by the clubhouse as a county process server, Al Smith advanced to become a municipal-court clerk, a state representative, the speaker of the assembly, Manhattan sheriff, and president of the New York City Board of Aldermen. Then, in 1918, he was elected to the first of four terms as governor.

Smith was certainly one of the most colorful politicians during the Roaring Twenties. And he earned the affection of the good-government types as well as the machine pols because he could get things done.

Indeed, his record was remarkable. Hospitals were built to care for crippled children, the deaf and the blind, tuberculosis patients, and disabled veterans. He established a state health laboratory, asylums for the mentally ill, and the state teachers' college. He created a network of parks and beaches from Long Island to Niagara Falls, and he oversaw construction of five thousand miles of roads. Social legislation was enacted that: eliminated sweat shops, regulated child and female labor, established the forty-eight-hour workweek, created workmen's compensation, developed housing projects, regulated milk prices, and consolidated school districts.

Cardinal Hayes became a good friend of Smith and from time to time asked him for a favor—though Smith was not always able to oblige. In January 1927, for example, the cardinal wrote to the governor on behalf of Magistrate Joseph E. Corrigan, who was "a candidate for the vacancy in the Supreme Court, occasioned by the death of the late Judge McIntyre". After endorsing Corrigan's candidacy, the cardinal wrote, "This I do in view of his long services on the bench and for the added reason of his blood relationship to my predecessor, the late lamented Archbishop Corrigan."[17] The magistrate did not get the post.

The cardinal also did his best to protect Governor Smith from potential anti-Catholic outbursts. In 1927, the pope wanted to bestow a papal honor on Smith for his kind reception of the Vatican's legate to the U.S. Eucharistic Congress, Giovanni Cardinal Bonzano (who as Archbishop John Bonzano had been the apostolic delegate to the United States). Governor Smith had welcomed the cardinal, kissed his ring in public, and made him an honorary citizen of New York State.

When asked his opinion on the matter, Hayes, remembering the flak Smith had caught for going down on bended knee before someone perceived by many non-Catholics as a foreign potentate, advised against the honor.

In Hayes' reply to a confidential letter from the apostolic delegate, Archbishop Pietro Fumasoni-Biondi, he wrote: "In my judgment, it would be very unwise for the Holy See to confer any ecclesiastical distinctions.... I fear the political effect of it, not only in this State, but throughout the country, Governor Smith being more than a potential candidate for President."[18]

By 1928, in his eyes and those of his New York supporters, Smith was ready for 1600 Pennsylvania Avenue. The question was whether the national party was ready for him. His heartbreaking experience at the 1924 Democratic National Convention convinced Smith that before the 1928 prize could be his, there was much hard political work to be done.

Democratic kingmaker Jim Farley once stated that "a political convention blows in and out like a ninety-mile gale".[19] In June of 1924 an ill wind fanned the prejudices of the fragmented Democratic Party in the city of New York. The Democratic National Convention, held at Madison Square Garden, was attended by scores of Klansmen and Prohibitionists as well as more sensible rank-and-file delegates.

The convention's highlight came when the polio-stricken Franklin D. Roosevelt, struggling on his crutches, rose to the podium before a stunned and silenced audience that marveled at his courage. The Hudson valley patrician, fully aware of the rigidity and bigotry of many of the delegates, boldly placed in nomination the name of a graduate of the Lower East Side's Fulton Fish Market. He spoke with admiration and closed with these soaring words:

> He has a power to strike error and wrongdoing that makes his adversaries quail before him.... He has a personality that carries to everyone here not only the sincerity but the righteousness of what he says. He is the "Happy Warrior" of the political battlefield ... Alfred E. Smith.[20]

One onlooker recalled that a band struck up "The Sidewalks of New York" and "the crowd just went crazy. Oh, it was stupendous, really stupendous!" But there were those who marched to another song:

> United we stick,
> Divided we're stuck.
> The better we stick
> The better we Klux![21]

These Grand Goblins and Exalted Cyclops proclaimed "America for Americans" and believed that African-Americans, Catholics, and Jews were so many knives pointed at their country's heart. They were particularly appalled when a prince of the Whore of Babylon, Cardinal Patrick Hayes, gave the invocation at the beginning of the convention.

Hayes was well aware of the threat the Klan posed. When he returned to the United States after receiving his red hat only weeks before the Democratic Convention was called to order in New York, he made a statement that generated large front-page headlines in the *New York American*:

INTOLERANCE IS A FOE ALL GOOD AMERICANS SHOULD FEAR
Cardinal Hayes Declares This Evil Must Not Be Allowed to Grow in U.S.

Hayes went after the Klan saying:

> If America now feels compelled to resort to lawless methods against and abuse of the stranger within her gates, such methods as have been advocated and begun by certain groups of the intolerant among us, then she has reached a point of weakness which no patriot has deemed a possibility and which is a more alarming danger signal than anything these foreigners within our gates could show.
> If the Ku Klux Klan is needed, then the faith which is the vast promise of the nation, which has thrilled and splendidly sustains the souls of true American patriots, must be accepted as unjustified.
> I refuse to think that this is true![22]

It was this atmosphere of hate that caused the Democratic Convention to drag on for 103 ballots (and to reject condemnation of the Klan by a vote of 543 to 542).

To break the deadlock between the two leading candidates, Smith and William Gibbs McAdoo, the convention turned to corporate lawyer John W. Davis—who, as historian Robert Murray put it, was "not a Catholic or a machine politician or a believing Protestant or an enthusiastic prohibitionist".[23] In fact, he wasn't much of anything, and the results proved it—in the general election he got 28.8 percent of the vote.

But the problem was not only his lackluster candidacy. Millions of inner-city Catholics and Jews, insulted by the Klan activities at the convention, deserted their party. While some went for Republican Calvin Coolidge, many cast their vote for the Progressive candidate, Robert M. La Follette.

The Klan, meanwhile, was not confined to the backwoods of the Deep South. Chapters appeared in many Northern and Midwestern cities. In New York's second-largest city, Buffalo, the Klan's activities in 1922 had caused significant religious and racial tensions. An imperial official who visited the city that year threatened to help elect the Klan's kind of mayor and told the media:

> Klansmen don't doubt the loyalty, integrity and bravery of Catholics, Jews, negroes [sic] and foreign born persons. We realize that these classes proved themselves good and brave Americans during the recent war and we are not against them. Catholics bar themselves [from the Klan] by their allegiance to the Pope; the Jews because they do not believe in the birth of Christ and negroes [sic] because of their color. We want only Caucasians, who, so far as their allegiance is concerned, have it all confined within the boundaries of the United States. That does not mean that we are opposed to them. We are organized to maintain American principles and are opposed only to lawlessness and lack of Americanism.[24]

In the archdiocese of New York, the chancellor, Monsignor Joseph Dineen, had alerted the New York Police Department in March of 1923 that local Klansmen were "writing threatening letters stating they intend to burn up Catholic churches and schools".[25] To aid the police, several local Catholics joined the KKK "for the purpose of obtaining inside information".[26] With the help of these Catholics, members of the NYPD detective division learned the passwords and secret handshakes and were able to infiltrate meetings. The password in 1922 was "White Supremacy" and in 1923, "American Native".[27]

Though the Klan did not have a significant presence in New York City, it was making inroads in the surrounding counties. In October 1923, Hayes received word that a cross was found burning on the steps of St. Joseph's Church in Middletown, in a rural area seventy-two miles north of the city.[28]

Reacting to such hostilities, State Senate Majority Leader James J. Walker (a future mayor of New York City), with Governor Smith's approval, introduced a bill that would require all secret societies annually to file lists of members, bylaws, and oaths with the New York secretary of state. The proposed law provided a heavy penalty for failure to comply.

While Archbishop Hayes made it a point to avoid publicly lobbying for the legislation, he did make this carefully worded comment when asked about Klan activities in New York: "As a Catholic I do not worry because of the Klan. But as an American citizen I am both ashamed and alarmed. The Catholic Church can stand the Klan but Americans cannot stand the Klan."[29]

The Walker Bill was passed and signed into law by Governor Smith. Although menaced by angry Klan members, New York's highest tribunal, the court of appeals, upheld the constitutionality of the law.

New York's passage of the Walker Bill had a salutary effect all over the United States. It helped discredit the Klan, which by 1929 was in rapid decline.

Meanwhile, Northern and Midwestern Democrats were angry that the aging Southern-populist William Jennings Bryan wing of the Democratic Party had embarrassed them again in the 1924 election. And for them, their urban hero, Al Smith, was the man to lead their party out of the desert and on to victory.

By late 1927, most Democratic pros conceded that the 1928 presidential nomination was Smith's for the taking. His easy 1926 reelection to a fourth term as governor—plus the fact that the national party was financially broke and held minority status in the U.S. Senate, the House of Representatives, and the governorships—made Smith appear invincible.

But just because Smith's 1928 nomination seemed to be in the bag, it did not mean that everyone—including many Democrats—was pleased. Supporters of Governor Smith were accused of forming an "alien Catholic conspiracy to overthrow the Protestant, Anglo-Saxon majority under which the country has achieved its independence and its greatness".[30]

The gauntlet was first thrown publicly by New York corporate lawyer and Episcopalian Charles C. Marshall in an April 1927 *Atlantic Monthly* article, "An Open Letter to the Honorable Alfred E. Smith".

In the essay, Marshall quoted reams of ancient papal encyclicals and bulls that included pronouncements on the Church's temporal and spiritual authority over her members. Marshall asked Smith to explain to Americans how these doctrines would affect his public-policy decisions. He also asked how a Smith presidency would handle Catholic parochial schools, nonchurch marriages, and foreign-policy conflicts with Catholic nations.

Smith's first reaction was to ignore the article. He told his staff, "I've been a devout Catholic all my life and I never heard of these bulls and encyclicals and books."[31] But Smith's senior advisors successfully argued that the Marshall article could not go unchallenged.

For help in drafting a reply Smith turned to his Jewish friend Judge Joseph M. Proskauer, who insisted on the help of a knowledgeable Catholic priest. Although Hayes had said, "I would give almost anything to see Al Smith President of the United States but I can take no part in a political campaign",[32] he did give the green light for Father Francis Duffy to give Smith a hand.

Hayes also read the text of the reply and said it was "good Catholicism and good Americanism".[33] To give the Vatican a heads-up, he sent a copy before its publication to his friend Cardinal Bonzano, a member of the Curia. The former apostolic delegate to the United States pronounced it *un capolavoro*—"a masterpiece".[34]

The May 1927 issue of the *Atlantic Monthly* published Smith's essay, titled "Catholic and Patriot: Governor Smith Replies". Smith refuted Marshall's charge that there existed "a conflict between his religious loyalty to the Catholic faith and his Patriotic loyalty":

What is this conflict about which you talk? It may exist in some lands which do not guarantee religious freedom. But in the wildest dreams of your imagination you cannot conjure up a possible conflict between religious principle and political duty in the United States, except on the unthinkable hypothesis that some law were to be passed which violated the common morality of all God-fearing men. And if you can conjure up such a conflict, how would a Protestant resolve it? Obviously by the dictates of his conscience. That is exactly what a Catholic would do. There is no ecclesiastical tribunal which would have the slightest claim upon the obedience of Catholic communicants in the resolution of such a conflict.[35]

As Cardinal Gibbons said of the supposition that "the Pope were to issue commands in purely civil matters." As to choosing between a conflicting political and religious duty, Smith said: "I have taken an oath of office nineteen times. Each time I swore to defend and maintain the Constitution of the United States.... I have never known any conflict between my official duties and my religious beliefs."[36]

And Smith summed up his credo as an American Catholic politician with these sentiments:

My personal attitude, wholly consistent with that of my church, is that I believe in peace on earth, good will to men, and that no country has the right to interfere in the internal affairs of any other country. I recognize the right of no church to ask armed intervention ... merely for the defense of the rights of a church.... I believe in the worship of God according to the faith and practice of the Roman Catholic Church. I recognize no power in ... my Church to interfere with the operations of the Constitution of the United States for the enforcement of the law of the land. I believe in absolute freedom of conscience and equality of all churches, all sects, all beliefs before the law.... I believe in the absolute separation of Church and State.... I believe that no tribunal of any church has any power to make any decree of any force in the law of the land, other than to establish the status of its own communicants within its own church. I believe in the support of the public school as one of the cornerstones of American liberty,... [and] in the right of every parent to choose whether his child shall be educated in the public school or in a religious school supported by those of his own faith.... And I believe in the common brotherhood of man under the common fatherhood of God.

In this spirit I join with fellow Americans in a fervent prayer that never again will any public servant be challenged because of his faith.[37]

Though the essay was well received in many political circles, Smith was premature in concluding that it would "end all whisperings and innuendo".[38]

At the 1928 Democratic Convention in Houston, Franklin Roosevelt nominated the Happy Warrior for the second time. Smith received more than two-thirds of the delegate vote on the first ballot and selected "dry" U.S. Senator Joseph Robinson of Arkansas as his running mate.

The convention, however, was not completely harmonious. While the platform contained a "dry" plank, Smith made it clear that he was "wet" and would support modifications of the Volstead Act.

The campaign of 1928, which matched Smith against Herbert Hoover, was one of the most vicious in American history. Because he was Catholic and of tenement origins, Smith had to endure virulent attacks across America from people of every walk of life. In the South and the West, Smith was portrayed as the first citizen of America's leading brothel—the city of New York. As historian Lawrence Fuchs put it, "New York was to millions of Americans the home of sin. It was where Catholicism, Tammany and liquor coalesced in the person of Al Smith. Smith was an acknowledged drinker, ring-kisser and a proud and loyal son of Tammany."[39]

Smearing the character of Smith and his family was also a popular tactic. In pamphlets and sermons, Smith was often described as a drunkard. Rumors were spread that he was loaded when he delivered his speech accepting the Democratic nomination. During campaign stops, word spread that he was inebriated before he got up to speak. Cardinal Hayes found himself dragged into the campaign when an anti-Smith tract appeared that contained a photo of Smith and Hayes on the steps of the cathedral during some public event. The caption under the photo read:

> Picture published in a Roman Catholic newspaper, showing Cardinal Hayes and Governor Alfred E. Smith, with a priest supporting the Governor from behind.[40]

The implication was that Smith was drunk and had to be held up. In fact, the priest was innocently walking behind Smith on crowded church steps.

Hayes would also, from time to time, authorize his secretary, Father Stephen Donahue, to answer on his behalf letters from people around the country concerning Al Smith's relations with the Church.

A typical letter, dated September 28, 1928, was from R. C. Woodward the principal of Haviland Rural High School in Kansas. He asked the cardinal for "an authoritative statement concerning the following assertions":

1. Mr. Smith had to get permission of the Pope before he could be a candidate for President of the United States.
2. The Catholics have arms stored in their churches in preparation for the time when they will be told by the Pope to rise against the Protestants.
3. Mr. Smith as President will be bound first by allegiance to the People and the Catholic Church rather than by his duty as President and as an American citizen.[41]

In his reply, dated October 4, 1928, Father Donahue stated that the cardinal was impressed by Mr. Woodward's "quest for the truth" and "will depart from his general policy of refraining from saying anything connected with the presidential campaign". Donahue went on to write that he was authorized to give these answers to the three questions:

1. This is as absurd as it is false. The Pope has nothing whatsoever to do with the candidacy of Governor Smith, either before his nomination, during the campaign, or after the election.
2. This, again, is as absurd as it is false. Our Churches are wide open to the public for investigation at any time.
3. Governor Smith, if elected, will be bound in conscience by his oath of office just as much as President Coolidge. Mr. Smith's allegiance will be just as

true, as lofty, and as complete as Mr. Coolidge's. In fact, his Catholic faith obligates him in conscience to be loyal in his allegiance to his Country, and any violation of that allegiance would be a sin against the law of God.[42]

The Great Commoner of the Urban Masses fought valiantly to the end, but he could not turn back the tide of religious prejudice. And on Tuesday, November 6, 1928, Smith lost to Hoover, 40.77 to 58.20 percent. Hoover carried the Electoral College 444 to 87.

Though Smith was hurt, angry, and depressed by his rejection at the polls, a careful analysis of the results showed that all was not bleak in his unsuccessful quest for the presidency. Al Smith's 15,000,185 votes significantly exceeded those received by every previous Democratic presidential nominee. In fact, he had double the average of the votes received by other late-nineteenth- and early-twentieth-century Democratic candidates thanks to the turnout of Catholics and Jews in America's inner cities.

The day after the election, Cardinal Hayes sent Smith a handwritten letter in which he said:

> As you stood in the shadow of political defeat, the nobility of your moral stature and the inspiration of your rare statesmanship made a stronger appeal to us all than ever before. . . .
>
> Your historic and memorable campaign is in my judgment more enduring than any [service] you might render, even in the Presidency, in view of the political opposition that necessarily should arise. . . .
>
> You have suffered a temporary loss through your uncompromising loyalty and love of Christ. Rather would you be true to Him than be elevated to any position of honor among men, no matter how exalted.
>
> With assurance of deep affection and with a blessing on Mrs. Smith and yourself, I am, my dear Governor, faithfully yours . . .[43]

Smith, apparently touched by the letter, wrote back to Hayes on November 10:

> Your letter of November 7th came to me as a wonderful word of cheer. I have great faith that the will of God is to be done on earth and I accept the decision, entirely satisfied.
>
> I believe that I justified my nomination by the Democratic Party in the kind of battle that I waged. It was not to be, and I am content. . . .
>
> In the meanwhile, with love and affection of all the family, I am, sincerely . . .[44]

Hayes versus Birth-Control Advocates

As we have seen, Archbishop Hayes was shy and avoided publicity as much as someone in his position could. But when circumstances demanded action, he was willing to enter the arena.

On November 13, 1921, during the meeting of the First International Birth Control Conference, held at Town Hall on West Forty-Third Street in Manhattan, a squad of police arrived and attempted to break up the assembly. The keynote speaker, eugenicist Margaret Sanger, a lapsed Catholic who boldly proclaimed "more children for the fit, less from the unfit", was arrested with several other women on charges of disorderly conduct.

Three thousand women who were in and around the hall followed the police and marched on the station house where Sanger was booked. Later that evening a night-court judge released the prisoner, citing lack of evidence.

The incident made front-page news and included accusations that Monsignor Joseph T. Dineen, secretary to Archbishop Hayes, called the local police captain and insisted the meeting be disbanded.

Though Dineen was present outside town hall and told the press that he was "delighted and pleased" with the arrests and that "decent and clean-minded people would not discuss a subject such as birth control in public",[45] it was never determined if he instigated the raid.

Five days later, Sanger gave her speech, "Birth Control: Is It Moral?" at the Park Theater surrounded by a police guard. Archbishop Hayes had declined Sanger's invitation to send a priest to debate her, but he did not remain silent.

In a statement released to the press on November 21, Hayes denounced the aims of Sanger's American Birth Control League. "As a citizen and a Churchman," he said, "deeply concerned with the moral well-being of our City, I feel it a public duty to protest against the use of the open forum for the propagation of birth control. This I do in no sectarian spirit but in the broader one of the commonwealth."

After refuting the tenets of the Birth Control League, he closed with these comments:

> Our public policy, in the spirit of "safety first," must set its face against the methods of birth-control propaganda....
>
> Confronted with such social problems as the gangster, the drug addict, girl traffic and the like, our welfare agencies, public and private, are sadly depressed to see tolerated for a moment the danger of spreading among our unmarried youth of both sexes the immoral lure of passion and irresponsibility lurking in the present birth control advocacy that aims at making the marriage relation more lustful and less fruitful. Social evils hardly imaginable will follow in quick order and with terrible consequences.
>
> The Catholic Church's condemnation of birth control, except it be self-control, is based on the natural law, which is the eternal law of God applied to man, and commanding the preservation of moral order and forbidding its disturbance. Therefore, the church has but one possible thing to do—namely, to accept and obey the will of the Supreme Lawgiver.[46]

Several weeks later, Mrs. Sanger replied to Hayes' statement, using an argument that baptized Catholic abortion advocates would still use in the late twentieth century:

> There is no objection to the Catholic Church inculcating its doctrines to its own people, but when it attempts to make these ideas legislative acts and enforce its opinions and code of morals upon the Protestant members of this country, then I do consider its attempt an interference with the principles of this democracy, and I have a right to protest.[47]

This clash was not to be the last battle between Hayes and birth-control advocates. In January 1929, after Republican Assemblyman John Remer of Manhattan introduced a bill to legalize contraceptives, Hayes encouraged the National Council of Catholic Women to organize a march on Albany. On February 19, the day of the bill's committee hearing, more than one thousand women opposing the legislation invaded the halls of the capitol.

Father William J. Duane, S.J., the president of Fordham University, testified against the bill and reported to Cardinal Hayes about his meeting with Governor Franklin Roosevelt and the Bronx political boss who was also New York's secretary of state, Edward J. Flynn.

"With both," he wrote in a letter to Hayes, "I urged that they use their influence to kill the Remer bill. The Governor told me that he was, himself, opposed to such a bill. So also is Mr. Flynn, who assured me that he would speak to [key legislators] and engage their support against the measure. I told both the Governor and Mr. Flynn that your Eminence was very much interested in this question. This fact will, I think, urge them to be more diligent in managing the Committee to which the bill has been referred."[48]

The Remer Bill got nowhere in 1929.

Cardinal Hayes took on Margaret Sanger and her followers again in 1935, after the American Birth Control League held a convention at Carnegie Hall on December 2. The delegates passed a resolution "that all agencies administering family relief inform mothers on relief where they may secure medical advice as to family limitations in accord with their religious convictions".[49]

One social worker urged that poor parents who "were too dull to be taught birth control" should be persuaded to accept "voluntary sterilization".[50] Rabbi Sydney Goldstein, chairman of the Commission on Social Justice of the Central Conference of American Rabbis, "deplored the refusal of the Catholic Church to participate in the conference".[51]

Reacting to the convention, Cardinal Hayes did something out of the ordinary for him. He spoke from the pulpit at the cathedral the following Sunday. He described the attendees of the convention as smug "Prophets of Decadence" who "would fly in the face of God and bring ruin and disaster to the land and to the civilization that some among us, at least, still cherish".[52] He continued:

> Who are these people that sit in soft garments and offer affront to the poor? Are they a race apart, superior beings with a special commission to order the lives of others less fortunate in worldly goods than themselves? And the women among them, who would enjoin the poor from motherhood, are they taking over from the poor the responsibilities of motherhood because they are the better able to bear the burden? You know that they are not. The true lover of the poor today and the true social scientist knows that the right approach to the whole problem is not to keep people from having children, but is so to reorder our economic and social structure as to make it possible for people to have children and to rear them in keeping with their needs. Therein lies true social leadership; in birth prevention lies social degradation.[53]

Hayes on the Moral Responsibility of Lawmakers

On another occasion, Hayes unexpectedly made national headlines. It was during a trip in March 1931 to participate in the two hundredth anniversary of the founding of San Antonio by Catholic missionaries.

The senate of the Lone Star State, pleased that a prince of the Church was visiting, by unanimous vote invited Hayes to address the body. From the podium of the packed chamber, the cardinal began his remarks by observing, "You know, I am also a Senator, a member of a Senate which has been at work over one thousand years.... I am proud to say that as I sit in the Senate of the Church, as one of the seventy Cardinals from all parts of the Christian world, under my Cardinal's robe my heart pulsates with true gratitude, because I am also an American citizen, born under the stars and stripes."[54]

After describing the role and influence of prominent Catholics in the American experiment, he reminded the senators that the missionary padres who settled in Texas and laid the foundations of order there "were not animated by any motive nor desire for conquest or worldly gain, but desired simply to serve humanity".[55]

In his closing comments, for which he received a standing ovation, the cardinal seemed to be laying the groundwork for what would become, the following year, the New Deal platform of his friend Franklin Delano Roosevelt:

> No legislation should be formulated which has not for its object, love for others, like unto God's love for us. It should be tinged with mercy, tenderness and consideration of our brothers. In the economic crisis which we are now facing, a stern responsibility is placed upon the lawmakers' shoulders. The problems which are before you must be considered from a humanitarian standpoint, if the democracy to which we aspire, as a nation, is to be realized.[56]

Hayes, the Great Depression, and the New Deal

Seven months after Herbert Hoover was sworn in as president in 1929, the stock market collapsed, and America's economy fell into the greatest and longest depression in the nation's history.

Contributions to Catholic Charities dropped significantly, and the cardinal strove to find ways to do more with less. He also turned to former Governor Al Smith to head up a Special Gifts Committee to solicit donations from the city's wealthy donors, corporations and nonreligious philanthropic foundations.

Despite the hardship, Hayes managed to supply the financial resources to open the Frances Schervier Home and Hospital in Riverdale in 1932, and in 1934 St. Clare's Hospital on West Fifty-First Street in Manhattan.

Hayes, who had solid friendships with both Franklin Roosevelt and Al Smith, stayed out of their battle for the Democratic presidential nomination in 1932. He did try to improve the relations between the two when they sat on either side of him on the dais of the Catholic Charities luncheon that year.

On Inauguration Day, March 4, 1933, Roosevelt told a desperately frightened nation that "the only thing we have to fear is fear itself—nameless, unreasoning, unjustified terror which paralyzes needed efforts to convert retreat into advance."

During the early days of the New Deal, many Catholics voiced support for FDR's programs and argued that they were consistent with traditional Catholic social thought and with positions expressed in recent papal encyclicals. Cardinal Hayes spoke for the Church when he said FDR was "crystallizing the sentiments of the Country in meeting the grave problems [of the depression]". At a Manhattan

College commencement in June 1934, Hayes told the graduates, "We ought to rejoice that everything [Roosevelt] tries to do ... will come to a happy success."[57]

America's Catholic press followed the hierarchy's lead. The conservative *Brooklyn Tablet* described the New Deal as "motivated by a Christian philosophy which moves forward in the right direction".[58] The liberal *Commonweal* declared that "all Catholics who desire to give practical effect to the principles of social justice laid down by Pope Pius XI will see that Roosevelt's opportunity to lead ... is likewise the Catholic opportunity to make the teaching of Christ apply to the benefit of all."[59]

Roosevelt knew that Catholics totaled one-sixth of the nation's population and that they represented the largest bloc of voters in many of America's major cities. Hence, to keep these Catholic voters within his political coalition, FDR stayed in close touch with their political and religious leaders.

When FDR arrived on the campus of Catholic University on June 14, 1933, to receive an honorary doctorate at the commencement ceremonies, he was greeted by his old friend Cardinal Hayes. Before presenting him with his degree, Hayes praised the president for "moving forward with courage and intelligence" in tackling the Depression and said his policies "sprung from one motive, namely, the advancement of the Common Good".[60]

The cardinal went on to deliver a major address on the concept of the common good that reads like a rationale for the programs of the New Deal and an endorsement of the expanded role of the federal government:

> When a major catastrophe endangers the good of all, neither government nor industry nor family life can proceed along the orderly lines of precedent. It is the genius of our government that in times of crisis we can centralize authority and the power to act effectively and quickly. Our people have come to realize that in national crises, as at a fire, one clear, confident voice can save hundreds from panic.
>
> Freedom thus abridged does not mean freedom denied. Power thus delegated does not mean the abandonment of democracy. Rather does it renew our faith in the American form of government, for it means that democracy is able, when necessary, to organize efficiently for an emergency. It gives us another proof that democracy can safeguard the rights of its people and can promote the Common Good even in the face of disaster.[61]

To enhance further his relations with the White House, Hayes invited FDR, in October 1933, to be the keynote speaker at the nineteenth annual meeting of the National Conference of Catholic Charities and the Centenary Celebration of the Society of St. Vincent de Paul, held in New York.

Hayes went on to endorse the ill-fated National Recovery Administration (NRA) enacted in June 1933, stating that it was instituted "to banish the want of recent years and to insure wider employment".[62] He hailed the 1935 Social Security Act, saying, "The security program of our President is ... taking into consideration the preservation and conservation of those principles of action so vital to a man's liberty and man's happiness here on earth."[63]

In league with Cardinal Mundelein, Hayes tried to shut down one of FDR's most outspoken critics, the Reverend Charles Coughlin of the Shrine of the Little Flower in Royal Oak, Michigan. Coughlin, who had a radio program that reached an audience of forty million, had been a strong supporter of Roosevelt in 1932, but by 1936 he was disenchanted. He frowned upon FDR's recognition of the Soviet Union and criticized New Deal programs for being too modest in their aims, and he threatened to topple the president from office in 1936.

As Coughlin's charges escalated, Roosevelt refused to raise the cleric's profile by making any public comments. This did not stop FDR's friends in the hierarchy from speaking out, however. Cardinal Mundelein, with Hayes' blessing, took the lead when he stated that Coughlin "is not authorized to speak for the Catholic Church nor does he represent the doctrine or sentiments of the Church".[64]

However, Coughlin's bishop, Michael Gallagher of Detroit, supported him, and the hierarchy elected not to risk schism by any attempt to discipline him. Coughlin was finally reined in after a meeting between Cardinal–Secretary of State Eugenio Pacelli, Boston Auxiliary Bishop Francis Spellman, and FDR in Hyde Park, in November 1936.

Hayes the Internationalist: Mexico

In 1917, Marxists took control of Mexico and imposed what has been called the Jacobin Constitution. Article 3 of the document declared that the Church was separate from the state but subject to it.

The constitution banned clerics and religious from teaching in secular or Catholic schools and permitted the government not only to define religious worship but also to determine which priests could serve and where.

The government did not immediately enforce these measures, because Mexican authorities feared that doing so would stall official U.S. recognition. But once that recognition was secured in 1923, the new president, Plutarco Calles, started a reign of terror.

First, he tried, albeit unsuccessfully, to create a government-controlled Nationalist Catholic Church headed by a "Patriarch of the Mexican Catholic Church". The dupe who accepted this post, Padre Perez, could convince only two priests and a few hundred laymen to join his schismatic church.

Reacting to the failure of this tactic, the government announced in June 1926 the Ley Calles (Calles Law), a new oppressive penal code that went into effect on July 31. The new law called for the rigorous enforcement of the anticlerical articles of the constitution. Priests could not wear clerical garb or exercise the duties of their office without government approval. Bishops either died in jail or were expelled. Their physical presence in the country was made a capital crime. Only 293 priests were recognized—about one for every 100,000 Catholics. More than 5,000 priests and lay activists were killed. In his novel *The Power and the Glory* Graham Greene said that this suppression of the Church was "the fiercest persecution anywhere since the reign of Elizabeth I."

In the United States, Catholics were appalled by the persecutions. Cardinal Hayes went against his parochial inclinations and took the most active role in preparing the American Church's response.

When the apostolic delegate to Mexico, George Caruana—an American by birth—was falsely charged with entering Mexico illegally and expelled by President Calles in June 1926, Hayes sent separate telegrams to President Coolidge and

Secretary of State Frank B. Kellogg. He urged them to use their influence "with the government of Mexico to prevent the unjust deportation of Archbishop Caruana— himself an American citizen now in Mexico".[65]

Hayes also appealed to prominent Catholic laymen to convince "the American Federation of Labor to withdraw all association from Mexican labor unions". The AFL's participation in a parade in Mexico City, he argued, "committed [it] to [an] antireligious program and by implication commits American Federation to same". Severing ties, he believed, would "go far to stop persecutions".[66]

When the bishop of San Antonio, Arthur Drossaerts, pleaded for help to find parish work in the Northeast for many Mexican priests who had escaped and "flooded our city and Diocese", Hayes made serious efforts to place priests in dioceses across the country.[67]

On July 16, 1926, Cardinal Hayes sent a letter to all the priests of his archdiocese describing the "distressful and dreadful crisis with which the Church in Mexico is confronted". He quoted extensively from a communication he had received from the Vatican secretary of state, Cardinal Pietro Gasparri, and ordered his letter to be read at every Mass on July 25.

In accordance with the instructions of Pope Pius XI, he directed his priests on August 1, the feast of St. Peter in Chains, to recite the Litany of the Saints after the principal Mass, to have the exposition of the Blessed Sacrament after the principal Mass until evening, to invite the faithful to pray in their private devotions for the intention of the Holy Father, and to offer Holy Communion for the Church in Mexico.[68]

The distinguished New York lawyer William D. Guthrie was retained by Hayes in September 1926 to analyze the Mexican constitution. A fifty-three-page booklet penned by Guthrie and approved by the cardinal, called *Church and State in Mexico*, was published on November 26.

Guthrie concluded that the Mexican constitution, illegally imposed on the country's people in 1917, and the 1926 presidential decree enforcing the antireligious constitutional provisions were "in violation of long-established rules of international law and the fundamental principles of liberty and justice which are recognized in all civilized countries, as well as in violation of fundamental and essential principles of constitutional law, as that term is understood among Americans, in that they conflict with American elementary conceptions of liberty, private property, free exercise of religion, and freedom of speech and of the press."[69]

The legal analysis was used in the preparation of a pastoral letter on Mexico that Hayes vigorously pushed for. It was issued on December 16, 1926, by the U.S. hierarchy. Condemning the suspension of God-given rights, the U.S. bishops concluded:

> Because of the fact that the persecution in Mexico is directed against all the principles of religion, we should speak as the servants of God; . . . because it is unloosed particularly against the religion of the majority of the people of Mexico, we should speak as Catholics; there are grave reasons, too, why we have a duty to speak as Americans attached to the institutions of our country and loving them for the benefits they have conferred upon us all. The government of Mexico has, indeed, by its actions in our very midst, made it necessary that we should no longer guard silence, for it has carried its war on religion beyond its own boundaries through organized propaganda in many countries, but especially in our own.[70]

Back in Mexico, when a petition signed by two million Catholics was ignored by the government and a national boycott failed, Anacleto González Flores organized and, in January 1927, led the Cristeros in guerrilla warfare. He took this course of action because he believed "the country is a jail for the Catholic Church.... We are not worried about defending our material interests because these come and go; but our spiritual interests, these we will defend because they are necessary to obtain salvation."[71]

González Flores was captured, tortured, and then executed on April 1, 1927. His last words were: "I die but God does not die." He was beatified by Pope Benedict XVI in 2005.

After the assassination of former president Álvaro Obregón in July 1928, Calles, fearing for his life, began negotiations with the Church. An American priest, Father John J. Burke, secretary general of the National Catholic War Conference, headquartered in Washington, D.C., served as mediator.

Calles agreed to retire, and Emilio Portes Gil took over as chief executive. The *arreglos* (arrangements) of 1929 between Gil and the Church promised the reopening of churches and seminaries, respect for the property of the Church, and general amnesty for the Cristeros. In addition, the president agreed that the anticlerical laws would not be rigidly enforced.

The improved church-state relations were short-lived. Gil stepped down in 1930, and Lázaro Cárdenas, a socialist and mason, became president in 1934. On January 1, 1935, he decreed that all schools must teach the marvels of socialism or be closed. When Catholic parents refused to put up with the requirement and kept their children from school, Cárdenas ordered the enforcement of the anti-Catholic penal laws.

Angered by reports that the Mexican government was once again murdering priests and religious, in July 1935 the Knights of Columbus, led by Supreme Knight Martin H. Carmody, delivered a petition with five hundred thousand signatures to the White House demanding that the United States "make representations to the government of Mexico that unless evils ... are ended forthwith, further recognition of the Mexican government will be withdrawn and diplomatic relations severed".[72]

Always cognizant of the importance of the Catholic vote, President Roosevelt trod softly on this issue. Because there was no agreement or treaty between the United States and Mexico, there was not much the administration could do. The United States, as historian George Flynn wrote, "had no power to act in this case, since it would be an unwarranted intervention in Mexico's domestic affairs".[73]

Trying to make the best of a bad situation, FDR cancelled a planned summer trip to Mexico, and while in San Diego—near the Mexican border—on July 17, 1935, stated that every person should "enjoy the free exercise of his religion according to the dictates of his conscience".[74]

Unimpressed, Catholic newspapers accused FDR of supporting Mexico's anti-Catholic policies. Meanwhile, Cardinal Hayes and Cardinal Mundelein, who had both been very active during the mid-1920s Mexican crisis, stayed on the sidelines this time and tried to limit the damage to their friend in the White House.

Roosevelt's statements on religious freedom sufficed for Hayes, who said, "We have a president who believes in religion and wants his fellow citizens to [do] likewise."[75]

At the University of Notre Dame on December 9, 1935, Roosevelt, who was receiving an honorary doctorate, was publicly praised by Mundelein. The cardinal dismissed the Knights of Columbus' run-in with the president and stated that no one group spoke for all American Catholics. The Washington bureau chief of the *New York Times*, Arthur Krock, "interpreted the entire [Notre Dame] affair as a Catholic endorsement of President Roosevelt and a repudiation of the [Knights of Columbus'] campaign".[76]

The public comments of Hayes and Mundelein helped mute Catholic criticism. When it came to Mexico, they now settled for encouraging words and little action. The frustration of Cardinal Hayes would be even greater in confronting communism.

Hayes and the Soviet Union

The Roman Catholic Church had been steadfast in its condemnation of atheistic communism and the Soviet Union's brutal totalitarian rulers Lenin and Stalin. Prayers were said after every Mass for the "conversion of Russia". And when the White House floated a trial balloon on recognizing the Soviet Union, the bishops used the editorial pages of their diocesan newspapers to express their displeasure. America's premier Catholic newspaper, the *Brooklyn Tablet*, led the charge. When surplus cotton was sold to the Soviet government, the paper vigorously objected. "Dealing with Russia", wrote the *Tablet*, "is a blunder materially, morally and patriotically."[77]

The Knights of Columbus and the National Council of Catholic Men also opposed recognition. They warned their members that a godless state could never be trusted. In Massachusetts these organizations gathered six hundred thousand signatures on petitions condemning recognition.

At the request of the American bishops, a prominent Jesuit, the Reverend Edmund Walsh, prepared a report for the president on religion in the Soviet Union. Walsh warned that "the Soviet Government undertakes to abolish religion itself, the God-idea in its every form and manifestation."[78] He concluded that if the United States recognized Russia without receiving some concessions on the religious-liberty issue, it "would have the practical effect of helping the perpetual conditions that are a matter of public record".[79]

Cardinal Hayes was a staunch anticommunist. As early as April 1921 he had signed the Declaration against the Recognition of the Soviet Union, sponsored by the National Civic Federation, that was presented to President Harding. The declaration's preamble read: "We believe that recognition of Soviet Russia would be a repudiation of all that our national life has represented for a hundred and fifty years, and of all the spiritual ideals for which modern civilization has striven for two thousand years."[80]

During the summer of 1933, when FDR was testing the waters on recognition, the apostolic delegate to the United States, Archbishop Amleto Cicognani, turned to Hayes for information and advice. To convey privately his and Cicognani's concerns to the president, the cardinal turned to the most prominent Catholic in the Roosevelt administration, Postmaster General James Farley.

One such letter, dated July 19, 1933, asked if "the sending of our Minister [to] Sweden, Mr. Steinhardt, to Russia on a special mission is a step toward recognition".[81]

Farley, in a July 27 reply to Hayes—typed on his stationery as chairman of the Democratic National Committee, not his government stationery—gave this evasive answer: "[The President] told me to advise you that Mr. Steinhardt went over there with strict instructions to do nothing except take care of the duties assigned to him in the country which he represents. He, of course, is to keep his eyes and ears open and pass along to the President any information which might be of interest and value to him."[82]

When it appeared recognition was inevitable, Hayes sent his secretary, Monsignor Robert F. Keegan, to meet the President on November 1, 1933, to present a memorandum that covered four topics: "freedom of conscience for Russians and foreigners; freedom of worship, public and private; liberation of those imprisoned for their faith; and cessation of propaganda against God".[83]

A young auxiliary bishop from Boston, Francis Spellman, who was a close friend of Cardinal–Secretary of State Eugene Pacelli, himself got word to the White House that the Vatican would be pleased if FDR would seek assurances from Moscow that it would tolerate religious liberty for the Soviet populace. The ever-confident Roosevelt let Hayes and Spellman know that he was a good horse trader and promised to consider their concerns.

Notes made during a meeting between FDR and the Soviet commissar for foreign affairs, Maxim Litvinov, stated that "the Soviets agreed to permit American Citizens in Russia free exercise of their religion."[84]

While many Catholics were not happy with this bone Litvinov threw FDR, Hayes considered it a victory. Monsignor Keegan, in a letter to the president, congratulated him, writing that "the masterly fashion in which you championed sacred principles which we Americans hold so dear is clear."[85]

It appears, however, that the Vatican was not pleased with the outcome. The apostolic delegate, in a confidential and somber letter dated December 31, 1933, states bluntly the Vatican's reaction:

Your Eminence:

I have just received a letter from Archbishop Pizzardo, Secretary of the Sacred Congregation for Extraordinary Ecclesiastical Affairs, in reference to the recognition of Soviet Russia by the United States Government.

The letter laments the fact that recognition on the part of the United States increases notably the prestige of the Soviet Government and its activities, among which is the propagation of atheism throughout the world. The example of the United States has led the public press of other countries, ex. Gr., Brazil and Czechoslovakia, to urge recognition of Russia along similar lines.

It was hoped that the president, who just prior to the opening of the conferences expressed publicly his appreciation of the moral and religious values of Christianity, would be able to obtain from the Soviet Government guarantees of freedom of conscience and worship and of cessation of atheistic propaganda.

What was actually obtained, restricted as it is to American citizens, is very little indeed, and will have effect only if gradually a certain number of American priests betake themselves to Russia. It is hoped that priests of other nations may be induced to do likewise.

The Holy Father explicitly instructed Archbishop Pizzardo to have me consult Your Eminence as to what steps may be taken to organize, even gradually, the work of spiritual assistance agreed upon in the conferences.

I understand that there will be a large staff of secretaries assigned to the American Embassy in Russia. Perhaps Your Eminence would undertake to suggest to the President that at least one of the secretaries assigned to the Embassy be a member of the Catholic Faith.[86]

On January 16, 1934, a nervous Hayes wrote back that it would be difficult to approach the president directly at this time about a Catholic staff member because "it was quite plain that [FDR] hoped for a favorable comment [from the Holy See] on his earnest efforts which he had made and an appreciation of the assurances which he had secured from Litvinov."[87]

Hayes feared that if he brought up embassy appointments, the president would ask again for the Vatican's reaction, and the cardinal did not want to be the bearer of bad news.

"I am truly at a loss", he concluded, "to know how we could gracefully approach the President with the request."[88]

It would appear, however, that Cardinal Hayes lost a little sleep over this matter, because he sought another route to the president, writing again to Postmaster General Farley.

Six days after his gloomy letter to the apostolic delegate, Hayes happily informed him that Farley had spoken to the president, and he had agreed that a Catholic should be on the Moscow embassy staff and had directed Ambassador William Bullitt to appoint one. In addition, Farley told the cardinal that "in his conference with Mr. Bullitt, the latter seems ... most willing to have a native American priest assigned to take care of the Catholics who may be at this Embassy or any other Catholics in Moscow."

Hayes concluded his letter to Archbishop Cicognani with these optimistic sentiments: "I gathered in the course of the conversation with Mr. Farley that the president is very sincere in his insistence that the Guarantees with regard to Religious Worship be carried out."[89]

The Final Years

In 1932, while attending the International Eucharistic Congress in Dublin, which celebrated the fifteen hundredth anniversary of St. Patrick's conversion of Ireland, Cardinal Hayes suffered a heart attack.

Although he recovered, the heart attack did take its toll, and Hayes began to curtail his activities. He turned to Monsignor Lavelle, the archdiocese vicar-general, and to his own longtime secretary, the Reverend Stephen Donahue, who would become an auxiliary bishop in May 1934 at the age of forty-one. The chancellor, Father Francis McIntyre, handled most of the day-to-day administrative matters.

By 1938 his health was in serious decline, and he spent much of his time convalescing at St. Joseph's Camp in Monticello, Sullivan County. In June, for the only time in his administration, he declined to ordain the Dunwoodie class of 1938. His last public appearance was on June 19, when he presided over a service celebrating the fiftieth anniversary of the death of Father John Christopher Drumgoole, who was known as the patron saint of homeless New York City newsboys.

The cardinal's last official function was at St. Joseph's Camp on August 15, when he said a few words honoring the golden jubilee of the Reverend Mother

Polycarpa, O.P. The cardinal presented to the sister, who managed the camp and the school, a gift of a pearl cross from Pope Pius XI.

On the evening of Saturday, September 3, 1938, Cardinal Hayes retired to his bedroom at St. Joseph's Camp. His priest-secretary found him dead the next day when he went in to awaken the cardinal for his morning Mass. Cardinal Hayes was seventy-one and had served as a priest for forty-six years, twenty-four of them as a bishop and fourteen as a cardinal.

Reacting to his death, the editors of the *New York Times* wrote on September 5, 1938:

> The sincerest tribute which can be paid to the memory of any man is to be mourned by the poor. Cardinal Hayes will be so mourned. He had them always in his heart. He rose from among them and went back among them again and again, ever on errands of mercy and charity. The cold, mechanical benevolence of government charity he deplored. To him donor and recipient must both be bathed in the mystical spirit of love and understanding. His was the understanding bred of poverty itself. The leader of the richest and most influential See in the world, he passes as the great democrat among the Catholic hierarchy of America.[90]

President Franklin Roosevelt said in a statement released from the White House:

> I am deeply sorry to hear of the passing of his Eminence Cardinal Hayes. I had the privilege of his friendship for many long years. His great spiritual leadership has had a deep influence on our generation and all of us who knew him and had sincere affection for him will feel his loss.[91]

The remains of Cardinal Hayes left St. Joseph's on Monday, September 5, at noon, accompanied by Bishop Donahue, who served as administrator of the archdiocese during the interregnum.

On September 6, his body was conveyed to St. Patrick's Cathedral, where he lay in state until the morning of Friday, September 9. Over 350,000 filed past his coffin.

On Tuesday evening the Divine Office was chanted by the priests of the archdiocese. On Wednesday morning a Mass was celebrated for the children of the archdiocese. On Thursday at 10:30 A.M., a Solemn Mass was celebrated by the members of religious orders in the archdiocese. Monsignor Lavelle preached.

The Solemn Pontifical Mass was held on Friday. The main celebrant was Hayes' boyhood pal, Cardinal George Mundelein. The homily was delivered by an old friend and former New York pastor, the Most Reverend Joseph Rummel, who was now archbishop of New Orleans. Rummel reminded the mourners of the important role Hayes had played during the dark days of the Great Depression:

> When the decade of depression and recession came, financial empires tottered and fell, kings of finance lost their crowns, captains of industry their commissions, and rich men became paupers overnight. Although free from neither anxiety nor embarrassment, the Cardinal Archbishop of New York preserved his calmness and confidence, met difficult situations with courage and generosity, and contributed not a little toward stabilizing general conditions, while he guided securely and preserved from disaster the great financial structure that encases the vast spiritual, educational,

and charitable empire called the Diocese of New York. And, incidentally, His Eminence of New York was a tower of strength, who inspired the leaders of the nation and his fellow citizens everywhere with new hope and spirit in their efforts to rebuild the moral as well as the economic life of the nation.[92]

After the Mass, Cardinal Hayes was interred with his predecessors in the crypt below the cathedral's main altar.

Patrick Hayes is justly remembered as the Cardinal of Charities. He devoted his priesthood to serving the poor because he had experienced their plight firsthand while growing up on the Lower East Side. He said of himself, "I was born among the very poor people in the lower part of New York, and my thought and love have always been with these unfortunates. I made up my mind years ago that if I could do anything to give them a new start I would be merely doing what God intended all of us to do."[93]

A month after his death, a young monsignor, Fulton J. Sheen, host of the radio show *The Catholic Hour*, devoted his talk to the memory of the cardinal who had made the inaugural broadcast eight and half years earlier.

Sheen reminded his listeners across the nation that, above all, Patrick Hayes was a priest, "a member of all families yet belonging to none; living in the world and yet not of it; serving the poor not as one giving but as one receiving; lifting man to God in the Consecration and bringing God to man in Communion; going to work from prayer and to prayer from work; being hard on oneself and easy on others; hating sin but loving the sinner; being intolerant about truth, but tolerant to persons; being a priest to others and a victim to Christ. What a vocation! That is the priesthood! That is Cardinal Hayes!"[94]

PART III

The City and the World

7

The Power Broker

Francis Joseph Spellman
Sixth Archbishop of New York
(1939–1967)

Cardinal Spellman greeted by Pope Pius XII in Rome

Francis Joseph Spellman had the good fortune to head the archdiocese during the golden age of the Church in the United States.

When Al Smith ran for president in 1928, Roman Catholics made up 16 percent of the U.S. population. In the post–World War II era, Catholics were major contributors to the baby boom; by 1956 their numbers had increased to 35 million, or 20 percent of the total population. And the Church prospered: more than 60,000 priests served in parishes, 150,000 nuns worked in schools and hospitals, and 12,000 religious brothers served in various ministries. Enrollment in Catholic grammar schools, high schools, and colleges was rapidly growing.

Catholic historian Michael Perko has described the Church in the golden age as "politically and economically powerful". It "exercised a role in American life previously unknown. No longer exclusively the preserve of a prosperous but insignificant minority, or of destitute immigrants, it had become a significant force of American society."[1]

Throughout his record-breaking twenty-eight-year administration, Cardinal Spellman leveraged this power to become the nation's leading religious spokesman and an advisor to presidents, governors, members of Congress, and mayors. His residence at 452 Madison Avenue was rightly called the Powerhouse, and politicians of every stripe visited to seek the cardinal's blessing on bended knee.

What is most interesting is that Spellman did all this even though he was neither a scholar nor a skilled orator—nor, at five feet five inches, plump, and balding, was he a person of impressive appearance or imposing bearing. Nevertheless, as Monsignor Florence Cohalan told the authors (and others who have written about the New York Archdiocese), Spellman's power did not come so much from what he saw in popes or presidents as from what they saw in him.

He had the advantage, Cohalan wrote,

> of being underestimated at first sight.... Only a very superficial observer could miss his intense awareness of his own authority and his determination that it be recognized and accepted by his subordinates on every level.... Few could miss his sense of duty, his capacity for work, his grasp of affairs, his willingness to settle things promptly, his quite exceptional confidence in his own judgment and in his ability to handle any problem that arose.... For the first time, New York had an archbishop who was not only able and willing, but determined to play a leading role in ecclesiastical matters on a national and international level and in public life.[2]

Another of America's leading Church historians, Monsignor John Tracy Ellis, in his memoir of Spellman, *Catholic Bishops*, agreed with Cohalan's analysis. "Beneath the commonplace exterior," he wrote, "there were qualities of a superior order, for example, high administrative talent, shrewdness to a marked degree, sharp intelligence in practical matters, all of which were employed in a dedication to the Church that was never in question."[3]

Early Life

Francis Spellman was born on May 4, 1889, in Whitman, Massachusetts, to William and Ellen Spellman, both the children of Irish immigrants. Whitman, which is twenty miles from Boston, was not an Irish ghetto. It was a classic New England Yankee town, and it did not even have a Catholic Church until 1898.

The Spellmans owned a second-generation grocery store that grew to become Whitman's largest supermarket. Young Francis (*Frank*, as he was known then) and his two brothers and two sisters worked in the store, stocking shelves, handling customers at the checkout counter, and making deliveries.

Frank Spellman grew up in a family that had achieved middle-class status and lived in a large home with a carriage house. The Spellman children attended public schools because there were no Catholic ones in Whitman. On Sundays, they traveled four miles to attend Mass at the Holy Ghost mission church.

Frank enjoyed photography and excelled at ice hockey, boxing, and baseball. He demonstrated early administrative ability when he managed the high school baseball team. For the most part, he was an indifferent student, although he did take an interest in writing and won the top award ($10) in the ninth grade for an essay on the Battle of Gettysburg.

When it came to choosing colleges, Frank turned down a scholarship to Notre Dame and instead chose Fordham University in the Bronx. The big city appealed to him more than rural South Bend. And his mother approved because she had a cousin, Katherine Conway, who lived in Brooklyn and could keep an eye on him.

When Frank tried out for the Fordham baseball team, he found the competition much tougher than at his high school, and he did not make the cut. So he turned to tennis, a sport he played throughout his life and found useful during his climb up the clerical ladder. He also joined the dramatic club and the debating club and wrote for the Fordham *Monthly*.

At the June 1910 commencement, Frank received the Archbishop John Hughes Award for religion. At his own graduation, on June 14, 1911, his bachelor of arts diploma was handed to him by another Fordham graduate, Archbishop John Farley.

After the ceremony, Frank told his parents that he had a vocation to be a priest, and his heart was set on going to the North American College in Rome for his training in theology and philosophy. Because he had already earned an undergraduate degree, he would be older than most incoming seminarians.

A distant relative, Father Michael Owens, opened doors for Spellman. He persuaded a Boston auxiliary bishop, Joseph Anderson, that Spellman had the intelligence and finances to succeed at the NAC, and Bishop Anderson procured the approval of the Boston archbishop, William O'Connell. To earn money for his trip, Spellman spent the summer of 1911 working as a trolley conductor on the Bay State Line, which ran from Grove Street in Boston to East Walpole, thirteen miles to the south.[4]

In September 1911, Spellman left the United States on the Cunard steamer R.M.S. *Franconia*. He was to spend the next five years in Rome.

The rector of the NAC, Bishop Thomas Kennedy, a priest from Philadelphia, did not take to Spellman. Kennedy viewed him as too affable, outgoing, and independent for a seminarian. Hence, he was denied early ordination and did not receive privileges that were bestowed on most other students.

This poor treatment did not stop Spellman from making friends with fellow students—many of whom went on to achieve high rank in the Church—and from ingratiating himself with professors at the Urban College de Propaganda Fide. He became particularly close to two clerics who would later hold major positions in the Curia, Don Domenico Tardini and Don Francesco Borgongini-Duca. He also made sure he met prominent Bostonians staying in Rome; he kept in touch with many of them for years to come.

Spellman was vacationing in Milan in August 1914, when the First World War broke out. Shortly thereafter, he fell ill with a kidney ailment and was confined to bed for six months. Fearful that the rector would send him home before he had completed his studies, Spellman got himself off the sick list even though he had not fully recovered. He was not as well prepared for his oral exams as he should have been, but he got through them thanks to his friend Tardini, who was on the board.

In 1916, Spellman completed his doctoral studies and on May 14 was ordained in Rome at the church of Sant'Apollinare by the Most Reverend Giuseppe Ceppetelli, the titular patriarch of Constantinople. A few weeks later, Father Spellman began the trip home to Boston via Lourdes and London.

When he arrived in Massachusetts, it quickly became apparent to Spellman that his archbishop, Cardinal O'Connell, did not care for him. The first assignment O'Connell gave the young priest, whom he called the "little popinjay",[5] was chaplain at St. Clement's Home, which served elderly women. Several months later he was named second curate at All Saints Church in Roxbury, where he was put in charge of Sunday school and confirmation classes.

When America entered the war in 1917, Spellman volunteered to join the chaplains. O'Connell approved his request—but to the navy, not the army. The cardinal likely knew that Spellman would be rejected because of his poor eyesight. Unwilling to give up, Spellman applied to the army and managed to pass the physical.

When a group of newly inducted chaplains, including Spellman, visited their archbishop for a farewell blessing, O'Connell, after giving some off-the-cuff remarks, sought out Spellman. "Did you understand what I said?" the cardinal asked. When Spellman answered yes, the cardinal ordered him to "go in the next room and write it out while you remember it." After he completed his assignment, O'Connell informed him, "I have decided that you will not be a chaplain after all. You are appointed to the staff of the *Pilot*."[6]

When he reported for duty at the archdiocesan newspaper, the editor, who had not been informed that Spellman would be joining the staff, was shocked that a priest was assigned the job of promoting subscriptions. Since there was no office space for him, Spellman used as his base of operation his rectory room at the Cathedral of the Holy Cross, where he had been reassigned as curate.

Another blow to Spellman was a letter he received from the cardinal's nephew, Monsignor James P. E. O'Connell, who served as chancellor and as the archbishop's hatchet man.

> I trust it will not be wasted advice to suggest to you that it may be well, while you are yet at the beginning of your career, not to allow yourself to get any false conception about your importance, or the importance of your particular work, thus leading you to either the one extreme, temerity, or the other, timorousness. I make this statement because one of your recent letters to me savored of arrogance, a quality which ill befits a subordinate. I passed it over without comment at the time because I attributed the display to your callow inexperience. A change in the attitude which you have so far displayed to my personal knowledge will have wholesome effects for yourself in the future.[7]

Spellman decided to make the best of a bad situation. He used his position to visit every parish, to befriend priests, and to take the political temperature of the neighborhoods that made up the archdiocese. He was also successful in boosting the circulation of the *Pilot*.

Instead of taking summer vacations, he studied Spanish and translated two books written by his Rome theology mentor Monsignor Borgongini-Duca. One volume, *The Word of God*, published in 1920, was read by the apostolic delegate to the United States, Archbishop Bonzano. Pleased with Spellman's efforts, he sent him a letter of congratulations. The second translation, *In the Footsteps of the Master*, appeared in print four years later.

In May 1922, Spellman was removed from the *Pilot* and was appointed to the lowly post of third assistant in the chancery. Once again, he made the most of the job, and his knowledge of Italian and Spanish proved to be useful.

After the first assistant died in the spring of 1924, Spellman, expecting a promotion, was told by his archbishop that his job in the chancery was terminated and he was now the diocesan archivist. With little to do in his basement office, Spellman decided to become the archdiocese's most knowledgeable priest by studying all the historical files.

To escape for a time from his place of exile, Spellman tried to get passage to Rome in 1925, which had been designated a Holy Year. Although O'Connell denied him permission to go on the first Boston-to-Rome pilgrimage, he managed to get a spot on the second trip, even though Auxiliary Bishop Anderson, who led the pilgrims, was not pleased.

The bishop's attitude changed, however, when the Boston entourage was greeted upon their arrival in Rome by Monsignor Borgongini-Duca of the office of the secretary of state. Anderson was impressed by Spellman's warm relationship with the monsignor and started giving the young priest some leeway.

When the pilgrims met Pope Pius XI in a private audience, Spellman scored more points by serving as translator of the pontiff's greetings to his guests. Both the pope and Bishop Anderson were pleased with Spellman's performance.

Borgongini-Duca, taking advantage of the situation, convinced the pope that the Boston priest should be appointed to the Secretary of State's Office to coordinate the Knights of Columbus' philanthropic activities in Rome.

After the pope confirmed the appointment of Spellman as the first American assigned to a Vatican post, a bystander asked, "Suppose his Eminence of Boston does not care to have him come to Rome?" Pius XI instantly replied, "Sopra di lui siamo Noi," "Above him are We."[8]

With a stroke of the papal pen, Father Spellman's banishment to the chancery basement ended and new vistas were open to him.

Spellman in Rome (1925–1932)

Because his main task was directing the construction of playgrounds financed by the Knights of Columbus, Spellman had plenty of time to ingratiate himself with the powers that be in the Vatican. He became particularly close to Cardinal–Secretary of State Pietro Gasparri; to Gasparri's successor, Cardinal Eugenio Pacelli; to three future cardinals, Giuseppe Pizzardo, Alfredo Ottaviani, and his old friend Domenico

Tardini; and to two laymen who were Vatican insiders: Francesco Pacelli, a Vatican lawyer and the elder brother of Eugenio Pacelli, and Count Enrico Galeazzi, the Knights of Columbus representative in Rome.

As the lone American in the Vatican State Department, he was called on to give his opinion on issues that affected his homeland. He was also assigned the duty of meeting and greeting important Americans who visited the Vatican. That's how he became a confidant of the very wealthy Nicholas Brady of New Jersey and Long Island, who spent winters at the palace Casa del Sole in Rome.

Spellman served as translator for members of the Curia who attended Brady dinner parties and as a tennis partner on the Bradys' courts. When the Bradys asked for a private chaplain, Spellman was given the job.

In August of 1928, after injuring his knee, Spellman checked himself into a hospital, where he contracted a mild case of tuberculosis. Fearing that he would be shipped back to the States, he again kept his illness under wraps. His friends, particularly the Bradys, covered for him, and by late September he was able to return to work. Several weeks later, he learned that the Holy Father had named him a monsignor—"supernumerary secret chamberlain". One year later he was promoted to domestic prelate.

During the negotiations between Cardinal Gasparri and Mussolini that led to the recognition of the Vatican as an independent city-state, Spellman had a ringside seat. He provided input and accompanied the Vatican delegation—in American automobiles provided by the Bradys—to the signing of the treaty at the Lateran Palace. Afterward, his friend and former teacher Monsignor Borgongini-Duca was named the first nuncio to Italy, with the rank of archbishop.

In September 1928, Monsignor Spellman took a vacation trip to Berlin and was greeted by the nuncio, Archbishop Eugenio Pacelli, who invited him to a luncheon the following day with the German president, Paul von Hindenburg. Spellman, who did not speak German, sat silently and observed.

During his five-day visit, Spellman impressed Pacelli, and upon the monsignor's return to Rome, Pacelli saw him off at the train station. Just two months later, when Pacelli arrived in Rome to take up the post of secretary of state, he was, in turn, met at the train station by his new good friend, Monsignor Spellman.

Cardinal Pacelli turned to Spellman for advice on many matters, particularly ones pertaining to America. The two also vacationed together. A trip to Switzerland in the spring of 1930 included mountain climbing and a retreat—but plenty of paperwork as well. Spellman also helped the multilingual Pacelli to learn English.

On February 12, 1931, Monsignor Spellman accompanied Pope Pius XI to the Marconi transmitting room, where Marquis Guglielmo Marconi personally supervised the Vicar of Christ's first radio address to the faithful throughout the world.

Spellman had a significant part in this historic event. After the pope completed his remarks and gave an apostolic blessing, the monsignor took to the microphone and gave a summary of the pontiff's comments in English. The Vatican bureaucrat instantly became a household name in Catholic homes across the United States, but particularly in Massachusetts.

Five months later Spellman was again to achieve international notoriety.

Pope Pius, disgusted with Mussolini and his Fascist government, was intent on releasing an encyclical condemning the atheistic, totalitarian regime. Fearing censorship, the pope and Cardinal Pacelli kept the document, *Non Abbiamo Bisogno* (We do not need), top secret. To avoid any leaks, the pope wrote the initial drafts longhand. To get the encyclical to the free world, Pacelli gave Monsignor Spellman the task of smuggling it to Paris.

Spellman left Rome quietly by train. He spent the travel time translating the encyclical into English. In case he was stopped by the police, he had official Vatican papers describing him as a diplomatic courier transporting papers to be delivered to the papal nuncio in Paris. Spellman also carried a letter of introduction from the Rome bureau chief for Associated Press, stating that members of the media could "have absolute confidence in the bearer".[9]

On July 4, 1931, Spellman successfully released the encyclical to the major press offices in Paris. The pope's critique made international headlines, and Il Duce was pummeled with criticism for suppressing religious liberties. Spellman's cloak-and-dagger mission made good copy, and his exploits were described in all the major U.S. newspapers. The headline in the July 12 *Boston Globe* read: "Monsignor Spellman 'The Nervy Kid From Whitman,' Who Flew [*sic*] from Rome to Paris with Pope's Message to Escape Censorship".[10]

Back in Boston, Cardinal O'Connell, fearing that Spellman's notoriety might result in his appointment as bishop coadjutor of Boston with right to succession, suggested to the Vatican that the monsignor be appointed to the vacant see in Portland, Maine.

The pope rejected the proposal, preferring to keep Spellman in Rome. Both the pope and Pacelli had come to appreciate Spellman's keen political antennae, his knowledge of finance (he had taken accounting courses), and his ability to handle the press. Pius XI also turned to Spellman for advice on appointments in New England. The bitter O'Connell said "the young man was swimming beyond his depth."[11]

Spellman, happy as a lark, continued to expand his network of contacts. Every U.S. bishop who arrived in Rome for his *ad limina* meeting with the Holy Father was first greeted and briefed by Monsignor Spellman.

He also met captains of industry and finance who visited his close friends the Bradys. Nicholas Brady died in 1930, but Mrs. Brady continued to offer hospitality. On Spellman's forty-third birthday, in 1932, she hosted a joint party honoring Spellman and the eighty-year-old Cardinal Gasparri. Spellman, in turn, planted the idea that led to Mrs. Brady's appointment as a papal duchess.

When Boston's auxiliary bishop, John Peterson, was named the ordinary of the Diocese of Manchester, New Hampshire, the pope decided—without consulting O'Connell—to appoint Spellman as the next auxiliary bishop. Pope Pius made it clear to Spellman that although he was not to be named coadjutor with right of succession, he would be the pope's pick for that job the day the Boston see became vacant. The consecration ceremony was to be performed by Cardinal Pacelli, not O'Connell. Co-consecrators were Archbishop Borgongini-Duca and Archbishop Pizzardo.

Borgongini-Duca gave Spellman an episcopal ring and suggested that Christopher Columbus' ship *Santa Maria* appear on Spellman's coat of arms. Pope Pius gave Spellman a pectoral cross and chose his motto: *Sequere Deum*—"Follow God."

On the big day, September 8, 1932, Spellman was consecrated in St. Peter's Basilica, wearing the same vestments Pacelli had worn when he became a bishop in 1917. Guests included Count Enrico Galeazzi, Marquis Francesco Pacelli, Cardinal

Lorenzo Lauri, diplomats from the American embassy, other diplomats, and a few friends from Boston.

Afterward Cardinal Pacelli and Bishop Spellman vacationed together for the last time, visiting Cannes and Chamonix. Before leaving for Boston, Spellman had a private audience with the pope that lasted two and a half hours.

Cardinal O'Connell, unhappy that an auxiliary had been imposed on him, put out a mean-spirited press statement:

> There have been so many exaggerated press statements in relation to the recent appointment of Msgr. Spellman as Auxiliary … that the office of the secretary to Cardinal O'Connell wishes to make a plain statement about the facts of the matter.
>
> Some years ago Cardinal O'Connell was consulted regarding the charge of appointing someone who could assist in the Secretary of State's office in Rome in the work of translating English documents into Italian and vice versa…. His task was merely to do the usual work given a cleric…. As soon as possible after consecration Bishop Spellman will return to Boston to take up whatever work Cardinal O'Connell designates for him to do in regard to the confirming of children in the archdiocese.[12]

While on the steamer *Rex* headed to New York, Spellman received this terse wire from his archbishop: "Welcome to Boston. Confirmations begin on Monday. You are expected to be ready."[13]

This "welcome" summarizes the chilly relationship O'Connell and Spellman would have during Spellman's six years as auxiliary. Why did O'Connell dislike Spellman so? Perhaps at least in part because he saw in the young priest a bit of himself in years past and resented an ambitious Roman-trained cleric encroaching on his turf.

O'Connell, like Spellman, had been educated and ordained in Rome, although he did not finish his doctorate because of illness. Later he became rector of the NAC and pushed his way into Vatican circles. He became particularly close to Pius X's secretary of state, Cardinal Rafael Merry del Val, who was to consecrate him in 1901 when he was named bishop of Portland, Maine.

Merry del Val sent him to Japan as a papal envoy in 1905. One year later he was named bishop coadjutor of Boston with right of succession. He succeeded to the see in August 1907 and became the first cardinal archbishop of Boston in November 1911.

Despite being a prince of the Church, the regal and pompous O'Connell was an unhappy cleric. His attempts to become a national spokesman for the Church in America failed, because he was disliked by most of his fellow U.S. bishops. His hopes to succeed Cardinal Gibbons in Baltimore were dashed. His bid to become archbishop of New York in 1918 also failed.

O'Connell was also miserable because after the death of Pope Pius X in 1914, Cardinal Merry Del Val was removed as secretary of state and succeeded by O'Connell's foe Cardinal Gasparri. For the remainder of his life, O'Connell had no influence within the papal court. And the fact that Vatican insiders turned for advice to another New Englander, Francis Spellman, was more than he could stand.

There may also be another reason for O'Connell's distaste for Spellman. The cardinal's nephew, Monsignor James O'Connell—the man who wrote that unpleasant

letter to the young Father Spellman—for several years split his time between Boston, where he was the chancellor of the archdiocese, and New York, where, as
"Mr. James Roe", he supported a wife and family. When word reached Rome
about this situation, Pope Benedict XV confronted Cardinal O'Connell, and he
denied the accusation. The pope challenged the denial by producing a copy of the
marriage certificate. The cardinal dropped to his knees and pleaded for forgiveness.
Shortly after Cardinal O'Connell returned to Boston, Monsignor O'Connell left
the priesthood, and "Mr. Roe" went on to become a member of the Manhattan
Board of Trade.[14]

The humiliated cardinal was convinced, without any proof, that Spellman was
one of the clerics who had conspired against him. The evidence suggests, however,
that this was not the case.

It was the apostolic delegate, Archbishop Bonzano, who after receiving information on the "Roe" matter from members of the American hierarchy, began his
own investigation and had the chancellor of the Archdiocese of New York, Monsignor John Dunn, hire a private detective. Bonzano received proof that Monsignor
O'Connell was legally married and that his wife lived at 102 East Thirty-Sixth
Street in Manhattan. It was he who turned the evidence, including the marriage
license, over to the pope.

Bishop Spellman in Boston (1932–1939)

When Bishop Spellman arrived in Boston to take up his duties, his archbishop did
not bother to give him a parish at first. He was told he could take a room at the
seminary. Some months later, after Spellman pushed for a parish assignment, he was
given a poor one, Sacred Heart in Newton Center.

A perturbed Spellman sent a letter to O'Connell acknowledging the appointment and stating that he would "cheerfully" perform his duties. He could not resist
pointing out, however, that he would "endure the humiliation of seeing some
priest appointed to a better parish than the auxiliary Bishop".[15]

As it turned out, Sacred Heart was just fine for Spellman. The parishioners were
excited to have a bishop as their pastor, and his rank enabled him to raise outside
money to pay down the parish's debt. Sacred Heart is the only church in America
that can boast that two of its pastors became cardinals—Spellman and the man who
succeeded him in 1939, Father Richard Cushing, who became archbishop of Boston in 1944.

For years Cardinal O'Connell did his best to ignore Spellman, and they rarely
met. The bishop was kept busy with confirmations, and during his tenure confirmed 177,000 children.

In the fall of 1936, Spellman learned from his friend Genevieve Brady that her
Long Island mansion, Inisfada, on Shelter Rock Road in Manhasset, was to serve
as Cardinal-Secretary of State Pacelli's vacation getaway. Mrs. Brady was dead set
against *any* public schedule for the cardinal, but Spellman realized that that was
not a good plan. Although it severely strained his relationship with Mrs. Brady, he
organized a nationwide tour for Pacelli that culminated with a visit to President
Roosevelt's home in Hyde Park, New York.

Spellman greeted Pacelli at New York Harbor when his ship arrived and served as tour guide and press spokesman. After spending a few days at Inisfada, the two men, on October 13, drove to the Knights of Columbus headquarters in New Haven and ended the day at Spellman's parish near Boston.

Pacelli said Mass at Sacred Heart Church using the chalice Pope Pius XI had given to Spellman as a parting gift when he returned to Boston. Later that day Pacelli met with Cardinal O'Connell at the seminary and dined at his residence. The grumpy O'Connell was not a great host.

On October 15, Pacelli said another Mass at Spellman's parish and went on to make visits during the next two weeks to New York, Philadelphia, Catholic University in D.C., Cleveland, Chicago, South Bend, Cincinnati, St. Louis, San Francisco, and Los Angeles. Reminiscing years later, Spellman said that during their cross-country flights, he persuaded the pilot to make various detours so that Pacelli could see some of the great natural wonders of America, especially Niagara Falls and the Grand Canyon.[16]

Since America was in the middle of a presidential campaign, a meeting between Pacelli and FDR was delayed until after the November 3 election. On November 5, two days after Roosevelt swept the nation, carrying forty-six states and receiving 61 percent of the vote, Bishop Spellman, Joseph P. Kennedy, and New York auxiliary bishop Stephen Donahue accompanied Cardinal Pacelli to the president's home along the Hudson in Hyde Park.

Serving as hostess was the president's mother, Sara Delano Roosevelt, who permitted the Irish-Catholic servants to meet the secretary of state and receive his blessing.

There were discussions about sending an envoy to the Vatican, and an agreement was reached to rein in the notorious Father Coughlin. Pacelli made it clear to FDR that Spellman was a trusted confidant who could serve as an intermediary between the White House and the Vatican.

Cardinal Pacelli left for Rome on November 7 pleased with his friend and former protégé. And their travels together had given Spellman a chance to expand his contacts throughout the United States, the key one being Joseph Kennedy, who would be appointed ambassador to the Court of St. James' in 1938. Spellman vacationed with Kennedy at his Palm Beach home in late November 1936.

Back in Boston, Cardinal O'Connell, who had had only a small role in the Pacelli visit, reconciled himself to the fact that Spellman had powerful friends in the Vatican and that it was time to make the best of a bad situation. He began to spend time with his auxiliary and appointed him a diocesan consultor.

Even so, he could not restrain himself when he learned, in 1938, that Boston College had decided to confer an honorary doctorate on Spellman. O'Connell promptly quashed the idea. Hearing of the incident, the president of Notre Dame, Father John O'Hara, decided that Spellman would be honored at his university's commencement. Spellman never forgot O'Hara's act of kindness. In later years he brought O'Hara to New York as an auxiliary bishop and engineered his appointments first as bishop of Buffalo and then as archbishop of Philadelphia.

In early 1938, it was rumored that the suburban counties on Long Island, Nassau, and Suffolk, were to be split off from the Brooklyn Diocese and encompass a new see, and that Spellman was to be the first ordinary. But the plans did not get off the drawing board because of the death of Cardinal Hayes on September 4. (In any event, Nassau and Suffolk remained in the Brooklyn Diocese until 1957.)

There was plenty of speculation as to Hayes' successor. Names included Bishop Donahue, Newark's Bishop Thomas Joseph Walsh, Hayes' friend Archbishop Joseph Rummel of New Orleans (a former New Yorker), and a dark horse—Bishop Spellman.

Spellman had mixed feelings about going to New York. He believed he was best suited to succeed O'Connell because he had come to know Boston like the back of his hand. Also, Pius XI had told Spellman when he was leaving Rome that he wanted him to get Boston, and the pope still held that position when he was considering candidates for New York.

It appears that the Holy Father had decided on a former New York pastor, the Most Reverend John T. McNicholas, O.P., then serving as archbishop of Cincinnati, to fill Hayes' shoes. All bets were off, however, when Pius XI died on February 10, 1939.

Cardinal O'Connell was vacationing in the Bahamas and Spellman was in Florida when they heard the news of the pope's death. O'Connell took the next steamer to Rome and told Spellman he was not needed back in Boston and could continue vacationing.

On March 2, 1939, after white smoke came out of the Sistine Chapel and it was announced that Eugenio Pacelli—who took the name Pius XII—would succeed to the throne of St. Peter, Spellman's life instantly changed. The new pope cabled him shortly after the conclave, and the White House frantically searched for the vacationing cleric.

The rumors that Spellman was to get New York abated, however, when word spread that three American cardinals had told Rome that Spellman was not the right man to succeed Hayes. The pope, however, ignored their advice. On April 12, 1939, Spellman received word privately from the apostolic delegate, Archbishop Cicognani, that he was to be tapped for the post. Twelve days later the official announcement was made that Francis Joseph Spellman was to be the sixth archbishop of New York. In a statement released by the archbishop-elect, he promised that he would dedicate himself to the welfare of children and said, "I shall welcome the participation of all in the doing of good things for God, for country, for the poor, the sick, the suffering and the under-privileged. For my part I shall give my all and do my best."[17]

Cardinal O'Connell, who had once coveted New York for himself, put out a lukewarm statement that summarized Spellman's career as a priest and concluded by stating, "I'm sure he has learned [in Boston] something of diocesan administration, for this Archdiocese is well-known to be one of the best organized Dioceses anywhere."[18] It was reported that O'Connell said privately, when he heard of the appointment, "Francis is an example of what happens when you teach a bookkeeper to read."[19]

Spellman in New York: The Early Years

On May 23, 1939, Spellman was installed by Archbishop Cicognani before a packed cathedral and greeted by fifty thousand onlookers outside on Fifth Avenue. The eighty-four-year-old rector of St. Patrick's, Monsignor Lavelle, read the required papal bulls. Afterward seven thousand people led by Al Smith attended a reception at the Commodore Hotel.

Spellman took command of an archdiocese that in 1939 had 1,695 priests, 374 churches, 218 parochial schools, and 10 Catholic colleges. He also learned that he was saddled with $28 million of debt. His predecessor, the Cardinal of Charities, had had to borrow to make ends meet because of the drop in collections at Mass during the Great Depression.

Appalled that the debt was financed at an annual interest rate of 6.50 percent, Spellman immediately began to negotiate for lower rates. When the archdiocese's bankers told him no deal, Spellman turned to their competitors for financing. Bankers Trust lent $10 million at 2.50 percent, and a consortium of Boston banks financed $18 million at significantly reduced rates. Spellman endeared himself to pastors when he informed them that he had achieved savings of half a million dollars annually by his new loan arrangements.[20]

In a letter to all archdiocesan priests announcing the refinancing, he also made this observation concerning parochial matters:

> In the future no priest will be appointed pastor of a new parish until he has been provided with a tract of land free of debt and a certain amount of unencumbered money placed at his disposal so that he and his parishioners may reasonably hope to have a church and a rectory not only built but paid for within a maximum period of fifteen years.
>
> Any parish priest who has a debt on his parish and at the same time has a credit balance greater than is prudently necessary for current or approximate expenses is expected to pay off as much of his debt as is possible and to pay it off at once to eliminate unnecessary interest charges. Parish priests are reminded that they are not to make purchases of any securities or to sell any of their present holdings without consultation with and authorization from the Chancellor.[21]

Unlike Cardinal Hayes, whose focus was primarily on charities, Spellman preferred to get a handle on the daily activities of the all parishes and facilities of his archdiocese. To achieve this end, he introduced over time a reorganization plan that not only saved money but increased efficiency, eliminated duplications, and provided competent and prudent oversight.

The first reform concerned the purchase of insurance. Father Walter Kellenberg (future bishop of Rockville Center) was named to head up the newly created Archdiocesan Service Corporation. Pastors would no longer procure the required coverage for their parishes. Instead, the Service Corporation was mandated to approach carriers for a group price that covered every facility in the archdiocese.

Other reform measures included creating the Building Commission, which centralized the bidding process for construction, and the Institutional Commodity Service, which made group purchases of goods and services.

Another important innovation was the Archdiocesan Reciprocal Loan Fund. Parishes and other facilities that could not procure loans from financial institutions for construction or repairs could borrow from the fund at favorable rates.

While some priests grumbled about their diminished authority, the reforms were successful. Spellman had not only saved money but had also made it clear that he was boss and expected his priests to work as hard as he did. To keep pastors on their toes, he made unexpected calls on parishes when driving around and asked pastors tough questions about their administrative and pastoral duties. A pastor out playing golf when the archbishop visited was called on the carpet. On the other hand, priests who excelled at their parochial work were justly rewarded. During his twenty-eight years as archbishop, Spellman secured from the Holy Father the promotion of more priests to the three ranks of monsignor and obtained more auxiliary bishops than all his predecessors combined.

Spellman ignored Cardinal O'Connell's advice that he clean house immediately. He kept the same chancery staff he inherited for some months in order to get a measure of each member.

The auxiliary bishop, Stephen Donahue, who had himself hoped to get the post of archbishop, had a poor attitude. He had made the mistake of appointing over a dozen pastors right before Spellman took office. Spellman rescinded the appointments and then immediately reappointed the priests. This action sent a strong message that he was in charge. Bishop Donahue was not to hold any regular position of authority during the Spellman years. He spent the remainder of his clerical life mainly performing confirmations.

On the other hand, the vicar-general, Father James Francis McIntyre, who had earlier opposed Spellman's appointment, threw his lot with him and enthusiastically aided him in executing the archdiocesan plans. McIntyre, who had become a priest later in life and had worked as a Wall Street investment banker, was Spellman's kind of priest. He became a New York auxiliary bishop in 1940 and later cardinal archbishop of Los Angeles.

Military Vicar Spellman and World War II

Archbishop Spellman needed a loyal and top-drawer staff in the chancery because, as the war in Europe spread into a world war, he was called on by the Vatican and the White House to be an active participant in international affairs.

Knowing that Spellman had the ear of Pope Pius XII, President Roosevelt turned to him frequently for advice and to serve as an intermediary.

Spellman, whom FDR referred to as his favorite bishop, also had discussions with the President during 1937 and 1938 concerning U.S. diplomatic recognition of the Vatican state.

In 1939, FDR, pleased that Spellman had been appointed to the New York see, sent him a handwritten letter that said: "I am deeply regretful that I cannot come to the installation—but my heart and my thoughts will be with you. A little later in the summer you must come to us at Hyde Park and incidentally start the good habit of staying with us when you come to see your flocks in Dutchess County."[22]

Over the next few years, the archbishop was to spend plenty of quality time at Hyde Park discussing pressing issues. One such discussion centered on Europeans—both Christians and Jews—seeking asylum in the United States and the need of formal contact with the Vatican to help deal with the issue.

While it was agreed that the United States needed a mission at the Vatican, defining it was a problem. When it became clear that Roosevelt was ready to name an ambassador, the striped-pants crowd at the Protestant-dominated State Department, while supportive of diplomatic relations, were opposed to an ambassadorial post. Anti-Catholic groups and bigoted members of Congress also objected and accused FDR of violating the Constitution.

The president, fearing a backlash, particularly in the Bible Belt—an integral part of his party's political coalition—found a back door to the Vatican. On Christmas Eve 1939, in a letter to the pope released to the press, he wrote:

> Because the people of this nation have come to a realization that time and distance no longer exist in the older sense, they understand that that which harms one segment of humanity harms all the rest. They know that only by friendly association between the seekers of light and the seekers of peace everywhere can the forces of evil be overcome.
>
> In these present moments, no spiritual leader, no civil leader can move forward on a specific plan to terminate destruction and build anew. Yet the time for that will surely come.
>
> It is, therefore, my thought that though no given action or given time may now be prophesied it is well that we encourage a closer association between those in every part of the world—those in religion and those in government—who have a common purpose.
>
> I am, therefore, suggesting to Your Holiness that it would give me great satisfaction to send to you *my personal representative* in order that our parallel endeavors for peace and the alleviation of suffering may be assisted.[23] [Emphasis added.]

Roosevelt had come up with the term "personal representative" to calm the political waters, but his appointee would be given the rank of ambassador.

Roosevelt's personal envoy to Pope Pius XII was Myron C. Taylor, an Episcopalian and former CEO of U.S. Steel. Taylor was confirmed and given ambassadorial status by the Vatican on February 28, 1940; he was to serve in the post until 1950.

Spellman, who was in on FDR's scheme, made these comments from the pulpit of St. Patrick's shortly after the pope's acceptance of Taylor's credentials:

> I express gratification that President Roosevelt, in his historic message of Christmas time, sent his personal representative to the Holy See with the rank of an Ambassador in order that "parallel endeavors for peace and the alleviation of suffering [may] be assisted."... Full of faith and hope and warning are the words in the message of the President saying that "unless there is some trust in a divine plan, nations are without light and peoples perish." ...
>
> There are those who have not been in favor of this action of our President.... The only reason which the non-approvalists seem to have is the shibboleth of separation of church and state.[24]

When Patrick Hayes became archbishop of New York near the end of World War I, he retained his rank as bishop-ordinary of the U.S. Armed Forces. After the outbreak of the new war in Europe in September 1939, some Catholic prelates urged the Vatican to move the vacant position to Washington, D.C., as a stand-alone ordinariate. But the pope thought differently and appointed Spellman military vicar.

To help him out, Spellman persuaded the Holy Father to appoint Notre Dame's Father John O'Hara, C.S.C., as a New York auxiliary bishop assigned to the military office. O'Hara, an order priest, preferring to serve out the remainder of his term as president of the university, tried to decline, but the apostolic delegate convinced him to accept.

As the war clouds darkened, Spellman began to take a more public role in his capacity as bishop-ordinary. He held Solemn Masses for the conquered people of Poland and France at St. Patrick's and supported FDR's proposal to institute a draft.

On the evening of December 7, 1941, Spellman put out this statement:

> As Archbishop of New York, I place all our resources, hospitals, institutions and personnel at the disposition of the Government. As Bishop in charge of the Catholic priests in the Army and Navy I can state that there are five hundred chaplains on duty at the present time. They have been an important factor in the building of the morale of our soldiers and sailors. They will be with them wherever they go and whatever they do. As an American and one of twenty-five million Catholic Americans I follow the identically glorious traditions of my country and my religion.[25]

Speaking as military vicar in a national radio address during Christmas week, he made the moral case for America's entry into the war: "The abandonment of Christ and His teachings, in personal life, [in] social life, in civic life and in international life, has brought us to the end of the world we have known. The way back to peace with justice through victory is in the identical order—personal righteousness, social decency, civic morality and international probity."[26]

In another national talk on March 23, 1942, Spellman turned up his rhetoric, saying:

> Americans are fighting for their God-given rights and every real American knows that he must fight, and, if necessary, die, for the principles that have had their noblest exemplification in history in the Government of the United States. I hold no enmity toward any people. Hatred has no place in my life. I love all men as brothers in Christ. But I am one of 130,000,000 Americans and millions and millions of other persons who are at war against any system of government which would destroy the things we cherish most. Franklin D. Roosevelt, more often than any other President, repeatedly has emphasized the truth that men who fulfill their duties to God are the pillars of a nation at war or in peace.[27]

In July 1942, preparing for his first of many trips to visit chaplains and troops, Spellman charged Bishop McIntyre and the vicar-general, Monsignor Joseph P. Donahue, P.A., with overseeing the archdiocese and making necessary decisions and appointments.

Racking up eighteen thousand miles in the summer of 1942, Spellman made stops in Seattle, Alaska, and the Aleutian Islands. He interviewed more than three hundred chaplains in ninety-two posts. In September he reported his findings to FDR and was invited to dine with Winston and Clementine Churchill at the White House. A collection of his speeches delivered on the trip, *The Road to Victory*, was published in October by Scribner's. *Commonweal* called it "a rousing rallying war cry to American Catholics",[28] and *America* said, "There is much sound, sane thought in the book, none of it, to be sure, new—but truths are not new. The statement of them, though, is here manly and forthright, unmistakably direct and challenging."[29]

In the first week of February 1943, Spellman reviewed his plans for another trip with the president and received his approval to visit troops in Britain, Africa, and the Middle East. After meeting with the president, he shared his itinerary with the apostolic delegate, who alerted the Holy Father via a coded message.

On hearing the news, Pope Pius requested that Spellman make a stop at the Vatican. FDR approved this side trip and ordered the State Department to get permission from the Italian government for the archbishop to travel through enemy territory. The official request stated that Spellman's visit to the Vatican was strictly limited to Church business. On this trip, which was to take six months, Spellman planned to make stops in forty countries, including Portugal, Spain, Algeria, Libya, Malta, Tunisia, Egypt, Palestine, Turkey, Iraq, Iran, Kenya, Rhodesia, and Nigeria.

The Nazis were the first to break the Spellman story, and they made absurd claims that he was FDR's pawn and his mission was to split the Axis by convincing Italy to abandon its Pact of Steel with Germany. The Nazi propaganda machine also told the German people that Spellman was going to Moscow to negotiate a treaty between the Vatican and the Soviet Union, and that afterward he was going to whisk the pope to a safe haven in Brazil. The Vatican Secretariat of State formally denied the assertions.[30]

While in Spain, Spellman met with the caudillo, Francisco Franco. In their two-hour discussion, Franco made the point that communism was the real evil but stated that he would stay neutral because Germany could not win. When questioned later by the liberal press about the propriety of meeting with Franco, Spellman, who was accused of being "a servant of Vatican intrigue",[31] stated: "Whatever criticism has been made of General Franco (and it has been considerable), I cannot doubt that he is a man loyal to his God, devoted to his country's welfare and definitely willing to sacrifice himself in any capacity and to any extent for Spain."[32]

From Barcelona, the archbishop made his way to the Vatican. During his ten-day visit he spent much time with the pope and leading members of the Curia. When the press inquired about his talks with the pontiff, the tight-lipped Spellman had "no comment". When he bade farewell to Pius XII, the pope's parting gift to him was the pectoral cross he was wearing that day.

From the Vatican, Spellman went on to Gibraltar and then to North Africa. He arrived in Tunisia shortly after the American and British forces were defeated at Kasserine Pass.

General Dwight Eisenhower met with Spellman and permitted him to visit troops at field hospitals. Spellman helped the wounded write letters home and authored many of them himself. It is estimated that by the end of the war the archbishop sent several thousand handwritten notes to parents and wives of our GIs. In a formal address to the troops, he told them that our war objectives are based on the Natural Law. "They clearly agree", he said, "with the traditional teaching of the Church and are in accord with the Christian life and the allocutions of His Holiness, Pope Pius XII."[33]

Spellman celebrated Mass near the front lines on St. Patrick's Day. A large contingent of Irish-Americans from New York and Massachusetts cheered him.

He went on to Istanbul, where he made the acquaintance of the apostolic delegate, Archbishop Angelo Roncalli—the future Pope John XXIII. During his stay in

Iran, he met the shah, Mohammad Reza Pahlavi, and said Mass for three thousand exiled Polish soldiers stationed at an RAF airfield.

Spellman cut his trip short when he received word that the president and the pope both wanted him to return home because of developments in Italy. The Axis forces in North Africa had surrendered in May after a series of crushing defeats, and the home front was in chaos because of Allied bombing and crippling shortages of food and fuel. Then on July 9 the Allies invaded Sicily. On July 26, King Victor Emmanuel dismissed Mussolini and appointed Marshal Pietro Badoglio to succeed him; that same day the king had Il Duce arrested. Ridiculous rumors circulated throughout Europe that Spellman was responsible for the change in the Italian leadership because he had had a meeting with the marshal while in Rome.

After twenty-four weeks on the road covering 45,585 miles, Spellman arrived back in New York on August 1. On August 3, he consecrated the new bishop of Ogdensburg, Bryan J. McEntegart, who had played a leading role in Archbishop Hayes' consolidation of Catholic Charities. Spellman then spent the rest of the month catching up on archdiocesan matters. On September 2, he traveled to Washington and briefed the president on his findings. He also dined that night at the White House with FDR and Winston Churchill.

In a two-page typed summary that Spellman wrote after his White House session, which covered such topics as the Big Four, the League of Nations, and the countries of Eastern Europe, he made these interesting observations concerning Russia and Poland:

> *Russia*: An interview with Stalin will be forced as soon as possible. [FDR] believes that he will be better fitted to come to an understanding with Stalin than Churchill. Churchill is too idealistic, he is a realist. So is Stalin. Therefore an understanding between them on a realistic basis is probable. The wish is, although it seems improbable, to get from Stalin a pledge not to extend Russian territory beyond a certain line. He would certainly receive: Finland, the Baltic States, the Eastern half of Poland, Bessarabia. There is no point to oppose these desires of Stalin, because he has the power to get them anyhow. So better give them gracefully.
> *Poland*: Poland, if re-established, would get Eastern Prussia.[34]

It appears that Roosevelt had formulated the territorial boundaries of Europe seventeen months before the Yalta Conference.

Spellman's special relationship with Roosevelt and Churchill permitted him to articulate to them the Vatican's position on the fate of Rome as the Allies fought their way north in Italy. After several "targeted" raids on Rome's freight yards, in which stray bombs had hit residential neighborhoods, the Vatican complained, and Spellman worked on his highly placed contacts. The result: In August 1943, the Allied Combined Chiefs of Staff ordered Supreme Commander Eisenhower to cease the attacks. While there was another bombing in November 1943, Rome was essentially spared by the Allies.

The Vatican, meanwhile, in September 1943 appointed Spellman the apostolic visitor to Sicily and occupied territories in Italy. He was empowered to review these areas and to report back to the pope on the condition of the Church and develop revitalization plans. He never had the opportunity to take up these duties,

however, because the rapid advance of the Allies made it possible for Vatican officials to travel freely and study the situation in liberated provinces for themselves.

After D-Day in June 1944, Spellman traveled to Europe and arrived in Rome on
July 22. He denied rumors that Pius XII was negotiating an armistice with Germany
and said Mass for thousands of GIs packed into the Church of the Gesù, the mother
church of the Society of Jesus. He also visited troop installations throughout Italy
and ministered to the needs of the wounded.

While he was visiting Lieutenant General Mark Clark's Fifth Army headquarters,
King George VI arrived, and, as the *Catholic World* reported, "the Archbishop was
the first person introduced to the King by General Clark."[35]

From Rome, Spellman traveled to liberated Paris and said Mass for three thousand American soldiers at the Cathedral of Notre Dame. He then crossed into
Germany and visited the First Army, commanded by General Courtney Hodges.

While making his way through Allied-held territory to Rome, Spellman learned
that former governor Al Smith had died on October 4. The archbishop ordered that
Smith was to lie in state in St. Patrick's Cathedral. (This was a great honor. The
only layman to lie in state there since Smith was Robert Kennedy in 1968.) At
the Requiem Mass, Bishop McIntyre was the main celebrant, and Monsignor
Donahue delivered the eulogy. Spellman said a Memorial Mass for Smith at the
American Church of Santa Susanna.

Spellman's stay in Rome was interrupted when word reached him that FDR
required his presence back in the United States. Spellman reported to the White
House on October 18 and learned that the president was concerned that the scarcity
of food in Italy could lead to civil unrest. At Spellman's urging, Roosevelt expedited visas for priests representing the War Relief Services of the National Catholic
Welfare Conference to go to Italy to perform relief work.

In April 1945, shortly before Roosevelt's death, Spellman was becoming disenchanted with the president's postwar plans concerning Eastern Europe. Agreeing
with the pope's plea for "Peace and Justice", Spellman, over dinner at the White
House, questioned the decision to give part of Poland to Russia. "Your decision",
Spellman said, "cannot cause a part of Poland to become Russia except by driving
the population off their land. It is immoral to uproot people like that and take away
their homes and their churches and even their cemeteries."[36]

When FDR lectured Spellman that he could handle Stalin, who, he said, "is just
another practical man who wants peace and prosperity", Spellman disagreed. "He
is not just another anything", the archbishop said. "He is different. You can't trust
him. He'll never cooperate."[37]

Upon hearing of Roosevelt's death on April 12, 1945, Spellman immediately
sent a telegram to Mrs. Roosevelt: "No words can express my grief at the death
of the President and the loss to the world, the nation and yourself. I offer you
my prayers."[38]

With peace restored to the world in 1945, Archbishop Spellman was able to look
proudly on the contribution of the Military Vicariate. More than 3,200 American
priests served as chaplains (150 from the Archdiocese of New York) throughout
all the theaters of war. Thirty-eight were killed in battle, and thirty-three others
died while serving the spiritual needs of our troops. Over eight hundred decora-
tions were awarded to five hundred chaplains. Historian George Flynn, reviewing

Catholic participation in the war, concluded that Catholics' patriotism was "so shining that never again would anyone dare to question their Americanism".[39]

The Postwar Golden Years

At the end of the Second World War, the Catholic population of the Archdiocese of New York stood at 1.180 million—down from 1.325 million in 1920. The decline came to a halt in the postwar era, and the number grew to 1.8 million by 1965, for two reasons: Returning GIs married and gave birth to what became known as the baby-boom generation. Next, the number of Puerto Ricans settling in the Bronx and Manhattan exploded. By the mid-sixties that population stood at more than five hundred thousand.

Reacting, Archbishop Spellman began a monumental building campaign. In the two decades after the war, he opened 32 new parishes and razed and rebuilt 24 old ones. The number of parochial grammar schools grew from 214 to 254; high schools from 32 to 48. The archdiocese's construction budget was second only to New York City's construction budget.

By 1964 there were 222,000 students in archdiocesan schools, versus 119,000 in 1939. The number of teachers doubled over the same period, to 7,120. The parochial schools in New York City constituted "the second largest school system in the state, topped only by the City's mammoth public school system".[40] Throughout the 1950s and early 1960s, Spellman reminded presidents, governors, and mayors, time and again, that if the archdiocese's parochial-school system did not exist, educating all those extra children would have cost governments more than $27 million annually.

A prolific fund-raiser, Spellman charmed New York's rich and powerful into financing his building plans. He also cultivated the upwardly mobile Catholics who, thanks to the GI Bill of Rights, had earned college degrees and were making their way to the top in finance, banking, and real estate.

Spellman began a major renovation program at St. Patrick's Cathedral that cost $3 million. The Lady Chapel, the rectory, and the archbishop's residence received needed repairs. The main altar was replaced, and the cathedral's wooden entrance doors were replaced with bronze ones.

Spellman then turned his attention to his favorite charitable activity, caring for needy children—as he had promised when first named archbishop. He persuaded his friend Joe Kennedy to purchase through his family foundation a parcel of land on Pelham Parkway in the Bronx and to finance what became known as the Lieutenant Joseph P. Kennedy Jr. Home. It initially housed 280 orphaned children.

To support services for homeless, abandoned, and mentally disturbed children, Spellman created, in 1946, the Annual Christmas Luncheon at the Waldorf-Astoria, which averaged more than three thousand attendees.

To increase awareness of the plight of homeless children, Spellman wrote a novel, *The Foundling*, published in 1951. This Literary Guild selection sold over five hundred thousand copies in hard and soft cover. All royalties went to support services for children. Spellman said he was inspired to write the story by "the love of my heart for little children and for all mankind".[41]

Spellman also built on his predecessor's creation, Catholic Charities. By 1960, the archdiocese was raising $5 million annually and receiving tens of millions from the federal, state, and city governments to help support 192 health and welfare agencies.

To minister to the rapidly growing Puerto Rican population, Church-sponsored social-welfare facilities were opened in their neighborhoods. Spellman established the Office of Spanish Catholic Action and funded language courses for priests and seminarians. More than two hundred priests in one hundred parishes ministered to the Puerto Rican faithful.

Spellman also helped improve the Catholic educational structure in the Commonwealth of Puerto Rico. In 1948 he helped build the Catholic University of Puerto Rico. The school, which today educates ten thousand students and has achieved pontifical status, named Spellman the university's "godfather".

Though African-American Catholics in New York were few in number, this did not prevent Spellman from speaking out on civil-rights issues. Spellman, who had a lifetime membership in the NAACP, in February 1964 made an "appeal to the conscience of New York" before a meeting of the Metropolitan New York Conference on Religion and Race. The cardinal said:

> I pray that the full light of God's truth will shine into the heart of each of us, the priceless truth that we are all His children and brothers one to another, and that each equally should share the benefits of those rights for which our forebears lived, fought and died. May history be allowed to record that in this our time the conscience of New York awakened fully, reacted strongly, and purged from our beloved city every last vestige of discrimination against Negroes.[42]

Spellman and Catholic Higher Education

Unlike Cardinal Hayes, Spellman took an immediate interest in Dunwoodie. After years of neglect, new life was instilled in the seminary.

Three weeks after he was installed as archbishop, Spellman made his first official visit to the seminary and sent a strong message to the staff and the students that there were to be major changes. His first move was in September 1939, when he removed the "Scrooge" procurator, Father John Donovan. Eight months later, on May 2, 1940, during an unannounced visit, Spellman informed the rector, Arthur Scanlan, that he was to become the pastor of St. Helena's parish in the Bronx and that his replacement was a professor of moral theology, Father John M. Feans.

One year later, on the twenty-fifth anniversary of his ordination, Spellman, after saying a Mass of Thanksgiving at the seminary, announced that a new infirmary and gymnasium were to be constructed.

After the war, Spellman continued his Dunwoodie building spree, spending more than $4 million on renovations and new construction. The new library, dedicated to Archbishop Corrigan in 1953, housed over sixty thousand books and the archdiocesan archives.

Spellman also turned his attention to two other centers of education—the financially troubled Catholic University of America and the North American College in Rome.

As a member of Catholic U's executive board, Spellman used the power of his office to reorganize the school and its balance sheet. On behalf of the university, he negotiated with McGraw-Hill a contract to issue a new *Catholic Encyclopedia* to replace the one sponsored by Cardinal Farley. All royalties would go to the university.

When the NAC, which had been closed during the war, reopened in 1948, Spellman served as treasurer of the governing board. Though the board and the rector, Bishop Martin J. O'Connor (who hailed from Scranton, Pennsylvania), agreed that a new facility was required, there were different opinions as to the scope of the construction plans for the new NAC on top of the Janiculum Hill in Rome.

Spellman frequently clashed with O'Connor over the proposed size of the new building and the costs. At times Spellman was ruthless and petty with O'Connor, particularly after O'Connor's larger vision for the NAC was adopted by the board. Despite all the infighting, however, the project was finally completed, and the new NAC was officially dedicated to Pope Pius XII on October 14, 1953. Spellman did not attend the ceremony.

Out of favor with Spellman, O'Connor never came back to the States as an ordinary. After he left the NAC in 1964, he held various Vatican posts, and he served as nuncio to Malta from 1965 to 1969. In 1980, at the age of eighty, he moved back to Pennsylvania; he died in Wilkes-Barre in 1986. In the 2012 introduction to *The Second Founder: Bishop Martin J. O'Connor and the Pontifical North American College*, by Monsignor Stephen M. DiGiovanni, Cardinal Raymond Burke observed, "The manner in which Bishop O'Connor was treated at the end of his years of service to the College is one of the saddest chapters in her history."[43]

The 1946 Consistory

Because the Church was officially in mourning during World War II, Pope Pius XII did not name any new members to the College of Cardinals. As a result, the number of cardinals dropped to thirty-seven in 1945, a modern historical low.

When word leaked out of Rome on December 23, 1945, that the pope was to hold a consistory in early 1946, no one was surprised to learn that Spellman was on the list of thirty-two cardinals-elect. Other Americans honored were Archbishops Edward Mooney of Detroit, Samuel Stritch of Chicago, and John Glennon of St. Louis.

But the national focus after the announcement was on Spellman. He even landed on the cover of *Life* magazine. The feature story, "Spellman: Close Up", declared that "a high degree of personal charm, a thorough knowledge of men and their temporal affairs and an abundance of other talents—spiritual, intellectual, executive and political—has made Archbishop Spellman the No. 2 man among [the] 350,000,000 Roman Catholics of the world.... Spellman is the Pope's personal envoy and reporter-at-large, his intimate friend and probably his most influential adviser."[44]

Rumors circulated that Spellman was to be recalled to Rome to fill the vacant post of secretary of state. Pius XII made it clear, however, that he was to be his own secretary, with the aid of Archbishop Giovanni Battista Montini (the future Pope Paul VI) and Spellman's old friend Archbishop Domenico Tardini.

Two chartered planes took Cardinal-Elect Spellman and his guests to Rome. While stopping to refuel in Ireland, Spellman said Mass at St. John's Cathedral in

Limerick and attended a reception hosted by Taoiseach (Prime Minister) Éamon de Valera.

On February 20, 1946, in a semiprivate consistory, the pope bestowed on Spellman the red biretta. The next day, in a public ceremony at St. Peter's Basilica, the new cardinals took the oath of the Sacred College and received from the pope the cappa magna. The hat placed on Spellman's head was the same galero Pius XI had given to Cardinal Pacelli in 1929.

At a secret consistory held on February 22, the new cardinals were given rings and were assigned their titular churches in Rome. The pope named Spellman to the Church of Santi Giovanni e Paolo—the same one the pope himself had received when he was named cardinal.

On the way back to New York, Cardinal Spellman stopped in Spain to attend a reception organized by the country's hierarchy. He had a tussle with the press concerning Franco, who was expected to attend the event. Spellman denied he was carrying any secret messages from the pope. At one point he lost his temper and told a persistent reporter from the *New York Herald Tribune*, "Don't ask me foolish questions."[45]

After additional stops in Portugal and the Azores, Cardinal Spellman flew back to LaGuardia Airport on March 5, 1966.

A huge motorcade led by Mayor William O'Dwyer accompanied the cardinal to St. Patrick's, where tens of thousands had gathered to greet him. After a ceremony of thanksgiving at the cathedral, more than four thousand people attended a reception at the Metropolitan Opera House on Thirty-Ninth Street. Spellman told the assembled:

> I would not even be remotely worthy of this honor were it not that I am aware that its greatest glory lies in its opportunity for service. This I have said before, and again I say, that in these days of chaos and crises while mankind is still engulfed in war-heated hatreds and bigotries, honors can be weighed, measured and considered only in terms of opportunity to serve. And service to the utmost and to the end I shall give. To serve my brother and share with him all honors bestowed upon me, all burdens imposed upon him, is the foundation of my faith and love for my fellowman....
>
> I pledge myself anew to love God and to serve Him only, striving ever to emulate Christ's Vicar on earth, unsparingly to spend myself for the spiritual and temporal welfare of you, my people.[46]

Spellman the Cold Warrior

During the Red Scare, Catholics took pride in displaying their anticommunist sympathies. They reminded Protestants that, historically, the Church was the foremost foe of the Marxist movement. They enthusiastically pointed to papal pronouncements denouncing godless, materialistic communism going back all the way to 1848. Having been treated for decades as political aliens, Catholics were delighted to lead a cause that could be viewed as Catholic *and* American.

Catholic groups, particularly the Knights of Columbus and the Catholic War Veterans, spoke out against communist infiltration in America and communist tyranny in occupied Europe. The imprisoned Archbishop Aloysius Stepinac of Yugoslavia and Cardinal Joseph Mindszenty of Hungary became American Catholic heroes. At a 1948 World Peace Rally, Cardinal Spellman declared that Stepinac's only crime was "fidelity to God and Country". In one year Spellman raised over $4 million to build a high school named after the embattled archbishop. From the pulpit of St. Patrick's Cathedral, Spellman told his congregation that Mindszenty was the prisoner of "Christ-hating Communists", and on February 6, 1949, the New York Archdiocese sponsored a day of prayer for Mindszenty. More than four thousand Catholic Boy Scouts marched down Fifth Avenue as they participated in the ceremony. Classes that day at Fordham University were halted and three thousand students prayed aloud the Rosary.

In 1948, Democrats who opposed President Harry Truman's hard line against the Soviet Union defected from the party and formed a new Progressive Party, which picked as its presidential candidate an extreme leftist, former Vice President Henry Wallace.

Most Catholics, including Cardinal Spellman, looked with horror on the Progressive Party's platform. They viewed Henry Wallace as a troublemaker and a pawn of the Reds. The Association of Catholic Trade Unionists condemned the Progressive Party as "a new front for American Communists", and the hierarchy publicized Wallace's statements accusing the Roman Catholic Church of being the key culprit in "stirring up trouble with Russia".[47]

Throughout 1948, Truman followed a plan to attract the Catholic vote. One important date in his plan was March 17. At the annual Friendly Sons of St. Patrick Dinner in New York City, over four thousand men in tuxedos gathered to honor their patron saint and to hear the keynote speaker, President Harry Truman. The presiding cleric, Cardinal Francis Spellman, warmed up the crowd with a rousing anticommunist speech, saying, "It is not alone in defense of my faith that I condemn atheistic Communism, but as an American in defense of my country, for while Communism is an enemy of Catholicism, it is also a challenge to all men who believe in God and in America."[48]

Truman followed the cardinal and, playing to his audience, bluntly stated: "I do not want and will not accept the political support of Henry Wallace and his Communists. If joining them or permitting them to join me is the price of victory, I recommend defeat. These are days of high prices for everything, but any price for Wallace and his Communists is too much for me to pay. I'm not buying."[49]

While his Republican opponent, Thomas Dewey, was picking wallpaper for the White House and Wallace was vehemently denying any domestic communist threat, Truman barnstormed the nation and forged a bond with Catholics.

The Election Day results stunned the pollsters, the pundits, and the Republicans: Truman beat Dewey 49.51 to 45.12 percent. Wallace received only 1.15 million votes, or a little over 2 percent. Catholics overwhelmingly voted for Truman, who in New York exceeded Al Smith's showing in 1928.

As America's leading Catholic cleric and as military vicar, Spellman led the charge against the communists. In July 1946, he wrote an article in *America* magazine, "Communism Is Un-American". "I believe", he wrote, "in America, her freedoms, ideals, traditions. I believe that communism violates these freedoms, is opposed to these ideals, transgresses these traditions, is weakening our nation's unity and wrecking our American way of life. If communism triumphs, Americanism will die."[50]

Spellman sent a similar message in a November 1946 essay, "Do We Want a Soviet Peace?" in *Cosmopolitan* (which at that time was a serious literary magazine). If we commit to a Soviet peace plan, he claimed, "we will commit our children to serfdom."[51]

At Knights of Columbus and American Legion conventions, in university commencement speeches, in his travels to Europe and to Korea, Japan, Okinawa, Labrador, Greenland, Baffin Island, and the Philippines, visiting troops as military vicar, Spellman reminded his listeners of the dangers of communism and the "price of freedom".

Supporting America's involvement in Korea and later in Vietnam, Spellman subscribed to the domino theory and frequently quoted Lenin's vision of communist world domination:

> First we will take Eastern Europe; then the masses of Asia. Then we will encircle the United States of America, which will be the last bastion of Capitalism. We will not have to attack it; it will fall like an overripe fruit into our hands.[52]

After Senator Joseph McCarthy of Wisconsin made the front pages of America's newspapers for exposing the communist "threat from within", many Catholics, particularly of Irish, German, and Polish descent, enthusiastically supported him. Cardinal Spellman was no exception. He defended McCarthy in the public square, saying, "He is against communism and has done and is doing something about it."[53]

While Spellman was not, in his own words, a "wildly enthusiastic McCarthyite",[54] he dismissed criticism from New York's liberal press, mainline Protestants, and left-leaning Catholic publications such as *Commonweal* and *America*. "Anguished cries and protests against 'McCarthyism'", he promised, "will not deter America from trying to root Communists out of the government."[55] In April 1954 Spellman was not afraid to appear with McCarthy on the dais at the New York Police Department's annual Communion Breakfast, attended by six thousand cops. In fact, photographs captured the cardinal basking in the rousing ovation he received. After the senator spoke, the cardinal told the assembled policemen: "McCarthy has told us about the Communists and about the Communist methods. I want to say I'm not only against Communism—but I'm against the methods of the Communists."[56]

Spellman's reputation did not take any hits, either nationally or locally, after McCarthy was censured by his Senate colleagues later that same year. After McCarthy's death in 1957, there was celebrated, for decades, an annual Memorial Mass for the repose of his soul at St. Patrick's Cathedral.

Spellman's Efforts for Aid for Catholic Schools

Cardinal Spellman constantly complained that Catholics who sent their children to parochial schools were treated as second-class citizens because they had to pay both school taxes and tuition. He made it a top priority to lobby federal and state officials to obtain financial aid for students who attended religious schools.

Aid to children attending religious schools had been a hot issue for decades. Catholics had scored a number of victories, the first in 1930 when the U.S. Supreme Court permitted local governments to provide nonreligious textbooks to students attending private and parochial schools. The next victory was the School Lunch Act of 1946, which "included parochial schools in its grant-in-aid programs to the states".[57]

After the Supreme Court ruled by a 5–4 vote in *Everson v. Board of Education* in 1947 that it was permissible for the state to reimburse "parents who paid school bus expenses either to public schools or to Catholic parochial schools",[58] secularists and many Protestants went off the deep end.

Anti-Catholics rallied around Justice Wiley Rutledge's dissenting comment that such aid "exactly fit the kind of evil which Madison and Jefferson struck".[59] Headlines read: "Methodist Bishops Attack Catholics", "Baptist Convention Told Wall between Church and State Is Being Attacked", "Presbyterians Condemn Catholic Demands for School Aid".[60] The court decision gave birth to an organization called Protestants and Other Americans United for the Separation of Church and State, known as POAU, which would give John F. Kennedy plenty of grief when he ran for president in 1960.

Outraged by the bigoted attacks, Spellman struck back in his Fordham University commencement address on June 11, 1947. Speaking to four thousand people, Spellman denounced Protestant groups for a "crusade of bigotry against the Catholic Church in which the patriotism of Catholics is being impugned".[61] He continued:

> Much fearful criticism has been directed at the Supreme Court because of its decision in this case. In high indignation some of our leading newspapers have denounced the decision as a dangerous departure from American principles, an egregious blunder which will lead to union of church and state, an attack upon our cherished free American public schools, the opening wedge in breaking down the wall between church and state.
>
> And with complete disregard for the absolutely clear language of the New Jersey law, which says that transportation shall be provided for children attending both sectarian and non-sectarian private schools, several papers condemned the court for showing favoritism to the Catholic Church.[62]

Responding to attacks by the Reverend Dr. Charles Clayton Morrison, a Disciples of Christ minister who opposed the busing decision and declared that "no pulpit can be silent on the issue", the cardinal said, "No believing Christian of any denomination who respects the church as a place of worship, and whose earnest prayer is for charity and love to all mankind, can let this suggestion go unchallenged. The results of this un-American and un-Christian attitude are now being felt in many small American communities where until recently ministers and priests had worked together in fellowship on community projects."[63]

This was not to be Spellman's last clash in the national public square over aid to schools.

In May 1949, a bipartisan aid-to-education bill that would provide $300 million to "equalize educational opportunities among the states" and that permitted the allocation of funds to private and parochial schools, was passed by the U.S. Senate 58 to 15.

After hearings in the House, however, the Senate bill was altered to limit funds solely to public schools. Congressman Graham A. Barden of North Carolina, who served as chairman of a subcommittee of the Education and Labor Committee, championed the restriction. Shortly thereafter, Cardinal Spellman devoted a talk at Fordham University to articulating his reaction to Barden's bill.

The cardinal denounced Barden as a hypocrite for including parochial-school students in head counts when calculating federal-aid formulas while denying their schools any financial benefits. Spellman concluded his remarks by describing the congressman as a "new apostle of bigotry" who was leading a "craven crusade of religious prejudice against Catholic children and their inalienable rights".[64]

Press coverage of the Fordham talk woke up leading members of Congress, particularly Catholic ones. John McCormack of Massachusetts, the House majority leader, declared that the Barden bill was "grossly unfair" to Catholic and African-American children. The chairman of the House Committee on Labor and Education stated that the bill was "dripping with bigotry and racial prejudice" and predicted it would not be approved by his full committee.[65]

Spellman versus Eleanor Roosevelt

The issue took on a new life when Mrs. Eleanor Roosevelt decided to weigh in and devoted the first of three nationally syndicated columns to the matter on June 23, 1949. After announcing her opposition to aid for private schools, she claimed:

> The controversy brought about by the request made by Francis Cardinal Spellman that Catholic schools should share in Federal aid funds forces upon the citizens of the country the kind of decision that is going to be very difficult to make.... The separation of church and state is extremely important to any of us who hold to the original traditions of our nation. To change these traditions by changing our traditional attitude toward public education would be harmful, I think, to our whole attitude of tolerance in the religious area. If we look at situations which have arisen in the past in Europe and other world areas, I think we shall see the reasons why it is wise to hold to our early traditions.[66]

Catching a lot of flak for her comments, Mrs. Roosevelt took another shot at the question in her July 8 column:

> I would like to make it clear once and for all that I believe in the right of any human being to worship God according to his conviction, and I would not want to see this right taken away from anyone.
>   Sometimes, however, I think church organizations are foolish because they do things that lead people to believe that they are not interested mainly in the spiritual side of the church, but that they have a decided interest also in temporal affairs. This may be harmful to the church's spiritual influence.[67]

Mrs. Roosevelt damaged her cause even further when she admitted in a third column on July 15 that she had not read the Barden bill "carefully" and that she "had been rather careful not to say if I am for or against any particular bill or bills".[68]

Brooding for weeks over Mrs. Roosevelt's commentaries, Cardinal Spellman struck on July 21 in a seventeen-paragraph letter to the former First Lady that was released to the public on July 22. In the scathing letter, Spellman went on the offensive:

When, on June 23rd in your column *My Day*, you aligned yourself with the author and other proponents of the Barden Bill and condemned me for defending Catholic children against those who would deny them their constitutional rights of equality with other American children, you could have acted only from misinformation, ignorance or prejudice, not from knowledge and understanding. It is apparent that you did not take the time to read my address delivered at Fordham University; and in your column of July 15th you admitted that you did not even carefully read and acquaint yourself with the facts of the Barden Bill—the now famous, infamous bill that would unjustly discriminate against minority groups of America's children....

I had intended ignoring your personal attack, but as the days passed and in two subsequent columns you continued your anti-Catholic campaign, I became convinced that it was in the interests of all Americans and the cause of justice itself that your misstatements should be challenged in every quarter of our country where they have already spun and spread their web of prejudice.

After articulating the Church's position on aid to parochial schools, the cardinal, in his final comments, went past the point of no return:

Now my case is closed. This letter will be released to the public tomorrow after it has been delivered to you by special delivery today. And even though you may again use your columns to attack me and again accuse me of starting a controversy, I shall not again publicly acknowledge you. For, whatever you may say in the future, your record of anti-Catholicism stands for all to see—a record which you yourself wrote on the pages of history which cannot be recalled—documents of discrimination unworthy of an American mother![69]

The letter made national and international headlines. While members of America's Church hierarchy in official statements, and priests across the nation speaking from the pulpit, came to Spellman's defense, leading Democrats and members of the liberal media assaulted the cardinal.

New York's Democratic governor, Herbert Lehman, led the charge, stating: "I am deeply shocked at the attack of Cardinal Spellman on Mrs. Roosevelt.... Her every act has been a matter of record. In that splendid record I do not know of a single act or word that would in the slightest degree indicate bias or prejudice against any religion or any race."[70]

Archibald MacLeish, the Pulitzer Prize–winning poet and noted leftist, whom FDR had appointed as Librarian of Congress, published a vicious rhyme titled "I Shall Not Again Publicly Acknowledge You":

> Have you forgotten, Prince of Rome,
> Delighted with your Roman title,
> Have you forgotten that at home
> We have no princes? ...
>
> Prince of the church, when you pretend
> By rank to silence criticism
> It is your country you offend.
> Here man's the faith and rank's the schism.[71]

Reacting in her column, Mrs. Roosevelt sarcastically wrote that she was certain Spellman had written "in what to him seems a Christian and kindly manner and I wish to do the same" and denied "ill feeling toward any religion".[72]

In a letter to Spellman dated July 23, 1949, and released on July 28, she denied charges of being anti-Catholic but managed to take a shot at the Church: "I cannot, however, say that in European countries the control by the Roman Catholic Church of great areas of land has always led to happiness for the people of those countries."[73]

As for the Church's promoting public policy, she said: "Spiritual leadership should remain spiritual leadership and the temporal power should not become too important in a Church."[74]

And in her closing statement she let Spellman have it:

> I assure you that I had no sense of being "an unworthy American mother." The final judgment, my dear Cardinal Spellman, of the worthiness of all human beings is in the hands of God.[75]

Looking to do damage control, Spellman ate some crow and wrote another letter, released on August 5, clarifying his views:

> We are asking Congress to do no more than to continue, in its first general aid-to-education measure, the non-discriminatory policy it has followed in the School Lunch Act and other Federal laws dealing with schools and schoolchildren. We do not want Congress, for the first time, to adopt a discriminatory policy in the field of education. This in no way undermines "the traditional American principle of separation of Church and State." We are asking only for what is constitutional and in accordance with America's previous policy and tradition.[76]

Mrs. Roosevelt admitted that "[I] read it and think it is a clarifying and fair statement."

Two weeks later, Spellman called on Mrs. Roosevelt at Hyde Park, and the two made peace. Both admitted there were "misunderstandings". In her column describing the meeting, Roosevelt wrote tongue-in-cheek: "The Cardinal had dropped in on his way to dedicate a chapel in Peekskill. We had a pleasant chat and I hope the country proved as much a tonic for him as it always is for me."

The story was not over, however. On March 6, 1950, Mrs. Roosevelt stuck it to Spellman one more time. She appeared with Congressman Barden at a luncheon in New York City sponsored by the Committee on Federal Aid to Public Education. In his speech to the 350 attendees, Barden, as the *New York Times* reported, "accused the Roman Catholic Church hierarchy of having tried for 30 years to break down the wall of separation of Church and State."[77] As for Cardinal Spellman, Barden condemned him for attacking "a great noble American lady and mother" and accused him of speaking as a "cruel authoritarian".[78]

Despite all the hyperbole, the Barden Bill went down in flames. Many of Barden's congressional colleagues turned on him when it was revealed that his home state of North Carolina had been contributing tax dollars to schools run by Protestant churches for years.[79]

While Spellman lost the public-relations battle, the question raised as to whether Eleanor Roosevelt harbored anti-Catholic sentiments was a legitimate one. Mrs. Roosevelt's distant cousin, the nationally syndicated columnist Joseph Alsop, explained her distaste for Catholics, particularly prelates: "Eleanor still believed the anti-Catholic nonsense she heard during her childhood."[80]

Mrs. Roosevelt's biographer and friend Joseph Lash revealed that he was "struck by her hostility" to the Catholic Church. "Somewhere deep down in her subconscious was an anti-Catholicism which was part of her Protestant heritage.... Her fear of the Church as a temporal institution was reawakened from time to time by its political operations.... Her distrust of the Church as a temporal institution was one of the reasons for her strenuous opposition later to John F. Kennedy's bid for the presidential nomination."[81]

Mrs. Roosevelt appears to have confirmed Lash's contention when she wrote to a friend on August 15, 1949, "The whole episode with Cardinal Spellman as far as I am concerned is only part of a much larger situation. I think they felt the time had come to form a Catholic party in this country and hoped it could be accomplished. It was a disappointment to them that it did not turn out quite the way they hoped."[82]

It says a lot about Mrs. Roosevelt's paranoia concerning the Church that she could entertain for a moment the absurd thought of the U.S. hierarchy organizing a national Catholic political party.

Spellman versus the Gravediggers

In the late 1880s labor unions that were formed to represent coal miners, steelworkers, and factory workers, among others, were dominated by Catholics. And, for the most part, the Catholic hierarchy blessed these new unions for attempting to improve the lot of the faithful. In his book *Our Christian Heritage*, Cardinal Gibbons "supported the right of workers to organize unions, condemned child labor and attacked monopolies".[83]

The 1891 publication of Pope Leo XIII's encyclical *Rerum Novarum* was a great victory for Cardinal Gibbons and other bishops who defended organized labor's agenda. According to Leo, the state must exercise a positive role in protecting not only the rights of property owners but also those of workers. In calling for regulations to humanize the workplace, the encyclical insisted that the state should "save unfortunate working people from the cruelty of men of greed".

Leo acknowledged the right of laborers to form unions and concluded that such associations can serve the common good. Unions, he explained, have intrinsic value and can offer "the means of affording ... many advantages to the workmen ... [and] should become more numerous and more efficient". On the subject of strikes, he wrote: "When working people [have] recourse to a strike, it is frequently because the hours of labor are too long, or the work too hard, or because they consider their wages insufficient."

To prevent strikes and labor-management conflicts, Leo called on governments to enact laws that would "forestall and prevent such troubles from arising; they should lend their influence and authority to the removal in good time of the causes which lead to conflict between employers and employees."[84]

On May 5, 1931, the fortieth anniversary of *Rerum Novarum*, Pope Pius XI released *Quadragesimo Anno* (In the fortieth year), which expanded on Leo XIII's positions. Pius made clear that "unions and the practice of collective bargaining can serve as a practical and highly effective means for implementing the principle of subsidiarity in contemporary society."[85]

As archbishop, Spellman had extensive relations with New York's organized labor. His postwar construction projects were paying on average $30 million annually in wages to union members in the building trades. On the subject of labor unions, Spellman publicly promoted Church teachings. "Labor", he declared, "has the right and duty to expand its service and usefulness to the social body and to progress through orderly processes."[86]

When it came to strikes, however, Spellman's position was relatively conservative. In a speech he delivered at the 1948 New York Federation of Labor convention, he said:

> In fair collective bargaining rests America's greatest hope for future peaceful labor relations, but in its processes men must guard themselves against selfish, domineering minority groups opposed to our democratic form of government, groups that refuse to solve their problems through this just device and use strikes as smokescreens to wage political war against America. In no business, nor profession, nor craft, nor institution in America, is there any room for a man with a divided allegiance.[87]

Even though religious organizations in New York were exempt from laws pertaining to unions, the cardinal permitted, and indeed encouraged, the archdiocesan cemetery workers to join the United Cemetery Workers Local 293. The local, serving as bargaining agent, won a number of concessions, and by 1947 its members' wages were $59.04 a week, versus the national average of $54.77.[88]

When the union met with officials of the archdiocese in 1949 to negotiate a new contract, it demanded a 30 percent pay increase and a cut in the workweek from forty-eight to forty hours. The archdiocese offered an 8 percent raise and rejected the forty-hour-week proposal because many burials took place on Saturdays. With the two sides at loggerheads, the union issued a strike order to its 240 members effective January 13, 1949.

The cardinal, appalled by the strike, became belligerent after he was informed that the United Cemetery Workers were affiliated with the communist-infiltrated Congress of Industrial Organizations (CIO). Any settlement, he insisted, would include a change in the local's parent organization from the CIO to the American Federation of Labor, which had broken with the CIO precisely over the communist issue.

With strikers unwilling to budge and negotiations getting nowhere, and with more than one thousand bodies awaiting burial, the cardinal retaliated. In a public announcement he said: "Thus have the men and the union made their decision. And now I must make mine. This evening I shall go to Dunwoodie and suspend classes in the Seminary, releasing all physically able seminarians to assist in the corporal work of mercy of burying the dead!"[89]

On March 3, 1949, the cardinal-archbishop of New York led over two hundred seminarians, with shovels in hand, past picketing strikers, and supervised as they dug graves in the soil still hard from winter.

This effort, which Spellman described as "the most important work of my ten years in New York",[90] was a public-relations disaster. The press ridiculed the cardinal, and the tabloids published photos of students knee-high in graves with Spellman inspecting their work.

In the course of this controversy, Spellman lost not only public backing but also the support of the Association of Catholic Trade Unionists (ACTU), many of his diocesan consulters, and several seminary professors. When the ACTU criticized the cardinal for "union-busting", Spellman boasted, "I admit to the accusation of strikebreaker and I am proud of it. If stopping a strike like this isn't a thing of honor, then I don't know what honor is."[91]

One of the dissenting clerics, the prominent Catholic social thinker and future archdiocesan secretary of education and family-life director, Monsignor George A. Kelly, made this observation: "Pitting the seminarians, sons of workingmen, against workers no better off than their own fathers was not viewed by priests as an appropriate way of confronting a disagreeable labor situation.... [Spellman's] blunder in the Calvary strike was picking on little people."[92]

After six weeks without pay, the strikers began to crack. To placate the cardinal on the communist issue, the gravediggers made this pledge at their meeting hall: "We here as Catholic gentlemen, declare that we are opposed to Communism and all it means in all walks of life. Be it recorded, however, that Communism is not the basic issue here."[93]

On March 11, 1949, the gravediggers agreed to end the strike. They settled for an 8.3 percent raise and agreed to affiliate with the AFL. As for the workweek, both sides agreed to turn the issue over to an independent mediator. To help heal the breach, Spellman dug into his personal savings and sent every gravedigger $65.

Spellman and the Making of a President—1960

Having met during the 1936 Pacelli visit, Spellman and Joseph P. Kennedy became fast friends. Kennedy frequently invited Spellman to his home in Bronxville, in an affluent section of the archdiocese. Spellman officiated at the marriage of several Kennedy children and baptized a few of the grandchildren. The two men took advantage of each other to achieve various ends.

When Kennedy was out of favor with FDR because of his support of British Prime Minister Neville Chamberlain's appeasement policies, he used Spellman as a back door to the White House. (But he never fully got on board with FDR and Churchill's conduct of the war. He frequently spouted off to Spellman, particularly against the Allies' "unconditional surrender" policy.) Kennedy also leaned on Spellman to gain access to John J. Reynolds, a leading New York commercial-real-estate broker who had close ties to the Church. As Kennedy biographer David Nasaw wrote, "With the City's premier broker working for him, [and his] connections to the Catholic Church ... Kennedy ended up defying his own expectations and making at least as much money from [New York] real estate as he had from trading stocks."[94]

Spellman, on the other hand, frequently turned to Kennedy for donations to fund various projects and programs, and he would seek Kennedy's advice on investments.

Another reason Joe Kennedy valued his close relationships with Spellman and other leading prelates, particularly Archbishop Cushing of Boston and Chicago's

Cardinal Albert Meyer, is that he knew that if his son Jack was to have any chance of being elected president, he would need the overwhelming support of urban Catholics.

Although the Harvard-educated John F. Kennedy "possessed the affectation of a Brahmin", he had gained an understanding of the social conservatism of his Roman Catholic constituents while representing Massachusetts in both the House of Representatives and the Senate. Biographer Thomas Maier points out that JFK "acted as a stalwart supporter of the Church, both for calculated political reasons and out of his own convictions". In a speech he gave in 1950 at Notre Dame, Kennedy sounded like a Thomistic scholar when describing the nature of man: "You have been taught that each individual has an eternal soul, composed of an intellect which can know truth and a will which is free.... Believing this, Catholics can never adhere to any political theory which holds that the state is a separate, distinct organization to which allegiance must be paid rather than a representative institution which derives its powers from the consent of the governed." He also cautioned the graduates about "the absorbing hands of the great Leviathan" and warned against the "ever expanding power of the federal government". He even made a lucid statement on the principle of subsidiarity, when he said that "control over local affairs is the essence of liberty."[95]

But when Kennedy had his eye on national politics, he could be equivocal on certain popular Catholic issues. After the public brawl between Cardinal Spellman and Eleanor Roosevelt over the merits of direct federal aid to parochial schools, Kennedy took a middle position in order to avoid offending supporters on either side of the issue. To please liberals, he opposed such aid as unconstitutional. To placate the Church and his conservative constituents, he vigorously argued that Catholic students should receive direct aid for health services, transportation, and textbooks.

During his campaign for the presidency in 1960, the Catholic issue haunted him. In early August, Protestant organizations in Michigan and Kentucky announced their opposition to electing a Catholic president. Later in the month, twenty-five Baptist, Methodist, and Pentecostal ministers promised to "oppose with all powers at our command, the election of a Catholic to the Presidency of the United States".[96] Numerous other groups representing tens of thousands of Protestants voiced similar anti-Catholic opposition to Kennedy.

To stop the political hemorrhaging, Kennedy decided to confront the issue at a meeting of the Greater Houston Ministerial Association on September 12:

> I believe in an America where the separation of church and state is absolute—where no Catholic prelate would tell the President (should he be Catholic) how to act, and no Protestant minister would tell his parishioners for whom to vote—where no church or church school is granted any public funds or political preference—and where no man is denied public office merely because his religion differs from the President who might appoint him or the people who might elect him.[97]

Though the speech did appear to allay the fears of many Protestants, it did not sit well with all Catholics, particularly Spellman. He was not pleased that by reinventing himself and currying favor with liberals, Kennedy had discarded issues such as aid to parochial schools. The cardinal was also perturbed by Kennedy's attempt to sever any connections between one's religious and political creeds. He agreed with the observation of the Jesuit political philosopher John Courtney Murray that "to make religion merely a private matter was idiocy. Murray played on the Greek work *idiotes* which originally signified a private person with no responsibility for public affairs and gradually came to mean a person who is irresponsible".[98]

Joe Kennedy was livid that Spellman and other members of the hierarchy were silent on his son's candidacy. He had expected that, at the very least, Spellman would have given directions to parishes, *sotto voce*, to get Catholics to the polls to support one of their own.

One reason for Spellman's lack of support was fear of a Protestant backlash. According to Kennedy biographer Thomas Maier, Spellman "adopted a position in 1960 that he considered best for the Church rather than the interests of one family. Spellman believed Richard Nixon would be more flexible to the Church's needs than Jack Kennedy [because Nixon] was not handcuffed by his own words on the separation of church and state. All the issues pressed by the Catholic hierarchy— funding for parochial schools, a U.S. ambassador at the Vatican, tough stands on communism and sexual morality—would be likely pushed by Nixon."[99]

Angry that Spellman was not loyal to his family, Jack Kennedy had to be dragged to the October 1960 Al Smith Dinner, which the cardinal hosted and at which Richard Nixon was slated to appear. The annual dinner had been instituted by Spellman in 1945 to honor the former governor and to raise funds for the Alfred E. Smith Memorial Foundation. To this day, an invitation to sit on the dais is considered a command performance for politicians—including presidents of the United States.

Kennedy, who had the Irish touch for delivering humorous lines, charmed the audience and managed to tweak his host. His opening line was: "Now that Cardinal Spellman has demonstrated the proper spirit, I assume that shortly I will be invited to a Quaker dinner honoring Herbert Hoover." He went on to say, "Cardinal Spellman is the only man so widely respected in American politics that could bring together amicably, at the same banquet table, for the first time in this campaign two political leaders who are increasingly apprehensive about the November election— who have eyed each other suspiciously and who have disagreed so strongly, both publicly and privately—Vice President Nixon and Governor Rockefeller."[100]

Toward the end of the campaign, Spellman did give Kennedy a helping hand. In late October, after the bishops of Puerto Rico issued a statement directing Catholics not to vote for Governor Luis Muñoz Marín and instead to vote for the candidate of the Christian Action Party, Spellman quelled the fears of Protestants, stating "that Catholic voters who did not obey the bishops' directive would not be committing a sin".[101]

Although John F. Kennedy was elected president, neither Joe nor his family ever forgave Spellman for putting the Church ahead of their political interests. Writing to his and Spellman's friend in the Vatican, Count Enrico Galeazzi, Joe said:

> I have a very strong feeling that the time for friends to be together is when you need them the most. I have never asked for many things, but I needed all the help I could get in this campaign. I don't think [Spellman] gave the help he should have and I think we did as badly in New York amongst the Catholics as we did anywhere in the country. He was asked to do two or three things and he just didn't deliver. In my

book we are all even for past services and I haven't any interest in the future.... As far as I am concerned, I am through working for them or with them, with the exception of Cushing in Boston.... Don't think that I am irrational or too mad about the situation. I am just fed up with the whole crowd.[102]

After the count made an effort to mend fences between the two men, Joe Kennedy wrote to him, "I am sorry to say, I am less in the mood then ever to 'straighten the matter'.... I know that I should be more charitable in my old age, but I seem to get worse instead of better."[103]

Being shunned by the Kennedys did not stop Spellman from fighting for Church principles. Three days before JFK was sworn in as president, Spellman attacked Kennedy's Task Force on Education, which called for federal aid to public schools but not to Catholic schools. He declared "that its recommendations are 'blatantly discriminating against' parochial school children depriving them of freedom of mind and freedom of religion."[104] In a January 17, 1961, front-page article, the *New York Times* declared that Spellman had "rarely ... taken so strong a stand on a legislative proposal".[105]

Later in 1961 Spellman used his influence to kill the Kennedy proposal. The powerful Democratic congressman from Queens, James Delaney, a ranking member of the House Rules Committee, was persuaded to join Republicans to defeat the federal aid-to-education bill. It is interesting to note that Protestants and Other Americans United for the Separation of Church and State, which had viciously opposed Kennedy's election, now supported his legislation. It put out a statement saying, "We hope that the American people will support President Kennedy against the Bishops of his Church."[106]

Spellman the Power Broker

There is no question that Francis Cardinal Spellman was the most influential U.S. Catholic cleric on both the national and international stages in the history of the nation. Roosevelt, Truman, and Eisenhower took his calls and sought his advice, and he carried out delicate diplomatic missions for them. As he traveled the world visiting our troops as military vicar, doors of foreign leaders were always open to him.

Spellman was able to get the attention of political leaders, captains of industry, and the media for two key reasons. First, as the leading voice for the Church in America, Spellman would use his pulpit at St. Patrick's Cathedral to influence millions of the faithful. Secondly, he had a special relationship with Pope Pius XII that no other member of the universal Church hierarchy could rival.

In the United States in general, and in New York in particular, Spellman pursued the interests of the Church quietly through back channels to public officials. He often served as the intermediary between the Vatican and the White House. Also, through his travels as military vicar and his oversight of such organizations as the Catholic Near East Welfare Association, he would garner information that presidents, secretaries of state, and secretaries of defense found invaluable. From the pulpit he did not fear taking on the communists, pro-birth-control legislation, or films that he considered immoral or blasphemous. Criticism from New York's intellectual and cultural elites just rolled off his back.

Despite public controversies, Spellman remained very popular with Catholic laity. In August 1957, in honor of the twenty-fifth anniversary of his consecration as a bishop, four cardinals, eighteen archbishops, over eighty bishops, and fifty thousand laymen gathered at Yankee Stadium, where he celebrated Mass. (Today only papal visits attract such Catholic crowds at The House That Ruth Built.) When Spellman celebrated the fiftieth anniversary of his ordination in May 1966, ABC-TV produced a documentary, *Cardinal Spellman: The Man*, that was broadcast on national television during prime time.

Spellman also used his special relationship with Pope Pius XII to restructure the Church in New York and in the nation. When he arrived in New York in 1939, there were two auxiliary bishops, and when he died in 1967 there were ten. He had more priests elevated to monsignor than all his predecessors. He was known to inform favored priests of such promotions before Rome knew of them. He would bypass the apostolic delegate and would present lists of monsignors to Pope Pius directly for after-the-fact approval during trips to the Vatican. At his death in 1967, about 25 percent of the archdiocese's priests were monsignors. "When I go to a parish and don't have any prepared remarks," he told one audience, "I make the pastor a monsignor."[107]

Spellman had the ability to spot and attract bright priests to help him manage the archdiocese. One priest who worked with him closely observed, "There was a *mystique* about [him], a sort of benign aloofness that produced reverence, affection and unshakeable loyalties. Spelly was a shrimp in size, but you always talked up to him."[108]

Priests who were loyal and competent, known as "Spelly's Boys", were promoted, and many became ordinaries throughout the nation. Here is a listing of them:

- James Francis McIntyre (1886–1979): Spellman's first chancellor went on to become an auxiliary bishop of New York, archbishop-coadjutor of New York, and cardinal-archbishop of Los Angeles.
- John O'Hara (1888–1960): Auxiliary bishop of the Military Ordinariate; bishop of Buffalo; cardinal archbishop of Philadelphia.
- William McCarty (1889–1972): Auxiliary bishop of the Military Ordinariate; bishop of Rapid City, South Dakota.
- Bryan J. McEntegart (1893–1968): Executive director of Catholic Relief Services; bishop of Ogdensburg; archbishop of Brooklyn.
- Thomas McDonnell (1894–1961): Auxiliary bishop of New York; bishop coadjutor of Wheeling, West Virginia.
- Patrick O'Boyle (1896–1987): Executive director of New York Catholic Charities; cardinal archbishop of Washington, D.C.
- Fulton J. Sheen (1895–1979): Auxiliary bishop of New York; bishop of Rochester.
- Walter P. Kellenberg (1901–1986): Auxiliary bishop of New York; bishop of Ogdensburg; bishop of Rockville Center.
- John Maguire (1904–1989): Auxiliary bishop of New York; bishop-coadjutor of New York.
- Christopher Weldon (1905–1982): Secretary to Spellman; executive director of New York Catholic Charities; bishop of Springfield, Massachusetts.

- Francis Reh (1911–1994): Chancellor of the Archdiocese of New York; rector of St. Joseph's Seminary; bishop of Charleston, South Carolina; bishop of Saginaw, Michigan.

- George Guilfoyle (1913–1991): Auxiliary bishop of New York; bishop of Camden, New Jersey.

- John Ryan (1913–2000): Chancellor of the Military Vicariate; archbishop of Anchorage, Alaska; first archbishop for the Military Services.

- Thomas Donnellan (1914–1987): Secretary to Spellman; rector of St. Joseph's Seminary; bishop of Ogdensburg; archbishop of Atlanta.

- Terence Cooke (1921–1983): Auxiliary bishop of New York; cardinal archbishop of New York.

The most famous of the "Spelly" bishops, Fulton J. Sheen, also had one of the most famous falling-outs with his mentor in U.S. Church history.

Sheen and Spellman

Fulton John Sheen was born over his father's hardware store in El Paso, Illinois, on May 8, 1895. An outstanding student, Sheen attended St. Victor's College in Bourbonnais, Illinois, and later, realizing he had a religious vocation, entered St. Paul Seminary in Minnesota.

Ordained a priest on September 25, 1919, he was not assigned a parish but was sent to the Catholic University of America for graduate studies. Upon earning his master of arts degree, he traveled to Europe for additional education, earning a doctorate of philosophy from the University of Louvain.

During this period, his reputation as a preacher and Catholic apologist grew, and invitations to speak and preach throughout the nation poured in. In 1930 the American bishops invited him to represent the Church on NBC's nationally broadcast radio show *The Catholic Hour*, and he appeared on that show until 1951, when he switched from radio to television, with a new show called *Life Is Worth Living*.

Sheen accomplished much besides. He produced at least one book a year, wrote two weekly newspaper columns, became national director of the Society for the Propagation of the Faith, and edited two magazines. Also, he was instrumental in numerous conversions, including those of Clare Boothe Luce, Henry Ford II, ex-communists Louis Budenz and Elizabeth Bentley, and violinist Fritz Kreisler.

Sheen caught Spellman's eye, and in 1948 the cardinal invited the monsignor to accompany him on a trip to Melbourne, Australia, to participate in the centenary of its archdiocese. Their travels, which included visits to missions and military bases, permitted Spellman to judge whether the two could work together.

Shortly thereafter, in 1950, Spellman, in his capacity as national president of the Society for the Propagation of the Faith, engineered Sheen's appointment as national director of the organization. One year later, Sheen was consecrated auxiliary bishop of New York.

In 1952, Spellman approved Sheen's appearing on what was to become his award-winning television show, *Life Is Worth Living*. Taped in Manhattan's Adelphi

Theater, it was the first (and possibly only) religious show sponsored by a major corporation (Admiral, the television-set manufacturer). *Life Is Worth Living* was up against *The Milton Berle Show*. Every week America asked, "Shall we watch Uncle Miltie or Uncle Fultie?" Sheen's ratings skyrocketed, and Mr. Television was knocked off the top of the ratings chart.

The show continued until 1957 and had an estimated audience of thirty million. The bishop, who covered a wide range of subjects, from psychology to Irish humor to Stalin, received between eight and ten thousand letters a day.

All of Sheen's income from the show and royalties from related books went to the Society for the Propagation of the Faith. His fame from the show helped him raise tens of millions for the charity. During his tenure as national director (1951–1966), Sheen raised approximately $200 million.

The feud that commenced between Spellman and Sheen, which destroyed their friendship and shook the very foundations of the Archdiocese of New York, was over money.

To finance favored oversees projects, Spellman would call Sheen and demand that he cut a check on the Society for the Propagation of the Faith's account. If Sheen refused, citing the need for board approval, Spellman—who was used to getting his own way—fulminated.

Their disagreements over the allocation of Society funds came to a head in 1957 when President Eisenhower turned over to Spellman surplus powdered milk for the poor. Spellman, in turn, gave it to the Society and demanded that the archdiocese be paid for it. Sheen refused and looked to Rome for protection.

To settle the matter, Pope Pius XII called both men to Rome and asked each to give his version of events. After Vatican conversations with the White House revealed that Sheen was right in his account of where the powdered milk had come from, the pope ruled in his favor. Spellman, who had distorted the truth in reporting to the pope, was humiliated.

Sheen's biographer, Thomas Reeves, notes that Spellman "reportedly said to Sheen, 'I will get even with you. It may take six months or ten years, but everyone will know what you're like'".[109]

And he did. Sheen was barred from preaching on Christ's Seven Last Words on Good Friday at St. Patrick's Cathedral, and his show was cancelled after the 1956–1957 season.

In later years, fearful that Sheen would be named his successor in New York, Spellman arranged with Rome, after much clerical juggling, Sheen's appointment as bishop of Rochester, which took place in 1966. As Reeves wrote:

> Rochester was a good choice, not only because of its location but because it was ripe for change. Bishop Edward Kearney was nearly eighty-two years old and had led the diocese since 1937. To pave the way for Sheen, Spellman quietly had the Vatican, on March 9 (a month before Fulton was summoned to Rome), transfer the auxiliary bishop of Rochester, Lawrence Casey, to Paterson, New Jersey. Bishop John Joseph Boardman, who had accepted the position in Paterson three days earlier, found the offer retracted. Spellman had a long acquaintance with both Kearney and Casey, and knew that the bishop was highly dependent upon his young auxiliary. Once Casey was gone, Kearney would retire willingly.[110]

Bishop Sheen was ill-suited to be an ordinary, and, after serving only three years in Rochester, he resigned. Pope Paul VI accepted his resignation and named him archbishop of the Titular See of Newport, Wales.

Sheen was to spend the final decade of his life living and preaching in New York City. When he died, on December 9, 1979, one could say he got the last laugh: Spellman's successor, Cardinal Cooke, announced that Sheen's Requiem Mass was to be held in St. Patrick's and that he was to be buried in the crypt under the main altar, right next to Cardinal Spellman.

Vatican II

In the fall of 1958, Spellman left New York Harbor on the Greek ship T.S.S. *Olympia*, leading eight hundred New Yorkers on a pilgrimage that was to include stops in Lourdes and Rome. While sailing by Gibraltar on October 6, the cardinal received word that Pope Pius had suffered a stroke.

The cardinal led the pilgrims in prayer for the ailing pope, and when a telegram for Spellman arrived on Tuesday, October 7, saying that it appeared that he was recovering, Spellman sent this reply:

> EXCELLENCY DELLACQUA—VATICAN CITY
> PILGRIMS SORROWSTRICKEN HOLY FATHERS ILLNESS OFFERING MASSES AND HOLY COM-
> MUNIONS FOR HIS HOLINESS MAINTAINING TWENTY-FOUR HOUR VIGIL OF PRAYERS
> BEFORE THE BLESSED SACRAMENT.
>
> CARDINAL SPELLMAN[111]

The next morning, this telegram arrived from Castel Gandolfo, where the pope was in residence when he took ill:

> WEDNESDAY OCT. 8TH
> HIS EMINENCE FRANCIS CARDINAL SPELLMAN
> ARCHBISHOP OF NEW YORK S.S. OLYMPIA
> WE FEEL CONSOLED AND COMFORTED IN OUR ILLNESS BY THE PRAYERFUL MESSAGE
> WHICH YOU HAVE SENT TO US AND WITH THE ASSURANCE OF OUR SINCERE GRATITUDE
> WE IMPART TO YOU AND YOUR PILGRIMS OUR PATERNAL APOSTOLIC BLESSING.
>
> POPE PIUS XII[112]

Several hours later the pope died.

An old acquaintance of the cardinal, General George Dany, the commander of the U.S. Air Force Base at Terceira, made flight arrangements for him to be taken to Rome. Upon arriving, he immediately went to Castel Gandolfo and prayed at the pope's deathbed.

Afterward, the pope's gatekeeper and the cardinal's close friend, Mother Pasqualina, met with him and described the pontiff's final hours. The nun also gave him a number of papal mementos: the last white cassock Pius had worn and the white zucchetto she had placed on his head after he died. (Pasqualina, who was removed from the papal household by the Curia after Pius was buried, was cared for by Spellman. He had an apartment built for her at the North American College.)

Spellman stayed on in Rome for the papal funeral and the subsequent conclave. On October 28, after the eleventh ballot, white smoke came out of the Sistine Chapel announcing the election of a new pope. The College of Cardinals, after a stalemate, chose a compromise candidate, Cardinal Angelo Roncalli, the patriarch of Venice, who took the name John XXIII.

The death of Pius XII was a serious blow to Cardinal Spellman. He lost not only a great friend but also the power that was associated with that relationship. With the new pope, Spellman no longer had the same degree of access and influence, particularly over appointments in the States and over foreign policy.

When Pope John XXIII announced there would be a second Vatican Council, Spellman was leery about the implications of the meeting. While his rank and seniority in the College of Cardinals required his appointment as a Council Father, he did not play a leading role in the proceedings. He did, however, make two significant contributions: First, he fought for the inclusion on the Council agenda of an item on religious liberty. The cardinal also insisted that his personal theologian at Vatican II, John Courtney Murray, S.J., be the lead drafter of the text of that item.

Murray was well known in U.S. political and philosophical circles for his book *We Hold These Truths*, published in 1960. In that work, Murray, as historian Patrick Allitt put it, "sought to convince skeptical America that [the] Catholic Tradition shared the basic premises of the Declaration of Independence and on the other hand tried to convince the Vatican that it need have no fear of Americanism but rather should acknowledge the U.S. constitutional system as the ideal modern setting for the Church".[113]

At the Council, Murray was the primary author of the Declaration on Religious Liberty, which was approved by a vote of 2,308 to 70 on December 7, 1965. The document was a great victory for Catholics in America, because it reflected the First Amendment to the Constitution, which prohibits "impeding the free exercise" of religion. The Vatican document declared "that the right to religious freedom has its foundations in the very dignity of the human person as this dignity is known through the revealed word of God and by reason itself.... This right of the human person to religious freedom is to be recognized in the constitutional law whereby society is governed and thus it is to become a civil right."[114]

The second influence Spellman had on the Council concerned the Jewish people. In fact, Rabbi James Rudin of the American Jewish Committee has publicly stated that the "Cardinal's efforts were indispensable during the final efforts of the Vatican Council to adopt the Nostra Aetate declaration on the Jewish people."[115]

The 642-word statement reminded Catholics that the Church "believes that by His cross Christ, Our Peace, reconciled Jews and Gentiles making both one in Himself". It went on to state, "in her rejection of every persecution against any man, the Church, mindful of the patrimony she shares with Jews and moved not by political reasons but by the Gospel's spiritual love, decries hatred, persecutions, displays of anti-Semitism, directed against Jews at any time and by anyone." Finally, the document rejected Jewish culpability for the death of Christ.

Regarding other Vatican II decisions and their aftermath (the "Spirit of Vatican II"), Spellman was unhappy with the radical changes in the liturgy of the Mass. He preferred the Latin Mass over the English Mass. "The Latin language," he said, "which is truly the Catholic language, is unchangeable, is not vulgar, and has for many centuries been the guardian of the unity of the Western Church."[116]

While he followed the guidelines that came into use after Vatican II and arranged for the liturgy to be conducted in English, he was critical of priests who had a "zeal for novelties" and misinterpreted the "spirit" of Vatican II. Spellman especially despised novelties such as the so-called Hootenanny Masses, which included guitar playing. As for other post-Vatican II changes, as Monsignor George Kelly wrote, by the time of his death in 1967, they "were in place in New York—new ecumenical relations, the updating of religious life, a priests' senate, and better consultation procedures".[117]

Cardinal Spellman did convince Pope John XXIII, in 1962, that the Church should have a presence at the upcoming World's Fair, to be held in New York City's Flushing Meadow Park in 1964–1965. Pope John approved the building of a Vatican Pavilion and offered Michelangelo's *Pietà* as "the outstanding work of art he could send for it".[118] The *Pietà* was the fair's biggest single attraction, with twenty-seven million people viewing it.

The Sixties: Changing Times

After a short but eventful tenure, John XXIII died of stomach cancer on June 3, 1963. The man who succeeded him to the papacy on June 21 was not a close buddy of Spellman. Giovanni Montini, who took the name Paul VI, had often clashed with Spellman on foreign-policy matters when he was Vatican deputy secretary of state under Pius XII. In particular, Montini took a conciliatory attitude toward the Soviet Union, while Spellman was the Church's number-one Cold Warrior.

Their icy relations did not stop Spellman from rolling out the red carpet when Pope Paul made a visit to New York in 1965. Spellman greeted the pope on the tarmac at LaGuardia Airport upon his arrival on October 4. The pope's first words to the assembled crowd of the faithful and political dignitaries were: "Greetings to you, America. The first Pope to set foot upon your land blesses you with all [his] heart."[119]

The cardinal accompanied the pope in a bubble-top limousine on a route to Manhattan lined with millions of cheering New Yorkers. Arm in arm, the cardinal and the pope waved to the tens of thousands standing outside St. Patrick's Cathedral. After a time of prayer, the pope attended a luncheon hosted by Spellman.

Later in the afternoon, Paul had a private meeting with President Johnson at the Waldorf-Astoria, and from there he went to the United Nations, where he told the General Assembly: "Peace.... It is peace which must guide the destinies of peoples and all mankind."[120]

Before departing for Rome that night, the pope and the cardinal celebrated Mass in a packed Yankee Stadium. The pope stressed, once again, that "you must love peace.... You must serve the cause of peace.... Peace must be based on moral and religious principles which must make it sincere and stable."[121]

Spellman had never made up with the Kennedys after their falling out in 1960, and he remained banished from the White House until after President Kennedy's tragic death in November 1963. Lyndon Johnson, however, welcomed the cardinal with open arms.

As a fervent anti-communist, Spellman supported Johnson's escalation of the war in Vietnam and his invasion of the Dominican Republic in 1965. Called the Bob Hope of the Clergy, the cardinal regularly visited our fighting troops in Vietnam, and newspapers frequently printed photos of him blessing GIs as well as airplanes and weapons. His Christmas card in 1965 had a photo of him standing in front of a fighter plane.

Unlike the "good war" waged against the Nazis and the Japanese imperialists, the conflict in Southeast Asia drew plenty of opposition. Spellman was appalled in December 1965 when student protesters marched outside the Powerhouse at 452 Madison Avenue, condemning Spellman's public support of Johnson's war policies. A year later, on Sunday, January 22, 1967, protesters displaying posters that accused Spellman of being a warmonger disrupted the eleven o'clock Mass.

When the two Berrigan brothers—the Jesuit Daniel and the Josephite Philip— circulated a petition called a Declaration of Conscience, which opposed the bombing of North Vietnam and compared the war to racism in the United States, Spellman used his influence through back channels to get Philip transferred from Newburgh, New York, to Baltimore, Maryland, and Daniel to Latin America.

Spellman did his best to ignore Pope Paul's opposition to the war. He was not happy that Vatican diplomats were making direct contacts with Ho Chi Minh, the communist leader of North Vietnam. Spellman refused to bend and continued visiting our troops at Christmas. The fearless cleric told Catholic troops they were fighting "Christ's war against the Vietcong and the people of North Vietnam" and that "any solution other than victory is inconceivable."[122]

Nonetheless, when Paul VI had his chance to send a strong message to the Church in America concerning the Vatican's change in attitude toward the Cold War, he took a pass. Spellman's mandatory resignation letter, sent to the Vatican when he turned seventy-five in 1964, was rejected by the Holy Father.

Meanwhile, on the home front, President Johnson supported policies close to the cardinal's heart. The Higher Education Facilities Act, which the president signed into law in 1963, permitted Catholic colleges to receive building-construction grants.

Sometimes the Johnson policies had unintended consequences, however. When Great Society money started pouring into New York City, unfortunately Spellman succumbed to temptation and supported urban-planning programs that had the effect of destroying old Catholic neighborhoods. For instance, to build Lincoln Center on Manhattan's Upper West Side, master builder Robert Moses knew he would have to eliminate several Catholic parishes and their environs through the power of eminent domain. "Don't let's spend too much time with an individual pastor who thinks his jurisdiction and membership may be somewhat reduced", Moses lectured his planners. "There must be adjustments in the churches to keep pace with adjustments of the general population."[123]

To undercut Catholic protests, Moses sought the support of Cardinal Spellman and the Jesuits of Fordham University, and New York's churchmen actually went along with his cynical view. In exchange for their acquiescing to his plans to take the land needed to build Lincoln Center, Moses offered Fordham the chance to build a Manhattan campus in the Lincoln Center complex. The cost of the property to Fordham? One dollar. The real cost of the property? The dislocation of seven thousand mostly Catholic families along with the destruction of St. Matthew's parish on West Sixty-Eighth Street, which was bulldozed to make way for Fordham's graduate school, which included a school of theology.

State Aid to Parochial Schools

Cardinal Spellman's last battle in the public square was in support of state aid to parochial schools.

As described in the chapter on Archbishop Corrigan, Protestants in the late nineteenth century, fearing the growing number of Catholic state legislators, sought to prevent them from appropriating money to underwrite the Church's educational system. To meet this end, the 1894 New York State constitutional convention, controlled by Protestant "good government" types, adopted the Blaine Amendment, which "prohibited direct or indirect aid to educational institutions under the direction of a religious denomination".[124]

As mentioned earlier, every twenty years New Yorkers must vote on whether they want to convene a state convention to review and, if they deem it appropriate, revise their constitution. More often than not, they vote against such a gathering, but in 1965, 53 percent of the voters decided it was a good idea.

Sensing an opportunity, Spellman called in his chits with the political establishment to include, as one of the proposed constitutional revisions, the repeal of the Blaine Amendment. Republican Governor Nelson Rockefeller, who had presidential ambitions, was sympathetic, as was the Catholic Democratic Speaker of the Assembly, Anthony Travia—who hoped one day to be governor.

Travia, who controlled a majority of the convention delegates, visited the cardinal at the Powerhouse to explain his agenda. The repeal of the Blaine Amendment would be one of a number of proposals that would be packaged together and placed before the voters in November 1967. These included a conservation bill of rights; the assumption by the state of all welfare costs; the elimination of redistricting by the legislature and the establishment of a nonpartisan apportionment commission; and the elimination of the requirement that state debt not be incurred unless approved by the voters. Travia argued that presenting all these proposals to the voters in a take-it-or-leave-it proposition would gather enough special-interest voting blocs to ensure victory on Election Day. On paper this approach seemed to make sense, and Spellman gave it his blessing.

After word leaked about this meeting, Rockefeller sent as his emissary to the Powerhouse Lieutenant Governor Malcolm Wilson, one of the most devout Catholic pols in New York. Wilson urged that repeal of the Blaine Amendment should not be included in such a package. With many New Yorkers trending to the right, he feared that a backlash against Great Society–type leftist social-engineering policies could spell defeat at the polls for the Travia package. The better approach would be for the convention to approve putting repeal on the ballot as a stand-alone proposition.

Speaker Travia, however, disagreed and stuck with his all-or-nothing approach. When Republican delegates tried to separate out the Blaine repeal, their motion was voted down.

Realizing he was boxed in, the cardinal continued to support the Travia package. After all, there were over nine hundred thousand non-public-school students in

New York State, and their parents could prove to be a decisive voting bloc in an off-year election in which voter turnout was expected to be light.

What Spellman and Travia underestimated, however, was the potential voting power of diverse special interests that opposed the Blaine repeal. First, there were the anti-Catholic groups such as POAU and the ACLU, which hated parochial schools. Next, there was Mayor John Lindsay and teachers'-union officials, who feared that the public schools would lose tens of thousands of students if the state in any way subsidized private ones. Then there were groups such as the American Jewish Congress, which, as Monsignor George Kelly wrote, "saw the repeal of Blaine as a concession to the bigotry of white parents who did not want their children to sit with blacks".[125] (They held this position despite the fact that in 1967, while only 18 percent of New York City's Catholics were minorities, 52 percent of Catholics enrolled in Manhattan parochial schools and 30 percent of those in the Bronx were minorities.[126])

Finally, the five-year-old New York Conservative Party opposed the other constitutional revisions in the package. The party, which had been founded by two Irish Catholics, J. Daniel Mahoney and Kieran O'Doherty, and whose membership was overwhelmingly blue-collar Catholic, campaigned against the liberal welfare provisions and the elimination of voter approval for long-term bonded debt, claiming it was a "prescription for fiscal disaster".

Despite the odds, the cardinal decided to fight. He raised large sums of money to promote the message on television and in print media that the new constitution would be "a document worthy of support by the people in New York State". Parochial-school children brought home literature urging their parents to vote yes. A great rally was held at Madison Square Garden, for which Catholic students and parents were bused in from all over the state. Spellman, Bishop Sheen, AFL-CIO president George Meany, Congressman Hugh Carey, Senator Eugene McCarthy, and William F. Buckley Jr. all addressed the packed arena. The Sunday before Election Day, a pastoral letter from the New York bishops was read from every pulpit in the state, and Knights of Columbus members handed out flyers after every Mass at every parish.

On November 7, 1967, ballot question 1, which read, "Shall the proposed new constitution adopted by the Constitutional Convention and the resolution submitting the same, be approved?" went down in flames. Those voting no totaled 3,487,513 (72 percent); those voting yes totaled 1,327,999 (28 percent).

Spellman's Final Days

That defeat signaled the end of the Spellman era. Twenty-five days later, on December 2, 1967, the most influential Catholic cleric in America's history, the man who personified the golden age of the Church, was dead.

On December 3, Spellman was laid out in the cathedral. For the next four days, 3,600 people per hour walked by the casket to pay their final respects.

President Lyndon Johnson, who was the first sitting U.S. chief executive to attend the Requiem Mass of a cardinal archbishop, said in a statement, "The Lord has called a man who served Him and all His children well.... The race of man mourns him now, for mankind was his ministry.... His voice was heard on the smallest parish street and in the highest councils of his Church. He was both pastor and statesman.... Cardinal Spellman was my close and cherished friend of many years. I pray that the American family, as my own, will be consoled by this truth: As God has taken him away this day, He has given us the blessings of his disciple's work for all our days."[127]

The *New York Times* editors, however, could not help themselves. They went after the cardinal for standing up for Church principles in the public square. In an editorial dated December 4, 1967, they asserted that Spellman, "a conservative and a traditionalist ... exercised his formal authority and personal influence on behalf of the familiar and the narrowly orthodox.... In political affairs and in public debate he often tended to speak in a commanding tone and to don a mask of authoritarianism which, however appropriate in some other time and some other place, was ill-suited to a pluralist democracy."[128]

The Catholic magazine *Commonweal*, which was moving to the left in the Sixties, also took a shot at the dead cardinal:

> He stood for a kind of Catholicism, oriented toward bureaucratic efficiency, money raising and good public relations, which we felt symbolized the social success and power of the Church at the same time as it symbolized the spiritual failure of Catholic Christians in New York.[129]

The Jesuits' *America* was much kinder to an alumnus of one of their universities:

> The marvel is not that Cardinal Spellman was a man of his time, but that he showed himself as open and flexible as he did. Granted, he was never described by the press as the darling and the champion of the "liberal faction" in the Catholic Church; yet amid the crashing alternations of recent years he displayed notable calm modesty, good sense. He encouraged liturgical renewal, he appointed Episcopal vicars, he refrained from reactionary pronouncements, he functioned quietly and wisely, he maintained— and without hidden power plays—a truly remarkable peace in his sprawling, brawling Archdiocese. No one denies that the cardinal was an authentic friend to the Negro, the Puerto Rican, the Jew, to the men in uniform, to the poor....
>
> This Review, whose editorial freedom Cardinal Spellman always respected, prays that he may enjoy eternal refreshment, light and peace.[130]

At 6:30 P.M. on Sunday, December 3, New York's auxiliary bishops, led by Archbishop-Coadjutor John Maguire and the consultors of the Archdiocese, sang a Mass in the cathedral for the repose of the cardinal's soul. The next day, more than 2,400 children, representing the archdiocese's 250,000 parochial-school students, attended a Memorial Mass. On Tuesday, December 5, there was a Mass for the archdiocesan nuns and on Wednesday for the representatives of the U.S. Armed Forces.

On Thursday, December 7, President Johnson, Vice President Hubert Humphrey, members of the U.S. Cabinet, New York's senior elected officials, and over 50 Protestant and Orthodox churchmen attended the Pontifical Requiem Mass at St. Patrick's, which was televised nationwide. The procession into the cathedral included more than 1,000 priests and 100 archbishops and bishops. The main celebrant was Pope Paul's representative, Archbishop Luigi Raimondi. Nine cardinals concelebrated.

Flags throughout the city were at half-mast, and at 1:00 P.M., when the Mass was to begin, trading on the floor of the American Stock Exchange was halted for a minute of silence.

The homily was delivered by Fordham President Robert Gannon, S.J., a close friend of the cardinal and his biographer. Gannon said of Spellman that, "in spite of a disarming simplicity of manner, he was complex and a very positive character, the wrong man to cross when he decided he was right and you were wrong."[131]

Ironically, the Mass itself was the first said entirely in English for a deceased cardinal. The traditional "Dies Irae" (Day of Wrath) was not sung. Instead the choir proclaimed "Happy are those who die in the Lord." It was a simpler and shorter ceremony than the traditional one—two hours, versus three hours for Cardinal Hayes in 1938.

At the end of the Mass, Archbishop Raimondi, in the name of the pope, declared: "We have lost a spiritual leader, a father—and a dear friend. However, he will, I am sure, pray for us. May his devotion to our Church and to his fellow man continue to be a source of inspiration to us. May his brave, Christ-like, priestly soul rest in peace."[132]

8

The Equalizer

FIAT VOLUNTAS TUA

Terence James Cooke
Seventh Archbishop of New York
(1968–1993)

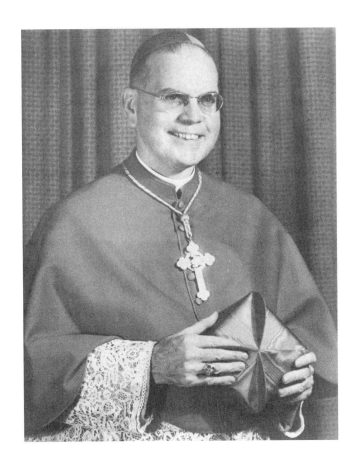

Cardinal Cooke with soldiers in Vietnam

John Joseph Maguire, Archbishop-Coadjutor of New York, expected that he would succeed Cardinal Spellman. So did his family, his friends, and most of his fellow priests.

Maguire had earned Spellman's trust while serving, successively, as assistant chancellor, vice chancellor, chancellor, and vicar-general. He was delegated significant authority, particularly over education, and he initiated the Spanish Apostolate, low-income-housing projects, marriage counseling, and the Christian Family Movement. It was his idea to build the twenty-one-story Catholic Center, located at 1011 First Avenue and completed in 1975, to house under one roof all the administrative offices of the archdiocese.

Maguire was named an auxiliary bishop in 1959 and Archbishop-Coadjutor in 1965, succeeding the previous coadjutor, Francis McIntyre, who had moved on to become cardinal archbishop of Los Angeles. Maguire's "particular skill", Catholic intellectual Monsignor George Kelly observed, "was finding reasonable answers to tricky problems, whether they concerned priest personnel, the division of parishes, new Church programs, or diocesan finances".[1]

Six months before his death, sitting next to Maguire at a meeting of the board of consultors, Spellman prophesied, "I can tell you this. When my time comes to go, the Holy Father this time, unlike 1939, will not have to look outside for my successor."[2] Hence, no one was surprised when, within hours after the passing of Spellman, the priest-consultors elected Maguire administrator of the archdiocese during the interregnum.

Nonetheless, John J. Maguire's wish to be the seventh archbishop of New York was not to be realized. Instead, on March 8, 1968, the Vatican announced that the position was to go to the vicar-general, forty-seven-year-old Terence James Cooke, who had been named an auxiliary bishop only two years earlier.

What happened? There are a number of explanations. First and foremost is that Spellman was displeased with Maguire for instituting too quickly some of the Vatican II liturgical changes. When Spellman was in Vietnam visiting troops during the 1966 Christmas season, Maguire decided that he did not want to be seen celebrating the televised Midnight Mass at St. Patrick's with his back to the faithful just one year after the closing of the Vatican Council. As Edward Fiske wrote in the *New York Times Magazine*, "He solved the problem by shifting the candles around and conducting the Mass from *behind* the main altar—the option now used routinely. Cardinal Spellman, who apparently had little enthusiasm for some of the post-Vatican II innovations, was said to have been furious."[3]

The other reason is that Cooke, who had become Spellman's priest-secretary in 1957, vice chancellor in 1958, and chancellor in 1961, had formed a close relationship with the cardinal. Cooke was not only a competent administrator but also a very kind and gentle man, who took care of the cardinal as his health declined in the mid-1960s. According to one priest, Cooke, in Spellman's final years, gave "Spelly his Post Toasties in the morning and ate dinner alone with him at night".[4] Cooke "loved the old man, who reciprocated the affection", as Monsignor Kelly put it, "to the extent this was possible for a Boston Yankee".[5]

Though Spellman could not get Cooke named coadjutor with right to succession, he did make it known in no uncertain terms to the apostolic delegate and to Pope Paul VI himself that his vicar-general was his preferred choice for his successor. The pope, who had been impressed with Cooke's organization of the events during his October 1965 trip to New York, granted the final request of a loyal and dedicated son of the Church.

The Early Years

Terence James Cooke was born on March 1, 1921, on La Salle Street in Manhattan's Morningside Heights. He was the third child of an Irish immigrant couple, Michael and Margaret Cooke, and was named after the Lord Mayor of Cork, Terence MacSwiney, who had died in an English jail in 1920 as the result of a hunger strike. Terence Cooke was baptized at Corpus Christi Church on 121st Street.

Terence's father, who was a lay member of the Third Order of St. Francis, climbed the economic ladder, working as a chauffeur, a construction worker, and a civil servant.

When Terence was four, his family moved to St. Benedict's parish in the Throgs Neck section of the Bronx. Five years later his mother died of peritonitis, and his aunt Mary Gannon, who worked at Wanamaker's department store in Manhattan, took over the job of rearing him and his brother, Joseph, and sister, Katherine.

After his grammar-school education, which he received from the Dominican Sisters of Blauvelt, in Rockland County, Terence, believing he had a vocation, entered the minor seminary, Cathedral College, to which he commuted every day from the Bronx. During the summer breaks, he worked at a second-hand furniture store, Berger's, at 146th Street and Third Avenue in the Bronx.

Terence was a good student who followed the rules. He took up the violin and served as the editor of the *Chimes*, the Cathedral College newspaper. After completing the prescribed six years of study, Cooke advanced in September 1940 to St. Joseph's Seminary, Dunwoodie.

During his five years at Dunwoodie, Cooke became manager of the seminary bookstore and helped organize the summer programs at Badger Camp, a Catholic facility in New Rochelle. He also was active in Casita Maria, an outreach program for Puerto Rican youth, which provided various family-counseling services.

Terence Cooke was ordained by Archbishop Spellman on December 1, 1945. His first assignments as curate in two parishes in Harlem, Mount Carmel and St. Thomas the Apostle, were brief, because his archbishop decided that he was to begin graduate work at the University of Chicago in the spring of 1946. That assignment was also short-lived. Upon his arrival in Chicago, Father Cooke contracted a painful eye ailment that prevented him from reading. Forced to abandon his studies, he returned to New York in early 1946 and was assigned to a South Bronx parish, St. Athanasius.

His eye infection persisting, Cooke was moved in March 1947 to Nanuet—near the hamlet of Blauvelt, where he had gone to school—to serve as chaplain of St. Agatha's Home for Children. During the six months he resided at the orphanage, he took an active role in organizing programs and projects for the children.

With Cooke's eyesight finally improving, the cardinal sent him to the Catholic University of America in the fall of 1947 to pursue studies in the School of Social Work.

At Catholic U., Cooke did well academically. His master's thesis, "Thomistic Philosophy in the Principles of Social Group Work", not only received a top grade but was published and widely read. As Benedict Groeschel and Terrence Weber wrote in *Thy Will Be Done*, "The readership was by no means confined to Catholic institutions. Schools of social work in Europe wrote for copies and schools in South America translated it into Spanish."[6]

Returning to New York after graduating in 1949, Cooke was assigned to the youth division of Catholic Charities. He lived at the retreat house of the Cenacle of St. Regis on West 140th Street, helped out with the Masses at St. Jude's parish on West 204th Street, and began teaching a course at Fordham University's School of Social Services.

Father Cooke took his responsibilities at Catholic Charities very seriously. For him, social workers were "apostles, apostles of kindness working with the mind of Christ under the protection of the Blessed Mother".[7]

The hardworking Cooke caught the eye of Cardinal Spellman, who in January 1954 appointed him procurator of St. Joseph's Seminary. Although he was sorry to leave his job with the youth of the archdiocese to take on a nuts-and-bolts maintenance job, nevertheless he proved to be an able manager with an eye for detail. And the job did have one advantage: He was able to get to know and assess future priests.

To Cooke's surprise, he received a call in January 1957 informing him that he was to report to the Powerhouse as secretary to the cardinal. What followed was a rapid climb up the clerical ladder. In August 1957 he was named a papal chamberlain; in June 1958 he was appointed vice chancellor; in November 1958 was elevated to domestic prelate; and in June 1961 he became chancellor of the archdiocese.

In his last years as archbishop, Spellman basically split the responsibility for running the day-to-day activities of the archdiocese. Bishop John Maguire, who served as vicar-general, devoted most of his energies to the educational system. According to Monsignor Kelly, he "approved all subsidies for educational efforts, authorized all of the construction of schools, and dealt with most of the major superiors whose communities staffed diverse educational apostolates".[8] He also dealt with priest-personnel issues.

Monsignor Cooke, as chancellor, devoted most of his energies to tracking the finances of the archdiocese. He also had the job of being the aging cardinal's friend and gatekeeper. He was a tireless worker who managed to balance his administrative duties with the difficult task of managing the cardinal's daily activities. Over time, the relationship developed into that of a father and son.

Reflecting years later on this time he spent with his mentor, Cooke said, "It was a rich experience and an educational one being around [Spellman]. His memory was incredible. He knew how to take the best of the past and the present. His consideration was unfailing and so was his courtesy. I can still see him helping every visitor on with his or her coat and accompanying them to the door."[9]

On September 15, 1965, the Vatican announced that Monsignor Cooke had been named an auxiliary bishop of New York and titular bishop of Summa (a see that was located in what is now Algeria). There was, however, no time for celebrating. The actual consecration by Spellman was put off until December 15 because of the pending visit to New York by Pope Paul VI.

Cooke was assigned the huge task of coordinating all the events surrounding the trip. Behind the scenes he dealt with the office of President Lyndon Johnson, the United Nations staff, the U.S. Secret Service, the offices of Governor Nelson Rockefeller and Mayor John Lindsay, the New York Police Department, and local, national, and international media outlets. He also had to oversee the planning of the papal events at St. Patrick's Cathedral and Yankee Stadium. Cooke's attention to detail paid off; the pope's whirlwind tour of New York went off without any major hitches.

On December 2, 1967, two years after his consecration as bishop, Cooke, who resided at 452 Madison Avenue, was present when Spellman suffered a major stroke, and he administered the sacrament of extreme unction. He was also present a few hours later when the cardinal died at St. Vincent's Hospital in Greenwich Village.

Less than three months after Spellman's death, the Vatican informed Bishop Cooke that he was to be the seventh archbishop of New York.

Archbishop Cooke

Right before the announcement became public on March 2, 1968, Cooke took a walk around the blocks surrounding St. Patrick's with his friend Monsignor Patrick Ahern, a future auxiliary bishop of New York who had also served as Spellman's secretary. Cooke told Ahern that he was to be the next archbishop. After the shocked Ahern hugged and congratulated his old friend, Cooke said to him:

> Nobody knows the situation better than I. I know the finances of the diocese and they're not good. I also know that all of the troops are jumpy, especially the priests. Everyone is in a very upset frame of mind and the guy who gets this job is going to catch all the flak that they have suppressed. It's going to be terrible, but that's what [my motto] "Fiat Voluntas Tua" [Thy Will Be Done] means.[10]

Cooke's comment to Ahern on East Fiftieth Street in front of Burger Heaven was truly an epiphany—a sudden manifestation of the essential nature of a situation.

The end of the Spellman era marked the beginning of a cultural and religious revolt brewing among an important segment of America's Catholic population.

Immigrants who had brought with them from the Old World a commitment to the rock-solid doctrines of the Catholic faith were now bombarded by zealous innovators, who, "in the spirit of Vatican II", discarded, tampered with, revised, or eliminated ceremonies and doctrines that had been practiced and cherished for generations.

Bishops, priests, nuns, theologians, and canon lawyers questioned Catholic certitudes and papal authority. Some declared independence from the Magisterium and interpreted Church doctrine according to their whims. They questioned all matters, even the divinity of Christ.

There were young priests who believed that their call was to eliminate social injustice, not to save souls. Instead of praying and tending to parishioners, many pursued careers as activists in the civil-rights movement, the War on Poverty, and the antiwar movement. They stood by César Chavez and his United Farm Workers of America, formed the Catholic Campaign for Human Development, and generally launched the Church's equivalent of the Great Society.

Ethnic Catholics whose families had supported Catholic higher education for more than a century were shocked in July 1967 when twenty-six educators from ten Catholic colleges signed the so-called Land O' Lakes document, declaring their independence from the Vatican in running their schools. Crucifixes were taken down from classroom walls, and dissent was the order of the day. Faculty members took pride in questioning Church doctrine in the classroom.

Those bishops desperate to appear "with it" allowed dissenters within their dioceses to subvert the Church. Apostasy was fostered, with dissenters condemning or ridiculing papal and ecclesiastical teachings on contraception and, later, on ordination of women and on homosexuality.

Vacillating bishops, rebellious priests and nuns, and revisionist theologians caused great confusion in parishes, in Church grammar schools, and on Catholic campuses. It has been estimated that in 1960, 75 percent of America's forty million Catholics went to Mass weekly and 85 percent made their annual Easter duty. By the time of Terence Cooke's death in 1983, the statistics had changed markedly:

- Only twenty-five million Catholics attended Mass every Sunday, 37 percent less than in 1960, even though by virtue of natural increase the Catholic population was 25 percent larger.
- The sacrament of penance was virtually neglected, evidence of a lessened sense of sin.
- There were fewer than six thousand seminarians studying for the priesthood, one-quarter of the 1960 number.

First Crises

Cooke was not to have a honeymoon. On March 13, 1968, before he took office, members of the archdiocese's Senate of Priests sent a twenty-five-hundred-word memorandum of priorities to the archbishop-elect. The *New York Times*, in a front-page story, ran this headline, along with subheadings: "Priests Here Ask Cooke to Initiate Sweeping Change—Advisory Unit Petitions Archbishop in Naming of Leaders—Financial Data Sought—Full Statements and Talks on Budgets Requested—Racial Justice Stressed".

The *Times* printed the entire text of the memorandum and reported that Cooke met for thirty minutes with the priest-representative who presented the document. In a nutshell, the priests urged the new leadership to:

- Issue "full and understandable financial statements".
- Give priests a voice in the selection of auxiliary bishops and other top officials.
- Create an archdiocesan pastoral council of laymen, priests, and religious that would have the power of prior consultation on "all proposed programs and their budgets".
- Establish a "centralized department of urban affairs" that would initiate and coordinate programs in the areas of housing, race relations, and other urban problems.[11]

The cover letter stated that the memo was not a "routine and superfluous protestation of loyalty" but an attempt to initiate "responsible collaboration in the mission of the Church between bishops and priests".[12]

This was not the first strike by a subset of priests after Spellman's death. In January, they had sent a letter to Pope Paul VI asking for a say in the selection of the new ordinary. The Vatican did not reply to the request.

The battle for the soul of the Church in New York had begun. And Cooke, not looking for a public brawl that could mar his new administration, punted. A spokesman for the archdiocese said that Cooke was pleased with the meeting and that "in general [the memo] expressed the things he had in mind".[13]

Cooke faced his next crisis on April 4, 1968—the day he was installed at St. Patrick's. At 6:01 that evening, the Reverend Martin Luther King Jr. was shot by an assassin outside his motel room in Memphis. One hour later he was declared dead at St. Joseph's Hospital.

Reacting to the murder, African-Americans took to the streets and rioted in several major cities, including Washington, D.C., Baltimore, Chicago, Kansas City, and Louisville.

Upon hearing the news, the archbishop left a reception at the Waldorf-Astoria and went to a Harlem parish to pray with the faithful for the repose of Dr. King's soul.

At a press conference, Archbishop Cooke called for calm in the city, which was experiencing some mild looting in Bedford-Stuyvesant and Harlem, and said, "Dr. King died in the cause of racial justice and peace, the cause for which we must all pray and work unceasingly." He announced that Masses and prayers would be offered for King on April 6 in the archdiocese's 412 parishes.[14] Cooke also contacted elected officials and offered his assistance to help defuse racial strife. He then flew down to Atlanta, Georgia, to attend King's funeral on April 9.

Fifty-seven days after King's funeral, New Yorkers received another jolt—their junior senator, Robert F. Kennedy, was gunned down by an assassin shortly after midnight on June 5 after declaring victory in the California Democratic presidential primary. He died at 1:44 A.M. on June 6.

Archbishop Cooke's offer that Kennedy's body lie in repose in St. Patrick's Cathedral was accepted by his family. When Kennedy's casket arrived on Air Force One at LaGuardia Airport at 9:00 P.M. on June 6, the archbishop prayed over the slain senator on the tarmac. One hour later the coffin was carried into St. Patrick's.

Thousands waited outside the cathedral, in a line that stretched for a mile and a half; they were permitted to start entering the cathedral to pay their respects at 5:30 A.M. on June 7. The viewing continued nonstop until 5:00 A.M. on June 8.

At 10:00 A.M., Archbishop Cooke celebrated a Solemn Pontifical Mass in a packed cathedral. Presiding were Pope Paul VI's vicar-general, Cardinal Angelo Dell'Acqua, and Cardinal Richard Cushing of Boston. Leonard Bernstein conducted parts of Mahler's Fifth Symphony, and Andy Williams sang "The Battle Hymn of the Republic".

Archbishop Cooke, in his sermon to the huge congregation, which included the Kennedy clan, President Johnson, Vice President Humphrey, Richard Nixon, Coretta Scott King, César Chavez, Walter Reuther, and Barry Goldwater, said:

Today in simple realism we salute the sense of purpose which gave direction to Robert Kennedy's life. We salute the sacrifice which answering the call demanded of him each day.... In death Robert Francis Kennedy has joined the immortals of America and will be remembered with honor wherever the history of our nation is recorded. May he be joined also with those immortals from every land and nation who live forever with God in heaven.[15]

Reacting to the King and Kennedy assassinations, President Johnson appointed a commission headed by Dr. Milton Eisenhower, the former president's brother, to examine the "causes, the occurrences and the control of physical violence across the nation, from assassination that is motivated by prejudice and ideology and by politics and by insanity; to violence in our streets and even in our homes".[16] Archbishop Cooke was appointed a member of the panel.

On July 25, forty-seven days after the Kennedy funeral, Cooke had to deal with another event that would bring turmoil to his flock—this one from Rome. Pope Paul VI's encyclical *Humanae Vitae* reconfirmed the Church's opposition to the use of artificial contraception.

Reaction from the Left was dismissive or indifferent. "One hopeful sign is that educated Catholics are not going to pay any attention to this statement", said a Jesuit philosopher, the Reverend Robert Johnson.[17]

Cooke was in Puerto Rico, making pastoral visits to churches and schools, when he was informed of the papal statement. Knowing that some of the faithful and even some of his priests in New York would be unhappy with *Humanae Vitae* did not stop Cooke from pledging his support. From Puerto Rico he sent this cable to Paul VI:

> Most Holy Father:
> Thou art Peter. Where ever Peter is there is the Church. United with you in your paternal care to safeguard the holiness of marriage and the human family. Assure you of our prayerful pastoral efforts in fulfilling this urgent responsibility.
>
> Your devoted son,
> Terence Cooke[18]

When he returned to New York, he penned a pastoral letter that was read from 412 pulpits after every Mass on Sunday, August 11. "You may be sure", Cooke declared, "that I share the concerns of Pope Paul for the difficulties which this teaching involves for those who are married.... I pray that God will give them strength to bear their burdens bravely and to draw inspiration from their pure and noble love for each other. I urge them most earnestly to receive the sacraments often."[19]

Putting His Imprint on the Archdiocese

Despite the numerous crises Cooke had to face immediately after his installation, he did make a series of decisions that would put his personal imprint on the archdiocese.

Unlike his predecessor, Cardinal Spellman, who adhered to the view that at times one had to break a few eggs to make an omelet, Cooke shunned controversy and confrontation. Some, like the New York Catholic historian Monsignor

Florence Cohalan, would go so far as to say that while Cooke was perfect as a number-two man—one who could execute the boss' decisions brilliantly because of his excellent administrative abilities and his fine eye for detail—he was less well suited to be number one because, Cohalan wrote, he was "by nature inclined to prefer persuasion to command.... He disliked anything approaching public confrontation, and was prepared to go a surprising length to head off or to refuse it.... Above all, Cooke intended to be a reconciler rather than a ruler."[20]

To defuse the ticking time bomb of radical antiestablishment sentiment in the archdiocese, Cooke clearly spelled out his approach in his installation homily: "We seek to achieve a happy wedding of the new and the old. Our task is to perfect and adopt what we have and at the same time move forward into new areas of concern. Progress builds, it does not destroy."[21]

On April 16, 1968, Cooke announced the creation of a nonsectarian committee of sixteen experts in finance and education to oversee a survey of the archdiocese's 432 schools. Members included Cyrus Vance, who had served as secretary of the army and deputy secretary of defense; Daniel Lufkin, chairman of the investment-banking firm of Donaldson, Lufkin and Jenrette; Dr. James Perkins, president of Cornell University; and Dr. Robert Goheen, president of Princeton University.[22]

In announcing the panel, the archbishop made it clear that "money very frankly is a problem."[23] He instructed the members to "develop all the facts pertinent to the entire scope of Catholic education in the Archdiocese, evaluate the policies and objectives with our available resources; propose revisions in our educational endeavors as dictated by the facts; analyze the choices available to us; set forth the advantages of each; and use the best judgment to provide a solid basis for action".[24]

In 1968 there were 333 elementary schools and 99 high schools in the archdiocesan system; total student enrollment was 215,000. Of the 7,850 teachers, 4,405 were religious and 3,451 were laymen.

Because the number of teaching sisters had been dropping in the 1960s, the schools had been hiring more lay teachers, whose salaries and benefits were more costly. As a result, the system was running a deficit, and more than one hundred schools were not self-supporting. Meanwhile, the archdiocese was adamant about keeping schools open in poor minority neighborhoods—more than 50 percent of parochial-school students in Manhattan were African-American or Puerto Rican—and this further increased the financial burden.

Summarizing the problem, Cooke's secretary, Monsignor Eugene V. Clark, put it this way: "We're not at the point of hocking things, but it is true there is no cash around.... Until five or so years ago, the Archdiocese was banking money. Now money earned by sound investments is going into operating expenses, rather than new investments."[25]

Next, Cooke turned his attention to the clergy in his charge. In early May he sent a letter to his 1,265 priests requesting that they send him a confidential list of recommendations of priests to be appointed to "various diocesan offices".

In a letter dated May 7, 1968, he wrote, "Since my recent appointment, I have stressed my reliance on you to help me fulfill my responsibilities.... At this time I would appreciate your judgment on those priests you consider qualified to assume the responsibilities of various diocesan offices.... I shall personally review these names and your nominations and comments will be held confidentially."[26]

While this action was unprecedented, there were mumblings among some of the more liberal clergy. One priest complained "that the Archbishop is implying that he does not feel bound by what we say. He just wants to hear us, which is gratuitous."[27]

Members of the Senate of Priests complained that Cooke "was bypassing the formal organizations that have been set up to reflect the priests' views". The president of the senate, Father John Byrne, argued that the letter circumvented "the principle of formal collegiality, or shared government in the Church".[28]

Others applauded the archbishop's request. "I think it's a great day in the tradition of the Church in New York that we would be asked our opinion", said one Manhattan pastor, Monsignor James Wilson. "It's certainly flattering and gratifying, and I feel the Archbishop is being very humble in reaching out for our suggestions."[29]

To further placate his outspoken priests, Cooke instituted weekly staff meetings to hear a variety of opinions on policy matters. He also approved a proposal, backed by the Senate of Priests, to establish a personnel commission made up of "elected priests to advise on the placement and transfer of priests".[30]

Cooke pledged that no priest would be given a new assignment without prior consultation. He encouraged priests to drop him a line or to set up an appointment with him to discuss their individual concerns or problems.

Cooke established a committee to assist Harlem priests in executing their outreach to African-Americans. He appointed, in July 1968, the first black pastor, Father Harold Salmon, to Harlem's largest parish, St. Charles Borromeo on West 141st, and also named Salmon a vicar for the area. (Cooke presided—uncomfortably—over a jazz Mass at the installation of Father Salmon.) Another African-American, Father Emerson Moore, was named the director of the day camp attended by five hundred Harlem boys on the grounds of St. Joseph's Seminary. In 1982 Moore was named an auxiliary bishop.

Other new ventures approved by Cooke included Project Equality, which was dedicated to promoting "Equal Employment Opportunity practices", and a fifty-member Social Justice Task Force, whose major accomplishment was, according to the *New York Times*, a "decision not to purchase California grapes in order to show support for the campaign to unionize grape pickers".[31]

As for seminary training, Cooke, the first Dunwoodie graduate to become archbishop of New York, announced, in a letter to priests on June 4, 1968, a reorganization plan. Cathedral College, which educated prospective priests for six years—four years of high school and the first two years of college—was now to be a high school only and was renamed Cathedral Preparatory Seminary. Undergraduate training was to take place at the Brooklyn Diocese's Immaculate Conception Seminary College in Douglaston, Queens. Four years of postgraduate work before ordination would be provided by Dunwoodie. A scholarship program was established for the training of Hispanic and African-American seminarians.

Cooke also announced, with the bishops of Brooklyn and Rockville Centre, the consolidation of seminary education for the three dioceses in the metropolitan region, believing it would enhance the various institutions academically.

Cooke made it clear that he had acted on the recommendations of a committee that "included representatives of St. Joseph's Seminary and Cathedral College, the new priests' senate and the administrative offices".[32]

Amid all this administrative activity, in his first months as archbishop Cooke managed to visit churches in each of the ten counties that made up the archdiocese. He also addressed the increasing problem of troubled marriages among Catholic couples. Cooke endorsed, in September of 1968, "a simplification of legal procedures in marriage cases but stopped short of endorsing an entirely new system".[33] In a statement he made it clear, however, that "the indissolvable bond of marriage is basically a matter of divine law" and that any revisions in annulment procedures must be carried out "within the limitations imposed by the divine law".[34]

This declaration was a rebuke of one of his priests, Monsignor Stephen Kelleher, a canon lawyer who had served on the archdiocese's marriage tribunal for twenty-five years. Kelleher had publicly recommended that "Catholics in 'intolerable' marriages be permitted to decide for themselves whether they are morally free to remarry."[35] He also argued that Church teachings on troubled marriages "lack[ed] Christian love and compassion" and recommended that marriage tribunals be "abolished entirely".[36]

Shortly after Cooke clarified the position of his archdiocese, he called Kelleher into his office and personally informed him that he was being removed from the marriage tribunal and transferred to a parish in Scarsdale, in Westchester County. Though Cooke had proven in his first five months as archbishop that he was open to some changes and innovations inspired by the Second Vatican Council, Kelleher, in Cooke's judgment, had pushed "the spirit of Vatican II" too far. This would not be the last time that Cooke—the "unlikely warrior", as Monsignor Cohalan called him—would stand up and publicly defend and enforce fundamental Church teachings.

Back on May 5, Pope Paul had formally appointed Archbishop Cooke military vicar for Catholics serving in the U.S. armed forces. In mid-December, Cooke left from JFK Airport to visit troops stationed around the world. Stops on his trip included Frankfurt, Teheran, Bangkok, Manila, Seoul, Tokyo, and Saigon. For Christmas, he celebrated Midnight Mass in South Vietnam at Tan Son Nhut Airbase outside the capital city of Saigon.[37] He returned in January in time to give the benediction at the presidential inauguration of Richard Nixon on January 20, 1969.

To top off the busy first year of his administration, Cooke learned in April 1969 that he was to be elevated to the College of Cardinals at a papal consistory to be held on April 28. At forty-eight years of age, he was not only the youngest American ever to become a cardinal but was also the youngest of the thirty-three prelates named that year by Pope Paul VI.

Looking back on Cooke's first year as archbishop, Cardinal Edwin O'Brien, who would later serve as the archdiocese's director of communications and as Cooke's secretary, said:

> He dealt with many trying situations that would get other people down. Just dealing with the priests in those days with almost rebellion throughout the church. Certainly in his own flock, people dissatisfied either with the pace of counsel that was not being fulfilled or they wanted more, or they wanted to go slower. He had to address everyone and keep their eyes fixed on what the church is—the body of Christ. On

the reality of the human condition. We [do not] have a perfect world here, a lasting city, but he knew there was one awaiting and that this was Christ's promise to him.

He was able to motivate other people in those difficult days. As I think an extraordinary leader would hope to do. He did it and he did it almost effortlessly. I think it was because of the hope that he had.[38]

Cooke left for the consistory on April 25, 1969, on a TWA plane that had painted on its fuselage a three-foot-by-two-foot copy of his coat of arms. He was accompanied by his family and twenty members of his 1945 ordination class.

Greeted by more than three hundred Americans at the Rome airport, Cooke said to them, "To see the Pope is a great source of joy to me, particularly for the honor he has chosen to give to the people of New York through my person and for having offered me the chance to serve my neighbors better."[39]

After receiving the red biretta and a cardinal's ring from Pope Paul VI, Cooke celebrated Mass in his titular church in Rome, Santi Giovanni e Paolo.

On the way home, his entourage made a pilgrimage to the hometown of Cooke's parents in County Galway, Ireland. The cardinal celebrated Mass in the parish of his ancestors.

Upon arriving at JFK Airport on May 7, Cooke was greeted by a huge crowd of well-wishers. He rode to St. Patrick's Cathedral in a bubbletop limousine that permitted him to wave to the crowds gathered along the route.

At the cathedral he was greeted by political dignitaries including Governor Nelson Rockefeller, Mayor John Lindsay, and U.S. Senators Jacob Javits, Charles Goodell, and Edward M. Kennedy. U.S. Secretary of Transportation John Volpe represented President Nixon. After thanking the welcoming committee, Cooke walked to the barricades on Fifth Avenue and worked the crowd for half an hour.

Afterward he celebrated his first Mass in the cathedral as cardinal archbishop. In his homily, reflecting on his motto, "Thy will be done," he told the assembled, "Today and tomorrow and for whatever time God chooses that I remain as Archbishop of New York, I must devote all my efforts to doing God's will, being a good bishop serving my fellow men.... If God's will is to be done we must have the will to chart a course of action that is independent of all fears."[40]

Returning to Fifth Avenue to greet more of the faithful, Cooke told one group of Irish-Americans of his experiences in the Emerald Isle: "Years ago I was in Ireland as a young priest, and I found I had dozens of cousins. Then when I went as a bishop I found I had hundreds of cousins. And when I went as a Cardinal I found I had thousands of cousins. That's how it is in Ireland."[41]

In his first year as archbishop of New York, Terence Cooke had demonstrated that when it came to managing the inner workings of the archdiocese he ably filled Spellman's shoes. The jury was still out, however, as to whether he was capable of maintaining the Church's authentic mission while simultaneously controlling or tempering those radical forces within his archdiocese clamoring for instant change regardless of Church teachings or the potential consequences of their agenda. Cooke would be tested almost every day in the 1970s on the battlefield of what was to become known as the Culture War.

Cooke in the Public Square

While Cardinal Cooke was grappling in 1970 with the management of his archdio-cese, a public-policy issue suddenly surfaced and caught him and his fellow bishops throughout the state off guard. The issue was abortion. On March 18, 1970, Senate Majority Leader Earl Brydges, a practicing Catholic, permitted a no-restrictions abortion bill sponsored by an upstate member, Senator Clinton Dominick, to come to the floor for debate. Brydges, an ardent foe of abortion who for years had bottled up various bills that would have removed restrictions on it, decided he could pla-cate some of his critics by permitting a vote on a piece of legislation he was certain would be defeated.

After five hours of fierce debate, however, Senator Brydges realized he had mis-calculated, but by then it was too late. The bill, which repealed the anti-abortion law that had been on the books since 1830, managed to pass with a vote of 31 to 26. Senator John Marchi of Staten Island, a leading debater against the bill, was shocked that it received such support. "Abortion had barely entered into the pub-lic dialogue", Marchi said. "I remember attending the [state] Constitutional Con-vention of 1967, and there wasn't a single bill on the subject, nor was there any advocacy." Mike Long, a leader of the New York State Conservative Party, also admitted that his party was caught napping: "Abortion was a non-issue up until then.... We first put a pro-life plank in the party platform in 1968, and we had a big internal fight about it ... [because] nobody, and I mean nobody, expected this to become a reality."[42]

Hoping to stop the bill in the assembly, Cooke and the other ordinaries in New York made public statements opposing abortion, and the New York Catholic Con-ference was directed to use its influence to persuade wavering legislators, particu-larly Catholic ones, of the evil of the legislation.

When the bill hit the assembly, it was amended to restrict abortions after twenty-four weeks' gestation. On March 30, proponents failed by three votes to get the needed majority. Another roll call took place on April 9, and when it was announced that the vote was seventy-four to seventy-four, a Democrat from a predominantly Catholic area in upstate New York, Assemblyman George Michaels, took to the floor and stated that he was changing his vote to "Aye" because one of his sons had called him "a whore" for his earlier vote against the measure.

Republican Speaker Perry Duryea, who had remained silent on the bill, then announced he would vote "Aye". The final talley was seventy-six for the abortion legislation, seventy-three against.

Because the assembly bill differed from the senate version, the senate needed to vote again. All the stops were pulled by interested Catholics and the leaders of the Conservative Party to change the minds of several senators.

Suddenly a rumor began to circulate around the halls of the state capitol that Governor Rockefeller and Cardinal Cooke had cut a deal. Allegedly, Cooke would look the other way on the abortion bill in return for approval of a bill for mandated services reimbursement for private and parochial schools.

A number of legislators actually believed that the cardinal had sold out for a few pieces of silver and that they were off the hook. As a result, on April 10, the Senate approved the assembly bill by a vote of thirty-one to twenty-six. Before he ended the debate, a weeping Senator Brydges read from *The Diary of an Unborn Child*. Reacting, Cooke and his fellow bishops issued a statement that read in part:

> It is difficult to express our shock and distress over this event particularly since it seems destined, God forbid, to lower respect for all human life—the aged, the sick, the unwanted. We cannot forget that this Bill was endorsed by many because it would help parents rid themselves of unwanted children.
>
> The Law of New York may be changed, but that does not change the Law of God. Abortion is a heinous crime and remains a crime against man's nature even though it may no longer be a crime against man's law in New York.
>
> We believe life, all life, is God's gift. We urge our people to rededicate themselves to its protection in the face of the present attacks against the aged, the neglected, the unwanted, the abandoned and the unborn.[43]

Their plea fell on deaf ears. Governor Rockefeller signed the legislation into law.

The first round had been lost, but the fight continued. In the 1970 elections, Catholics and other pro-lifers came out in force and defeated three key legislators who had sold out on the abortion bill, Senator Dominick and Assemblymen Michaels and Baletta. In addition, Catholics helped to send to Washington two men who would become national leaders on the life issue: Congressman Jack Kemp of Buffalo and Senator James L. Buckley. Senator Buckley, who was elected solely on the Conservative Party line in a three-way race, went on to author and introduce the Human Life Amendment after the *Roe v. Wade* decision was handed down by the U.S. Supreme Court.

In 1971–1972, Cardinal Cooke led the charge to repeal the abortion law. And in May 1972, the state legislature did just that and reinstated the 1830 statute. To prevent complete repeal, Rockefeller tried to broker a compromise that would reduce the period to procure an abortion, but the Catholic and pro-life groups rejected it.

On May 10, 1972, the day the state senate voted thirty-one to twenty-six for repeal, Cardinal Cooke received support for his efforts from an unexpected quarter. President Richard Nixon addressed a letter to the cardinal clearly stating his views on the controversy:

> Dear Cardinal Cooke:
>
> I read in the *Daily News* that the Archdiocese of New York, under your leadership, has initiated a campaign to bring about repeal of the state's liberalized abortion laws. Though this is a matter for state decision outside Federal jurisdiction, I would personally like to associate myself with the convictions you deeply feel and eloquently express. . . .
>
> Your decision, and that of tens of thousands of Catholics, Protestants, Jews, and men and women of no particular faith, to act in the public forum as defenders of the right to life of the unborn, is truly a noble endeavor. In this calling, you and they have my admiration, sympathy and support.
>
> Richard Nixon[44]

Governor Rockefeller, who would serve that fall as chairman of the New York committee to reelect President Nixon, was not moved. He vetoed the repeal of the liberalized abortion law on May 13, 1972.

Despite this latest setback, Cardinal Cooke continued fighting for the rights of the unborn for the remainder of his life. In addition to issuing pastoral letters condemning abortion as a "fundamental moral evil", he inaugurated the annual Respect Life Week in New York, established Birthright, a service to help women who want to avoid an abortion, and took on the job of chairman of the United States Conference of Catholic Bishops' Pro-Life Activities Committee after the Supreme Court legalized abortion nationwide in *Roe v. Wade* on January 22, 1973.

The noted Catholic social thinker Monsignor George Kelly has written that one of Cardinal Cooke's "finest hours was his work as Chairman of the Pro-Life Activities Committee for the U.S. Bishops.... No one in the hierarchy was more committed to Catholic principles and priorities than the New York Archbishop. He did not carry the day on the national scene ... [but] he stood tall on the issue."[45]

Cardinal Cooke understood "the proper hierarchy of values" and rejected the "seamless garment" argument promoted by his fellow cardinal Joseph Bernardin of Chicago. Cooke publicly proclaimed: "Improving the quality of life is surely a laudable purpose, but the quality of life movement becomes insidious and dangerous when it equates the quality of life with life itself."[46]

New York's Homosexual Rights Movement

In the 1970s, New York elites began to press a political and educational agenda that aimed to eradicate the influence of Judeo-Christian principles on public policy. Beginning in 1971, for example, and every year thereafter until it finally passed in 1986, a so-called homosexual rights bill was introduced in the New York City Council to amend the administrative code to outlaw discrimination due to one's "sexual orientation or affectional preference".

Such legislation, if enacted, would bestow privileges based on sexual proclivity. Homosexuals' historical plea for privacy in the bedroom was discarded in favor of a radical program of public celebration of homosexual culture, especially in the city's classrooms.

Cardinal Cooke publicly opposed so-called homosexual-rights legislation and stood by Church teaching that homosexuality is "a more or less strong tendency ordered toward an intrinsic moral evil, thus the inclination itself must be seen as an objective disorder".[47]

Attempts at passage failed no fewer than twelve times thanks to the city council's Democratic majority leader, Thomas Cuite; the chairman of the General Welfare Committee, Councilwoman Aileen Ryan of the Bronx; and Brooklyn councilman-at-large and Conservative Party leader Michael Long.

Councilman Long spoke for many blue-collar Catholics and cultural conservatives when he articulated his party's position:

> We are committed to the concept of equal opportunity for all people regardless of sex, race and religion in all areas of life.
>
> We reaffirm and continue to support traditional civil rights protection for all and continue to oppose discrimination, reverse discrimination, quotas and the creation of preferential classes. Thus, we most certainly oppose this bill, which would have the effect of creating a new protected class of homosexuals, who given the interpretive

propensities of certain of our eminent jurists, would eventually ... require affirmative action programs, preferential status in hiring [and] housing, and other benefits under this expanded definition of civil rights.[48]

To help defeat the legislation, Cardinal Cooke would call wavering councilmen and explain over and over again the Church's position.

Most years, before a committee vote, Cooke would push the reluctant ordinary of the Brooklyn Diocese, Bishop Francis Mugavero, to sign with him a joint statement opposing the legislation.

One typical statement, released on April 17, 1978, said:

> If the bill has an underlying purpose, to advocate and gain approval of homosexual behavior and lifestyle, then there is no way in which the Catholic Church in the City of New York may find it acceptable. And there is no way in which we can remain silent on the issue.
>
> The Catholic Church's moral teaching differentiates between "orientation" and "behavior" for both homosexuals and heterosexuals. While a person's orientation is not subject to moral evaluation, there is no doubt that a person's behavior is subject to evaluation. Homosexual behavior and an attendant homosexual life style [are] not in accord with Catholic moral teaching and [are], in fact, harmful to all persons who become involved; heterosexuality is the norm for human behavior.[49]

On another occasion, the assistant director of the archdiocesan Office of Communications, Father Kenneth Jadoff, in a *Daily News* op-ed piece (July 18, 1977) expressed the Church's position in this fashion: "Religious people maintain unequivocally that homosexual activity is gravely immoral, violating the order of human sexuality ordained by the Creator. Without any unkindness toward homosexuals, the Jewish and Christian parents are conscience-bound to keep children in their formative years free from homosexual associations and influences. Parents' rights are unchallengeable in this regard."[50]

Despite the cardinal's efforts, the political clout of the homosexual rights movement grew. Shortly after Edward Koch was sworn in as mayor in January 1978, he issued a "gay-rights ordinance", an executive order prohibiting discrimination against homosexuals in municipal hiring. He also proclaimed annually a Gay Arts Festival Month and approved of and marched in the annual Gay Pride March.

Cardinal Cooke caught a lot of flak for his unwavering opposition to the "gay" political agenda. And during the June 28, 1981, Gay Pride March on Fifth Avenue, many of the fifty thousand marchers expressed their anger as they marched by St. Patrick's Cathedral. Gay militant atheists chanted, "Smash the state, smash the Church, death to the Church." A man in a nun costume with an upside down cross screamed, "Pope John Paul, are you gay?" Others sang, "Two, four, six, eight, how do you know the pope is straight?" and "Cardinal Cooke, Cardinal Cooke, where are you, where are you? Hiding in the closet, hiding in the closet. Shame on you, shame on you."[51]

Participants stood on the steps of the cathedral waving placards that read, "Ignorance and Immorality Taught Here", "Tax Churches—No Subsidies for Oppressors", and "God is Gay".[52] Celebrators threw thousands of condoms on the sidewalk in front of St. Patrick's.

Despite all the abuse, Cardinal Cooke refused to back off on the issue, and the so-called gay-rights bill did not pass during his tenure as archbishop of New York.

Issues of War and Peace

As military vicar, Cooke, like his predecessor, took the job seriously. But unlike Spellman, over time, he became troubled over the conflict in Vietnam.

Archbishop Cooke made his first trip overseas as military vicar in December 1968 and said Christmas Mass for the troops in Vietnam. In his sermon he reminded the troops:

> There are critics today who scoff at the idea that our military forces are interested in peace, but you are more deeply interested in peace than any group I know or with whom I have been in contact.... Today, we again celebrate the birthday of the Prince of Peace and pray together before his altar that peace may quickly come to a world weary of conflict. Above all, we pray for inner peace, the peace of the soul. That was the peace experienced by the Holy Family in spite of their surroundings of hostility. That is the peace that is our heritage as followers of the One who came to speak "peace to the nations." May this peace be yours.[53]

He would go back to Vietnam in 1969 and in 1970, always telling the troops of America's gratitude "for the work they are doing in the cause of freedom".[54] But like many Americans, his views on the protracted conflict began to change. Unlike Spellman, he did not want to be closely associated with the war; hence, in December 1971 he chose to go to Bethlehem, not Vietnam, to say Christmas Mass. In that sermon, he was not a crusading Cold Warrior:

> Let us then work for justice in the world so that the nations of the earth will be moved to draw back from ominous arms races and unbalanced concentration on the tools of war, from the terrifying proliferation of nuclear weapons and from senseless quarrels and insane hatreds. Let us turn our united efforts instead to true human development throughout our world, and to the betterment of all our brothers. Let us pray on this Christmas night that all the nations of the earth may turn away from the ever present sounds of conflict and hear the angels' clear invitation to peace through love of God and neighbor.[55]

In May 1972, while there were ongoing secret peace negotiations between President Nixon's top foreign-policy advisor, Dr. Henry Kissinger, and representatives of North Vietnam, the communists commenced an Easter offensive that routed many of the forces of the Republic of Vietnam. Reacting, Cardinal Cooke sent a pastoral letter to his flock on May 19, 1972, expressing his dismay that "hostilities have flared anew and our hopes for a quick solution have been placed in jeopardy."

While recognizing that the war had "divided and polarized our people", he did not condemn the interventionist policies of the United States: "For my part I do not think that our national purpose in Vietnam has all along been ignoble, selfish and dishonorable. On the contrary, I am convinced that our country committed itself to this struggle to help our fellow men achieve the blessings of peace and liberty against the forces of tyranny and oppression."[56]

He went on, however, to call for the creation of an international commission of people of every relevant discipline "in the service of all mankind to study and plan for the prevention of war". The cardinal feared that if there was not some world-wide action, "the bomb which might explode at any time could destroy all of us, friend and foe alike."[57]

Throughout his time as military vicar, Cooke walked a fine line between the hawks and the doves within the Church. Yet he did not fear taking on his fellow bishops when he decided they were too extreme. Hence, when Seattle's Archbishop Raymond Hunthausen in 1981 announced his support for unilateral U.S. disarmament, called "nuclear deterrence idolatry", and urged Catholics to refuse to pay 50 percent of their federal income tax to stop "nuclear murder", Cooke publicly disagreed.

In his December 7, 1981, annual letter to military chaplains, he stated that "a strategy of nuclear deterrence can be morally tolerated if a nation is sincerely trying to come up with a rational alternative." Relying on the just-war analysis of nuclear weapons that was promulgated by Pope Pius XII, Cooke made it clear the Church "considers the strategy of nuclear deterrence morally tolerable; not satisfactory, but tolerable".[58]

As for the call of some to freeze or drastically to cut U.S. military spending, Cooke insisted, "We must be very careful about assuming that reductions in defense spending would automatically or completely solve such problems as poverty, hunger and disease in our nation or in the world."

While Cooke agreed that the Church must continue to seek nonviolent ways of maintaining peace, he argued that "as long as we have good reason to believe that another nation would be tempted to attack us if we could not retaliate, we have the right to deter attack by making it clear that we could retaliate."[59]

"Every nation", the cardinal concluded, "has a grave moral obligation to reduce and finally get rid of [nuclear] weapons altogether, but the Church points out that this must be done gradually, with all nations cooperating, and with prudence."[60]

Cooke's letter caused an uproar in many circles, both nationally and in his arch-diocese. A thousand-word letter saying he was "contradicted by the developing position of his fellow bishops" was signed by a number of his own priests. The signatories, "who wish to separate ourselves from this teaching", included the Reverend Richard Dillon, a professor of sacred Scripture at St. Joseph's Seminary; the Reverend Robert Ritchie, director of the Catholic Youth Organization; and the Reverend Paul Dinter, the Catholic chaplain at Columbia University.[61]

While Cooke made it clear to his critics that he "abhorred the arms race" and that it was morally necessary to make efforts "toward disarmament and the reduction and eventual elimination of all weapons of mass destruction",[62] he maintained his just-war explanation, particularly during the 1981–1983 drafting of the U.S. bishops' Pastoral Letter on War and Peace, titled *The Challenge of Peace: God's Promise and Our Response*.

Cooke questioned a draft of the pastoral letter that endorsed a nuclear freeze, condemned nuclear war absolutely, opposed America's targeting doctrine, and questioned the morality of nuclear deterrence. The proposed pastoral letter, Cooke warned his colleagues in November 1982, has "great potential ... for seriously dividing our Church and our nation". While he agreed that "the world must work toward the elimination of nuclear arms, and indeed, of all instruments of mass destruction", he argued that there was concern "that the moral teaching of the Church on the traditional concept of the just war and defense against unjust aggression not be intertwined with political strategic, military speculation".[63] One member of the drafting committee who appreciated Cooke's concerns was the new auxiliary bishop of the Military Vicariate and the retired chief of navy chaplains, Bishop John J. O'Connor.

The final version of *The Challenge of Peace*, which was presented to the bishops for a vote on May 3, 1983, condemned a defensive policy "based either on first use of 'counterforce' nuclear weapons or on second-strike 'counter value' attacks, each of which ... by threatening the lives of millions, violated Jesus' peaceable injunctions and the principles of Catholic just-war theory".[64] It passed by a vote of 238 to 9.

After the adoption of the pastoral letter, Cooke sent a letter to his military chaplains explaining that the condemnation of nuclear weapons "did not conflict with their roles in the military".

He pointed out that the bishops did not intend "to create problems for Catholics in the military" but stressed that "every profession ... has its specific moral questions and it is clear that the teaching on war and peace developed in this letter poses a special challenge and opportunity to those in the military profession."

The bishops' statement, he concluded, "reaffirms the Church's traditional clear and unequivocal teaching that a country has the right and obligation to defend its citizens against unjust aggression, using armed forces, if necessary, as a last resort. It does question, however, the morality of some strategies of defense and requires us to examine our individual consciences and our 'national conscience.' "[65]

Catholic Education

When Cooke became archbishop of New York in 1968, it cost parochial schools $200 a year to educate a child versus $1,400 in the public-school system. Education costs, at parochial schools, however, were projected to increase every year because of the need to hire more lay teachers every year to replace religious sisters. The Church historian Monsignor Thomas Shelley has pointed out that "between 1968 and 1983 fully three-quarters of the [8,955] sisters who were engaged in teaching in the Catholic schools either died, retired or left the classroom (and often religious life as well) for other fields of endeavor."[66]

In addition, there was the ever-growing need to update aging school buildings. Most electrical systems, boilers, and classroom furniture needed to be upgraded or replaced.

To get a handle on the situation, Cooke, in his first weeks in office, created the McDonnell Committee, chaired by Wall Street mogul T. Murray McDonnell, to examine school finances. The blue-ribbon panel was requested to "develop all the facts pertinent to the entire scope of Catholic education in the Archdiocese" and to "propose revisions in our educational endeavors as dictated by the facts".[67]

The final report presented to Cooke was titled *A Financial Study: The Catholic School System of the Archdiocese of New York*. To eliminate the annual high-school deficit of $2.5 million, to aid the hundred parish schools that were not self-supporting, and to implement cost controls, the committee recommended the establishment of a central financial office. The report also called for the consolidation of underused schools—a very touchy subject in many parishes. In addition, the analysis provided the framework to implement better money-management procedures and to calculate realistic tuition payments.

While the committee understood the need to solicit financial support from federal, state, and local governments, it did give this warning: "Over the long term, the infusion of public funds into Church-related schools could result in such secularization of the schools that the Church would have little remaining motive to operate them. Public aid could prove to be an attenuated way of ending the Church's school system."[68]

Heeding the calls to find revenue streams to balance the education budget, Cooke took an initial step that proved to be lackluster at best. His expansion of the annual Catholic Charities appeal—established by Cardinal Hayes to include education needs—failed to make a serious dent in reducing school deficits.

Cooke did proceed to create other programs that forestalled the closing of schools in poor minority neighborhoods. The first was the Commission for the Inter Parish Finance, which developed a method to tax parishes. The initial tax was 6 percent of annual parish income, and the proceeds were dedicated to helping deficit-ridden parishes keep their heads above water. Though many pastors grumbled about having to subsidize other parish schools, the program was a success; it helped save over 25 percent of the archdiocese's ailing parish schools by providing, during Cooke's tenure, a total of $41 million in aid.[69]

To help defray the tuition costs for poor minority students (Manhattan's parochial-school population when Cooke took office was 60 percent African-American or Hispanic), he created in 1971 the Inner-City Scholarship Fund (ICSF), a not-for-profit corporation that provides tuition assistance to low-income families.

Since its inception, the ICSF has raised hundreds of millions, and eighty-five cents of every dollar goes to minority students. Today the ICSF awards approximately eight thousand scholarships annually to students in seventy-four elementary and nineteen secondary Catholic schools. High-school graduation rates in Archdiocesan schools are 98 percent versus 65 percent in city schools.

Cooke also turned his attention to the Confraternity of Christian Doctrine (CCD) programs for Catholics attending public schools. To upgrade the caliber of volunteer teachers, he instituted a Catechetical Institute at the seminary to train them.

While Cooke understood the dangers of government interference in the Catholic educational system if it relied too heavily on state aid, nevertheless he continued to pursue all avenues to procure for parents some form of state financial support to help defray tuition costs. In a letter to Governor Nelson Rockefeller in 1971, the cardinal reminded him of "the grave economic plight of non-public education".

In addition to calling for the repeal of the state constitution's Blaine Amendment, he requested the passage of legislation "establishing a meaningful program of state aid structured in such a way as to comply with the limitations of the First Amendment".

Cooke advocated a Parents' Aid Bill similar to the very successful and popular Scholar Incentive Program approved by the legislature in the 1960s, which helped parents to cover tuition charges in public and private colleges, "including those under religious auspices".⁷⁰ While the governor and many legislators—particularly Catholic ones—agreed that such aid to parents was constitutional, unfortunately it never got off the ground.

No one could question the cardinal's devotion to preserving New York's Catholic educational system. Nevertheless, the changing demographics, the increasing costs, and the increasing number of baptized Catholics falling away from the Church took their toll. During his fifteen years as archbishop, the elementary-school population dropped from 167,000 to 88,000, forcing Cooke to close thirty-one schools.

The 1970s: Crisis Decade

Cardinal Terence Cooke was described by many of his closest clerical colleagues as a "pragmatic conservative". By this they meant that he supported papal decrees to the letter and that he was solid on the documents of Vatican II but tolerated or looked the other way when priests promoted the "spirit of Vatican II", which contradicted or ignored the conciliar documents.

Among other things, Cooke tolerated experimental liturgies that included folk and jazz Masses and liturgical dancing in church aisles. He tolerated dissenters who ignored his pastoral letter on *Humanae Vitae* and who preached that using contraceptives was not sinful or that parishioners need only follow their consciences, without explaining the need to have an informed conscience based on Church teaching. He put up with community-organizing priests who employed Saul Alinsky's radical techniques and who supported Alinsky's extremist social agenda.

Cooke, who had made it clear from day one that he would be a good listener, proved to be just that. He would sit patiently for hours on end listening to rabble-rousers, members of the Senate of Priests who questioned priestly celibacy or called for women's ordination or wanted the archdiocese to make public statements on the federal budget and spending on B-1 bombers. Some of his priests called him "the group worker" because of "his ability to sit with groups, listen, and with remarkable skill, steer his audience toward an acceptable conclusion".⁷¹

Not much of a public person, Cooke preferred to work behind the scenes. He worked long hours, and thanks to his ability to absorb mounds of details, he knew the archdiocese like the back of his hand. "He loves annual reports", said one chancery priest. "He can sit with a 70-page memo on how to rescue the hospitals and master it. He has a terrific memory for such things."⁷² Church historian Monsignor Florence Cohalan agreed: "The Cardinal can do many things very well. He was on every rung of the ladder himself. When you bring him a problem, he has such a phenomenal memory that his mind goes back to when he was in your job."⁷³

But he also disliked confrontation. "He had no stomach for controversy", said a close associate.⁷⁴ "He doesn't like to admit the existence of problems", said Monsignor Cohalan. "He is the most ebullient man you'd meet."⁷⁵

Critics of all theological stripes complained that his distaste for confrontation often led to no decision at all or to a decision that pleased no one. It also led to situations in which a priest would ignore a request from the cardinal, knowing he would not be called on the carpet. For instance, when Cooke told Father Louis Gigante—a relative of the notorious Genovese crime family and brother of alleged mobster Vincent Gigante—not to run for a South Bronx City Council seat, Gigante ignored him and won the election in 1973. Gigante went on to spend a week in jail when he claimed that a conversation he had with reputed mobster James "Jimmy Nap" Napoli was under the seal of the confessional.

To placate younger priests, Cooke agreed to retire priests at seventy-five and to limit pastors to two terms totaling twelve years. This soon added to the growing clerical problem in New York. Many seasoned priests who knew how to run a parish, both pastorally and financially, and were still physically fit were unnecessarily put out to pasture and were replaced by inexperienced ones—some of whom were more concerned with community organizing and rabble-rousing.

Though "absolutes about age and terms", wrote Monsignor George Kelly, "were no more helpful to apostolic parish life than the absolute permanency of earlier decades ... they did absolve the Bishop of personal decision-making and of explaining why he allowed one man to stay but insisted that another man go".[76]

Cooke's flexibility with his priests did not have a discernible effect on the clerical crisis. Every year in the late sixties and early seventies, about a dozen men in New York would leave the priesthood. Many just took a walk without being laicized. This situation, plus the increased number of retirements, caused the rolls of active priests, which stood at 1,252 in 1969, to drop to 1,069 by 1978; by the time of Cooke's death in 1983, the total was 777.

At Dunwoodie, there was dissatisfaction among the administrators and professors. The first rector Cooke appointed in 1968 was one of his classmates, Father Edward Montano, a professor of philosophy. He proved to be ill-suited for the job, particularly during those rebellious times.

Like his mentor, Montano disliked confrontation, and this led to his tolerating professors who were not orthodox. But when a group of Dunwoodie teachers openly complained about colleagues who questioned Christ's knowledge of His divinity, some action had to be taken. Those faculty members eventually "found their way out of Dunwoodie (with a little help from Cooke)," as Monsignor Kelly put it, "but not before they disparaged the competence of those who supported traditional Catholic reading of the scriptures".[77]

In February 1969, a rambunctious Dunwoodie student council delivered to the rector a *Report on Seminary Life* that called for significant changes in the rules that applied to seminarians. The fifty-seven-page report concluded that "there is general dissatisfaction based on a lack of spirit of *aggiornamento* in this institution."[78]

The council members complained about their professors and demanded that students receive theological instruction at Catholic colleges in the region. It also called for a legislative body consisting of faculty and students that would be empowered to determine seminary policies and practices and would be "an appellate board in the manner of discipline and community affairs".[79] One item that generated a *New York Times* front-page story was the answer to a poll taken among the seminarians that indicated that a majority wanted daily Mass to be optional.

To placate the students, Montano permitted them to have automobiles and allowed them more time off campus. According to Catholic historian Thomas Shelley, " 'Quiet' replaced 'Silence' as the rule above the first floor; students were permitted to visit one another's rooms; attendance at meals became optional; a black suit replaced the cassock as the proper attire for most functions."[80] Montano also permitted the seminarians to drink beer in the lounge.

In 1973, a battered Montano stepped down and was replaced by Monsignor Austin Vaughn, a noted orthodox theologian. To bring peace within the ranks of the Dunwoodie clergy—whose differences were described by the archdiocese's education secretary, Monsignor Joseph O'Keefe, as "basically ideological—not necessarily theological"[81]—a faculty handbook that clearly described various responsibilities was developed. However, the handbook, released in 1976, contributed little to ending disputes. The tense situation eventually resolved itself when frustrated and angry dissident professors quit or moved on to different assignments.

As a result of the internal battles, the seminary's academic standing suffered. St. Joseph's became a second-rate educational institution.

On the positive side, Cooke did make some contributions to addressing the drop in vocations and enhancing seminary life. He wisely ended the combined college seminary program with the Brooklyn and Rockland Centre Dioceses at the Douglaston Cathedral College in Queens County. That Douglaston center was viewed as out of control theologically and in terms of oversight and discipline. In its place Cooke created the St. John Neumann Residence, which served as a house of formation and collaborated with a local Catholic university where seminarians took courses in philosophy. Cooke also renovated and restored the chapel at Dunwoodie to its original design.

The administrative problems and theological disputes at Dunwoodie did not help the problem of declining vocations. Yearly ordinations in the 1970s were down 50 percent from the 1960s. The trend did not improve in Cooke's final years. Six men were ordained in 1980, eleven in 1981, and ten in 1982. In Cardinal Cooke's last year as archbishop there was a spike—the class of 1983 had eighteen men ordained to the priesthood.

New York City's Crisis

The postwar boom had lifted New York City from its Depression-era fiscal malaise. As early as the 1950s, however, the ideological seeds were planted that eventually destroyed the city's financial base.

It was Mayor Robert F. Wagner Jr. (in office from 1954 to 1965) who expressed the political view that prevailed from the 1950s through the early 1970s. He stated: "I don't propose to permit our fiscal problems to set the limits of our commitments to meet the essential needs of the people of the City."[82] This philosophy, promoted by Wagner and his successor, Mayor John Vliet Lindsay (1966–1973), created a government dominated by social engineers who destroyed the city's very social fabric.

In the name of urban development, neighborhoods of single-family homes were bulldozed and replaced with "projects"—huge apartment buildings that became breeding grounds for crime and drug use.

Worse yet was the social-welfare spending spree that destroyed the family structure among low-income New Yorkers by encouraging men to abandon their wives and children. Big, expensive activist government failed to achieve the expected social and financial equity. Instead, it created a permanent underclass.

In 1960, 4 percent of the city's population received welfare benefits. That number had doubled by 1965, and by 1969 it had grown to 13 percent. Expenditures for welfare programs rose from $400 million in 1965 to more than $1 billion by 1970.

It became so easy to apply for welfare that the *Daily News* called the city's welfare commissioner "Come and Get It Ginsburg".

Lindsay used every imaginable financial gimmick. He increased nuisance taxes, water rates, and sewer taxes, and he instituted the city income tax. In 1969, Budget Director Fred Hayes admitted: "We're going broke on $6.6 billion a year."

All the budgetary tricks, phantom revenues, and capitalizing of expenses led to a situation in which 56 percent of locally raised taxes went either to debt service or to pension and welfare payments. Short-term debt, which in 1965 was $536 million, ballooned to $4.5 billion—36 percent of total debt. By 1976, these abuses had caused the financial markets to close their doors to the city and the state to take over the city's finances, complete with a default-on-debt decree from the state legislature.

"The rollovers, false revenue estimates and plain lies", journalist Ken Auletta wrote, "have robbed taxpayers of literally billions through excessive borrowings to cover up excessive fraud."[83]

Viewing the results of the city's great social experiment in the mid-1970s, liberal journalist Murray Kempton observed: "the air is fouler, the streets dirtier, the bicycle thieves more vigilant, the labor contracts more abandoned in their disregard for the public good, the Board of Education more dedicated to the manufacture of illiteracy than any of these elements ever were under Wagner." And Kempton cited another liberal, Jack Newfield, who quipped that Lindsay "gave good intentions a bad name".[84]

To avoid bankruptcy, drastic measures had to be taken at the state capital in Albany. Governor Hugh Carey imposed an independent control board to direct city finances. The city also agreed to a ceiling on the size of its budget; a moratorium on additional taxes, wage freezes, and reductions in the capital budget; and the dismissal of thousands of municipal workers, the elimination of thousands of positions from the city's budget, and a freeze on new hiring.

By means of attrition, retirements, resignations, and layoffs, New York City lost 20 percent of its teachers, 14 percent of police, 14 percent of firefighters, 33 percent of sanitation workers, and 25 percent of Parks Department workers. Scores of programs and departments were reduced or eliminated. Capital-project spending came to a halt. Governor Carey said it best when he told New Yorkers, "The days of wine and roses are over."

Cardinal Cooke took a great interest in the city's crisis, believing it threatened the common good. Over the years Catholic Charities had partnered with the city to provide human services to poor, abandoned children and to the aged.

Acknowledging that the city was poorly managed, that it spent excessively, and that it wasted resources, he urged that

> prior abuses and mismanagement of resources cannot blind our leaders ... from accepting their challenging task in a spirit of commitment to human priorities, so that the final solution will take into account the human dimension and that it will be beneficial to human brotherhood and true community. This will only happen if they have a true respect for all life and for personal dignity of all men and women who live in New York City, and if they are dedicated to an improvement of the moral climate of life for New York's citizens and their families. To this end they must receive adequate citizen support.[85]

The financial crisis and the recession of the early 1970s took its toll on Cooke's flock: a million people, many of them Catholics, fled the city for New Jersey, Connecticut, and New York's suburbia. Solid Catholic areas such as the Bronx turned into municipal deserts. Tens of thousands of apartments were abandoned; crime, arson, and drug abuse were rampant.

While the financially broke state and city governments ignored the plight of inner-city neighborhoods, Cooke refused to give up hope. He called for "courage in the defense of basic morality and in the preservation of human life". He argued that New York City could not be solely "defined in terms of new systems and analyzed master plans", and he urged his flock to focus on "what happens to them and to their children on *their* block".[86] The cardinal, whose friend Auxiliary Bishop Patrick Ahern described him as "a boy from the Bronx with an accent to prove it", urged his flock to champion the basis of Catholic thought, subsidiarity.

It was the local parish priests who led the charge to protect and enhance the lives of those who stuck it out in burned-out neighborhoods. Cooke encouraged the clergy to join neighborhood coalitions that helped renovate abandoned apartment buildings and single-family homes and that built new housing. Studying the results, the noted Bronx historian Jill Jonnes concluded, "The Catholic Church quietly emerged as the institution most committed to preserving and resurrecting the blighted South Bronx."[87]

Cooke: The Final Years

Pope Paul VI died in August of 1978, and later that month Cardinal Cooke traveled to Rome to participate in the conclave that elected the new pope, Albino Luciani, who took the name John Paul to honor his two predecessors. Five weeks later, Cooke found himself flying back to the Vatican to bury the "September Pope", who had died after only thirty-three days in office. In the October conclave, Cooke cast his vote for Cardinal Karol Wojtyla, the first non-Italian pope since Adrian VI, who had died in 1523.

The high point of the Cooke administration was Pope John Paul II's two-day visit to New York in October 1979. Cooke oversaw many of the arrangements himself. Having directed Pope Paul's trip for Spellman in 1965, he knew firsthand the potential pitfalls.

Arriving at LaGuardia Airport, the pope went to the United Nations, where he told the General Assembly, "The progress of humanity must be measured not only by the progress of science and technology, which shows man's uniqueness with regard to nature, but also and chiefly by the primacy given to spiritual values and by the progress of moral life."[88]

Afterward, accompanied by Cardinal Cooke, the pope went to Yankee Stadium, where he said Mass for seventy-five thousand. On their way to the Bronx, the pope and the cardinal stopped at St. Charles Borromeo parish in Harlem, where they were greeted by Monsignor Emerson Moore and a packed church. Moore said to the pope, "We see in your visit here your support and encouragement for our continuing struggle for justice and human rights, not just in our own community, but in all the Harlems in America."[89]

The entourage also stopped at Morris Avenue and 151st Street in the Bronx for the pope to bless the ground on which two apartment houses sponsored by the archdiocese were to be built. As John Paul began to speak, the lighting system failed, and Cardinal Cooke held a flashlight to the pope's text. In Spanish, John Paul told the crowd, "I came here because I know the difficult conditions of your existence. I know the sorrow that takes place in your lives. For this reason, you deserve particular attention on the part of the Pope. My presence here signifies an appreciation of what the Church has done and continues to do."[90]

The vicar for the South Bronx, Father Neil Connolly, who was the guiding hand in the housing and anti-arson programs, told the pope before he departed for a visit to Cardinal Hayes High School, "Your presence here tonight means that we count."[91]

The pope spent the night at the cardinal's residence, and the following morning he addressed a rally of nineteen thousand Catholic schoolchildren at Madison Square Garden. The pope was presented with various gifts, including a pair of jeans. Cooke told one of the authors that John Paul tried on the dungarees backstage after the event.

Despite a heavy rainstorm, tens of thousands lined the sidewalks to greet the pope as he rode in an open car for a ticker-tape parade. Cardinal Cooke dutifully held an umbrella over John Paul to free the pope's hands to bless the crowds. The final events included a time of prayer at St. Patrick's Cathedral and a farewell rally at Shea Stadium. Before departing for Philadelphia, John Paul blessed those assembled and said, "Keep Jesus Christ in your hearts, and you will recognize His face in every human being. You will want to help Him out in all his needs: the needs of your brothers and sisters."[92]

Failing Health

Few people knew the physical toll the pope's trip took on Cardinal Cooke. For that matter, few knew how his sixteen-hour workdays and his overseas trips as military vicar were taxing him physically. That's because the ever-cheerful cardinal kept to himself his serious health problems.

Shortly before Cooke was consecrated an auxiliary bishop by Spellman in December 1965, he underwent surgery for removal of lymphatic tissue in his neck. Even though he was told at the time that he might have only three years to live, that did not stop his advancement in the Church hierarchy.

Ten years later, generalized lymphoma was diagnosed. The cardinal had an obstructing lesion removed from his mouth and received chemotherapy that continued for four years. The chemotherapy was then stopped because of "bone marrow depression secondary to the drugs", as the Cardinal's physician, Dr. Kevin Cahill put it.[93]

From 1979 to 1983, Cooke suffered, according to Dr. Cahill, "frequent infections due to an inadequate number of white blood cells and had received various steroids and multiple transfusions to maintain adequate blood cell and platelet counts". After he suffered a urinary-tract infection in early 1983, a bone-marrow test revealed that he had leukemia.[94]

Cooke insisted that his condition be kept under wraps as long as possible, and he insisted on business as usual. In preparation for what was to be his last St. Patrick's Day celebration, the cardinal had the unpleasant duty of informing New Yorkers in February that he disapproved of the choice of Michael Flannery as the parade's grand marshal. Born in Ireland in 1900, Flannery had been an Irish Volunteer during the Rebellion. After serving time in prison, he moved to the United States in 1927. As of 1983 he was still an active supporter of the IRA and of NORAID, an underground group that allegedly engaged in gunrunning to Northern Ireland.

When the parade committee refused to replace Flannery as grand marshal, the cardinal on March 9 once again condemned "indiscriminate violence" in Northern Ireland and called IRA activities "futile and immoral".[95] He also said that the discord over the choice of grand marshal had distracted from the "religious, cultural and family richness of the celebration".[96]

On March 17, no one was sure what the cardinal was going to do. Before the morning Mass at the cathedral, Cooke met privately with Flannery in a room off the main altar. While the discussion was cordial, the two agreed to disagree.[97]

In his homily, Cooke once again explained his position, and afterward the great bronze doors of the cathedral remained closed until Grand Marshal Flannery had marched by. Only then did the cardinal step outside and take his traditional place on the steps of St. Patrick's to meet, greet, and bless parade participants. The cardinal took in stride an organized group that booed him.

One month later, on April 8, 1983, Cooke had the much more pleasant task of leading the celebrations to mark the 175th anniversary of the creation of the New York Diocese, at the first Catholic church in New York State, St. Peter's on Barclay Street in Lower Manhattan. The cardinal announced: "It all began here, so far as the Church of New York is concerned.... Thank the Lord for all the blessings of these 175 years."[98]

Business as usual ended in August 1983, after the cardinal and his doctors concluded that his medical condition could no longer be concealed. The chancery announced on August 26 that the sixty-two-year-old Terence Cooke was terminally ill with cancer and had only a few months to live. Monsignor Peter Finn, director of communications for the archdiocese, told the media, "The prognosis is that the disease is terminal.... It's severe and it's moving quickly." Finn explained that the cardinal would be treated for myelomonocytic leukemia at his residence, not in a hospital. Finn also said the pope was aware of the situation.[99]

On the day of the announcement, Pope John Paul called Cooke at 2:00 P.M. EDT. A memo written by a witness to the conversation stated:

> The Holy Father spoke in a loving, fraternal way and expressed his deep personal concern for the Cardinal, whom he regards as a close friend and brother. He referred to the love of His Eminence for the Church and for the Pope. And he expressed gratitude for his pastoral service to God's people in his years as a faithful priest and bishop.
>
> The Cardinal told His Holiness what a joy it has been to serve under his leadership as the Vicar of Christ on earth. He spoke of his profound gratitude to Almighty God for the gift of the Priesthood and the opportunity of carrying out his pastoral responsibilities as Archbishop of New York and as Military Vicar.

His Eminence spoke to the Holy Father of his illness and assured him that the pastoral care of the people of the Archdiocese and of the Military Vicariate will be provided for by his collaborators with his encouragement and that he would be guided by the wishes of His holiness for the future.[100]

New Yorkers were stunned by the news. The state's senior U.S. senator, Daniel Patrick Moynihan, said: "This is a time for prayer. There is not a man in New York who would be so much missed."[101]

The clamor for information forced the archdiocese's Communications Office to release a statement from Dr. Kevin Cahill, in which he said:

> Cardinal Cooke has acute myelomonocytic leukemia, complicating a chronic lymphoma condition. After reviewing the various treatment options available, Cardinal Cooke has chosen to receive future medical management in the privacy of his home. A system of protective isolation has been established in his rooms. His Eminence can walk about, eat normal meals and carry on a limited schedule of spiritual and administrative activities. He does have a nurse in attendance to assist with the necessary infusions and medications. He has accepted his illness in a spirit of peace and equanimity.[102]

One man who took an interest in the cardinal's health condition was the fortieth president of the United States, Ronald Reagan. Upon hearing the news, he phoned the residence at 7:45 P.M. on Sunday, August 28. According to an archdiocese memorandum describing the call, the president "spoke of the heartfelt prayers that he and Nancy were offering on the Cardinal's behalf and thanked the Cardinal for the prayers and encouragement the Cardinal offered the Reagans in their time of need".[103] The president went on to express his gratitude for the friendship that had developed between them.

Cardinal Cooke and the Reagans were genuine friends. On December 10, 1980, Reagan, on his first trip to New York as president-elect, paid a call on Cooke at his residence. Cooke's secretary, Father Edwin O'Brien, told the media that "the talk had been substantive, not just ceremonial".[104]

On March 13, 1981, while the president was meeting with city officials, Mrs. Reagan lunched with the cardinal at his residence. When she left 452 Madison Avenue, she told the assembled press that she and the cardinal "discussed inner-city schools, which I was very impressed with when I went to visit them, and the drug problem, which I'm very much interested in".[105]

The assassination attempt on President Reagan came just seventeen days later. While he was recovering from his wounds, his top aide, Michael Deaver (a former seminarian), arranged for Cooke to meet with the president on April 12 in the residential part of the White House. During their meeting, Reagan, reflecting on his medical comeback, said to the cardinal, "I have decided that whatever time I have left is for Him."[106]

One month later, minutes after Reagan heard that Pope John Paul had been shot by Mehmet Ali Agca, he called Cooke and asked him to convey to the Vatican that he was praying for the pope.[107]

In September 1983, as the cardinal lay dying, President and Mrs. Reagan indicated that they would like to pay him a final visit. Told that it was touch and go whether the cardinal would be up to meeting the First Couple, they decided to take their chances and arrived at 452 Madison Avenue on Sunday, September 25, at 2:30 P.M.

Greeted by Monsignor Joseph Murphy, Monsignor Charles McDonagh, and Father O'Brien, the Reagans were taken to the third-floor chapel, where they were met by Cooke's good friend Cardinal William Baum, archbishop of Washington, D.C. After a short prayer service, the group proceeded to the cardinal's bedroom, on the second floor.

In a memo written immediately after the visit, Monsignor McDonagh stated:

The Cardinal spoke of his high regard for the Reagans and of his gratitude for their solicitude at this time of sickness. Mrs. Reagan reminded the Cardinal that he came to them in their time of need and they have never forgotten that kindness and so many others to them.

His Eminence assured President and Mrs. Reagan of his prayers for them and for the people of the Nation. He encouraged the President to pursue the cause of world peace and multi-lateral disarmament.

The First Lady asked the President to share the good news he had for the Cardinal. Mr. Reagan then said that after lunch he and Secretary General Pérez de Cuéllar of the United Nations had just finished speaking to President Gemayel of Lebanon by telephone and that a ceasefire in Lebanon has been reached. His Eminence suggested that this was the best medicine he has had in many days, and was truly delighted. He reminisced and made an analogy with his experience as a boy in the bleachers of Yankee Stadium as he watched Babe Ruth circling the bases after a home run....

The Cardinal went on to thank the President for his strong stand on behalf of tuition tax credits and said that the President's reasons for support are many and well stated.

The Cardinal thanked the President for his stand on behalf of human life and noted that President Reagan, among all the Presidents, is the only one to take so clear and strong a stand for the right [to] life of the unborn. The Cardinal offered the view that years from now, when so much else has been forgotten, President Reagan would be known (and loved by God) for his courageous Pro-Life stand. The President, in speaking on abortion, referred to a recent legal case in which a pregnant woman was attacked. Though she survived, the unborn child was killed, and the defendant was charged with murder.[108]

Before the Reagans departed, the cardinal gave the president a St. Patrick's Cathedral medallion and gave Nancy Reagan a Celtic cross. Reagan thanked him and spoke of the beauty of "the Cathedral in the midst of the City". The president ended the visit by relating "the story of the Protestant minister who, after asking an Irish taxi driver to bring him to 'Christ Church,' was brought to St. Patrick's with the assurance that if Christ were not here, He was surely out of town".[109]

In a handwritten note dated September 28, Monsignor McDonagh, on behalf of the cardinal, thanked the president for the visit and said:

It was a warm meeting of friends in an atmosphere of love, concern and faith. The affection which you, Mr. President and Mrs. Reagan, have for the Cardinal and which he has for both of you, was very obvious as you prayed together—for one another, for the people of our Nation and for peace in the world.... As an expression of the heartfelt appreciation of the Cardinal and all of us, I can only repeat the words of the blessing shared in the Prayer Service: "May the Lord bless you and keep you.... May He look upon you with kindness and give you His peace."[110]

On October 4, thirty-nine days after the announcement that Cooke was terminally ill, Monsignor Peter Finn told the media that the cardinal was close to death. "As for the question of when," said Finn, "that's in the hands of God. It could be in a few hours, it could be in a few days."[111] Two days later, at 11:30 A.M., Finn announced, "Terence Cardinal Cooke, 10th Bishop, 7th Archbishop, 5th Cardinal of the See of New York and Vicar to Military Service, Veterans Administration hospitals and Government service overseas, completed his work on earth and was called home by Almighty God to Heaven this morning at 4:45 A.M."[112]

A farewell letter signed by Cooke was read in all the parishes of the archdiocese on Sunday, October 9. In his dying declaration, this leader of the pro-life movement reiterated the fundamental Church belief that every life was precious regardless of one's physical condition because it was a gift from God.

We are made in God's image and likeness, and this fact gives a unique dimension to "the gift of life." We have even more reason to be grateful. It is tragic that in our time, concepts which are disastrous to the well-being of God's human family—abortion, euthanasia and infanticide—are falsely presented as useful and even respectable solutions to human, family and social problems. Human life is sometimes narrowly viewed in terms of being inconvenient or unwanted, unproductive or lacking arbitrarily imposed human criteria.

From the depths of my being, I urge you to reject this anti-life, anti-child, anti-human view of life and to oppose with all your strength the deadly technologies of life-destruction which daily result in the planned death of the innocent and the helpless. Together we must search for ways to demonstrate this conviction in our daily lives and in our public institutions. In doing so, we must never be discouraged or give up. Too much is at stake—"the gift of life" itself.

The "gift of life," God's special gift, is no less beautiful when it is accompanied by illness or weakness, hunger or poverty, mental or physical handicaps, loneliness or old age. Indeed, at these times, human life gains extra splendor as it requires our special care, concern and reverence. It is in and through the weakest of human vessels that the Lord continues to reveal the power of His love....

At this grace-filled time of my life, as I experience suffering in union with Jesus, Our Lord and Redeemer, I offer gratitude to Almighty God for giving me the opportunity to continue my apostolate on behalf of life. I thank each one of you, my sisters and brothers in the Archdiocese of New York and throughout our nation, for what you have done and will do on behalf of human life. May we never yield to indifference or claim helplessness when innocent human life is threatened or when human rights are denied.

With you, I entrust our efforts to the care of Our Lady, who, from the moment of her Immaculate Conception to the present, has been the refuge for the poorest and most forgotten among God's people. I assure you of a special share in the prayerful offerings of my sufferings to the Father, in union with Jesus and through the Spirit of Love Who is ours in abundance.

May God bless you always and give you His peace.[113]

Bishop Joseph T. O'Keefe, who was elected administrator during the interregnum, released excerpts from the late cardinal's last will and testament:

> I thank God for the wonderful gift of the priesthood and for the happiness that I have found united with Jesus in the Church in the service of my brothers and sisters in God's human family. It has been a joy to live among priests, religious and laity, to have the opportunity of serving them, to experience the warmth of friendship, to watch their devoted labors and sacrifices and to know and feel the encouragement and strength of their prayerful support. I deeply appreciate their kindness and I am sorry for any failure on my part in doing the will of our Heavenly Father.
>
> I wish to thank my brothers and sisters in God's family with whom I have come in contact during the days of my life for their friendship, for their generous assistance in my pastoral work and for overlooking my faults. I trust that all, in their charity, will secure for me by their prayers, pardon from God for my failures.
>
> With gratitude I accept whatever manner of death God wills for me and despite my unworthiness, with faith in God's grace and plan, I hope for eternal life in the company of the Risen Savior.
>
> May God bless you with His peace![114]

The outpouring of grief was remarkable. Millions were struck by his example of a holy death. Others pointed out how he never forgot his Bronx roots and that he was the son of Irish immigrants. "He was a humble man, good to the poor. He visited the sick. What more could you ask?" said one mourner.[115]

Hundreds of thousands viewed the casket; tens of thousands attended the daily Masses at the cathedral. The annual Columbus Day parade down Fifth Avenue was canceled in his honor.

The Requiem Mass on October 11 began with a forty-five-minute entrance procession which included seven cardinals, fifteen archbishops, eighty bishops, and one thousand priests. Representing Pope John Paul was Cardinal Baum, who said in his homily that Cooke was "a steady, strong and cheerful pastor of his people.... [He] combined the heart and spirit of a real New Yorker. He loved the City tenderly and deeply."[116]

The main celebrant of the Mass, Archbishop Pio Laghi, the apostolic delegate to the United States, described the cardinal as an "example of faith".

President Reagan's representative, the director of the Central Intelligence Agency, William J. Casey, delivered to Bishop O'Keefe a personal letter from the president. "Nancy and I", Reagan wrote, "share in the grief of the people and the clergy of the New York Archdiocese at the passing of His Eminence Terence Cardinal Cooke.... [He] will always be remembered for his tireless defense of the right to life. And he deeply believed it was God's will that all human life, even in the womb, deserved respect and protection."[117]

Cardinal Edwin O'Brien had this to say about his friend and mentor when he gave testimony on Terence Cardinal Cooke's cause for canonization.

> Cardinal Cooke, at whatever stage of life he found himself, was an extraordinarily single-minded man focused on the church and his responsibilities to the church. Seeking to imitate Christ in carrying out his pastoral responsibilities, he was unwavering. The more I think of it, the more I realize how difficult those days of his tenure

as Archbishop were. He didn't swerve, he didn't complain, he never doubted and led others through it all with tremendous strength of resources.[118]

In 1993, Cooke's successor, Cardinal John O'Connor, appointed a commission for the Cardinal Cooke beatification process after the Vatican approved his cause for sainthood.

Whether Cooke exhibited the qualities required for sainthood is for others to decide. But what can be said is that during the most difficult and turbulent period in the history of the Roman Catholic Church in America, Cardinal Terence Cooke managed to hold down the lid of the archdiocese's boiling cauldron while protecting and enhancing the spiritual life of his flock.

9

The Admiral

John Joseph O'Connor
Eighth Archbishop of New York
(1984–2000)

The future Cardinal O'Connor in his naval uniform

When the forty-seven-year-old Terence Cooke was named archbishop of New York in 1968, it was expected that he would hold that office well into the 1990s. When, instead, he died at age sixty-two in October 1983, there was something of a succession crisis. Because none of Cooke's team of senior associates was considered seasoned enough to take over, most clerical insiders expected someone from outside the archdiocese to be appointed.

One man who had impressed Cooke was his former auxiliary bishop in the Military Vicariate, John J. O'Connor, who had become bishop of Scranton, Pennsylvania, in May 1983 and who many assumed was being groomed to become archbishop of his home diocese, Philadelphia, when Cardinal John Krol retired.

As Pope John Paul II reviewed candidates for the position, it was apparent that he too was impressed with O'Connor, who was not only theologically sound and loyal to the Holy See but had the grit to manage New York and represent the Church nationally.

John Paul had met O'Connor a few times, but it was during the *ad limina* luncheon the pope hosted for New York bishops in 1981 that he had an opportunity to size up O'Connor. John Paul quizzed him for about forty minutes concerning the U.S. bishops' proposed pastoral letter on war and peace. The following day the pope approached O'Connor, who had just given a lecture to a roomful of clergy, and said, "That was a very interesting discussion we had yesterday. I would like you to tell [Vatican Secretary of State] Cardinal [Agostino] Casaroli what you told me."[1]

Apparently O'Connor passed muster, because on January 3, 1984, only three months after Cooke's death, Rome announced that John J. O'Connor, age sixty-three, was to become the eighth archbishop of New York. He was also named apostolic administrator of the Military Vicariate. This was to be a temporary job until the new Military Archdiocese was operational in Washington, D.C., and its first archbishop, Joseph Ryan, officially became the ordinary.

The Early Years

John Joseph was born the fourth child of Thomas and Dorothy Gumpel O'Connor, on January 15, 1920, in a working-class row house in southwest Philadelphia. In April 2014, the O'Connor family announced that genealogical research revealed that Dorothy was born Jewish and "converted to Catholicism before she met and married Thomas".[2] John's sister Mary O'Connor Ward said that when they were "growing up ... she surmised her mother was a convert, but ... the family never discussed the matter".[3]

Tom O'Connor made his living as a gold-leaf craftsman, applying decorative coating to the walls and ceilings in hotels, theaters, and churches. He was, as his son would constantly remind audiences later in life, a proud union man.

During World War I, Tom served as supervisor of six thousand workers at the Hugg Island shipbuilding plant in Philadelphia. It was in this period of his life that Tom learned to "look suspiciously at the wealthy". According to John, "[Dad] had no time at all for those he felt had made their money on the backs of working men, or in some shady way. He wanted nothing to do with them."[4] John inherited from his father this suspicion of the rich and in later life was known not to treat them preferentially—indeed, on some occasions, to treat them with contempt. (This attitude was at times to hurt fund-raising drives for his archdiocese.)

Tom and Dorothy did not wear their Catholicism on their sleeves, but they were stalwarts who said the Rosary with their children on Friday evenings during Lent. Dorothy O'Connor was a shy, humble, low-key person who enjoyed entertaining John's friends and loved taking him out to dinner. When she suddenly went blind, young John served as her guardian angel. Although she recovered her sight, the experience sparked in John a lifelong interest in helping the disabled.

As a boy, John played baseball and football and had after-school jobs. He sold produce for a truck farmer and worked in an ice house. He also worked in a bicycle-repair shop and delivered telegrams for Western Union. His family did not need government relief during the Depression, but John helped the less fortunate by delivering food baskets.

Because the nearest parochial school was too far away from the O'Connors' home, the children attended public schools. Then at age thirteen John entered West Philadelphia Catholic High School for Boys, which was run by the Christian Brothers. He began thinking about the priesthood soon afterward and later said he owed his vocation to the brothers. "All of the brothers there were dedicated", he said. "They gave us evidence of no outside interest whatever. They were there to work, to pray and to deal with us kids. They were tough men."[5]

From West Philadelphia Catholic, John O'Connor went on to St. Charles Borromeo Seminary, where he earned his bachelor's degree in theology and philosophy. In 1941 the rector informed him that he had been chosen to go to Rome for seven years to earn a doctorate at the North American College (NAC). The move to Rome was canceled, however, once the Axis powers declared war on the United States; the NAC was closed during the remainder of Mussolini's reign as Il Duce. Instead, O'Connor earned a master's degree in ethics at Villanova University.

On December 15, 1945, O'Connor was ordained, and his first assignments were as a curate in St. Gabriel's parish in Chester, Pennsylvania, and as an English, civics, and religion teacher and guidance counselor at St. James High School. In 1948 he earned his second master's degree, in theology, from St. Charles Borromeo.

In the late 1940s, he spent time teaching courses at St. John's night school and working in local hospitals, in a psychiatric ward, and at an institute that helped retarded children. He also spent time in Georgia, helping out a former Philadelphia priest who now served as bishop of Savannah. Father O'Connor ran a small mission in Valdosta and volunteered at a camp for underprivileged children in Savannah.

Back in Philadelphia, O'Connor made his debut as a weekly commentator on WVCH's Catholic radio program. He also directed the Delaware County Catholic Players, which performed dramatic pieces every week on the air.

When the Korean War broke out in 1950, Father O'Connor wanted to answer Cardinal Spellman's call to join the chaplaincy, but his archbishop, Cardinal Dennis Dougherty, denied his request. Two years later, the new archbishop, Cardinal John O'Hara—who had been an auxiliary bishop attached to the Military Vicariate— gave O'Connor the green light to join the U.S. Armed Forces.

O'Connor originally signed up for two years but agreed to stay on for an additional two years working in the Washington office of the chief of chaplains. During this period he came under the eye of Bishop Bryan J. McEntegart, who headed the Catholic University of America. (A future ordinary of the Brooklyn Diocese, McEntegart was the man who three decades earlier had headed Cardinal Hayes' effort to reform Catholic charitable institutions in New York.) McEntegart asked O'Connor to join the faculty at Catholic University after his military stint ended. O'Connor declined the offer because he had decided to join the regular navy after Cardinal O'Hara asked him to stay on for at least another year.

That one additional year in the service extended into a twenty-seven-year career.

O'Connor embraced the chaplaincy as his priestly vocation because it "provided an opportunity ... to provide pastoral care for those trained in the things of war.... The chaplain's job is to try to generate the idea that you have to teach people to love even if you have to kill."[6]

In the course of his military service, O'Connor said Mass for troops in the Mediterranean, the North Atlantic, and the Caribbean, as well as on Okinawa. While stationed in Washington and at Quantico, Virginia, he continued his education, earning an M.A. from Catholic University in clinical psychology and a Ph.D. in political science from Georgetown University. At Georgetown, he became a favorite student of Dr. Jeane Kirkpatrick, who would be ambassador to the United Nations during the Reagan years.

In 1965, O'Connor landed in Vietnam with the first Marines assigned to that war-torn country, with the rank of regimental chaplain. He was later promoted to divisional chaplain of the Third Marine Division, and he made additional visits to Vietnam later in 1965 and in 1967. In 1966, he received a Legion of Merit decoration for outstanding performance in Vietnam. He was to be awarded the Legion of Merit two more times for developing a moral-leadership program for the navy and the marine corps and for leadership with a cruiser-destroyer unit.

In 1968, when protests against U.S. involvement in the war were growing throughout the nation, O'Connor wrote *A Chaplain Looks at Vietnam*, for which he received the Alfred Thayer Mahan Award for Literary Achievement. The introduction, written by a leading war hawk, U.S. Senate Republican leader Everett Dirksen of Illinois, stated: "The moral implications of the conflict in Vietnam and the United States' involvement there have not, to my knowledge, been presented clearly to the American people—until now."[7]

Vice President Hubert Humphrey also praised O'Connor's efforts in a dust-jacket blurb. Saying that O'Connor was eminently qualified because he "served in combat with U.S. Marines and observed some of the bloodiest fighting", the vice president recommended the book "as imperative reading for every concerned American".[8]

The dust jacket stated that Chaplain O'Connor wrote the book because he was gravely troubled by the "mounting attacks on the United States' moral position in Vietnam" and that it "threatened to tear the country asunder and to destroy the prestige of the United States abroad".[9]

O'Connor defended U.S. military participation in Vietnam as morally just and frowned upon those who took to the streets condemning President Johnson's handling of the war: "I must confess a feeling of revulsion for those who chant 'LBJ, LBJ, how many babies have you killed today?' Such a charge is an assumption that the Administration actually wants war. Nothing in my experience warrants such an assumption. On the contrary, I am convinced that the administration has opted to accept the tragedy of war as the only available road to meaningful peace."[10]

As for the Vietcong terrorists, O'Connor condemned their tactics as immoral and defended U.S. motives, which were based on "defense of a nation that asked for our help, defense against aggression in Southeast Asia, resistance to Communist aggression throughout the world, our own justifiable interest".[11]

O'Connor also opposed an immediate withdrawal of our troops from South Vietnam because he believed "there would be the retaliatory slaughter ... [and] virtually everything we have done to secure rivers and streams—extremely important to Vietcong transportation—would be lost. Vietcong could again prey, maraud and terrorize at will."[12] The acts of brutality after South Vietnam fell to the communist North bore out O'Connor's predictions.

Why did he write this book at a time when public opinion was rapidly turning against the war? Some suggest that, having served with troops who endured horrific living and fighting conditions in the jungles of Vietnam, and having witnessed brave men die on the battlefield, he was compelled to justify morally America's role in the war. Others claim that he wrote it as an ambitious officer eager to enhance his reputation with the White House and bolster his military career. Years later, when out of uniform, O'Connor repudiated *A Chaplain Looks at Vietnam* as "a bad book" and insisted, "It was written too early, and I was too close to it."[13]

Whatever his motivations for writing the book, in the post-Vietnam era, O'Connor's career soared. In 1972, Captain O'Connor was the first Catholic priest to be named senior chaplain of the U.S. Naval Academy at Annapolis, Maryland. In that position, he was assigned a mansion with seven bedrooms. His niece, Joanne, lived with him while she attended college in the area.

O'Connor reached the top of the navy's greasy pole three years later, when he was promoted to the rank of rear admiral (two stars) and navy chief of chaplains. He claimed that he accepted the promotion reluctantly because, "as a priest and as a person, I am not used to the pomp and trappings" that came with the post.[14] Until his retirement from the navy on June 1, 1979, O'Connor spent most of his time traveling to the far corners of the world while visiting naval installations.

Shortly before his tour of duty was up, O'Connor visited his archbishop in Philadelphia, Cardinal Krol, and told him he wanted nothing more than a small debt-free suburban parish in his home diocese. Six weeks later, when he was at Quantico holding Lenten services, he received a call from Cardinal Cooke's priest-secretary, Father Larry Kenney. After the usual pleasantries, Kenney turned the phone over to the cardinal, who asked O'Connor to visit him in New York, ASAP. O'Connor replied, "Well, Your Eminence, tomorrow is Holy Thursday and the next day is Good Friday."

Cooke said, "I know, John; I'm aware of that", and insisted that the admiral report to 452 Madison Avenue the next day.

Meeting O'Connor at the appointed hour, Cooke cut to the chase. "You'd better sit down", he said. "The Holy Father wants to make you a bishop." John Paul had decided to name O'Connor a New York auxiliary bishop assigned to the Military Vicariate. Recalling that day, O'Connor later said, "I couldn't believe it. I was never so stunned until the day I heard I was going to New York."[15]

On April 24, 1979, the Vatican announced that the fifty-nine-year-old O'Connor was named an auxiliary bishop of New York and titular bishop of Cursola. Four weeks later Pope John Paul II personally consecrated him in Rome.

Arriving in New York, O'Connor took up residence in the rectory of Holy Family Church on East Forty-Seventh Street, near the United Nations building. Most of his time was spent on the road, ministering to the needs of U.S. troops and their families at military installations throughout the States and the world. He did find time to write a book, published in 1981, *In Defense of Life*, which described the Church's teaching on just war.

O'Connor was soon to receive national attention as a member of the U.S. bishops' committee that worked on the Pastoral Letter on War and Peace. Although viewed suspiciously by many of his fellow bishops as the token pro-military cleric on the committee, O'Connor took his responsibilities very seriously.

In an early draft, the bishops proposed language that went so far as to question America's defense policy: "the deterrence relationship which prevails between the United States, the Soviet Union and other powers is objectively a sinful situation because of the threats implied in it ... [yet] we reluctantly tolerate the American government's reliance on nuclear deterrence because unilateral withdrawal from this reliance has its obvious and grave risks."[16] Monsignor George Kelly, who served as research professor of Contemporary Problems at St. John's University and as a consultant to the Holy See, observed at the time that the statement on deterrence "placed the Bishops on record as maintaining the immorality of the mere possession of a vast nuclear arsenal because of the implied threat that it would be used, if necessary, to kill innocent Russians".[17]

Many of the bishops were pushing to take a stand that was even contrary to the public position of Pope John Paul II. At the United Nations in June 1982, the Holy Father told the General Assembly: "In current conditions *deterrence* based on balance, certainly not as an end in itself but as a step on the way toward a progressive disarmament, may still be judged morally acceptable."[18]

O'Connor (joined, as we saw in the last chapter, by Cardinal Cooke) took on the majority doves appointed by the well-known liberal Cardinal Joseph Bernardin, who served at that time as president of the Bishops' Conference.

As the most knowledgeable member of the committee on the moral questions surrounding the use of military weapons, O'Connor tried to steer the bishops away from their extreme pacifist position. As to the proliferation of nuclear weapons, he tried but failed to persuade them to use the word "curb" instead of "halt".

The Challenge of Peace: God's Promise and Our Response was published on May 3, 1983. Thanks to the efforts of O'Connor and Cooke, "the document no longer contained a reference to deterrence as a tolerable evil. Instead, the statement provided "a strictly conditional moral acceptance of nuclear deterrence".[19]

Reflecting on the time he spent on the committee, O'Connor said, "I was billed as the Genghis Khan of the committee. The resident barbarian. The token militant.... The two and a half years I served on the committee were fascinating, agonizing. The deliberations were often anguished. What we were doing was so important that we had to be absolutely honest with each other. And that would have been impossible without conflict, tension, misunderstanding, intense debate."[20]

In the end, O'Connor's beliefs that there was no "official teaching that suggests that our military people are engaged in immoral activities in carrying out their responsibility"[21]—and that it would be immoral if the United States disarmed unilaterally and left its people vulnerable to attack—prevailed. While he was not pleased with all the language, he was comfortable that the final document was basically in line with the teachings of Pope John Paul, and he cast his vote in favor of adoption.

John O'Connor was proud of the efforts he and his fellow bishops had put into the pastoral letter. At the University of Chicago in November 1984, he explained why:

> It seems to me that if the pastoral letter on war and peace may be used as a criterion, the bishops of the United States, *mutatis mutandis*, appear convinced that they *do not have the right to divorce politics from the realm of faith and morals*.... [Emphasis added.]
>
> The bishops speak because they cannot remain silent: the evil and danger of nuclear proliferation and the lurking possibility of nuclear war involve our nation in decisions that transcend the military and political. Fundamental *moral* choices are at stake and these choices must be informed by rational moral discourse, given the numbing awareness that "we are the first generation since Genesis with the power virtually to destroy God's creation."[22]

The argument that clerics "do not have the right to divorce politics from the realm of faith and morals" would serve O'Connor well in his future battles in the public square over abortion and other social issues.

On May 10, 1983, exactly seven days after the Bishops' Conference released the Pastoral Letter on War and Peace, the Vatican announced the appointment of John O'Connor as the seventh bishop of the Diocese of Scranton, Pennsylvania.

Critics of O'Connor saw the appointment to that see, which encompassed eleven counties in the rust-belt region of the Keystone State and had about 350,000 Catholics, as a demotion because of his hawkish views. Others believed it was to serve as a prelude to a bigger appointment—perhaps archbishop of Philadelphia.

O'Connor learned about the appointment on the last day of the committee's work, right before he was to deliver prepared remarks on the pastoral letter. Archbishop Pio Laghi approached him in the hotel and said, "I want to tell you that the Holy Father loves you very much." O'Connor, preoccupied with the speech he was about to give, said, "That's very gratifying but I'm about to make the intervention." Laghi, appearing not to be concerned, then said, "The Holy Father has appointed you the Bishop of Scranton." O'Connor was floored. He later confessed, "Everything went out of my head. I mean that literally. I got up, and when I spoke I was a blithering idiot. All I could think of was: I'm finally going to be a pastor. It was a slightly bigger parish than I'd anticipated, but my roots were in Pennsylvania, I knew Scranton, and I was overjoyed. But my speech about the changes I wanted to see in the pastoral was awful."[23]

Installed as bishop on June 23, 1983, O'Connor, not being a local boy, spent several months getting to know the layout and assessing the priests and lay employees of the diocese. Shortly after Labor Day, he sent a memorandum to his priests titled, "First Impressions and Initial Observations".[24] This remarkable memo was most revealing about its author. O'Connor bluntly stated his views and intentions, coming across more as the admiral than as the bishop.

To the priests in his charge he gave this warning: "There can be no such thing as 'I will not accept that assignment.' Nor may any pastor arbitrarily say: 'I will not accept that assistant.' The priest who will not accept any assignment could find himself without any assignment. The pastor who will not accept any assistant could find himself without an assistant."

As for the deportment of children in Scranton's parochial schools: "It may seem trivial or old fashioned to some, but I hope that our school system is such that if a sister or a priest walks into a classroom, the entire class stands in greeting. I hope that our school system is such that if a sister or priest passes on the sidewalk outside a Catholic school when students are leaving classes, they greet him or her respectfully. Are these things really trivial?"

As for the treatment of teachers, O'Connor revealed his "union man" side: "It is absolutely essential that we assure a just wage for our teachers. I do not pretend to know at this time where the money is to come from, but I have very strong feelings about this matter.... I want to make it very clear that every teacher in every Catholic school must be completely free, without harassment or pressure of any sort, to join any one of the appropriate teachers associations.... At the same time, I will categorically resist any pressure on any teacher to join any association to which he or she does not belong."

On pro-abortion politicians: "I will give no support, by word or action, that could in any way be construed in favor of any politician, of any political party, who professes either a specific pro-abortion position, or takes refuge in a so-called 'pro-choice' position."

As for homilies during Mass, O'Connor, who was known to speak too long on some occasions, gave this warning:

> I consider preaching our most important responsibility next to the offering of the Eucharistic Sacrifice itself.... People plead for bread; we may not give them stones. Our preaching must be clear, it must be scripturally oriented, it must be intelligible and meaningful for the people, and it must be delivered plainly and audibly. The pulpit is not the place for theological speculation. Our people are crying for fundamentals. We must remember that, for the most part, our people receive *no* religious instruction except what they receive at Mass on Sunday. Too often, we let the schedule of Masses and parking problems determine the length of sermons.... Many of [our people] watch television by the hour. Why must we rush them out of Mass as though forty-five minutes were a sacred restriction?

Finally, he declared that most music played during Mass was "abominable", and that too many people in the sanctuary were dressed in clothes "more fitting for outdoor barbecues".

Whether his marching orders to the clergy and religious would have been followed was never to be known, because on January 26, 1984, after only seven months in Scranton, he was named the eighth archbishop of New York.

Archbishop O'Connor

The conventional wisdom is that John O'Connor was named archbishop of New York because Pope John Paul II wanted a man much like himself in the nation's premier see. The historian Monsignor Florence Cohalan explained it this way: "There are not many lions or eagles around these days. Many bishops are like second or third level civil servants. Social workers actually. They wouldn't think of rocking a boat. They wouldn't know how to rock a boat if they wanted to. But O'Connor is strong. He's the kind of man who can say no and make it stick.... The Pope saw that O'Connor was a man who could say no, and yes, too, and give reasons for both."[25]

In meetings, O'Connor, who was referred to as the Boss or the Admiral, could be brutal to his staff members. Being unprepared or going against the grain would get one a sarcastic tongue-lashing. And the cardinal's humor could, at times, be very cruel. On the other hand, priests and laymen who called on him to discuss personal matters would find him to be compassionate. He would do whatever he could to help them. Monsignor Cohalan put it this way: "The Cardinal thought of himself as the chairman of the board.... The man is captain of the ship. This, I think, is communicated immediately to the passengers."[26]

There were other contradictions. On the one hand, he would say time and again that he always wanted to be nothing more than a parish priest helping troubled children or a Trappist monk removed from the world. On the other hand, he exhibited the driving ambition that was essential for any man to achieve the ranks of naval admiral and prince of the Church.

When stationed at Annapolis as senior chaplain, O'Connor claimed that when he heard rumors that "I would be promoted to Rear Admiral and go to Washington ... I honestly didn't want it, and all the folderol that goes with it".[27] Well, one does not reach the highest ranks of the military by being a wallflower. While stationed in the Washington, D.C., area, for instance, he earned from Georgetown a Ph.D. in political science. That's not exactly the education path of the average parish priest.

As for his advancement in his post-military career to auxiliary bishop, ordinary, archbishop, and cardinal, is it plausible that an unambitious person who truly wanted nothing more than a small suburban parish could achieve these posts?

There was also a split in O'Connor's public persona. Right-wingers, whether Catholic or not, revered O'Connor because of his public defense of Church teaching on the hot social issues of the times, and he played up to them.

George Marlin witnessed such an occasion when he was executive director of the Port Authority of New York and New Jersey. In 1996, O'Connor visited the 1 World Trade Center headquarters of the Port Authority to receive an award from the Authority's police department. Marlin, who served as M.C. for the event, was given a Waterford crystal U.S. flag that had the word "Conservative" engraved on it, because he was a prominent member of New York's Conservative Party and had run for mayor under the party's banner in 1993. After O'Connor received his award, playing to the assembly, he asked why "Conservative" was not engraved on *his* Waterford gift. The audience roared with laughter and gave him a standing ovation.

Meanwhile, O'Connor would make it clear to leftists that he was not a conservative; rather, like John Paul, he was theologically orthodox and a progressive on social-justice issues. Hence his episcopal motto: "There is no love without justice." O'Connor claimed he had inherited his father's "passion for justice"[28] as well as his unswerving support for labor unions.

Time and again, to emphasize that he was a humble common man, he would remind people that he was "one of five kids who grew up in row houses in Philadelphia" and that he had always felt "very comfortable with ordinary people".[29] To further that image he would claim that he was uncomfortable living in the cardinal's residence at 452 Madison Avenue.[30] In later years he told the *New York Times*, "I think I should have moved into and lived in a poor parish, or a poor section of the South Bronx, Central Harlem, East Harlem, rather than live in a swanky house attached to the Cathedral." He claimed, "It would have been wise."[31]

The man whom Pope John Paul sent to the city that he described as "the Capital of the world" was as complex as his new hometown. In his dual roles as militant admiral and humble social worker, he would enthrall and infuriate New Yorkers in every walk of life for the next sixteen years.

O'Connor in New York: Opening Salvos

At his March 19, 1984, installation, which was attended by more than one thousand priests, one hundred bishops, nineteen archbishops, and five cardinals, O'Connor proved to be very different from his twentieth-century predecessors. Unlike them, he was a skilled orator with a fine sense of humor who enjoyed engaging with the news media and using the pulpit in St. Patrick's Cathedral as a bully pulpit.

The general public loved O'Connor's opening act at his installation. The three thousand people packed into the cathedral roared with approval when O'Connor summoned to the pulpit a Bronx ten-year-old named John Joseph O'Connor, who was attired in cassock and surplice, and placed his miter on the boy's head.

The young O'Connor had sent the cleric a letter wishing him luck and pointing out that they had the same name and that "the day when you become an Archbishop is my granddad's anniversary and the day before my birthday."[32] Touched, O'Connor invited the boy to the installation to serve as an altar boy and to carry the cross during the procession. "I never thought it would come out like this", the young O'Connor said after the ceremony.[33]

The faithful also laughed heartily when O'Connor donned a Yankees cap.

O'Connor hit the sidewalks of New York running. Like his predecessor, he too had to confront a series of public controversies in his first year as archbishop. But unlike Cooke, who had to deal with events that were beyond his control (e.g., the King and Kennedy assassinations), O'Connor brought on many of his own challenges.

The troubles began on June 24, 1984, when the archbishop said during a press conference, "I do not see how a Catholic, in good conscience, can vote for an individual expressing himself or herself as favoring abortion."

This comment did not sit well with New York's governor, Mario M. Cuomo. The governor, who in the early 1970s was publicly pro-life, had changed his tune after losing a primary for lieutenant governor in 1974 and a race for mayor in 1977. To advance his career, Cuomo promoted the line that although he was personally opposed to abortion, as an elected official it would be wrong for him to impose his religious beliefs on the general public.

Reacting to the archbishop's June 24 comment, Cuomo launched, as the *New York Times* interpreted it, "an unusual challenge to the Catholic Church by a Catholic politician".[34] An unhappy Cuomo told the *New York Times*, "The Church has never been this aggressively involved [in politics]. Now you have the Archbishop of New York saying that no Catholic can vote for [Mayor] Ed Koch, no Catholic can vote for [City Comptroller] Jay Goldin, for [City Council President] Carol

Bellamy, for [U.S. Senator] Pat Moynihan or Mario Cuomo—anybody who disagrees with him on abortion.... The Archbishop says, 'You, Mario, are a Catholic
who agrees with me that abortion is an evil.' ... The Archbishop says, 'OK, now
I want you to insist that everybody believe what we believe.' "[35]

Cuomo did not stop there; he described to *Newsday* what he believed were the
potential implications of O'Connor's remark:

> So I'm a Catholic governor. I'm going to make you all Catholics—no birth control,
> you have to go to church on Sunday, no abortion.... What happens when an atheist
> wins? Then what do I do? Then they're going to start drawing and quartering me.[36]

Responding to the governor's statement, O'Connor appeared, at first, to be
backing off when he told the Brooklyn *Tablet*, "I have never said, anywhere, at any
time, that 'no Catholic can vote for Ed Koch.' "[37] He added: "My sole responsibility is to present ... the formal official teaching of the Catholic Church. I leave to
those interested in such teachings [to judge how] the public statements of office-
holders and candidates" match up.[38] In a *New York Magazine* interview he further
explained his position:

> I think there's a deep disquiet in the national consciousness about this issue. People
> know it's wrong. They know we're killing. It's not a matter of arguing the pre-
> cise moment when a fetus becomes a baby—people *know* that thousands of real live
> human babies are being killed every day ... and they don't know what to do. They're
> confused, upset about it. To me, that anguish is the only reasonable explanation of
> why I can utter a simple statement, a simple answer to a simple question—I don't
> see how a Catholic in good conscience can vote for a politician who explicitly favors
> abortion—and immediately it becomes enormous news.[39]

O'Connor was not backing off, and the matter for him was far from over.

After the Democratic National Convention nominated the first woman vice-
presidential candidate, Italian-American Congresswoman Geraldine Ferraro of
Queens, a so-called pro-choice Catholic, O'Connor publicly criticized her for
saying "things about abortion relevant to Catholic teaching which are not true".
He said, "The only thing I know about her is that she has given the world to
understand that Catholic teaching is divided on the subject of abortion.... As an
officially approved teacher of the Catholic Church, all I can judge is that what has
been said about Catholic teaching is wrong. It's wrong."[40]

On September 10, after the congresswoman denied she had ever misinterpreted
Church teaching, O'Connor released a copy of a letter Ferraro had signed and sent
two years earlier to fifty Catholic congressmen concerning a group called Catholics
for a Free Choice. In the letter she wrote "[Catholics for a Free Choice] shows us
that the Catholic position on abortion is not monolithic and that there can be a
range of personal and political responses to the issue."[41]

In a twenty-five-minute phone conversation with Ferraro after the release of the
letter, O'Connor reemphasized that there is "simply no room for a 'free choice' on
the matter of abortion and that the Second Vatican Council, Pope Paul VI, Pope
John Paul II and the bishops of the United States had made that abundantly clear".[42]
Afterward, in a statement, Mrs. Ferraro said the conversation was "cordial, direct

and helpful". She added that "when bishops speak out they are doing their duty as Church officials.... When I speak out I am doing my duty as a public official and my foremost duty as a public official is to uphold the United States Constitution, which guarantees freedom of religion. I cannot fulfill that duty if I seek to impose my own religion on other American citizens. And I am determined to do my duty as a public official."[43]

The liberal establishment was appalled by what it viewed as O'Connor's meddling. The *New York Times* took this shot at him: "It might as well be said bluntly:... [the] effort to impose a religious test on the performance of Catholic politicians threatens the hard-won understanding that finally brought America to elect a Catholic President a generation ago."[44]

Senator Ted Kennedy accused O'Connor of "blatant sectarian appeals" and argued that not "every moral command could become law."[45]

Governor Cuomo refused to sit on the sidelines. On September 13, he flew to America's best-known Catholic university, Notre Dame in South Bend, Indiana, to answer O'Connor in a talk titled "Religious Belief and Public Morality: A Catholic Governor's Perspective".[46] Cuomo described himself to his audience as "an old-fashioned Catholic who sins, regrets, struggles, worries, gets confused, and most of the time feels better after confession". "The Catholic Church", he added, "is my spiritual home."

"I accept the Church's teaching on abortion", he continued. But then he asked, "Must I insist you do?" Cuomo went on to argue that one cannot impose one's moral views. "Our public morality then—the moral standards we maintain for everyone, not just the ones we insist on in our private lives—depends on a consensus view of right and wrong. The values derived from religious belief will not and should not be accepted as part of the public morality unless they are shared by the pluralistic community at large by consensus."[47]

He appealed to Cardinal Bernardin's "seamless garment" position, saying "Abortion has a unique significance but not a preemptive significance." "Abortion", he contended, "will always be a central concern of Catholics. But so will nuclear weapons. And hunger and homelessness and joblessness, all the forces diminishing human life and threatening to destroy it."[48]

Arguing that a consensus to ban abortion did not exist, Cuomo concluded: "I believe that legal interdicting of all abortions by either the federal government or the individual states is not a plausible possibility and, even if it could be obtained, it wouldn't work. Given present attitudes, it would be Prohibition revisited, legislating what couldn't be enforced and in the process creating a disrespect for law in general."[49]

Of Cuomo's attempt to protect his political flanks, historian Richard Brookhiser wrote: "Cuomo had found, in consensus and prudence, a way of having religion when he wanted it and not having it when he didn't."[50]

The consensus argument was even too much for the very liberal bishop of Albany, Howard Hubbard:

While I support wholeheartedly the governor's position on capital punishment, there is no consensus in our state or nation on this matter. Quite the contrary. The polls show that 60 percent to 70 percent of the population favors the death penalty.

Also polls indicate that the vast majority of the citizens in New York are opposed to recent legislation about the mandatory usage of seat belts. Yet contrary to citizen consensus, the governor supports such legislation because it would save several hundred lives a year. Why not a similar concern about saving the thousands of human lives which are terminated annually through abortion on demand?[51]

The renowned theologian Monsignor William B. Smith, academic dean of St. Joseph's Seminary, agreed:

The governor's style was smooth and slick, but the content was specious and misleading. He is obviously a competent man, but a couple of points were horrendous, one being the complete ignoring of the human rights issue. Human rights do not rest on consensus. Respect for the human rights of blacks, Jewish people—any minority—does not rest on consensus. This is why we call them inalienable rights. He relied on the 15-year-old rhetoric of Planned Parenthood [that] we're trying to impose our morality on others. The Supreme Court didn't establish a consensus; it destroyed one. The laws in the 50 states weren't there because the Catholic Church put them there.[52]

One month later, on October 18, Archbishop O'Connor, in a speech before a Catholic medical group—with Mother Teresa of Calcutta sitting on the stage— challenged the Cuomo thesis:

You have to uphold the law, the Constitution says. It does not say that you must agree with the law, or that you cannot work to change the law....

There are those who argue that we cannot legislate morality. The reality is that we do legislate behavior every day.... It is obvious that law is not the entire answer to abortion. Nor is it the entire answer to theft, arson, child abuse, or shooting police officers. Everybody knows that. But who would suggest that we repeal the laws against such crimes because the law is so often broken?[53]

O'Connor ended by reasserting his original public stance. "I have the responsibility of spelling out ... with accuracy and clarity what the Church officially teaches.... I have simultaneously the obligation to try to dispel confusion about such teaching wherever it exists, however it has been generated, regardless of who may have generated it.... I recognize the dilemma confronted by some Catholics in political life. I cannot resolve that dilemma for them. As I see it, their disagreement, if they do disagree, is not simply with me [but] with the teaching of the Catholic Church."[54]

Many Catholics declared John O'Connor a national hero. After years of bishops sitting on the sidelines, finally there was someone standing up and challenging whether "Catholic politicians could separate their personal convictions from their public stance" on abortion.

"I think", said New York auxiliary bishop Patrick Ahern, "John O'Connor upped the ante on abortion all by himself. He started the ball rolling, and the other bishops have been forced to follow along. I think, too, that it is an act of great courage, because they're going to *flay* him over this before he's finished."[55]

All the national and international press, plus the public accusations by the liberal media that he was shilling for Ronald Reagan's reelection, did not ruffle the archbishop. In fact, he was laid-back about it. He told *New York Magazine* reporter Joe

Klein that he was "surprised by all the fuss". He pointed out that "I'm saying the same things I've always said."

O'Connor went on to tell Klein that other social issues did concern him. For instance, in September 1984 he had made a public statement during a hospital strike that received little press coverage: "No Catholic hospital could hire substitutes for the striking workers or threaten them in any way", he had said.

But despite his concern for numerous social issues, he rejected the "seamless garment" approach. "I simply don't see the rationale in saying that a politician is for better housing, a lower rate of unemployment, a more rational foreign policy—and the only thing wrong is that he supports abortion, so it's okay to vote for him. You have to go back to the basic question: What is abortion? Do you think it's the taking of innocent human life or don't you? If you do, then translate it: How can we talk about a rational foreign policy or the horrors of nuclear war if we hold the position that you can take innocent human life?"[56]

Abortion was not the only issue O'Connor took on in the public square during his first year in office. In December, at a joint press conference with Mayor Koch concerning a low-income-housing proposal on which the two men agreed, O'Connor was asked his position on Koch's 1980 Executive Order 50, which forbade any city contractors for social services from discrimination in employment based on "sexual orientation or affectional preference". His answer—"We will not sell our souls for City contracts"[57]—generated major headlines. And he went on to state that if the archdiocese lost the suit it had filed challenging the validity of the order, he was prepared to reject the $72 million in government funds.

After the mayor interrupted O'Connor, saying that his position was "impossible", the archbishop went on to say, "We have said repeatedly that we have no problem whatsoever in employing people admitting to or not admitting to homosexual inclinations. If an individual avows engagement in homosexual activity, then we want to be able to say whether or not we will employ that person in this particular job, and we feel this is a perfectly appropriate thing for any agency. You know, we have 5,700 youngsters in the child-care agencies, and they are the ones currently at issue."[58]

Once again the Left went ballistic, particularly since the Brooklyn Diocese, on the other side of the East River, disagreed. The ordinary, Bishop Francis Mugavero, and his auxiliary, Bishop Joseph Sullivan, two very liberal trained social workers (the Brooklyn Diocese under Mugavero was known as the Reno of the Catholic Church for annulments), claimed they could "sign the pledge [Order 50] as a matter of secular employment practice without implying any doctrinal approval of homosexuality".[59]

The editorial writers at the *Times* slammed O'Connor. If he carried out his threat, they complained, "the poor and the children will be the losers."[60]

Times columnist Sydney Schanberg also took a shot at O'Connor. In his December 18 column, titled "Put Up Your Dukes", he accused O'Connor of being divisive and picking fights "only to sharpen a difference with others rather than to soften and resolve one".[61]

Archbishop O'Connor answered his critics in an essay published in the January 17, 1985, issue of *Catholic New York*. He began by describing Church teachings on homosexual behavior:

Homosexual inclination, in our theology, is not morally wrong. Homosexual behavior is. We bear no malice toward homosexually active persons. We abhor their being harassed or persecuted in any way. At the same time, we do not believe that homosexual behavior should be declared lawful or that such behavior should be elevated to a protected category.[62]

He went on to state that the Catholic Church in New York does "not believe that religious agencies should be required to employ those engaging in or advocating homosexual behavior.... We believe ... that only a religious agency itself can properly determine the requirements of a particular job within that agency and whether or not a particular individual meets or is reasonably likely to meet such requirements."[63]

Finally, O'Connor pointed to one section of Order 50 that was overlooked by the media: a mandate "that agencies such as ours 'actively recruit' members of all protected groups for all positions". To yield to this order, O'Connor concluded, "would constitute an exceedingly dangerous precedent and invite unacceptable governmental intrusion into and excessive entanglement with the Church's conducting of its own internal affairs".[64]

O'Connor's first major battle with city hall did not end until June 1985, when New York's Court of Appeals ruled, in a six-to-one decision, in favor of the archdiocese and its coplaintiffs, Agudath Israel and the Salvation Army. The court struck down the phrase in the executive order "sexual orientation or affectional preference", stating that "no matter how well intentioned his actions may be, the mayor may not unlawfully infringe upon the legislative powers reserved to the City Council."[65]

Although O'Connor won the executive-order battle, however, the war over homosexual rights continued.

His Eminence

In his first year as archbishop of New York, O'Connor had made his voice heard not only in the Empire State but across the nation, and apparently Pope John Paul II approved. In April 1985, the Vatican announced that John Joseph O'Connor was to be elevated to cardinal at a consistory to be held on May 25. The *New York Times* reported that at a luncheon the cardinal-elect told the audience, "In deepest humility, I must confess it does have a nice ring to it."[66]

Archbishop John O'Connor was one of twenty-eight churchmen elevated to the College of Cardinals on May 25. New Yorkers who attended the ceremony included Governor Cuomo's wife, Matilda, and Mayor Ed Koch.

Afterward Cardinal O'Connor revealed to the New York press his scarlet socks. He said that he would never dare to wear them back in New York. At a reception that night for five hundred people at a Hilton hotel, Mayor Koch, who had donned a bright-red tie, proclaimed, "New York City is once again the international capital of the world now that we have our Cardinal back."[67]

Upon his return from the Vatican, the cardinal was greeted by huge crowds inside and outside the cathedral. "I missed you", he told the faithful, and he assured them that he had not changed. "Before I went to Rome I wore a 6⅞ hat size", he said. "That is the size of my [red] biretta. I plead with you to pray that I will never need a larger size."[68]

Cardinal O'Connor in the Public Square

In a 3,500-word *New York Times* profile of Cardinal O'Connor in February 1986, sociologist Peter Berger pointed out that the cardinal "brought a fresh assertiveness to the role of Archbishop of New York and has expanded the influence of the Roman Catholic Church on the life and politics of the City, government and Church".[69]

In addition to expressing the Church's position on abortion, labor, housing, homosexual rights, and the homeless, Cardinal O'Connor, according to Auxiliary Bishop Patrick Ahern, "is mobilizing public opinion within the Church and outside the Church. He is carrying the message to everybody, the same as the Pope."[70]

The cardinal's new good friend, Mayor Koch, agreed with Ahern's observation: "I think he's enhanced the image of the Archdiocese in the public perception and in fact, he is a smart man who has commitment to withstand whatever pressures are out there."[71] Conceding that he did not "agree with him on some matters", Koch said he respected him and that he was a "tough and effective adversary".[72]

Working together on issues on which they agreed, Koch and O'Connor developed a genuine friendship and became known as "the temporal and ecclesiastical Odd Couple". Claiming that two people who sue each other can indeed be friends, the cardinal stated: "The Mayor has never made an effort to force me to bend morally. He's not attempted to use me for his political interests, and I have no intention of losing my friendship with the Mayor to advance the interests of the Church."[73]

In August 1987, the two announced that they would coauthor a book to be titled *His Eminence and Hizzoner*. O'Connor made it clear that his primary interest for agreeing to the book was "to assess from a moral, spiritual and religious perspective those public policy issues of critical concern to people". Koch said the book would not be "a kissy-huggy book" and would "tell it as it is". Royalties would be split between Catholic Charities and the city's Meals on Wheels program.[74]

When the book was published in March 1989, the media focused more on Koch's part of the book. Koch, who described himself as a "sane liberal", revealed, the *Times* reported, "his queasiness about abortion on demand, his support of tuition tax credits with children in parochial schools, his opposition to racial and ethnic quotas", and his support of "a proposed Constitutional amendment permitting prayer in public schools".[75] The cardinal's portions of the work were well researched and crisply described the Church's position on a host of issues, including the natural law, education, health care, AIDS, drug abuse, racism, homosexuality, and abortion.

Meanwhile, O'Connor's relations with Governor Cuomo remained somewhat frosty. Their first clash, during the 1984 presidential race, was not to be their last. In 1986, for instance, to put some heat on the governor, the New York bishops, led by O'Connor, initiated a postcard campaign in parishes to urge Cuomo to stop Medicaid financing of abortion. Cuomo's office was inundated with more than fifty thousand cards, signed by Catholics, that said: "I will hold all elected officials accountable who do not support my conscientious objections."

Despite their serious differences, Cuomo realized that at times it was important to have the cardinal standing at his side. When promoting his housing program, for instance, Cuomo reached out to O'Connor to help him get it through the legislature. "In the end," Cuomo conceded, "that's going to make a difference, because they respect him, they know he's not trying to win a race; he's trying to help people."[76]

In addressing the question of his public persona, O'Connor once again displayed his split personality. On the one hand, it was obvious that he relished being outspoken in the public square and using his position to move public opinion and to pressure politicians. To build a stage off the main altar in St. Patrick's in order to hold press conferences after celebrating Sunday Mass, to host a local television show, and to have his Sunday homilies broadcast on WMCA, one must enjoy the limelight.

In addition, O'Connor truly believed that he had to be assertive to ensure that Catholics were not treated badly in the public square. "I get increasingly distressed", he told the *Times*, "that when Catholics express their views as citizens, there are in some sectors a claim that we are attempting to impose our views on the rest of society. But when other communities demand legislation that may be in conflict with Church teaching this seems at times to be considered appropriate. Catholics are not second-class citizens."[77]

As for complaints that he was crossing the line and "imposing" his abortion views, he told a gathering at Harvard Law School in April 1986:

> Why would we *not* be "imposing our morality" on others when we oppose rape, but "*imposing* our morality" on others when we oppose abortion? What a strange democracy it would be that would encourage bishops to cry out their convictions so long as these were popular, but to remain mute when so ordered.[78]

Yet, on the other hand, O'Connor tried to downplay his role, feigning that he did not enjoy it. When asked about the inherent influence the resident of 452 Madison Avenue possesses, he demurred, "I abhor the concept of [the] Powerhouse because it smacks of the use of money, manipulative approaches, threats, rewards, of knowing big people, prominent people who are able to bring leverage to bear, to punish and reward."[79]

One must ask if O'Connor really believed that statement. When he told Mayor Koch that he would terminate contracts with the city if the Church was compelled to comply with Executive Order 50, one could argue that he was "bringing leverage to bear".

O'Connor may not have had the type of power Spellman possessed, in the form of a network of the wealthy and the politically connected; nevertheless, he did possess power due to his communication skills. When he spoke from the pulpit or from the front steps of 452 Madison Avenue, friend and foe alike listened and reacted— often cautiously, so as not to offend. That is power.

Throughout his tenure, Cardinal O'Connor continued to fight many battles and speak out on many issues in the public square. Here are some of the most pressing issues he confronted.

The Abortion Battle

In January 1986, in a letter read at all Masses in the archdiocese on the anniversary of the *Roe v. Wade* decision, O'Connor described that day in 1973 as one of "national infamy". From the pulpit in St. Patrick's Cathedral, he told the faithful, "In 1984, when I talked strongly on the issues, I was accused of doing so because the national election campaign was in progress. I said then, 'I'll be talking about this in 1985 and 1986 and until the day I die.' "[80] And so he did.

For the rest of his life, he continued to stress that, unlike those who took the "seamless garment" approach, he strongly believed that the right to life superseded all other issues, because without life the other issues didn't matter.

And O'Connor continued to critique the thin-skinned Mario Cuomo. In February 1986, he said, "I flat out think [Cuomo's] wrong. I don't think that makes him evil. It makes him wrong. He makes a serious effort to theologize his way through it and I think he's been unsuccessful."[81] O'Connor was referring to Cuomo's argument, repeated ad nauseam, that as an elected official he should not impose his religious views on the electorate.

The cardinal said that whereas Cuomo "has a great deal to offer on other issues, he [is] misguided about abortion". O'Connor specifically criticized Cuomo for supporting Medicaid funding for abortion "without any constitutional requirement to do so".[82]

The public envelope was pushed further in August 1986 when a routine newsletter signed by the vicar-general, Bishop Joseph O'Keefe, arrived at 410 parishes containing this paragraph, which was directed toward pro-abortion politicians and spokesmen:

> Great care and prudence must be exercised in extending invitations to individuals to speak at parish-sponsored events, e.g., Communion breakfasts, graduations, meetings of parish societies, etc. It is not only inappropriate, it is unacceptable and inconsistent with diocesan policy to invite individuals to speak at such events whose public position is contrary to and in opposition to the clear, unambiguous teaching of the Church. This policy applies, as well, to all Archdiocesan owned or sponsored institutions and organizations.

The pro-abortion crowd and New York's liberal establishment vociferously objected to the announcement. Catholics for a Free Choice protested that the archdiocese had "nailed [the door] shut to prevent its members from being heard".[83]

A *New York Times* editorial described the directive as a "revival" of the argument between O'Connor and Cuomo "about how fervently Catholics in public office must oppose abortion".[84]

Initially, Governor Cuomo declined to comment, saying he had not read the statement. But a member of his press office coyly said that it "doesn't seem to apply to the Governor", who "is totally within the confines of Church teaching".[85]

Defending the policy, Bishop O'Keefe said he was not denying free speech. "I'm not saying we shouldn't listen. I'm not afraid to listen to anybody's opinion. But when you are bringing together a church society, it is inappropriate to invite people who divide your community."[86] The bishop added that when he decided to issue the directive, "I never even thought of the Governor."[87]

On September 4, Cuomo, who was in the midst of a reelection campaign, went on the offensive. "We lay people have a right to be heard", he declared. "It is very difficult to see how this [directive] would be implemented."[88] In typical Cuomo fashion he raised a host of questions to confuse the issue. "From what I'm told, it applies to Church teaching. But what is Church teaching? When are you teaching infallibly and when aren't you? What people, which people will decide who agrees with Church teaching? Will you have ecclesiastical courts?"[89]

Reacting, Monsignor Peter Finn, director of communications for the archdiocese, dismissed Cuomo's comments, saying they were "nonsense". "I hardly think", Finn continued, "our local synagogue would be about to invite a P.L.O. [member] to their seder any more than a church in Harlem would invite Mr. Botha [the president of South Africa] to their supper. So I don't understand. What's the problem? In a response to a request from many people about what the guidelines should be for inviting people for speaking, a guideline was given. Period.... I think it's very clear as far as the Church is concerned, what it means by 'differing with the Church's teachings' ".[90]

Bishop O'Keefe joined the fray, ridiculing Cuomo's Notre Dame speech as "the encyclical by Mario". He also said that "under no circumstances would I invite [Cuomo] to speak to young people at a graduation" because "he would confuse young people."[91]

Cuomo did, however, concede to a *Times* reporter that "the Church has the right to make rules for itself, there's no doubt about that. The Church has the right to make rules. It can say, 'If you want to belong these are the rules.' But depending on what the rule was, one can say whether it was wise or whether it was unwise."[92]

The September 11 issue of *Catholic New York* published the cardinal's response to Church critics in a column titled "A Matter of Common Sense". O'Connor threw down the gauntlet, asking, "How much further are the nonsensical allegations going to go on?"

Imitating Cuomo's rapid-fire approach, the cardinal asked, "So what is all this furor about? What is all this fuss about? What is the nonsense I read about squelching 'free speech'? Where is the deep, dark sinister political motivation that some choose to see? When did common sense, or a sense of appropriateness, become unconstitutional or un-American? Why the hysterics that leads a columnist to speak of the 'thought police' of the Archdiocese of New York? (A rather nasty Nazi-like implication there, wouldn't you say?)"[93]

The cardinal also addressed Cuomo's inquiries as to who decides who will be heard: "Who is supposed to make the judgment in such matters? Our pastors, with the guidance of our Vicar General, are charged by Church law and by my delegation to provide guidance. Are we to have a Church in which everyone's judgment is equal to everyone else's? That's not a Church, it's chaos."[94]

The cardinal's column was not his final word on the subject.

After a Bronx assemblyman, John Dearie, complained that he was banned from speaking at his home parish, St. Raymond's, because he had voted for Medicaid funding and because the archdiocese was acting "in anticipation of the elections", O'Connor replied in a letter that Dearie's statement had been "grossly untrue, deeply insulting, and morally libelous".[95]

In early October, Dearie met with the cardinal at his office at 1011 First Avenue for an hour and fifteen minutes and agreed to keep "communications open".[96]

Dearie, at first, was not repentant. After that meeting he told journalist Nat Hentoff that he still believed the cardinal wanted to harm him politically. "It was like a warning—'We're letting you know, we're watching you.'"[97]

He did, however, take the cardinal's advice to pray over the matters discussed—and in later years he became pro-life. Dearie described his reversal this way:

> I did pray and I did think a lot. I began thinking about going with my wife, Kitty, and seeing those sonograms of our son in the womb. It had a profound impact, the notion of life and what it meant. And I did change my position. There was some feeling that, "Oh, it was just a matter of time before O'Connor's politics got to him." But it was the Cardinal's *thoughts* that got to me.
>
> After I changed my position, the Cardinal had my wife and me to dinner at his residence. He had a remarkable way of showing his thanks. As stern as he was in the beginning, there was a great feeling of love about him. And he was concerned about what my decision would mean to me in both a political and a personal sense.[98]

In November 1989, the cardinal took two active steps in support of his words. First, he became chairman of the U.S. Bishops' Committee for Pro-Life Activities. That same month he urged the founding of a new order of nuns, the Sisters of Life, who would take an additional vow to defend human life against abortion and euthanasia. Nine women took up his challenge in June 1991 and cofounded the order, which thrives to this day (106 sisters including those in formation).

On January 31, 1990, O'Connor defended his auxiliary bishop, the vicar of Orange County, New York, Austin Vaughan, who had spent ten days in an Albany jail for protesting in front of an abortion clinic. While incarcerated, Vaughan stated that Governor Cuomo was "in serious risk of going to hell" because of his "active support of abortion rights and government financing of abortion".[99]

In his *Catholic New York* column, later quoted in the *New York Times*, the cardinal, describing Vaughan as "one of the finest theologians I know," continued:

> I read in the newspapers that His Excellency, the Auxiliary Bishop of New York, had "cursed" His Excellency, the Governor of New York, "to hell." Indeed, the Governor is quoted as saying: "I get condemned to hell for not agreeing [on abortion]."
>
> "Not so," Bishop Vaughan told me, "very much not so," when I spoke with him after his release from prison. He went on to say that he is well aware that he has no power whatsoever to condemn anyone to hell. He would agree with the Governor completely that such an unpleasant task is exclusively the prerogative of a much higher and wiser power.
>
> He told me, too, that despite the newspaper reports, he had never suggested for a moment that he would be happy to see me refuse the Governor Holy Communion. In fact, he says he was asked by the press whether he, Bishop Vaughan, would excommunicate the Governor, and replied that he had no authority to do so and would not think it a good idea anyway.
>
> That out of the way, would anyone deny that the Bishop has the right and even the obligation to warn any Catholic that his soul is at risk if he should die while deliberately pursuing any gravely evil course of action, and that such would certainly include

advocating publicly, as the Bishop puts it, "the right of a woman to kill a child." What the Bishop told me he actually said was that the Governor is "quite possibly contributing to the loss of his soul." To me that sounds significantly different from "cursing" or "condemning" the Governor to hell. . . .

I do have one major concern, however, and it's not the highly confused report on who said what in the newspaper stories. It's that such stories tend to distract from the real issue, that abortion, as the Second Vatican Council puts it, is an "abominable crime." That, neither political fortunes nor ecclesiastical sanctions, is the bottom line.[100]

Reacting to O'Connor's column, Cuomo had a terse reply: "The Cardinal says the Bishop was misquoted, I'm glad."[101]

A June 14, 1990, special edition of *Catholic New York* contained a twenty-thousand-word Q&A written by O'Connor that addressed almost every conceivable subject concerning abortion, including suggestions to doctors, lawyers, educators, and parents "to advance the cause of life". What caused headlines was this statement:

> Where Catholics are perceived not only as treating Church teaching on abortion with contempt, but helping to multiply abortions by advocating legislation supporting abortion or by making public funds available for abortion, bishops may decide that . . . such Catholics must be warned that they are at risk of excommunication. If such actions persist, bishops may consider excommunication the only option.[102]

O'Connor went on to state that, at the same time, "the Church does not want to make 'martyrs' of individuals by punishing them. It is up to the local bishop to use his best judgment concerning particular cases."

Of the "personally opposed" position, O'Connor stated that it "says, in effect, 'In public life I will act indistinguishably from someone who sees abortion as a positive social good, but please know that I will do so with personal regret.' This regret is hardly effective, since it serves the agenda of those who actively favor abortion."

While the archdiocese's communications director, Joseph Zwilling, said that O'Connor's Q&A was "not written with anyone in mind", the *New York Times* reported that Governor Cuomo "appeared to take it personally".[103] Cuomo told the *Times*, "It is difficult to discuss it. It is upsetting. I don't like to hear it. How could you? This is something very fundamental to our family."

Cardinal O'Connor kept up the battle on abortion for the rest of his life. One notable instance occurred on June 13, 1992. After celebrating the 8:00 A.M. Mass at the Church of St. Agnes on "Fulton Sheen Place"—the block of Forty-Third Street east of Grand Central—the cardinal led a group down Lexington Avenue to the Eastern Women's Center Abortion Clinic at 38 East Thirtieth Street. He made it clear to the general public that "there will be no material distributed, and there will be no confronting anyone. We will simply be praying."[104] In front of the clinic, O'Connor joined those assembled in praying the Rosary.

On April 10, 1996, President Clinton upped the ante by vetoing Congress' ban on partial-birth abortion. The following Sunday, April 14, O'Connor forcefully condemned the veto from his pulpit. He described the practice of partial-birth abortion as "barbarous": it "is actually killing babies who are virtually out of their mothers' wombs".[105] He went on to say that, "of course, there will be those who accuse us of crossing the line—meaning the line between the spiritual and the political, between church and state. That's nonsense. The line has been crossed—a crucial line—between life and death."[106]

The cardinal was not alone in his criticism; Pope John Paul described Clinton's decision as "a shameful veto that in practice is equivalent to an incredible brutal act of aggression against innocent humans".[107]

A year later, in March 1997, O'Connor and the other U.S. cardinals sent a letter to President Clinton urging him to sign recently passed legislation that would ban partial-birth abortion. The letter pointed out that the "public were misled by a prominent abortion-rights advocate [Ron Fitzsimmons] last year when he said the procedure ... was very rarely used and only in cases where the mother's life was in danger".[108] Fitzsimmons, executive director of the National Coalition of Abortion Providers, admitted that he had "lied through his teeth".[109]

After reading the letter during Sunday Mass at St. Patrick's, the cardinal told the faithful, "I plead with you to pray that this horror of infanticide will be once and for all banned from our land."

Clinton once again vetoed the bill.

O'Connor later told George Marlin that nothing had angered him more than Clinton's vetoes of the bills. He made it clear that Clinton would never be invited to the annual Al Smith Dinner and would never be welcomed to St. Patrick's Cathedral so long as O'Connor was archbishop of New York.

The Archdiocese's Foster-Care Program

In the 1970s the American Civil Liberties Union (ACLU) filed a suit against New York City—the *Wilder* case—"alleging that religiously-operated agencies were discriminating against black Protestant children", as Cardinal O'Connor summarized it, because "non-Catholic children are not placed in the best institutions, which are Catholic and Jewish."[110] The city's practice for decades had been to assign Catholic children to Catholic-managed child-care agencies and Jewish children to Jewish agencies, and so forth.

Although the ACLU at one point dropped the charges of minority discrimination against Church-related foster agencies, the case continued because it also alleged that children in Catholic foster-care programs were denied family-planning information and birth-control and abortion services.

After years of fighting the ACLU, Mayor Koch, who frequently stated that the case was ridiculous and had no merit, suddenly settled in October 1986. The terms of the agreement included these provisions:

- "Religious matching placements" would be discontinued, but parents could designate a religious preference.
- Special Services for Children "shall ensure that all children have meaningful access to the full range of family planning information, services and counseling to be provided either by the agency or by a suitable outside source or both.... The tenets of any religion with regard to family planning will not be conveyed to a child other than in the course of providing religious counseling." In other

words, the archdiocese would have to cooperate in providing contraceptives and abortion services.

- "Religious symbols that are present in the child's room shall be permitted so long as they have been requested by the child. Agencies shall not display excessive religious symbols."[111]

O'Connor would not tolerate these overreaching provisions, and on January 22, 1987, he announced, "I have chosen to reject the contracts [that expire on June 30] rather than to accept this agreement.... We will lose in the neighborhood of $100 million a year.... $100 million is not worth one baby."[112]

While most political observers were shocked by the announcement, which would affect four thousand children, Mayor Koch said he agreed with the cardinal's reaction. As the *Times* reported, he "called the stipulation 'bad' and said the City agreed to it only to avoid a court fight that could have led to a ban on religious agencies providing any publicly financed foster care."[113]

After Sunday Mass at the cathedral on January 25, 1987, O'Connor made it clear to the press that "the door is always open" for negotiations, particularly since the mayor called the stipulation "bad". "It would be inappropriate", he said, "for me to say they couldn't come up with something."[114]

In his column in the January 29 issue of *Catholic New York* he described the implications of the city's capitulation: "How many realize the extent of this A.C.L.U. victory? Will it end with the city of New York? In my judgment, it will sweep the United States. Will it end with driving the church out of child care only? Who's kidding whom?"

The following week Mayor Koch announced that he expected the archdiocese to discontinue providing foster-care services because "I know of no way out."[115]

At the end of March, O'Connor agreed to join the United Jewish Appeal-Federation of Jewish Philanthropies in filing a suit objecting to the requirements, and the city agreed to a six-month extension of current contracts while the case was pending. But once again, O'Connor insisted that, "If the day comes that the requirement is that to receive a contract, we must violate our Catholic principles, then we will not accept any city contracts."[116]

Six weeks later, on May 7, 1987 the Federal District Court denied the archdiocese's request "to postpone the implementing of the [stipulations] while the issue was being tested in the higher courts".[117]

On June 9, 1988, the U.S. Court of Appeals for the Second Circuit upheld the lower court's settlement but acknowledged "that some of the provisions pose a risk of excessive entanglement" and ordered redrafting of various stipulations.[118]

The archdiocese and the city began negotiations and in August announced "new contract language that would allow the Church to continue operating in a matter consistent with its moral teachings".[119] Despite the court rulings, the cardinal had successfully held his ground.

Looking back on this church-state battle, he said, "I sincerely fear government intervention.... All government funding that helps the Church meet the needs of society is both welcomed and deserved. When used to control, to modify values, to divert the Church from its appointed purpose, it must be feared and feared mightily. There is no room for a Trojan Horse in the City of God."[120]

Homosexuality and the AIDS Crisis

In November 1985, a new city council was elected that pundits agreed was more liberal than its predecessor, particularly on social issues. In addition, long-time Majority Leader Tom Cuite, who, with the help of the Archbishop of New York, had engineered the defeat of the gay-rights bill in the city council no less than a dozen times, had retired. As a result, supporters of the legislation were confident that in 1986 it would finally reach the desk of Mayor Koch, who would sign it into law.

While cognizant of the change in the political landscape, O'Connor, who became archbishop in 1984, did not back down. At a news conference on Sunday, January 12, 1986, he said he still opposed legislation that would "ban discrimination on the basis of sexual orientation because it could turn homosexuals into 'an exempt or preferred class'" and might lead to "the introduction of practices we believe are harmful to society". The cardinal was meeting with lay groups and urging them to organize to defeat the legislation.

O'Connor was taking nothing for granted, and he worked hard to convince the bishop of Brooklyn, Francis Mugavero—who was soft on the issue—to join him in signing a joint statement opposing the legislation.

"We believe it is clear", the February 6 statement said, "that what the bill primarily and ultimately seeks to achieve is the legal approval of homosexual conduct and activity, something that the Catholic Church, and indeed other religious faiths, consider to be morally wrong. Our concern in this regard is heightened by the realization that it is a common perception that whatever is declared legal by that very fact becomes morally right."[121]

With the pressure building to pass the bill, the Episcopal bishop of New York, Paul Moore Jr., publicly endorsed passage and took a shot at O'Connor, saying his position was "immoral". The *New York Times* reported on February 8 that in an interview O'Connor "offered a cool response". He said, "The [Episcopal] Bishop feels the need to make public comments about my sense of morality. I don't feel the same need. I can only assume he's following his conscience.... My inclination is not to call people I think are wrong immoral."[122]

Several days before the city council was scheduled to vote, Moore struck again, condemning the actions of Catholics and Orthodox Jews to defeat the bill. "Passage of this bill is a simple and urgent matter of justice", he said.[123]

Responding from the pulpit of St. Patrick's on March 16, O'Connor told the faithful that the legislation was "an affront to Judeo-Christian values". The claim that "you can do whatever you please, because love takes care of everything", he said, "betrays an ignorance of certain moral absolutes". "Divine law cannot be changed by federal law, state law, county law or city law, even by passage of legislation by the City Council. This changes nothing in terms of divine law."[124]

The cardinal received a standing ovation after he completed his homily.

On March 20, the New York City Council passed the so-called homosexual-rights bill with twenty-one voting yea and fourteen voting nay.

The measure was approved for several reasons: First, the voting population in the city had moved to the left because of the exodus of many blue-collar Catholics to suburbia or to greener economic pastures in the South and the Southwest. The new speaker of the city council, Peter Vallone, a Catholic who was elected to his post by a margin of only one vote (eighteen to seventeen), agreed to bring the bill to the floor for a vote and, unlike Tom Cuite, would make no effort to stop passage. And, finally, Cardinal O'Connor, despite his public pronouncements, did not work behind the scenes and, unlike Cardinal Cooke, did not make personal calls to wavering legislators.

While O'Connor opposed the free distribution of condoms and syringes to curb AIDS, he was most compassionate about the victims of the disease and, at the Vatican's AIDS conference in November 1989, urged his fellow churchmen not to treat people with AIDS as "outcasts".[125]

O'Connor himself served as a volunteer at St. Clare's Hospital and ministered to the needs—both medical and spiritual—of AIDS patients. He helped wash and comfort thousands of them and helped Mother Teresa open an AIDS hospice in the Bronx.

In January 1987, O'Connor overruled the rector of the cathedral and permitted a man dying of AIDs to be married there. The cardinal stood in a pew and watched as the thirty-eight-year-old David Hefner and his bride, Maria, exchanged vows on St. Valentine's Day. Hefner died on Sunday, May 3.

O'Connor's compassion for the victims of AIDS was noted by President Reagan, who appointed him to the President's Commission on the HIV Epidemic. The homosexual community, however, was outraged over the appointment; homosexuals began standing in protest during O'Connor's Sunday Mass in the cathedral. Others would hold insulting banners.

Eventually, the protests got out of hand. On Sunday, December 10, 1988, as O'Connor was beginning his sermon, demonstrators started shouting, "You bigot, O'Connor, you're killing us!" Members of the militant homosexual group ACT-UP sat in the aisles, and some chained themselves to pews. At least one desecrated a consecrated Communion Host by tossing it on the floor and stomping on it. Police arrested over forty protesters in the cathedral, and many who refused to budge were carried out on stretchers. Outside the cathedral were over forty-five hundred protesters, shouting obscenities and chanting, "We will fight O'Connor's bigotry." The four hundred police stationed on Fifth Avenue locked up approximately seventy people.

O'Connor, who was stoic during the disruption (the admiral in him came out), told his congregation, "Never respond to hatred." He told the media that it was "kind of ironic that I'm accused of not doing enough", particularly since he had argued for more government spending on AIDS research and care, and 12 percent of the archdiocese's health-care budget was devoted to AIDS patients.[126]

As for the protest itself, the cardinal said, "I pray that this doesn't happen again. But if it happens again and again and again, the Mass will go on, or I will be dead." No demonstration, he warned, "is going to bring about a change in Church teaching, and it's certainly not going to bring about any kind of yielding on my part. I don't say that with any bravado; I'm your basic coward. But I'm the Archbishop of New York, and I have to preach what the Church teaches."[127]

The invasion of the cathedral backfired; political leaders of every stripe condemned the desecration. It was too much even for the *New York Times*, whose editors wrote:

The demonstrators ... mostly brought discredit on themselves for demonstrating in a way that obstructs consideration of their arguments.

There is plenty of room for controversy over church positions on homosexuality, AIDS and abortion. No one can quarrel with a peaceful demonstration outside St. Patrick's, and John Cardinal O'Connor did not do so.

But some of the demonstrators turned honorable dissent into dishonorable disruption. They entered the cathedral and repeatedly interrupted the service. They lay down in the aisles, chained themselves to pews and sought to shout down Cardinal O'Connor as he said mass. One protester is reported to have disrupted even the administering of communion with an act of desecration that deeply offended worshipers.

New Yorkers generally expect protesters to respect the rights of others, even those with whom they disagree. To deny clergy and laity alike the peaceful practice of religion grossly violates a decent regard for the rights of others, let alone the law. Far from inspiring sympathy, such a violation mainly offers another reason to reject both the offensive protesters and their ideas.

Arguments over AIDS, homosexuality and abortion are not going to be advanced by hysterics, threats or the disruption of religious services. They might be advanced by serious argument that reflects conviction. The demonstrators who entered St. Patrick's Cathedral Sunday invite the public to think about a different kind of conviction.[128]

Other actions O'Connor took during his tenure included ordering, in March 1987, the Jesuits at the Church of St. Francis Xavier on West Sixteenth Street to stop having special Masses for the homosexual group Dignity, which champions gay sexual activity; refusing to permit "instructions about condoms in AIDS education in the schools, hospitals and youth programs of the Archdiocese";[129] and opposing in 1998 city council legislation that would "make domestic partners the legal equals of married couples, calling it a violation of natural law and a blow to traditional marriage".[130]

In the late 1980s and early 1990s, gay and lesbian organizations were denied permission to march with their banners in New York City's annual St. Patrick's Day Parade by the group that had sponsored the parade for over a century, the Ancient Order of Hibernians. (No attempt was made to keep individual gays and lesbians from marching.)

In 1993, Mayor David Dinkins, Ed Koch's successor, tried to impose a different approach. Arguing that the St. Patrick's Day Parade had to be inclusionary, he leaned on Police Commissioner Raymond Kelly to award the 1993 parade permit to a new group, the St. Patrick's Day Parade Committee, that had pledged to allow gay groups to march, and Kelly complied.

Upon hearing of this decision, Cardinal O'Connor, speaking from the cathedral pulpit, asked, "Do the Mayor and the Police Commissioner agree to this arbitrary transformation from the religious to the political? Will other religiously related activities become equally vulnerable to arbitrary politicization in this land which boasts of its tradition of separation of church and state?"[131] The cardinal made it clear that the position of the archdiocese was not rooted "in antagonism toward homosexual persons but in the right of religious bodies to express their own devotions in accordance with their own tenets without interference or harassment by others".[132]

The Hibernians filed suits in state and federal courts challenging the city's decision to deny the permit. Eyebrows were raised when the New York State Supreme
Court judge assigned to the case, Alice Schlesinger, sought and obtained permission
from her judicial superiors to meet with O'Connor to discuss it. Meanwhile, as the
suits were pending, scores of Irish and Catholic organizations threatened to boycott
the parade if the Hibernians did not regain sponsorship under the old terms.

In an expedited decision, the court ruled in favor of the Hibernians, declaring
that the parade was a "religious procession" and its organizers were constitutionally
protected.

On the day of the parade, Irish gay-rights groups staged a protest. About ninety
participants blocked Fifth Avenue by sitting in the street; when they refused to
disband, they were arrested.

On December 14, 1994, the St. Patrick's Day Parade chairman, John Dunleavy,
announced that the grand marshal of the 1995 parade would be Cardinal John
O'Connor. He was the first New York archbishop to lead the marchers up Fifth
Avenue. Many viewed his participation as a victory lap.

The Jewish Community and the Middle East

Shortly after arriving in New York in January of 1984, O'Connor was taken aback
when several Jewish leaders objected to his likening abortion to the Holocaust.

To make amends, O'Connor began to reach out to the Jewish community and
to articulate his abhorrence of anti-Semitism and his "commitment to the survival
and security of the State of Israel, understanding the evil of the Holocaust, and support for the freedom of Soviet Jewry".[133]

That May, as the keynote speaker at the American Jewish Committee's annual
meeting in New York, he pledged "to make constructive Catholic-Jewish relations
a centerpiece of his work as Archbishop".[134]

He also told Jewish leaders that in the navy he had, as Rabbi James Rudin
reported, "been traumatized by a visit he had made to the Nazi concentration camp
in Dachau, near Munich". This confrontation with evil, he said, "changed my
life forever".[135]

In 1988, on the fiftieth anniversary of the Kristallnacht pogrom, O'Connor spoke
at a New York City synagogue and conceded "that centuries of systematic anti-
Jewish Christian teachings helped create the poisonous seedbed for Nazism".[136]

When dealing with American and Israeli Jews, things did not always break
O'Connor's way, however. In 1986, he got into hot water with the Vatican and his
Jewish friends concerning his travels to the Middle East.

On Thursday, June 12, Cardinal O'Connor traveled to Lebanon for three days
in his capacity as president of the Catholic Near East Welfare Association. His
announced plan was "to review the circumstances of various humanitarian activities
supported by Catholic Near East and to see what further help may be needed at this
time". The Vatican made it clear that his trip was not a peace mission for the Holy
See but "was designed to show solidarity with the country's besieged Maronite
Christians".[137]

After meeting with Christian leaders and churchmen, O'Connor met with President Amin Gemayel on June 14 in Beirut. He said afterward, as the *Times* reported,

"that he was hopeful there would be a break in the case of five American hostages held by Muslim extremists".[138] The next day he paid a call in West Beirut to Sheikh Hassan Khaled, the spiritual leader of Lebanon's Sunni Muslims. O'Connor discussed the situation in Lebanon and conveyed greetings from Pope John Paul and the head of Lebanon's Maronite Catholics, Patriarch Nasrallah Sfeir.

Before departing for Rome to report his findings to the pope, O'Connor "emphasized that reconciliation and coexistence between Christians and Muslims was the safest way out of the Lebanese problem".[139]

While in Rome, the cardinal made public comments in which he called for a homeland for Palestinians, many of whom were in refugee camps "living in the most wretched circumstances imaginable".[140]

Back in the States, many Jewish leaders, concerned about his comments about the Palestinians, engineered an official invitation for O'Connor to visit Israel. The cardinal accepted and said he would arrive on December 27.

On Christmas Eve, the Vatican put a damper on the trip when it informed O'Connor that the Vatican secretary of state wanted him to cancel the official meeting scheduled with the Israeli head of state and cabinet members in Jerusalem. The reason: the Vatican did not, at that time, recognize Jerusalem as the capital of Israel. A senior Vatican diplomat said, "It would be very unfortunate if the confusion and emotion generated by [O'Connor's] trip somehow blurred the Holy See's very carefully developed positions on the complex Mideast issues. Confusion of any kind in that region tends to set back the cause of peace."[141]

Not wanting to cancel the trip, O'Connor emphasized that he was not on a mission for the Holy See; he explained that the trip was a "personal initiative" and that "he had every expectation and hope of visiting informally with various representatives of the Israeli government".[142]

Throughout the trip he spoke carefully. When visiting a Palestinian refugee center in Jordan, he said, "When I speak of the needs and rights of the Palestinians, I'm concerned about the needs and rights of the Israelis as well."[143]

During the Mass on New Year's Day at St. Savior's Church in Old Jerusalem, Cardinal O'Connor made an apology to his hosts for ignoring diplomatic formalities:

> It is fitting and it behooves me to say that I deeply regret and certainly apologize to those who govern Israel.... I failed to be sufficiently thorough in my preparations. I failed to familiarize myself with the protocols normally surrounding a visit by a member of the College of Cardinals. Because of that error on my part, unfortunately, it is quite understandable that the people of Israel and those in the government might well have construed some deliberately intended offense.... Whatever compensation can be made during my visit will be made within the restrictions that bind me.[144]

O'Connor later admitted to the *New York Times* that he had made a mistake and "hoped that his relationship with the Jewish community in New York did not depend on his never making a mistake".[145] He went on to say, "I want to be a friend to the Jewish community, I want to do everything I can to be supportive, but that doesn't mean I do everything your way. You can't write the script for me."[146]

And O'Connor did prove to be a friend. In December 1993, he was credited with being a key architect in the establishment of diplomatic relations between the Vatican and the state of Israel.

Dealing with Labor Unions

As previously mentioned, Cardinal O'Connor frequently reminded New Yorkers that his father was a union man and that he was a strong supporter of labor's goals. "Anything less on my part", he once said, "would have been a complete betrayal of the father I loved".[147] Every year in his homily during the Labor Day Mass, he would welcome union officials, saying "You are always welcome in this cathedral. You built it, your presence is an honor."

In his 1989 sermon, he clearly described his position:

> You have the right, and I will defend it to the death, to engage in collective bargaining. And if all peaceful and reasonable means are exhausted then you have a right to engage in a strike—a non-violent strike, of course. I will never attempt to deprive anyone of that right. I will never engage in any reprisals or disciplinary measures against people for demanding a just wage and for taking appropriate means to try to see that they get it.... I have to say to you at the same time that I cannot bankrupt the Church, cannot close down hospitals and health care systems. I cannot close our schools.... I must always find the right balance.... If you consider me unjust ... picket me. Picket my residence.... Picket everything but my Masses.... There will be no reprisals against anyone ever for picketing anywhere."[148]

O'Connor lived by those words. In his first year, he had warned his administrators, during a Catholic hospital strike, that they were forbidden to hire substitutes. A decade later, in November 1994, he pledged that striking nurses at Mercy Hospital in Port Jervis, New York, would not lose their jobs. On one occasion in December 1990, O'Connor addressed a rally outside the East Forty-Second Street building of the *Daily News* in support of the paper's striking workers.

Cardinal O'Connor went so far as to meet and appear on platforms with members of the leftist fringe. He met with the Reverend Jesse Jackson to discuss improvements in working conditions for health-care workers. He even appeared at rallies with the noted huckster the Reverend Al Sharpton. Many of the cardinal's most vocal and prominent supporters, however, believed that, no matter how generous the impulse, appearing with such people diminished his office and empowered professional rabble-rousers.

The cardinal did take on organized labor in January 1990, when he learned that a pro-abortion resolution was to be voted on at an upcoming AFL-CIO executive meeting. In a *Catholic New York* column, which was reprinted in the February 8, 1990 edition of *Origins*, he wrote that he was "heartsick" that the union was under pressure "to go pro-abortion". To become a stronger union by getting more women members, he lamented, would be "at the expense of the weakest of the weak, the blameless unborn". He added, "Might we even see the sorry spectacle of union members required to permit a portion of their union dues to go into anti-life, pro-abortion activities? ... Will union workers who are 'personally opposed' to abortion be nonetheless required to support it with their dues?"[149]

Heeding the cardinal's words, the AFL–CIO sidestepped the issue at its February meeting by postponing a vote. On August 1, the executive council rejected a proposal to "abandon its traditional neutrality on abortion and take a pro-abortion stance".[150]

Poverty, Housing, and Racial Issues

Six months after he became archbishop, O'Connor—who made housing for the poor a top priority—established an Office of the Homeless to assist with food and shelter programs. Believing that housing is a basic human right, he joined Ed Koch in August 1985 when the mayor signed a moratorium on demolition of the single-room-occupancy hotels that housed many of the poor.

In May 1988, the cardinal launched the Affordable Home Ownership Program to provide two thousand homes for low-income families in the South Bronx. That same year he announced additional plans for housing in the Highbridge section of the Bronx, a 750-unit renovation for low-income families.

Nine years later, O'Connor led a procession through Highbridge to bless a youth center and to celebrate the revitalization of the neighborhood, which included the rehabilitation of 29 buildings with 917 apartments. "This is not just housing—bricks and mortar", said Monsignor Donald Sakano, president of the Highbridge Community Housing Development Corporation. "This is needed social services, job opportunities, day care, health care—the ingredients that make a successful and viable community."[151]

The cardinal, impressed with the progress, said, "I can hardly believe the difference. It's been truly astonishing.... This has been a careful collaboration of the Church and the public sector. No one has tried to take undue credit. We've all worked together. We're all proud."[152]

To bring attention to the plight of the poor and downtrodden, O'Connor lobbied every year in Albany for funding of antiviolence and antidrug programs managed by priests in the South Bronx. In August 1986, he led an antidrug vigil on Fifth Avenue. More than a thousand people with lighted candles gathered in front of St. Patrick's "to pray and to exhort their neighbors and public officials to bring about a drug-free New York", as the official announcement of the vigil put it.[153]

O'Connor also did his part to ease racial tensions in New York. In May 1990 he appeared with Mayor David Dinkins and Governor Mario Cuomo at a unity rally. Afterward, from the pulpit, he condemned racism as a "sin and an outrage" and asked the congregation to take a pledge against bigotry.

After clashes between blacks and Jews in the streets of Crown Heights in August 1991, the cardinal released a statement denouncing the violence.

On February 4, 1999, a twenty-three-year-old immigrant from Guinea, Amadou Bailo Diallo, was killed by four plainclothes policemen in the Soundview section of the Bronx. The police fired forty-one rounds, nineteen of which hit Diallo. The police had stopped him because they thought he matched the description of a notorious rapist. After they identified themselves, Diallo reached into his jacket pocket. One of the cops yelled, "Gun!" and all four commenced shooting. The NYPD investigators did not find any weapons on Diallo; it appeared that he had reached for a wallet. The Diallo death sparked numerous protests, and many feared racial violence. On March 25, the four officers were indicted by a Bronx grand jury on charges of second-degree murder.

Attempting to calm the waters, Cardinal O'Connor mediated a meeting at his office at 1011 First Avenue between police-union officials and black business and community leaders. While he explained that he would attempt to come up with recommendations to improve relations, he warned his guests that he did not have "any smoke and mirrors". "I happen to be in a very visible position," he added, "but that doesn't make me a genius."[154]

The cardinal persuaded the participants to sponsor a prayer service for racial harmony. Afterward James Savage of the Patrolmen's Benevolent Association told the media, "The idea of the meetings is to try to work out jointly instead of screaming at one another over the barricades. We sort of needed a mediator like the Cardinal, somebody who was trusted by both sides."[155]

"There are a great number of black people and other people of color in the New York area who sincerely believe that they are far more vulnerable to the police than white people are", O'Connor told the *New York Times*. "I have tremendous respect for our police force, but clearly we have problems, and we have to get at those problems."[156]

Three weeks after the meeting, O'Connor celebrated a Mass for the Police Department Holy Name Society at St. Patrick's Cathedral. In his homily, he pleaded for an end to the "hostile rhetoric between city officials and leaders of the daily protests against the police."[157] "We cannot have reconciliation", he said, "if talks begin with the assumption that the Police Department is rotten to the core."[158] But he also added that "if there has been discrimination against blacks and Latinos and Asians, then we do no good by denying those injustices. As long as those perceptions are there, they must be dealt with. And it is rare that perceptions have no basis in reality."[159]

On April 6, the cardinal met with Amadou Diallo's parents. "I'm so privileged to take the meeting," O'Connor said. "I'm so sorry for your loss." Later his spokesman Joseph Zwilling indicated that "there is still a need for healing." Cardinal O'Connor hoped that the interfaith service he would hold at St. Patrick's on April 20 would "be a beginning on the road toward reconciliation".[160]

The two-hour service dedicated to healing and reconciliation was held in a packed cathedral. The finest moment was after the Reverend Calvin Butts of Harlem's Abyssinian Baptist Church completed his talk and hugged the man he had previously denounced as a racist, Mayor Rudolph Giuliani. "Nothing unites us like the humble, simple act of prayer", Butts said.[161]

The mayor, who was not slated to speak, was asked by O'Connor to make a statement after this extraordinary moment. Giuliani simply said, "Our similarities are much greater than our differences. We're children of the same God. The Mayor needs to recognize that. The police do. And the citizens of the City do."[162]

Addressing the congregation, O'Connor reminded them that "there is a time for protest and a time for prayer. Today is a time for prayer."[163]

In a city that could have been ripped apart by this tragic killing, Cardinal O'Connor played a major role in restoring racial harmony.

O'Connor and His Archdiocese

When John O'Connor was installed as archbishop in March 1984, the New York Archdiocese had 1.84 million faithful, 777 active priests, 411 parishes, 51 missions, 256 parochial elementary schools with 85,956 students, and some money in the bank. At the time of his death in May 2000, the total Catholic population was 2.39 million, and there were 561 active priests, 412 parishes, 228 parochial elementary schools with 76,763 students, little money in the bank, and a general operating budget with a significant structural deficit.

Part of the problem during the O'Connor years had to do with a changing demographic: the number of cafeteria Catholics as well as those who completely abandoned their faith grew annually. Another part of the problem was O'Connor's management and fund-raising style.

Because of his national and international activities and his membership in a host of papal commissions and committees, John O'Connor was not a hands-on administrator like his predecessor, Terence Cooke. Instead, he ran the archdiocese as he had run the Naval Chaplain Corps: he delegated most of the day-to-day management to his subordinates. In the archdiocese, these included Bishop O'Keefe, who would go on to become the bishop of Syracuse; Bishop Henry Mansell, who would become the bishop of Buffalo and, later, archbishop of Hartford; Bishop Robert Brucato; and Bishop Edward M. Egan—O'Connor's eventual successor, who before being named archbishop of New York spent twelve years as bishop of Bridgeport.

When in Manhattan, O'Connor would begin a typical day with morning prayers at 7:10 A.M. in his chapel with his priest-secretaries and other clerics who lived at 452 Madison Avenue. At 7:30 he would say Mass in St. Patrick's followed by breakfast with key aides or visitors. From there he would go to his office at 1011 First Avenue. On most nights, O'Connor, a chronic insomniac, would read and write into the late hours.

He relied on trusted aides just as Spellman had when he traveled the world on behalf of the Church. But that's where the comparison stops. Despite the time he spent outside his archdiocese, Spellman—a numbers man—always had his finger on the financial pulse of his see and had a knack and an enjoyment for fund-raising. Spellman knew that, to finance his massive construction budget in the forties, fifties, and sixties, the man wearing the red hat had to do most of the begging. To get captains of industry and finance to open up their wallets, the cardinal archbishop personally had to charm and cajole them.

While Spellman thrived on fund-raising, O'Connor did not. Historian Monsignor Cohalan put it this way: "One of the most obvious differences between O'Connor's work in New York and his work in the Navy was the financial problem: ordinary expenses were met by the Navy and the Chaplains' Aid Society. The incessant hunt for funds, a major task of the Archbishop of New York, was not something he knew well."[164]

There were other reasons: he just didn't like fund-raising, and he was uncomfortable with the rich. Some of his priests believed his reluctance to ask for money was due to his pride over being the son of a blue-collar union member. Other priests have suggested that he disliked dealing with the wealthy because he thought they had grown up with silver spoons in their mouths and led leisurely, superfluous lives. What he failed to understand is that many Catholics who achieved financial success were themselves the sons and daughters of blue-collar workers. They were proud that their hard-working parents had sacrificed so that they could get a decent education and work their way up various ladders to success.

Unfortunately, several prominent Catholics who visited with the cardinal intending to hand him a large donation walked out with the check still in their breast pocket because they were offended by his "silver spoon" cracks.

Despite these faults, O'Connor was passionately devoted to enhancing the spiritual, social, and financial conditions of his flock.

O'Connor's Synod

To rejuvenate his archdiocese, O'Connor announced in May 1987 that he intended to hold the first synod in fifty years and swore in seventy-eight priests, religious, and laypeople to prepare the agenda. Eleven months later the list of 243 delegates, half of whom were laymen, was released.

In May 1988, the cardinal personally opened the synod and lectured the participants on the importance of the sixty-six proposals that were before them. As he observed after the synod had ended, "The one challenge that emerged from our synod reflections as both overriding and undergirding all others was expressed as a constant plea: 'Give us the word of God.' It was virtually a cry of anguish. It said: Give us the word of God clearly, straightforwardly, unambiguously, and we will use it to address every other need.... With the word of God, we can meet every challenge; without it, we are a dead body that only calls itself Catholic."[165]

Shortly after the synod officially closed in January 1989, O'Connor unveiled a five-year plan he hoped would "pump new life" into the archdiocese. Recommendations included giving top priorities "to programs for young people, to extending religious education to youth outside Catholic schools and to adults, and welcoming black and Hispanic Catholics to parish life.[166]

To meet the synod's goal of widening the role of the laity, new advisory boards, recruitment efforts, training programs, and fundraising projects were to be established. Every parish that did not already have a parish council was to start one within the next year.

Stating that the parish councils were an "indispensable key" to the plan, the cardinal admitted, "If a year from now we don't have a truly active parish council, we won't be able to implement the synod." Calling the plan "my work for the next five years", the cardinal conceded, "This will pretty much shoot my bolt. Then they'll wrap me up and send me to the glue factory."[167]

One immediate problem he faced was that many pastors were unaware of the synod's work. "There were", he said, "a significant number of pastors for whom the synod is still something in outer space."[168] Unfortunately, there was very little follow-through, and as a result the synod had little impact on the laity of the archdiocese.

Catholic Education

The education of Catholic youth was a key concern of the synod and a top priority for the cardinal. The problem was, as always, financing parish schools in poor neighborhoods.

Because of changing demographics, the number of schools classified as poor inner-city ones stood at 140 in 1992, up from 79 in 1981. To cover the deficits of these schools, the archdiocese was subsidizing them to the tune of $20 million a year—an unsustainable figure.

Though the archdiocese's Inner-City Scholarship Fund was a great help, the annual donations were not enough. To raise $100 million over three years from the business and financial communities, O'Connor created the Partnership for Quality Education in 1991. The annual goals, however, were never reached. In the program's first year, for instance, $23 million was pledged, and only half of that amount was actually received. The appeal failed for two reasons: the tough economy at that time and the cardinal's distaste for fund-raising. Monsignor Thomas Bergin, who for a time was vicar for education, described the problem this way: "He was uncomfortable with money people. If we had an event for wealthy patrons in the residence, he'd circulate for fifteen minutes or so and would slip upstairs. I think the people knew he was uncomfortable around them. He would tell them, 'We don't want your money, we want your soul.' And those of us who set up the event would groan."[169]

Unable to raise the additional funds, the archdiocese had to announce that the $20 million in annual subsidies would be cut in half. This meant that schools that had experienced significant drops in enrollment would have to be closed.

While members of the education staff knew in 1991 that at least twenty to thirty schools were in serious trouble, in April it was announced that no more than five would be closed at the end of the academic year. One year later, a list of forty-one schools set for closing was reduced to fifteen. And not all the announced closings came to pass. Pleas from parents who, from time to time, met with the cardinal to ask for a reprieve worked. After a meeting with the pastor and the parish council of St. Jerome's parish at Alexander Avenue and 138th Street in the Bronx, for example, O'Connor relented. "The next day," as the *Times* reported, "the Cardinal's office told the school that it would be given another chance to get its financial house in order."[170]

St. Jerome's was not the only parish to get a reprieve. Only about thirty schools in all were closed or consolidated during the O'Connor years. However, supporting a score of schools with shrinking enrollments and underutilized facilities that were in need of expensive infrastructure repairs put a huge strain on the operating budget of the archdiocese. By 2000, church real estate was being sold to make up the annual operating deficit, and the toughest choices were left on the plate of O'Connor's successor.

St. Joseph's, Dunwoodie

Early in his tenure, O'Connor turned his attention to St. Joseph's Seminary in Dunwoodie. He soon discovered that there were serious deficiencies in the training that seminarians were receiving in philosophy and history. He did not believe it was possible for priests adequately to "impart the theological truths of our faith ... without a familiarity with the modern philosophies and their history as well with the history of our church".[171]

Monsignor Edwin O'Brien—a future cardinal—was appointed rector by O'Connor in 1985 and was given the tasks of expanding the faculty and various Dunwoodie programs, revitalizing the *Dunwoodie Review*, and bringing in visiting scholars every year.

The Catholic historian Monsignor Thomas J. Shelley related that O'Brien took his marching orders from O'Connor very seriously:

> During O'Brien's rectorship other academic changes also took place. A week of work-
> shops was introduced at the beginning of each semester; the curriculum was revised;
> the dormant M.A. program was revived; and an affiliation was established with the
> University of St. Thomas Aquinas in Rome enabling the students to obtain [an] S.T.B.
> [Bachelor of Sacred Theology] degree after three years of theological studies.[172]

O'Connor expanded the Archdiocesan Catechetical Institute at Dunwoodie, which granted graduate degrees in theology to parish catechists and schoolteachers. To make it more convenient for interested students, satellite programs were opened in Manhattan, Staten Island, and Orange County.

The cardinal also took an interest in the St. John Neumann Residence, which housed seminarians who were pursuing undergraduate studies. A new wing, which cost $3.9 million and doubled the size of the residence, was dedicated by him in 1990.

O'Connor at St. Patrick's

O'Connor started making changes at St. Patrick's Cathedral on the day he took possession of the archdiocese. He ordered that the altar be moved to just behind the steps of the sanctuary so that he could say Mass nearer to the congregation. He also announced that he intended to celebrate High Mass every Sunday and, whenever possible, to say a weekday morning Mass. And he would give the sermon on Christ's "Seven Last Words" every Good Friday.

Over the ensuing years, the cathedral underwent renovations, including the refurbishment of the hundred-year-old wooden doors of the transept entrances. A new bronze statue of St. Jude was put in place.

O'Connor promoted and expanded the cathedral volunteer program that Cardinal Cooke had initiated in 1975. "There were ten separate programs," as Thomas Young wrote, "in which volunteers contributed more than one thousand hours each week."[173] The volunteers served as tour guides, helped at special events, manned the cathedral's information desk, and worked with the elderly, poor children, and the homeless.

Security in the cathedral had to be seriously upgraded after a series of incidents. Before a concert in April 1985, a man announced he had a bomb in a bag he was holding. After two hours of negotiations with the police, the man surrendered and was sent to Bellevue Psychiatric Hospital. (The "bomb" turned out to be a clock.)

That November, gunmen stole $7,000 from the cathedral safe.

The worst incident was in September 1988, when a deranged man entered the cathedral, took off his clothes, grabbed a metal prayer plaque, and used it to strike and kill John Winters, an usher, who was trying to subdue him. A police officer who arrived at the scene was struck unconscious; another officer shot and killed the murderer.

On a much happier note, in May 1996, the cardinal had permitted the first Pontifical Tridentine Mass since November 1969 to be celebrated at St. Patrick's. The Mass was sung by Cardinal Alfons Maria Stickler of the Vatican. And in 1998 O'Connor instituted twenty-four-hour adoration of the Blessed Sacrament in the cathedral's Lady Chapel on the first Friday of each month. A side door of the cathedral remained open so the faithful could make visits throughout the night.

But Cardinal John O'Connor will be best remembered for using the cathedral's pulpit to defend and promote the teachings of the Church. For example, in 1995 and 1996, he delivered a number of sermons explaining the fundamentals of the new *Catechism*.

And, of course, as we have seen throughout this chapter, he fearlessly addressed issues of public policy on which it was his duty as archbishop to proclaim Church teaching—issues ranging from abortion and homosexuality to racial bias.

In September 1994, Cardinal O'Connor was gravely disappointed when he had to announce that a papal visit to New York that year had to be canceled. John Paul, who was in declining health, needed more time for a broken leg to heal.

Although the pope promised to make the trip the following year, neither he nor the cardinal could be certain that his health would permit the arduous journey or that the seventy-four-year-old O'Connor would still be archbishop of New York. O'Connor would turn seventy-five in January 1995 and, according to canon law, would have to send a letter of resignation to the Vatican.

As it turned out, the pope asked O'Connor to remain in his post "until other provisions were made" and announced that he would make his visit to New York in October.

On Wednesday, October 4, 1995, Pope John Paul arrived at Newark Airport for a four-day pilgrimage and was greeted by President Bill Clinton and senior U.S. prelates. An excited O'Connor told the media, "You have to understand, I'm a kid from an ordinary family in Philadelphia. Never in my wildest fancy did I dream that I would host a Pope. That is all kind of Alice in Wonderland stuff for me."[174]

From Newark, the pope took a helicopter to the Wall Street heliport, where he was greeted by Mayor Rudy Giuliani and other political heavyweights. From there he went up to the cathedral, where he was greeted by the faithful, chanting, "John Paul II, we love you!"

The pope spoke to the UN General Assembly and pleaded for a new global order where freedom, trust, and acceptance would prevail. He concelebrated Mass with O'Connor on the Great Lawn in Central Park, at Aqueduct Raceway, and at Giants Stadium. He also paid a visit to St. Joseph's Seminary.

On October 7, after he recited the Rosary at St. Patrick's, the pope shocked his security detail and delighted onlookers when he suddenly took a stroll around the block. "He's walking! He's walking!" one person shouted.[175] The six thousand people behind the barriers cheered. The pope worked the line until, as the

Times reported, "scrambling police officers and Secret Service agents caught up and formed a protective ring around him."[176]

As for the critics who wondered how much longer O'Connor would be permitted to remain archbishop, Pope John Paul disappointed them when he said during the Mass in Central Park, "Cardinal O'Connor will need all of you, and especially you young people, to help the Church enter the Third Millennium."[177]

A tragedy occurred when, on the night of July 17, 1996, TWA Flight 800 went down off the coast of eastern Long Island, killing all 230 passengers and crew. At the time, George Marlin was executive director of the Port Authority of New York and New Jersey, the agency that operates the metropolitan area's three major airports, as well as many of the bridges and tunnels that commuters use to reach them. He had the task over the next nine days of caring for the families of the flight victims at a hotel on the grounds of JFK Airport.

Information on the fate of victims was slow in coming from the federal authorities in charge of the investigation, and the hundreds of family members who congregated in the hotel's ballroom, particularly those who were related to a group of French Club students from Montoursville, Pennsylvania, were getting angrier by the moment.

While Marlin was trying to calm them, Cardinal O'Connor tracked him down on his cell phone and asked if there was anything he could do to help. "Eminence," Marlin said, "I have a potential riot on my hands. Get here as soon as you can." As it turned out, Montoursville High School was in the Diocese of Scranton. The spiritual connection the cardinal made with the parents and classmates of the victims was the most moving moment of this tragic period.

On Friday, July 19, after it was announced that a memorial service would be held at JFK's Hanger 12 on Sunday, Marlin asked Cardinal O'Connor to preach, and he agreed. When Secret Service agents showed up at JFK, and word spread that President Clinton, who was up for reelection that November, was going to attend the service, Marlin felt obligated to give O'Connor a heads-up. In no uncertain terms, the cardinal made it clear that he would not attend if Clinton was on the guest list. He said he was repulsed by Clinton's veto of the partial-birth-abortion ban and made it clear to Mr. Marlin that he would not appear with the president if Clinton came to the airport. Marlin made known the cardinal's position, and soon after learned that the Secret Service detail had disappeared.

In August 1996, Cardinal O'Connor celebrated at St. Patrick's a "Month's Mind" Mass (that is, a Requiem Mass about a month after the death or deaths) for those who died on Flight 800. On the day of the Mass, Clinton, who was coming to New York to celebrate his fiftieth birthday at a fund-raiser, asked to attend the Mass. The cardinal said no. Clinton did not manage to get into the cathedral until O'Connor was dead. The president attended the cardinal's funeral with his wife, senatorial candidate Hillary Clinton.

The Predator-Priest Crisis

Beginning in the 1980s and continuing into the the twenty-first century, the Catholic Church in America had to deal with the disaster of clergy sexual abuse. The predator-priest scandals have to date cost the Church billions of dollars and driven eleven dioceses into bankruptcy. In 2002 the American bishops felt compelled to impose a zero-tolerance policy.

The term "predator-priest crisis" has been chosen with care—in contrast to the label "pedophile priest" popularized by the *National Catholic Reporter* when the issue first surfaced. This term was not accurate and may have compounded the sexual-abuse problem.

To this day, most people believe that the priests who were charged with sexual abuse of minors committed acts of pedophilia, which means having sexual contact with children who have not reached puberty. However, the 2011 independent report by the John Jay College of Criminal Justice, *The Causes and Context of Sexual Abuse of Minors by Catholic Priests in the United States, 1950–2010*, commissioned by the USCCB's National Review Board and the Office of Child and Youth Protection, dismisses the pedophile assumption. After reviewing the case files, the report concluded that "it is inaccurate to refer to abusers as 'pedophile priests'" because fewer than 5 percent of predator-priests fit that diagnosis. The report also stated that "the majority of priests who were given residential treatment following an allegation of sexual abuse of a minor also reported sexual behavior with adult partners."

Taking that conclusion and relating it to a 2004 John Jay study, Dr. William A. Donohue, a noted sociologist and president of the Catholic League for Religious and Civil Rights, wrote a twenty-four-page analysis in which he said:

> Now we know from the first John Jay study ... that 81 percent of the victims were male, and that almost as many were postpubescent. If we can extrapolate from this, it suggests that acts of abuse were not only mostly of a homosexual nature (pedophilia being largely ruled out), but that the abusive priests also had sexual relations; the partners, as will become evident, were mostly of the same sex.[178]

Cardinal Timothy Dolan would come to a similar conclusion. In an interview with the authors in 2014, he said that although he found the "data of John Jay to be good", he added, "I'm afraid [the report] is politically correct as it is. It's very difficult to avoid the conclusion from the John Jay report that there is a connection between homosexual promiscuity and the abuse of minors. I'm quick to add that a homosexual does not have a propensity for the abuse of minors—no more than a heterosexual. So, [the report] seems to be reluctant."

The problem for the Church in dealing with predatory priests in the late twentieth century was the mistaken assumptions that most were pedophiles and that the sickness was treatable. Dr. Philip Jenkins, in his highly regarded work *Pedophiles and Priests*, published by Oxford University Press in 1996, pointed out that in the 1960s and 1970s therapists and America's so-called enlightened intellectual circles held that pedophilia was treatable. "Officials in the Catholic Church", Jenkins wrote, "embraced the reigning orthodoxy ... and ... when the tide turned in the 1980s—when a more litigious approach gained favor—those same officials were seen as culprits, men who had sought to treat a problem that demanded a more punitive approach."[179]

But even after that change began, bishops throughout the nation, including Cardinal O'Connor, signed on with the approved therapeutic procedures. They were assured that priests who committed predatory acts could be cured and returned to ministry.

For example, Dr. L. M. Lothstein of the Institute of Living in Hartford, Connecticut—a premier psychiatric hospital to which many problem priests were sent—in a paper delivered before the National Diocesan Attorneys' Association on April 30, 1990, said, "The fact is that many priests who are labeled as child molesters are treatable and can return to ministry."[180]

Lothstein, who boasted that the Institute of Living had "established a model program that addresses the psychological, theological, vocational, and legal issues surrounding return to ministry",[181] concluded that "to date, approximately 60% of priests treated at three treatment centers have been successfully returned to active ministry."[182] While conceding that "in a few cases the decisions were wrong,"[183] he reemphasized that "most sexually addicted priests can be returned to a successful active ministry after treatment."[184]

In "Ways Cited to Treat Priests Who Abuse" by James L. Franklin, the *Boston Globe* reported on July 19, 1992, that "officials of three of the four leading centers that treat priest sex offenders—Southdown near Toronto, St. Luke Institute in Maryland and the Institute of Living in Hartford—said in interviews last week that improved treatment yields great success with as little as a 10 percent recidivism rate. They and other specialists said many offenders can be returned to active ministry so long as the clergy and their supervisors accept lifelong restrictions and follow-care."

During the O'Connor administration, the archdiocese had to contend with its share of predator-priest cases. One of these hit the front page of the *New York Post* in December 1989; it concerned the founder of Covenant House, Father Bruce Ritter.

Father Ritter, a Franciscan priest, founded Covenant House in the Times Square area in 1972 as an institution to help teenage runaways. What started as a nickel-and-dime operation had grown by 1988 to an $87 million one funded mostly by private donations and managed by a board of directors made up of New York's captains of industry and finance. Its shelter sponsored highly praised programs that included helping youths infected with the AIDS virus and drug addicts and providing long-term housing and education for motivated teenagers. In his 1984 State of the Union Address, President Reagan hailed the efforts of Covenant House in aiding troubled youths.

In December 1989, Ritter was accused of giving gifts to a former male prostitute in return for sexual favors. Ritter denied the allegations, and Cardinal O'Connor, who had spoken with him, said he had complete confidence in the priest.

Shortly thereafter, other accusers surfaced. The Manhattan district attorney began an investigation, and Covenant House's board of directors ordered its own probe, which was led by former New York Police Commissioner Robert McGuire.

As more and more salacious details made front-page news, including stories in the *New York Times*, which had previously praised Ritter's work, the board turned to Cardinal O'Connor for help in March 1990. Calling the situation at Covenant House "a mess", O'Connor appointed two of his priests to serve as temporary administrators in place of Ritter, who had resigned in late February, and he agreed that the archdiocese would pay their salaries during this interim period. "It is no longer a question of guilt or innocence, but of public perception", he said.[185]

On August 3, 1990, the Covenant House board released its report, which gave detailed evidence "that Father Ritter used his position to facilitate sexual relationships between himself and young men who came under Covenant House's care".[186] The report substantiated the allegations of four young men who claimed Ritter had had sex with them, and it revealed other evidence "indicating a pattern of sexual misconduct on Ritter's part".[187]

Ritter resigned from the Franciscan Order and moved to India to work with the poor; he eventually returned to the States and lived quietly in Upstate New York until his death in 1999. Covenant House was restructured and continues successfully to aid troubled youth.

While Covenant House was an independent 501(c)(3) and not part of the archdiocese, Cardinal O'Connor did demonstrate leadership by pushing Ritter out and finding a successor who stopped the hemorrhaging. Nevertheless, the scandal gave a black eye to the Church in New York, which was about to face other revelations concerning the behavior of its priests.

In March 1992, thirty-one-year-old Father Daniel A. Calabrese, a priest of the archdiocese, was charged with sodomizing a sixteen-year-old boy in the rectory of St. Mary's Catholic Church in Poughkeepsie. Removed by O'Connor from his post, the priest pleaded guilty on July 22 and was sentenced to ninety days in jail and five years' probation, one year in a treatment center, and community service.

A year later, in April 1993, Father Edward Pipala was accused of sexually abusing teenage boys for years at parishes in Monroe and Goshen. In June, O'Connor personally installed the new pastor in St. John the Evangelist parish in Goshen as a show of support and concern in the wake of the abuse allegations. The next month Father Pipala pleaded guilty to federal and state charges. He was defrocked and served seven years in a federal prison. The archdiocese was sued for $900 million and settled for an undisclosed amount.

Other cases were to follow.

Responding to this crisis, O'Connor devoted a number of his columns in *Catholic New York* to "lamenting sexual misdeeds by priests and warning that more local cases might emerge".[188] He stated bluntly in his May 22, 1993, essay that "a grenade could explode at any time, and another and another."

O'Connor also made it clear in a column that he would provide victims and their families with "pastoral assistance, professional counseling, therapy or whatever other help is desired and possible." But he also stated that he was prepared "to defend the Archdiocese legally" against "excessively punitive measures or lawsuits [meant] to teach the Church a lesson".[189] "Lawsuits based on an assumption that the Church is a bottomless financial well are simply unjust", he wrote.[190]

Six weeks later, on July 1, O'Connor announced new investigatory and disciplinary procedures and policies. "The Church is one of the final bastions of trust and some [abuse cases] have put its credibility at risk", he declared in a preface to the procedures. "It is long since time to get down on our knees, to beat our breast, to ask God's mercy." The cardinal also stated emphatically: "I will not knowingly permit a single act of abuse to be covered up or excused, and I will involve myself in the process of healing any wounds that have been opened."[191]

The policy document itself stated that:

- All allegations would be channeled for investigation to the Office of Priest Personnel.
- The identity of accusers would be kept confidential "to the extent possible and desired".
- Accusers could talk directly to the director of Priest Personnel.
- Accusers would be advised that they could report the matter to civil authorities, and "Church officials who fall into the categories legally required to report allegations—like school principals or therapists—will be required to do so."[192]
- A priest who admits charges are true will immediately be removed from his ministry and referred for evaluation and treatment.

In the preface to the document, O'Connor warned that all bishops "must remain balanced [and] prudent" and not panic over newspaper headlines concerning unsubstantiated charges. He acknowledged that in earlier times "the Church had often treated sexual abuse as a moral failure rather than a deep disorder. It was assumed that the priest 'had learned his lesson' by being caught, reported and embarrassed", O'Connor wrote. "Many transfers were made in good faith, based on ignorance, and in an effort to do what was thought to be the right thing to do at the time for everyone involved. Was that really a cover-up? Some bishops today have inherited the result of actions that took place 15, 30, 40 years ago, when the whole world had different ideas. But now we have to live with those results and try to do our best by the victims."[193]

It is interesting to note that two days after the release of the document, on July 4, 1993, a *New York Times* editorial praised the cardinal, stating that "these welcome announcements suggest that the Church is beginning to climb to recovery from what has been a wrenching issue for Catholics everywhere." Highlighting that a "priest who admits allegations are true will be immediately removed from ministry, referred for evaluation and treatment", the *Times* concluded, "This comes as good news, not just for Catholics but for Americans of all faiths.... The actions of the Cardinal ... won't make the problem of sexual abuse disappear, but they are surely a comforting first step."[194]

In the 1980s O'Connor and many other prelates, like the *New York Times*, had bought into or, as Cardinal Edward Egan told the authors, were ordered by the Vatican to buy into the prevailing medical opinion that treatment was a viable prescription and would in most cases lead to rehabilitation.

O'Connor's Final Years

During the 1999 Lenten season, Cardinal O'Connor, in a letter to his priests, wrote, "I don't want to sentimentalize this, but it is obvious that this may well be my final Chrism Mass as Archbishop of New York. Your participation with as many of your parishioners as possible would, therefore, be especially welcomed."

O'Connor's prediction came to pass, not because Pope John Paul wanted to replace him, but because of an illness that would prove to be fatal.

In August 1999, feeling nauseated and weak, O'Connor checked himself into Memorial Sloan Kettering Hospital for tests. His director of communications, Joseph Zwilling, insisted that the cardinal was in "very good health" and asked that the media not read anything into his choice of hospital.[195] There was no reason, said Zwilling, to believe he had cancer or was being treated for it.[196]

Tests did reveal that there was a small tumor on O'Connor's brain, and it was removed the first week of September. Following the operation, he was to receive radiation therapy regularly for the remainder of the month. The archdiocese stated that the doctors had "determined that no other areas of the body were affected".[197] His stay in Sloan Kettering lasted ten days.

The cardinal made his first public appearance following the operation on September 12, when he celebrated a delayed Labor Day Mass. He told the twenty-five hundred people in the cathedral that "after days of examination ... [the doctors] said, 'We have good news for you.' What's that? 'Nothing's wrong with you but your head.' I said a lot of New Yorkers have known that for a long time."[198]

On October 18, suffering from fatigue due to the therapy, O'Connor readmitted himself to the hospital to check if he was on the road to recovery. The doctors found thrombosis in his left leg and installed a filter to prevent clotting. He returned to the residence two days later.

For the first time since becoming a bishop, the cardinal missed the mid-November annual conference of U.S. prelates in Washington. A letter from him that many viewed as a farewell was read to the attendees. "Although I have no word whatsoever from our Holy Father ... it would seem to me to be the height of presumptuousness, in view of my becoming an octogenarian on the forthcoming 15th of January, to anticipate continuing in office much longer." He went on to thank his fellow bishops for their friendship, and wrote, "I cannot recall a single difference or conflict that we have not worked our way through in the best interest of the Church universal and of the Church in the United States." While O'Connor did not refer to his health, many bishops assumed that his ailments were the catalyst for the letter.

The cardinal continued to say his Sunday Mass when he was up to it, although he stumbled on several occasions when leaving his chair or when walking up the altar steps.

At Christmas he gathered the energy to say Midnight Mass. While his legs were weak and his face was puffy from the radiation treatments, he got through the service. He did not attempt to climb the stairs to the pulpit but instead delivered his homily from his chair. In a low-key speaking style, the cardinal reminded his flock that Jesus "suffered to make it possible for each of us to love. Without that suffering, there would be no way of our truly understanding and loving one another.... But could anything, in the final analysis, really mean more than that we love one another with a gentleness, with a true profound love?"[199]

On January 15, 2000, over fifteen hundred people attended an eightieth-birthday bash for O'Connor at the Waldorf-Astoria. Five million dollars was raised for Catholic Charities and to endow a chair in Jewish studies at St. Joseph's Seminary. After a sustained standing ovation, the cardinal promised not "to fade into the woodwork", although he added, "I will go one day. Some wonder how soon."[200]

Even his old adversary Mario Cuomo paid tribute to him. In a January 17 *New York Times* op-ed piece, the former governor wrote:

> I have felt the force of the cardinal's strong advocacy on the subject of abortion, but I also know about his equally vigorous efforts on behalf of the rest of the Catholic agenda. Over the last decade and a half, his New York Archdiocese has educated, housed, cared for, comforted and counseled hundreds of thousands of Catholics and non-Catholics. None of the great American philanthropies have done more for the most vulnerable among us. And in some cases the archdiocese has led the way for the rest of the private charities....
>
> And, of course, there are personal deeds that tell us even more about the cardinal: unpublicized visits to AIDS patients to comfort them in their last hours; long, personal letters to Catholic leaders, filled with humble admissions of his own imperfection and gentle attempts to save them from committing what he thought were grave and dangerous errors of judgment; scores of homilies to small groups of communicants at daily Mass.
>
> All of these were private acts of conscience and compassion by an extraordinary prince of the Church who has always been a priest first.[201]

As the cardinal's health continued to decline, his two vicars-general, Auxiliary Bishops Robert Brucato and Patrick Sheridan, oversaw the operations of the archdiocese. From time to time O'Connor would attend a cabinet meeting, but he worked mostly from the residence. Because the vicars-general also resided at 452 Madison Avenue, they were able to keep O'Connor fully briefed and get his sense of things. "We know his policies", Sheridan said. "We know his mind. His authority is vested in us, to implement what he would want implemented."[202]

On February 9, O'Connor flew to Rome to have a farewell audience with Pope John Paul II. It was "a very personal trip, and he had a private and personal meeting with his Holy Father", said Communications Director Joseph Zwilling.[203]

Upon his return, O'Connor gave a sermon at St. Patrick's on the "power of suffering". As for his meeting with John Paul, he said, "It was amazing to watch the Holy Father, because there was so much love being radiated. One could not help but be deeply moved."[204] Journalists were disappointed when the cardinal remained mum on whether he had disclosed to John Paul a preferred candidate to succeed him.

Experiencing bouts of weakness, O'Connor did not celebrate Sunday Mass for the remainder of the month. On Sunday, March 5, he officiated but did not celebrate; instead, Auxiliary Bishop William McCormack said the Mass. The cardinal's only comment to the congregation was that he had "the great privilege of being here with [McCormack] and with you".

The next day, O'Connor received a proclamation from U.S. Senator Charles Schumer awarding him the Congressional Gold Medal, Congress' highest civilian honor. President Clinton, who signed the proclamation on Sunday, March 5, said, "For more than fifty years, Cardinal O'Connor has served the Catholic Church and our nation with constancy and commitment."[205]

On Friday, March 17, the cardinal did not celebrate the St. Patrick's Day Mass and did not view the parade from the front steps of the cathedral. Spokesman Joseph Zwilling told the public that O'Connor's "sense of humor is there as always, but he was very weak".[206] The cardinal's hearing and eyesight were rapidly declining.

One month later, it was announced that Cardinal O'Connor would be unable to celebrate Mass on Easter Sunday, April 23.

The cardinal's last foray into the public square concerned the presidential candidacy of Texas Governor George W. Bush. On February 2, 2000, Governor Bush addressed the student body at Bob Jones University in South Carolina, an institution known to promote anti-Catholic prejudice. The school's website contained rhetoric that disparaged the Catholic Church as the "mother of harlots" and as an "ecclesiastic tyranny". The pope was described as the "Archpriest of Satan".

At first the Bush campaign defended the appearance, despite receiving criticism from both Democrats and Republicans. The candidate's own silence on the subject annoyed a Roman Catholic congressman from Long Island, Peter King, who complained to the *New York Post* that "by going to [Bob Jones University] and being silent, [Bush] gives approval."[207]

Suddenly, Dan Rather, Tom Brokaw, Al Sharpton, Alan Dershowitz, and Maureen Dowd found, as the *Wall Street Journal* put it, "the ugly specter of anti-Catholicism lurking in Republican showdowns".[208] Democrats suddenly came to the defense of Catholics, despite the fact that over the years many of them had refused to criticize the desecration of the Communion Host by homosexuals in protests at St. Patrick's Cathedral or the anti-Catholic smears made by pro-abortion groups. Kate O'Beirne wrote in the *Wall Street Journal* that "Democrats have discovered anti-Catholicism. Seeing a chance to exploit tensions in the Republican base and to make a play for Catholic swing voters, they have been tarring Republicans as anti-Catholic bigots."[209]

Bush's opponent for the Republican presidential nomination, Arizona Senator John McCain, took advantage of this chaos and approved a Catholic Voter Alert phone campaign in the heavily Catholic state of Michigan. "The voice", according to columnist Robert Novak, "claimed Governor Bush sought support from anti-Catholic bigots in winning the South Carolina primary."[210] The Catholic Voter Alert probably accounted at least in part for the underdog McCain's unexpected eleven-point victory in the February 22 Michigan primary.

To avoid offending Evangelical Christian voters before the February 19 South Carolina primary, the Bush camp had remained silent on the Bob Jones flap. But after the Michigan primary defeat and the release of a *Wall Street Journal* poll that "showed the GOP trailing among Catholics in both the presidential and congressional votes", the Bush campaign went into damage-control mode.[211]

Turning to Mike Long, the Roman Catholic chairman of the New York Conservative Party, Bush operatives asked for help in getting a letter of apology to the ailing O'Connor. On February 27, one week before the critical New York primary, the letter was delivered to the cardinal:

Your Eminence:

A few weeks ago, I visited Bob Jones University in South Carolina to address its students and outline the reasons I'm seeking the presidency. Some have taken—and mistaken—this visit as sign that I approve of the anti-Catholic and racially divisive views associated with that school....

Criticism should be expected in any political campaign. What no American should expect—and what I will not tolerate—is guilt by association. I reject racial segregation—in our laws, in our hearts and in our lives. And I reject religious intolerance—because faith is defined by grace and hope, not fear and division. . . .

In my speech to the students, I emphasized that I am a uniter, not a divider, and that Americans can work together for the good of all. On reflection, I should have been more clear in disassociating myself from anti-Catholic sentiments and racial prejudice. It was a missed opportunity, causing needless offense, which I deeply regret.[212]

And at a press conference in Austin, Texas, that same day, Mr. Bush said:

I got back off the road. I thought long and hard about the speech I gave. . . . I started thinking about the impressions about me that just weren't true. I couldn't believe that anybody would think I'm an anti-Catholic bigot. I regret not having got up there and spoken from my heart.[213]

Although the cardinal did not publicly comment on the letter, New York Catholics were proud that, even in his final days, he was still recognized as America's top prelate by the national media and a leading candidate for president.

On Wednesday, May 3, 2000, Cardinal John O'Connor died at 8:05 P.M. of cardiopulmonary arrest. Making the public announcement, Joseph Zwilling said that the cardinal had "completed his earthly journey and gone home to God". Zwilling added that the cardinal's death was "the result of the tumor and the cancer that he was suffering from".[214]

The cardinal had lost consciousness that afternoon. At the time of his death, his sisters and other relatives and close friends, including Cardinal Bernard Law of Boston and the priests who lived in the residence, were at his side.

Upon hearing the news, former Mayor Ed Koch summed up the views of millions of New Yorkers when he said: "What was extraordinary about him was his willingness to say what had to be said insofar as Catholic teachings were concerned and at the same time demonstrate extraordinary compassion for the sinner. I'm not Catholic—everybody knows I'm Jewish and very proud of my faith—but I loved him as a brother and a mentor. I will miss him."[215]

Pall bearers carried the body of John O'Connor into the cathedral on the afternoon of Friday, May 5. He would lie in state until the Requiem Mass on Monday, May 8. Masses and prayer sessions were held on Saturday and Sunday for Catholic schoolchildren, the disabled, employees of the archdiocese, New York's religious brothers and sisters, and friends and former colleagues from the armed services, the Archdiocese of Philadelphia, and the Diocese of Scranton.

Those lined up to walk by the casket and pay last respects included people from across the nation. When the cathedral opened its doors on Saturday, May 6, the crowds, as the *Times* put it, "snaked around onto 50th Street, then back to Madison Avenue, where they doubled back again to Fifth Avenue and redoubled back toward Madison. And they kept getting larger."[216]

The procession at the beginning of the Mass of Christian Burial on Monday, May 8, was led by Pope John Paul's representative, Cardinal Angelo Sodano, who would be the main celebrant, and fourteen cardinals, more than three hundred bishops, and thirteen hundred priests and religious. The front pews to the left of the center aisle were packed with political dignitaries, including President and Mrs. Clinton (who was running for U.S. senator from New York), Vice President and

Mrs. Gore, former President George H. W. Bush, and Governor and Mrs. George W. Bush of Texas.

Members of the cardinal's staff described to George Marlin the difficult negotiations with the White House concerning the appearance of the nation's First Couple. The president's staff had hoped President Clinton could process into the cathedral with the clergy and religious. The chancery made it clear, however, that the president would have to be in the cathedral sitting with the other dignitaries before the ceremony commenced, and there would be no opportunity for greeting mourners.

In his homily, Cardinal Law beautifully described John O'Connor with these words:

> God gifted him with a keen and subtle intellect, an uncommon rhetorical skill, a knack for the dramatic gesture, a sharp wit and an outrageous sense of humor, all of which he used in the service of preaching. No one proclaimed what Pope John Paul II has called the gospel of life with greater effectiveness than Cardinal O'Connor. It was in proclaiming that gospel of life that he became a national and international public figure.
>
> Inevitably there is an effort to categorize public figures as conservative or liberal. Cardinal O'Connor, like the Church herself, defies this type of categorization. He was eloquent and unremitting in his defense of the life of the unborn as well as his support of the value of human life to the moment of natural death. Perhaps his most lasting testament in support of life will be the work of the Sisters of Life, a religious community he founded and loved so dearly.
>
> As he was dying last Wednesday as a result of a disease with terrible consequences, he bore witness one last time to the moral evil of euthanasia and physician-assisted suicide.
>
> He preached most powerfully, by his example, the necessity of seeing in every human being, from the first moment of conception to the last moment of natural death and every moment in between, particularly in the poor, in the sick, in the forgotten, the image of a God to be loved and to be served.[217]

Law's next line produced an extraordinary response.

> What a great legacy he has left us in his constant reminder that the Church must always be unambiguously pro-life.

Spontaneously almost every person in the cathedral jumped to his feet and began applauding wildly. After a two-minute ovation, Law, to more applause, said, "I see he hasn't left the pulpit."

The few who did not stand and applaud were in the political-dignitary pews. Two couples who remained seated were the Clintons and the Gores, who looked perplexed and nervous at the outpouring. New York's Governor George Pataki, a baptized Catholic who was pro-abortion and had signed the state's so-called gay-rights bill into law, tried to have it both ways. He remained seated but applauded lightly. (After the Mass, Pataki's communication director tried to explain away his applause by saying the governor clapped "out of respect for the Cardinal and the principles of the Catholic Church".[218])

At the end of the Mass, Cardinal Sodano sprinkled the casket with holy water and, as the *Times* reported, "led the coffin up the center aisle and down the side as the choir and the congregants sang, 'May the Angels Take You into Paradise.' Behind him walked other cardinals and a few members of Cardinal O'Connor's family, including his two sisters, Mary Ward and Dorothy Hamilton, and his brother, Thomas."[219] They then accompanied the casket down into the crypt under the main altar, where the cardinal was interred.

In one of his columns in *Catholic New York*, O'Connor wrote: "I regularly go down to the crypt under St. Patrick's Cathedral and look at the tombs of my predecessors.... Right in the center is the next marble block with no inscription. That's reserved for me. And all that's important when I move into that crypt is that I have served New York as a good priest."

No archbishop since Dagger John Hughes had been as steeped in controversy as was Cardinal John O'Connor, but one thing his critics and his admirers agreed on was that for sixteen years he had "served New York as a good priest".

PART IV

The Church in Crisis

10

The Realist

Edward Michael Egan
Ninth Archbishop of New York
(2000–2009)

Cardinal Egan with Pope Benedict XVI at Yankee Stadium

In August 1999, when it was announced that Cardinal O'Connor had entered Sloan Kettering, clerical, political, and media observers began speculating about whom Pope John Paul II would appoint to succeed him.

The names frequently mentioned included three priests who had started out in the Archdiocese of New York: Military Archbishop Edwin O'Brien; Theodore McCarrick, Archbishop of Newark; and Henry Mansell, Bishop of Buffalo. Others on the list were Archbishop Justin Rigali of St. Louis, Bishop Donald Wuerl of Pittsburgh, and Archbishop Charles Chaput of Denver.

It was well known that the sixty-nine-year-old McCarrick, a favorite of extreme-leftist churchmen, longed for the post. But the archbishop was not a favorite of O'Connor. Archbishop O'Brien, who had served as O'Connor's secretary, rector of Dunwoodie, and auxiliary bishop, and was a fellow veteran, dropped out of the running and went on to become archbishop of Baltimore in 2007. Most Church insiders believed O'Connor wanted Bishop Mansell to succeed him.

Prior to the cardinal's death, one name missing from the public discussion was that of the Chicago-born, Vatican-trained former New York auxiliary bishop who had been bishop of Bridgeport since 1988, Edward Michael Egan.

Egan's name did not surface in the media until the day after O'Connor's death. Here is how the *Times* described him in a May 5 article:

> In Bridgeport, Bishop Egan has gained attention for his ability to produce home-grown Catholic priests, with some 26 priests ordained in his diocese over the last five years, despite the absence of a major seminary to train them. His success in bringing young men into the priesthood, per capita, has ranked among the best in the northeast, outpacing both the New York and Boston archdioceses....
>
> In Bridgeport, he reorganized the school system, much as the cardinal did in New York, so that the financing of schools was shared in common by the entire diocese, and poorer parishes no longer had to carry the cost of their neighborhood schools alone. He also closed schools that were dilapidated or poorly attended, thereby strengthening the 38 that remained open, according to local Catholic leaders who observed the process.[1]

And then the *Times*, editorializing, added this comment: "Perhaps equally important, at 68, Bishop Egan would presumably have time to reorganize the church in New York, while the Vatican could simultaneously groom a Hispanic leader to succeed him."

On Sunday, May 7, it was reported that the focus continued to be on Egan. "Some Church officials", the *Times* wrote, "have virtually confirmed Bishop Egan's appointment, saying that an announcement as early as Tuesday or Wednesday is likely."[2] Also, word soon got around that Auxiliary Bishop Patrick Ahern told his parishioners during a Mass that it was to be Egan.

One could see priests and laymen pointing at Egan on Sunday, May 7, when he was at the memorial service attended by those who had worked with O'Connor and when he processed on Monday, May 8, with fellow bishops up the cathedral's center aisle at the Solemn Requiem Mass.

On Thursday, May 11, the Vatican made it official: Egan was the pope's choice to be the ninth archbishop of New York. It was New York's shortest interregnum in more than a hundred years.

The Early Years

Born on April 2, 1932, Edward Michael Egan was the third of four children born to Thomas and Genevieve Costello Egan. Thomas, whose parents were born in Ireland, was one of nine children; two of his brothers, Edward and William, would go on to earn degrees in medicine. Genevieve Costello was third-generation American, her grandparents having immigrated from Ireland. Thomas and Genevieve lived with their children, Marian, Thomas, Edward, and James, in a western suburb of Chicago called Oak Park.

The Egans were a solid Midwestern middle-class family. Thomas was a regional sales manager for Emerson Electric, a manufacturing company based in St. Louis, Missouri. Its products were distributed primarily by two Chicago-based companies, Sears Roebuck and W. W. Grainger.

Genevieve, a schoolteacher before she married, was a graduate of DePaul University. The Costello family had settled in Chicago after Genevieve's grandparents lost their Iowa-based business, a hat company, during the depression of the 1890s.

Edward and his three siblings attended St. Giles Parish Grammar School, which was managed by the Dominican Sisters of Sinsinawa, Wisconsin.

When Edward was in the third grade, he and his older brother, Thomas, contracted polio and were bedridden for close to two years. Mrs. Egan homeschooled them during this period, and they passed the official exams of the Chicago Archdiocesean school system.

Egan attributes his recovery to the "Sister Kenny Method", which was recommended to his parents by a March of Dimes physician. Despite protests from the boys' physician uncles, who were the family doctors, for eighteen months hot woolen blankets were wrapped around the patients' legs for twelve hours a day. This was to protect the affected muscles from tightening or withering away. (Sister Elizabeth Kenny [1880–1952], a lay Australian nurse, was lionized in a 1946 movie starring Rosalind Russell.) Sister Kenny's approach was ridiculed by the American medical profession until it was proved effective prior to the development of the Salk vaccine.

Having a vocation to the priesthood, Edward turned down a scholarship to Fenwick High School and entered Quigley Preparatory Seminary on the north side of Chicago. During his five years at Quigley, he served as editor of the school newspaper and the yearbook and was elected president of his senior class. Because of physical problems related to his bout with polio, Edward limited his participation in sports to swimming and tennis.

Summer jobs included clerking at a music store, delivering mail for the Oak Park post office, and counseling at the Stella Maris boys' camp in Oostburg, Wisconsin.

Edward also took up the piano. He received lessons at first from a neighborhood music teacher and later from a retired concert pianist. The archdiocese, believing he exhibited talent, paid for him to study music theory at a conservatory. Although considered by many to be a first-rate pianist, he has admitted in interviews that "thanks to wise counsel from my professor of harmony, I realized that the piano would never be anything more in my life than a much-loved avocation."[3]

Moving on to St. Mary of the Lake Seminary, Egan excelled academically, scoring a three-year report-card average of 98.6 percent—the top grade at the seminary. Recognizing his academic prowess, the archbishop of Chicago, Cardinal Samuel

Stritch, decided Egan should continue his studies at the Pontifical North American College in Rome after completing his bachelor's degree in philosophy at St. Mary of the Lake.

When Egan left for Italy on the S.S. *Constitution* in July 1954, he learned that the cardinal, who had also intended to travel to Rome, had canceled his plans and had given Egan his first-class ticket. A fellow seminarian on board from the Diocese of Rochester, James M. Moynihan—future bishop of Syracuse—convinced the bursar to permit him and four other men bound for the NAC to visit Egan's suite on the sundeck so they could all enjoy the first-class amenities.

When they reached Rome, Egan and his shipboard confreres reported to the NAC rector, Bishop Martin J. O'Connor, and took up residence in the new facility, which had just been completed in 1953. Although there were six professors at the NAC, most of Egan's course work was at the Pontifical Gregorian University, run by the Jesuits.

One task Bishop O'Connor assigned to Egan was to play piano for visitors. Impressed by Egan's skill, the rector informed him one evening that he was to attend Rome's Pontifical Institute for Sacred Music to study organ. When Egan made it clear that he was not all that interested in pursuing organ lessons, the rector firmly responded, "I have spoken with the Director of the Institute. You will start next Tuesday, Edward. Good evening."[4]

Edward M. Egan was ordained by Bishop O'Connor on December 15, 1957. His parents, who had come over on the S.S. *Independence*, were present for the event and attended his first Mass at Cardinal Stritch's titular church, the Basilica of St. Agnes Outside the Walls. Afterward Egan and his parents spent ten days together touring Switzerland and France.

In the subsequent six months, Egan studied intensely for his written and oral finals at the Gregorian. In July 1958 he was awarded a license in sacred theology, magna cum laude. Before returning to the United States, he and eight classmates spent three weeks touring Jordon, Syria, and the Holy Land.

When Father Egan arrived in Chicago in September, he was assigned as the ninth curate at Holy Name Cathedral and as a chaplain at Wesley Memorial Hospital.

A few months later, Chicago's new archbishop, Albert Meyer, informed Egan during lunch at the cathedral that he was to become his secretary and was to live in his residence. Egan attributed the appointment, after being back in his home diocese for such a short time, to pure luck. The archbishop wanted a priest working for him who could speak fluent Italian and knew the ins and outs of the Vatican—and young Father Egan was the only one who fit the bill.

Egan was to serve as secretary, master of ceremonies, and assistant chancellor. In that last job he learned the basics of finance, insurance, and administration from a lay finance officer, Joseph Klupar. Klupar taught Egan how to develop requests for proposals from private-sector vendors for construction projects, insurance coverage, and various other services.

As secretary to Archbishop Meyer, who was named a cardinal by Pope John XXIII in 1959, Egan had to eat dinner with him every evening. Egan told the authors that most evenings Meyer would not say one word during dinner, and he would occasionally read a book while eating. A big treat on Saturday evenings would be listening in silence to classical music on the radio. When Egan had his own priest-secretaries in later years, he gave them a pass from this duty and insisted they have a life outside the chancery.

One morning in August 1960, Cardinal Meyer walked into Egan's room in the residence and informed him that he was appointed to the faculty of the NAC. Meyer advised Egan to send a telegram "to your friend Archbishop O'Connor" to tell him that he was pleased to accept the job. While Egan was explaining that he was not a close pal of Martin O'Connor and that the only contact he had had with him since he left Rome was to congratulate him on his promotion to archbishop, Meyer brusquely turned away and stormed out of the room.[5]

During Egan's assignment at the NAC, it had a full house of seminarians, around three hundred. He was one of six faculty members and had the title of repetitor. In the evenings, he assisted seminarians taking courses at the Gregorian University in moral theology, canon law, and Latin. He also managed the music program and the infirmary. Working around this schedule, he also managed to earn a doctorate in canon law and completed doctoral course work in moral theology.

Egan's stint in Rome coincided with the Second Vatican Council, and like the young John Farley in the 1870s at Vatican I, he had a ringside seat. He had the opportunity to become acquainted with the apostolic delegate and the American cardinals, all of whom were staying at the NAC during the Council sessions. He also had the privilege of meeting Pope John XXIII on three occasions.

In June 1965, the new archbishop of Chicago, John P. Cody—the successor to Cardinal Meyer, who had died in April—called Egan back to Chicago to serve as his priest-secretary. The former Archbishop-Coadjutor of New Orleans had met Egan when serving as one of the Council Fathers during the Vatican II sessions.

In addition to the secretary job, Cody directed Egan to create two commissions, one for ecumenism and interfaith relations, and the other dedicated to social justice and racial equality in housing and employment.

It should be noted that Chicago was the home of the professional rabble-rouser Saul Alinsky (1909–1972). Rejecting American liberalism and the labor-union movement because they merely hoped to reform capitalism, Alinsky called for the training of professional revolutionaries to infiltrate cities and use "whatever works to get power to the people" in order "to advance from the jungle of laissez-faire capitalism ... [to a point] where the means of economic production will be owned by all of the people instead of just a comparative handful." His 1971 book *Rules for Radicals: A Pragmatic Primer for Realistic Radicals* shaped generations of leftists, many now running America's social programs.

When Alinsky began his career as an urban agitator near the Chicago stockyards, in the neighborhood known as Back of the Yards, he managed to form an alliance with the Archdiocese of Chicago, which helped him start his Industrial Areas Foundation. To this day IAF holds community-organizing workshops for aspiring radicals. (Barack Obama is an alumnus of IAF.)

Many influential Catholics embraced Alinksy's political vision. Bernard J. Sheil, then auxiliary bishop of Chicago, called Alinsky's first book, *Reveille for Radicals* (1946), "a life-saving handbook for the salvation of democracy", and the great French Catholic philosopher Jacques Maritain called it "epoch making" and convinced the archbishop of Milan, Cardinal Giovanni Montini—the future Pope Paul VI—to hire Alinsky organizers.[6]

In the 1950s, Father John Egan (no relation to Edward) of the Chicago Cana Conference met Alinsky through Maritain. Impressed with Alinsky's hands-on experience and confrontational style, he convinced Cardinal Stritch to hire IAF to advance various social projects. According to Church historian Steven Avella, Cardinal Stritch and his successor, Cardinal Meyer, funded Alinsky's community-organizing operations for years because Alinsky persuaded them that the "Church could be a very powerful social force in ... Chicago if it could only mobilize itself for action."[7]

Alinsky trained scores of young priests who later took on major responsibilities within the Church bureaucracy, including the U.S. Conference of Catholic Bishops. Thomas Pauken, President Reagan's director of the ACTION agency, which had been giving grants to many radical groups, holds that "the radicalization of elements of the Catholic clergy turned out to be one of Saul Alinsky's most significant accomplishments."[8]

Part of Father Edward Egan's job for Archbishop Cody was to wind down several of the fringe elements of the Church's Alinsky activities, such as the Organization for a Better Austin, "Austin" referring to a Chicago neighborhood. So Egan developed A Parish Program for Community Life, whose mission was "to educate the Catholic community in ecumenism, interfaith relations, social justice, and—above all—racial justice". Egan spent many evenings addressing the faithful in parish halls, urging them to participate in the program—and he did not always have friendly audiences.

One evening, Monsignor John Egan took Father Edward Egan to dinner to meet Alinsky. Finding Alinsky to be vulgar and intemperate—particularly in his views on the Church—Father Edward left the restaurant before dinner was served.[9]

As vice chairman of Chicago's Conference on Religion and Race, Egan worked with other religious leaders to promote racial harmony. When Dr. Martin Luther King arrived in Chicago in 1966 to lead marches demanding open housing projects, Cardinal Cody appointed Egan and Auxiliary Bishop Aloysius Wycislo to give welcoming remarks before a huge crowd at Soldier Field. Egan and his Protestant and Jewish counterparts worked with King and his lieutenant Andrew Young to coordinate the role of religious organizations in the King demonstrations. Egan appeared at twenty-two of the twenty-three protest marches, urging neighborhood residents to remain peaceful.

When a high fever forced Dr. King to bed, the more radical elements, led by a young Jesse Jackson, took over. At one point Jackson declared, "They can buy tanks and they can arm every child but we are going to Cicero"[10]—a primarily white suburban community on the border of Chicago that had experienced race riots in 1951.

Daily vigils in Cicero heightened racial tensions, and reports of violence caused Egan's boss, Cardinal Cody, "with a heavy heart", to call on August 10 "for a moratorium on demonstrations to prevent loss of life".[11] The cardinal went on to declare, however, "They [the marchers] have not been guilty of violence and lawlessness, others have. It is truly sad, indeed deplorable, that the citizens should ever have to be asked to suspend the exercise of their rights because of the evil doings of others. However, in my opinion and in the opinion of many men of goodwill, such is the situation in which we now find ourselves."[12] Historian Taylor Branch pointed out that "his [Cody's] edict exonerated the marchers."

Nonetheless, Mayor Richard Daley's Democratic machine, fearing a white backlash at the polls in November, welcomed the cardinal's comments and pressed to end the protests. Egan said the result was "the collapse of the open-housing campaign in Chicago".[13]

Two years later, immediately after it was reported that Dr. King had been assassinated in Memphis, Tennessee, Father Egan found himself in a car with Cardinal Cody and Mayor Daley driving toward the west side of Chicago, which was already beset by riots, violence, and arson.

Negotiations with leaders of the African-American neighborhoods led to an agreement that brought peace to the area and established the Leadership Council for Metropolitan Open Communities. Egan, who served as vice chairman of the council, stated that "the major commitment of the religious community was that all congregations would adopt a program similar to the archdiocese's A Parish Program for Community Life. Sadly, however, few followed through, as the assassination and the rioting lost their hold on the attention of the public."[14]

Egan was named co-chancellor of the archdiocese in 1969, and in 1971 he received the additional assignment to straighten out St. Leo's parish on the South Side of Chicago. The eleven months he spent as the administrator of this predominantly African-American parish, Egan later said, "were among the happiest of my life".[15] He fixed its problems, named a new principal to the school, caused an uproar in some bureaucratic circles when he refused to use the new religion textbooks, which he found to be problematic with regard to Catholic teaching, and turned over to a new pastor a revitalized and growing parish. (Forty years later, in 2013, Cardinal Francis George decided that St. Leo's parish was to be closed and invited Egan to return to Chicago to celebrate the final Mass in the church.)

In 1970, Cardinal Pericle Felici, prefect of the Supreme Tribunal of the Apostolic Signatura and former general secretary of the Second Vatican Council, paid a visit to Cardinal Cody in Chicago. Because Egan was fluent in Italian, he was assigned to serve as tour guide. Apparently, the cardinal was impressed, for one year later Egan received a call from the apostolic nuncio, Archbishop Luigi Raimondi, notifying him that he had been named a judge of the Tribunal of the Second Roman Rota, the highest appellate court in the Church. Pointing out that he had not worked on the Chicago tribunal, he asked the archbishop if he could visit him in Washington to discuss the appointment. The nuncio bluntly replied, "You can come to see me if you wish, but your assignment is to the Rota."[16]

Egan left for Rome in December 1971. Years later he learned that Cardinal Felici, on the plane back to Rome after his Chicago trip, asked an American priest companion for Egan's full name and announced that he would soon be back in Rome.[17]

In addition to his position as judge, Egan taught canon law at the Gregorian University and civil and criminal procedure at the Studium Rotale, the Rota's law school. And he served as a consultor to the Commission for the Clergy, as a commissioner of the Congregation for Divine Worship and the Discipline of the Sacraments, and as a weekend pastor at the mission church Sant'Angelina di San Francesco.

When he assumed the office of judge, Egan was automatically promoted to Right Reverend Monsignor, Protonotary Apostolic, the highest grade of monsignor, whereby one is an "actual" prelate though not a bishop. (In America, "Right Reverend Monsignor" is an honorary title.)

On the Rota, Monsignor Egan went against the prevailing practice of granting annulments for newly (and wrongly) devised reasons. In a paper he delivered before the Fellowship of Catholic Scholars in 1988, Egan said:

> I have personally seen any number of sentences, that is, judicial decisions, in which Church tribunals have declared marriages invalid because the man in question was found to be selfish or the woman in question was found to be grasping, and it was concluded that such persons had to be at the time of their marriage unable "to give themselves to one another," and "especially to do this totally." If you wish just one example, I might refer you to a decision given at the Roman Rota "coram Egan," as they say, on March 29, 1984, which reversed the judgment of a diocesan tribunal that had pursued this manner of argument.[18]

About his experiences as a judge in dealing with annulments, Egan said that a key issue was the psychological incapacity for marriage. He concluded that "the discussion had lost all balance well before my assignment to the Curia." He went on to say, "My reaction to all this was quite negative and even a bit angry. This of course [did not endear] me ... to many of the Rota lawyers and not a few of the judges who were striving at all cost to uncover new bases for freeing unhappy couples from the bond of matrimony."[19]

Egan's time at the Vatican also included a diplomatic sojourn. Shortly before the collapse of the Iron Curtain and at the direction of Cardinal Agostino Casaroli, the Vatican secretary of state, Egan traveled to Zagorsk, a district outside Moscow that is considered the Vatican of the Russian Orthodox Church. Accompanied by a Vatican-appointed interpreter, he visited Patriarch Pimen, who was the fourteenth patriarch of Moscow and head of the Russian Orthodox Church from 1970 to 1990 and a member of the Supreme Soviet.

After meetings with the patriarch and a dinner with the patriarch and a group of Orthodox hierarchs, Egan was given numerous gifts, including icons and Bibles with mother-of-pearl covers.

Upon his return to Rome, Egan gave Cardinal Casaroli and his staff a detailed report and passed along the gifts. The purpose of the visit had been to get a sense of Pimen's attitude toward the Roman Catholic Church and to weigh the reactions of the patriarch's clerical staff to the presence of a Roman prelate in the sanctum sanctorum of their church.

In 1981 Egan was fortunate enough to be appointed one of the five canonists chosen to work on the final draft of the new *Code of Canon Law*. This job gave him plenty of time alone with Pope John Paul II, who had a great interest in the project. Not only did Egan get to go over sections of the new *Code* line by line with the pope before it was released in 1983, but he also enjoyed many luncheons and dinners with the pontiff and got to know him on a personal level.

Bishop Egan

In April 1985, Cardinal Bernardin Gantin, the prefect of the Congregation of Bishops, summoned Egan to his office to tell him that he was to be named an auxiliary bishop of New York. Egan's initial reaction was that the cardinal had called in the wrong person—after all, a Chicago guy becoming a New York auxiliary did not make much sense. Shortly after this meeting, he bumped into the secretary of the Congregation of Bishops, Archbishop Lucas Moreira Neves, who told him, as Egan later recalled, that Gantin "was mystified by my reaction". Egan explained that his "comportment had been an effort to avoid embarrassing the cardinal, who had evidently called the wrong person to his office". The archbishop laughed and told Egan, "Go back and see His Eminence again. You're on your way to New York."[20]

Why did Egan wind up in New York? As he admitted, he had not endeared himself to confreres at the Rota because of his opposition to finding new grounds for declaring marriages invalid. Also, he may have annoyed some powerful churchmen by rightly opposing annulment requests that were considered "politically sensitive". A promotion to a post back in the United States may have been viewed as the best political solution.

There was, however, one problem with that plan: The very liberal archbishop of Chicago, Cardinal Joseph Bernardin, did not want the orthodox Egan back in his home diocese as an auxiliary. So with Plan A failing, Plan B was executed, and Cardinal O'Connor was informed that he had a new auxiliary.

O'Connor, who would have preferred to recommend one of his own priests for the post, was not thrilled. He made it clear that Egan, as the *New York Times* put it, "had been foisted on him by the Vatican".[21] In a letter he sent to his clergy, he explained that Egan "was not his choice and that any one of them would have been just as qualified".[22]

Edward Michael Egan was consecrated a bishop in Rome on May 15, 1985—ten days before the consistory that elevated Archbishop O'Connor to the College of Cardinals. Cardinal Gantin served as the principal consecrator with O'Connor and Egan's close friend Bishop John Keating of Arlington, Virginia, as co-consecrators.

Afterward, at a celebratory dinner at the Hotel Villa Pamphili in Rome, the new bishop found himself on the receiving end of O'Connor's cutting deadpan humor. After saying that Egan was "Chicago's revenge on New York", O'Connor pointed out that Egan played piano and said, "He has indicated that he'll be needing very large quarters [for his piano], and I have found them—across the river, in Newark."[23] Glancing around at the guests assembled in the ballroom, the archbishop took this shot: "It is clear that Bishop Egan has an enormous number of friends in the Vatican—who will go anywhere for a free meal."[24]

A week later, at a dinner at the Grand Hotel in Rome celebrating John O'Connor's elevation to the cardinalate, Egan was asked to give the invocation. Determined not to appear intimidated, Egan walked slowly to the podium and delivered the invocation slowly. As he left the podium, Mayor Ed Koch shouted, "If you're coming to New York, you better learn to walk faster and talk faster than that." Egan quickly replied, "Don't be concerned—I'm from Chicago, where we think faster."[25]

Act I in New York: 1985–1988

When Bishop Egan arrived in Manhattan, he took up residence in a facility on First Avenue and Thirty-Fourth Street that housed fourteen retired priests. O'Connor gave him the job of vicar for education, which included oversight of the archdiocese's elementary and high schools, the catechetical programs, campus ministry, vocations, and the pro-life and family-life departments. Although he was named to the board of the junior seminary in Douglaston, Queens, which served the archdiocese and the dioceses of Brooklyn and Rockville Centre (Long Island), he had no duties or authority at the major seminary in Dunwoodie.

During his tenure as vicar for education, Egan demonstrated his skills as a negotiator in dealing with the two unions that represented the teachers of the archdiocesan school system. He worked diligently with one of the unions to renew its expiring contract with an agreement that was fair to both sides. The other union, led by an activist who was more interested in making headlines than negotiating, eventually succumbed to the demands of rank-and-file membership and signed on to a similar deal. Egan's approach—"Keep calm, avoid grandstanding, and say only what needs to be said"—paid off.

The vicar for education also had to confront New York elites who were pressing a political and educational agenda that would eradicate the influence of Judeo-Christian principles on public policy. Behind the scenes, in meetings with members of the city's board of education, he successfully presented arguments for not imposing liberal sex-ed programs on public-school children.

It is fair to say that during Egan's three years as auxiliary bishop, he and O'Connor did not have a close relationship. Besides staff meetings, and one meeting in O'Connor's office about school contracts and another in the residence about the appointment of a chaplain, Egan spent very little time with his archbishop.

In October 1988, at an *ad limina* meeting of New York bishops led by Cardinal O'Connor, Pope John Paul was surprised to see his old friend Edward Egan in the delegation. The pope had thought Egan was the ordinary of a diocese.

One month later, the papal nuncio, Archbishop Pio Laghi, called Egan and told him that the Holy Father had appointed him bishop of the Diocese of Bridgeport in Connecticut. "The call", Egan said in an interview with the authors, "brought an end to a rather awkward situation."

On a snowy December 14, in a ceremony at St. Augustine Cathedral, Archbishop Laghi installed Edward Egan as the third bishop of Bridgeport.

The Bridgeport Years: 1988–2000

When Egan took the reins in Bridgeport, which had 99 parishes and 360,000 Catholics, he quickly learned that the diocese was in a state of fiscal distress. It was so bad that his predecessor, Bishop Walter W. Curtis (1961–1988), had sold the bishop's residence to meet operating expenses.

Egan borrowed $60,000 to pay current bills as a prelude to designing a financial-recovery plan. Next, he spent weeks on the road visiting parishes, schools, and charitable institutions throughout the diocese. During this period, he lived free of charge in a small hotel in Trumbull, Connecticut. He finally got a home when the Connecticut courts awarded the diocese a small two-bedroom ranch in Stratford. Egan later pointed out that this "humble abode afforded me privacy and a remarkably effective setting in which to beg visitors for financial support of the diocese, its schools, and its charities."[26]

In Bridgeport, Egan demonstrated his administrative skills in reorganizing the diocese and employed a management approach he would later apply in New York.

He believed the focus should be on pastors and that the parish should be the center of activities. "Bishops and their staffs", he said, should be "servants to the Community of Faithful."[27]

But Egan also believed that a bishop should not be the center of attention and should not seek press coverage. The chancery should be in the background, serving as a back office that provides support and services to help pastors carry out their duties. Egan had learned this approach when he served in the Chicago chancery of Cardinal Meyer. The cardinal spent his time visiting the parishes and encouraging pastors to make the parish the center of life for the faithful.

The model priest for Bishop Egan was Monsignor L. W. Frawley, pastor of his childhood parish, St. Giles. Frawley not only was a shrewd administrator who built a new church, rectory, convent, and three school buildings that are operating to this day but was also "a devoted shepherd of souls" who worked hard in his parish and among the people.

Frawley and his curates made yearly visits to every parishioner's home. He had a pulse of the parish. He shared the sorrows and joys of the faithful and would provide a helping hand for troubled souls. And, when necessary, he was not afraid to put the fear of God into his congregation.

Egan recalled how impressed he was when Frawley announced from the pulpit "that he was that very afternoon going to visit Dr. and Mrs. Percy Julian to welcome them to our community after someone had thrown a lighted can of gasoline through their living room window".[28] (Dr. Julian, an African-American who was a world-famous chemist, was allegedly denied a Nobel Prize because of his race.) Frawley's actions restored racial harmony in the neighborhood.

Egan made some tough decisions about the fiscal health of his diocese and devoted much time and energy to fund-raising. He reached out for help to captains of finance and industry, such as Jack Welch of General Electric, and his efforts paid off. He stopped the financial hemorrhaging, paid down the debt, and began funding new projects. During Egan's tenure in Bridgeport he:

- stabilized the education finances by regionalizing the school system so that all parishes now contribute to the funding of the school system
- started the Inner-City Foundation for Charity and Education
- built four new parishes, two assisted-living homes for the elderly, the first retirement home for priests, and new facilities for various charitable agencies

Egan also acquired properties, including one tract of 135 acres, for future diocesan expansions. Another purchase, an Episcopal cemetery next to Catholic St. Michael's Cemetery in Greenwich, caused an interesting incident. Bishop Egan received a phone call from President George H. W. Bush shortly after his mother, Dorothy Walker Bush, died. The president explained that his mother had hoped to be buried in the Greenwich Episcopal Cemetery, but he thought that that was no longer possible because it was now owned by the Catholic diocese. Egan quickly explained that the transfer of title did not change anything, and that the Bush family had nothing to worry about. Egan said he would personally make sure that Mrs. Bush's request was carried out. The grateful president and Egan became fast friends.[29]

Egan also instituted new programs for the expansion of priestly vocations, including the founding and construction of the St. John Fisher pre-seminary in Trumbull. As the numbers of men considering the priesthood grew, he constructed another, larger facility in Stamford. He created apostolates for the growing Hispanic, Haitian, and Asian communities, and he gave Mother Teresa's Missionaries of Charity a convent. He also helped the Sisters Minor of Mary Immaculate establish a retreat center.

The Priest-Predator Crisis—Bridgeport

Bishop Egan inherited nine sexual-abuse cases from the preceding administration. After consultations with lawyers, doctors, and clergy, he decided "to deal one by one with the cases in which there had been a confession or unassailable proof of guilt".[30]

Egan paid his own way to fly to the West Coast to see a priest who was accused of having committed abuse years earlier. The priest admitted his guilt and signed a prepared document requesting that he be defrocked by the Holy See. Once again on his own dime, Egan flew to Rome to have the request approved by the appropriate Vatican official.

Egan hoped to handle the other cases in a similar, successful fashion. However, the Holy See had ruled that ordinaries must embark on an approved "process" with accused priests. Like Cardinal O'Connor in New York, Egan had to send the accused for psychiatric evaluation and then abide by the directives of the psychiatrists.

Following the Vatican's directive, Egan established a policy that required any priest accused of sexual misconduct "to be sent immediately to one of the most prominent psychiatric institutions in the nation for evaluation".[31] And it was the institution, not the bishop or any other Church official, that certified whether individual clerics could return to active ministry.

In Egan's judgment, the treatments conducted by these institutions, which were praised by the *New York Times* and other leaders of public opinion, proved for the most part to be futile. He said later, "I lost all confidence in the analysis and forecasts of even the most highly esteemed exponents of the psychiatric community."[32] Egan would tell the *New York Times* in August 2002:

> If you take it out of the context of the times right now I have less and less confidence in depending upon the medical and the psychiatric community to tell me if the person can control this sort of thing or has controlled it. My experience is that sometimes they're right and sometimes they're wrong. They're probably right more than they're wrong, but it's too dangerous, it seems to me, to do anything now but to play always on the side of safety. My first consideration has to be protection to see there is no harm done. While I will be sending these people to institutions or whatever, maybe not the same ones, my trust in their ability to analyze and figure it out and forecast is significantly diminished.[33]

With lawyers suing for damages on behalf of alleged victims, Egan found himself spending many hours consulting lawyers himself. Despite the fact that the alleged abuses by the nine priests had all taken place well before Egan arrived in Bridgeport, he still had to sit through depositions answering questions about them. When those 1997 depositions were released in 2002, pundits, led by Father Andrew Greeley in his syndicated column, claimed that Egan had used a legal notion that priests in his diocese were "independent contractors". An examination of the transcript, however, reveals otherwise.

The plaintiff's lawyer deposing Egan strove to get the bishop to say that a curate in a parish works for and is employed by his bishop rather than his pastor. This line of inquiry led to questions about income taxes. Egan said that under the "federal law of the Internal Revenue Service, every priest, like every rabbi, like every minister, is self-employed; he pays his income tax four times a year."[34]

Later in the deposition, he added: "Yes, it's one of those things that our government gets into: By federal law, I am like any other professional, a priest is like any other professional, I am self-employed; four times a year I have to send into IRS one fourth of what it's anticipated I will owe the next year. This, if I wanted to pay once a year, I would not be allowed to by law because I am self-employed."[35]

As to a curate's status and duties, Egan stated:

He [the curate] remains self-employed even though he's working under the direction of the pastor, very much like a curate in the Episcopal Church, or I would imagine, like a lawyer in a firm. He is directed by the pastor to do this, and to do that, and to do the other, and examples would be, you are to say the nine o'clock Mass on Sunday, you are to hear confessions on Saturday at 3 o'clock, you are to be in charge of the women's society, you are to visit the hospital, everyone in our parish that's in St. Vincent's Hospital, every week, and so forth.[36]

This line of questioning continued for some time, and, in trying to sum up, the plaintiff's counsel asked:

Q. And I want to know this, if—in regard to this setup, which sounds a lot like franchising or independent contractors, where everybody is self-employed, okay—
A. I have to say right off I don't know about franchising, and I don't know about—the independent contractors....
Q. I am talking about priests now, okay?
A. Okay.
Q. I am talking about priests who are dealing with parishioners.
A. Well, there is no franchising.[37]

After a March 17, 2002, article in the *Hartford Courant* claimed that Egan had mishandled the priest-predator cases in Bridgeport, he released a letter that was distributed at the churches of the Archdiocese of New York, of which he was by then archbishop. Here are key excerpts:

First, in every case discussed in the article, the alleged abuse occurred prior to my appointment as Bishop of Bridgeport.
Second, the policy and practice that I established for the Diocese and followed in every instance required that any clergy accused of sexual misconduct with a minor was, after preliminary diocesan investigation, to be sent immediately to one of the

most prominent psychiatric institutions in the nation for evaluation. If the conclusions were favorable, he was returned to ministry, in some cases with restrictions, so as to be doubly careful. If they were not favorable, he was not allowed to function as a priest.

Third, in all of the cases, the plaintiffs were already adults represented by attorneys and seeking financial settlements from the Diocese. These cases were well publicized, and a matter of the public record at the time. At no time in these discussions did any representative of the Diocese discourage the plaintiffs or their attorneys from contacting civil authorities.

Fourth, inasmuch as they were represented by legal counsel, direct communications between myself and the plaintiffs were precluded.

In December 2009 the Supreme Court of Connecticut ordered the Diocese of Bridgeport to release files to the public related to allegations of sexual abuse of minors by five clergy during the tenure of Bishop Curtis. The Archdiocese of New York, on behalf of Egan, put out this statement, which reiterated his position expressed in 2002:

> Of the five priests, one died prior to Bishop Egan's appointment. The remaining four were all sent for expert evaluation and professional treatment to the most highly regarded psychiatric institution in the New England and Greater New York area, which had no affiliation with the Church. They were ultimately returned to ministry only upon the specific recommendation of the aforementioned institution, along with the advice of experienced clergy and laity. This was the recognized evaluation-and-treatment protocol for sexual misconduct cases at the time. It was widely embraced and implemented by the psychiatric community and commended in an editorial of the *New York Times*.
>
> After their return to ministry, new information was received about misconduct prior to Bishop Egan's appointment to the Diocese of Bridgeport on the part of the remaining four priests mentioned above. In response, two had their authority to exercise ministry removed indefinitely. The third, who had suffered a brain injury, was permanently retired from ministry. And the fourth, whose misconduct was never firmly established during Bishop Egan's years in Bridgeport, was permitted to continue in a restricted ministry as an assistant chaplain in a home for the aged, while residing in a convent of religious women.
>
> Three additional priests, who are not mentioned in the case before the Connecticut Supreme Court, were accused during Bishop Egan's tenure in Bridgeport of engaging in sexual misconduct with minors prior to Bishop Egan's assignment to the Diocese. In response, Bishop Egan secured a declaration from the Vatican removing one from the priesthood, while the cases of the remaining two were handled according to the evaluation-and-treatment protocol. One of the two was evaluated and treated in another highly regarded psychiatric institution located near where he was residing. It too had no affiliation with the Church.[38]

After Bishop Egan was named Archbishop of New York in May 2000, he met with the newly elected administrator who would manage the Bridgeport Diocese during the interregnum, Monsignor Laurence Bronkiewicz, and with the diocese's chief financial officer to discuss the civil claims concerning priests who were accused of sexual abuse during the Curtis years. Given the much improved financial condition of the diocese, Bronkiewicz was advised and agreed to settle all cases out of court for approximately $8 million in order to give Egan's successor an altogether clean slate when he took over as ordinary.

Archbishop Egan

Edward Egan knew weeks in advance of the May 11, 2000, Vatican announcement that he was to become the ninth archbishop of New York. "In fact," Egan said in an interview, "some weeks before the Cardinal's death, I had been told [by the Vatican] to go into New York on a Monday so as to have a press conference about the appointment on the following Tuesday, when the appointment was to be announced. As my priest-secretary and I were driving to New York from Connecticut, however, the cardinal–secretary of state telephoned us in our car and directed us to return home and await instructions."[39] It is the authors' understanding that O'Connor had requested that his successor's name not be released until after his death.

When the announcement did become official, the *New York Times*, in an article titled "Man in the News: Secure at the Helm", described Egan and contrasted him with O'Connor:

> Those who have tracked Bishop Egan's 43-year career in the church say that he is a man who likes to take charge.
>
> In Bridgeport, he had his hands in everything from the pension plan to celebrating the confirmation Masses for nearly every child confirmed in the diocese. His supporters praise him as a hands-on administrator, a successful fund-raiser, a lively intellectual and a talented homilist....
>
> People who have known both Bishop Egan and Cardinal O'Connor say that the two men are temperamental opposites, with very different styles and skills. Where Cardinal O'Connor was spontaneous and blunt, Bishop Egan is cautious and measured....
>
> Where the cardinal was more interested in ministering than in managing the business affairs of the enormous corporation that is the New York Archdiocese, Bishop Egan involved himself in everything from architectural plans for churches to building the endowment of the diocese.[40]

A *Times* editorial commenting on the appointment took a similar approach: That "given the financial and managerial challenges facing the archdiocese, Bishop Egan's demonstrated administrative skills may have appealed to the pope every bit as much as his doctrinal reliability."[41]

In this the *Times* was correct. Pope John Paul II was aware of New York's financial difficulties, and this explains, at least in part, why he rejected the list of recommendations and reached out for Egan. The apostolic nuncio, Archbishop Gabriel Montalvo, in his official Vatican statement confirming the Egan appointment, said that a part of his mission was to restore the financial condition of the archdiocese.

Egan's installation at St. Patrick's, on June 19, 2000, was attended by eight cardinals, eighteen archbishops, one hundred bishops, nine hundred priests, and three thousand of the faithful. But soon after the festivities, reality set in. In his first days in office, Egan learned that for several years the archdiocese had been running an annual operating deficit in excess of $20 million, and it was projected that the *deficit* for the fiscal year 2000 budget (of $500 million) might well top $23 million. In addition, the archdiocese's common fund, which held the deposits of parishes and religious communities, was $47 million short, and the archdiocese's hospital system owed creditors more than $300 million.

To get a better handle on the finances, Egan brought down from Bridgeport his numbers guy, Bernard Reidy, whom he named delegate for finance and administration, and he later hired, as chief financial officer, William Whiston, a senior vice president of Allied Irish Banks.

Egan, Reidy, and Monsignor Gregory Mustaciuolo, the archbishop's secretary, proceeded to review all the audits and financial documents related to the key offices and agencies of the archdiocese. Egan also ordered an independent audit of all the real estate.

Next, he established an archdiocesan finance council, for which he recruited top laypeople from the finance, insurance, and real-estate industries, to advise him on every important fiscal decision he had to make. The council, which grew to thirty-five members, was divided into three subcommittees: investment, audit, and real estate. The council members received every document available to make their assessments. Every month, each member received a booklet describing all the financial actions taken by the archdiocese.

Based on the council's recommendations, a new system of accounting was installed. Associate directors of finance were hired to work in twelve areas of the archdiocese in order to assist archdiocesan personnel in executing their financial duties. An internal-audit department was created to catch management mistakes. Finance officers held training courses for pastors and associate pastors. The insurance department was reorganized, and in 2001 the archdiocese hired the Catholic Mutual Group of Omaha, Nebraska, to handle all of its property and casualty insurance. Premiums declined by 35 percent.

When Governor George Pataki, a baptized Catholic, signed into law a 2001 bill that would force Catholic institutions to provide birth control in healthcare coverage for employees, Egan blasted it as "un-American". As a result, the archdiocese became self-insured.[42]

Departments at the 1011 First Avenue headquarters were ordered to cut their budgets, and the cathedraticum, the annual contribution by parishes to the archdiocese, as required by canon law—which had been suspended by Cardinal O'Connor—was restored. These revenues were used to fund general expenses of the archdiocese and to subsidize struggling parishes.

Egan took advantage of the city's bullish real-estate market and raised millions to support archdiocesan services by selling air rights and leasing properties that weren't currently being used for archdiocesan activities.

The reorganization, the cost-cutting measures, and Egan's fund-raising permitted the archdiocese to balance the operating budget by the third year of his administration. By his eighth year in office, Egan had paid off all the debt of the archdiocese.

To impatient journalists who were accustomed to O'Connor's constant availability to them, Communications Director Joseph Zwilling explained over and over that the new archbishop, "with little flash and fanfare ... had been acquainting himself with his new territory". He was involved with the big picture, "studying the nuts and bolts of his jurisdiction, through presentations by people who run the Archdiocese departments, schools and hospitals". The goal: to give Egan "a handle on where everything is, where everything stands".[43]

In addition to tending to financial matters, Egan met during his first year in office with groups of his priests and held a picnic for all of them on the grounds of St. Joseph's Seminary, Dunwoodie. He began visiting parishes. In some case he would dedicate new buildings, as he did at Our Lady of the Sacred Heart parish in Rockland County. By the end of his second year in office, Egan had visited 150 of his 413 parishes.[44]

On Labor Day, 2000, he spoke from the pulpit, emphasizing his support of labor's right to organize, and he met privately with various union leaders. On Respect Life Sunday (October 1), Egan condemned the FDA approval of the abortion pill, RU-486. And, like his predecessors, he stood outside the cathedral greeting participants in the St. Patrick's Day, Hispanic Day, Labor Day, and Columbus Day parades.

What quickly became obvious to all New Yorkers was that Egan was very different from Cardinal O'Connor. His model was not Dagger John Hughes, but Hughes' successor, Cardinal McCloskey. Egan did not strive to become a national spokesman for the Church. He ceded that role to others, because he preferred to confine himself almost exclusively to ecclesiastical affairs. He viewed his role as a behind-the-scenes facilitator who devoted all the resources at his disposal to the parishes and other archdiocesan institutions. For Egan, it was the parish that carried out the mission of the Church to serve the spiritual needs of New York's two million Catholics.

In January 2001, Pope John Paul II announced that Archbishop Egan would be one of forty-four priests elevated to the College of Cardinals in a consistory to be held on February 21. Two other Americans were named to receive red hats that day: former New Yorker Theodore McCarrick, by then Archbishop of Washington, D.C., and the renowned theologian Father Avery Dulles, S.J., who taught at Fordham University.

Because of the archdiocese's fiscal problems, Egan kept the celebratory events in Rome to a minimum. "If I seemed to not be overdoing it," he told the press in Rome, "it is because, as I see it, I am here as a servant to the 413 parishes of New York."[45] To keep down costs, Egan stayed free of charge at a hotel owned by an old friend. On the day of the public consistory, there were about eight hundred New Yorkers in attendance, including former Governor Hugh Carey. That evening, Cardinal Egan hosted a small dinner for about forty friends and relatives at his favorite restaurant, the family-owned Abruzzi. In the days following he presided over larger events for the other pilgrims and celebrated Mass at the church in Rome assigned to him, Santi Giovanni e Paolo.

It was a busy time, and Egan told the press, "I think the Archdiocese sees itself as honored by this event; that's exactly the proper way to see it." He said, "Cardinals choose the pope, the successor of Peter, and I think everybody likes the idea that their particular religious leader would be involved in the choice. It is an honor, and people treat you in a very loving way, but really, the honor is to the Archdiocese."[46]

Egan also learned during the consistory that the pope had appointed him to be the rapporteur—the person in charge of an upcoming synod of bishops concerning the office and duties of bishops. Egan tried to beg off, citing all the challenges he faced in New York—but his pleas were ignored. Much to his chagrin, this lofty position required him to fly to Rome several times during the fall of 2001.

September 11, 2001

On the morning of September 11, while having breakfast at 452 Madison Avenue with his priest-secretary and the archdiocesan chancellor, the cardinal received an urgent call from Mayor Rudy Giuliani. The mayor explained that "we have been attacked in Lower Manhattan" and that a police car would shortly arrive at the cardinal's residence to pick Egan up. Giuliani wanted the cardinal to go to Chelsea Piers on the West Side, where a temporary morgue had been established, to help receive the dead.

As the patrol car was nearing the piers, the mayor called again to say that it made more sense for Egan to go to St. Vincent's Hospital on West Fourteenth Street. "It's better that he is there for the injured", Giuliani said.

Before going back uptown, the driver dropped off one of the policemen riding in the car near the World Trade Center site. While waiting for another officer to join them, Egan, in the back seat with Monsignor Mustaciuolo, witnessed the second tower crash to the ground.

At St. Vincent's, Egan put on scrubs, was handed a gas mask, and began ministering to the injured and anointing the dying and dead. One of the early victims to arrive, whom Egan personally anointed and absolved, was a Catholic chaplain of the New York Fire Department, Monsignor Marc Filacchione, who was successfully resuscitated.

"What happened next", Egan said in an interview, "is a mass of confusion in my mind and memory, as is virtually all that happened over the next five days in Lower Manhattan."[47]

Egan spent the better part of that time near Ground Zero, at St. Vincent's Hospital, or at the morgue at Chelsea Piers. "Smoke and ash were coming from above and below", he recalled. "I opened black plastic body bags so as to absolve and anoint the persons inside. I knelt to absolve and anoint others, both conscious and unconscious, who had been struck by falling beams and debris or who were overcome by the thick, stifling air. The horror that engulfed us defied description."[48]

In addition to ministering to the needs of the 9/11 victims, Egan celebrated Masses for the city and the nation at St. Patrick's Cathedral. In one homily he referred to Ground Zero as "Ground Hero". At the request of the mayor, he also took on the job of chairman of a committee charged with organizing an interfaith service at Yankee Stadium, and on September 23, Egan delivered the opening prayer at that service.

When President George W. Bush came to Ground Zero, he stood on top of a crushed fire truck and shouted down to Egan, "Say the prayer, Cardinal." Fearful that he would not be heard over the surrounding noise, Egan, as he later put it, "just aimed my voice into the sky and shouted my prayer". When the prayer was completed, the president asked over a loudspeaker, "Why doesn't my Methodist minister pray that way?"[49]

For weeks thereafter, the cardinal celebrated two or three funeral Masses a day at St. Patrick's or in the outer boroughs. He also celebrated the Requiem Mass at St. Francis of Assisi on West Thirty-First Street for Father Mychal Judge, the sixty-eight-year-old Franciscan who was killed on the morning of 9/11 as he ministered to fallen firefighters at Ground Zero. During the Mass, which was attended by three thousand, including former President Bill Clinton and Senator Hillary Clinton, the Franciscan provincial, Father John Felice, said, "Mychal died doing what he loved among the people he loved, his firefighters. He would not want this any other way."[50]

In an interview, Egan described an experience that he believed "captured the spirit of the human side of the tragedy". In front of St. Vincent's on 9/11, he saw a young doctor in scrubs trembling, and Egan asked what was the matter. "He replied that his father was killed when the second tower was attacked. I invited him to come inside the hospital, where the sisters had left tea and coffee for me in a little room next to the main door. 'Thank you,' he said, 'but this is my place. I am a doctor, and more who have been injured will soon be here.'" Some months later when Egan was in Rome, in the course of a conversation during lunch with Pope John Paul II, he told him about the young doctor. The pope asked if he had completed his studies, and Egan replied that he still needed to do an internship and a residency. "Find out how much that will cost," the Holy Father said, "and I will send him a gift to assist him." A few months later, Archbishop Leonardo Sandri, the substitute (assistant) secretary of state, joined the doctor and Egan at Ground Zero to present the doctor a check from the Holy Father, as the three of them stood in front of the celebrated "9/11 Cross", which was formed by two pieces of steel rising above the rubble.[51]

One week after the attack, Lord Peter Levene, who would later become chairman of the British insurance market, Lloyd's of London, called on Egan at his residence. During the meeting, he told the cardinal that the London banking community wanted to perform some acts of charity to show their support and sympathy for the families that had lost loved ones. Egan suggested that they pay the tuition of all the children in Catholic schools who had lost parents in the 9/11 attack. Levene agreed, and all tuitions were paid for hundreds until they graduated.

On September 29, Cardinal Egan flew to Rome for the synod of bishops that the pope had appointed him to lead. Upon arriving, he went to see Cardinal Sodano, the Vatican secretary of state, and explained that he had to be excused because he "was needed and expected back with the people I had been appointed to serve". While Sodano agreed and said Egan could leave right after his opening address, the pope disagreed. Egan was told by John Paul's secretary, Monsignor Stanislaw Dziwisz, that he was to remain in Rome.[52]

The cardinal told the Associated Press that having to stay away from New York during that period was "one of the saddest things that ever happened to me in my life". He went on to say, "I feel that whatever grace I gained by going through that, I said to the Lord, use for anybody who was hurt in the tragedy."[53]

For years, Egan later admitted, he and Monsignor Mustaciuolo would not talk about those post-9/11 days. "It was too much of a horror", he said.[54] But at a September 6, 2011, interfaith service at the World Trade Center Plaza, he did speak, saying:

On September 11, 2001, I had been ordained for 45 years. I was a preacher, and I had preached in Illinois, Connecticut, New York and Rome. However, on 9/11 and the days that followed I became a member of the congregation. The preachers were many, but none preached more powerfully than "New York's Finest," the Police Department of the City of New York, from the chiefs down to the rank-and-file members.

Their sermon was about total sacrifice of self for others. With incredible courage they labored for hours on end in swirling soot and smoke, guiding, protecting, and saving their fellow human beings, while counting the cost to themselves not at all. "No greater love has anyone than to give his life for his friends," a Galilean Preacher proclaimed 2,000 years ago. On September 11th, 23 police officers preached that sermon with immense power by giving their lives for persons whom they had never even met; and 50 more died since that horrendous day. How could I not be inspired by their unspoken but magnificent homily? It was easily the most eloquent I have ever known.[55]

Later that week, at an assembly of New York City firefighters gathered at Avery Fisher Hall at Lincoln Center to commemorate the tenth anniversary, Egan, who was scheduled to speak, bumped into the new fire commissioner, Salvatore Cassano. "I have always been wanting to tell you this, Cardinal", he said. "On the day after 9/11, I was hit by a falling object and lying on the ground semi-conscious. You approached me, knelt down, and shouted into my ear that you were absolving me of my sins and anointing me, too. It was dark. So I couldn't see you but I knew it was you." "How did you know?" Egan asked. Laughing, the commissioner replied, "Everyone knows your voice."[56]

The Priest-Predator Crisis—New York

In the first quarter of 2002, there appeared in the press across the nation a slew of stories concerning sexually predatory priests. Many of the reports were vicious, and editorial writers, particularly at the *New York Times*, had forgotten how they had praised bishops in the past for utilizing the best psychiatric care available for troubled priests and how psychiatrists had pronounced many offenders "cured" and had urged their return to active ministry.

As soon as he arrived in New York, Egan had met with those assigned to handle sex-abuse cases. After seeking the advice of priests, psychologists, and lawyers, he decided to hire a law firm to examine the files of every priest of the archdiocese going back fifty years to identify any and all cases. The investigation took a year and a half, and the district attorneys in the eight affected counties served by the archdiocese were given the relevant files, all of which previously had been officially closed.

While the legal review was proceeding, Egan spoke out publicly on the crisis. In a statement released on March 19, 2002, he denounced "sexual abuse of children as an abomination". It "is not only immoral," he said, "it is also illegal." He went on to say, "Along with the District Attorneys, I believe that allegations of abuse should be reported to the proper civil authorities, and I urge anyone who has an allegation to bring it immediately and directly to the civil authorities. If such allegations are made first to the Archdiocese, we will encourage the person making the allegation to report that allegation to the proper civil authorities."[57]

Four days later, in a letter to the faithful, Egan reiterated his position that abuse is an abomination and that he "will not tolerate it". He told his flock that they could be "assured that I will continue to do everything in my power to ensure the safety and security of every child in this Archdiocese. Should any priest sexually abuse a child, he will be removed from pastoral ministry. My heart goes out to any and all victims and their families."

The cardinal added: "The explosive headlines of the last few weeks have focused everyone's attention on the issue of sexual abuse of minors by a small number of clergy. The overwhelming majority of our good and dedicated priests, who do splendid work day after day, have found their reputations unfairly tarnished by the terrible misdeeds of a few."[58]

In his March 24 Palm Sunday sermon, which the New York Times called an "extraordinary homily",[59] Egan told his flock: "Today we walk into Jerusalem with [Christ]. A time of great suffering for the Church: Acts have been committed against our children by those who have been called and ordained to care for all with total self-sacrifice and with the utmost respect.... The cry that comes from all hearts is to see to it that no such horror is ever visited upon our young people, their parents, their loved ones, and the Body of Jesus Christ, His Church. I join that cry."

"I have taken steps for this here in the Archdiocese", he added, promising: "This evil will be stamped out with all the fervor the Lord and the Lord's people expect and demand."[60]

Preaching two days later at the Holy Week Chrism Mass held at St. Patrick's, with over three hundred priests attending, Egan said that, like the Lord Jesus Christ, they are anointed for others. "For it is this 'for others' that most marks the priests of the Archdiocese. In all my years as a priest and bishop, I have seen no group so utterly and enthusiastically forgetful of self and committed to serving others.... And all facing a society that is no longer just uncomfortable with Church teachings, but openly, even bitterly opposed to them."

After listing the spiritual and social problems many of the faithful face in the archdiocese, the cardinal praised his priests for being there with them "at every step along the way—with wisdom, professional excellence, incredible self-sacrifice".

Then he added that he could not conclude without addressing a situation that was on the minds of all: "Once again, I join you in condemning any misconduct with minors by any persons whatever, and especially by clergy. Such misconduct is an abomination, a scandal, an outrage. We reject it with all the strength of our being. We will do everything in our power to see to it that it does not take place in our midst. This we proclaim to the faithful whom we serve and as well to the wider community in which we live and work."[61]

In April, Pope John Paul II summoned all the American cardinals to Rome to discuss the U.S. priest-predator crisis. When embarking on this trip, Egan stated in a letter addressed to the faithful of the archdiocese dated April 20:

The abuse of children and young people is a terrible crime. It must always be for us a top priority to care for them and to protect them. I will do everything in my power to ensure, as much as humanly possible, that such abuse by clergy will never happen again. You should expect nothing less of me, and the other leaders of our Church.

Over the past 15 years, in both Bridgeport and New York, I consistently sought and acted upon the best independent advice available to me from medical experts and behavior scientists. It is clear that today we have a much better understanding of this problem. If in hindsight we also discover that mistakes may have been made as regards the prompt removal of priests and assistance to victims, I am deeply sorry....

As we focus our efforts towards effectively addressing this problem, I also ask you to remember the goodness and dedication of the overwhelming majority of our priests. I am sure that you will agree that during these difficult times they have not faltered in their commitment to serve you. They need our prayers, support, and encouragement. May our Faith sustain all of us throughout this crisis.[62]

In Rome, Egan described to the press the grueling discussions with the pope. "What we're mainly interested in right now is how we're going to deal with these particular cases when they come forward", he said. "What I think has been most important here is that the Holy See, the pope and his top officials have had a chance to explain to us their reaction to all of this in great detail, and we've had a chance to explain our understanding to them."[63]

One month later, on May 15, Egan released a revised addendum to the archdiocese's Policy Relating to Sexual Misconduct: "Under the revised addendum, when the Archdiocese has reason to suspect that a priest abused a minor, it will report the complaint to the appropriate District Attorney's Office without review by any advisory committee."[64]

In June 2002, the American bishops met in Dallas to act on the priest-predator crisis. The result was the Dallas Charter, which called for "zero tolerance" and "for the suspension of any priest credibly accused of abusing a child under the age of eighteen".[65]

In his book *The Faithful Departed*, the Catholic journalist Philip F. Lawler explained the bishops' decision this way:

The logic of the "zero-tolerance" approach was based on the American bishops' new-found understanding that a priest who molested young people could not be trusted to amend his ways. In the past, bishops had been convinced that a priest could learn to master his sexual impulses through prayer, penance, and ascetical struggle. More recently therapists had persuaded the bishops that a regimen of counseling and treatment would make the offender safe for a new pastoral assignment. Now the American hierarchy had learned, in the most painful way possible, that any such assurances were mistaken. A priest who committed sexual abuse would always be a threat to commit sexual abuse again and his bishop would be liable for the consequences.[66]

In his August 2002 column in *Catholic New York*, Egan reported that the overall policy of the archdiocese reflected the recommendations approved by the U.S. bishops in Dallas. All priests "who are to be removed definitively from ministry [will be asked] to seek what is called 'laicization,' that is, a dispensation of the Holy See from the obligations of priestly celibacy and daily recitation of the Breviary, so as to begin new lives unencumbered by commitments made at ordination". He did, however, caution that laicization is granted only if the clergyman requests it of his own free will. "Some may, unfortunately, refuse to make the request."[67]

The independent John Jay Commission, empowered by the U.S. bishops, concluded that between 1950 and 2002 approximately 4 percent of priests in the nation were accused of sexual abuse. In the Archdiocese of New York, the number was less than 1 percent. In an interview with the authors, Cardinal Egan said, "Throughout my tenure as Archbishop of New York, there was no known case of the sexual abuse of a minor by a priest of the Archdiocese, though there was one accusation which was tried judicially at the direction of the Holy See and concluded with a verdict of innocent for the priest in question."[68]

Two incidents concerning priests of the archdiocese were revealed during Egan's tenure; both took place before his arrival in New York. The first concerned Bishop James McCarthy, who was an auxiliary bishop in Cardinal O'Connor's time. After a sexual scandal with a woman became public, McCarthy left the active priesthood. He is listed in *Annuario Pontificio 2013*, the official Vatican directory, as a retired auxiliary bishop.

The other incident involved Monsignor Charles Kavanagh, who was accused of having sexually abused a minor. At the direction of the Vatican, that case was heard and decided by a tribunal of the Archdiocese of New York. Kavanagh was convicted, and the decision was upheld in two subsequent ecclesiastical appeals, one in Erie, Pennsylvania, and another in Chicago, Illinois.

In his *Bicentennial History of the Archdiocese of New York*, Monsignor Thomas J. Shelley pointed out: "The Archdiocese spent $8.2 million for settlements and legal costs, and mostly for psychological counseling for victims of sexual abuse, all of which occurred before Cardinal Egan's tenure. More than half of the money came from the Archdiocesan Self-Insurance Fund and the rest from operating funds and investments. By contrast, when the Archdiocese of Los Angeles settled some 500 cases of clerical abuse in 2007, the total payments came to $660 million."[69]

Improving the Archdiocese's Infrastructure

In addition to having to deal with budget deficits, Egan had to make tough decisions concerning the future of many parochial schools and parishes: changing enrollment demographics, declining revenue streams and student populations, aging facilities; aging priests and declining vocations.

Having been vicar of education, the cardinal was ahead of the learning curve when it came to the Office of Education. His first important decision was to choose a new vicar. For this job he turned to the superintendent of archdiocesan schools, Dr. Catherine Hickey. A former public- and parochial-school teacher, she had also served as principal of a Catholic school.

Hickey and her staff were given the arduous task of determining "which schools needed to be expanded, which needed to be merged, and which needed to be discontinued, always with the stated goal of keeping the total enrollment in schools of the archdiocese growing".[70]

To this end, twenty-five elementary schools were closed or merged with nearby schools, and St. Helena's High School in the Bronx was closed. Eight schools were closed or merged in Manhattan, two in the Bronx, one in Staten Island, and fifteen north of the city's borders.

Additional elementary schools that were initially slated to be closed but were kept open were Guardian Angel, Holy Cross, St. James, St. Joseph, and Mount Carmel in Manhattan and Holy Rosary and St. Jerome in the Bronx. Owing to the efforts of Egan, the business community, and the students' parents, the necessary funds to keep the doors open were secured. Eleven other schools continued operating thanks to the creation of the Archdiocesan Elementary School Corporation, which placed them under a financial umbrella that treated them as one entity.

Two new schools were opened during Egan's administration: the Academy of St. Joseph, an elementary school in Manhattan, and the Montfort Academy, a high school in Katonah, Westchester County.

To help finance archdiocesan high schools, Egan mandated in 2008 that local boards, consisting of laymen and clergy, be established for each institution to help raise money. By 2012, the hard work of those boards had permitted the archdiocese to reduce its subsidies by 50 percent.

The cardinal also spent plenty of time with New York's business, financial, and labor leaders, begging on behalf of the schools and promoting various programs that would help finance the schools and award scholarships.

The Inner-City Scholarship Fund raised more than $140 million during the Egan years. The endowment for the Inner-City Education Fund topped $100 million in 2009. The Cardinal Egan Scholarships offered by the Tri-State Italian-American Congress since 2004 have been paying half the tuition of six hundred students of Italian descent. The Patrons Program covers the operating deficits of various schools every year. The Young Executives Serving Our Schools program provides $350,000 annually to repair the infrastructure of schools. The Student-Sponsor Partnership and the Student Friendship Program award several thousand scholarships every year.

The Catholic Alumni Program (CAP), which raises money from graduates, was developed in 2006 by hedge-fund titan Bob Wilson, who had become friendly with Egan through their mutual interest in music. Wilson, who died in December 2013 and professed to be an "ardent atheist", said he supported Catholic education because "the future of our nation and our world rests on whether or not we teach the generations to come the moral law—what is right and what is wrong—and Catholic schools in their religious lessons are proudly and professionally doing precisely that."[71] Wilson gave gifts to Catholic schools in excess of $45 million.

In November 2001, the teachers in ten archdiocesan high schools represented by the Lay Faculty Association went on strike, demanding large pay raises and a new pension system. Having negotiated new contracts during his time as vicar for education, Egan, as archbishop, was in a position to guide his negotiators.

The archdiocese's chief negotiator was Paul Ward, the deputy schools superintendent, who met regularly with the union leaders who represented the three hundred striking teachers and guidance counselors at nine high schools. When the Lay Faculty Association took to the streets and complained publicly about Egan's staying in the background, archdiocese spokesman Joseph Zwilling said, "Does the cardinal know what is going on? Yes. Does the cardinal approve of what Dr. Ward is doing? Yes."[72]

Tom Drohan, who had been Egan's spokesman in the Bridgeport Diocese, explained Egan's style to the *New York Times*: "He strongly believes it is not his place to get between the people negotiating the contract and the union. At the same time, he will not be intimidated by public expression of antipathy by the union."[73]

Meanwhile, the archdiocese was quietly negotiating with the other, much larger teachers' union that represented 3,200 teachers at 235 schools; a contract accord was announced on December 10. "Leaders of the Federation of Catholic Teachers", the *Times* reported, "appeared happy with the 11 percent salary increase, which is more than the 6 percent that the archdiocese initially offered but less than the 15 percent that some union officials said they were seeking."[74]

The settlement with the larger union weakened the position of the smaller one, and upon hearing of the deal, "Henry Kielkucki, a leader of the Lay Faculty Association, softened his stance on the pension accord. He said in an interview that the union would consider dropping the proposal if the archdiocese improved the existing pension plan."[75] The Lay Faculty Association soon settled, on terms similar to those agreed to by the larger union.

The cardinal's union-negotiation tactics worked this time, just as they had when he was an auxiliary bishop. In a 2010 lecture he gave at St. John's University School of Law, Egan explained his approach to dealing with labor-management issues:

> If both sides truly want a fair and acceptable resolution, the "locus" of their discussions is often key. Carry them out in the media, and the result may well be very much less than ideal. It is far better to get together, talk, and find a way forward, away from the glare of cameras. Reporters and television announcers may be upset and may even retaliate, but so be it. If the controversy is of real consequence, this is a small price to pay for a favorable outcome.[76]

When Cardinal Egan retired in 2009, total student enrollment in Catholic schools had risen by 15,400, and of those attending the 115 inner-city schools, 65 percent came from families living below the federal poverty line. The students were scoring higher on state-sponsored exams than public-school students in New York City and the surrounding suburbs.

In the archdiocese's high schools, 96 percent of students were graduating in four years, and 95 percent were going on to college. This dramatically bested New York City's public high schools, which spent significantly more per student, but from which only 50 percent graduated in four years and just 30 percent went on to college.

As early as 1992, Cardinal O'Connor had convened a planning committee to study the status of the archdiocese's parishes. The committee concluded that, to make the most effective use of limited financial resources, a number of parishes should be closed or merged. Because O'Connor could not bring himself to pull the trigger at any point in the final eight years of his administration, it was up to his successor to revisit the recommendations.

In early 2003, Egan appointed his vicar-general, Auxiliary Bishop Timothy McDonnell, to initiate a new realignment study. McDonnell analyzed sacramental, demographic, and financial data and gained additional information from questionnaires answered by thousands of parishioners.

Auxiliary Bishop Dennis Sullivan, who took over the project after McDonnell became Bishop of Springfield, Massachusetts, visited parishes to determine "which should be considered for expansion, merger, or closure and those properties of the archdiocese which would be suitable for new [buildings] and schools".[77]

Egan held weekly meetings to review the latest data, and when preliminary recommendations were available, he turned them over to the Realignment Advisory Panel—a diverse group of people recommended by area pastors and staff members—for further analysis.

After the panel's revised recommendations were received, Egan and his staff refined the proposals, which were then presented to the Archdiocesan Priests' Council for its review.

In announcing the results, Egan wrote an open letter to his flock dated January 20, 2007, in which he said:

> While some parishioners may be concerned or even upset by the realignment decisions, they have my assurance that all will be faithfully served in the parishes where they will be members, and warmly welcomed members at that. As a result of realignment, there will be closures, mergers, new parishes, and expanded facilities for established parishes; and all of this will be accomplished in such a way that all of the Lord's people will be cared for, both effectively and lovingly.[78]

During Egan's tenure he closed eight parishes—two in Manhattan, four in Westchester County, one in Dutchess County, and one in Staten Island. Two additional parishes were in the process of closing when he retired. Meanwhile, three parishes in Manhattan were merged: Our Lady of Guadalupe into St. Bernard; the Church of the Resurrection into St. Charles; and Sacred Heart of Jesus and Mary with St. Stephen/Our Lady of the Scapular.

Egan made it a policy when closings were required to make sure that "a nearby parish was easily available to the faithful who were displaced".[79] Nevertheless, he did catch flak from some parishioners in targeted churches and from the media. The *New York Times*, in particular, made its objections front-page news. One closing that received plenty of coverage was that of the Church of Our Lady of Vilnius, on Broome Street, near the entrance to the Holland Tunnel.

This parish was established in 1909 as a national church for the families of Lithuanian longshoreman who worked the piers on the Lower West Side. By the end of the twentieth century, the congregation had dwindled and the church was in serious disrepair. A damaged support beam in the roof forced the clergy to celebrate Mass in the basement. In addition, no services in the Lithuanian language had been celebrated since the 1970s.

These facts did not stop protests. First, the president of Lithuania, Valdas Adamkus, went on a mission to Rome in April 2007 to appeal personally to Pope Benedict to stop the closing. His mission failed. Next, parishioners went to the courts and received a restraining order to prevent the church's demolition. After a five-year court battle, the New York Court of Appeals ruled unanimously in December 2011 that the archdiocese possesses the authority to demolish the church and that the petitioners were not entitled to have any say in the fate of the structure.

Cardinal Egan also closed a number of mission chapels in rural parishes, some of which did not even have running water and had heat supplied only by pot-bellied stoves. "The pastors", Egan noted, "felt that in an era of the automobile the missions were no longer needed."[80]

Finally, three churches were assigned to serve mainly new ethnic congregations. In the Bronx, St. Mary's became a Korean parish, and St. Valentine's became Syro-Malabar. In the Blauvelt section of Rockland County, the Church of the Queen of Peace also became Syro-Malabar.

Proceeds from the leasing of church property and gifts from donors Egan had developed were used to renovate existing churches and to build new ones. During his tenure, thirteen churches were totally renovated, six churches were expanded, seven new churches were constructed or begun, and eight parishes expanded their facilities, including schools, parish centers, and rectories.

At St. Patrick's, the Lady Chapel was completely renovated at a cost of $5 million. The main altar and its baldachin (canopy) were restored, as was all the woodwork in the sanctuary.

Catholic Charities and Outreach Programs

Cardinal Egan also revamped Catholic Charities and expanded outreach programs. The long-time executive director of the agency, Monsignor James Murray, retired and was replaced by Monsignor Kevin Sullivan. The former chairman and CEO of the New York Stock Exchange, John J. Phelan, took over as chairman and revamped the board. Egan also created a Catholic Charities junior board, whose membership included up-and-coming professionals from various fields.

The name and focus of the cardinal's Committee of the Laity were changed. The newly named Cardinal's Committee for Charity, as Egan put it, "brought Catholic Charities into a new era of garnering support.... Various Catholic Charities initiatives [that] were organized, advertised and conducted improved beyond all expectations, and the result was a significant growth in revenues and a significant improvement in the morale of the staff and the board, too."[81]

The newly empowered board reviewed Catholic Charities' ninety-eight agencies and institutions, with the objective of making them more efficient and responsive. After much discussion and analysis, the board announced in 2005 that the various components under its oversight would be organized in five divisions, charged with:

- protecting mothers and children
- feeding the hungry and sheltering the homeless
- strengthening families and resolving their crises
- assisting the physically and emotionally challenged
- integrating immigrants into the life of their communities

This division of services permitted participants to be more focused and creative in pursuing their missions.

In 2007, at Egan's request, the board inaugurated an annual Catholic Charities dinner at the Waldorf-Astoria. The event, whose costs are underwritten by several donors, has been a successful fund-raiser every year since. Attendees have come from the financial, legal, insurance, business, and entertainment industries and have donated millions.

During the Egan administration, the annual budget of Catholic Charities had increased by 126 percent. It was serving over six million meals annually to the hungry. An immigration office was established with a staff that speaks ten foreign languages, and it took responsibility for managing the New York State Immigration Hotline, with a staff that speaks seventeen languages.

The cardinal himself, in addition to facilitating fund-raising, made visits every year to havens for mothers and children, prisons, homes for physically and emotionally challenged children, soup kitchens, halfway houses, homeless shelters, and residences for troubled teenagers. In an interview, Egan said the success of Catholic Charities was one of the greatest blessings of his tenure as archbishop.

ArchCare, instituted in 2007, was given the authority to oversee all of the archdiocese-controlled hospitals, nursing homes, and neighborhood clinics. It opened new clinics in the Bronx, Harlem, and Staten Island, and, as Egan reported, it "has succeeded in putting all of [the archdiocese's] traditionally struggling health-care institutions into the black."[82]

The mission of the Hispanic Apostolate, under the direction of the episcopal vicar for Hispanics, was expanded to give assistance to the Education Department and Catholic Charities. It has also guided the charismatic movement, which has grown to more than twenty-five thousand attending prayer services.

On the local scene, in December of 2001, Cardinal Egan joined Mayor Rudy Giuliani and Secretary Mel Martinez of the United States Department of Housing and Urban Development in a project to build two-family homes and senior housing in the troubled Highbridge area of the South Bronx. On that occasion, the cardinal said, "I stand behind this wonderful effort with delight. We are focused on strategies that improve the social and economic conditions of our people."[83] In October of 2003, he joined Mayor Michael R. Bloomberg in celebrating the completion of the project and announcing further developments of it.

In 2005, the cardinal demanded "a just and fair wage" for home-health aides in a rally sponsored by Catholic Charities and community groups in Harlem, and throughout his tenure he worked to advance safe and affordable housing for the needy of the city with a coalition of construction workers and construction companies, which annually presented him with a check of between $400,000 and $500,000 for the maintenance of two Catholic elementary schools for children with special needs.

Religious congregations that were received into the archdiocese by Egan to perform charitable and educational works included the Pax Christi Sisters, the Sisters Minor of Mary Immaculate, Le Suore Missionarie del Catechismo, Los Misionarios de Madrid, and the Oratory priests.

Egan and the Clergy

Like all his predecessors, Cardinal Egan had friends and foes among the clergy of the archdiocese. Some viewed him as a tough taskmaster, while others viewed him as a competent manager who strove to provide the clergy with the resources needed to carry out their priestly mission.

When it came to his relations with his priests, Egan adhered to advice he received from a Vatican cardinal shortly after he was named an auxiliary bishop. "If one day they make you the bishop of a diocese," the Italian cardinal told him, "love your priests with all your heart and soul. But do not forget that you are their 'father in the Lord' and will at times have to make demands of them and insist upon their fulfillment. This is all part of the episcopal office, and you have nothing to do but accede to it with total trust in Your Divine Savior. If you cannot do this, decline the appointment."

When he was named bishop of the Diocese of Bridgeport three years later, he received a letter from his cardinal friend. It read as follows: "Remember what I told you during our luncheon before you left Rome. Love your priests with all your might, but do not hesitate to guide them and to expect them to follow your guidance, which must always be the fruit of humble prayer. Be assured that I will be remembering you and your priests at the altar as long as the Lord gives me breath."[84]

This meant that Cardinal Egan, unlike Cardinal O'Connor, did not spend every Sunday morning preaching at St. Patrick's High Mass. Instead, he preferred to take the pulse of the archdiocese by visiting parishes. "I made it my business", Egan has written, "to be in a parish, preaching, celebrating Mass, meeting with the parishioners at a reception or dinner, and chatting with the pastor and his collaborators. I wanted to be informed about the parish. I wanted to know what it needed. And I wanted to be regularly on the scene to encourage, to rejoice in success, and to express my admiration and gratitude for what was being achieved."[85]

As for priestly formation, he provided a new facility for the St. John Neuman pre-seminary. The facility, originally constructed by Cardinal O'Connor for $11 million to be an archive for the archdiocese, had never been opened, and Egan had it retrofitted to be a pre-seminary residence with funds donated by one benefactor.

Cardinal Egan later admitted that his greatest disappointment was his failure to increase the number of young men seeking ordination to the priesthood. That he had considerable success at this during his tenure as bishop of Bridgeport made the New York situation doubly painful. Still, during his years in New York the ordination numbers did not decline from what they had been in the decade before his appointment.[86]

With a donation from one family, Egan built the John Cardinal O'Connor Residence in Riverdale for retired priests. A similar but older facility also in Riverdale, Our Lady of Consolation Residence, for elderly priests in need of nursing care, was restored and updated.

As in the Cardinal Cooke years, there were unhappy priests who whispered to the media their complaints about Egan, often to the *New York Times*, which was ever eager to listen. In October of 2006, a Philadelphia blog, *Whispers in the Loggia*, posted an anonymous letter critical of Egan. The letter called for a clerical vote of no confidence in the archbishop. Although no priest took credit for the letter, the *New York Times* turned it into a major news story.

Archdiocesan Communications Director Joseph Zwilling said the cardinal took the letter seriously. "An anonymous letter of this kind can potentially do great damage to the church."[87]

While the *Times* kept the story of the unsigned letter alive for weeks, most priests dismissed it. In a letter to the *New York Times* published on October 21, a leading liberal priest, Monsignor Harry Byrne, wrote:

To the Editor:
    Most of us priests of the New York Archdiocese are appalled at the letter critical of Cardinal Edward M. Egan from "A Committee of Concerned Clergy for the Archdiocese of New York" because of its anonymity (who constitutes it, and how many?) and its overblown rhetoric, written in anger and articulating emotional judgments, generalized and uncharitable. (News article, October 15.)
    Many of us priests would welcome more open communication and participation in ecclesiastical policy formation, local and Vatican-initiated. But this letter does not advance the reform that would benefit all concerned.[88]

New York's Priests' Council, a clerical advisory board, issued a statement on October 16 saying, "We are also upset and dismayed that our archbishop has been personally vilified in this manner. At today's meeting, the members of the Priests' Council reiterated their support for His Eminence. We stand with him in confidence, and look forward to his continued ministry to the clergy, religious and laity of the Archdiocese of New York."[89]

In a letter to the priests of the archdiocese dated October 20, 2006, Cardinal Egan wrote:

> The recent anonymous letter criticizing my pastoral service to the Archdiocese has done immense harm largely because it has been so shamelessly exploited by the media. At the core of the letter ... are stories that are being told by priests who have been found guilty of sexually abusing minors after thorough treatment of their cases according to well-established Archdiocesan procedures.
>
> Many claim that they have been the victim of unjust treatment, deception and lack of understanding. Unfortunately, no one challenges what they have to say. And the reason is clear: the Archdiocese has always been careful to respect their privacy.
>
> This situation cannot be allowed to continue, as the recent episode of the anonymous letter ... and other negative statements to the media have amply proved. Thus it is that I believe we need to address this matter head on....
>
> When a priest has been found guilty of sexually abusing a minor and appropriate action has been taken in his regard, if he is reported to be speaking untruthfully about the matter, he will be called in to see me and invited to write a letter correcting his statements and offering his apology. His letter will then be made public.
>
> If he refuses to write the letter, he will be asked to appear before a panel of six priests—three members of the Presbyteral Council and three Vicars—to make his case. Thereafter, officials of the Archdiocese will make our case. The panel will study the matter and issue a report of the Presbyteral Council....
>
> Confident that all cases of the sexual abuse of minors by priests that have been treated during my tenure have been handled properly, I have no doubt what the conclusion of the panel will be. The conclusion, however, will be theirs.
>
> The faithful will then be informed of what has happened and the road to savaging the Archdiocese and its Archbishop with falsehoods about cases regarding the sexual abuse of minors will be definitely closed.

Some thought the cardinal's letter was a mistake because it kept the story alive, while others, as a *Times* article reported, "praised him both for calling out his detractors as abusive priests and for taking action against them". Monsignor Joseph Servodidio, a Staten Island priest, put it this way: "He just wants to get the record clear from the way he sees it and I think a number of us see it in the same way."[90]

Subsequent to the controversy, there was never an allegation by any priest of the archdiocese that he was treated unjustly by Cardinal Egan, and, as he explained to the authors of this book:

> There were a number of serious situations to be addressed when I came to the archdiocese as archbishop, and dealing with them inevitably entailed decisions that were not welcome by all. Any bishop has to expect something of this sort and decide, hopefully in prayer, how he should proceed. It was always my intention to act in justice, fairness, and compassion, as the shepherd of a community of faith must do

before his God. Some found my approach too formal and demanding, and they may well have been right. Others told me that they felt that I was usually on target in my dealing with the faithful and especially with the clergy. It is my hope and prayer that the success or failure of my approach will be judged on the basis of results: "Did he leave things better than he found them?" That, of course, will be decided by others over the years that lie ahead.[91]

Egan in the Public Square

Egan did not seek to be a national spokesman for the Church, nor did he speak publicly on every issue in the news. He did not let self-promotion get in the way of fulfilling the essential duties of his office. "A wise and conscientious bishop", he wrote, "must regularly ask himself whether what he is doing is being done to gather applause or attention to himself. If it is, adjustments need to be made and made immediately."[92]

While the cardinal stated, "I don't believe in getting into politics. I don't believe in getting into political conflict", he also said, "I do believe in getting into matters of morality and ethics"[93]—and he did speak publicly on such matters when he determined it was necessary.

In March 2001, Egan led a group of pro-life advocates to Albany to protest the bill, mentioned earlier in this chapter, "that would force religious medical in-stitutions to include birth control in health-care coverage for their employees".[94] For the next year, he fought for "conscience clause" exemptions for religious insti-tutions. But in February 2002, Republicans in the state senate surrendered. They approved an assembly bill that prohibited a "refusal clause" (the Left's latest phrase to make the Right appear unreasonable) at any health center.

Reacting to what they labeled "health care totalitarianism", New York State's Catholic bishops issued this protest:

> We, the Catholic Bishops of New York State, are united in the view that legislation passed today in the state Senate that would force Catholic employers to provide cov-erage for contraception in employee health insurance plans is a clear and unprece-dented violation of religious liberty. By providing a religious exemption for parishes while forcing Catholic education, health, and human-service ministries to violate the teaching of our faith, the Senate is legislating what is and is not Catholic. This is a grave and unconstitutional encroachment by government into the realm of religion.

On March 12, 2002, when Cardinal Egan made another journey to Albany to urge a gubernatorial veto, Governor Pataki excelled at doubletalk. *New York Times* reporter Shaila Dewan described his posturing this way:

> Earlier in the day, at his own news conference, Governor Pataki, who is a Roman Catholic, would not take a stand on the conscience clause, saying that if the Senate and the Assembly agreed on a bill, he would sign it. But later, standing next to Cardinal Egan, he said he would sign the bill if it included a conscience clause, but he declined to say whether that meant he would veto a bill that did not include the clause.[95]

On September 17, 2002, Governor Pataki stuck it to his own Church and signed the bill forcing religious employers to pay for contraceptive prescriptions. (As we saw earlier, to circumvent what the Brooklyn *Tablet* called "the most anti-Catholic piece of legislation ever passed in the state", Egan had the archdiocese become self-insured, and at least for the archdiocese, the problem was solved.)

Cardinal Egan also traveled to Albany with students lobbying for tax credits to pay for private or parochial schools. The proposal, if approved, would have given "parents who live in failing school districts ... up to $500 per child to use for any educational purpose".[96] Promoting the legislation, Egan said, "We're talking about giving the middle class the opportunities that the wealthy have." The bill, he added, would permit parents to send their children to "schools of their choice and to find the very best of education that is available—academically, spiritually, morally".[97] Unfortunately, the powerful public-school teachers' unions have kept this legislation bottled up for over a decade.

Time and again, from his pulpit and at the annual March for Life in Washington, D.C., Egan spoke out forcefully against abortion, which he said "continues to erode the honor of our country".[98]

On March 24, 2008, the Speaker of the House, Nancy Pelosi, made this remark to Tom Brokaw on NBC's *Meet the Press*: "As an ardent practicing Catholic, [abortion] is an issue that I have studied for a long time. And what I know is, over the centuries, the doctors of the church have not been able to make the definition.... St. Augustine said at three months. We don't know. The point is, is that it shouldn't have an impact on the woman's right to choose."

Egan, after hearing her comment, was quick to respond. "What the Speaker had to say about theologians and their positions regarding abortion was not only misinformed; it was also, and especially, utterly incredible in this day and age", he said.

"Crystal clear photographs and films of babies in their mothers' wombs make it impossible", he explained, that any person with "the slightest measure of integrity or honor" could fail to concede what these "marvelous beings manifestly, clearly and obviously are, as they smile and wave into the world outside the womb. In simplest terms, they are human beings with an inalienable right to live, a right the Speaker is bound to defend at all costs for the most basic of ethical reasons. They are not parts of their mothers, and what they are depends not at all upon the opinions of theologians of any faith."[99]

Egan also worked successfully with the New York Catholic Conference and other Church allies to keep "no-fault divorce" and "same-sex marriage" bottled up in the state legislature throughout his tenure.

One public stand Egan took that upset New York's neoconservatives was his opposition to the 2003 war in Iraq. On January 26, 2003, in a World Peace Day homily at the cathedral, Egan made his opposition to the preemptive invasion of Iraq clear in the presence of the U.S. ambassador to the United Nations and over eighty other ambassadors and staffers. "We must not jump to conclusions", he said. We must "carefully study the issue. And we may not attack unless we are sure that those whom we are attacking have ceded rights by their behavior."[100]

Three days later, the cardinal, in a live intercontinental webcast organized by the Vatican, said that "U.N. weapons inspectors must determine that Iraq poses a clear and present danger before military action can be justified against the country." Egan admitted that the UN's task was difficult, but insisted that "the truth of the danger must be established beyond any doubt."[101] And he reminded the audience of Pope

John XXIII's warning, "If clear and present danger cannot be demonstrated, justice requires that no conflict be engaged."[102]

Mostly, Egan forged relationships with New York's political class quietly, behind closed doors. He had understandings with most major pro-abortion Catholic politicians that they would not embarrass the archdiocese, particularly at St. Patrick's Cathedral, by marching up to the altar rail. The only pol to violate the agreement was the thrice-married Rudy Giuliani, who received Communion during Pope Benedict's papal Mass at the cathedral in April 2008.

After learning about the incident, the cardinal released a statement saying, "I deeply regret that Mr. Giuliani received the Eucharist during the papal visit here in New York." Egan made it clear that he had reached an understanding with Giuliani in 2000 that he "was not to receive the Eucharist because of his well-known support of abortion".[103] Giuliani put out a contrite statement, saying he agreed with the cardinal and that he was misguided by a layman at the cathedral.

As for the most renowned Catholic event held annually in New York, the Alfred E. Smith Memorial Foundation Dinner, Egan was cautious. While presidents and major-party presidential nominees have attended and spoken at the dinners since its inception in 1945, nevertheless, Egan made sure that no Catholic pro-abortion politician would address the gathering.

In 2004, Egan did not invite the presidential contenders to sit on the dais because Democrat John Kerry, a baptized Catholic, was pro-abortion. Instead he had former President George H. W. Bush represent the Republicans and former New York Governor Hugh Carey represent the Democrats.

When some criticized Egan for inviting Al Gore and Barack Obama as speakers, he pointed out that because they were not Catholics, their views on abortion were not the Church's responsibility.

Death Comes for the Pope

On April 2, 2005, Pope John Paul II died, having served as the Supreme Pastor of the Church for twenty-six years, five months, two weeks, and three days. Flags were lowered at St. Patrick's Cathedral, and at the 5:30 P.M. Mass, Egan reminded the faithful about the pope's visit to an Italian prison in 1983 to forgive the man who had attempted to assassinate him in 1981. "The scene", the cardinal said, "is dramatic but it is more than dramatic; it is supremely holy."[104]

At a Memorial Mass celebrated at St. Patrick's on April 3, which the UN secretary general and many of New York's elected officials attended, Egan, reflecting on John Paul's final days, said, "He was a humble giant who grew to his loftiest stature when he couldn't raise his head, lift his eyes or whisper a prayer."[105]

As Egan prepared to go to Rome to attend John Paul's Requiem Mass and the conclave to elect a new pope, New York's pundits reported that the cardinal would "wield considerable influence among his 116 colleagues as they withdraw to the Sistine Chapel to choose the next pope".[106] David Gibson, author of *The Coming Catholic Church*, said, "His skill makes him a valuable person in the conclave."[107]

When speaking to the media, Egan recalled that he had been a judge of the Rota during the conclaves that elected Popes John Paul I and John Paul II. For centuries, it was understood that the judges of the Rota were to be present as "protectors of the cardinals in conclave" until the cardinals entered solemnly into the Sistine Chapel for the voting. And he confessed that when Cardinal Pericle Felici announced that Karol Cardinal Wojtyla had been elected to the See of Peter, Egan and his colleagues were as surprised as anyone else.

He declined to say whom he would support in the 2005 conclave. Egan told a press conference that he hoped the focus of the next pope "would be on local communities of faith. The parish is the central unit that must be served."[108]

In a short, four-ballot conclave, the College of Cardinals chose John Paul II's long-time collaborator, Cardinal Joseph Ratzinger, who took the name Benedict XVI. When asked about the selection, Cardinal Egan told the media that he was certain that Ratzinger was the right choice. "I believe that the Lord has something to do with it.... This man is going to do a splendid job."[109]

The Archdiocesan Bicentennial and Benedict XVI's Visit

To celebrate the two hundredth anniversary of the creation of the diocese by Pope Pius VII in 1808, Egan asked the noted Catholic historian Monsignor Thomas Shelley to write a history of the archdiocese. In that volume, Shelley described how the parish became the center of life for millions of immigrants. In the introduction, Egan wrote, "The parish was the place where [immigrants] could practice their faith and gain spiritual strength. It was the safe haven where they could gather and adjust to a strange new world. The Mass, the Sacraments, the clergy who came with them, spoke their language and understood their needs, and the unique sense of community that the parish engendered all gave newcomers a much-needed sense of society and belonging."[110]

The Museum of the City of New York, meanwhile, had a year-long exhibition on the history of the archdiocese; it held seminars and published a book edited by Terry Golway titled *Catholics in New York: Society, Culture, and Politics.*

The Cardinal's Bicentennial Campaign raised $230 million for the renovation of parish facilities. The chancery covered all the costs of the campaign, and all proceeds raised were for the parishes. In fact, 80 percent of the funds stayed in the parishes in which they were raised, with 20 percent to be distributed by an elected committee of pastors to parishes that were in particular need.[111] The campaign, which exceeded its stated goal by $30 million, contributed to major renovations in more than 85 percent of parish physical plants.

A closing Mass for the campaign was celebrated on April 8, 2008. Afterward, the cardinal hosted a dinner attended by hundreds of clergy, religious, and laity representing the nineteen vicariates of the archdiocese.

But the high point of the yearlong celebration was a three-day apostolic visit by Pope Benedict. On April 18, the pope addressed the United Nations General Assembly, reminding its members that human rights were a gift from God and not the state. He also visited a synagogue and held an ecumenical service at the traditionally German St. Joseph's parish in Yorkville, Manhattan. He dined at the cardinal's residence with the American cardinals and the bishops of New York State.

The next day, Benedict celebrated Mass for clergy and religious with Egan at St. Patrick's. Afterward he met with a group of disabled children and their parents. Later that day, Benedict greeted over forty-three thousand teenagers at St. Joseph's Seminary.

One of the most moving moments of the pope's trip was his visit to Ground Zero on April 20. He knelt and prayed on a prie-dieu overlooking the site, blessed the ground, and lit a candle. He met with family members of victims and with surviving first responders.

At Yankee Stadium, Benedict concelebrated Mass with Egan before sixty thousand of the faithful. Before the pope departed that evening from JFK Airport, Vice President Dick Cheney presided over a farewell ceremony.

The First Archbishop to Retire

When Cardinal Edward Egan turned seventy-five on April 2, 2007, he submitted his resignation to Pope Benedict, as required by canon law. He was the first in the archdiocese to retire, since the rule about mandatory resignation had been in place only since the time of Paul VI, and Egan's three predecessors during that time had died in office. As expected, the pope permitted him to keep his post until after the completion of the bicentennial celebrations and the observance of the fiftieth anniversary of his ordination.

Egan's resignation did not become effective until February 23, 2009, when Benedict named Milwaukee Archbishop Timothy Dolan to be the tenth archbishop of New York. Egan, who joked that he was "the first spiritual leader of New York's 2.5 million Catholics to get out of town alive", served as apostolic administrator of the archdiocese until Dolan was officially installed on April 15.

Egan's final *Catholic New York* column, on March 26, 2009, was devoted to saying thank you:

> I look back over these ... wonderful years and prayerfully thank the Lord that my hopes have been fulfilled beyond all that I might have expected....
>
> On numerous occasions over the last ten years ... I have declared with pleasure that, in my judgment, the priests of our Archdiocese are the best in the nation. They are wise and disciplined men of God who willingly sacrifice themselves for the people whom they serve, and have never ceased to be a source of both encouragement and pride for the Archbishop whom they warmly received into their ranks. To each of them, my sincere and heartfelt thanks....
>
> Our parishes are spiritual families of faith, hope and love that have never ceased to amaze me as I visited them and prayed with them as their Archbishop. Somehow I believe that they know how deep are my esteem and affection for them....
>
> All who know me realize how enthusiastic and uncompromising is my commitment to Catholic education on all levels. Our elementary schools, our high schools and the many institutions of Catholic higher learning that serve our community of faith have always been "the apple of my eye." ...
>
> Permit me to conclude by simply assuring the People of God of the Archdiocese of New York that I will never celebrate a Mass without mentioning them by name to the Lord. To have served as their bishop has been an honor and privilege beyond anything I might have ever imagined.

Upon retirement, Egan decided to stay in New York and moved into a new rectory attached to the Chapel of the Sacred Hearts of Jesus and Mary that he had had built in 2009 on Manhattan's East Thirty-Third Street.

After stepping down as archbishop, Egan did not slow down. He sat on a number of Vatican committees, including the Supreme Tribunal of the Apostolic Signatura, the Prefecture for the Economic Affairs of the Holy See, and the Pontifical Council for the Family. He also assisted his successor in numerous ways. He performed confirmations, filled in for Dolan at various events, and continued his fund-raising activities. He raised more than $40 million for inner-city schools.

At the February 2014 consistory in which the members of the College of Cardinals discussed with Pope Francis the pastoral challenges of marriage and family, Egan spoke out after a controversial speech was delivered by Cardinal Walter Kasper. He pointed out that Kasper, in his speech "La famiglia come ecclesia domestica" (The Family as Domestic Church), failed to mention the role of the parish. Egan went on to expound on a theme he had promoted throughout his clerical career:

> No one questions that the various "comunità ecclesiali" make a valuable contribution to the life of the Church. The contribution of the parish, however, is unique and essential and must be accorded pride of place. The parish is the stable, ongoing community of faith that proclaims the Gospel to the People of God directly and regularly, makes available to them the means of salvation day in and day out, and leads them in matters of justice, compassion, and peace by word, yes, but also, and most importantly, by deed.
>
> It is through the parish that all in a certain area or of a certain background are brought to Jesus Christ officially and systematically. It is, moreover, through the parish and its pastor that the faithful are bonded to their bishop spiritually and institutionally. Diminish the parish, and I am not sure what of power, presence, and permanence will remain.

Back in New York, Cardinal Dolan praised Egan's comments from the pulpit in St. Patrick's Cathedral.

Shortly before Pope Benedict retired, Cardinal Dolan and Cardinal Egan met with the pontiff. In the course of the conversation, Dolan said to the pope, "Cardinal Egan is my best auxiliary bishop." Egan told Benedict that he hoped to be of assistance however he could and as long as he could. Benedict replied, "Bravo, Eminenza, bravo."[112]

11

The Evangelist

AD QUEM IBIMUS

Timothy Michael Dolan
Tenth Archbishop of New York
(2009 to the Present)

Cardinal Dolan distributes food on Ash Wednesday

When Cardinal Egan turned seventy-five on April 2, 2007, Catholic observers did not begin debating a long list of potential successors. For the next two years, the chatter largely focused on just one man: Timothy Michael Dolan, who had been archbishop of Milwaukee since 2002.

The clerical buzz centered on Dolan for two reasons. Cardinal Egan knew him well and, as chairman of the North American College in Rome, had recommended him as the next rector when that position became vacant in 1994. Also, Dolan's archbishop when he was an auxiliary bishop of St. Louis, Justin Rigali, had become a cardinal who served on the Vatican's Congregation for Bishops—the committee that recommends candidates to the pope.

Hence, most Church insiders were not surprised when the Holy See announced on February 23, 2009, that Dolan, who had been on the clerical fast track since he was ordained a priest in St. Louis in June 1976, was to be the tenth archbishop of New York.

The Early Years

Timothy Michael Dolan was born on February 6, 1950, in the St. Louis, Missouri, metropolitan area. When he was four, his parents, Robert and Shirley Dolan, bought a home for $11,000 in Baldwin, a newly developed St. Louis suburb populated heavily with World War II veterans who received their education and their first mortgage under the GI Bill of Rights. Robert, who was to die suddenly at fifty-one in 1977, was an administrative supervisor at Emerson Electric and later at McDonnell Douglas. Shirley was a full-time wife and mother.

Dolan later described his parents as "meat and potatoes" Catholics who would "never miss a Sunday Mass, who would never miss grace before meals, who would never break a Lenten fast—who would sacrifice to see their children went to Catholic school.... But they were typical Catholic Americans who didn't wear their religion on their sleeves."[1]

Tim and his two brothers and two sisters were quintessential middle-class baby boomers. They grew up in the golden age of the Church, when the parish was the center of life for Catholics. Looking back on his grammar-school days at Holy Infant School, run by the Sisters of Mercy from Drogheda, Ireland, Dolan said, "I can never remember a time I didn't want to be a priest."[2]

Friends, teachers, family, and the Dolans' pastor, Father Jeremiah Callahan, a former chaplain, encouraged Tim to pursue his dream, and after he completed the eighth grade in 1964, he entered St. Louis Preparatory Seminary in Shrewsbury, Missouri. Later he earned his bachelor's degree from the archdiocesan senior seminary, Cardinal Glennon College, and was selected as the member of his class to continue his studies at the North American College.

For the next four years, he studied theology at the Pontifical University of St. Thomas Aquinas (the Angelicum) and received his bachelor in sacred theology. (Dolan told the authors of this book that Cardinal Carberry of St. Louis had advised him not to go to the Jesuit-run Gregorian University because he believed it was heretical.) Having a strong interest in Church history, Dolan had the good fortune while residing at the NAC to meet and become friends with America's leading Catholic historian, Monsignor John Tracy Ellis.

Timothy Dolan was ordained on June 19, 1976, by the auxiliary bishop of St. Louis, Edward O'Meara—formerly a protégé of Archbishop Fulton Sheen and future ordinary in Indianapolis. Dolan was assigned as curate to Immacolata parish in Richmond Heights, where he was to serve for three years before being sent to the Catholic University of America to earn a Ph.D. in Church history.

As a seminarian and a young priest, Dolan lived through the period when many American Catholics wrongly interpreted Pope John XXIII's *aggiornamento* as a call to dismantle the very foundations of the Roman Catholic Church. Although he knew priests and seminarians who left the Church, he never doubted either his own faith or the authority of the institutional Church. In an interview with Catholic reporter John L. Allen Jr., he said, "I don't have the antipathy to those years that some have. I know they were an era of excesses and sometimes I'll now say about some loopy idea, 'Oh, that's so Sixties-ish or Seventies-ish.' Unfortunately in the Sixties and the Seventies there were some liturgical abuses and catechetical pollution that we still have to clean up."[3]

At Catholic University, Dolan was mentored by Monsignor John Tracy Ellis and wrote his doctoral thesis on Archbishop Edwin V. O'Hara (1881–1956). O'Hara, a social activist, was the defendant in the suit *Stettler v. O'Hara*, in which the U.S. Supreme Court upheld the minimum wage in 1917. O'Hara became bishop of Kansas City, Missouri, in 1939 and was a champion of rural workers and founder and director of the National Catholic Rural Life Conference.

Back in St. Louis in 1983, Dolan did not get the teaching post he hoped for at the seminary. Instead, for two years he served as a curate in the Curé of Ars parish in Shrewsbury and in 1985 was transferred to Little Flower parish in Richmond Heights. In 1987, he was informed that he would be moving back to Washington, D.C., to serve as a secretary to the Holy See's Apostolic Nunciature.

For the next five years Dolan was an insider, dealing with bishops throughout the nation. He learned firsthand how the Vatican chooses bishops, and he developed a network of influential clerical friends in the Vatican and throughout the United States. One of these friends was Justin Rigali, who served in the Curia and would become archbishop of St. Louis in 1994. Another was the bishop of Bridgeport, Connecticut, Edward Egan. As Chairman of the NAC's board of governors, Egan had considerable say in the appointment of the rector, as did another friend of Dolan, Cardinal Pio Laghi, who would give up the job as nuncio in Washington in 1990 to become head of the Vatican's Congregation for Catholic Education. When there was a vacancy at the NAC in 1994, Egan and Laghi agreed on Dolan, who was then serving as vice-rector of the Kinnick-Glennon Seminary in St. Louis.

Dolan, who had come to know and admire Egan while at the Nunciature, said, "It was he who went after me to become NAC rector.... It was [Egan] who lobbied [for] me and got it through. The wisdom, the advice he gave me when I became rector of NAC in '94 was priceless. He was close by my side during these happy seven years. I was thrilled when he was made Archbishop of New York."[4]

During his NAC tenure (1994–2001), Dolan was a popular rector. His exuberant personality and his enjoyment of good food, wine, beer, whisky, and cigars helped endear him to his students, while he was also an orthodox priest and teacher who saw eye to eye with Pope John Paul II and with his theological collaborators.

In addition to his duties at the NAC, he taught theology at St. Thomas University and Church history at the Pontifical Gregorian University, and he found time to assemble a book titled *Priests for a Third Millennium*. In this collection of lectures to NAC students, he advised, "We priests can bring out the best in one another. When we visit, share a drink, meal, day off or vacation, discuss things, let off steam with one another, challenge one another as a brother if something's bothering him, or pray together, we enhance one another's priestly identity."[5] He also held that "the intimate bond between a bishop and his priests is a theological necessity, which is to be a human reality. There is not a bishop I know who does not have the welfare of his priests as a top priority. As I have in the past, I encourage you to remain in close contact with your bishop."[6]

Shortly after the book's publication, Dolan was given the opportunity to practice what he preached: he was named an auxiliary bishop of St. Louis in June 2001 and was consecrated on August 15, 2001, by Archbishop Rigali.

When he returned to St. Louis, Bishop Dolan took over the diocese's Stewardship of Catholic Education and the Vocations Department. But when the vicar of clergy, Auxiliary Bishop Michael Sheridan, was named coadjutor of the Diocese of Colorado Springs, Dolan was appointed in January 2002 to take over the personnel job—just as the predator-priest crisis was making national headlines.

Dolan, who said he "was consumed by the sexual-abuse controversy",[7] led a campaign urging victims to contact him. On television and radio he asked those who alleged they had been abused to come forward.

The *St. Louis Beacon* reported that Dolan met with victims, and, in Rigali's name, "the just minted bishop dismissed abusive priests." Also in Rigali's name, "he visited lay parishioners to talk about the removal of their often well-liked priests at masses just before the removal news was made public.... Two of the men he relieved of their priestly ministries over sex abuse allegations were the two priests that shared [Our Lady of] Sorrows rectory with him that winter of 2002."[8]

Dolan's assignment was grueling—he worked eighteen hours a day. It was, however, short-lived. On June 25, 2002, ten months after being consecrated an auxiliary bishop, Dolan was appointed archbishop of Milwaukee. He relates that he found out about the appointment during a trip to the District of Columbia. He accepted a dinner invitation from Archbishop Gabriel Montalvo, the nuncio in Washington, for what he thought would be an evening to talk about old times. After Dolan declined a drink and a cigarette, the archbishop informed him he was going to Milwaukee. A shocked Dolan responded by saying, "I'll have that drink and cigarette now."[9]

The Milwaukee Years

Some in clerical circles saw the appointment as a huge and speedy promotion for a job well done in St. Louis, plus recognition of the fact that he was a solid John Paul II priest. Others suggested Dolan was being moved from the frying pan into the fire.

Timothy Dolan was installed on August 22, 2002, to lead an archdiocese that was considered a hotbed of radical, unorthodox Catholicism.

The man who had led the Archdiocese of Milwaukee for twenty-five years, Archbishop Rembert Weakland, had tendered his resignation when he turned seventy-five on April 2, 2002. Several weeks later, it was revealed that the archbishop had paid his former lover, Paul Marcoux, $450,000 out of diocesan funds to prevent a sexual-abuse lawsuit. While no criminal charges were filed, the disgraced Weakland urged the Vatican quickly to accept his resignation. This it did on May 24.

During Weakland's long tenure in Milwaukee, he had implemented a radical agenda. He endorsed a married priesthood and, in 1980, established an annual lecture titled "Homosexuality and Its Impact on the Family". The priest who delivered the first talk in this series served as a chaplain of the dissident Catholic group Dignity, which rejects Catholic teachings on the issue.[10]

While chairman of the Bishops' Committee on the Liturgy in 1980, Weakland tampered with the words of consecration at his own Masses in Milwaukee. He excluded the phrase "for men" because he considered it sexist.[11] He permitted homosexual activists, who redefined the family as people "sharing", to be members of the archdiocesan Commission for the Plan of Pastoral Action for Family Ministry.[12] Confessionals had cobwebs, because general absolution had become the norm.

"Weakland made no bones about being proud that he was at odds with the Holy See", Dolan said. He had created an atmosphere in which anything that came from Rome was suspect and anything done prior to the Second Vatican Council needed to be rejected.[13]

Dolan expected to be harangued by clergy who had been running wild for years. "The major obstacle I was going to face", he said, "was the perception that I am some flame-throwing right-winger who is going to come in and have a scorched-earth policy." His first job, he concluded, "was to win the trust of the Milwaukee priests and to love them".[14]

Meeting with his priests for the first time, he gave them what he later called a "spiritual and lofty" talk in which he stated that they must approach the "crisis as a call to integrity, as a call to holiness, as a call to humility". Dolan then asked for questions. As he recounted to reporter John Allen, one priest raised his hand and said, "Yeah. Are we still going to be able to live wherever we want? Are you going to keep the salaries the highest in the country, and can we still retire at sixty-eight?" Dolan thought to himself, "What is this, a damned Teamsters meeting?"[15]

However, Dolan was not a bull in a china shop. While frankly stating that "there was bizarre experimentation [in Milwaukee] after the council", he did not want a civil war, and so moved slowly in undoing the questionable policies and practices of the Weakland years, emphasizing "the positive instead of the negative".[16] One of his first moves was to rein in the practice of general absolution and promote a return to the confessional. To this end, during his first Advent in Milwaukee, he had services in each of the deaneries with "dozens and dozens" of confessors available. Over twelve thousand of the faithful attended, and Dolan believes that his "call back to the sacrament" worked because he accentuated the positive.[17]

Pointing out that he and his priests had a duty to "obey Church directives on the liturgy", he reintroduced kneeling during Mass and abolished preaching by nonordained people.[18]

He also established a rapport with his priests, meeting with them often in groups and sometimes one-on-one. His affable personality and his genuine concern for the welfare of his priests, however, did not completely calm the waters. In August 2003, for instance, 160 priests signed a letter addressed to the president of the United States Bishops' Conference, Wilton Gregory, demanding that the Church permit married men to become priests.

The priests who drafted the letter had told Dolan about their plans before releasing it. His spokesman said, "It was something that had come up in discussion.... He certainly hasn't said, 'You shouldn't do this.' He knows it's an emotional issue."[19]

A week later, Dolan answered the critics in the archdiocesan newspaper. He declared that he supported celibacy "wholeheartedly ... not because I'm 'supposed to,' or reluctantly 'have to' but because I want to".[20] He went on to write: "This is the time we priests need to be renewing our pledge to celibacy, not questioning it.... The recent sad scandal of clerical sexual abuse of minors, as the professionals have documented, has nothing to do with our celibacy commitment."[21]

The archbishop had also promised that a top priority would be addressing the predator-priest scandals. At a forum in October 2002, Dolan listened for hours to the heart-wrenching stories of more than two hundred victims of abuse, after which he said, "I find myself speechless; I find myself helpless on knowing what to do.... We can't do business as usual."[22]

Dolan attempted to handle the problems he inherited from Weakland honestly and openly, while always cognizant that he had an obligation not only to those under his care but also to the institutional Church. Dolan appointed a non-Catholic as the director of assistance to those who accused priests of sexual abuse, and he continued to meet with the accusers, many of whom he judged to be telling the truth. As for settlements, he made it clear that he would not tap into money that donors had intended for schools, cemeteries, charities, and so forth. He set up a separate fund for settlements, the money for which came from sales of Church-owned property, and he released the names of forty-three predator-priests, many of whom were dead. He refused, however, to release the names of accused priests in various religious orders, stating that he lacked authority to do so.

Although few lawsuits could be filed, because of the Wisconsin statute of limitations and a 1995 court ruling that "church and state separation barred lawsuits against religious organizations for negligent supervision of clergy",[23] Dolan believed it was important and, above all, just to compensate victims. During his tenure, the independent mediator paid out over $10 million for therapy and settlements to more than 170 victims.[24]

In 2007, however, the Wisconsin Supreme Court made it harder for the archdiocese by ruling that victims could sue for fraud on the grounds that predator-priests were assigned to new parishes without first informing parishioners. The implications of this ruling forced Dolan's successor in Milwaukee, Archbishop Jerome Edward Listecki, to file for bankruptcy in 2011.

Two decisions Dolan made in Milwaukee were to follow him to New York. The first was his request to transfer $57 million of restricted cemetery assets to a separate cemetery trust, which the Vatican approved. When Dolan's letter seeking approval became public in 2013, attorneys for the victims suing the archdiocese claimed he was trying to hide assets and prevent the money from being used for settlements. The lawyers focused on this sentence in Dolan's letter to the Vatican: "I foresee an improved protection of these funds from any legal claims and liability."

On this matter, the United States District Court sided with the archdiocese, ruling that the transferred monies were off limits to victim suits because the assets were restricted funds intended solely for cemetery-related purposes, such as maintenance. However, the Seventh U.S. Circuit Court and the Archdiocese asked the Supreme Court to review the decision. It was still pending in 2016.

The second Milwaukee case that followed Dolan to New York concerned charges that he paid off a priest to agree to seek laicization. Dolan pointed out in an interview that the moment a priest is laicized, he can no longer be covered by diocesan medical insurance. The priest in this case was one year away from being eligible for Medicare, and so he had to get private insurance, which he could not afford.

Dolan directed legal counsel for the Archdiocese of Milwaukee to cut a check for $10,000 to a private insurance company to pay for the ex-priest's health coverage. Although the latter claimed in a press conference that Dolan paid the money to get rid of him, Dolan insists that was not accurate. Paying the premium, he said, "was a simple act of charity, if not justice". He added that it also protected the archdiocese. "If that man had a stroke, he would have ended up on our doorstep. To protect [the archdiocese] I needed to make sure this guy had insurance."[25]

When accusations in these two matters and others were resurrected in 2013, *New York Times* columnist Frank Bruni called Dolan "a slippery operator".[26] Dolan, who publicly welcomed the opportunity to be deposed by lawyers, described the charges as "old and discredited": "While certain groups can be counted upon to take certain statements or events out of context, the documents released show plainly that the bishops have been faithful to the promises made over a decade ago: permanent removal from ministry of any priest who abused a minor; complete cooperation with law enforcement officials; and strict child-safety requirements."[27]

In a July 17, 2013, memo to the priests of the Archdiocese of New York, Dolan wrote:

> I always regret it when there is negative reporting about me in the media, as there was a couple of weeks ago. Even though I'm at peace knowing the charges are silly, scurrilous, and mean, and even though we put out yet another statement rebutting the groundless accusation, it's still a pain to all of you who have to field questions about "this stuff Dolan is supposed to have done in Milwaukee." I am sorry for the position this puts you in.

In February 2014, when it was announced that the St. Louis Archdiocese was about to obey a court order and "release documents regarding cases there of sexual abuse of minors", Dolan stated, "I would anticipate that my name will again be highlighted in the press." He continued, "I sure have nothing to hide and am very much at peace with law enforcement officials reviewing the files. In fact, we released all the documents to them a dozen years ago."[28]

"This will be, I suspect," the cardinal reminded the public, "a repeat of last year's attempt by the same tort lawyers to muddy my name. A year ago, they contended—remember?—that while Archbishop of Milwaukee I had 'hidden funds,' and they had even deposed me. Nothing, of course, ever came of it, although the ever-compliant press here gave me headlines about being deposed."[29]

Looking back on the scandals, Dolan said in an interview with the authors of this book on June 27, 2014:

> In general, I think there is a benign side to it and how it happened—obviously there is nothing benign about the facts, the malign side. The benign side—bishops, and I would say a majority of bishops, acted in accordance with the standards of the time. In other words, if there was an accusation of a priest abusing a minor, the bishops, in general, the majority of bishops, took that very seriously. [The bishop] would have called him in, confronted him. [He would have] first taken moral and spiritual remedies and secondly, assigned him to intense therapy; not willing to reassign him until the experts would say it is safe to do so.

Dolan told the authors that earlier in the day of that interview, he had spent six hours in a deposition covering the period during which he was an auxiliary bishop in St. Louis and was queried about the standards of that time. He said he told the lawyers that in the case of an accused priest, a judge had said in a letter that it would be "enough for me if [the priest] is sent away for psychological treatment". Dolan noted that there was also a letter from the police department saying, "If this man goes for residential treatment we will drop the sentence."

In Dolan's judgment, this demonstrated that the treatment approach "was not some backward perilous approach by just the bishops". It was used "by the Boy Scouts, by the Mormons, by everybody else".

He went on to say, "There was also, I'm afraid, and we cannot deny it—there was what happened among some bishops. They would have simply said—sadly, in the same way they treated alcohol—'Father, you have made a good confession. You have to make a good retreat. And we will move you from your parish, and you need a fresh start.' That's not good. It's not good at all."

"Tragically", the cardinal went on, "we were not the only ones doing that—foster care was doing that, public schools were doing that. So that seems to me—I think there was a drive to protect the image of the Church. Fear—if anything went public on this, it would scandalize the faithful. So, we have seen how stupid that was. There was never a greater scandal in the Church in the history of American Catholicism than that was. So that sure backfired."

Dolan rejected the view of many critics that the bishops' sole motive was to protect the money and the assets of the Church. "No", he said. "In those days there weren't such things as suits. So the protected aspect of it wasn't to protect the assets of the Church. It was to protect, I think, the good *reputation* of the Church.... But what I'm always upset about is the question of motive. I think the motive of most bishops was good. In no way was it malicious. In no way did they think they were putting children in danger. Looking back now, we know it was terribly misguided, and we deeply regret it."[30]

As for the situation in New York, he said he was grateful he inherited a clean archdiocese. "I thank God for Egan. I mean, he took very difficult steps, very blunt, very dramatic reform. He did it justly, quickly, and I thank God for it."[31]

When it was announced in February 2009 that Dolan was to become the tenth archbishop of New York, the media reported that most people in Milwaukee believed he was leaving their archdiocese in much better shape than it had been in when he arrived in 2002. Dolan's jolly, outgoing personality, his ability to reach out to people, and his work ethic had helped in Milwaukee to heal and reinvigorate an archdiocese that was rocked by scandal. The battles that many leftist priests predicted would happen did not happen. "He is with Rome on the big issues and on the little ones", said a Marquette University professor. "But he does not do it in a dictatorial fashion."[32]

An editorial in the *Milwaukee Journal Sentinel* best summed up Dolan's time as archbishop: "In many ways, he was a perfect match for Milwaukee: self-effacing, friendly, funny—a guy you wouldn't mind sharing a beer with, yet sympathetic and caring as a parish priest should be and still a man with clear intellectual depth.... Dolan brought a sense of renewal when he arrived in August 2002 and has reached out in a thousand different ways to Catholics and non-Catholics across the region. It was his personal touch that endeared him to so many."[33]

Dolan in New York

On February 23, 2009—the day the Vatican announced the appointment of the fifty-nine-year-old Timothy Dolan as the tenth archbishop of New York—he held a press conference with Cardinal Egan standing at his side. Dolan thanked Egan for his years of service and expressed his gratitude that he was inheriting an archdiocese that was "spiritually vibrant and financially secure".[34] He also said, "There's no intention to close any Catholic school in the archdiocese".[35]

As he had done in Milwaukee, Dolan made a point of saying that his first priority would be to spend time with his priests. "Our priests", he said, "are on the front line of an important ministry, so I'm here to help them. I'm their servant, I work for them, and I need them more than ever."[36]

Dolan avoided answering questions on proposed legislation in Albany that would "temporarily lift the statute of limitations to allow more victims of sexual abuse to file suits", saying he would have to study the proposal.[37]

When asked if he would deny Communion to pro-abortion Catholic politicians, he said he preferred to have a "trusting dialogue" instead of public confrontation.

The initial press reviews were for the most part excellent, although the *New York Times* lamented that Dolan did not speak Spanish and that a Hispanic had not been chosen. The article was titled: "Hoping for a Latino Archbishop, in Due Course".[38]

In assessing the Dolan appointment, Church historian Monsignor Thomas Shelley said, "He comes across as a very intelligent and gregarious and happy person, someone that's comfortable with people. He gives religion a good name."[39]

When asked in an interview with the authors if he was surprised by the appointment to lead New York's Catholics, Dolan replied yes. Admitting that many will think "it's obligatory humility", he told us he was genuinely surprised and thrilled by his various appointments, particularly to the Nunciature and as archbishop in Milwaukee and New York. While he knew his name was in the mix for New York, he did not spend much time thinking about the possibility, he said, calling this "Irish insurance against disappointment".[40]

Before taking over the archdiocese, Dolan flew to New York on two occasions to visit Egan and discuss the transition. The meetings were kept quiet. Egan arranged for someone to pick up Dolan at the airport, and he was brought into the residence by way of the cathedral to avoid media attention.

Dolan told the authors that during their sessions together Egan gave him a "great intro to the life of the archdiocese". He added that Egan "is a great source of wisdom. He's a perfect predecessor, and he said, 'I will never interfere but I'm here if you need me.' He is indefatigable—he keeps at it. He could have retired to isolation, which he well deserved. He could have gone to Florida, to his beloved Chicago, or he could have gone to Rome. To have him here is amazing."[41]

On April 14, 2009, the day before his official installation, Dolan made the ceremonial entrance to take possession of St. Patrick's Cathedral. He began the rite by rapping loudly with a hammer on the bronze front doors. The doors were swung open, and Dolan processed up the center aisle with much pomp and music and to the applause of the three thousand guests. To much laughter, he confessed in his remarks that upon hearing the news of his appointment, he said to the Lord, "I'm not your man. My Spanish is lousy and my English not much better. I'm still angry at New York for taking Favre and Sabathia from us in Wisconsin. The Yankees and Mets over the Cardinals and Brewers? Forget it."

In a more serious vein, he listed the challenges he would face as archbishop, including "threats to marriage and family, to the unborn baby and fragile human life at all stages".[42]

The following day at 1:30 P.M., more than a thousand priests began processing into the cathedral. The next to last in the procession was Cardinal Egan, followed by the new archbishop. The papal nuncio to the United States, Archbishop Pietro Sambi, read the document signed by Pope Benedict XVI appointing Dolan. Then Dolan was led to the archbishop's chair—the cathedra—and as metropolitan was welcomed by bishops from the New York province.

In his homily delivered during the Pontifical High Mass, he thanked Cardinal Egan for his leadership and said to him, "As the disciples on the Road to Emmaus asked the Lord, please, 'stay with us.'"

He then invited the faithful to take a stroll with him along the road to Emmaus, where Christ appeared to those two disciples after his resurrection. Dolan said:

We've just been through a litany of ways that the *rising* of Jesus radiates in the Church in this historic archdiocese. But we'd be naïve if we overlooked the *dying*, wouldn't we?

For indeed not only the Resurrection but the *cross*, the dying, of Christ goes on:

- as we are tempted to fatigue in our works of service and charity
- as we continue realistically to nurse the deep wounds inflicted by the horrible scandal, sin, and crime of sexual abuse of minors, never hesitant to beg forgiveness from God and from victim survivors and their families, committed to continue the reform, renewal, and outreach Pope Benedict encouraged us to last year, when, among many other places, he urged us in this very cathedral "to respond with Christian hope to the continuing challenges [of] this painful situation"
- as we struggle to keep our parishes and schools strong, and recognize that we need a new harvest of vocations to the priesthood, diaconate, religious life, and faithful, life-long, life-giving marriage

I say to you, my sister and brother disciples now on the road to Emmaus, let's not turn inward to ourselves, our worries, our burdens, our fears; but turn rather to *Him*, the way, the truth, and the life, the one who told us over and over, "Be not afraid!"[43]

After the Mass, Dolan processed around the cathedral shaking hundreds of hands and hugging scores of people. Outside on Fifth Avenue, he worked the crowd like an old-time Irish pol. He was outgoing and exuberant. Watching his performance, Bill Donohue, president of the Catholic League for Religious and Civil Rights, said that Dolan "is a gregarious down-to-earth man who will resonate well with New Yorkers".[44]

In his first week in office, Dolan raced around his archdiocese. He attended a Yankees game and a Mets game, visited a Bronx food pantry, and attended a Holocaust memorial service at St. Peter's Lutheran church in Manhattan.

In fact, he spent his first year as archbishop constantly on the move. He spent time with his priests—he even called them on their birthdays. He visited parishes throughout the ten counties of the archdiocese. After Masses he would linger, shaking hands with parishioners. Finding his waistline expanding from eating the local fare at parishes and washing it down with beer, he told one group of the faithful, "New York has grown on me."

For Dolan, communicating with New Yorkers is important. He started his own blog called *The Gospel in the Digital Age* and posted his first message, "God Is Everywhere, Even on the Blog", on October 6, 2009. Later he began tweeting at @CardinalDolan.

He also made a point of preaching at the 10:15 A.M. Mass on Sundays at the cathedral. Knowing that members of the press would often attend to hear what he had to say, Dolan explained that he wouldn't "pass up the chance to say the name of Jesus and to get the Church's teachings out there".[45]

Between excursions and sermons, Dolan did find time to sit behind his desk and begin studying the intricacies of his archdiocese's finances and the effects of the Great Recession on the bottom line. Concluding that he had inherited an excellent staff from Egan, he retained most of them, and he appointed as chancellor of the archdiocese Monsignor Gregory Mustaciuolo, who had been the priest-secretary to Cardinals O'Connor and Egan. Later Chancellor Mustaciuolo received the additional post of vicar-general.

From time to time, he spoke out on public issues; he was particularly vocal in his defense of Pope Benedict.

On March 29, 2010, at the end of his Palm Sunday Mass in the cathedral, Dolan asked the congregation to stay for a few minutes so that he could speak to them concerning "a tidal wave of headlines about abuse of minors by some few priests, this time in Ireland, Germany, and a re-run of an old story in Wisconsin".

"What deepens the sadness", he said, "is the unrelenting insinuations against the Holy Father himself, as certain sources seem frenzied to implicate the man who, perhaps more than anyone else, has been the leader in purification, reform and renewal that the Church so needs....

"Does the Church, and her pastor, Pope Benedict XVI, need intense scrutiny and just criticism for tragic horrors long past? Yes! He himself asked for it, encouraging complete honesty, at the same time expressing contrition and urging thorough cleansing."

Observing that Sunday Mass was "hardly the place to document the inaccuracy, bias and hyperbole" of the media, he asked the congregation to pray for the pope and concluded by saying, "All we ask is that it be fair, and that the Catholic Church not be singled out for a horror that has cursed every culture, religion, organization, institution, school, agency, and family in the world."[46]

The archbishop's comments brought the faithful in the packed cathedral to their feet, and they applauded for over a minute.

As for his approach to the media, on the one hand, he believes one must not be isolated, but, on the other hand, he would prefer to pick his shots and not be like Cardinal O'Connor, who was available to talk about almost any topic at any time. Dolan also admitted that mistakes could be made, because "sometimes bishops are a little naïve and trusting of the press". He slyly added: "We can learn a lot from politicians."[47]

While Dolan was still getting his feet wet in New York, something totally unexpected happened. On Tuesday, November 16, 2010, the American bishops elected Archbishop Dolan to succeed Cardinal Francis George as president of the U.S. Conference of Catholic Bishops. This event catapulted Dolan onto the national stage and gave him less time to spend on his archdiocese.

Dolan in the National and International Arenas

Dolan's selection was certainly a surprise. As the bishops had gathered for their annual meeting, it was presumed that the vice president of the USCCB, Bishop Gerald Kicanas of Tucson, would move up to the top spot, because that's how it had worked in the past.

This time, however, a majority of the bishops wanted a solid John Paul II bishop to lead them. On the second ballot, Dolan came out ahead with a plurality. In the runoff, Dolan was elected, with 128 votes versus Kicanas's 111 votes, or 54 to 46 percent.

To these bishops, Archbishop Dolan seemed to be the best suited to carry out the New Evangelization and to articulate the Church's teachings in the nation's protracted culture wars. Many of them believed that he had proved he had the mettle for the USCCB job when he stood up to the Catholic Health Care Association, a group representing hundreds of Catholic hospitals and other health-care institutions, and the Leadership Conference of Women Religious, a group of largely dissident nuns, in March 2010 after they endorsed the Senate version of the Affordable Care Act despite problems with provisions regarding abortion and the absence of language that would protect freedom of conscience for Catholic medical personnel. Catholics, Dolan said, should look to the bishops, not these groups, for guidance— because bishops are "not just one set of teachers in the Catholic community, but *the* teachers".[48]

Dolan had also impressed many in October when he took on the *New York Times*. After the paper rejected an op-ed he submitted that criticized it for anti-Catholic news coverage, he posted it on his blog. It said: "While we are not asking the *Times* or, for that matter, any media of communication to give special treatment to the church, we are asking that it be treated equally. Anti-Catholicism seems to be the only acceptable bigotry in our nation, and we as Catholics need to do all that we can to call those who engage in it to task."[49]

A week after he was elected to head the USCCB, the archbishop gave an interview to the *New York Times*, in which he listed as a top priority the New Evangelization. "We need to recover our vigor", he said, and to reach out to Catholics who have walked away from the Church. He expressed concern and sadness that studies have indicated that only half of younger baptized Catholics get married in the Church and only 35 percent of Catholics attend Sunday Mass every week, as opposed to 78 percent in the early 1960s.[50]

As for rumors that the Church was going to change her doctrine on birth control, Dolan told the reporter, "You get the impression that the Holy See or the pope is like Congress and every once in a while says, 'Oh, let's change this law.' We can't."

Finally, Dolan told the reporter that he would soon be leaving New York for three weeks to carry out a papal assignment, an investigation of the state of Irish seminaries in response to a report that indicated widespread predatory acts by priests committed against minors between 1975 and 2004. Dolan was to lead the apostolic visitation and to report his findings directly to Pope Benedict.[51]

Dolan's greatest challenge during his three-year term as president of the USCCB was dealing with the impact on Catholic institutions of the Affordable Care Act, which had been signed into law by President Obama on March 23, 2010.

The American bishops had some tough going during the congressional debate over Obamacare. They had caught lots of flak from media moguls, congressional leaders, and renegade Catholics because they dared to inform their flocks that portions of the health-care proposal violate Church teachings on the sanctity of human life.

For instance, syndicated columnist E. J. Dionne, a baptized Catholic, complained that the bishops were discarding "the flag of social justice" because they said the final bill was not abortion-neutral and undermined the Hyde Amendment, which prohibits using federal tax dollars to pay for abortion except in cases of rape and incest.[52]

Speaker Nancy Pelosi, also a baptized Catholic, demonstrated her ignorance of the Church's position regarding human freedom while dismissing the objections of the bishops: "I practically mourn the difference of opinion because I feel what I was raised to believe is consistent with what I profess, and that we are all endowed with a free will and a responsibility to answer for our actions. And that women should have the opportunity to exercise their free will."[53] Pelosi seemed blissfully unaware that true freedom is not an endorsement of bad moral choices.

Then there were other Catholics who simply thumbed their noses at the bishops. As mentioned above, the Catholic Health Association and the Leadership Conference of Women Religious broke ranks and supported the bill.

The *New York Times* and the *Washington Post* applauded these dissidents in front-page stories. Maureen Dowd, the *Times'* most prolific anti-Catholic polemicist (although a baptized Catholic herself), proclaimed that "the nuns provided the Democrats with cover" to procure the last votes needed for House passage. She was right—eighty-four of the ninety-three Catholic Democrats in the House of Representatives voted for the bill. (All thirty-seven Catholic Republicans voted against.)

The fact that the U.S. bishops had for a hundred years called for "reform of our healthcare system so that all may have access to the care that recognizes and affirms their human dignity" did not matter in the national debate. Because the bishops did not embrace, without question, a health-care agenda at variance with several basic American principles, they were portrayed as being out of touch, stepping over the line, and violating separation of church and state.

What these critics failed to grasp is that bishops, as shepherds, have a duty to their flocks to offer guidance on the Church's moral teachings. They also have an obligation to correct any person—Catholic or not—who misleads or sows confusion about Church doctrine. Clergy of all faiths explain to their coreligionists how their religions apply in the temporal world. Catholics are no different.

It was a rough patch, but it got rougher on Dolan's watch.

The original Obamacare legislation had left many of the details to the discretion of the Secretary of Health and Human Services. In August 2011—more than a year after the law was passed and signed—Secretary Kathleen Sebelius, yet another Catholic, issued an "interim final rule" stating that most insurance plans would have to include "preventive health services" for women, including contraception. Objections were swift and sharp, not only from the bishops and Catholic health-care providers, but also from many non-Catholic employers who provided insurance coverage for their employees. The Obama administration spent some time "evaluating" these objections.

Then in January 2012 Secretary Sebelius caused a firestorm when she announced the "final rule". Ignoring conscience objections, the administration ordered all employers to amend their health-care plans by August 1, 2012, to include birth-control services (among them abortion-inducing drugs and sterilization procedures) or be subject to millions of dollars in fines and penalties. Nonprofit employers—including Catholic schools, hospitals, and charities—were given an additional year to comply.

Prominent Catholics from across the political spectrum were aghast.

E. J. Dionne, who had supported the renegade Catholic health-care organizations back in March 2010, denounced the president for throwing "his progressive Catholic allies under the bus". Sean Michael Winters, a dogged foe of Church conservatives, accused the president of "dishonoring your own vision by this shameful action" and vowed not to vote for him in the fall.[54]

One need not agree with Catholic teaching on birth control to understand that it is, indeed, a matter of core principle—flowing directly from an understanding of human personhood and sexuality to the conclusion that contraception dehumanizes its users and debases love both physically and spiritually. Nor need anyone be deceived by the administration's pseudoscientific rationales. The ruling was a brute-force assertion of a particular ideology onto the entire nation.

Most perturbed was the president of the USCCB. Dolan vociferously condemned the announcement. "In effect," he said, "the president is saying we have a year to figure out how to violate our own consciences. . . . Never before has the federal government forced individuals and organizations to go out into the marketplace and buy a product that violates their conscience. This shouldn't happen in a land where free exercise of religion ranks first in the Bill of Rights."[55]

The archbishop felt he had been sandbagged, because the previous November, in an "extraordinarily friendly" forty-five-minute meeting in the Oval Office,

President Obama, whom he found "very open and very sensitive", gave him assurances that Obamacare would not infringe on Catholic teachings.

At the end of that session, Dolan reviewed his understanding of the president's position: "I've heard you say, first of all, that you have immense regard for the work of the Catholic Church in the United States in health care, education and charity.... I have heard you say that you are not going to let the administration do anything to impede that work and ... that you take the protection of the rights of conscience with the utmost seriousness.... Does that accurately sum up our conversation?"

Obama said, "You bet it does."[56]

Dolan told the president that at the completion of their White House meeting he would be going to the U.S. bishops' meeting, and he sought permission to pass on this summary of their conversation to them. The president replied, "You don't have my permission, you have my request."[57] After being briefed, the former president of the USCCB, Cardinal George of Chicago, who also had unsatisfactory dealings in Illinois with Obama as U.S. senator, and then as president, warned Dolan, "Trust but verify."

In an interview with the authors, Dolan said that at that meeting with Obama, the president conceded, "You are winning the pro-life battle." Dolan continued, "When it comes to the real pro-life battles of winning the hearts and souls of the American people, the president had to say begrudgingly that 'you people have victory there' ".[58]

When the president called the archbishop to give him a heads-up about the scheduled HHS mandate announcement, Dolan told him: "Mr. President, I appreciate the call. Are you saying now that we have until August to introduce to you continual concerns that might trigger a substantive mitigation in these mandates?"

The president said, "No, the mandates remain. We're more or less giving you this time to find out how you're going to be able to comply."

Dolan replied, "Well, sir, we don't need the [extra time]. I can tell you now we're unable to comply."[59]

Unnerved by the public backlash against his mandate, the president called Dolan on February 10, 2012, at 9:30 A.M. and said, "You will be happy to hear religious institutions do not have to pay for this, that the burden will be on the insurers."

The message was, in effect, a presidential decree, because he was not asking for Dolan's advice; he was just informing him. Two hours later, Obama announced the administration's so-called accommodation.[60]

Not wanting to appear to be rushing to judgment, the seething Dolan said publicly, "We welcome this initiative, we look forward to studying it, we hope that it is a decent first step, but we still have weighty questions."[61]

The following day, Dolan made it perfectly clear that the "compromise" did not cut it. In a public statement and in a letter to his fellow bishops he declared: "We have grave reservations that the government is intruding in the definition of who is and who is not a religious employee. Our concerns remain strong that the government is creating its own definitions of who is 'religious enough' for full protection.... It is the place of the Church, not of government, to define its religious identity on ministry."

Dolan emphasized that the issue was not over contraception per se but over religious liberty, and that the government does not have the right to burden the consciences of religious believers. "We remain fully committed to the defense of our religious liberty and we strongly protest the violation of our freedom of religion that has not been addressed."[62]

Several hours after blasting "Obama's bitter pill", as the *New York Post* put it, Dolan left for Rome—to receive his red hat from Pope Benedict.

When Benedict had announced in October 2010 that he would elevate twenty-four priests to the College of Cardinals on November 20, 2010, Dolan's name was not on the list. His exclusion was not a papal snub. Since Cardinal Egan was still eligible to vote in a conclave to elect a pope until he turned eighty years old in 2012, giving New York a second vote was considered granting an unfair advantage or undue influence. Hence, Dolan was excluded.

But Dolan's name was included on the list that Benedict released on January 6, 2012, even though Egan would not turn eighty until three months later. Dolan was "fast-tracked", said Catholic commentator Robert Royal, because "the leaders of the Church believe the crisis of religious liberty in America is that pressing."[63]

Of his elevation to the cardinalate, the cardinal-designate said, "As a kid I just wanted to be a parish priest, and to think that now the pope has named me a cardinal—that is awesome." Patting his belly, he said he hoped his new rank would elevate "my message—not my weight or blood pressure".[64]

The archbishop emeritus, Cardinal Egan, praised Dolan's appointment, saying he was impressed the first time he met Dolan as a young priest and "earmarked him for success". Egan recalled that when he had recommended Dolan to be rector of the North American College, "I wanted a guy that could hit the baseball farther than anybody. I wanted a guy who was very buoyant. At that time, I saw he was the man. A man that would handle men very well.... He filled the bill."[65]

Before leaving for Rome, Dolan said he was concerned about two things: "Letting my mother loose on the Via Condotti with those very expensive shops" and an address on the New Evangelization he was to deliver before the pope and the cardinals two days before the consistory.[66]

In that speech, after thanking the Holy Father "for your patience with my primitive Italian", he went on to say that the "towering challenge to both the *missio ad gentes* and the New Evangelization today is what we call secularism."

> The New Evangelization is urgent because secularism has often choked the seed of faith; but that choking was sadly made easy because so many believers really had no adequate knowledge or grasp of the wisdom, beauty, and coherence of the Truth.
>
> Thus, our mission, the New Evangelization, has essential catechetical and ecclesial dimensions.
>
> This impels us to think about Church in a fresh way: to think of the Church as a mission. As John Paul II taught in *Redemptoris Missio*, the Church does not "have a mission," as if "mission" were one of many things the Church does. No, the Church is a mission, and each of us who names Jesus as Lord and Savior should measure ourselves by our mission-effectiveness.[67]

Chatting with the press corps that followed him around Rome, he joked about his waistline and dieting. "I actually have a Ph.D. in dieting", he said. He pointed out that in Rome, "the temptations are going to be the rich, creamy pastas. You don't like to come to Rome without trying out your old favorites."

After eating at a favorite restaurant of clerics (including Cardinal Egan), the Abruzzi on the Piazza dei Santissimi Apostoli, he told a crowd of media, "They've got the greatest cannelloni I've ever had. They have a wonderful abbacchio alla romana, that's lamb. They have fresh spinach and a tiramisù that's worth the flight. And some pretty good red wine."[68]

On the day he was given his red biretta, more than one thousand of his friends, including fifty priests and bishops, watched in St. Peter's Square. After the ceremony, Dolan hosted receptions for the pilgrims and celebrated Mass for them at the church in Rome the pope had assigned to him, and which would bear his coat of arms, Our Lady of Guadalupe in Monte Mario.

Upon returning to New York, Cardinal Dolan presided over a service of thanksgiving. In his thirteen-minute homily before a packed cathedral that included elected officials and representatives of the city's major religious denominations, Dolan insisted that his elevation to the cardinalate was "an honor not only to him and the Catholic Archdiocese of New York, but to the entire city and the expansive greater New York community".[69]

Afterward he hosted a reception at the Sheraton Hotel on Seventh Avenue for all who had attended the service.

When asked by reporters that day about his opposition to the Obamacare mandate on religious institutions, he said, "We will worry philosophically that nothing's been done to temper what seems to be to us and to a good swath of people an unwarranted and unprecedented intrusion into the integrity of the churches."[70]

In the aftermath of the red-hat hoopla, Cardinal Dolan turned his attention back to designing a plan of action to combat the HHS mandate. On March 2, he sent a letter on the matter to his fellow American bishops. First, he congratulated them and the faithful "for our unity in faith and action as we move forward to protect our *religious freedom* from unprecedented intrusion from a government bureau, the Department of Health and Human Services".

Next he declared that two things had been certain since the restrictive rules were announced on January 20: "religious freedom is under attack, and we will not cease our struggle."

Then he pointed out that he was pleased that this was not solely a Catholic issue. He quoted former Arkansas Governor Mike Huckabee, a Baptist minister, who said, "In this matter, we're all Catholics."

As to what to do now, he wrote:

- The USCCB will continue in "our strong efforts of advocacy and education," and
- The USCCB will pursue legislation in the Congress and 'explore our legal rights under the Constitution and the Religious Freedom Restoration Act' to remedy Obamacare's fundamental flaws.

Dolan also confessed that the invitation from President Obama to "work out the wrinkles" was getting nowhere. "The White House Press Secretary", Dolan noted, "had informed the nation that the mandates are *fait accompli*."

Given this climate, he warned, "we have to prepare for tough times", but he concluded that the courts might "offer the most light". He cited the unanimous

U.S. Supreme Court ruling in *Hosanna-Tabor Evangelical Lutheran Church and School v. Equal Employment Opportunity Commission*, which "defended the right of a church to define its own ministry and services".

The *Wall Street Journal* editorial page congratulated Cardinal Dolan on the frankness of his "Liberty Letter". It also stated that as a study in ideology and power, the attitude of the White House was "chilling," and "it was compounded by all the recent claims by Democrats and liberals that Catholics who actually abide by their faith are opposed to modernity. Such prejudice is supposedly defunct in contemporary America except when it's practiced against religion."[71]

In an interview on a local New York talk show on Friday, April 27, the host asked Dolan whether the Church would petition the court over the HHS mandate. Dolan replied, "I think we are going to have to. What recourse does any citizen have? Like any other citizen that feels aggrieved, we go to the judiciary, and I don't think we'll be reluctant to do that."[72]

On Monday, May 21, the Church struck: forty-three Catholic institutions filed suits against Obamacare's birth-control mandate. The plaintiffs included the Archdioceses of New York and Washington, D.C., Catholic University of America, and the University of Notre Dame.

The suits claimed that the HHS mandate violated the free-exercise clause of the First Amendment and the 1993 Religious Freedom Restoration Act. The Notre Dame brief argued, "There is no apparent limit to government power if the government can force religious institutions to violate their beliefs in such a manner."[73]

The *New York Times* defended President Obama in an editorial, claiming the lawsuits were "a dramatic stunt, full of indignation but built on air". Insisting it was a "clear partisan play", the *Times* harked back to a Mario Cuomo idea: "The real threat to religious liberty comes from the effort to impose one church's doctrine on everyone."[74]

This was too much for the left-leaning (non-Catholic) political columnist Michael Goodwin, who wrote in the *New York Post*, "Do the *New York Times*' attacks on the Catholic Church have any limits? Do the paper's editorial writers have any sense of decency?" The editorial "is a new low, disgraceful in its assault on religious freedom and the integrity of some of the finest people and institutions in America. Shame on the *New York Times*."[75]

When the U.S. Supreme Court ruled in favor of Obamacare in a 5–4 decision the next month, the USCCB stated that it would continue its fight in the courts to remedy "fatal flaws" in the 2,700-page legislation. It also pointed out that the bishops did not join "in seeking to have the whole law overturned"[76] but voiced opposition to "Congress' failure to exclude coverage for abortion; its failure to provide conscience protections; and its refusal to allow immigrant workers to buy coverage in the new insurance exchanges to be established under Obamacare even using their own money".[77]

In the midst of the 2012 Obamacare battle, the major political parties held their national conventions. The Democrats renominated President Obama, and the Republicans chose former Massachusetts governor Mitt Romney. After it became public that Dolan was to deliver a closing prayer at the Republican Convention in Tampa, Florida, there were accusations that he was a shill for the GOP. The archdiocesan Communications Department told the media that "Cardinal Dolan is going to pray, not to engage in partisan politics. He made it clear when he accepted the invitation that he would accept an invitation from the Democratic National Committee to offer a prayer at their convention should they ask."[78]

Catholic Vice President Joe Biden and other Democratic leaders were fearful that the HHS mandate suits and Obama's recent endorsement of gay marriage would drive into the arms of the GOP many older and blue-collar Catholic Democrats in key Midwestern swing states. And so the DNC took Dolan up on his offer and invited him to give a closing prayer at their convention in Charlotte, North Carolina. To even things out, however, the DNC also slated as a speaker Sister Simone Campbell, executive director of the liberal lobbying group Network, which claims to be Catholic but enthusiastically supports Obamacare.

At the GOP convention in the last week of August, Dolan prayed for "the sacred and inalienable gift of life" and added, "We ask your benediction upon those to be born, and on those who are about to see you at the end of life." Alluding to marriage, he said, "May we know the truth of your creation, respecting the laws of nature and nature's God, and not seek to replace it with idols of our own making."[79]

At the Democratic gathering the following week, Dolan's invocation had a slightly different tone. He asked for God's "benediction on those waiting to be born, that they be welcomed and protected". About marriage, he said, "Show us anew that happiness is found only in respecting the laws of nature and of nature's God. Empower us with your grace so that we might resist the temptation to replace the moral law with idols of our own making, or to remake those institutions you have given us for nurturing of life and community."[80]

Meanwhile, Dolan found himself caught up in a political slugfest when it was announced in August that both Obama and Romney had been invited as keynote speakers at the annual Al Smith Dinner to be held at the Waldorf-Astoria Hotel on Thursday, October 18, 2012. The cardinal received a slew of angry letters and e-mails from Catholics and other Christians objecting to his decision to invite a pro-abortion president who supported gay marriage and was at that very time challenging religious liberty.

Of course, Obama had been invited by Cardinal Egan to speak at the dinner four years earlier, as was his opponent, John McCain. The rule observed over the years is that it is permissible to invite non-Catholics who might be pro-abortion to speak at this charitable fund-raiser. It is not a political gathering, but rather an evening to put aside political differences and to have a few laughs. Cardinal Cooke invited Jimmy Carter in 1976 and 1980 and, in the O'Connor years, Democratic presidential nominee Michael Dukakis spoke in 1988, as did Vice President Al Gore in 2000.

Dolan wrote on his blog that he invited the presidential contenders to be civil. "If I only sat down with people who agreed with me, and I with them, or with those who were saints, I'd be taking all my meals alone."[81] He also explained that "an invitation to the Al Smith Dinner is not an award, or the provision of a platform to expound views at odds with the Church". The dinner is "an occasion of conversation", an "evening of friendship, civility, and patriotism, to help those in need, not to endorse either candidate".[82]

At the dinner, which raised $5 million for thirteen charities, Obama referred to his poor performance in the first presidential debate, saying, "It turns out that millions of Americans focused in on the second debate who didn't focus in on the first debate, and I happen to be one of them."

Romney, who had been caricatured by the media as a regal rich guy, made fun of the formal white tie and tails he was required to wear for the occasion, saying, "A campaign can require a lot of wardrobe changes—blue jeans in the morning perhaps, suits for a lunch fundraiser, sport coat for dinner, but it's nice to finally relax and to wear what Ann and I wear around the house."[83]

Dolan, in his remarks, described the first Catholic presidential candidate, New York Governor Alfred E. Smith, as a man who had "a tear in his Irish eye for what we call the 'uns' of the world—the unemployed, the uninsured. The unwanted. The unwed mothers. The innocent fragile unborn baby in the womb. The undocumented. The unhoused. The unhealthy. The undereducated." He stressed that religious liberty is the core value of our nation but that government must have a role. "Government, Al Smith believed, should be on the side of these 'uns.'"[84]

Electing a New Pope

On Monday, February 11, 2013, the world awakened to the news that eighty-five-year-old Pope Benedict XVI had decided to resign at the end of the month. He was the first pope to resign the office since Gregory XII in 1415. A conclave to elect a new pontiff was scheduled to commence in early March.

Cardinal Dolan learned of the decision in a very early phone call from his communications chief, Joseph Zwilling. "Sorry to disturb you," Zwilling said, "but I thought you should know that there are rumors that Pope Benedict has just announced his resignation." A skeptical Dolan replied, "Go get a Bloody Mary and go back to bed." Minutes later Zwilling called back and said, "It's been confirmed the Holy Father has resigned."[85]

On that hectic day, between numerous television appearances to discuss the pope's decision, Dolan managed to keep his appointments to dedicate a chapel in Rockland County and to lead a Bronx prayer meeting.

In a press statement, Dolan said, "The occasion of his resignation stands as an important moment in our lives as citizens of the world. Our experience impels us to thank God for the gift of Pope Benedict. Our hope impels us to pray that the College of Cardinals, under the inspiration of the Holy Spirit, choose a worthy successor to meet the challenges present in today's world."[86]

During a press appearance, when asked if he would be *papabile*—a possible papal candidate—Dolan replied, "I'll tell them they have the wrong guy. Don't bet your lunch money on that one. Bet on the Mets".[87]

Most Vatican watchers, meanwhile, considered it unlikely that the College of Cardinals would elect anyone from the United States. That's because many European and South American clerics are not all that fond of Americans, whom they perceive as upstarts on the international stage.

Before departing for the conclave in Rome on Tuesday, February 26, Dolan described the kind of person he believed should occupy the Chair of St. Peter: "Somebody who just seems to radiate the love, the tenderness, the mercy, the truth of Jesus". He added, "In my recent memory, the Holy Spirit's not let us down, because popes with whom we've been blessed have been a great icon of Jesus Christ, and I'm confident that the next one will be as well."[88]

At a morning Mass for Catholic Center staff members the day he caught his plane to Rome, he said that the conclave should also give cardinals an opportunity to reflect and to repent. "All you got to do is listen to the radio, watch TV or read the newspapers to find out how much we need contrition, repentance, conversion of heart. We are all conscious of the old Latin saying 'Ecclesia semper reformanda,' the Church is always in need of reform, always."[89]

As Dolan was flying across the Atlantic, the buzz in Rome was growing that the archbishop of New York was indeed papabile.

A senior Vatican reporter, Sandro Magister of *L'Espresso* magazine, predicted that Dolan would get "quite a few votes" on the first ballot and might just break the hold of the "feudal lords of the Roman curia".[90]

The buzz grew louder in the Italian newspapers after the eighty-two-year-old Cardinal Camillo Ruini—who was prevented by age from participating in the conclave—said Dolan would be a "dream" candidate.

The daily paper *La Repubblica* called Dolan a "shadow candidate" who could be an alternative if the conclave was deadlocked and reported that Cardinal Tarcisio Bertone, the Vatican secretary of state, was "quietly working behind the scenes lobbying others to push for Dolan".[91]

Meanwhile, Dolan tried to play down all the buzz, saying, "You know, listen, all the cardinals are really embarrassed to talk about that, and we'd be uncomfortable about it, so I'll leave it at that."[92]

When Matt Lauer, the host of NBC's *Today* show, asked Dolan if he would vote for himself, he answered: "No. Crazy people cannot enter the conclave."

Two days before the conclave began, on the fourth Sunday of Lent, which is known as Laetare (Rejoice) Sunday, all the cardinals said Mass at their titular churches in Rome. In his homily delivered at Our Lady of Guadalupe in Monte Mario, Dolan tried to change the subject, telling the parishioners, "What I like about being here is that I do not stand before you as a bishop or as a cardinal but as a priest sustained by your prayers. I will take your prayers with me into the conclave."[93]

The debate over Dolan continued in the press. Some argued that his outgoing, friendly style, his experiences in three dioceses, and his knowledge of Rome from his NAC days, were all pluses. Others claimed that he lacked gravitas and pointed out that he was not a theologian and had not mastered Italian or Latin.

Robert Royal, President of the Faith and Reason Institute, writing in Rome for the *Catholic Thing* during the conclave, gave this assessment:

> Dolan has multiple weaknesses as a papal candidate. He really speaks no languages other than English, and by default, Italian is the lingua franca in the Vatican. That lack alone would hamper him in carrying out the administrative reform and close supervision of the Curia everyone agrees the next pope must undertake.
>
> He's of course a charming and bighearted man, but I myself am not quite sure that the worldwide gathering of cardinals is ready for that much charm and that large a heart. Also, his shtick, to employ a technical theological term, is better suited to Manhattan and the surrounding boroughs than it is to the Roman Urbs, to say nothing of audiences *in partibus infidelium* to use a popular expression.[94]

On the morning of Monday, March 12, 2013, Cardinal Timothy Dolan boarded a bus that took him and his fellow American cardinals from the Domus Sanctae Marthae—a hotel within the walls of the Vatican built at John Paul's direction to house electors during a conclave—to the Sistine Chapel. "Our cell phones and computers were taken. Our bags were X-rayed", Dolan reported. "Yes, confidentiality and security were taken seriously."[95] The shutters in the assigned rooms were also locked to prevent any outside communication.

The next day Dolan processed with 115 confreres to the Sistine Chapel and took his oath. Then the master of ceremonies announced, "*Extra omnes*" (Everyone out), the doors of the chapel were locked, and the conclave began.

Cardinal Jorge Bergoglio, Archbishop of Buenos Aires, was elected pope on the second day of the conclave, March 13, on the fifth ballot.

"After the final ballot had been counted," Dolan wrote, "everything moved very quickly. When Cardinal Bergoglio said 'accetto'—that is, 'I accept'—we once again broke into applause. When asked, 'By what name will you be called?' he told us he was taking the name Francis, immediately adding, 'I choose the name Francis in honor of St. Francis of Assisi,' a beautifully inspired choice."[96]

As to whether any votes were cast for him in the rounds of balloting, Dolan gave this cagy answer: "Of course, everyone wants to know who came in second place. It's a natural curiosity, and I'm grateful people are so interested in the whole process. Obviously there *were* other candidates, or it wouldn't have taken more than one ballot to elect the pope. But as you know, I'm unable to say anything about that."[97]

In a statement to the American people on Francis' election, Dolan said, "The bishops of the United States thank God for the guidance of the Holy Spirit and the inspired choice of the College of Cardinals. With joy in our hearts, we declare 'Ad multos annos!' (For many years!)"[98]

Back to the Wars

Meanwhile, in the United States, the health-care battle continued.

The Department of Health and Human Services' final rule on the birth-control mandate, issued on June 28, 2013, did not change anything. In categorizing religious institutions, it still distinguished between houses of worship, which were exempt from the mandate, and ministries of service, which were not.

Speaking for the USCCB, Cardinal Dolan said that a preliminary review of the 110-page document "has not discovered any new changes that eliminate the need to continue defending our rights in Congress and the courts".[99] He did express gratitude for the five-month extension granted to review further and respond before huge fines would be levied for noncompliance.

During the disastrous rollout of Obamacare in the fall of 2013, Dolan made overtures to the White House offering to be helpful if the president would give religious institutions mandate exemptions—at least until the courts ruled—such as those given to numerous other employers. Dolan told the administration, "Look, you're in big trouble. We can be on your side here and philosophically at least arguing for more comprehensive health care."[100] Dolan's offer fell on deaf ears.

Dolan scored his first major victory in the courts in December—on the eve of the mandate's enforcement—when Judge Brian Cogan of the United States Eastern District Court in New York ruled in *The Roman Catholic Archdiocese of New York v. Kathleen Sebelius* that the mandate violated the First Amendment and the Religious Freedom Restoration Act. He issued a permanent injunction halting implementation.

Cogan was the first judge to rule that the Obamacare mandate was a significant burden on the free practice of one's religion. The mandate, Cogan declared, "directly compels plaintiffs, through the threat of onerous penalties, to undertake actions that their religion forbids.... There is no way the court can, or should, determine that a coerced violation of conscience is of insufficient quantum to merit constitutional protection." He added, "It is not the court's role to say that plaintiffs are wrong about their religious beliefs."[101]

In a statement released by the archdiocese, Communications Director Joseph Zwilling said the Church in New York "welcomes and applauds Judge Brian Cogan's thoughtful decision and order that holds that so-called non-exempt religious agencies have religious freedom rights.... The court has correctly cut through the artificial construct which essentially made faith-based organizations other than churches and other houses of worship second class citizens with second class First Amendment protections."[102]

Dolan in the Hothouse of New York

Like all his predecessors, Dolan has to speak out on public issues and controversies and remind New York's political class—particularly its Catholic members—and the public of the teachings of the Church. In August 2010, for instance, he condemned a rash of racially motivated attacks on Hispanics in heavily Catholic Richmond County (Staten Island).

Over several months, a neighborhood populated by Mexican immigrants had been the target of over a dozen attacks. As the *New York Times* reported, "the attacks underscored long-simmering tensions between Hispanic immigrants and blacks."[103] Parishioners on Staten Island were reminded by Dolan that "God is our father. He wants us all to be his children. He wants to gather us together in the unity of the Kingdom."[104]

That same month he offered to serve as a mediator in the mosque controversy in lower Manhattan. Many New Yorkers, particularly the families of victims of the terrorist attack on the World Trade Center, were angered over plans to build a thirteen-story Islamic center and mosque two blocks from Ground Zero.

The city became polarized over the issue. Proponents—including Mayor Bloomberg and President Obama—claimed that it was a matter of religious liberty and that construction should proceed. Opponents, on the other hand, argued that it was inappropriate and an insult to those who died on 9/11, given that all the hijackers had been Muslim.

After a meeting at Covenant House, the cardinal told the press that he prayed for a compromise on the mosque question. The *New York Times* reported that though "he had no strong feelings about the project, he might support finding a new location for the center".[105]

He reminded the media that in 1993, after listening to the protests of Jewish leaders, Pope John Paul II had ordered nuns to find a new location for a convent they had been planning to build near Auschwitz, the former Nazi death camp in Poland. "[John Paul] was the one who said 'Let's keep the idea, and maybe move the address.' It worked there; might work here."[106]

Later in the day, while defending the religious liberty of Muslims, he told WCBS radio, "Those who wonder about the wisdom of the situation of the mosque, near such a wounded site, ask what I think are some legitimate questions that I think deserve attention."[107]

Dolan's offer fell on deaf ears. The owners of the parcel did, however, slow down the project. As a compromise, the new Islamic center would occupy four thousand square feet of renovated space in the old building on the site. It was opened to the public in September 2011 with an exhibit containing 160 portraits of immigrant children of various ethnicities. The lower level was carpeted as a prayer room. In April 2014 Sharif El-Gamal, the center's developer, announced that the building would be demolished and in its place a three-story museum of Islamic culture would be built.

On November 2, 2010, Andrew M. Cuomo, son of Mario M. Cuomo, was elected New York's fifty-sixth governor. Like his father, Andrew is a baptized Catholic who graduated from a Catholic grammar school, high school, and college and is to the far left on many issues that concern Catholics. But unlike his father, Andrew has not attempted to put a Catholic philosophical veneer on his positions. Instead, his convictions appear to be based on polls and on what he believes will serve him best in his wish to occupy 1600 Pennsylvania Avenue.

Cuomo's approach to governing has led to clashes with the archbishop of New York of an intensity that has not been seen since Cardinal O'Connor tangled with the senior Cuomo in the 1980s. Since the days when O'Connor bested Mario in the public square on social issues, New York's political, religious, and social structures have changed significantly, leaving Dolan with new challenges never contemplated by O'Connor or, for that matter, Mario Cuomo.

After Andrew Cuomo took office in January 2011, his first assault on the Catholic Church was against her teaching that marriage is between a man and a woman. He was embarrassed, he said, that his state had been "surpassed by many ... countries which have legalized same-sex marriage including the Netherlands, Belgium, Spain, Canada, South Africa, Norway, Sweden and Portugal; as well as by many states." "Marriage equality", he declared, "is a question of principle, and the state shouldn't discriminate against same-sex couples who wish to get married." He promised to "fight to make sure all couples have equal marriage rights under the law".[108]

Dolan told the authors of this book that, in a meeting with the governor, Cuomo was "pretty blunt" with him. The governor said, "I will fight for gay marriage and I know you're going to be at my throat, as you should be."[109]

The governor played classic political hardball, reassuring several wavering Republican state senators—sadly, all baptized Catholics—with promises of appointments if voters should turn them out of office.

Cuomo won over the GOP state senate leader Dean Skelos, who had previously promised Cardinal Dolan that he would never permit the same-sex-marriage bill to make it to the floor of the upper chamber. According to Dolan, "What happened is factually we were assured it was not going to go anywhere by our [Republican] friends. Skelos said, 'You don't have to worry about it, this is not going to go anywhere.' "[110]

But Skelos broke his word and permitted a roll call, knowing the bill would pass. Skelos' rationale that the days of bottling up bills are over was absurd. Every year, at least 90 percent of all legislation introduced is bottled up and dies in committee *by design.*

After Cuomo signed the bill into law amidst ruffles and flourishes, the cardinal admitted in an interview that he was "betrayed" by members of the state senate who had given him their word. "I think we were a little too trusting of the political process", he said.[111] "We got a little stung, and it could be as much our fault as anyone else's."[112] He added, "We would have probably been a lot more vigilant had I not had those assurances."[113]

The rookie archbishop (he had been in office less than two years) did not realize that when dealing with Albany legislators of whichever political party, one cannot just take them at their word and go home. One must constantly stay in touch with them over issues that matter and maintain pressure at all times.

While Dolan claimed that the Church and her leaders throughout New York "were pretty aggressive" and that he "was rather proud of my fellow bishops",[114] many Catholic activists hold that the Church failed to organize the faithful in parishes to make their views known to wavering legislators—particularly ones in upstate districts. The faithful in those economically depressed rust-belt cities tend to be older practicing Catholics who subscribe to traditional Judeo-Christian principles, live out those beliefs in their daily lives, and expect the same of public officials. Their beliefs transcend economic issues. And if those Catholics had been organized to come out in force to make their views known, the three Catholic legislators who provided the margin of victory for the bill might have thought twice before casting their yea votes.

Summing up the gay-marriage battle in an interview with the authors, Dolan said, "Number one, I believe Cuomo and the others said, 'These bishops can huff and puff all they want but when push comes to shove, their people are not going to listen to them, and even if they do listen and oppose it, this isn't going to direct their vote.' Second, there's the realization that in some ways Catholics are political eunuchs, and we have no one to blame but ourselves."[115]

Dolan was upholding the Church's teaching in the *Catechism* that "homosexual acts are intrinsically disordered.... They are contrary to the natural law.... Under no circumstances can they be approved."[116] But he also adheres to Church teaching that homosexuals "must be accepted with respect, compassion, and sensitivity" and that "every sign of unjust discrimination in their regard should be avoided."[117]

His approach to the subject was evident in an interview he granted to the ABC show *This Week* on Easter, 2013. He stressed that marriage was "one man, one woman, forever, to bring about new life", and he defended that belief. He went on to tell his host, George Stephanopoulos, however, that "we've got to do better to see that our defense of marriage is not reduced to an attack on gay people. And I admit, we haven't been too good at this. We try our darnedest to make sure we're not anti-anybody."[118]

When asked what he would say to homosexuals who feel excluded from the Church, Dolan answered, "Well, the first thing I'd say is: I love you, too. And God loves you. And you are made in God's image and likeness. And—and we—we want your happiness. But—and you're entitled to friendship. But we also know that God told us that the way to happiness, that—especially when it comes to sexual love— that is intended only for a man and a woman in marriage, where children can come about naturally."[119]

A year later when asked on *Meet the Press* if he was uncomfortable with civil unions for homosexual couples, Dolan answered that he was and went on to say, "I don't think—marriage, between one man and one woman forever leading to life and love, that's not something that's just a religious, sacramental concern. You bet it is that, and that's how God has elevated it, to making [it] a sacrament. But it's also the building block of society and culture. So it belongs to culture. And if we water down that sacred meaning of marriage in any way, I worry that not only the church would suffer, I worry that culture and society would."[120]

Dolan's answer to a follow-up question did, however, raise the eyebrows of many Catholics:

Question: Michael Sam, from your home state, the football player—revealed that he was gay, first in the NFL. And you saw the celebration from the President, the First Lady, and they were saying what a courageous step that was. How did you view it?

Answer: Good for him. I would have no sense of judgment on him. God bless you. Look, the same Bible that tells us, that teaches us well about the virtues of chastity and the virtue of fidelity and marriage, tells us not to judge people. So I would say, "Bravo."

Using the phrase "Good for him" and concluding with "Bravo" seemed to go too far.

When asked by the authors about his comments, Dolan admitted it was not his best moment. He said he was caught off guard and had never heard of the football player. He explained that he "would certainly eliminate the first and last lines and make the distinction that while we can never judge the interior disposition of a person's soul, we can judge the morality of acts".

The cardinal added, "It irritates the life out of me, [the media are] always saying we're hung up on sex, but they're the ones always asking [about] it."

In retrospect, Dolan said his answer should have been, "I don't know who that gentleman is. I would remind you of the *Catechism*'s distinction between homosexual acts and the state of homosexuality. Whoever he is, if he has same-sex attraction, he deserves dignity and respect, but we must still say that homosexual activity would be contrary to the divine plan."[121]

The cardinal was impelled to speak out on the subject when, in November 2013, a scheduled lecture at Cardinal Spellman High School in the Bronx by a priest from Courage, a Church ministry for gays, was suddenly canceled because of protests by the media and homosexual groups. Dolan believed that the complaints could not go unanswered because the cancellation was wrong. In a *Daily News* op-ed, he defended Courage, "which assists and supports people with same-sex attraction to live chaste lives":

> Imagine my surprise and disappointment when I learned of the cancellation of a talk by a retired priest of the archdiocese (a remarkably gentle and holy man, by the way), active in Courage, that was to be given, at their request, to parents of Catholic high school students, intended to help and support those parents whose children may sense a same-sex attraction. The reaction to the planned lecture at Cardinal Spellman High School is a shame—one that distorts the very meaning of "tolerance."
>
> It seems that no one can talk of virtue anymore without, at the very least, being labeled out of touch with reality, and in this case, accused of far worse—spreading hatred....
>
> One thing must be made clear. Courage is not against anyone or anything. Having been a supporter of Courage for many years, and now serving as chairman of its episcopal board, I know what it is unwaveringly for: for the person, for the faithful expression of God's love and mercy, for helping people who are seeking Jesus to live full, happy, integrated lives. There is never an intention to impose on anyone, but always to extend an invitation to those who wish to respond.
>
> "Who am I to judge?" Pope Francis asks. How sad that those who claim to be in favor of tolerance have pre-judged and blocked a message of love and acceptance from being delivered, tarnishing the reputation of a splendid group and a school which has as one of its goals to help our youth live out their faith.[122]

With the federal courts knocking down state laws that had limited marriage to the union of one man and one woman, Dolan has made it clear that he disagrees with some bishops and theologians who have suggested that the Church give up her civil authority in performing marriages and preside only over the religious ceremony. "We would be capitulating to the secularists to say we'll take care of the religious side and you take care of the civil and cultural side."

Dolan argues that it's not good for the culture if the state dilutes marriage. "I try to say all the time, we're against anything that dilutes the sacred natural timeless meaning of marriage. We're against frivolous divorce. We're against cohabitation. We're against husband and wife who don't live in loving fidelity. We're against marriage of two people of the same sex. Anything that dilutes it, we're not for it.... We're not anti-gay, we're pro-marriage."[123]

The 2015 St. Patrick's Day Parade

Cardinal Dolan became embroiled in another homosexual-rights controversy when he agreed to serve as grand marshal of the 2015 St. Patrick's Day Parade. In itself, that news would be unremarkable, since Cardinals Egan and O'Connor had previously accepted the honor. But this time it was different because, at the NYC St. Patrick's Day Parade and Celebration press conference designating Dolan as figurehead, it was also announced that, after years of controversy concerning the exclusion of organized homosexual marchers, the committee had decided that one such "LGBT" group, Out@NBC Universal, would be given a place in the parade. (The parade is broadcast in New York by a local NBC affiliate.)

Cardinal Dolan said at the press conference, "I have no trouble with the decision at all. I think the decision is a wise one."[124] Dolan also told the press that "neither he nor his predecessors have ever told the St. Patrick's Day parade organizers who could or could not march."[125]

It is true that the head of the Church in New York is not ipso facto the head of either the Ancient Order of Hibernians, former organizers of the parade, or the current Parade and Celebration Committee. His predecessors have often taken strong positions, however—as described in earlier chapters—against past attempts to politicize the event. Cardinal O'Connor rejected demands for the inclusion of gay organizations, declaring in a sermon during the 1993 St. Patrick's Day Mass, "Neither respectability nor political correctness is worth one comma in the Apostles' Creed."

In addition, during the O'Connor years, the New York State Supreme Court declared that the parade was a "religious procession", and therefore its organizers were constitutionally protected from including any group that represented views in opposition to those of the Church.

Cardinal Egan told George Marlin shortly after the decision was announced that he not only disagreed with it, but had also declined to announce at the press conference the name of the grand marshal as he had done for many years. He also made it clear that no important decision was ever made by the organizers without consulting the archbishop of New York and that he would have strongly advised them to thank NBC for its years of service and to find another station to cover the parade on television.

Supporters on both sides of the issue were unhappy with the decision.

The president of the Catholic League for Religious and Civil Rights, Bill Donohue, contended that the parade organizers surrendered to outside pressure. "The political pressure", he said, "came from people like [Mayor] de Blasio, the economic pressure came from Guinness [Brewing]. The corporate Wall Street gang, they're all lined up with the gay-rights agenda."[126]

The spokeswoman for "Irish Queers", Emmaia Gelman, told the *Wall Street Journal* that "allowing the NBC group, which isn't affiliated with Irish heritage, to march demonstrates that parade organizers are more concerned with corporate connections than its relationship with the Irish community". She continued, "My interest in marching in the St. Patrick's Day Parade is to celebrate my identity and community as an Irish LGBT person."[127]

Overall, Cardinal Dolan received only faint praise from supporters of gay inclusion. In its coverage of the decision, the *New York Times* called the Church "hostile" and characterized the parade organizers' decision as a "retreat". It said of Dolan that he represents "changing attitudes in the hierarchy of the Roman Catholic Church"—a remark that only further confused practicing Catholics, particularly since the Magisterium had not changed.[128]

One week after the decision was made public, the Catholic League, which had marched in the parade for twenty years, announced that it would not participate any longer. Bill Donohue's reason for withdrawing: "I asked them to pledge that a pro-life Catholic group would also be permitted. I was told that a formal change in the rules had been approved and that a pro-life group would march. Now I am being told that the list of marching units is set and that no pro-life group will march

in next year's parade. Accordingly, I have decided to withdraw our participation."
He added: "My reasons for withdrawing from the parade have nothing to do with
Cardinal Dolan or with gays. It has to do with being betrayed by the Parade Committee. They not only told me one thing, and did another, they decided to include
a gay group that is neither Catholic or Irish while stiffing pro-life Catholics. This is
as stunning as it is indefensible."

Donohue also expressed the view of many Catholics who opposed the decisions
when he said in his statement "The goal of some in the Irish community is to neuter
the Catholic element in the St. Patrick's Day Parade. They want it to be an ethnic
celebration."[129]

With many Catholics calling on Dolan to step down as grand marshal, he wrote a
column in *Catholic New York* (September 18, 2014), explaining his decision to accept
the honor. Admitting that he had received "much fiery mail and public criticism",
he nevertheless reaffirmed that, the "archbishops of New York have never been 'in
charge' of the parade" and that he "did not make the decision". He added, "I did
not oppose the former policy; nor did I push, condone, or oppose the new one."

But, he concluded, "the committee's decision allows a group to publicize its
identity, not promote actions contrary to the values of the Church that are such
an essential part of Irish culture. I have been assured that the new group marching
is not promoting an agenda contrary to Church teaching, but simply identifying
themselves as 'Gay people of Irish ancestry....' If the Parade Committee allowed
a group to publicize its advocacy of any actions contrary to Church teaching, I'd
object.... In fact, the leaders of the Parade Committee tried to be admirably sensitive to Church teaching.... I found their sensitivity wise, and publicly said so. If in
doing do, I have shown an insensitivity to you [people who object] I apologize."

On Tuesday, March 17, 2015, even as Out@NBC Universal marched past St.
Patrick's Cathedral on Fifth Avenue carrying a banner that read, "Lesbian, Gay,
Bisexual, Transgender and Straight Ally Employees Alliance", protests continued
against the organizers of the parade. Leading political officials, including Mayor Bill
de Blasio, boycotted the event, because Irish gay marchers were excluded.

On a Fifth Avenue sidewalk, protestors held a fifty-foot banner that read, "Let
Irish Gays into Irish Parade" and "Boycott Homophobia". The city's Irish Queers
chapter complained that the inclusion of a corporate gay group "is actually an
exclusion for the wider community". In a statement, Irish Queers said that "the
demand has always been for Irish LGBTQ groups to march under banners that
say who we are without *shame*—not corporate groups marching behind an 'Out'
banner."[130]

When asked about the newcomers in the parade, Grand Marshal Timothy Cardinal Dolan said, "I'm glad everyone is welcome here. There's no distinction.
They're all welcome and I'm glad they are."[131]

Politics and More Politics

On the Albany front, Governor Cuomo continued to promote a radical agenda.
His next move was to propose legislation to expand abortion rights. In his 2013
State of the State Address, he pandered to the pro-abortion lobby by screaming at
the top of his lungs four times, "It's her body; it's her choice!"

For years, New York has been the Abortion Capital of the nation. It has had on the books since 1970 the nation's most liberal abortion statute. In fact, if *Roe v. Wade* were suddenly overturned, it would have no impact on the state of New York, short of a constitutional amendment banning abortion.

Figures released by New York City's health department in 2011 revealed that the number of abortions performed in the Big Apple the previous year was twice the national average. Forty-one percent of all pregnancies—about ninety thousand— were terminated.

The breakdown by minority groups is frightful. The abortion rate for African-Americans is 60 percent and for Hispanics 41 percent. The city's poorest borough, the Bronx, had the highest number of abortions, followed by Brooklyn, Queens, Manhattan, and Staten Island. An alarmed Reverend Ruben Diaz Sr., a state senator from the Bronx, warned a group of ministers that abortion is an attack on minorities: "They are killing black and Hispanic children."[132]

Cardinal Dolan refused simply to "shiver over these chilling statistics". In a press conference with prominent Jewish, African-American, and Hispanic religious leaders announcing the formation of a new outreach program for young women, Dolan said that for the first time since becoming archbishop he was "embarrassed to be a member of a cherished community I now ... call home".[133]

"We've been hearing for many years", the cardinal said, "from pro-choice supporters that abortion should be 'safe, legal and rare.' Well, if that's the goal, we've clearly abysmally failed—especially here in New York City."

Archbishop Dolan reaffirmed the pledge of his two predecessors, Cardinals O'Connor and Egan, "that any woman who is pregnant and in need can come to the Archdiocese for assistance". He also named a Pro-Life Commission for the archdiocese that included Father Joseph Koterski, Kathryn Jean Lopez, Sean Feiler, Michael and Maria Lewis, Annette Rein, and Mother Agnes Mary Donovan.[134]

Despite those gruesome statistics, Cuomo's legislation would, if enacted, make matters even worse. It would repeal the state's twenty-four-week limit and permit late-term abortions if the mother's health is in danger or if the fetus is deemed not viable.

"The mother's health" may sound like a reasonable criterion, but, according to Cuomo's legislation, the factors that could be considered in determining the state of a mother's health include age, emotional maturity, and economic and social status. Under these terms, an abortion would essentially be permissible at any time for almost any reason.

In addition, health-care practitioners who are not licensed physicians would be permitted to perform abortions. "This dangerous and extreme change", the New York Catholic Conference has observed, "clearly puts women's health at risk and mirrors a national abortion strategy to permit non-doctors to perform abortions due to the declining numbers of physicians willing to do so."[135]

The legislation would codify abortion as a "fundamental right of privacy"—a classification even the U.S. Supreme Court has rejected. Under this provision, New York could no longer enforce regulations requiring parental consent or at least notification, and it could not limit or abolish taxpayer-funded abortions.

New York's abortion law would also be reclassified. Instead of being part of the state's penal code, it would come under public-health laws.

The Catholic Conference has publicly stated that such a proposal is "unnecessary, extreme and dangerous" and would threaten the religious liberty of Catholic institutions. The limited conscience protection in the legislation is ambiguous. It does not offer protection for "institutional providers such as religious hospitals and other agencies that do not wish to be involved with abortion". There would be no "discrimination" against a woman's fundamental right to an abortion in the "provision of benefits, facilities, services or information". This could be interpreted to mean that state regulators could insist that state-licensed or state-funded health-care institutions make abortion procedures available.

Learning from his experience with Senator Skelos on same-sex marriage, Cardinal Dolan refused to take seriously Governor Cuomo's assurance, expressed to him in a private meeting, that "the women's rights bill is not going anywhere." ("I said to myself, I've heard that one before", Dolan told the authors.)

Blasting Cuomo's abortion-expansion plans, Dolan said, "I am hard pressed to think of a piece of legislation that is less needed or more harmful than this one.... It's as though, in [lawmakers'] minds, our state motto, 'Excelsior' [Ever upward], applies to the abortion rate."[136]

Promising "vociferous" and "rigorous" opposition, Dolan and his fellow bishops in the New York province empowered the state's Catholic Conference to fight against passage, which it did, working along with other pro-life groups. They succeeded in stalling the legislation in 2013, 2014, 2015, and 2016.

Dolan has learned that he will always have to be vigilant and will have to organize opposition every year, because Planned Parenthood and other groups never rests on *their* laurels. They are back year after year in the halls of the capitol in Albany pushing their radical agenda.

Dolan admitted that he "bristled a little" when Evangelical friends at a meeting "suggested that perhaps the Catholic Church and the bishops of New York were not aggressive enough". Dolan told them, "You know, let's talk frankly here. We don't need to be lectured on this issue when it comes to pro-life or defense of marriage. I'm happy for your company, but, admit it, you're pretty Johnny-come-lately. This all started decades ago when marriage was attacked because of easy divorce. And the whole pro-life stuff [started] decades ago [in response to] easy access to contraceptives and the acceptance of the contraceptive mentality. We were the only ones talking back then.

"You didn't provide much comfort to us on contraception. So let's be pretty blunt here.... We're grateful for your company and we need you more than ever.... But I don't think we need to be lectured on a lack of enthusiasm for this cause, because we have been rather enthusiastic about it for half a century and pretty much by ourselves."[137]

Cuomo made his next foray on Friday, January 17, 2014, on *The Capital Press Room*, an Albany radio talk show. He said the following about a large segment of New York voters: "Who are they? Are these extreme conservatives who are right-to-life, pro-assault-weapon, anti-gay? Is that who they are? Because if that's who they are and if they are the extreme conservatives, they have no place in the state of New York, because that's not who New Yorkers are."

In an unguarded moment Governor Cuomo stated publicly what many on the Left have been privately thinking for years: that pro-life and pro-traditional-marriage Americans are Ku Klux Klan–like bigots who should either shut up or get out.

Cuomo not only wrote off millions of New York Christians and Jews (among others) as unfit to be citizens; he also yanked the welcome mat from under half the nation's population, who, public-opinion polls indicate, oppose abortion and same-sex marriage. By claiming that people who disagree with his cultural views "have no place in the state of New York", Cuomo has joined those whom historian Richard Hofstadter described as "totalitarian liberals"—people who employ illiberal means to achieve so-called liberal reforms.

Cuomo's comment caused an uproar—not only in New York but across the nation. Many Catholics were outraged that they were spoken of in that way simply because they adhere to Church doctrine. And not a few Catholics were also surprised that the person who would be at the top of the list of those who "have no place in the state of New York", Cardinal Dolan himself, did not immediately respond.

After five days, Dolan finally broke his silence, saying that the governor's remarks were "unfortunate at best; inflammatory and outrageous at worst". Dolan added that the "extremists are really on the other side. The extremists are those who want to radically expand abortion, are not happy with the way things are, resist the constitutionally legal restraints that have been reasonably placed upon abortion."[138]

The Question of Communion

Meanwhile, although pro-lifers admired Dolan's toughness on abortion itself, they were leery of his position on giving Communion to pro-abortion Catholic politicians—for example, when they heard him say, at his first press conference after being named archbishop, that he preferred "trusting dialogue" instead of public confrontation.

When asked by the authors what precisely was his position on giving Communion to Catholic officials who publicly disagree with Church teachings, Dolan replied:

> Scandal is when the actions or words of a particular person make it easier for other people to sin.... Scandal is being given because prominent Catholics who are blatantly at odds with core Church teachings are still saying, "I'm a faithful Catholic, I'm within the fold, and there's nothing wrong with what I'm saying." That is scandal.
>
> Now, of course, whenever you deal with scandal you have the whole question of prudential judgment. What is the best way to handle it? I guess—I don't know if it's my Irish roots—you see, one of the things your gut would want to [do is] to take firm action and just say, "You should not approach Holy Communion." Actually, I mean, to say publicly: "You are radically at odds with the Church and it would be tough to justify saying you're still a faithful Catholic."
>
> So my gut might want to do that in certain circumstances. [But] my instincts would say ... it will be counterproductive.... Politicians used to dread [an] over-the-glasses stare from the occupant of [452 Madison Avenue]. Right now they welcome it. [I'd be] playing right into their hands.

Dolan cited the example of Leo Maher, who was the bishop of San Diego from 1969 to 1990. During a special election for a vacant California State Senate seat in

1989, Maher denied Holy Communion to the Democratic candidate, Lucy Killea, because, as Maher put it, her "media advertisements and statements advocating the 'pro-choice' abortion position in the public forum" were "in complete contradiction to the moral teaching of the Catholic Church".[139] As it turned out, Killea won the election in a heavily Republican district, and her victory was attributed in part to Maher's public rebuke.

Dolan was hoping to avoid the "Maher factor", but he admitted that a bishop must think "long and hard what to do here". He cited Cardinal Burke, whom he says he admires and loves, and other bishops whose judgment "calls for being very strong here, and God bless them—what an act of courage. [But] other bishops would say ... I agree that this person is very much on thin ice when it comes to Catholic allegiance, but prudential judgment would say—if we are dealing with scandal here—that the scandal of taking a very definitive action might outweigh the [original] scandal."

But whatever the decision about rebuking an individual, "Never should we generically stop speaking about it ... [saying] here is what the Church teaches. That's what I admire [about Cardinal] John O'Connor.... He made it very clear, heroically clear. He said, 'Look, politics is not my business; the integrity of the Catholic Church is. If I have a candidate who is telling you this is what the Church is teaching, Catholic or not, my job is to correct what he or she is saying.' I admire that immensely, and that was a turning point, I think, in the whole communications process."[140]

Dolan's position was tested when Vice President Joe Biden, who is pro-abortion and pro–gay marriage, attended the 10:15 A.M. Mass at St. Patrick's Cathedral on March 24, 2013—Palm Sunday.

When asked about that day by the authors, Dolan said, "First of all, I am grateful anyone comes to Mass." He pointed out that when dealing with the Obama White House, he felt "personally closer to the vice president.... We have our arguing, but I think he is sincere in his desire to help." Among other things, Biden had been the contact man who asked Dolan to give the closing prayer at the 2012 Democratic Convention.

Dolan did not talk directly with Biden or his staff before the Mass, but he passed on a message that Biden was welcome. Dolan told the authors that "the question of Holy Communion was not asked" and that he wasn't sure if Biden actually received Communion.[141] (Biden did receive Communion. Photographs reveal that he received the host from a priest standing next to Dolan at the sanctuary steps.)

The vice president's people, meanwhile, had made it clear that he wanted no acknowledgment or special seating. However, from the pulpit Dolan welcomed him and said, "You have a place in our thoughts and prayers." Afterward Biden stopped in at the residence and had coffee with the cardinal.[142]

When it comes to bishops dealing with issues in the public square, Dolan admitted that it "irks" him when "those on the Left say we should withhold the thunderbolts [but they then] applaud the famous Archbishop of New Orleans, [Joseph] Rummel, who excommunicated three Catholic segregationists [in 1962]. And the *New York Times* could not have had a bigger editorial applauding that. [Rummel was] a brave prophetic bishop, who used the full force of the Church to remind the Catholic politicians that she and he are completely out of the bounds of Catholic propriety. Alleluia—he should be made a Cardinal. [But] then if we dare to do it for the protection of unborn life in the womb, we are bigoted right-wing flakes, flame throwers."

Dolan adds that it is easy for bishops to address issues such as racism, poverty, nuclear weapons, and immigration. But "when you speak up on the hot-button issues—protection of marriage, protection of the baby in the womb—you expect scars from the very people who applaud you" on those other issues.[143]

Fighting for Catholic Schools

Dolan's next battle with Albany concerned help for the financially troubled Catholic school system.

For years, proponents of parochial and private schools have pushed for passage of an Education Investment Tax Credit, which would permit "individuals, with certain well-defined limits, to donate money for education and receive a tax credit for doing so". It is believed that such a credit would encourage more donations to help eliminate the operating deficits of Catholic schools, which educate 215,000 children throughout the state. Proponents were optimistic that the bill, which had the support of trade unions and business leaders, would finally be part of the 2014–2015 state budget.

Although Governor Cuomo, who was up for reelection in 2014, had promised Dolan that it was a done deal, the cardinal took nothing for granted and went on the offensive. In interviews and op-ed pieces, he promoted the tax credit as an essential element in the battle to save Catholic schools and to help parents who send their children to other nonpublic schools.

"Anything we can do to help education, to help our kids, we want to do it as vigorously as possible. And I don't know of a bill that does that better than the one that we've got now", Dolan said at a press conference held at Manhattan's Cathedral High School.[144]

His efforts included a trip to Albany in late March "for one last push before the state's April 1 budget deadline".[145] But even so, when Albany's smoke-filled rooms were cleared on Sunday, March 31, it was learned that the governor, who has huge executive authority over the budget process, had permitted the provision to be dropped.

In a *New York Post* op-ed piece titled "State Leaders Betray Catholics, Others on Education Tax Credits", Cardinal Dolan wrote that "assurances from state leaders that passage of the proposal was a 'no brainer' in fact turned out to be empty, and, once again, Catholic school kids get kicked to the curb along with children attending other faith-sponsored schools and even the other private and public schools that would have benefited". He added: "I get disappointed and frustrated—and, to be honest, angry—when the children in our Catholic schools are treated like second-class citizens again and again. State leaders missed a great opportunity to show their real commitment to the education of all students across New York. Sadly, once again, they've divided our kids into winners and losers."[146]

Dolan, however, refused to give up. Since the legislative session for 2014 would not close until the end of June, there was still a chance the bill could be passed in the final hours, when there is always a lot of horse-trading between legislative leaders and the governor. He even released a TV commercial in which he and a group of Catholic schoolchildren called on the governor to keep his word. "Governor Cuomo, don't let us down", the children chanted. In the TV spot, Dolan reminded the public that "when the state budget was done, we were left out" and added, "Now's the time to get it done."

The television commercial got through to the governor, who called Dolan several hours after the first airing and requested a meeting.

In that session, Dolan reported to the authors, Cuomo told him the TV commercial was effective and admitted that he had let the cardinal down. Dolan asked him why the tax credit had not been added to the budget, "which the governor had assured us would be ... the easy, no-brainer way to do it".

Cuomo told Dolan that there was more opposition than he had expected and that "the entrenched opposition of the Speaker [Democrat Sheldon Silver] and the threats of the teachers' union had intimidated a good number of people."

Cuomo repeated that he had let Dolan down and suggested that they try again next year. He also suggested that Dolan "scale down the money you would settle for".[147]

In a last-ditch effort, a letter signed by all the bishops of New York was distributed after every Mass throughout the state on the weekend of June 14, 2014, and every student in parochial school was given a copy to take home to his parents. The statement reminded the faithful of Cuomo's unfulfilled assurances and added:

> As the legislative session ends in Albany this coming week, we pray that Governor Cuomo won't let us down. We ask that you join us in that prayer. Pray that Governor Cuomo will put children ahead of politics and fight for the Education Investment Tax Credit.
>
> We also ask that you contact him immediately with the same message. You can send a message to the governor through the website of the New York State Catholic Conference.
>
> Time is short. Please act today. God bless you.

On Friday, June 20, the New York State Legislature adjourned for the year, having failed to act on the tax-credit legislation. An op-ed by Dolan was published the next day in the *New York Post* titled "The Abandoned Kids: State Leaders' Broken Vows". The cardinal reminded the public that both Cuomo and Senate Leader Dean Skelos had assured him that passage would be a "no-brainer". After pointing out that the only public opposition came from the public-school teachers' union and Assembly Speaker Sheldon Silver, he took aim at Albany's pols:

> The hundreds of thousands of families for whom we have been advocating are right to be disappointed. I know I am.
>
> I am frustrated because the governor and state legislators have bypassed multiple opportunities to help these families.
>
> Yet they stayed up all night in Albany talking about marijuana—but not a word about supporting our kids by finally passing the EITC.
>
> The EITC would have been a lifeline to our schools, so the painful exercise of closing could be avoided. (It seems that the only time a politician takes notice of our schools is when they are trying to get a child into one of our schools, or when there

are not enough parents able to pay tuition and a school has to close—then there is plenty of handwringing and grandstanding by political leaders about the "mean bishop" closing a school!)

Rest assured, this issue will be kept front and center by me and my brother bishops, along with the broad coalition of supporters for the EITC and the children it would help.

We're not giving up.[148]

Dolan continued the fight for the tax credit in 2015. He was more confident that the initiative would finally be approved because the governor proposed $100 million in tax benefits for the initiative in his 2015–2016 budget and linked it to the Dream Act Bill that would give college tuition subsidies to undocumented immigrants—a proposal that was popular with assembly Democrats.

In a March 20, 2015, *New York Post* op-ed piece, Dolan complimented Albany politicians "on what appears to be a united, promising, hopeful and significant effort: improving educational opportunities for New York's school kids". He observed that the state senate had already approved the Education Investment Tax Credit and that an assembly version cosponsored by the new speaker, Carl Heastie, had majority support.

The cardinal's optimism, however, was short-lived. Succumbing to political pressure during budget negotiations in late March, Governor Cuomo yanked the tax credit from the proposed state budget.

Dolan stated publicly that Cuomo had told him "the best way to pass the credit was to include it in the state budget".[149] The cardinal expressed "discouragement" and told the *New York Post*, "It's time for a vote.... Please it's time for some action. This has gone on for too long."[150]

Though he made it clear that he was "in the business of hope" and that he still had "enough trust in people who I firmly believe put the education of our kids first", Dolan added, "When I keep getting disappointed like this, I can see why people get cynical.... If this doesn't work out, there's a lot of blame to go around."[151]

With the tax credit out of the budget, lawmakers would have to vote on a stand-alone bill. In the past this had been the death knell for the tax credit because, as the cardinal informed the *Post*, assembly Democrats who are supported by teachers' unions "lack sensitivity" toward students who attend parochial schools.[152]

In March of 2015, Cardinal Dolan announced the creation of a political action committee called Catholics Count, an initiative to promote issues such as the tax credit and to organize Catholics to exercise influence on government officials. "In essence," William McGurn wrote in a *Post* op-ed, "the new PAC is an attempt to restore sanity to education policy by rewarding success and punishing failure in a state capital that does just the opposite."[153]

One of the PAC supporters, Robert Flanigan, a founder of Educate LLC, which serves as a technology consulate to schools, said that the PAC will permit the Catholic Church to "have a voice in Albany commensurate with our numbers and with the contributions our church makes to our state and our communities. Especially in education."[154]

One of the Cardinal's educational initiatives that seemed successful, concerned New York City's pre-K program that commenced in September 2014. The city agreed to pay Catholic schools in the archdiocese to provide prekindergarten classes for approximately three thousand students. But there was a price for the infusion of municipal cash: All religious symbols had to be removed from the pre-K classrooms, and there could be no Catholic instruction. Some critics wondered if accepting the restrictions defeated the purpose of Catholic education.

Where Angels Fear to Tread

On July 17, 2014, New York City police officers approached Eric Garner, a six-foot, three-inch African-American on Bay Street in the Tomkinsville part of Staten Island. Garner, who was selling illegal "loosie" cigarettes that were untaxed, told the officers, "Get away [garbled] for what? Every time you see me, you want to mess with me. I'm tired of it. It stops today. Why would you...? Everyone standing here will tell you I did nothing. I did not sell nothing. Because every time you see me, you want to harass me. You want to stop me [garbled] selling cigarettes. I'm minding my business, officer, I minding my business. Please just leave me alone. I told you last time, please just leave me alone."[155]

When Officer Daniel Pantaleo tried to handcuff him, Garner told him, "Don't touch me please." The cop proceeded to chokehold Garner and brought him to the ground facedown. Garner said, "I can't breathe."[156] As he lay motionless on the ground, an ambulance was called, but while he was being transported to Richmond University Medical Center, Garner suffered a heart attack and was pronounced dead on arrival by hospital officials.

The New York City Medical Examiner's Office determined that Garner's death was the result of his asthma, obesity, and heart disease and the "compression of neck, compression of chest and prone positioning during physical restraint by police". Mr. Garner's death was ruled a homicide.[157]

A protest led in Staten Island by the Reverend Al Sharpton was held on July 19, and another was planned for August 23. On August 19, Staten Island District Attorney Dan Donovan announced that the Pantaleo case would go before a grand jury, and the next day Mayor de Blasio, almost certainly for political reasons, asked Cardinal Dolan to host a meeting with him, the police commissioner, and religious leaders before the August 23 protest in hopes of healing the community-wide rift and avoiding violence.

Cardinal Dolan agreed to help, but instead of holding the meeting at his offices at 1011 First Avenue, he invited attendees to his residence behind St. Patrick's Cathedral.

To visit the residence at 452 Madison Avenue is considered a great honor, and the archbishops of New York have used it judiciously. For instance, in 1984, when President Reagan was running for reelection, he paid a courtesy call at the residence, and when he left, Cardinal O'Connor walked out with him to the front steps for a press conference and photo opportunity. When the Democratic presidential nominee, Walter Mondale, called on O'Connor, the meeting was held at the 1011 First Avenue Catholic Center offices. The cardinal bid farewell to Mondale at the nineteenth-floor elevator bank. No photo-op, no happy chatter with the press. Having those meetings at the different venues sent a strong message to the general public.

The unintended consequence of having the August 20 meeting at the residence was the elevation in the public's eyes of the status and respectability of one invitee—Al Sharpton. He made sure he had center stage at the press conference on the steps of the residence with the cardinal looking on. Sharpton, who came to fame during the infamous Tawana Brawley case and had never been welcomed into the residence by Cardinals O'Connor and Egan, now publicly boasted after the meeting, "When I was at the Cardinal's residence...." From the hustler who had exploited Miss Brawley, Sharpton had become a senior sage and peacemaker, in his own mind anyway.

Whether the meeting had an impact on the behavior of the protestors in Staten Island that Saturday is unknown. Nevertheless, there were no violent incidents reported.

The city cooled down, but the flames were reignited on December 3, when the grand jury announced that no indictment would be brought against Officer Pantaleo.

Protests occurred in New York and around the country. Hundreds were arrested in New York for blocking traffic and disrupting retail stores on December 3 and 4.

Tensions between the police union, the mayor, and the police commissioner intensified, and the bombastic rhetoric and fingerpointing appeared to be getting out of hand. So Cardinal Dolan wrote an op-ed piece for the *Daily News* titled, "Demonizing NYPD or City's Leaders Won't Unite New York". The cardinal contended that "when our understandable anger leads us to become inflammatory and accusatory", it distracts from the "renowned character" of New Yorkers. He added that "it's only pouring kerosene on the fire when some upset leaders caricature our dedicated police officers as bigots.... It is equally unfair and counterproductive to dismiss our mayor and other leaders as enemies of the police."[158]

Just as the city was quieting down during the approaching Christmas holidays, tragedy struck again on Saturday, December 20. Ismaaiyl Abdullah Brinsley, a twenty-eight-year old African-American, allegedly seeking revenge for the Eric Garner death, murdered two on-duty police officers in the Bedford-Stuyvesant section of Brooklyn. Fleeing the scene, Brinsley committed suicide at a nearby subway station.

Hoping to calm the city, Dolan once again took a public role. At a Mass at St. Patrick's on the Sunday after the murders (attended by Mayor de Blasio, Police Commissioner Bratton, and NYPD Chief James O'Neill), His Eminence called the murders of Officers Rafael Ramos and Wenjian Liu "brutal and irrational".

> As we mourn the brutal and irrational execution of two young officers ... as we tear up thinking about their heartbroken families, as we are in solidarity with our police officers, who themselves experienced a death in the family, and yes, as we worry about a city tempted to tension and division, good news this morning might seem distant, difficult, even somewhat discreet. Here we are anticipating the joy of Christmas, and we feel like we're nearer to Good Friday.

Then Dolan looked directly at Bratton and O'Neill and said, "Would you tell your officers that God's people gathered at St. Patrick's Cathedral this morning, thundered with prayer, with and for them?" He received a standing ovation. He also asked the officials that they tell members of the NYPD "that we love them very much, we mourn with them, we need them, we respect them and we're proud of them and we thank them".[159]

Dolan and Archdiocesan Finances

When Timothy Dolan took possession of the archdiocese in April 2009, the operating budget was balanced and there were no outstanding debts, and during his predecessor's tenure there had not been one known case of sexual abuse of a minor by an archdiocesan priest. Nevertheless, Dolan faced plenty of challenges: an aging priesthood, declining vocations, and less money in the collection baskets, a problem exacerbated by the 2008 financial and economic meltdown.

Dolan made it a priority to reach out to his priests in a series of formal and informal meetings. He initiated summer "town meetings" and "retreat pilgrimages" with groups of priests in Assisi, Rome, Mexico, and the Holy Land. He also reinstated the rule that a priest's term as pastor would be six years and could be renewed for another six years. No priest would serve more than twelve years as the pastor of a particular parish, and no priest over the age of eighty could serve as a parish administrator.

While the Priests' Council approved this measure by a 2–1 majority, Dolan relates that, on many occasions, priests came to him complaining about an impending move to a new parish and seeking an exception. He turned them all down. When told that Cardinal O'Connor would have listened to their reasoning and probably not have moved them, Dolan replied, "I think it is a wise policy, and, no, I can't make exceptions."

The cardinal finalized a joint operating agreement with the Brooklyn and Rockville Centre Dioceses to create a single program for the training of seminarians. This was to address the expenses at the major seminary at Dunwoodie as well as problems in the education and the priestly formation of seminarians. The agreement, which had been in negotiation during the Egan administration, provided that after completing their undergraduate studies, seminarians from all three dioceses would reside at Dunwoodie for advanced training and degrees in theology.

Bishop Gerald Walsh, who had been serving as rector of Dunwoodie, stepped down in June 2012 and was succeeded by Monsignor Peter Vaccari of Brooklyn on July 1, the beginning of the new academic year. Walsh would later serve briefly as vicar-general of the archdiocese.

Meanwhile, the Cathedral Seminary Residence program for undergraduates contemplating the priesthood was to be located at the Brooklyn Diocese's Immaculate Conception Center in Douglaston, Queens. This program was established in 2012 with Monsignor Robert Thelen as the first rector of the residence, which houses about eighty students from the three dioceses. Its purpose, the rector explained, is to be a college residence "developing Christ in the young man". The men, he emphasized, "are encouraged to live among their peers, with special emphasis on prayer and communal living as they discern whether God is calling them to lives of service as priests".[160]

Turning to the financing of the parochial-school system, which was hard hit by the Great Recession, Dolan concluded that changes had to be made, which would include closing and consolidating schools and cutting back on subsidies. In interviews with the authors, Dolan pointed out that the root of the problem was the Inter-Parochial Fund (IPF) created by Cardinal Cooke, which dispensed archdiocesan money to poor parochial schools. He explained that Cardinal Egan did an excellent job in economizing, but there was still more that had to be done.

In Dolan's first year at the helm, the IPF dispensed $48 million. But, after the financial meltdown, the archdiocese's operating budget was, once again, running in the red, so Dolan concluded, "We can't give away that kind of money."

Another reason for cutting back on school subsidies is that Cardinal Dolan was hearing from people throughout the archdiocese that he should increase spending in other areas. People have told him, he explains, that the archdiocese needs "more good priests on college campuses. Or that we need better religious education; or that we have to up our technology; or that we have to get more involved in halfway houses; or that we have to get more hardened in our pro-life efforts."[161]

To address so many problems, the archdiocese unveiled on October 5, 2010, a three-year strategic plan for Catholic schools called Pathway to Excellence. A key component of the plan was a School Reconfiguration Committee made up of pastors, principals, and archdiocesan representatives empowered to address declining enrollment, "which undermines a school's financial stability and often necessitates unsustainable levels of financial subsidies from both the archdiocese and its parish".[162]

On November 9 of that year, the Reconfiguration Committee made its preliminary recommendation, which designated thirty-one grammar schools and one high school that were at risk of no longer receiving significant financial subsidies from the archdiocese. These grammar schools enrolled 4,451 students out of a total of 53,281 in the parochial-school system; the high school enrolled 110 students out of a total of 26,501. "These schools", the committee reported, "have seen a decline in enrollment of 34 percent over the past five years." The archdiocese's superintendent of schools, Dr. Timothy McNiff, reaffirmed Dolan's position, saying, "These under-enrolled schools require significant financial support from the archdiocese that cannot be sustained indefinitely. We need to allocate our resources where they can do the most good, and support schools that can sustain themselves over time."[163]

After the Reconfiguration Committee analyzed the sustainability plans filed by each of the schools that were deemed at risk, the final recommendations were given to the archbishop, who approved them. Twenty-seven of the thirty-two schools were to lose archdiocesan subsidies and were to close at the end of the academic year, in June 2011. Three of these schools were in Manhattan, six in the Bronx, four in Staten Island, nine in Westchester and Putnam Counties, and five in the remaining upstate counties.

The number of students in the closing elementary schools totaled 3,652, and those schools' decline in enrollment in the previous five years had been 71 percent—more than double the decline for all the at-risk schools studied by the committee. The one high school to be closed taught only 110 students.

Closing the twenty-seven schools would reduce the financial deficit by $10 million, and archdiocesan subsidies to Catholic schools were expected to be down to $13 million (from $48 million) in the next academic year. In April 2011, the archdiocese announced that a transition package totaling $7 million was to be distributed to teachers who were slated to lose their jobs.

The remaining parochial schools were consolidated into groups based on region, with oversight powers given to regional boards. Pastors were no longer to be directly responsible for the management and maintenance of the schools located on the grounds of their parishes. Pastors might serve on the regional board, however, and were to remain responsible for the sacramental life of the students. To finance the schools, a new archdiocesan tax was levied on each parish within a school region. And students in schools that were slated to close were given the opportunity to register in another Catholic school within their region.

Dolan took a similar approach with the 368 parishes he inherited.

"Making All Things New"

The archdiocese, in Dolan's judgment, could no longer prop up parishes with small congregations that couldn't support themselves. He turned to Auxiliary Bishop Dennis Sullivan, whom he calls "the real patriarch of parish planning",[164] to oversee the review.

Sullivan began the process of gathering data and holding town-hall meetings. He hired demographers and sociologists to analyze the data. But before the project was completed, he was named the bishop of Camden, New Jersey. In early 2013, Dolan hired the consulting firm he believed had "the best batting record" and would best carry on Sullivan's work, the Reid Group of Seattle, Washington, and Waukesha, Wisconsin.

The consulting firm worked with sixty-five clusters of parishes to gather all relevant data on the life of each parish. Dolan referred to the clusters as the grassroots of the archdiocese, because membership included priests, deacons, religious, and laypeople from each of the cluster parishes.

The findings and recommendations for the project, which was named Making All Things New, were turned over to a forty-person advisory group in February 2014. The group was charged with reviewing the cluster findings and then returning its suggestions and recommendations to the clusters for further evaluations. According to an archdiocesan spokesman, these recommendations could include:

1. Collaboration, where parishes in a given cluster area will be renewed and strengthened by avoiding duplication and sharing in ministries, pastoral programs and community outreach;
2. Consolidation, where several parishes will come together to form a new parish community, with the financial assets of the former parishes going to the new consolidated parish;
3. Closings, where the remaining parishioners from parishes that close will be invited to join surrounding parishes, with the financial assets being distributed equally among those surrounding parishes.

In addition, the planning process will likely result in the expansion of existing parishes, and even the possible establishment of new parishes, to better meet the needs of the people in currently under-served areas of the Archdiocese.[165]

The revised cluster reports were delivered to the advisory group in early summer 2014, and it met in late June to make final recommendations to the Presbyteral Council—the council, made up of priests, that aids the archbishop in governing the archdiocese.

The council met in early July to review the reports, to debate the issues, and then to vote on whether each parish on the list should remain open or be closed. The results of the council's vote were forwarded to Cardinal Dolan, who had the final say on the future of the parishes and was expected to announce his decisions after Labor Day.

Meanwhile, throughout the review process, rumors were rampant around the archdiocese that "Making All Things New" was just a fancy name and process concocted by consultants to mask what was already decided: that fifty to seventy parishes were to be closed.

"Some people are really upset, and they say they may not attend a Catholic service ever again. Others say, I'll choose where I want to go, and no one will tell me where to go", said one cluster committee member, a Ms. Ali of Harlem's Church of All Saints—which can seat a thousand but on any given Sunday has only about one hundred in the pews.[166]

Others complained that Dolan didn't like approaching rich New Yorkers to raise funds and that, as a result, many parishes were to be closed solely to sell valuable real estate and use the proceeds to balance budgets and pay off debt. Still others argued that selling irreplaceable real estate to fix today's financial difficulties would hurt the institutional Church and hamper future archbishops.

Cardinal Dolan had a very different perspective. "I know", he said in an interview with the authors, "everyone thinks I have a list in my desk [of parishes to be closed]. I have not seen any list, and I purposely kept hands off." He had taken this approach because "the wisdom of it [has] got to come from the grassroots"—that is, the clusters. Dolan conceded, however, that at the end of the process the "buck will stop with me".

After being handed the final recommendations of the Presbyteral Council, Dolan knew that he was "going to have to be the one to make the very tough decisions" and that "they're not going to be easy." He also expected his "honeymoon" in New York to come to an abrupt end after he announced his decisions.[167] As for complaints that it was all about money, Dolan insisted that his plan "is *not* solely based on money".

He explained that Cardinal Egan did "a masterful job in bringing stability, frugality, tightening things up, stopping the hemorrhage." But when he took over New York, Egan told him, "You still have a long way to go."[168] And now he is continuing the course Cardinal Egan started.

As for the future use of Church property, the cardinal has developed what he calls the Dolan Doctrine, which holds that selling real estate should be the last option; leasing is better. Next, proceeds from sales will not be used to cover operating expenses.

If a church is sold, the money from the sale will go to help build and expand parishes where "the great-grandkids of the families who originally donated to build that church now live"—in the bedroom communities outside the city.[169]

As for schools, Dolan used the example of the old St. Agnes High School in midtown Manhattan, which was sold for about $50 million. "Because it was built as a seminary high school," he explained, "the money belongs to the seminary."[170] The $50 million will be deposited in an endowment, and the seminary will live off the return on investments. Dolan hopes the endowment will throw off about $2.5 million annually. That income will permit him to cut the seminary expense from his operating budget and help eliminate the deficit.

As for Church property that is leased, half the rental income will go to helping other Catholic institutions in need, and half will remain in the parish.

"When I got here," Dolan said, "a lot of pastors were eager to close their schools. Not only would they not have the drain of money, but they could rent the building and then be on easy street."[171]

He cited the example of St. Michael's parish high school on West Thirty-Fourth Street, whose buildings are now rented by the New York City Board of Education. "The high school is closed—wise decision. The income from that is $1.7 million a year to the parish. [The] Dolan Doctrine says half goes to the neighboring Catholic schools."[172]

Dolan has also made it clear that he is not letting off the hook pastors who owe money to the archdiocese. In a January 24, 2014, memo to his priests, he wrote:

> In the delicate and stressful duty of financial administration, a pastor is often tempted to ignore the parish's debts to the *archdiocese*! Heat, water, electricity, salaries are automatically paid—rightfully so—while pension, insurance, education assessment, and *cathedraticum* are not. This is unfair. Our people get the idea that "the rich old archdiocese" can wait, and hardly needs their debts paid. This is sloppy stewardship, and—I admit I'm hardly unbiased here—unjust to us, as we try to pay our bills, and assist parishes in genuine stress.
>
> Just recently I was at a beautiful parish in a rather affluent area. I asked the pastor (among other things) how the parish was doing financially. He smiled and replied, "We're in the black—except for the $200,000 we owe you!" Needless to say I did not smile back.

Many pastors complained, however, that a significant amount of money received from the archdiocese to meet parochial-school expenses and payrolls, was not loans but grants and that Dolan had now reclassified them as loans.

After several delays on Sunday, November 2, 2014, the archdiocese released its Making All Things New decisions.

"This time of transition in the history of the archdiocese", Cardinal Dolan said, "will undoubtedly be difficult for people who live in parishes that will merge. There will be many who are hurt and upset as they experience what will be a change in their spiritual lives, and I will be one of them. There is nobody who has been involved in Making All Things New who doesn't understand the impact that this will have on the Catholic faithful. It will be our responsibility to work with everyone in these parishes so as to help make the change as smooth as we possibly can."[173] In his *Catholic New York* column that same week, he admitted, "There will soon be a real sense of grief.... I wish it could be different."

The official announcement disclosed that 112 parishes were to be merged to create 55 new parishes. By August 2015, 31 of those parishes would no longer hold services and would in effect be closed. The breakdown: 6 in the Bronx, 9 in Manhattan, 6 in Westchester and in Rockland, Dutchess, Sullivan and Ulster Counties 6 would be closed. The other merged parishes would continue to hold services in both churches, but would be administered from one parish.

The *New York Times* reported in a front-page story on Monday, November 3, titled "Tears for New York's Catholics as Church Closings Are Announced", that "there were gasps and tears at Sacred Heart in Mount Vernon, congregants shared mournful embraces. And at our Lady of Peace on the East Side parishioners pledged a fight."[174] Nevertheless, the initial reaction in the media was somewhat muted because the federal and state elections held on Tuesday, November 4, dominated the news.

However, as the news of the closings sank in, angry rumblings among some of the faithful became public. The liberal "Catholic" nonprofit Call to Action–Metro NY hosted a workshop for parties interested in fighting the closures. There were complaints that the merger approach took advantage of loopholes in the Church's *Code of Canon Law*. Some alleged that Dolan escaped going to Rome to seek permission to close parishes by calling them mergers. Others claimed that in a merger, the proceeds from the sale or lease of property could be kept by the archdiocese and used for general expenses. In an official closing by the Vatican, any proceeds must be expended in the immediate area surrounding the former parish to maintain the intent of original donors.

Another criticism was that a merger really didn't save all that much money. Although one staff might administer two churches the major expenses—insurance, utilities, upkeep, security, et cetera—would not go away.

In his November 11, 2014, *Catholic New York* column, "The Best Is Yet to Come", Dolan addressed some of the concerns.

"Why do we have to reduce our numbers of parishes from 360 to about 305? ... Shortages in the number of priests and in the available money to support struggling parishes are, indeed, a part of the answer to the question." The other part of the answer, he admitted, "our people aren't coming anymore."

Although the Catholic population in the archdiocese continues to rise (it is currently around 2.8 million), Cardinal Dolan insisted that "the stats tell us that only somewhere between 15 and 28 percent of our folks show up."

"The best is yet to come", Dolan proclaimed, because "with, yes, fewer, but now stronger, fuller, more vibrant parishes, better served by more available priests, in new communities no longer straitjacketed by demands of maintenance of huge, half-empty, in-need-of-repairs buildings, we can unleash a *new evangelization!* ... Let's go from *shortages*—of priests, resources, and people—to a surplus!"[175]

In mid-December, a *New York Times* headline read "Archdiocese Appears Likely to Shutter More Churches: Cardinal's New Proposals Detailed in Documents". The article claimed another thirty-eight parishes were to be merged to create sixteen new ones with eleven closing. Archdiocese spokesman Joseph Zwilling made it clear to the *Times* that "these are just proposals. They are not decisions." The parishes in question were told they had to respond to the proposals by March 1,

2015, and that the cardinal wanted "honest feedback" before he would make any final decisions.[176]

The announcement that the Church of St. Thomas More on the fashionable Upper East Side of Manhattan—once the parish of Jackie Kennedy—was on the chopping block angered its wealthy parishioners. Many were outraged that, with 3,500 parishioners and $1.5 million in reserves, their church might be merged with neighboring parish St. Ignatius Loyola on Eighty-Third Street and Park Avenue.

The most outspoken parishioner was *Wall Street Journal* columnist and former President Reagan speechwriter Peggy Noonan. In a December 27, 2014, column she called on the cardinal, "Please spare this Church".

Asserting that St. Thomas More "is not empty, it is vital and alive" and not in need of repairs and not a financial drain on the archdiocese, she went on to say: "Our cardinal, my friend Timothy Dolan, being from Milwaukee, *would not know, and the members of his many clusters and advisory boards would not know,* that St. Thomas More is another root of spiritual life of the Catholics on Manhattan's Upper East Side. They're not talking about the closing of a church but the destroying of a world" (emphasis added).

Noonan even stated what she called an "uncharitable thought" of some parishioners: "Is it possible, they ask, the archdiocese is driven by what drove Henry VIII [the executioner of St. Thomas More]; politics and real estate?" She went on to assert that the parishioners of the affluent St. Thomas More parish are victims because the cardinal fears he will be severely criticized if he closes only poor parishes. Instead of selling her parish for "$50 million, maybe $100 million", she suggested, the cardinal should sell his Madison Avenue mansion.[177]

Noonan's accusatory column did not go unchallenged. On January 4, 2015, the *New York Post* published as an op-ed piece a reply by Auxiliary Bishop John O'Hara, the director of Making All Things New. O'Hara explained that Noonan's column was "sadly full of misinformation and half-truths" and that no decision was made to merge St. Thomas More. It was "one of 16 proposals that the cardinal has asked be considered throughout all parts of the archdiocese".

O'Hara dismissed her notion that the "proposal is nothing more than an attack on the rich and a move against excellence (which begs the question in Noonan's mind: Is 'excellence' only to be found among the well-to-do?) and an attempt to cash in on real estate."

Making All Things New, O'Hara pointed out, was a plan to make all remaining parishes vibrant. In any merges, "the assets and liabilities are combined into the newly formed parish, for the further pastoral care of the people". He added, "To claim that the Making All Things New process is motivated by 'what drove Henry VIII...' would be insulting if it weren't so farcical."

O'Hara also refuted Noonan's snide comment about "the cost, the past 20 years, of all the settlements and legal fees associated with sex scandals". Unlike Boston, which had to sell real estate to pay high sex-abuse settlements, New York (as we explained in this book's chapter on Cardinal Egan) did not make large settlements and did not sell any property to meet those expenses.

After picking apart Noonan's arguments, O'Hara concluded "The facts are clear, though her vision is not."[178]

Cardinal Dolan also weighed in on the Noonan matter. In his January 8, 2015, *Catholic New York* column, he assured the faithful that "if there are any proceeds from unused properties, the revenue would not go to that mean, selfish, money-hungry archdiocese, so that Dolan can maintain his mansion (part of the Cathedral itself, and which actually makes money each year hosting fundraisers for our schools and charities), or pay off that boondoggle Cathedral repair (which, in advance gifts alone, is already over halfway funded), or pay off the bills from that clergy sex abuse scandal (there are none), but would by Church law, go to the new parish."[179]

Despite the participation of parishioners throughout the archdiocese on the Making All Things New committees, a subset of the faithful continued to complain that the process lacked transparency and demanded to see the decrees that approved the mergers. On Wednesday, February 11, 2015, the day after the *New York Times* made inquiries about the formal decrees, the archdiocese posted them on its website.[180]

The Vatican's Congregation for the Clergy announced in March 2015 that it will take up the appeals of parishioners from St. Elizabeth of Hungary on East Eighty-Third Street and Our Lady of Peace on East Sixty-Second St.

The archdiocesan spokesman defended the cardinal's decision on the parish mergers saying, "We believe that not only did we meet the requirements to merge parishes [but] once the congregation has had a chance to fully review the matter they will support the decisions made by Cardinal Dolan."

While it is likely that Dolan will prevail in any canon law or civil legal procedures or appeals, the cardinal correctly predicted that Making All Things New would end his honeymoon with New York's faithful.

Sprucing up St. Patrick's and Catholic Arts

Dolan faces other financial woes. The rehabilitation of St. Patrick's Cathedral is expected to cost $180 million. Since its dedication in 1879, there have been periodic repairs, the most extensive in the late 1970s, when Cardinal Cooke spruced it up to celebrate the cathedral's hundredth anniversary. More recently, the Lady Chapel was completely restored in 2002–2003.

The present project involves repairing and restoring the entire interior and exterior of the cathedral and the exterior of the rectory and the archbishop's residence. On St. Patrick's Day 2012, Dolan began what he described as a "great" fund-raising campaign. In June 2013, it was reported that the restoration fund had $70 million, and by late 2014 it had grown to $90 million—still 50 percent shy of the total estimated costs.

As the *New York Times* reported, the restoration was complicated by the fact that the "cathedral had to remain open during the rehabilitation. That means tourists and worshipers enter under a sidewalk bridge, and inside, scaffolding begins at the narthex at the Fifth Avenue entrance, blocking the great rose window. The scaffolding runs east through the sanctuary to the transepts that spread north and south."[181] Walking through the cathedral is like walking through a war zone.

As of early 2015, although most of the work on the outside of the cathedral had been completed, crews of laborers and artisans continued working on scaffolds inside. Dolan anticipated the restoration would be completed in time to welcome Pope Francis when he visited New York City in September 2015.

Another project initiated by Dolan has sparked some controversy: the Archbishop Fulton J. Sheen Center for Art and Culture, at Elizabeth and Bleecker Streets on Manhattan's Lower East Side. Holding that the New Evangelization encourages engagement with the culture, Dolan has spent in excess of $18 million to renovate Our Lady of Loreto Church and soup kitchen, which had been closed for years, and turn the space into a center that "includes an exhibition area, several conference rooms that are able to be opened into one large conference room, a 'black box' theatre, which holds 93 people ... ; [another] theatre that holds 250 people; and a chapel for those who visit the center and want to sit, converse and pray with the Lord."[182]

Though there has been much grumbling that the center is an extravagance that the archdiocese can ill afford when parishes and schools are being closed, Cardinal Dolan believes it is a worthy project that will "present the heights and depths of human expression in thought and culture" and that acknowledges that "the glory of God is man fully alive." As he wrote in his June 16, 2014, *Catholic New York* column, the Sheen Center will "proclaim that 'life is worth living' especially when we seek to deepen, explore, challenge, and uplift ourselves, Catholic and non-Catholic alike, intellectually, artistically and spiritually."[183]

The center, which was dedicated by the cardinal in September 2014, is managed by an executive director and an experienced staff. It is governed by a "board of directors comprised of clergy and religious, executives and academicians, and those who are engaged in the arts to ensure its success and its allegiance to the mission."[184] Sadly, the first overseer of the project, Monsignor Michael Hull, S.T.D., took a walk from the Church, married, and moved to Italy with his new wife.

Dolan believes that the center will eventually be profitable, once there is a full line of Catholic entertainment. In the meantime, the studios and theater will be available for interested parties to rent for recitals and shows.

To fund the renovations at St. Patrick's and the Sheen Center, as well as other infrastructure projects that Cardinal Dolan has in mind, plenty of outside funding will be necessary. And the cardinal's fund-raising efforts to date have been lackluster, at best.

The cardinal readily admits that there is a challenge in stewardship. "I came from two dioceses, St. Louis and Milwaukee, where the annual appeal is almost what we get [in New York] with one-fourth of the Catholics. So when I got here, Ed Egan told me, 'Timothy, you have a poor archdiocese.' And he said, 'Your greatest foe will be everybody, including your priests, who think you're rolling in dough and we ain't.'"[185]

When queried by the authors about concerns that he was not banging on the doors of New York's upper crust begging for money to fund projects and to subsidize schools, as Cardinal Egan had, he replied: "I would say I wouldn't have the talent of my predecessor. He was excellent at that. He enjoyed it. He knew where the money was. He was excellent in getting people's trust. The wealthy people appreciated him and loved him."[186] And despite the fact that Dolan and Egan both grew up in middle-class neighborhoods and that both their fathers worked for Emerson Electric, he said of Egan, "He himself came from a higher grade of society than I did.... So, he was a pro at it [raising money], and it's tough for me to do it."[187]

The perception that Pope Francis is down on the wealthy is also hampering Dolan's fund-raising efforts. A bold headline on the front page of the January 1, 2014, *Daily News* read: "IN GREED THEY TRUST: Fat Cats Revolt. Francis' Rap on Rich May Cost St. Pat's". Ken Langone, the cofounder of Home Depot, said he and a few other wealthy Catholics were threatening to withhold their financial support of the St. Patrick's renovation project because of the pope's comments concerning economics in his first apostolic exhortation, *Evangelii Gaudium*. These disgruntled donors thought he was against democratic capitalism and people who strive to succeed.

Langone told Cardinal Dolan, "Your Eminence, this is one more hurdle I hope we don't have to deal with. You want to be careful about generalities. Rich people in one country don't act the same as rich people in another country."

Dolan replied that Francis was being misunderstood: "The pope loves poor people. He also loves rich people. He loves people.... We've got to correct to make sure this gentleman understands the Holy Father's message properly." Pope Francis, Dolan added, believes "money itself is morally neutral. Money, our wealth is a gift from God. And the morality comes in the way we use it.... If it became a god, if it becomes an idol, Pope Francis is saying, then it's wrong because there is only one God."[188]

Death Comes to a Retired Archbishop

Throughout his years in retirement, Cardinal Edward Egan kept his word to Pope Benedict that he would be active in helping the universal Church and the Archdiocese of New York "however he could and as long as he could".

Egan kept a busy calendar, raising money for parochial schools and serving on various New York and Vatican boards and committees.

After Pope Benedict announced his retirement, Egan flew to Rome to attend the Congregation of Cardinals, the preparation meeting before the conclave to elect a new pope. Because Egan was over eighty and therefore was not eligible to enter the conclave to vote, he agreed to fly back to New York to handle the media for Dolan after the election of the 266th successor of St. Peter.

Egan was on NBC-TV with Brian Williams when Cardinal Jorge Bergoglio walked out onto the balcony overlooking St. Peter's Square as Pope Francis. Unlike most American clerics, Egan actually knew Bergoglio. They collaborated at the 2001 synod of bishops, and Egan was able to describe to American viewers the background of this little-known prelate from Argentina.

During the 2001 synod, when Egan served as rapporteur general, he met and became good friends with Jorge Cardinal Bergoglio, the deputy rapporteur. During downtime, the two prelates discussed, in Italian, their mutual interest in classical music. Later, when Egan learned that Bergoglio was an admirer of his longtime friend Renée Fleming of the New York Metropolitan Opera, he persuaded her to send him a recording of *La Traviata*.

Egan admitted in a paper he delivered at St. John's University School of Law in 2014 that the "Cardinal Bergoglio I knew in 2001 was, I must confess, quite different from the Pope Francis I know now". By this he meant that the Bergoglio he worked with and got to know at the synod was a quiet, thoughtful man, "a classic Jesuit professor, wise, learned, and endowed with a kind heart and an authoritative manner."[189]

When Egan had opportunities to meet with Bergoglio at the preconclave meetings *and* since his election as pope, he admitted that "on these occasions he came across as much more lively, humorous, spontaneous, and enthusiastic than he was in 2001. It was almost as though I now know two Jorge Bergoglios, both of whom I liked immensely."[190]

While Egan applauded Pope Francis' actions to reform the Vatican Curia, he was leery about the chatter concerning matters of sexual and marital morality. Concerning the Fall 2014 Extraordinary Synod on the Family, he told the authors that he was appalled by the leaks, which he explained broke Vatican protocols. Dissenters, he said, "believe they are above the rules". He also made clear to the authors his opposition to Cardinal Walter Kasper's proposal that the rules be changed to allow divorced Catholics to receive Holy Communion and held to his position that he had expressed in a paper he delivered to St. John's University in October 2014 that "the seriousness of Church deliberations of marital invalidity is, in my judgment— and that of many others—questionable at best." Egan hoped to attend the 2015 synod to support Cardinal Gerhard Müller and to defend traditional Church teaching on marriage.

During the summer and fall of 2014, Egan limited his activities to taking care of his health. He had a cancer scare that turned out to be negative. He was also having trouble with his legs, so affected by childhood polio, and was receiving leg therapy. He began using a cane.

Doctors told the cardinal that there appeared to be signs of a relapse of the polio. Egan explained to the authors that he was not the only person at his age to have a mild relapse. The late Cardinal Avery Dulles, who had infantile paralysis, also had a recurring bout in his eighties. Such re-occurrences had been rare because most people who had been infected with the disease did not live into their ninth decade.

Throughout the winter of 2014–2015, Egan continued to work on his legs, particularly after he took a serious fall in his apartment in early January.

In a letter to George Marlin, dated February 5, 2015, Egan wrote, "I decided not to go to Rome for the meeting about the Curia. The legs are still too unsteady. There is much I would like to say, but I feel the trip would get in the way of bringing the legs back to something near normal."

On March 4, 2015, Cardinal Egan wrote to Marlin on a personal matter— something many other busy people might simply have ignored—which Marlin had raised with him several days before. Knowing that Marlin had been at the Vatican that week attending to matters concerning a Catholic charity he chairs, Egan wrote: "Hopefully, all went well in Rome. You missed a lot of terrible weather here. Take care of yourself."

The following day, Thursday, March 5, 2015, Cardinal Egan slumped over shortly after having lunch in his apartment with his priest-secretary, Father Douglas Crawford. He was rushed to NYU Langone Medical Center, where he was pronounced dead of cardiac arrest at 2:20 P.M. Cardinal Egan died a month shy of his eighty-third birthday.

Announcing the death of the first archbishop of New York to retire from office, Cardinal Dolan said to the people of New York, "Join me, please, in thanking God for his life, especially his generous and faithful priesthood. Pray as well that the powerful mercy of Jesus, in which our Cardinal had such trust, has ushered him into heaven."[191]

Cardinal Egan's body was received into St. Patrick's on Monday, March 9, and the public visitation commenced at noon. A Vigil Mass for the deceased was celebrated that evening, and on Tuesday afternoon the Mass of Christian Burial was celebrated by Cardinal Dolan.

Egan had left instructions that his Requiem Mass was to be simple and the attention should be on the Church, not on him, and he requested that Dolan give the homily.

The procession that began at 1:30 P.M. included more than four hundred priests, a hundred bishops and eight cardinals. Dolan was the principal celebrant, and his concelebrants were the other cardinals and the Apostolic Nuncio to the United States, Archbishop Carlo Maria Vigano.

In his homily, Cardinal Dolan described Egan as a dedicated churchman. And when describing a meeting he had with the Egan family the previous day, he said that one of them told him: "We loved him as our uncle, and he us as his family ... but the Church was his real family."

Dolan continued:

Indeed it was. He met Jesus in the Church; he learned of Jesus in the Church; he was united to Jesus in the sacraments; he served Jesus as he loved and served the children, the sick, the families, the poor, the elderly through the Church.... And now this Church thanks God for him and commends his noble priestly soul to the everlasting mercy of Jesus."[192]

After Communion, Egan's longtime friend and favorite operatic soprano, Renée Fleming, sang "Ave Maria".

At the end of Mass, Cardinal Dolan and the other prelates and priests escorted Egan's coffin through the cathedral and into the crypt under the main altar, where Egan was entombed with his eight predecessors.

Pope Francis' Visit to New York

When the Vatican confirmed in November 2014 that a trip to the United States by Pope Francis the following September would include a stop in New York, the archdiocese and its ever-ebullient archbishop began preparations. Cardinal Dolan never doubted the value of the papal visit. As he would say several weeks ahead of the pope's arrival, "While the visit of Pope Francis to New York will be relatively brief—only about thirty-six hours or so—I am confident that his presence among us will have a profound and lasting impact on all New Yorkers."[193]

The pope arrived in Washington, D.C., on September 22, 2015, after completing a visit to Cuba. His Washington itinerary included a visit to the White House, an address to Congress, a meeting with U.S. bishops at St. Matthew's Cathedral, and a Mass in Spanish on the campus of the Catholic University of America, during which the eighteenth-century missionary Junípero Serra was canonized.

From Washington, Francis would fly to New York on September 24 and go directly to St. Patrick's Cathedral, where he would lead vespers. The next day he would address the United Nations, attend an interdenominational prayer session at the 9/11 Memorial at Ground Zero, visit a Catholic school in East Harlem, say Mass at Madison Square Garden, and drive in his popemobile through Central Park to greet and bless the faithful—a long day, to be sure, for the seventy-eight-year-old pontiff. On September 26, the pope would fly to Philadelphia to attend the World Meeting of Families.

Any papal trip requires the archbishop of New York to devote a great deal of time to organizing and raising money to pay for the various events. When Pope Benedict XVI came to New York in 2008, Cardinal Egan was able to keep the archdiocese's costs down to $3 million, in part because George Steinbrenner did not charge the archdiocese a dime for the use of Yankee Stadium for the Papal Mass.

Dolan told the *Wall Street Journal* that the total cost for the visit of Pope Francis would be approximately $2.8 million and that Madison Square Garden came at "no cost".[194] For contrast, consider that Philadelphia archbishop Charles Chaput was required to raise more than $40 million in 2015 to cover Church and government expenses for the papal visit to his city.

Dolan and his aides attended scores of meetings with Vatican, federal, state, and city officials just for security—as the cardinal was simultaneously pushing for the completion of the $170 million renovation of St. Patrick's Cathedral. He was determined to have all the scaffolding removed from outside and inside the cathedral before Pope Francis arrived.

All previous papal visits to the Big Apple have had an effect on the city—that "profound and lasting impact" of which Cardinal Dolan spoke, although some of the impact is superficial and transient. Political leaders, including those who oppose the Church on abortion, same-sex "marriage", and state aid or tax credits for parents who send children to Catholic schools, clamor for tickets to events, hoping for a photo opportunity with the pope. But there was also an avalanche of donations to the archdiocese, including $40 million to fund student scholarships and 150 new beds in a Bronx homeless shelter.

When asked by the *Wall Street Journal* about the public expectations for the pope's visit, Dolan said, "You've got the one poll—and thanks be to God [that] is dominant—namely excitement, thrill, high interest. You've got the other poll of a built-in disappointment, too. The limited amount of time he is here doesn't allow either him or us to give him the accessibility to people that he wants and that we want."[195]

The pope's plane landed at JFK Airport at 5:00 P.M. on Thursday, September 24. An hour and a half later the pope arrived at the scaffold-free St. Patrick's. The faithful, packed in the nave, gave Pope Francis a rousing reception as he processed up the center aisle.

In his welcoming message to Pope Francis, Cardinal Dolan said:

> Once you entered those famous doors on Fifth Avenue, you became an official New Yorker.... This great Cathedral in the middle of midtown Manhattan—geographically and spiritually we are here in the heart of New York City.

New Yorkers and people from all over the world come to St. Patrick's Cathedral to pray, to cry, to rejoice, to sense God's love and grace and mercy, and the Mass and the sacraments. And this evening ... [we] come to pray with you and for you.

Now, for the past three years we have all worked very hard to repair and renew and restore our beloved St. Patrick's Cathedral. Thanks to the workers, whom you saw outside, and the extraordinary generosity and leadership of so many people here, we have seen this repair and restoration as an invitation from Jesus to the spiritual renewal of ourselves and his Church as you have asked.

Your presence this happy evening renews all of us and provides a special blessing to all our work for this Cathedral we so love.

And now we ask you, Holy Father ... to bless our repaired Cathedral. Thank you for stopping by and come back soon.[196]

At the UN on Friday, the Holy Father gave a wide-ranging speech before the General Assembly, touching on poverty, human suffering, and environmental destruction. He reminded the representatives of 193 nations of the "painful situation" in the Middle East, where Christians and other religious minorities "have been forced to witness the destruction of their places of worship, their cultural and religious heritage, their houses and property".[197]

Afterward, accompanied by Cardinal Dolan, Pope Francis visited the National September 11 Memorial and Museum in lower Manhattan and led a prayer service with Hindu, Sikh, Buddhist, Christian, and Muslim religious leaders. At the memorial pool, the pope placed a rose on the stone that contained the names of the 9/11 victims.

The pope told service attendees, "It is a source of great hope that in this place of sorrow and remembrance I can join with leaders representing the many religious traditions which enrich the life of this great city.... I trust that our presence together will be a powerful sign of our shared desire to be a force for reconciliation, peace, and justice in this community and throughout the world."[198]

Later in the day, Pope Francis made a stop at Our Lady Queen of Angels School in East Harlem, where he met with schoolchildren. This was followed by a Central Park procession. Eighty thousand people greeted the Holy Father, who drove around the park grounds in the popemobile blessing all who were gathered there.

The finale of his visit was the Mass attended by twenty thousand people at Madison Square Garden. After Cardinal Dolan said that Catholics pray for their pope and "now here you are", the crowd cheered and gave a standing ovation that lasted several minutes. "It is clear", Dolan said, "how much we welcome you ... how much we love you."[199] At the end of the Mass, Pope Francis presented Dolan with a chalice for St. Patrick's Cathedral to commemorate his visit.

Bidding farewell to the pope at JFK Airport on Saturday morning, a very happy Cardinal Dolan told the press that Francis was "fairly moved" by his time in New York. "Two days of blessing and grace and mercy, [the pope] was beaming." The cardinal said the pope had remarked on, "Friendly people, so many people".[200] Asked if he needed to rethink anything about the papal visit, Dolan replied, "It caused me to rethink that I need to take a nap."[201]

The cardinal's rest was short, however, because he had to pack his bags and leave just a few days later for the three-week Synod on the Family in the Vatican.

2015 Synod on the Family

The Fourteenth Ordinary General Assembly of the Synod of Bishops, the Synod on the Family, which convened in the Vatican on October 4, 2015, had a total of 270 delegates representing the universal Church. From the United States there were seven bishop delegates, one alternate delegate, and two members of the synod over-sight council: Cardinal Dolan and Cardinal Donald Wuerl of Washington, D.C. Two of the delegates—Archbishop Blase Cupich of Chicago and Bishop George Murray of Youngstown—were appointed by Pope Francis. The others had been elected by the U.S. Bishops at a November 2014 meeting of the USCCB.

In the aftermath of the preliminary synod in 2014, many members of the U.S. hierarchy were concerned that much confusion had been sowed by leftist media and dissident clerics about what actually constitutes authentic Church teaching on marriage and divorce. Archbishop Chaput (who was to be the major U.S. voice at the 2015 synod), had said of that earlier synod, "I was very disturbed by what happened. I think confusion is of the devil, and I think the public image that came across was one of confusion."[202]

There was also talk that the 2015 synod was being "packed" with delegates sympathetic to the proposal of German Cardinal Walter Kasper that divorced Catholics who remarried without annulment of their first marriages should be able to receive Holy Communion (called the Kasper Proposal)—an idea that had been rejected by both St. John Paul II and Pope Benedict XVI. Ordinarily the pope appoints about thirty delegates; but this time Francis appointed one hundred. The rules governing the synod were also changed. Priests drafting the synod documents were not elected but were appointed by the pope.

Fearful about the direction in which the synod was heading, Cardinal George Pell, former archbishop of Sydney and current prefect in charge of Vatican financial reforms, delivered a letter to the pope signed by him and a dozen other cardinals expressing "serious" concerns about the procedures of the synod. Cardinal Dolan was one of the signatories.

The letter, which was leaked to the media on October 12, was headline news throughout the world. Admitting the existence of the letter, Cardinal Pell said in a statement, that although "a private letter should remain private", he confirmed that "concerns remain among many of the synod fathers about the composition of the drafting committee of the final *relatio* [summary report] and about the process by which it will be presented to the synod fathers and voted upon." He added, "Obviously there is some disagreement because minority elements want to change the Church's teachings on the proper dispositions necessary for the reception of Communion.... Obviously there is no possibility of change in this doctrine."[203]

Here are key excerpts from the letter:

> The new synodal procedures will be seen in some quarters as lacking openness and genuine collegiality....
>
> Additionally, the lack of input by the synod fathers in the composition of the drafting committee has created considerable unease. Members have been appointed, not elected, without consultation. Likewise, anyone drafting anything at the level of the small circles should be elected, not appointed.

In turn, these things have created a concern that the new procedures are not true to the traditional spirit and purpose of a synod. It is unclear why these procedural changes are necessary. A number of fathers feel the new process seems designed to facilitate predetermined results on important disputed questions.

Finally and perhaps most urgently, various fathers have expressed concern that a synod designed to address a vital pastoral matter—reinforcing the dignity of marriage and family—may become dominated by the theological/doctrinal issue of Communion for the divorced and civilly remarried. If so, this will inevitably raise even more fundamental issues about how the Church, going forward, should interpret and apply the Word of God, her doctrines and her disciplines to changes in culture. The collapse of liberal Protestant churches in the modern era, accelerated by their abandonment of key elements of Christian belief and practice in the name of pastoral adaptation, warrants great caution in our own synodal discussions.

Your Holiness, we offer these thoughts in a spirit of fidelity, and we thank you for considering them.[204]

In unscheduled remarks, an unhappy Pope Francis addressed the synod fathers on the matter. According to the Vatican paper, *L'Osservatore Romano*, "The Pontiff emphasized that Catholic doctrine on marriage has not been touched and he cautioned against the impression that the only problem of the synod is that of communion for the divorced, appealing against a reduction in the horizons of the synod." The Vatican spokesman, Father Federico Lombardi, added, "The decisions of method were also shared and approved by the pope and, therefore, cannot be brought back into discussion."[205]

Cardinal Dolan publicly confirmed that he signed the letter that was drafted before the synod convened. According to Dolan, he was approached by Pell, who said, "Why don't we get together, we love the Holy Father, we trust him. He's urged us to be as honest with him as possible. Why don't we write him that we're worried." Dolan considered the letter noncontroversial and claimed to have "actually forgotten about it". Dolan listed what "troubled" the signers of the letter:

> We're worried first of all, if the *Instrumentum Laboris* [the presynod working document], which has a lot of good things, but we're kind of worried if that's the only document that we're going to be talking about the synod.
>
> Number two, we're a little worried about the process. There seems to be some confusion. And thirdly, we're a little worried about if we could have a say in the people who are going to be on the final drafting committee.[206]

Dolan went on to say that although the pope did not refer to the letter directly, Francis said, "'Hey everybody, I've heard from some of you that you've got some concerns,' and then the pope listed the concerns: And then he said, '... let me try to respond to that.' And I said 'Way to go Pope Francis' you told us to be honest, we were [and] you answered right to the heart. I'm grateful you paid attention. Let's get on with the work."[207]

Dolan glossed over the fact that the pope had actually rejected their concerns. According to a tweet by Antonio Spadaro, S.J., director of the Italian newspaper *La Civiltà Cattolica*, who was present, the pope told synod members, "not to give in to the conspiracy hermeneutic, which is sociologically weak and spiritually unhelp-ful".[208] This was not denied by the Vatican.

While concerns continued that the process was rigged by leftist clerics, Dolan claimed halfway through the synod that he was optimistic: "I think the process is extraordinarily candid", he declared. "I think it is working, and this is from one who likes to complain." He added that, despite "confusion", he was beginning to see light at the end of the tunnel, "as much as sometimes I hate to admit it".[209]

At the end of the synod, the final text of the consulting document did not address the issue of Communion for the divorced and remarried. "But", as Dr. Robert Royal reported in the *Catholic Thing*, "a couple of paragraphs in the final text—which received the highest number of negative votes—push far into 'discernment' of individual circumstances and invoke the 'internal forum' which is to say private direction by a priest or bishop, coming right up to the edge of Communion for the divorced or remarried, but not crossing over in so many words."[210] In other words, the Kasper Proposal.

While the pope spoke often of "dialogue" and "listening" he made it clear to the assembly that "the synodal process culminates in listening to the Bishop of Rome, who is called upon to pronounce as 'pastor and teacher of all Christians.' "[211] Many interpreted this to mean that "dialogue" it acceptable as long as, in the end, the pope's opinion prevails: his way or the highway.

The pope showed his dissatisfaction with the final document, stating, "It was also about laying bare the closed hearts, which frequently hide even behind the Church teachings or good intentions, in order to sit in the chair of Moses and judge, some-times with superiority and superficiality, different cases and wounded families."[212]

Writing in *Catholic New York* after he returned from Rome, Dolan put the best face he could on the outcome: "I am pleased that the final report of the synod was a vast improvement over the original working text.... A very refreshing consistent theme of the synod has been inclusion. The Church, our spiritual family, welcomes everyone, especially those who many feel excluded. Among those, I've heard the synod fathers and observers comment, are the single, those with same-sex attrac-tion, those divorced, widowed, or recently arrived in a new country, those with disabilities, the aged, the housebound, racial and ethnic minorities. We, in the fam-ily of the Church, love them, welcome them and need them."[213]

Looking toward the Future

Cardinal Timothy Dolan's administration is—God willing—far from over. Since he could be guiding the faithful for at least another ten years, he has ample time to put his personal imprint on the archdiocese.

To protect and enhance the spiritual well-being of his flock, he will have to keep reminding himself, as he wrote in a memo to his priests on September 24, 2013, that his "fulltime job" is in New York. And if he is to succeed at maintaining and growing the spiritual, educational, and social services the faithful need, he will have to devote time and energy to the important task—even though it is one that he finds difficult—of fund-raising.

As for issues in the public square, he will have to put in the time and effort nec-essary to organize his fellow bishops and their flocks throughout the New York province and remind them of his own words: "We are called to be very active, very informed and very involved in politics."[214]

But Dolan described in his 2012 Independence Day statement the greatest task that the archbishop and all New York Catholics must tackle:

The challenge, then, concerns the face of the Catholic faith that our fellow Americans encounter every day. *It is a question of evangelization.* Do we Catholics *practice* the faith we are working so hard to *defend*? What about its more difficult teachings, especially the one that exhorts us to love our enemies?

When done right, our Catholic faith creates a culture of true joy. People can see it in what we do, in how we talk, in the look in our eye. "This is how all will know that you are my disciples, if you have love for one another" (Jn 13:35). Amid the culture of death that we find all around us, our faith is something that our neighbors will find compelling and may even be something they want for themselves. We must show the culture that seeks to marginalize us that our faith is a living and life-changing reality. The more fundamental challenge needed for us to preserve our American ideals is to boldly live our faith, to boldly proclaim it, and to boldly love God and our neighbor. As Jesus taught, "Let your light shine before all."[215]

NOTES

INTRODUCTION

1. *New York Times*, February 23, 2009.

2. *New York Times*, June 10, 2014.

3. Thomas J. Reese, *Archbishop: Inside the Power Structure of the American Catholic Church* (San Francisco: Harper and Row, 1989), p. v.

4. Editorial, *Catholic World*, July 1939, p. 386.

PART I. BEFORE THE BEGINNING

Chapter 1. Hard to Kill

1. Rev. J. R. Bayley, *A Brief Sketch of the Early History of the Catholic Church on the Island of New York* (1870; New York: U.S. Catholic Historical Society, 1973), p. 15.

2. William Harper Bennett, *Catholic Footsteps in Old New York* (1909; New York: U.S. Catholic Historical Society, 1973), p. 18.

3. Edwin G. Burrows and Mike Wallace, *Gotham: A History of New York City to 1898* (New York: Oxford University Press, 1999), p. 31.

4. Bayley, *A Brief Sketch*, p. 21.

5. Frances G. Halpenny, s.v. "Bressani, François-Joseph" in *Dictionary of Canadian Biography*, vol. 1 (Toronto: University of Toronto Press, 1967).

6. David Lovejoy, *The Glorious Revolution in America* (Middletown, Conn.: Wesleyan University Press, 1987), p. 98.

7. Burrows and Wallace, *Gotham*, pp. 91–92.

8. Ibid., p. 93.

9. Ibid., p. 95.

10. Charles H. McCormick, *Leisler's Rebellion* (New York: Garland, 1989), p. 179.

11. John Tracy Ellis, *American Catholicism* (Chicago: University of Chicago Press, 1956), p. 10.

12. Ibid., p. 19.

13. Msgr. Thomas J. Shelley, *The Archdiocese of New York: The Bicentennial History, 1808–2008* (Strasbourg, France: Éditions du Signe, 2007), p. 24.

14. Ibid.

15. John Higham, *Strangers in the Land: Patterns of American Nativism*, quoted in Philip Jenkins, *The New Anti-Catholicism: The Last Acceptable Prejudice* (New York: Oxford University Press, 2003), p. 23.

16. *Wikipedia*, s.v. "Anti-Catholicism", last modified April 13, 2016, http://en.wikipedia.org /wiki/Anti-Catholicism/, quoting David Gibson, *The Coming Catholic Church* (New York, HarperCollins, 2004).

17. John Carroll to prefect of Propaganda, June 17, 1807, Archives of the Dominican Master General, Rome, Codex XIII, 731, quoted in Victor F. O'Daniel, O.P., "Concanen's Election to the See of New York", *Catholic Historical Review* 2, no. 1 (April 1916): 20.

18. Shelley, *Archdiocese of New York*, p. 44.

19. R. Luke Concanen to William O'Brien, February 22, 1800, Archives of the Archdiocese of New York (hereafter cited as AANY), St. Joseph's Seminary, Dunwoodie.

20. Thomas F. Meehan, "Catholic Literary New York, 1800–1840", *U.S. Catholic Historical Society* 4, no. 4 (January 1919): 399.

21. R. Luke Concanen to John Carroll, December 20, 1803, AANY.

22. John Talbot Smith, *The Catholic Church in New York*, vol. 1 (1905; New York: Cosimo, 2008), p. 38.

23. Victor F. O'Daniel, "The Right Rev. Richard Luke Concanen, O.P., the First Bishop of New York, 1747–1810", *Catholic Historical Review* 1 (January 1916): 401.

24. Shelley, *Archdiocese of New York*, p. 46.

25. O'Daniel, "Right Rev. Concanen", p. 401.

26. Shelley, *Archdiocese of New York*, p. 47.

27. Victor F. O'Daniel, O.P., "Concanen's Election to the See of New York", *Catholic Historical Review* 2, no. 1 (1916): 31.

28. Edward Cardinal Egan, "Our History: Humble Beginnings", *Catholic New York*, April 13, 2006.

29. J. Wilfred Parsons, "Rev. Anthony Kohlmann, S.J. (1771–1824)", *Catholic Historical Review* 4, no. 1 (April 1918): 38.

30. Robert E. Scully, S.J., "The Suppression of the Society of Jesus: A Perfect Storm in the Age of 'Enlightenment'", *Studies in the Spirituality of Jesuits* 45, no. 2 (Summer 2013): 2–3.

31. Henry de Courcy and John Gilmary Shea, *The Catholic Church in the United States* (New York: P.J. Kenedy, 1904), p. 366.

32. Jason K. Duncan, *Citizens of Papists?: The Politics of Anti-Catholicism in New York, 1685–1821* (New York: Fordham University Press, 2005), p. 116.

33. Parsons, "Rev. Anthony Kohlmann", p. 43.

34. *Wikipedia*, s.v. "Thomas Paine", last modified May 6, 2016, http://en.wikipedia.org /wiki/Thomas_Paine/.

35. Peter Schineller, "Thomas Paine and St. Patrick's Old Cathedral—200 Years Ago", *America*, June 8, 2009, http://americamagazine.org/.

36. Thomas F. Meehan, "Self-Effaced Philanthropist: Cornelius Heeney, 1754–1848", *Catholic Historical Review* 4, no. 1 (April 1918): 9.

37. William Sampson, *The Catholic Question in America* (New York: Edward Gillespy, 1813).

38. Most Rev. John M. Farley, *History of St. Patrick's Cathedral* (New York: Society for the Propagation of the Faith, 1908), p. 65.

39. John Gilmary Shea, *Life and Times of the Most Rev. John Carroll: Bishop and First Archbishop of Baltimore, Embracing the History of the Catholic Church in the United States, 1763–1815* (Rahway, N.J.: Mershon Press, 1888) pp. 664–67.

40. Shelley, *Archdiocese of New York*, p. 54.

41. Smith, *Catholic Church in New York*, p. 41.

42. W. Barry Smith, *Issues in Church Governance from a Cross-Border Perspective: The Case of Lay Trusteeism in Mid-Nineteenth Century Buffalo, New York* (New York: Canadian Society of Church History, 1996), p. 26.

43. Robert Emmett Curran, *Shaping American Catholicism: Maryland and New York, 1805–1915* (Washington, D.C.: Catholic University of America Press, 2012), p. 20.

44. Bill J. Leonard and Jill Y. Crenshaw, eds., *Encyclopedia of Religious Controversies in the United States* (Westport, Conn.: Greenwood Press, 1997), p. 804.

45. Ellis, *American Catholicism*, p. 46.

46. Smith, *Catholic Church in New York*, p. 79.

47. Richard Shaw, *John Dubois: Founding Father* (Yonkers, N.Y.: U.S. Catholic Historical Society, 1983), p. 105.

48. John Connolly to Leonard Neale, February 13, 1817, AANY.

49. Bayley, *Brief Sketch*, p. 84.

50. Ibid., p. 85.

51. http://www.scny.org/files/2016/08/SCNY-Only-For-Your-Love-2009.pdf/, p. 6.

52. Quoted in Bayley, *Brief Sketch*, p. 94.

53. *The Catholic Encyclopedia for School and Home*, s.v. "Brooklyn, Diocese of" (New York: McGraw-Hill, 1965), p. 93.

54. Richard H. Clarke, *Lives of the Deceased Bishops of the Catholic Church in the United States* (1872; New York: P. O'Shea, 1888), p. 202.

55. Ibid., p. 16.

56. Msgr. Florence D. Cohalan, *A Popular History of the Archdiocese of New York* (Yonkers, N.Y.: U.S. Catholic Historical Society, 1983), p. 40.

57. Bayley, *Brief Sketch*, p. 104.

58. Shaw, *John Dubois*, p. 19.

59. Ibid., p. 108.

60. Quoted in Shaw, *John Dubois*, p. 108.

61. Shaw, *John Dubois*, p. 110.

62. Bayley, *Brief Sketch*, p. 109.

63. Shelley, *Archdiocese of New York*, p. 92.

64. Shaw, *John Dubois*, p. 125.

65. Ibid., p. 137.

66. Richard Shaw, *Dagger John: The Unquiet Life and Times of Archbishop John Hughes of New York* (New York: Paulist Press, 1977), p. 105.

67. Shaw, *John Dubois*, p. 173.

PART II. THE RISE TO POWER

Chapter 2. The Gardener: John Joseph Hughes

1. John Hassard, *Life of the Most Reverend John Hughes* (New York: Cosimo [1865], 2008), p. 18.

2. "Fr. Robert Barron Comments on Religious Liberty", YouTube video, 8:38, posted by Bishop Robert Barron, May 16, 2012, http://www.youtube.com/watch?feature=player_embedded&v=sh9AiESvImM#!.

3. John Savage, *Fenian Heroes and Martyrs* (Dublin: Patrick Donahoe, 1869), p. 16.

4. Hassard, *Life of Hughes*, p. 13.

5. U.S. Department of Homeland Security, *2004 Yearbook of Immigration Statistics* (Washington, D.C.: U.S. Department of Homeland Security, Office of Immigration Statistics, 2006), http://www.dhs.gov/xlibrary/assets/statistics/yearbook/2004/Yearbook2004.pdf.

6. Hassard, *Life of Hughes*, p. 15.

7. Ibid., p. 16.

8. Richard Shaw, *Dagger John: The Unquiet Life and Times of Archbishop John Hughes of New York* (New York: Paulist Press, 1977), p. 14.

9. Hassard, *Life of Hughes*, pp. 19–20.

10. Shaw, *Dagger John*, p. 15.

11. *Life of Archbishop Hughes* (New York: American News Company, 1864), p. 7.

12. Carl Apone, "Archbishop's Life One of Turmoil", *Pittsburgh Post Dispatch*, May 2, 1978, p. C-15.

13. Henry A. Brann, *Most Reverend John Hughes: First Archbishop of New York* (New York: Dodd Mead, 1892), p. 26.

14. Ibid., p. 26.

15. Ibid., p. 28.

16. Shaw, *Dagger John*, p. 41.

17. Hassard, *Life of Hughes*, p. 47.

18. Joseph J. Ellis, *His Excellency: George Washington* (New York: Knopf, 2004), p. 225.

19. Dubois to Hughes, October, 1826, Archives of the Archdiocese of New York (hereafter cited as AANY), St. Joseph's Seminary, Dunwoodie.

20. Hassard, *Life of Hughes*, p. 55.

21. Ibid., p. 56.

22. Shaw, *Dagger John*, p. 46.

23. Hughes to Bruté, May 7, 1827, AANY.

24. Shaw, *Dagger John*, p. 49.

25. Ibid., p. 57.

26. Philip Hamburger, "Illiberal Liberalism: Liberal Theology, Anti-Catholicism, and Church Property", *Journal of Contemporary Legal Issues* 12 (2002): 704.

27. John J. Hughes and John A. Breckinridge, *Discussion of the Question: Is the Roman Catholic Religion, in Any or in All of Its Principles or Doctrines, Inimical to Civil or Religious Liberty?* (Baltimore: John Murphy, 1869), p. 301.

28. John Hughes and John Breckinridge, *Controversy Between the Reverend John Hughes, of the Roman Catholic Church, and the Reverend John Breckinridge, of the Presbyterian Church, Relative to the Existing Differences in the Roman Catholic and Protestant Religions* (Philadelphia: Joseph Whetham, 1833).

29. Hassard, *Life of Hughes*, p. 157.

30. Ibid., p. 325.

31. Ibid., p. 145.

32. Thomas W. Jodziewicz, "Bishop John England: A Catholic Apologist at the United States Capitol", *American Catholic Studies* 121, no. 1 (2010): 31.

33. Hassard, *Life of Hughes*, p. 146.

34. Ibid., p. 147.

35. Thomas J. Shelley, *The Archdiocese of New York: The Bicentennial History, 1808–2008* (Strasbourg, France: Éditions du Signe, 2007), p. 103.

36. Ibid., p. 104.

37. Vincent Peter Lannie, "Profile of an Immigrant Bishop: The Early Career of John Hughes", *Pennsylvania History* 32, no. 4 (October 1965): 370.

38. Dubois to Hughes, November 6, 1837, AANY.

39 Hughes to Purcell, February 24, 1838, Archives of Notre Dame University, quoted in Shelley, *Archdiocese of New York*, p. 108.

40. Shelley, *Archdiocese of New York*, pp. 107–8.

41. Ibid., p. 109.

42. Augustus Thébaud, S.J., *Three-Quarters of a Century* (New York: U.S. Catholic Historical Society, 1904), p. 287.

43. Carl Sandburg, *Storm over the Land* (New York: Harcourt, Brace, 1942), p. 87.

44. William J. Stern, "How Dagger John Saved New York's Irish", *City Journal*, Spring 1997, p. 84.

45. Don C. Seitz, *The James Gordon Bennetts: Father and Son, Proprietors of the New York* (New York: Bobbs-Merrill, 1928), p. 108.

46. Carl Sandburg, *Abraham Lincoln: The War Years*, vol. 1 (New York: Harcourt, Brace, 1939), p. 355.

47. Ibid.

48. Quoted in Henry J. Browne, "The Archdiocese of New York a Century Ago: A Memoir of Archbishop Hughes, 1838–1858", *Historical Record and Studies*, no. 39 (1952): 136.

49. Thomas F. O'Connor, "Pioneer Catholic Seminaries in New York", *New York History* 24, no. 2 (April 1943): 216.

50. Joseph J. McCadden, "Bishop Hughes versus the Public School Society of New York", *Catholic Historical Review* 50, no. 2 (July 1964):188.

51. Ibid., p. 189.

52. William O. Bourne, *History of the Public School Society of the City of New York* (New York: William Wood, 1870), p. 175.

53. McCadden, "Bishop Hughes versus the Public School Society", p. 190.

54. Henry J. Browne, "Support of Catholic Education New York", *Catholic Historical Review* 39, no. 1 (April 1953): 12.

55. Hughes to unknown recipient, August 27, 1840, AANY.

56. McCadden, "Bishop Hughes versus the Public School Society", p. 197.

57. Bourne, "Public School Society", p. 201.

58. McCadden, "Bishop Hughes versus the Public School Society", p. 202.

59. Browne, "Support of Catholic Education", p. 16.

60. George Potter, *To the Golden Door: The Story of the Irish in Ireland and America* (Boston: Little, Brown, 1960), pp. 414–15.

61. Browne, "Support of Catholic Education", p. 18.

62. Andrew P. Yox, "The Parochial Context of Trusteeism: Buffalo's St. Louis Church, 1828–1855", *Catholic Historical Review* 76, no. 4 (October 1990): 718.

63. Browne, "Archdiocese of New York", p. 137.

64. Ibid.

65. Patrick Carey, "The Laity's Understanding of the Trustee System", *Catholic Historical Review* 64, no. 3 (July 1978): 362.

66. Patrick J. Dignan, *A History of the Legal Incorporation of Catholic Church Property in the United States* (Washington, D.C.: Catholic University Press, 1933), p. 142.

67. Carey, "Trustee System", p. 373.

68. Father Gerald C. Treacy, S.J., "Evils of Trusteeism", in *Historical Records and Studies*, ed., 8:136–56 (New York: United States Catholic Historical Society, 1915), p. 141.

69. Ibid.

70. Robert F. McNamara, "Trusteeism in the Atlantic States, 1785–1863", *Catholic Historical Review* 30, no. 2 (July, 1944): 146.

71. Lawrence Kehoe, ed., *The Complete Works of John Hughes, D.D., Archbishop of New York*, vol. 1 (New York: Lawrence Kehoe, 1866), p. 314.

72. Ibid., p. 315.

73. Ibid., p. 316.

74. Ibid., p, 318.

75. Ibid., p. 320.

76. Browne, "Archdiocese of New York", p. 138.

77. Ibid., p. 139.

78. Shelley, *Archdiocese of New York*, p. 68.

79. W. Barry Smith, *Issues in Church Governance from a Cross-Border Perspective: The Case of Lay Trusteeism in Mid-Nineteenth Century Buffalo* (New York: Canadian Society of Church History, 1996), p. 30.

80. Ibid.

81. Shaw, *Dagger John*, p. 292.

82. Ibid., p. 93.

83. Margaret E. Fitzgerald, *The Philadelphia Nativist Riots* (n.p.: Irish Cultural Society of the Garden City Area, 1992), http://www.irish-society.org/home/hedgemaster-archives-2/history-events/the-philadelphia-nativists-riots.

84. Shelley, *Archdiocese of New York*, p. 126.

85. Hassard, *Life of Hughes*, p. 278.

86. Thomas J. Craughwell, *The Greatest Brigade: How the Irish Brigade Cleared the Way to Victory in the American Civil War* (Beverly, Mass.: Fair Winds Press, 2011), p. 5.

87. John, Bishop of New York, "TITLE", *Freeman's Journal*, May 11, 1844.

88. Shelley, *Archdiocese of New York*, p. 127.

89. Erastus Brooks and John Hughes, *The Controversy between Senator Brooks and †John, Archbishop of New York: Growing out of the Speech of Senator Brooks on the Church Property Bill ... March 6, 1855*, repr. ed. (Ithaca, N.Y.: Cornell University Press, 2010), p. 20.

90. Charles P. Connor, "Archbishop Hughes and Mid-Century Politics, 1844–1860", *U.S. Catholic Historian* 3, no. 3 (1983): 168.

91. Tyler Anbinder, *Nativism and Slavery: The Northern Know Nothings and the Politics of the 1850s* (New York: Oxford University Press, 1992), p. 134.

92. David J. Endres, "Know-Nothings, Nationhood, and the Nuncio: Reassessing the Visit of Archbishop Bedini", *U.S. Catholic Historian* 21, no. 4 (Fall 2003): 1.

93. Shaw, *Dagger John*, p. 277.

94. Hassard, *Life of Hughes*, p. 361.

95. Rena Mazyck Andrews, "Slavery Views of a Northern Prelate", *Church History* 3, no. 1 (March 1934): 60.

96. Ibid.

97. Alan J. Singer, *New York and Slavery: Time to Teach the Truth* (Albany: SUNY Press, 2008), pp. 82–83.

98. Lawrence Kehoe, ed., *The Complete Works of John Hughes, D.D., Archbishop of New York* (New York: Lawrence Kehoe, 1866), 2:595.

99. Connor, "Archbishop Hughes and Mid-Century Politics", p.176.

100. Patrick W. Carey, *Catholics in America: A History* (New York: Rowman and Littlefield, 2004), p. 43.

101. Andrews, "Slavery Views", pp. 61–63.

102. Walter G. Sharrow, "John Hughes and a Catholic Response to Slavery in America", *Journal of Negro History* 57, no. 3 (July 1972): 260.

103. Ibid., 261.

104. V. F. O'Daniel, "Archbishop John Hughes: American Envoy to France, 1861", *Catholic Historical Review* 3, no. 3 (1917): 338.

105. Kehoe, *Works of Hughes*, 2:372–73.

106. Sam Roberts, "New York Doesn't Care to Remember the Civil War", *New York Times*, December 26, 2010.

107. Quoted in Albon P. Man, Jr., "The Irish in New York in the Early Eighteen-Sixties", *Irish Historical Studies* 7, no. 26 (September 1950): 87.

108. Stern, "Dagger John Saved New York's Irish", p. 85.

109. "Death of Archbishop Hughes. His Sickness and Last Moments. Sketch of His Life", *New York Times*, January 4, 1864.

110. Ibid.

111. "Archbishop Hughes", *Harper's Weekly*, January 16, 1864, p. 44.

112. Charles G. Herbermann, et al., eds., *Catholic Encyclopedia* (New York: Encyclopedia Press, 1912), 11:21.

113. Sam Roberts, "At St. Patrick's, a Cornerstone That Has Long Eluded Searchers", *New York Times*, October 12, 2011.

114. Henry J. Browne, "Memoir of Archbishop Hughes", p. 153.

115. Ibid., pp. 155–57.

116. Ibid., p. 165.

117. Kehoe, *Works of Hughes*, 2:269.

118. *The Life of Archbishop Hughes with a Full Account of His Funeral [with] Bishop McCloskey's Oration* (New York: American News Company, 1864), pp. 20–21.

Chapter 3. The First: John Joseph McCloskey

1. John Cardinal Farley, *The Life of John Cardinal McCloskey: First Prince of the Church in America: 1810–1885* (New York: Longmans, Green, 1918).

2. John Tracy Ellis, review of *The American Pope* by John Cooney, *Catholic Historical Review* 72, no. 4 (October 1986): 676.

3. Michael Glazier and Thomas J. Shelley, eds., *The Encyclopedia of American Catholicism* (Collegeville, Minn.: Liturgical Press, 1997), p. 874.

4. John Talbot Smith, *The Catholic Church in New York* (1905; New York: Cosimo, 2008), 1:277.

5. See Joseph T. Durkin, *General Sherman's Son: The Life of Thomas Ewing Sherman, S.J.* (New York: Farrar, Straus, and Cudahy, 1959), pp. 10, 52, and 272.

6. Farley, *Life of McCloskey*, p. 345.

7. An online genealogy forum cites this credible note from the Genealogy Centre in Londonderry, in part: "Cardinal John McCloskey's parents were Patrick McCloskey of Killunaght and Elizabeth Hassan of Coolnamonan. These townlands are located in the civil parish of Banagher." "John McCloskey (Cardinal)", OurWebsite.org, http://ourwebsite.org/nevins/nevins-p/p228.shtml/.

8. Glazier and Shelley, *Encyclopedia of American Catholicism*, p. 874.

9. Letter from St. Peter's Church on the baptismal record of John McCloskey, November 29, 1898, Archives of the Archdiocese of New York (hereafter cited as AANY), "McCloskey", box A-33, St. Joseph Seminary, Dunwoodie.

10. Note of Bishop Farley, in ibid.

11. "The Boyhood of America's First Cardinal", undated, p. 1, in ibid.

12. Farley, *Life of McCloskey*, p. 14.

13. Ibid., p. 22.

14. Francis Beauchesne Thornton, *Our American Princes: The Story of the Seventeen American Cardinals* (New York, G. P. Putnam's Sons, 1963), p. 23.

15. Farley, *Life of McCloskey*, p. 16.

16. Thomas F. Meehan, "The First American Cardinal", *Catholic World* 90 (March 1910): 807.

17. Notes of Monsignor Hayes, AANY, "McCloskey", box A-33.

18. Jovana Rizzo, "Pierrepont: Seeing Great Potential across the River in Brooklyn", The Real Deal, July 30, 2008, http://therealdeal.com/.

19. Farley, *Life of McCloskey*, p. 14.

20. Thornton, *Our American Princes*, p. 21.

21. Ibid., p. 19.

22. Ibid.

23. Thomas Meehan, "Cornelius Heeney", in *Catholic Encyclopedia* (New York: Robert Appleton Company, 1910).

24. Thomas F. Meehan, "A Self-Effaced Philanthropist: Cornelius Heeney, 1754–1848", *Catholic Historical Review* 4, no.1 (April 1918): 9–10.

25. Farley, *Life of McCloskey*, p. 20.

26. Thornton, *Our American Princes*, p. 23.

27. Ibid., p. 22–23.

28. Ibid., p. 24.

29. Ibid., pp. 25–34.

30. Ibid., p. 34.

31. Photo no. 01012-001, AANY.

32. L. Fallon, "Concussion", in *Gale Encyclopedia of Children's Health: Infancy through Adolescence* (Farmington Hills, Mich.: Gale, 2006).

33. Farley, *Life of McCloskey*, p. 38.

34. Ibid., pp. 35–36.

35. Thornton, *Our American Princes*, p. 25.

36. Farley, *Life of McCloskey*, p. 40.

37. Ibid., p. 48.

38. Francis de Sales, *Introduction to the Devout Life* 2:2, Christian Classics Ethereal Library, http://www.ccel.org/ccel/desales/devout_life.txt/.

39. Mary E. Meline and Edward F.X. McSween, "Chapter 18: 1829" in *The Story of the Mountain*, Emmitsburg Area Historical Society, http://www.emmitsburg.net/archive_list /articles/history/stories/som/18.htm/.

40. Farley, *Life of Cardinal McCloskey*, p. 50.

41. Bertha Burnett, et al., *History of Bedford Academy* (Mt. Kisco, N.Y.: Press of the "Weekly", 1877), p. 1.

42. Farley, *Life of McCloskey*, p. 50.

43. "Rectors of the Seminary", Mount St. Mary's University website, http://www.msmary .edu/seminary/about/history/rectors-of-seminary.html/.

44. Farley, *Life of McCloskey*, p. 50.

45. Smith, *Catholic Church in New York*, p. 278.

46. Thornton, *Our American Princes*, pp. 25–26.

47. Farley, *Life of McCloskey*, p. 66.

48. Thornton, *Our American Princes*, p. 27.

49. Farley, *Life of McCloskey*, p. 74.

50. "Boyhood of America's First Cardinal", p. 4.

51. Ibid., p. 5.

52. Farley, *Life of McCloskey*, pp. 82–85.

53. Ibid., p. 86.

54. Ibid., pp. 94–95.

55. Ibid., p. 95.

56. Ibid., p. 98.

57. Ibid., p. 109.

58. Thomas J. Shelley, "Catholic Greenwich Village: Ethnic Geography and Religious Identity in New York City, 1880–1930", *Catholic Historical Review* 89, no. 1 (January 2003): 62.

59. Farley, *Life of McCloskey*, p. 128.

60. Thornton, *Our American Princes*, p. 31.

61. Ibid., pp. 32–33.

62. Ibid.

63. Farley, *Life of McCloskey*, p. 148.

64. Patrick W. Carey, *Orestes A. Brownson: American Religious Weathervane* (Grand Rapids: W.B. Eerdmans, 2004), p. 142.

65. Farley, *Life of McCloskey*, p. 160.

66. Thornton, *Our American Princes*, p. 35.

67. Farley, *Life of McCloskey*, pp. 169–70.

68. Very Rev. William H. Pape, "Within These Sacred Walls", website of the Cathedral of the Immaculate Conception, http://www.cathedralic.com/history.htm.

69. Farley, *Life of McCloskey*, p. 215.

70. Smith, *Catholic Church in New York*, p. 279.

71. Ibid., p. 202.

72. Copy of a letter to Cardinal de Reisach on why he does not wish to be considered for Archbishop of New York, January 1864, AANY, "McCloskey", box A-33.

73. Thornton, *Our American Princes*, pp. 36–37.

74. Farley, *Life of McCloskey*, pp. 239–40.

75. Msgr. Florence D. Cohalan, review of *A Cathedral of Suitable Magnificence: St. Patrick's Cathedral, New York* by Margaret Carthy, *Catholic Historical Review* 72, no. 3 (July 1986): 509.

76. Thornton, *Our American Princes*, p. 38.

77. Archbishop James Gibbons, *Funeral Oration on His Eminence John Cardinal McCloskey* (New York: Benziger Brothers, 1885), p. 9.

78. Smith, *Catholic Church in New York*, p. 285.

79. Bishop Henry Gabriels, *Historical Sketch of St. Joseph's Provincial Seminary* (1905; Ithaca, N.Y.: Cornell University Library, 2009), p. 7.

80. "Work Suspended by Order of Archbishop Hughes", *New York Times*, August 9, 1860, p. 8, quoted in Leland Cook, *St. Patrick's Cathedral: A Centennial History* (New York: Quick Fox, 1979), p. 58.

81. Most Rev. John M. Farley, *History of St. Patrick's Cathedral* (New York: Society for the Propagation of the Faith, 1908), p. 128.

82. *New York Times*, May 7, 1875, p. 8, quoted in Cook, *St. Patrick's Cathedral*, p. 58.

83. Reverend Frank J. Boland, *The Attitude of the American Hierarchy toward the Doctrine of Papal Infallibility at the Vatican Council* (Toronto: *Report 27* of the Canadian Catholic Historical Association, 1960), p. 44.

84. Thornton, *Our American Princes*, p. 40.

85. Farley, *Life of McCloskey*, p. 143.

86. Thornton, *Our American Princes*, p. 42.

87. Archbishop James Gibbons, *Funeral Oration*, p 6.

Chapter 4. The Roman: Michael Augustine Corrigan

1. Robert Emmett Curran, *Michael Augustine Corrigan and the Shaping of Conservative Catholicism, 1978–1902* (New York: Arno Press, 1978), p. 23.

2. John A. Mooney, *Memorial of the Most Reverend Michael Augustine Corrigan, D.D.: Third Archbishop of New York* (New York: Cathedral Library Association, 1902), p. 3.

3. Quoted in Curran, *Michael Augustine Corrigan*, p. 25.

4. Ibid., p. 23.

5. Ibid., p. 6.

6. Ibid.

7. Mooney, *Memorial of Corrigan*, p. 7.

8. Curran, *Michael Augustine Corrigan*, p. 31.

9. Joseph F. Mahoney and Peter J. Wosh, eds., *The Diocesan Journal of Michael Augustine Corrigan , Bishop of Newark, 1872–1880* (Newark: New Jersey Catholic Historical Records Commission, 1987), p. xii.

10. Mason Gaffney, "Henry George, Dr. Edward McGlynn, and Pope Leo XIII" (paper delivered to the International Conference on Henry George, November 1, 1997, Cooper Union, N.Y; revised March 12, 2000), http://www.masongaffney.org/publications/K18George_McGlynn_and_Leo_XIII.pdf/.

11. Mooney, *Memorial of Corrigan*, p. 39.

12. Curran, *Michael Augustine Corrigan*, p. vi.

13. Mooney, *Memorial of Corrigan*, p. 9.

14. Ibid., p. 11.

15. Glen Janus, "Bishop Bernard McQuaid: On 'True' and 'False' Americanism", *U.S. Catholic Historian* 11, no. 3 (1993): 53.

16. Ibid., p. 54.

17. Ibid., p. 56.

18. Mahoney and Wosh, *Diocesan Journal*, p. vii.

19. Ibid., p. viii.

20. Ibid.

21. Ibid.

22. Ibid., p. 6.

23. Mooney, *Memorial of Corrigan*, p. 20.

24. Ibid., pp. 24–25.

25. Mahoney and Wosh, *Diocesan Journal*, p. 248.

26. Ibid., pp. 250, 6.

27. Mooney, *Memorial of Corrigan*, p. 28.

28. John Talbot Smith, *The Catholic Church in New York* (New York: Hall and Locke, 1905), 2:415.

29. John Cardinal Farley, *The Life of John Cardinal McCloskey: First Prince of the Church in America: 1810–1885* (New York: Longmans, Green, 1918), p. 365.

30. Mooney, *Memorial of Corrigan*, p. 30.

31. Archbishop John Ireland, *The Church and Modern Society: Lectures and Addresses* (St. Paul: Pioneer Press, 1905), p. 53.

32. Marvin Richard O'Connell, *John Ireland and the American Catholic Church* (St. Paul: Minnesota Historical Society Press, 1988), p. 195.

33. Curran, *Michael Augustine Corrigan*, p. 71.

34. Henry A. Brann, *History of the American College of the Roman Catholic Church of the United States, Rome, Italy* (New York: Benziger Brothers, 1910), p. 345.

35. Curran, *Michael Augustine Corrigan*, p. 161.

36. Smith, *Catholic Church in New York*, 2:419.

37. Arthur J. Scanlan, S.T.D., *St. Joseph's Seminary Dunwoodie, New York: 1896–1921* (New York: United States Catholic Historical Society, 1923), p. 69.

38. Ibid., p. 79.

39. Ibid., p. 82.

40. Mooney, *Memorial of Corrigan*, p. 39.

41. CPI Inflation Calculator, Bureau of Labor Statistics, http://www.bls.gov/data/inflation_calculator.htm/.

42. Mooney, *Memorial of Corrigan*, p. 40.

43. Frank J. Cavaioli, "Patterns of Italian Immigration to the United States", *Catholic Social Science Review*, no. 13 (2008): 214–15.

44. Ibid., p. 215.

45. Stephen Michael DiGiovanni, *Archbishop Corrigan and the Italian Immigrants* (Huntington, Ind.: Our Sunday Visitor, 1994), p. 18.

46. Ibid., p. 19.

47. Ibid., p. 83.

48. Edward C. Stibili, *What Can Be Done to Help Them? The Italian Saint Raphael Society, 1887–1923* (New York: Center for Migration Studies, 2003), p. 36.

49. Ibid., p. 68.

50. Archbishop Michael A. Corrigan to Archbishop Camillo Mazzela, November 7, 1890, Archives of the Archdiocese of New York (hereafter cited as AANY), St. Joseph's Seminary, Dunwoodie, box G-28.

51. Anthony D. Andreassi, "The Cunning Leader of a Dangerous Clique? The Burtsell Affair and Archbishop Michael Corrigan", *Catholic Historical Review* 86, no. 4 (October 2000): 623.

52. Richard Burtsell papers, diary 1, March 30, 1865, AANY.

53. Curran, *Michael Augustine Corrigan*, p. 175.

54. Ibid., p. 176.

55. Leo XIII, *Humanum Genus*, April 1884, http://w2.vatican.va/.

56. Smith, *Catholic Church in New York*, 2:541.

57. Edward T. O'Donnell, "Soggarth Aroon: The Rise and Fall of Rev. Edward McGlynn", in *Catholics in New York: Society, Culture, and Politics: 1808–1946*, ed. Terry L. Golway (New York: Fordham University Press, 2008), p. 147.

58. Ibid.

59. Leo XIII, *Rerum Novarum*, May 15, 1891, par. 10, http://w2.vatican.va/.

60. "Letter to Pope Leo XIII", Henry George Foundation, http://www.henrygeorge foundation.org/the-science-of-economics/letter-to-pope-leo-xiii.html/.

61. Sylvester L. Malone, *Dr. Edward McGlynn* (New York: Dr. McGlynn Monument Society, 1918), p. 5.

62. See C. Joseph Nuesse, "Henry George and *Rerum Novarum*: Evidence Is Scant that the American Economist Was a Target of Leo XIII's Classic Encyclical", *American Journal of Economics and Sociology* 44, no. 2 (April 1985): 241–54.

63. Margaret Mary Reher, "A 'Call to Action' Revisited", *U.S. Catholic Historian* 1, no. 2 (Winter–Spring 1981): 55.

64. Robert Emmett Curran, review of *The Determined Doctor: The Story of Edward McGlynn* by Alfred Isacsson, *Catholic Historical Review* 84, no. 3 (July 1998): 587.

65. Curran, *Michael Augustine Corrigan*, pp. 199–200.

66. Archbishop Corrigan, "Pastoral Letter", *Freeman's Journal*, November 27, 1886.

67. Smith, *Catholic Church in New York*, 2:546.

68. Curran, *Michael Augustine Corrigan*, p. 239.

69. Smith, *Catholic Church in New York*, 2:553.

70. Philip Gleason, *Contending with Modernity: Catholic Higher Education in the Twentieth Century* (New York: Oxford University Press, 1995), p. 10.

71. Janus, "Bishop Bernard McQuaid", p. 53.

72. Ibid., p. 59.

73. Ibid., p. 61.

74. Thomas E. Wangler, "Americanist Beliefs and Papal Orthodoxy: 1884–1899", *U.S. Catholic Historian* 11, no. 3 (1993): 46.

75. Samuel J. Thomas, "Mugwump Cartoonists, the Papacy, and Tammany Hall in America's Gilded Age", *Religion and American Culture* 14, no. 2 (Summer 2004): 234, doi:10.1525/rac.2004.14.2.213.

76. Wangler, "Americanist Beliefs", p. 51.

77. Thomas E. Wangler, "American Catholic Expansionism: 1864–1894", *Harvard Theological Review* 75, no. 3 (July 1982): 383.

78. Smith, *Catholic Church in New York*, 2:555.

79. Ibid., p. 556.

80. Curran, *Michael Augustine Corrigan*, p. 512.

81. Leland Cook, *St. Patrick's Cathedral: A Centennial History* (New York: Quick Fox, 1979), p. 85.

82. "St. Patrick's Cathedral" in *Catholic Encyclopedia* (New York: Encyclopedia Company, 1913).

83. Cook, *St. Patrick's Cathedral*, p. 99.

84. Curran, *Michael Augustine Corrigan*, p. 512.

85. "Ordinaries of the Archdiocese of New York", "Archbishop Michael Augustine Corrigan (1839–1902)", AANY, http://archnyarchives.org/ordinaries-of-the-archdiocese-of-new-york/.

86. Smith, *Catholic Church in New York*, 2:557.

87. Curran, *Michael Augustine Corrigan*, p. 514.

88. Ibid.

89. Quoted in Smith, *Catholic Church in New York*, 2:561.

90. Mooney, *Memorial of Corrigan*, p. 61.

Chapter 5. The Builder: John Murphy Farley

1. Gibbons to Farley, November 23, 1988, Archives of the Archdiocese of New York (hereafter cited as AANY), St. Joseph's Seminary, Dunwoodie.

2. Thomas J. Shelly, "John Cardinal Farley and Modernism in New York", *Church History* 61 (1992): 352.

3. Ibid.

4. Ibid., 351.

5. James J. Walsh, *Our American Cardinals* (New York: D. Appleton, 1926), p. 133.

6. George J. Marlin, *The American Catholic Voter: Two Hundred Years of Political Impact* (South Bend, Ind.: St. Augustine's Press, 2004), p. 132.

7. Michael Novak, *The Rise of the Unmeltable Ethnics* (New York: Macmillan, 1972), p. 10.

8. Walsh, p. 141.

9. Ibid., p. 169.

10. Ibid., p. 139.

11. Msgr. Thomas J. Shelly, *The Archdiocese of New York: The Bicentennial History, 1808–2008* (Strasbourg, France, Éditions du Signe, 2007), p. 424.

12. Thomas J. Shelly, *Dunwoodie: The History of St. Joseph's Seminary* (Westminster, Md.: Christian Classics, 1993), p. 130.

13. Michael Davies, *Partisans of Error: St. Pius X against the Modernists* (Long Prairie, Minn.: Neumann Press, 1983), p. vii.

14. Ibid., p. xv.

15. Ibid., p. 104.

16. Walsh, *Our American Cardinals*, p. 144.

17. Farley and New York and New Jersey bishops to Pope Pius X, August 31, 1907, AANY.

18. Introduction to *The Catholic Encyclopedia*, vol. 1 (New York: Robert Appleton, 1907–1912).

19. Walsh, *Our American Cardinals*, p. 141.

20. Shelley, *Archdiocese of New York*, p. 427.

21. Shelley, *Dunwoodie*, p. 136.

22. From the prepublication brochure of the *New York Review: A Journal of the Ancient Faith and Modern Thought*, AANY.

23. Shelley, *Dunwoodie*, p. 144.

24. Shelley, "John Cardinal Farley", p. 357.

25. Falconio to Farley, January 15, 1908, AANY.

26. Shelley, "John Cardinal Farley", pp. 357–58.

28. Farley to Falconio, June 22, 1908, AANY.

29. Driscoll to Farley, March 6, 1908, AANY.

30. Shelley, *Dunwoodie*, p. 154.

31. Shelley, "John Cardinal Farley", p. 359.

32. Shelley, *Archdiocese of New York*, p. 429.

33. Shelley, *Dunwoodie*, p. 170.

34. Shelley, "John Cardinal Farley", p. 361.

35. Msgr. Florence D. Cohalan, *A Popular History of the Archdiocese of New York*, 2nd ed. (New York: U.S. Catholic Historical Society, 1999), p. 230.

35. Ibid., p. 229.

444 SONS OF SAINT PATRICK

36. Augustin McNally, *The Catholic Centenary, 1808–1908* (New York: Moffat, Yard, 1908), p. xxi.

37. Shelley, *Dunwoodie*, p. 165.

38. Francis Beauchesne Thornton, *Our American Princes: The Story of the Seventeen American Cardinals* (New York: G. P. Putnam's Sons, 1963), p. 81.

39. Walsh, *Our American Cardinals*, p. 153.

40. "Cardinal Farley", *Tablet*, June 30, 1917, p. 814.

41. *New York American* (November 1902).

42. Ibid.

43. G. J. Mar to Rev. P. J. Hayes, December 6, 1902, AANY.

44. Farley to William D. Guthrie, March 12, 1913, AANY.

45. Transcript from the *Los Angeles Examiner*, November 9, 1912, AANY.

46. Transcript from *Los Angeles Tidings*, December 1912, AANY.

47. Herman Bernstein to Farley, November 13, 1913, AANY.

48. Bishop Hayes to Henry Mitchell McCracken, moderator of the Presbytery of New York, March 16, 1915, AANY.

49. Proposed constitutional amendment introduced in State of New York Constitutional Convention, May 4, 1915, AANY.

50. George Gillespie to Bishop P. J. Hayes, May 5, 1915, AANY.

51. Minutes of the meeting of the Committee on Catholic Interests, February 8, 1915, AANY.

52. Ibid.

53. Memorial to the Sixty-Fifth Congress urging tax exemption for bequests, legacies, and gifts to education, philanthropy, and religion, AANY.

54. Wadsworth to Farley, June 3, 1917, AANY.

55. *The Truth about the Attack on the Charitable Institutions* (pamphlet published in 1916), p. 8, AANY.

56. William Farrell, *A Public Scandal: The Strong Commission* (pamphlet published in 1916), p. 10, AANY.

57. Peter Eisenstadt, ed., *The Encyclopedia of New York State* (New York: Syracuse University Press, 2005), p. 1008.

58. Guthrie to Hayes, December 27, 1915, AANY.

59. Guthrie to O'Brien, December 27, 1915, AANY.

60. Shelley, *Archdiocese of New York*, p. 437.

61. Farrell, *Public Scandal*, p. 11.

62. Transcript of Msgr. John Dunn's statement on the Strong Commission, AANY.

63. Ibid.

64. Ibid.

65. Cohalan, *Popular History*, p. 241.

66. McDonnell to Hayes, May 20, 1916, AANY.

67. Hayes to Bonzano, November 17, 1917.

68. David J O'Brien, *Public Catholicism* (New York: Orbis Books, 1996), p. 152.

69. Ibid.

70. Farley to Baker, June 13, 1917, AANY.

71. Baker to Farley, June 15, 1917, AANY.

72. Farley to Baker, June 19, 1917, AANY.

73. Farley speech to Catholic Clubs, undated, AANY.

74. *World*, July 9, 1918.

75. Stagni to Farley, March 2, 1913, AANY.

76. Farley to Stagni, March 4, 1913, AANY.

77. Donovan to Hayes, March 13, 1933, AANY.

78. Hayes to Donovan, April 3, 1933, AANY.

79. DiNapoli to Casey, March 26, 1934, and Casey to DiNapoli, March 27, 1934, AANY.

80. Hayes to Colonel A. G. Anderson, April 9, 1937, AANY.

81. Bonzano to Hayes, May 19, 1917, AANY.

82. Farley secretary to Bonzano, August 26, 1918, AANY.

83. Hickey homily, September 25, 1918, AANY.

Chapter 6. The Bureaucrat: Patrick Joseph Hayes

1. John B. Kelly, *Cardinal Hayes: One of Ourselves* (New York: Farrar and Reinhart, 1940), p. 78.

2. Thomas Sugrue, "Cardinal Shepherd", *New Yorker*, February 17, 1934.

3. Charles Morris, *American Catholic* (New York: Random House, 1997), p. 120.

4. Msgr. Florence D. Cohalan, *A Popular History of the Archdiocese of New York*, 2nd ed. (1983; New York: United States Catholic Historical Society, 1999), p. 257.

5. John Bonzano to Farley, December 26, 1915, Archives of the Archdiocese of New York (hereafter cited as AANY).

6. Ibid.

7. Hanna to Farley, undated, AANY.

8. Patrick J. Hayes, *Catholic World*, May 1923, p. 147.

9. Robert Kelgan, "A Survey and Its Aftermath", *Catholic Charities Review* 5 (1921).

10. *Catholic World*, May 1923, p. 148.

11. Ibid., p. 151.

12. Ibid., p. 152.

13. "The Cardinal's Crusade", *Commonweal*, February 1924, p. 449.

14. Thomas J. Shelly, *Dunwoodie: The History of St. Joseph's Seminary* (Westminster, Md.: Christian Classics, 1993), pp. 185–86.

15. Ibid., p. 186.

16. Ibid., p. 191.

17. Hayes to Smith, January 11, 1927, AANY.

18. Hayes to Fumasoni-Biondi, November 22, 1926, AANY.

19. George J. Marlin, *The American Catholic Voter: Two Hundred Years of Political Impact* (South Bend, Ind.: St. Augustine's Press, 2004), p. 176.

20. Ibid.

21. Ibid., p. 177.

22. "Intolerance Is a Foe All Good Americans Should Fear", *New York American*, June 6, 1924.

23. Robert K. Murray, *The 103rd Ballot* (New York: Harper and Row, 1976), p. 247.

24. Shawn Lay, *Hooded Knights on the Niagara* (New York: NYU Press, 1995), p. 43.

25. New York City Police Department commanding officer of bomb squad to William O'Neil, superintendent of police, Providence, Rhode, Island, March 5, 1923, AANY.

26. Ibid.

27. Ibid.

28. C. C. Young to Hayes, October 20, 1923, AANY.

29. *Catholic World*, August 1924, p. 693.

30. Peter H. Odegard, *Religion and Politics* (New York: Oceana Publications, 1960), p. 47.

31. Oscar Handlin, *Al Smith and His America* (New York: Little Brown, 1958), p. 4.

32. Msgr. Thomas J. Shelley, *The Archdiocese of New York: The Bicentennial History 1808–2008* (France: Éditions due Signe, 2007), p. 450.

33. Ibid.

34. Ibid., p. 452.

35. Alfred E. Smith, *Progressive Democracy* (New York: Hartcourt, Brace, 1928), pp. 254–69.

36. Ibid.

37. Ibid.

38. Marlin, *American Catholic Vote*, p. 183.

39. Arthur Schlesinger, ed., *History of American Presidential Elections*, vol. 7 (New York: Chelsea House, 1985), p. 2597.

40. Paul Winter, *What Price Tolerance* (New York: All-American Book, Lecture and Research Bureau, 1928), p. 183.

41. R. C. Woodward to Hayes, September 28, 1928, AANY.

42. Stephen J. Donahue to R. C. Woodward, October 4, 1928, AANY.

43. Hayes to Smith, November 7, 1928, AANY.

44. Smith to Hayes, November 10, 1928, AANY.

45. "Birth Control Raid Made by Police on Archbishop's Order", *New York Times*, November 14, 1921.

46. Statement of Archbishop Hayes addressed to the general public, November 21, 1921, AANY.

47. "Mrs. Sanger Replies to Archbishop Hayes", *New York Times*, December 20, 1921.

48. Duane to Hayes, February 8, 1929, AANY.

49. "Cardinal Hayes Speaks Out", *Commonweal*, December 20, 1935, p. 197.

50. Ibid.

51. Ibid., pp. 197–98.

52. Ibid., p. 198.

53. Ibid.

54. "Cardinal Hayes in Texas", *Commonweal*, March 31, 1931, p. 553.

55. George Anthony Kiener, "His Eminence, a Senator" *America*, March 21, 1931, p. 569.

56. Ibid.

57. George Q. Flynn, *American Catholics and the Roosevelt Presidency, 1932–1936* (Lexington, Ky.: University of Kentucky Press, 1968), p. 37.

58. *Brooklyn Tablet*, May 13, 1933.

59. Flynn, *American Catholics*, p. 42.

60. Ibid., p. 55.

61. Joseph Cardinal Hayes, "The Principles of the Common Good", *Catholic Mind* 31, no. 14 (July 22, 1933): 266.

62. Flynn, *American Catholics*, p. 79.

63. Ibid., p. 118

64. Thomas Maier, *The Kennedys: America's Emerald Kings* (New York: Basic Books, 2003), p. 109.

65. Hayes to Coolidge and Hayes to Kellogg, telegrams, ca. June 1926, AANY.

66. Hayes to John J. Burke, telegram, ca. June 1926, AANY.

67. Patrick J. Geehan, chancellor, Diocese of San Antonio to Hayes, March 16, 1926, AANY.

68. Hayes to pastors of the archdiocese, July 16, 1926, AANY.

69. William D. Guthrie, *Church and State in Mexico: Professional Opinion* (New York: Pandick Press, 1926), p. 2.

70. National Conference of Catholic Bishops; U.S Catholic Conference, *Pastoral Letters of the U.S. Catholic Bishops*, ed. Hugh J. Nolan, vol. 1, *1792–1940* (Washington, D.C.: USCCB Publishing Services, 1984), p. 339.

71. Newman C. Eberhardt, *A Summary of Catholic History*, vol. 2 (St. Louis: B. Herder, 1962), p. 790.

72. Flynn, *American Catholics*, p. 169.

73. Ibid., p. 164.

74. Ibid., p. 166.

75. Ibid., p. 175.

76. Ibid., p. 185.

77. Ibid., p. 127.

78. Ibid., p. 138.

79. Ibid.

80. Archbishop Hayes' secretary, Joseph P. Dineen, to Conde Pallen, April 12, 1920, and the National Civic Federation Declaration against the Recognition of Soviet Russia, AANY.

81. Hayes to Farley, July 19, 1933, AANY.

82. Farley to Hayes, July 27, 1933, AANY.

83. Flynn, *American Catholics*, p. 141.

84. Ibid., p. 144.

85. Ibid., p. 146.

86. Apostolic delegate Archbishop Amleto Cicognani to Hayes, December 31, 1933, AANY.

87. Hayes to Cicognani, January 16, 1934, AANY.

88. Ibid.

89. Hayes to Cicognani, January 22, 1934, AANY.

90. *New York Times*, September 5, 1938.

91. Archdiocese of New York press release on the life of Patrick Cardinal Hayes, ca. September 6, 1938, p. 7, AANY.

92. "Patrick Cardinal Hayes", *Catholic World*, October 1938, p. 15.

93. Ibid.

94. Transcript of eulogy by Msgr. Fulton J. Sheen, AANY.

PART III. THE CITY AND THE WORLD

Chapter 7. The Power Broker: Francis Joseph Spellman

1. Michael Perko, *Catholic America: A Popular History* (Huntington, Ind.: Our Sunday Visitor, 1989), p. 269.

2. Msgr. Florence Cohalan, *A Popular History of the Archdiocese of New York*, 2nd ed. (1983; Yonkers, N.Y.: U.S. Catholic Historical Society, 1999), pp. 317–18.

3. John Tracy Ellis, *Catholic Bishops: A Memoir* (Wilmington, Del.: Michael Glazier, 1984), pp. 94–95.

4. Warren Steibel, *Cardinal Spellman: The Man* (New York: Appleton-Century, 1966), p. 59.

5. John Cooney, *The American Pope: The Life And Times of Francis Cardinal Spellman* (New York: Times Books 1984), p. 23.

6. Robert Gannon, *The Cardinal Spellman Story* (New York: Doubleday, 1962), p. 36.

7. Cooney, *American Pope*, p. 25.

8. Gannon, *Cardinal Spellman Story*, p. 46.

9. Ibid., p. 75

10. Steibel, *Cardinal Spellman*, p. 24.

11. Gannon, *Cardinal Spellman Story*, p. 83.

12. Cooney, *American Pope*, p. 56.

13. Gannon, *Cardinal Spellman Story*, p. 90.

14. Charles Morris, *American Catholic* (New York: Random House, 1997), p. 122.

15. Gannon, *Cardinal Spellman Story*, p. 93.

16. Steibel, *Cardinal Spellman*, p. 29.

17. "New Archbishop of New York", *Catholic World*, June 1939, p. 363.

18. Gannon, *Cardinal Spellman Story*, p. 134.

19. Cooney, *American Pope*, p. 75.

20. Gannon, *Cardinal Spellman Story*, p. 249.

21. Ibid., pp. 250–51.

22. Ibid., p. 158.

23. Ibid., p. 164.

24. Ibid., p. 167.

25. Ibid., p. 189.

26. Ibid., p. 190.

27. Ibid., p. 191.

28. Edward L. Keyes, "The Road to Victory", *Commonweal*, November 13, 1942, p. 101.

29. "Insult to an Archbishop", *America*, June 5, 1943, p. 239.

30. "The Archbishop of New York", *Tablet* (February 27, 1943): 104.

31. "Insult to an Archbishop", *America*, June 5, 1943, 239.

32. "Archbishop Spellman on France", *Sign* (November 1943): 195–96.

33. Archbishop Francis Spellman, "America at War", *Catholic Mind* (April 1943): 3.

34. Gannon, *Cardinal Spellman Story*, pp. 223–24.

35. "Archbishop Spellman Overseas", *Catholic World*, September 1944, p. 562.

36. Gannon, *Cardinal Spellman Story*, p. 246.

37. Ibid.

38. Ibid., p. 248.

39. George Q. Flynn, *Roosevelt and Romanism: Catholics and American Diplomacy, 1937–1945* (Connecticut: Greenwood Press, 1976), p. 223.

40. Edward Watkin and Joseph Scheuer, *The De-Romanization of the American Catholic Church* (New York: Macmillan, 1966), p. 62.

41. Gannon, *Cardinal Spellman Story*, p. 262.

42. "An Appeal to the Conscience of New York", *Tablet* (March 1, 1964): 280.

43. Stephen M. DiGiovanni, *The Second Founder: Bishop Martin J. O'Connor and the Pontifical North American College* (New York: Trafford Publishing, 2013), p. xvi.

44. "Spellman: Close Up", *Life*, January 21, 1946, p. 102.

45. Gannon, *Cardinal Spellman Story*, p. 296.

46. "Cardinal Spellman Welcomed Home", *Catholic World*, April 1946, p. 82.

47. Richard J. Walton, *Henry Wallace, Harry Truman, and the Cold War* (New York: Viking Press, 1976), p. 48.

48. Proceedings of the Friendly Sons of St. Patrick's Dinner, March 17, 1948, p. 47.

49. Walton, *Henry Wallace*, p. 205.

50. Francis J. Cardinal Spellman, "Communism Is Un-American", *America*, July 1946.

51. Francis J. Cardinal Spellman, "Do We Want a Soviet Peace?", *Cosmopolitan*, November 1946.

52. Francis J. Cardinal Spellman, "The Price of Freedom", *Catholic Mind*, November 1954, p. 643.

53. Donald F. Crosby, *God, Church and Flag* (Chapel Hill, N.C.: University of North Carolina Press, 1978), p. 134.

54. Ibid.

55. Ibid.

56. David J. O'Brien, *Public Catholicism* (New York: Orbis Books, 1996), p. 221.

57. Alfred Kelly and Winfred Harbison, *The American Constitution*, 4th ed. (New York: Norton, 1970), p. 910.

58. Ibid., p. 911.

59. Gannon, *Cardinal Spellman Story*, p. 308.

60. Ibid., p. 309.

61. "Spellman Charges Protestant Bias", *New York Times*, June 12, 1947.

62. Ibid.

63. Ibid.

64. Philip A. Grant, Jr., "Catholic Congressmen, Cardinal Spellman, Eleanor Roosevelt, and the 1949–1950 Federal Aid to Education Controversy", *Records of the America Catholic Historical Society of Philadelphia* 90 (March–December 1979): 4.

65. Ibid., p. 5

66. Eleanor Roosevelt, "My Day" columns, June 23 and July 8, 1949, Eleanore Roosevelt Papers Project, https://www.gwu.edu/~erpapers/.

67. Ibid.

68. Ibid.

69. Gannon, *Cardinal Spellman Story*, pp. 316–17.

70. Allan Nevins, *Herbert H. Lehman and His Era* (New York: Charles Scribner's Sons, 1963), p. 309.

71. Joseph P. Lash, *Eleanor: The Years Alone* (New York: W.W. Norton, 1972), p. 161.

72. Ibid., p. 158.

73. Ibid., p. 159.

74. Ibid.

75. Ibid.

76. Gannon, *Cardinal Spellman Story*, p. 321.

77. Richard N. Parke, "Barden Denounces Spellman", *New York Times*, March 7, 1950.

78. Ibid.

79. Robert Leckie, *American Catholic* (New York: Doubleday, 1970), p. 339.

80. Geoffrey C. Ward, *A First-Class Temperament* (New York: Harper and Row, 1989), p. 252.

81. Mary Ann Glendon, "God and Mrs. Roosevelt", *First Things* (May 2010), https://www .firstthings.com/.

82. Lash, *Eleanor*, p. 160.

83. John Tracy Ellis, *The Life of James Cardinal Gibbons*, vol. 2 (Westminster, Md.: Christian Classics, 1987), p. 110.

84. Leo XIII, *Rerum Novarum*, May 15, 1891, http://w2.vatican.va/.

85. George Weigel and Robert Royal, eds., *A Century of Catholic School Thought* (Washington, D.C.: Ethics and Public Policy Center, 1991), p. 40.

86. Gannon, *Cardinal Spellman Story*, p. 274.

87. Ibid., p. 275.

88. Ibid., p. 276.

89. Ibid., p. 279.

90. Msgr. Thomas J. Shelley, *The Archdiocese of New York: The Bicentennial History 1808–2008* (France: Éditions due Signe, 2007), p. 518.

91. Ibid.

92. George A. Kelly, *Inside My Father's House* (New York: Doubleday, 1989), p. 60.

93. Cooney, *American Pope*, p. 195.

94. David Nasaw, *The Patriarch: The Remarkable Life and Turbulent Times of Joseph P. Kennedy* (New York: Penguin Press, 2012), p. 586.

95. Thomas Maier, *The Kennedys: America's Emerald Kings* (New York: Basic Books, 2003), p. 268.

96. George J. Marlin, *The American Catholic Voter: Two Hundred Years of Political Impact* (South Bend, Ind.: St. Augustine's Press, 2004), p. 254.

97. Ibid.

98. Ibid., p. 255.

99. Maier, *Kennedys*, pp. 348–49.

100. Ibid., p. 350.

101. Nasaw, *Patriarch*, p. 748.

102. Ibid., pp. 753–54.

103. Ibid., p. 755.

104. "A Regrettable Revival", *Christian Century*, February 1961, p. 131.

105. Nasaw, *Patriarch*, p. 754.

106. Maier, *Kennedys*, p. 400.

107. Edward B. Fiske, "A Visit to Archbishop Cooke's Domain", *New York Times Magazine*, October 13, 1968.

108. Ibid.

109. Thomas C. Reeves, *America's Bishop: The Life and Times of Fulton J. Sheen* (San Francisco: Encounter Books, 2001), p. 254.

110. Ibid., p. 288.

111. Gannon, *Cardinal Spellman Story*, p. 414.

112. Ibid.

113. Patrick Allitt, *Catholic Intellectuals and Conservative Politics in America* (New York: Cornell University Press, 1993), p. 35.

114. Paul VI, *Dignitatis Humane*, December 7, 1965.

115. James Rudin, *Cushing, Spellman, O'Connor: The Surprising Story of How Three American Cardinals Transformed Catholic Jewish Relations* (Grand Rapids: Eerdmans, 2012), p. 78.

116. Cooney, *American Pope*, p. 277.

117. Kelly, *Inside My Father's House*, p. 81.

118. Steibel, *Cardinal Spellman*, p. 10.

119. *New York Times*, October 5, 1965.

120. Ibid.

121. Ibid.

122. "U.S. Cardinal Calls for Victory in Vietnam", *Tablet*, December 31, 1966, p. 483, and "Cardinal Spellman under Fire", January 7, 1967, p. 24.

123. E. Michael Jones, *The Slaughter of Cities* (South Bend, Ind.: St. Augustine's Press, 2004), p. 373.

124. Peter Eisenstadt, ed., *The Encyclopedia of New York State* (New York: Syracuse University Press, 2005), p. 278.

125. Kelly, *Inside My Father's House*, p. 107.

126. Ibid.

127. Statement by President Lyndon Johnson on the Death of Cardinal Spellman, December 2, 1967. (Online by Gerhard Peters and John T. Woolley.)

128. Editorial, "Cardinal Spellman", *New York Times*, December 4, 1967.

129. "Cardinal Spellman", *Commonweal*, December 15, 1967, p. 348.

130. "Tribute to a Cardinal", *America*, December 16, 1967, p. 732.

131. *New York Times*, December 8, 1967.

132. Ibid.

Chapter 8. The Equalizer: Terence James Cooke

1. George Kelly, *Inside My Father's House* (New York: Doubleday, 1989), p. 68.

2. Ibid., 121.

3. Edward B. Fiske, "A Visit to Archbishop Cooke's Domain", *New York Times Magazine*, October 13, 1968.

4. Ibid.

5. Kelly, *Inside My Father's House*, p. 122.

6. Benedict Groeschel and Terrence Weber, *Thy Will Be Done: A Spiritual Portrait of Terence Cardinal Cooke* (New York: Alba House, 1990), p. 50.

7. Ibid., p. 60.

8. Kelly, *Inside My Father's House*, pp. 86–87.

9. Basic biography of Terence Cooke prepared by the Archdiocese of New York.

10. Groeschel and Weber, *Thy Will Be Done*, p. 93.

11. "Text of Priests' Memorandum Asking Cardinal Cooke for Sweeping Changes", *New York Times*, March 14, 1968.

12. Ibid.

13. Ibid.

14. Paul Hoffman, "National Political, Labor and Religious Leaders Mourn Dr. King", *New York Times*, April 6, 1968.

15. Text of Cooke's Eulogy of Senator Kennedy", *New York Times*, June 9, 1968.

16. "Transcript of Johnson Speech Naming Panel on U.S. Violence", *New York Times*, June 6, 1968.

17. John Leo, "Dissent Is Voiced", *New York Times*, July 30, 1968.

18. Ibid.

19. "Cooke Again Asks Catholics to Comply on Birth Encyclical", *New York Times*, August 9, 1968.

20. Msgr. Florence D. Cohalan, *A Popular History of the Archdiocese of New York*, 2nd ed. (1983; New York: U.S. Catholic Historical Society, 1989), p. 377.

21. Text of Archbishop Cooke's Sermon, *New York Times*, April 5, 1968.

22. M. A. Faber, "Nonsectarian Panel Is Named to Study Parochial Schools", *New York Times*, April 17, 1968.

23. Ibid.

24. Ibid.

25. Fiske, "Visit to Archbishop Cooke's Domain".

26. Ibid.

27. Ibid.

28. Ibid.

29. Edward B. Fiske, "Cooke Asks Priests to Advise on Posts", *New York Times*, May 8, 1968.

30. Fiske, "Visit to Archbishop Cooke's Domain".

31. Ibid.

32. Peter Kings, "Catholics Plan Seminary Change", *New York Times*, June 12, 1968.

33. Edward B. Fiske, "Cooke Supports Marriage Panel", *New York Times*, September 18, 1968.

34. Ibid.

35. Ibid.

36. Ibid.

37. "Cooke Leaves Tonight on World Journey", *New York Times*, December 18, 1968, and Sylvan Fox, "Christmas Celebrated around the World", December 25, 1968.

38. Transcript of Cooke canonization interview with Edwin Cardinal O'Brien.

39. Robert C. Doty, "Cooke in Rome for Elevation to College of Cardinals", *New York Times*, April 28, 1969.

40. Edward B. Fiske, "Cooke Welcomed Home as Cardinal", *New York Times*, May 8, 1969.

41. Ibid.

42. George J. Marlin, *Fighting the Good Fight: A History of the New York Conservative Party* (South Bend, Ind.: St. Augustine's Press, 2002), p. 169.

43. Groeschel and Weber, *Thy Will Be Done*, pp. 177–78.

44. Ibid., p. 181.

45. Kelly, *Inside My Father's House*, p. 176.

46. Ibid., p. 179.

47. Ibid., p. 223.

48. Marlin, *Fighting the Good Fight*, p. 299.

49. Joint statement of the Archdiocese of New York and the Diocese of Brooklyn, April 17, 1978.

50. *Daily News*, July 18, 1977.

51. *The Wanderer*, August 6, 1981, Report by Dr. Timothy Mitchell.

52. Ibid.

53. Groeschel and Weber, *Thy Will Be Done*, p. 133.

54. *New York Times*, December 21, 1969.

55. *Catholic Mind* (December 1971): 12.

56. Ibid., October 1972, pp. 51–54.

57. Ibid.

58. Pastoral Letter of the Military Vicar, December 7, 1982.

59. Ibid.

60. Ibid.

61. Kenneth A. Briggs, "Letter by Cooke on Arms Policy Prompts Protest", *New York Times*, December 18, 1981.

62. Ibid., April 30, 1982.

63. *Origins*, December 2, 1982, p. 404.

64. Patrick Allit, *Catholic Intellectuals and Conservative Politics in America, 1950–1985* (New York: Cornell University Press, 1993), p. 290.

65. Kenneth A. Briggs, "Cooke Letter on Arms Offers Advice to Catholics in Service", *New York Times*, June 8, 1983.

66. Thomas J. Shelley, *Dunwoodie: The History of St. Joseph's Seminary* (Westminster, Md.: Christian Classics, 1993), p. 241.

67. Kelly, *Inside My Father's House*, p. 138.

68. Ibid., p. 140.

69. Groeschel and Weber, *Thy Will Be Done*, p. 150.

70. Terence Cardinal Cooke letter to Governor Nelson Rockefeller on Government Aid to Nonpublic Schools, *Catholic Mind*, April 1971, pp. 4–5.

71. Kelly, *Inside My Father's House*, p. 195.

72. Kenneth A. Briggs, "Cooke: The Quiet Leader of New York's Catholics", *New York Times*, March 17, 1983.

73. Ibid.

74. Groeschel and Weber, *Thy Will Be Done*, p. 71.

75. Briggs, "Cooke: Quiet Leader".

76. Kelly, *Inside My Father's House*, p. 198.

77. Ibid., p. 201.

78. Shelley, *Dunwoodie*, p. 245.

79. Ibid.

80. Ibid., p. 247.

81. Ibid., p. 249.

82. Marlin, *Fighting the Good Fight*, p. 223.

83. Ibid., p. 225.

84. Ibid., p. 155.

85. Terence Cardinal Cooke, "A Statement on New York City's Financial Crisis", *Catholic Mind*, March 1976, p. 4.

86. Terence Cardinal Cooke, "City in Crisis: Election Day 1977, A Statement of Concern for New York City", *Catholic Mind*, January 1978, pp. 5–6.

87. Msgr. Thomas J. Shelley, *The Archdiocese of New York: The Bicentennial History 1808–2008* (France: Éditions due Signe, 2007), p. 585.

88. *The Pope in America* (Secaucus, N.J.: Chartwell Books, 1979), p. 10.

89. Shelley, *Archdiocese of New York*, p. 588.

90. Jill Jonnes, *We're Still Here: The Rise, Fall, and Resurrection of the South Bronx* (New York: Atlantic Monthly Press, 1986), p. 342.

91. Ibid.

92. *Pope in America*, p. 40.

93. Statement by Dr. Kevin Cahill, Archdiocese of New York news release, August 27, 1983.

94. Ibid.

95. Kenneth A. Briggs, "Cooke Appeals for a Parade of Peace", *New York Times*, March 10, 1983.

96. Ibid.

97. Groeschel and Weber, *Thy Will Be Done*, p. 128.

98. Kenneth A. Briggs, "Cooke Marks 175 Years of Diocese in New York", *New York Times*, April 9, 1983.

99. Kenneth A. Briggs, "Cardinal Cooke Is Terminally Ill with Leukemia", *New York Times*, August 27, 1983.

100. Memorandum on telephone call of His Holiness, Pope John Paul II, to His Eminence Terence Cardinal Cooke, Friday, August 26, 1983, at 2:00 P.M.

101. Briggs, "Cooke Is Terminally Ill".

102. Archdiocese of New York news release, August 27, 1983.

103. Memorandum on telephone call of President Ronald Reagan to His Eminence Terence Cardinal Cooke, August 28, 1983, at 7:45 P.M.

104. Maurice Carroll, "Reagan Visiting New York, Talks with the Cardinal and Top Blacks", *New York Times*, December 10, 1980.

105. Steven R. Weisman, "Reagan, Visiting City, Plans Westway Talks with Koch", *New York Times*, March 14, 1981.

106. Stephen F. Hayward, *The Age of Reagan: The Conservative Counter Revolution 1980–1989* (New York: Crown Forum, 2009), p. 142.

107. Robert Reinhold, "Reagan Says He Will Pray for the Pope", *New York Times*, May 14, 1981.

108. Memorandum of Meeting of His Eminence Cardinal Cooke with President and Mrs. Reagan, Sunday, September 25, 1983 at the cardinal's residence, New York City, written by Monsignor Charles G. McDonagh immediately after the visit.

109. Ibid.

110. McDonagh to President and Mrs. Reagan, September 28, 1983.

111. Joseph B. Treaster, "Cardinal Cooke 'Close to Death'", *New York Times*, October 5, 1983.

112. "Cardinal Cooke Dies at 62 after Fight with Leukemia", *New York Times*, October 7, 1983.

113. Letter of Terence Cardinal Cooke read at all Masses on Sunday, October 9, 1983.

114. "Excerpts from Testament", *New York Times*, October 7, 1983.

115. Sara Rimer, "Thousands Bid Goodbye to Cardinal", *New York Times*, October 9, 1983.

116. Kenneth A. Briggs, "Cooke Entombed in St. Patrick Rites", *New York Times*, October 12, 1983.

117. United Press International, "President Sent a Letter I P o C", *New York Times*, October 12, 1983.

118. Cause for Beatification and Canonization, Terence Cardinal Cooke, questionnaire for the witnesses by the Promoter of Justice.

9. The Admiral: John Joseph O'Connor

1. Nat Hentoff, *John Cardinal O'Connor* (New York: Charles Scribner's Sons, 1988), p. 76.

2. Claudia McDonnell, "Cardinal O'Connor's Mother Was Convert from Judaism, Family Research Reveals", *Catholic New York*, April 30, 2014.

3. Ibid.

4. An Interview with Archbishop O'Connor, February 24–25, 1984, Scranton, Pennsylvania, pp. 1–2, files of Archdiocese of New York, Respect Life Department.

5. Ibid., pp. 4–5.

6. Ibid., p. 8.

7. John J. O'Connor, *A Chaplain Looks at Vietnam* (New York: World Publishing, 1968), p. ix.

8. Ibid., book jacket.

9. Ibid.

10. Ibid., p. 4.

11. Ibid., p. 159.

12. Ibid., pp. 165–66.

13. Associated Press, "O'Connor: The Outspoken Cardinal", *Poughkeepsie Journal*, November 30, 1986.

14. Jim Castelli, *The Bishops and the Bomb* (New York: Doubleday, 1983), p. 71.

15. *Interview with O'Connor*, p. 10.

16. George A. Kelly, *Inside My Father's House* (New York: Doubleday, 1989), p. 343.

17. Ibid.

18. John Paul II, message to the UN General Assembly, June 7, 1982, https://w2.vatican.va/; *L'Osservatore Romano*, June 21, 1982.

19. Kelly, *Inside My Father's House*, p. 346.

20. Hentoff, *John Cardinal O'Connor*, p. 56.

21. Ibid., p. 57.

22. Ibid., p. 65.

23. Ibid., p. 67.

24. Excerpts that follow are from O'Connor's memo to Scranton priests, "First Impressions and Initial Observations", September 10, 1983.

25. Hentoff, *John Cardinal O'Connor*, p. 72.

26. Ari L. Goldman, "New York's Controversial Archbishop", *New York Times Magazine*, October 14, 1984.

27. *Interview with O'Connor*, p. 10.

28. Ibid., p. 2.

29. Joseph Berger, "The View from St. Patrick's", *New York Times Magazine*, March 26, 1989.

30. Ibid.

31. Joyce Purnick, "O'Connor Regrets His Quick Tongue, but Still Loves Leading Flock", *New York Times*, January 1, 1997.

32. Maureen Dowd, "O'Connor Brings Humility and Humor to a Day of Pageantry", *New York Times*, March 20, 1984.

33. Ibid.

34. Robert McElvaine, *Mario Cuomo: A Biography* (New York: Charles Scribner's Sons, 1988), p. 91.

35. Sam Roberts, "Cuomo to Challenge Archbishop over Criticism of Abortion Stand", *New York Times*, August 3, 1984.

36. *Newsday*, June 28, 1984.

37. *Brooklyn Tablet*, August 11, 1984.

38. Richard Brookhiser, *The Outside Story* (New York: Doubleday, 1986), p. 238.

39. Joe Klein, "Abortion and the Archbishop", *New York Magazine*, October 1, 1984, p. 39.

40. Brookhiser, *Outside Story*, p. 239.

41. Arthur Schlesinger, ed., *History of American Presidential Elections*, supplemental vol. (New York: Chelsea House, 1986), p. 302.

42. Gerald M. Costello, "No Room for 'Free Choice'", *Catholic New York*, September 13, 1984.

43. Ibid.

44. "A Faith to Trust", *New York Times*, September 15, 1984.

45. Kenneth J. Heineman, *God Is a Conservative* (New York: NYU Press, 1992), p. 141.

46. Mario Cuomo, "Religious Belief and Public Morality: A Catholic Governor's Perspective", in *More Than Words: The Speeches of Mario Cuomo* (New York: St. Martin's Press, 1993), pp. 32–51.

47. Ibid.

48. Ibid.

49. Ibid.

50. Brookhiser, *Outside Story*, p. 241.

51. Ellen McCormack, *Cuomo vs. O'Connor* (New York: Dolores Press, 1985), p. 73.

52. Tricia Gallagher and Gerald M. Costello, "The Governor's Speech", *Catholic New York*, September 20, 1984.

53. Brookhiser, *Outside Story*, p. 241.

54. Ibid.

55. Klein, "Abortion and the Archbishop", p. 38.

56. Ibid., p. 39.

57. Hentoff, *John Cardinal O'Connor*, p. 89.

58. Ibid.

59. "Catholics and the No-Bias Pledge", *New York Times*, November 7, 1984.

60. "A City-Church Dispute Enlarged", *New York Times*, December 15, 1984.

61. Sydney Schanberg, "Put Up Your Dukes", *New York Times*, December 18, 1984.

62. Archbishop John J. O'Connor, *Catholic New York*, January 17, 1985.

63. Ibid.

64. Ibid.

65. John Cardinal O'Connor and Edward I. Koch, *His Eminence and Hizzoner: A Candid Exchange* (New York: William Morrow, 1989), p. 123.

66. Richard Levine and Walter Goodman, "The Pope Appoints His Princes", *New York Times*, April 28, 1985.

67. John Tagliabue, "For New Cardinals, a Day of Awe and Pageantry", *New York Times*, May 26, 1985.

68. "Cardinal's Biretta Still Size 6 7/8", *New York Times*, June 1, 1985.

69. Joseph Berger, "O'Connor's Way: Assertive and Heard", *New York Times*, February 17, 1986.

70. Ibid.

71. Ibid.

72. Ibid.

73. Edwin McDowell, "'His Eminence and Hizzoner' to Write a Book", *New York Times*, August 23, 1987.

74. Ibid.

75. Richard Levine, "Koch, in Book with O'Connor, Traces a Conservative Shift", *New York Times*, March 7, 1989.

76. Berger, "O'Connor's Way".

77. Ibid.

78. Hentoff, *John Cardinal O'Connor*, p. 249.

79. Berger, "O'Connor's Way".

80. Hentoff, *John Cardinal O'Connor*, p. 114.

81. "Cuomo Opposes Cardinal on Abortion", *New York Times*, February 17, 1986.

82. Ibid.

83. Hentoff, *John Cardinal O'Connor*, p. 139.

84. Jeffrey Schmalz, "Cuomo and Cardinal Trade Quips", *New York Times*, September 13, 1986.

85. Ari L. Goldman, "Archdiocese to Bar Dissidents from Speaking in Its Parishes", *New York Times*, September 4, 1986.

86. Ibid.

87. Ibid.

88. Jeffrey Schmalz, "Cuomo at Odds with Archdiocese over Policy on Dissident Speakers", *New York Times*, September 5, 1986.

89. Ibid.

90. Ibid.

91. Hentoff, *John Cardinal O'Connor*, p. 144.

92. Schmalz, "Cuomo at Odds".

93. *Catholic New York*, September 11, 1986.

94. Ibid.

95. Hentoff, *John Cardinal O'Connor*, p. 145.

96. "Cardinal and Dearie Meet on Ban", *New York Times*, October 4, 1985.

97. Hentoff, *John Cardinal O'Connor*, p. 145.

98. Terry Golway, *Full of Grace: An Oral Biography of John Cardinal O'Connor* (New York: Pocket Books, 2001), pp. 70–71.

99. Sam Howe Verhovek, "Cardinal Defends a Jailed Bishop Who Warned Cuomo on Abortion", *New York Times*, February 1, 1990.

100. Ibid.

101. Ibid.

102. John Cardinal O'Connor, "Abortion: Questions and Answers", *Catholic New York*, June 14, 1990.

103. Ari L. Goldman, "O'Connor Warns Politicians Risk Excommunication over Abortion", *New York Times*, June 15, 1990.

104. Ari L. Goldman, "O'Connor's Vigil Signals a Shift in Abortion Fight", *New York Times*, June 13, 1992.

105. Frank Bruni, "Clinton Veto on Abortion Is Criticized by O'Connor", *New York Times*, April 15, 1996.

106. Ibid.

107. Noritmitsu Onishi, "O'Connor Backs Criticism of Clinton Abortion Veto", *New York Times*, April 22, 1996.

108. Melody Petersen, "O'Connor Calls on President to Sign Bill on Abortions", *New York Times*, March 10, 1997.

109. Ibid.

110. O'Connor and Koch, *His Eminence and Hizzoner*, pp. 125–26.

111. Ibid., pp. 126–27.

112. Joyce Purnick, "O'Connor Says He'll Drop Some Foster-Care Pacts with City", *New York Times*, January 24, 1987.

113. Ibid.

114. "Cardinal Assesses Foster-Care Dispute", *New York Times*, January 26, 1987.

115. Joyce Purnick, "Koch Sees Catholic Foster-Care Curb", *New York Times*, February 3, 1987.

116. Josh Barbanel, "New York Foster-Care Rules Upheld", *New York Times*, March 30, 1987.

117. Ari L. Goldman, "Foster Agencies Lose a Decision over Abortions", *New York Times*, May 8, 1987.

118. O'Connor and Koch, *His Eminence and Hizzoner*, p. 128.

119. Ibid.

120. Ibid., p. 130.

121. Joseph Berger, "Brooklyn Diocese Joins Homosexual-Bill Fight", *New York Times*, February 7, 1986.

122. Joseph Berger, "New York Church Leaders Divided over Homosexual-Rights Measures", *New York Times*, February 9, 1986.

123. Larry Rohter, "O'Connor Sees Council Bill Shielding Homosexual 'Sin'", *New York Times*, March 17, 1986.

124. Ibid.

125. Associated Press, "Vatican AIDS Meeting Hears O'Connor Assail Condom Use", *New York Times*, November 14, 1989.

126. Jason DeParle, "111 Held in St. Patrick's AIDS Protest", *New York Times*, December 11, 1989.

127. Todd S. Purdum, "Cardinal Says He Won't Yield to Protests", *New York Times*, December 12, 1989.

128. Ibid.

129. Ari L. Goldman, "Cardinal Won't Allow Instruction on Condoms in Programs on AIDS", *New York Times*, December 14, 1997.

130. Mike Allen, "Cardinal Sees Marriage Harm in Partners Bill", *New York Times*, May 25, 1998.

131. Raymond Hernandez, "Parade Permit Is Questioned by Cardinal", *New York Times*, January 11, 1993.

132. Ibid.

133. James Rudin, *Cushing, Spellman, O'Connor: The Surprising Story of How Three American Cardinals Transformed Catholic Jewish Relations* (Grand Rapids: Eerdmans, 2012), p. 120.

134. Ibid., p. 123.

135. Ibid., p. 127.

136. Ibid., p. 128.

137. E.J. Dionne, Jr., "Vatican Says O'Connor's Trip Is to Shore Up the Christians", *New York Times*, June 17, 1986.

138. Ihsan A. Hijazi, "O'Connor Hopeful on Lebanon Hostages", *New York Times*, June 15, 1986.

139. Rohter, "O'Connor Sees Council Bill Shielding Homosexual 'Sin'", *New York Times*, June 17, 1986.

140. Hentoff, *John Cardinal O'Connor*, p. 117.

141. Roberto Suro, "American Jewish Groups Say Cardinal Should Cancel Israel Trip", *New York Times*, December 30, 1986.

142. Hentoff, *John Cardinal O'Connor*, p. 119.

143. Ibid., p. 119.

144. Ibid., p. 121.

145. Ibid., p. 119.

146. Ibid.

147. *Origins*, February 8, 1990.

148. *Origins*, October 19, 1989.

149. *Origins*, February 8, 1990.

150. "Abortion History Timeline", entry for August 1, 1990, Catholic News Service, http://m.catholicnewsagency.com/.

151. Ian Fisher, "Blessings on Reborn Mile as Cardinal Walks through South Bronx", *New York Times*, June 13, 1997.

152. Ibid.

153. Glenn Fowler, "Cardinal Leads Antidrug Vigil on 5th Avenue", *New York Times*, August 8, 1986.

154. Kevin Flynn, "Cardinal Mediates Meeting on Police Role", *New York Times*, March 6, 1999.

155. Ibid.

156. Ibid.

157. Ginger Thompson, "Cardinal Urges a Dialogue to Rebuild Trust in Police", *New York Times*, March 22, 1999.

158. Ibid.

159. Ibid.

160. Jodi Wilgoren, "Cardinal Holds a Meeting with the Parents of Diallo", *New York Times*, April 7, 1999.

161. Jodi Wilgoren, "Under One Roof, Prayers for Diallo and a Hug for Giuliani", *New York Times*, April 21, 1999.

162. Ibid.

163. Ibid.

164. Msgr. Florence D. Cohalan, *A Popular History of the Archdiocese of New York*, 2nd ed. (1983; New York: U.S. Catholic Historical Society, 1999), p. 436.

165. *Commonweal*, November 17, 1989.

166. Peter Steinfels, "New York Catholic Synod Urges Bigger Role for Laity", *New York Times*, September 28, 1988.

167. Peter Steinfels, "Cardinal Promotes 5-Year Plan to Expand the Role of the Laity", *New York Times*, February 5, 1989.

168. Ibid.

169. Golway, *Full of Grace*, p. 193.

170. Ari L. Goldman, "Catholic Schools in Danger of Closing", *New York Times*, February 16, 1992.

171. Thomas J. Shelley, *Dunwoodie: The History of St. Joseph's Seminary* (Westminster, Md.: Christian Classics, 1993), p. 253.

172. Ibid., p. 254.

173. Thomas Young, *A New World Rising: The Story of St. Patrick's Cathedral* (New York: Something More Publications, 2006), p. 205.

174. Elisabeth Bumiller, "The Pope's Visit: The Cardinal", *New York Times*, October 8, 1995.

175. Robert D. McFadden, "Remembering John Paul II in New York", *New York Times*, April 14, 2008.

176. Ibid.

177. Bumiller, "Pope's Visit".

178. William Donohue, *John Jay 2011 Study on Sexual Abuse: A Critical Analysis* (New York: Catholic League for Religious and Civil Rights, 2011), p. 3.

179. William Donohue, "Philip Jenkins: Pedophiles and Priests", review of *Pedophiles and Priests* by Philip Jenkins, *Catalyst*, May 1996, http://www.catholicleague.org/.

180. L. M. Lothstein, "Can a Sexually Addicted Priest Return to Ministry after Treatment? Psychological Issues and Possible Forensic Solutions", *Catholic Lawyer* 34, no. 1 (1992): 89.

181. Ibid., p. 110.

182. Ibid.

183. Ibid.

184. Ibid., p. 111.

185. Kathleen Hendrix, "Bruce Ritter: A Puzzle for His Friends", *Los Angeles Times*, April 19, 1990.

186. *New York Post*, August 4, 1990.

187. Ibid.

188. Peter Steinfels, "1,000 Priests Told to Attend Talks on Sex", *New York Times*, May 26, 1993.

189. Ibid.

190. Ibid.

191. "Ending Abuse by Priests", *New York Times*, July 4, 1993.

192. Ibid.

193. Ibid.

194. "Ending Abuse by Priests".

195. Anthony Ramirez, "At 79, Cardinal O'Connor Is Hospitalized for Tests", *New York Times*, August 27, 1999.

196. Ibid.

197. Robert D. McFadden, "Cardinal O'Connor Has Tumor Removed from Surface of Brain", *New York Times*, September 5, 1999.

198. David Barstow, "Cardinal Ascends Pulpit for First Time Since Tumor Surgery", *New York Times*, September 13, 1999.

199. Jane Gross, "At Midnight Mass, a Thankful O'Connor Reflects", *New York Times*, December 26, 1999.

200. Diana Jean Schemo, "'Happy Birthday' to Cardinal, with Farewell between Lines", *New York Times*, January 17, 2000.

201. Mario M. Cuomo, "Compassion of a Cardinal", *New York Times*, January 20, 2000.

202. Diana Jean Schemo, "Cardinal's Light Hand as Leader Lets Archdiocese Adapt to Illness", *New York Times*, January 22, 2000.

203. Alessandra Stanley, "Cardinal Meets with Pope in Rome for Farewell Visit", *New York Times*, February 11, 2000.

204. Diana Jean Schemo, "An Ailing Cardinal Inspires with a Sermon on Suffering", *New York Times*, February 14, 2000.

205. "Congress Bestows Gold Medal on Cardinal", *New York Times*, March 7, 2000.

206. Diana Jean Schemo, "Even on Parade Day, Ill Cardinal Stays In", *New York Times*, March 18, 2000.

207. *New York Post*, February 17, 2000.

208. "Now Anti-Catholics Come Draped in Pashmina", *Wall Street Journal*, March 3, 2000.

209. Ibid.

210. Robert D. Novak, "... While McCain Foments a Schism", *Washington Post*, February 28, 2000.

211. *Wall Street Journal*, May 29, 2000.

212. Thomas M. DeFrank and Kenneth R. Bazinet, "Bush Apologizes, Sends Letter to O'Connor", *Daily News*, February 28, 2000.

213. Ibid.

214. Diana Jean Schemo, "Both Friends and Critics of the Cardinal Recall His Courage and Devotion to Duty", and Peter Steinfels, "Cardinal O'Connor, 80, Dies", *New York Times*, May 4, 2000.

215. Dan Barry, "Death of a Cardinal: The Reaction", *New York Times*, May 5, 2000.

216. Robert D. McFadden, "Death of a Cardinal: The Rites", *New York Times*, May 7, 2000.

217. "Death of a Cardinal", *New York Times*, May 9, 2000.

218. Ibid.

219. Ibid.

PART IV. THE CHURCH IN CRISIS

10. The Realist: Edward Michael Egan

1. Diana Jean Schemo with Laurie Goodstein, "Death of a Cardinal: The Challenges", *New York Times*, May 5, 2000.

2. Robert D. McFadden, "Death of a Cardinal: The Rites", *New York Times*, May 7, 2000.

3. Cardinal Edward Egan, interview with authors.

4. Ibid.

5. Ibid.

6. "ACORN's Problems—and the Church", *Catholic Thing*, September 23, 2009, https://www.thecatholicthing.org/.

7. Steven M. Avella, *This Confident Church: Catholic Leadership and Life in Chicago, 1940–1965* (Notre Dame, Ind.: University of Notre Dame Press, 1992), p. 246.

8. "ACORN's Problems".

9. Egan, interview with authors.

10. Taylor Branch, *At Canaan's Edge: America in the King Years, 1965–68* (New York: Simon and Schuster, 2007), p. 515.

11. Ibid.

12. Ibid.

13. Egan, interview with authors.

14. Ibid.

15. Ibid.

16. Ibid.

17. Ibid.

18. Edward M. Egan, "The Permanence of Marriage and the Mentality of Divorce" (paper delivered before the Fellowship of Catholic Scholars, Washington, D.C., 1988).

19. Egan, interview with authors.

20. Ibid.

21. Laurie Goodstein, "Archbishop-Elect Is a Man Who Takes Charge", *New York Times*, May 12, 2000.

22. Ibid.

23. John Tagliabue, *New York Times*, May 25, 1985.

24. Ibid.

25. Egan, interview with authors.

26. Ibid.

27. Ibid.

28. Ibid.

29. Ibid.

30. Ibid.

31. "Egan Letter Excerpts", *New York Times*, March 24, 2002.

32. Egan, interview with authors.

33. "'We Have to Put Our House in Order'", *New York Times*, August 16, 2002.

34. Transcript of Bishop Edward Egan deposition, July 23, 1997, p. 16.

35. Ibid., pp. 124–25.

36. Ibid., p. 127.

37. Ibid., p. 162.

38. "Statement of the Archdiocese of New York on Behalf of the Archbishop Emeritus", *Catholic New York*, December 3, 2009.

39. Egan, interview with authors.

40. Laurie Goodstein, "Man in the News: Secure at the Helm", *New York Times*, May 12, 2000.

41. "New York's New Archbishop", *New York Times*, May 13, 2000.

42. *New York Post*, March 14, 2001.

43. Gustav Niebuhr, "Archbishop Quietly Makes His Mark", *New York Times*, October 18, 2000.

44. Egan, interview with authors.

45. Alessandra Stanley, "For Cardinal-to-Be, a Busy Day in Rome", *New York Times*, February 20, 2001.

46. Ibid.

47. Egan, interview with authors.

48. Ibid.

49. "AP Interview: On 9/11, Cardinal Consoles a City", Fox News, August 31, 2011, http://www.foxnews.com/.

50. Msgr. Thomas J. Shelley, *The Archdiocese of New York: The Bicentennial History, 1808–2008* (France: Éditions due Signe, 2007), p. 603.

51. Egan, interview with authors.

52. Ibid.

53. "AP Interview: On 9/11, Cardinal Consoles a City", August 31, 2011.

54. Ibid.

55. Transcript of Egan talk, September 6, 2011.

56. Egan, interview with authors.

57. Edward Cardinal Egan, statement released by the archdiocese on March 19, 2002.

58. Edward Cardinal Egan, letter to faithful of the archdiocese, released and dated March 23, 2002.

59. David M. Herszenhorn and Elissa Gootman, "In Palm Sunday Homily, Cardinal Egan Says Evil of Sex Abuse 'Will Be Stamped Out'", *New York Times*, March 25, 2002.

60. Edward Cardinal Egan, Palm Sunday sermon delivered at St. Patrick's Cathedral, March 24, 2002.

61. Edward Cardinal Egan, Holy Week Chrism Mass sermon delivered at St. Patrick's Cathedral, March 26, 2002.

62. Edward Cardinal Egan, letter to the faithful of the archdiocese, dated April 20–21, 2002.

63. Daniel J. Wakin, "Scandal in the Church: The New York Cardinal", *New York Times*, April 25, 2002.

64. "Archdiocese Releases Revised Addendum to Its Abuse Policy" (statement released by Archdiocese Communications Department on May 15, 2002).

65. Philip F. Lawler, *The Faithful Departed: The Collapse of Boston's Catholic Culture* (New York: Encounter Books, 2008), p. 168.

66. Ibid., 166.

67. Edward Cardinal Egan, "A Policy in a Times of Crisis", *Catholic New York*, August 1, 2002.

68. Egan, interview with authors.

69. Shelley, *Archdiocese of New York*, p. 605.

70. Egan, interview with authors.

71. From statement of Cardinal Egan after the death of Wilson.

72. Daniel J. Wakin, "As Catholic Teachers Strike, Egan Takes Reserved Approach", *New York Times*, December 9, 2001.

73. Ibid.

74. Abby Goodnough, "Biggest Union of Teachers in Archdiocese Reaches Accord", *New York Times*, December 11, 2001.

75. Ibid.

76. His Eminence Edward Cardinal Egan, "Distinguished Lecture", *Journal of Catholic Legal Studies* 50, nos. 1–2 (2011): 62.

77. Edward Cardinal Egan, "The Very Best of Service", *Catholic New York*, February 8, 2007.

78. Egan letter to the faithful of the archdiocese, dated January 20, 2007.

79. Egan, interview with authors.

80. Ibid.

81. Ibid.

82. Ibid.

83. Mayor's Office press release, December 19, 2001.

84. Edward Cardinal Egan, "The Challenges of Episcopal Leadership Today", *Social Science Review* no. 18 (2013), p. 296.

85. From text of a speech Egan delivered at Harvard on March 6, 2012.

86. Egan, interview with authors.

87. Manny Fernandez, "Letter to Priests Is Critical of Archbishop's Leadership", *New York Times*, October 15, 2006.

88. Letter to the editor, *New York Times*, October 21, 2006.

89. Daniel J. Wakin, "Priests Support Cardinal in Matter of Critical Letter", *New York Times*, October 17, 2006.

90. Andy Newman, "Cardinal Egan's Angry Response to Priests' Critical Letter Revives Diocesan Dispute", *New York Times*, October 26, 2006.

91. Egan, interview with authors.

92. Egan, "Challenges of Episcopal Leadership", p. 291.

93. James Barron, "Egan Says Guiliani Broke 'Understanding' by Receiving Communion at Papal Mass", *New York Times*, April 29, 2008.

94. Kenneth Lovett, "Egan: Birth-Control Bill Is 'Un-American'", *New York Post*, March 14, 2001.

95. Shaila K. Dewan, "Cardinal Lobbies in Albany against Bill for Contraception Coverage", *New York Times*, March 13, 2002.

96. Jennifer Medina, "Students and Cardinal Call for Private-School Tax Aid", *New York Times*, February 15, 2006.

97. Ibid.

98. Edward Cardinal Egan, "Just Look", website of the Archdiocese of New York, October 23, 2008, http://www.archny.org/.

99. Edward Cardinal Egan, "Statement of His Eminence, Edward Cardinal Egan concerning Remarks Made by the Speaker of the House of Representatives", August 26, 2008, website of the Archdiocese of New York, http://archny.org/.

100. Gerard J. Hekker, "Truth, Justice, Compassion", *Catholic New York*, February 6, 2003.

101. Ibid.

102. Ibid.

103. Barron, "Guiliani Broke 'Understanding'".

104. Jim Dwyer, Colin Moynihan, Ann Farmer, and Andy Newman, "Krakow and Beyond: Prayers, Tributes and Awe", *New York Times*, April 3, 2005.

105. Robert D. McFadden, "John Paul II: Global Reaction", *New York Times*, April 4, 2005.

106. Andy Newman, "John Paul II: The New Yorker", *New York Times*, April 6, 2005.

107. Ibid.

108. Laurie Goodstein and Daniel J. Watkin, "Cardinal Hints at Profile of a New Pope", New York Times, April 10, 2005; http://www.nytimes.com/2005/04/10/world/worldspecial2/cardinals-hint-at-profile-of-new-pope-presence.html?_r=0/.

109. Ian Fisher, "German Cardinal Is Chosen as Pope", *New York Times*, April 20, 2005.

110. Shelley, *Archdiocese of New York*, p. 8.

111. Egan, interview with authors.

112. Timothy Cardinal Dolan, interview with authors.

11. The Evangelist: Timothy Michael Dolan

1. Cardinal Timothy Dolan, interview with authors.

2. Patricia Rice, "Dolan to Shepherd New York Catholics", *St. Louis Beacon*, February 23, 2009.

3. John L. Allen and Timothy M. Dolan, *A People of Hope* (New York: Image, 2011), p. 8.

4. Dolan, interview with authors.

5. Juliann DosSantos, "His Priests See Cardinal Dolan as True Shepherd", *Catholic New York*, February 12, 2012.

6. Ibid.

7. Dolan, interview with authors.

8. Rice, "Dolan to Shepherd".

9. Allen and Dolan, *A People of Hope*, p. 14.

10. Michael S. Rose, *Goodbye Good Men: How Liberals Brought Corruption into the Catholic Church* (Washington, D.C.: Regnery, 2002), pp. 195, 203.

11. George A. Kelly, *The Crisis of Authority: John Paul II and the American Bishops* (Washington, D.C.: Regnery, 1981), p. 59.

12. Ibid., p. 61.

13. Dolan, interview with authors.

14. Ibid.

15. Allen and Dolan, *A People of Hope*, p. 15.

16. Dolan, interview with authors.

17. Ibid.

18. Ibid.

19. Monica Davey, "Milwaukee Priests Seek End to Celibacy Rule", *New York Times*, August 20, 2003.

20. Laurie Goodstein, "Celibacy Issue Flares Again within Ranks of U.S. Priesthood", *New York Times*, September 5, 2003.

21. Ibid.

22. Jodi Wilgoren, "At Forum, Victims of Clergy Plead and Vent", *New York Times*, October 24, 2002.

23. Serge F. Kovaleski, "Complex Struggle: Prelate's Record in Abuse Crisis", *New York Times*, May 17, 2010.

24. Ibid.

25. Dolan, interview with authors.

26. Frank Bruni, "The Church's Errant Shepherds", *New York Times*, July, 6, 2013.

27. Dolan released letter, CBS News, February 20, 2014.

28. Ibid.

29. Ibid.

30. Dolan, interview with authors.

31. Ibid.

32. Michael Powell, "A Genial Conservative for New York's Archdiocese", *New York Times*, February 23, 2009.

33. "New York's Gain", *Milwaukee Sentinel*, February 23, 2009.

34. Laurie Goodstein, "New Archbishop Pledges to Look Out for His Priests and Increase Their Ranks", *New York Times*, February 23, 2009.

35. Ibid.

36. Ibid.

37. Ibid.

38. Paul Vitello, "Hoping for a Latino Archbishop, in Due Course", *New York Times*, March 3, 2009.

39. Goodstein, "New Archbishop Pledges".

40. Dolan, interview with authors.

41. Ibid.

42. Paul Vitello, "A Grand Entrance at St. Patrick's Cathedral", *New York Times*, April 16, 2009.

43. Most Rev. Timothy M. Dolan, homily during Mass of installation, St. Patrick's Cathedral, April 15, 2009, Archdiocese of New York website.

44. Clyde Haberman, "Welcome, Archbishop Dolan! Now Show Us What Ya Got", *New York Times*, April 16, 2009.

45. Dolan, interview with authors.

46. "Long Applause for New York Prelate Who Defends Pope", *Zenit News*, March 29, 2010.

47. Dolan, interview with authors.

48. George Marlin, "Why Bishops Need Dolan's True Grit", *New York Post*, November 22, 2010.

49. Ibid.

50. Laurie Goodstein, "A New Leader Confronts Catholics' Disaffection", *New York Times*, November 22, 2010.

51. Ibid.

52. "Obamacare and the Bishops", *Catholic Thing*, April 7, 2010, https://www.thecatholicthing.org/.

53. Ibid.

54. George Marlin, "Catholic-Bash May Be O's Undoing", *New York Post*, February 9, 2012.

55. Ibid.

56. James Taranto, "When the Archbishop Met the President", *Wall Street Journal*, March 31, 2012.

57. Ibid.

58. Dolan, interview with authors.

59. Taranto, "When the Archbishop Met the President".

60. Ibid.

61. Ibid.

62. Robert Royal, Op-Ed, *New York Post*, February 12, 2012.

63. Ibid.

64. Sharon Otterman, "New York's Next Cardinal", *New York Times*, January 6, 2012.

65. Christina Boyle, "Cardinal Egan's Advice for Archbishop Dolan: Hold On to Your Red Hat!", *Daily News*, February 7, 2012.

66. Stacey Stowe, "The Archbishop Prepares to Roll Out His Italian", *New York Times*, February 9, 2012.

67. *Inside the Vatican*, March 2012, p. 25–26.

68. Sharon Otterman, "A Test for Dolan in the Land of Pasta and Gelato", *New York Times*, February 15, 2012.

69. Colin Moynihan, "Celebration at St. Patrick's for Cardinal Dolan", *New York Times*, February 25, 2012.

70. Ibid.

71. "Bishop Dolan's Liberty Letter", *Wall Street Journal*, March 7, 2012.

72. Kate Briquelet, "Dolan's Supreme Strategy", *New York Post*, April 29, 2012.

73. "Catholics in Court", *Wall Street Journal*, March 24, 2012.

74. "Politics of Religion", *New York Times*, May 27, 2012.

75. Michael Goodwin, "Appeasing the Nuke Madman", *New York* Post, May 30, 2012.

76. "Bishops: 'Fundamental Flaws' Remain After Court Ruling on Health Care", *Long Island Catholic*, July 11, 2012.

77. "Catholics React to Supreme Court Decision", *OSV Newsweekly*, July 3, 2012.

78. Sharon Otterman, "Dolan to Give Benediction at Gathering of the G.O.P.", *New York Times*, August 22, 2012.

79. Jaweed Kaleem, "Cardinal Timothy Dolan's Benedictions at RNC and DNC (Full Text)", *Huffington Post*, updated September 7, 2012, http://www.huffingtonpost.com/2012/.

80. Ibid.

81. Sharon Otterman, "A Night of Laughs amid a Bitter Run for President", *New York Times*, October 18, 2012.

82. Cardinal Dolan, "Obama Invite Is Not an Award or Platform", *Long Island Catholic*, August 22, 2012.

83. Charlie Spiering, "Mitt Romney's Surprisingly Hilarious Speech at the Al Smith Dinner", *Washington Examiner*, October 18, 2012.

84. Sharon Otterman, "At Charity Dinner, Self-Deprecation and Plenty of Zingers", *New York Times*, October 19, 2012.

85. Cardinal Timothy M. Dolan, *Praying in Rome: Reflections on the Conclave and Electing Pope Francis* (New York: Image, 2013), introduction.

86. Statement of Timothy Cardinal Dolan on the resignation of Pope Benedict XVI, February 11, 2013, Archdiocese of New York website, http://archny.org/.

87. Sharon Otterman, "Dolan Is Seen as Long Shot to Be Pope", *New York Times*, February 13, 2013.

88. Michael Paulson, "Dolan Offers Role Model for Choosing New Pope", *New York Times*, February 24, 2013.

89. Sharon Otterman, "Dolan Says Papal Conclave Should Be Occasion of Repentance", *New York Times*, February 26, 2013.

90. Eric J. Lyman, "New York's Cardinal Dolan Says Mass ahead of Conclave", *USA Today*, March 10, 2013.

91. Michael Zennie, "Could Next Pope Be American?", *Daily Mail*, February 21, 2013.

92. Ibid.

93. Lyman, "Dolan Says Mass".

94. Robert Royal, "Day Four: The Great Game Begins", *Catholic Thing*, March 9, 2013, https://www.thecatholicthing.org/.

95. Dolan, *Praying in Rome*, p. 45.

96. Ibid., p. 57.

97. Ibid., p. 55.

98. Statement of Timothy Cardinal Dolan on the election of Pope Francis, March 13, 2013, Archdiocese of New York website, http://archny.org/.

99. "HHS Rule Still Requires Action in Congress, by Courts, Says Cardinal Dolan", United States Conference of Catholic Bishops (USCCB) website, July 3, 2013, http://www.usccb.org/.

100. Dolan, interview with authors.

101. Roman Catholic Archdiocese of New York, et al. v. Kathleen Sebelius et al., 12 Civ. 2542 (BMC), memorandum decision and order, December 16, 2013, p. 26.

102. Statement of Joseph Zwilling regarding decision by Judge Cogan, Archdiocese of New York website, December 16, 2013, http://archny.org/.

103. Associated Press, "Archbishop Dolan Speaks on Staten Island Attacks", *New York Times*, August 23, 2010.

104. Ibid.

105. Javier C. Hernández, "Archbishop Offers Mediation for Islamic Center", *New York Times*, August 19, 2010.

106. Ibid.

107. Ibid.

108. George J. Marlin, "Andrew Cuomo, the Catholic Anti-Catholic", *Catholic Thing*, April 9, 2014, https://www.thecatholicthing.org/.

109. Dolan, interview with authors.

110. Ibid.

111. Ibid.

112. Kenneth Lovett, "Cardinal Dolan Fumes: Albany 'Burned' Us on Gay Nuptials", *Daily News*, updated March 12, 2013.

113. Briquelet, "Dolan's Supreme Strategy", *New York Post*, April 29, 2012.

114. Dolan, interview with authors.

115. Ibid.

116. *Catechism of the Catholic Church*, nos. 2357, 2358, 2359.

117. Ibid.

118. Vivian Yee, "Dolan Says the Catholic Church Should Be More Welcoming to Gay People", *New York Times*, April 1, 2013.

119. Ibid.

120. Transcribed from *Meet the Press* program, March 9, 2014.

121. Dolan, interview with authors.

122. Timothy Cardinal Dolan, "The True Meaning of Tolerance", *Daily News*, November 25, 2013.

123. Dolan, interview with authors.

124. George J. Marlin and Brad Miner "The Ad Hoc Moral Theology of Cardinal Dolan", *Catholic Thing*, September 5, 2014, https://www.thecatholicthing.org/.

125. Ibid.

126. Matthew Chayes, "St. Patrick's Day Parade Ends Ban on Gay Groups", *Newsday*, September 3, 2014.

127. Michael Howard Saul and Sophia Hollander, "St. Patrick's Day Parade Allows a Gay Group", *Wall Street Journal*, September 3, 2014.

128. Marlin and Miner "Ad Hoc Moral Theology of Cardinal Dolan", *Catholic Thing*, September 5, 2014.

129. Bill Donohue, "The Politics of the St. Patrick's Day Parade", website of the Catholic League for Religious and Civil Rights, September 16, 2014, https://www.catholicleague.org/.

130. Megan Specia, "LBGT Group Makes St. Patrick's Day History, but Not Everyone Is Pleased", *Mashable*, March 17, 2015, http://mashable.com/.

131. Antonio Antenucci, Georgett Roberts, and Leonard Greene, "Openly Gay Group Makes History at St. Patrick's Day Parade", *New York Post*, March 17, 2015.

132. "The Abortion Capital of America", *Catholic Thing*, February 9, 2011, https://www.thecatholicthing.org/.

133. Ibid.

134. Ibid.

135. George J. Marlin, "Cuomo's 'Abortion Expansion Act'", *Catholic Thing*, March 21, 2013, https://www.thecatholicthing.org/.

136. Ibid.

137. Dolan, interview with authors.

138. George J. Marlin, "Andrew Cuomo: The Catholic Anti-Catholic", *Catholic Thing*, April 9, 2014, https://www.thecatholicthing.org/.

139. Timothy A. Byrnes, *Catholic Bishops in American Politics* (Princeton: Princeton University Press, 1991), pp. 139–40.

140. Dolan, interview with authors.

141. Ibid.

142. Antonio Antenucci, "Biden Time at St. Pat's", *New York Post*, March 25, 2013.

143. Dolan, interview with authors.

144. Al Baker, "Cardinal Dolan to Lobby for Tax Credit that Rewards Donations to Education", *New York Times*, March 17, 2014.

145. Ibid.

146. Timothy Dolan, "State Leaders Betray Catholics, Others on Education Tax Credits", *New York Post*, April 1, 2014.

147. Dolan, interview with authors.

148. Timothy Cardinal Dolan, "The Abandoned Kids—State Leaders' Broken Vows", *New York Post,* June 20, 2014.

149. Aaron Short, "Cardinal Dolan Pushes Albany to Pass Education Tax Credit", *New York Post*, March 27, 2015.

150. Ibid.

151. Kenneth Lovett, "Cardinal Dolan 'Discouraged' at Likely Exclusion of Tax Credit from State Budget", *Daily News*, March 26, 2015.

152. Aaron Short, "For God's Sake Act", *New York Post*, March 27, 2015.

153. William McGurn, "A Friend in Jesus: New York's New Catholic PAC", *New York Post*, March 13, 2015.

154. Ibid.

155. *Wikipedia*, s.v. "Death of Eric Garner, last modified June 23, 2016, https://en.wikipedia.org/wiki/Death_of_Eric_Garner/.

156. Ibid.

157. Ibid.

158. Timothy Cardinal Dolan, "Demonizing NYPD or City's Leaders Won't Unite New York", *Daily News*, December 15, 2014.

159. Timothy Cardinal Dolan, "After Our Darkest Day, the Light", *Daily News*, December 22, 2014.

160. Mary Iapalucci, "New York Has New Plan for Educating Priests, Lay Leaders", *Long Island Catholic*, May 2, 2013.

161. Dolan, interview with authors.

162. "Archdiocese of New York Announces Publication of Strategic Plan for Catholic Schools", Archdiocese of New York website, October 5, 2010, http://archny.org/.

163. "Reconfiguration Committee Announces Preliminary Determinations of 'At-Risk' Schools", *Catholic New York*, November 9, 2010.

164. Dolan, interview with authors.

165. "40-Person Advisory Group Named for Making All Things New", *Catholic New York*, February 6, 2014.

166. Josh Dawsey, "Archdiocese Moves to Close Parishes", *Wall Street Journal*, November 18, 2013.

167. Dolan, interview with authors.

168. Ibid.

169. Ibid.

170. Ibid.

171. Ibid.

172. Ibid.

173. "Making All Things New", press release of the Archdiocese of New York, November 2, 2014.

174. Sharon Otterman, "Heartache for New York's Catholics as Church Closings Are Announced", *New York Times*, November 2, 2014.

175. Cardinal Dolan, "The Best Is Yet to Come", *The Gospel in the Digital Age* (blog), November 11, 2014, http://blog.archny.org/.

176. Sharon Otterman, "New York Archdiocese Appears Likely to Shutter More Churches", *New York Times*, December 14, 2014.

177. Peggy Noonan, "Cardinal, Please Spare This Church", *Wall Street Journal*, December 27–28, 2014.

178. John O'Hara, "Holy Rights", *New York Post*, January 4, 2015.

179. Cardinal Timothy M. Dolan, "Mission, Not Maintenance, Should Be Our Focus", *Catholic New York*, January 8, 2015.

180. Sharon Otterman, "Parishioners See a System of Secrets", *New York Times*, February 13, 2015.

181. James Barron, "Spires at St. Patrick's Cathedral, Cleaned Up, Come Back in View", *New York Times*, June 18, 2013.

182. Cardinal Timothy M. Dolan, "The Archbishop Fulton J. Sheen Center for Art and Culture", *Catholic New York*, June 26, 2014.

183. Ibid.

184. Ibid.

185. Dolan, interview with authors.

186. Ibid.

187. Ibid.

188. "IN GREED THEY TRUST: Fat Cats Revolt. Francis' rap on rich may cost St. Pat's", *Daily News*, January 1, 2014.

189. Edward Cardinal Egan, "Pope Francis: Where He Would Lead the Church" (paper delivered at St. John's School of Law, New York, October 24, 2014).

190. Ibid.

191. Statement of Timothy Cardinal Dolan on the death of Cardinal Egan, Archdiocese of New York website, March 5, 2015, http://archny.org/.

192. Timothy Cardinal Dolan, homily at funeral Mass of Cardinal Egan, Archdiocese of New York website, March 10, 2015, http://archny.org/.

193. Statement of Timothy Cardinal Dolan on the release of the papal visit schedule, Archdiocese of New York website, June 30, 2015, http://archny.org/.

194. Melanie Grayce West, "High Hopes for Pope Visit", *Wall Street Journal*, September 21, 2015.

195. Melanie Grayce West, "Cardinal Dolan Prepares to Meet the Pope", *Wall Street Journal*, September 23, 2015.

196. Transcribed from EWTN recording of papal visit to St. Patrick's Cathedral, September 24, 2015.

197. "Pope Francis at United Nations", *Newsday*, September 26, 2015.

198. Ibid.

199. Ibid.

200. Lorena Mongelli and Yaron Steinbuch, "Hundreds Bid Pope Francis Farewell at JFK Airport", *New York Post*, September 26, 2015.

201. Ibid.

202. Hilary White, "Synod Confusion 'of the Devil': Archbishop Chaput", *LifeSiteNews*, October 22, 2014, https://www.lifesitenews.com/.

203. "Leading Cardinals Confront Pope Francis over Manipulation of Synod", *LifeSiteNews*, October 12, 2015, https://www.lifesitenews.com/.

204. Sandro Magister, "Thirteen Cardinals Have Written to the Pope. Here's the Letter", Chiesa, October 12, 2015, http://chiesa.espresso.repubblica.it/articolo/1351154?eng=y&refresh _ce/.

205. Ibid.

206. Lisa Bourne, "Cardinal Dolan Confirms He Signed Leaked Letter to Pope Francis: Provides More Details", *LifeSiteNews*, October 15, 2015, https://www.lifesitenews.com/news /cardinal-dolan-confirms-he-signed-leaked-letter-provides-more-details/.

207. Ibid.

208. Magister, "Thirteen Cardinals".

209. Inés San Martín, "New York Cardinal Dolan Sees Light amid the Synod's Confusion", *Crux*, October 15, 2015, https://cruxnow.com/church/2015/10/15/new-york-cardinal-dolan-sees-light-amid-the-synods-confusion/.

210. Robert Royal, "The Text and the Context", *Catholic Thing*, October 26, 2015, https://www.thecatholicthing.org/2015/10/26/the-text-and-the-context/.

211. Jonathan V. Last, "Rome's Obama", *Weekly Standard*, November 9, 2015, http://www.weeklystandard.com/romes-obama/article/1055639.

212. Royal, "Text and Context".

213. Cardinal Timothy M. Dolan, "Report on the Synod", *Catholic New York*, October 29, 2015.

214. Tim Stelloh and Andy Newman, "Dolan Urges Catholics to Become More Active in Politics", *New York Times*, March 3, 2012.

215. Cardinal Timothy M. Dolan, "Celebrating Our Independence", *Columbia* 92, no. 7 (July 2012): 10.

INDEX

Page numbers in italics represent images.